Perfecting Paradise

by Roger M. Showley
photo editor Richard Crawford

DEDICATION
Charles and Catherine

Dedicated to my children,
Charles and Catherine,
who along with the other children
of San Diego County and
Tijuana, will grow up to make
and write history in the 21st
century and third millennium.

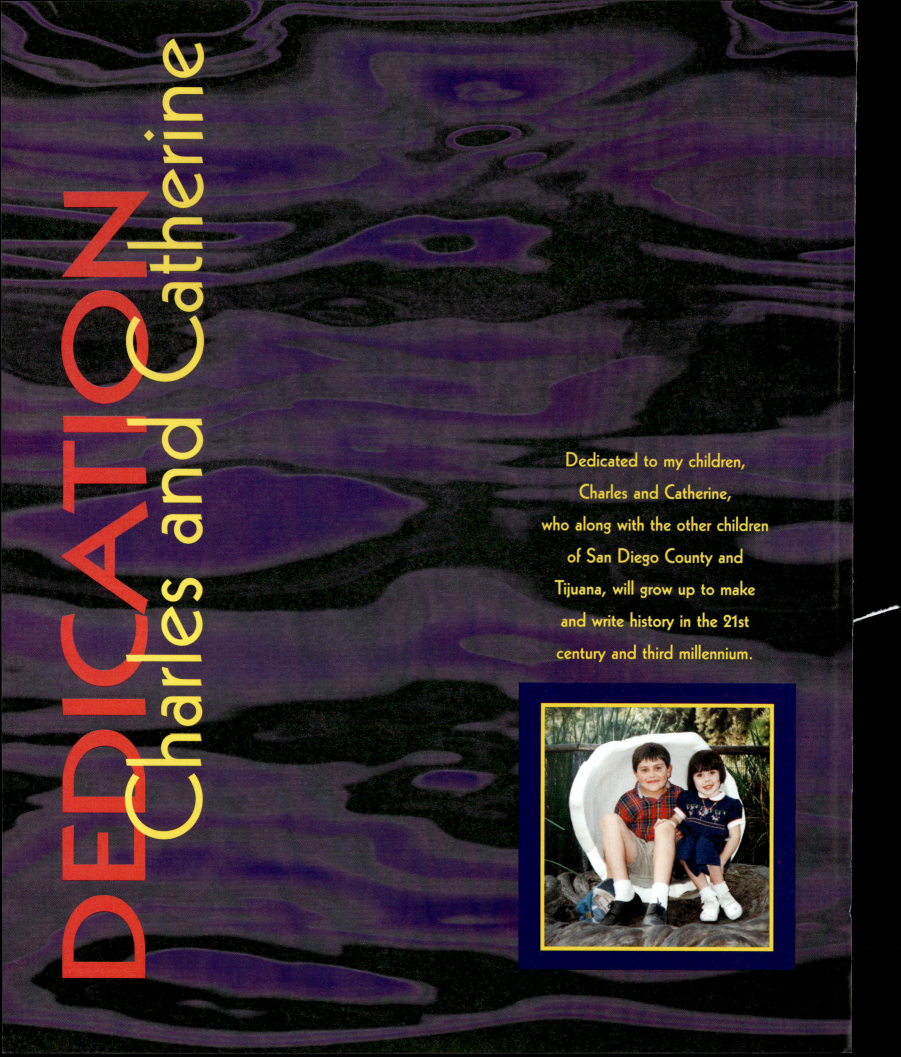

First Edition
Copyright©1999
by Heritage Media Corporation
All rights reserved. No part of this book may be
reproduced in any form or by any means,
electronic or mechanical, including photocopying,
without permission in writing from the publisher.
All inquiries should be addressed to Heritage Media Corp.
ISBN: 1-886483-24-8
Library of Congress Card Catalog Number: 98-073492

Text © *Roger M. Showley*
Photo Editor: *Richard Crawford*
Publisher: *C.E. Parks*
Editor-in-Chief: *Lori M. Parks*
VP/National Sales Manager: *Ray Spagnuolo*
VP/Corporate Development: *Bart Barica*
CFO: *Randall Peterson*
Managing Editor: *Betsy Blondin*
Production Manager: *Deborah Sherwood*
Art Director: *Gina Mancini*
Production Staff: *Jeff Caton, Sean Gates,
Andrea Giorgio, Brad Hartman, Dave Hermstead,
Jay Kennedy, John Leyva, Barry Miller, Norm Pruitt,
Chris Rivera, Steve Trainor*
Coordinating Editors: *Renee Kim, Betsy Lelja,
Elizabeth Lex, Sara Rufner, Adriane Wessels, John Woodward*
Profile Writers: *Karen Boyd, Joe Connor, Andrea Glass,
Linda Goldman-Foley, William Goodwin, Melissa Jacobs,
Donna Kordela, Neal Leavitt, Melissa McNulty,
William Mueller, Leslie O'Brien, Marce Parrish-Hanson,
Gerald Poindexter, Frank Sabatini Jr.*
Administration: *Juan Diaz, Cory Graham, Letty James,
Scott Reid, Ellen Ruby, Patrick Rucker*
Project Coordinator: *Kathee Finn*

Published by

Heritage Media Corp.
6354 Corte del Abeto, Suite B
Carlsbad, California 92009
www.heritagemedia.com

Printed by Heritage Media Corp. in the United States of America

San Diego photos in front section by Robert A. Eplett

Table of Contents

Foreword 6

Introduction 8

Prologue: *Paradise Discovered* 10

One: *Explorers and Exploiters* 16

Two: *Paradise Under New Management* 34

Three: *Heaven on Earth: The Horton Period* 54

Timeout: *The Nolen Plan* 80

Four: *Fairs, Wars, Smokestacks and Geraniums* 88

Five: *Growing Pains* 118

Timeout: *Temporary Paradise?* 144

Six: *Retooling for the 21st Century* 154

PARTNERS IN SAN DIEGO 180

Building a Greater San Diego 182

Business & Finance 222

Entertainment 232

Manufacturing & Distribution 244

Marketplace 272

Networks 322

Professions 340

Quality of Life 368

Technology 406

Chronology 432   End Notes 436   Index 440   Partners Index 447

Foreword

Since the establishment of Mission San Diego de Alcalá in 1769, planning in San Diego has been a governmental activity, a business and, some would say, a community sport.

The first European settlement in what is now Old Town was laid out in accordance with the Laws of the Indies, promulgated by King Philip II of Spain for the towns of the New World. The planning of San Diego has continued unceasingly ever since, and often, with inspired results.

Who would not applaud the creation of Mission Bay Park in the 1950s and the revitalization of Centre City that began in the 1970s and brought about the preservation of the Gaslamp Quarter? Then, there was the enlightened move to preserve open space, which also came into vogue in the 1970s and culminated in the Multiple Species Conservation Program in the 1990s. And let's not forget the construction of the San Diego Trolley in the 1980s, which, in itself, was no mean feat. These are but a few examples of how planning in San Diego has resulted in great benefit to us, and furthermore, our planning and development achievements have become models for other cities across the United States as well as for those throughout the world.

In the early 1900s, the country was caught in the "City Beautiful" movement and the nation's largest cities began to develop and adopt comprehensive plans. In spite of being a small town, San Diego started to follow the lead of the big cities. San Diego's leading businessman, George W. Marston, promoted the idea of a civic improvement committee, and in turn, John Nolen was hired to prepare a plan to guide San Diego's growth.

From 1906 on, formal city planning became an integral part of both the city structure and the regional structure. Planning has flourished; but, implementation has not always kept pace. Even though much has been accomplished, it has not been without a price; and, we paid through the nose for the growth management wars of the 1970s and '80s that sharply divided the community and defeated any unification of progressive attitudes toward the future of the region. Thankfully, the war is over now, and, under the banner of "Smart Growth," which took flight in 1999, a multitude of efforts are underway to plan for the future and assign responsibility for implementation. We can move forward with the expectation that we are successfully embarked upon building true community consensus about "what we want to be when we grow up."

As we look back over the last 100 years, it is evident that planning — both public and private — has produced the city we call "Paradise," albeit a paradise that is "temporary" and one that requires continuing vigilance and effort to attain perfection.

Building a city is akin to building a personal relationship. If it is to be of value, it must be nurtured continually. As San Diego has learned only too well, the best plan in the world is worthless if it is left to collect dust in the archives. The secret is implementation, implementation, implementation.

As George Santayana said, "Those who cannot remember the past are condemned to repeat it." With his book, Roger Showley has given us the prescription to ward off that curse. His medicine opens our eyes to how San Diego got to be the way it is and opens the door to the knowledge we need to bring our "Temporary Paradise" to permanence. Roger's "bedside manner" is just what the doctor ordered.

Michael J. Stepner, FAIA, AICP
Dean, Newschool of Architecture
July 1999

Introduction

This book is about America's Finest City, Heaven on Earth, The First Great City of the 21st Century. City in Motion. The Silver Gate. Sports town, USA. Home of the Super Computer and WD-40. The Plymouth Rock of the West Coast: Where California Began.

Any one of these monikers might have been suitable for the title. But I chose "Perfecting Paradise" because this story is about a centuries-long attempt to improve an already wonderful place provided by nature. In some years, San Diegans have made things better. At other times, things got worse.

Throughout its history, San Diego has planned its future and it is from two key, unofficial plans that I drew the title's words. Turn-of-the-century planner John Nolen used the word "perfect" in his 1908 comprehensive plan for San Diego, the first attempt to masterplan the region: "To beautify a city is to make it perfect — perfect as a city, complete in serving a city's purpose." Nearly 70 years later, urbanologists Kevin Lynch and Donald Appleyard evoked the word "paradise" in their reconnaissance report on what they considered San Diego's true dimensions — the San Diego-Tijuana metropolitan area. They warned explicitly that to the extent San Diego was a paradise, it would not remain one for long unless San Diegans altered their landuse policies and lifestyles.

In concentrating on the history of city-building, I have necessarily included less detail about San Diego's economic, political, artistic and social development. It would take a work much larger to cover all facets of the county. Every town, neighborhood, organization, ethnic group and business deserves a written history. Perhaps this book will inspire others to delve into those dusty archives and detail the story of each part of San Diego.

Some San Diego histories have told the region's story through pictures. And what a rich treasure trove we enjoy in the millions of photographs housed at the San Diego Historical Society photographic archives in Balboa Park! We could only include a sampling here, for there are millions more images available for enjoyment, education and commercial uses.

We have made one bow to the electronic Information Age in offering all or part of this book on the Internet, at least at the initial publication. A text-only with footnotes version on floppy disk is available from the author for researchers who wish to check the sources of various quotations. Perhaps the next history of San Diego can include a digital companion with video clips from contemporary news footage and family movies, audio clips from oral histories and hypertext links via the Internet to online text and visual sources.

Local history writers are a dedicated corps of researchers who select a topic of personal interest and often become obsessed with tracking down the truth. I came to an interest in San Diego history from my family. My grandparents — B. Guy Showley and Ruth Marchand Showley and William G. Mirow and Ruth Irwin Mirow — were key influences in what they did and passed along to me via my parents, Guy R. Showley and Vivian M. Showley. For the many stories of their childhoods and memories of San Diego, dating back to the horse-and-buggy days, I continue to be forever grateful. Many San Diegans are transplants from elsewhere and have had to learn local history on the run. I count myself lucky that I grew up here a "native" and learned by osmosis from friends and family firsthand.

The second source of local history has been my job in local journalism. First in high school and college newspapers and then at the *Evening Tribune, The San Diego Union* and *The San Diego Union-Tribune*, I have watched and reported history in the making for more than 30 years. The wonderful newspaper clip files, yellowing and turning brittle in a windowless storage room in the company's printing plant

and Acknowledgments

building, made for many hours of enjoyable research as I looked up the background of many events in the course of preparing stories for the paper. My longest assignment has been in the Homes section of the U-T and my editors — Bill Parry, Joan Taylor, Liz Poppens, Mike Crowell and Carl Larsen — indulged my interest in San Diego history as I veered off the real estate industry path to connect the present to the past. My continuing "Smokestacks and Geraniums" monthly column provided the basis for many of the stories included in this book. For that freedom to explore our past, I thank my editors, our diligent librarians and my other newspaper colleagues, many of whom share my historic bug.

For this particular project, I had leaned on many personal and professional friends who agreed to read all or part of the chapters. Even as she was suffering from lung cancer, San Diego County historian Mary Ward willingly read one chapter after another and offered suggestions. She died in early-1999 but saw the final manuscript over Christmas and offered her encouragement and blessings. San Diego's past could not be easily preserved and promoted if it were not for dedicated researchers like Mary who remind the rest of us what's fact and what isn't.

Philip Klauber, retired businessman and dedicated watchdog over San Diego's history, read every word and offered many suggestions in both style and substance, most of which have been incorporated. University of San Diego history professor Iris Engstrand helped ensure that her latest historical research was reflected in the sections on the Spanish, Mexican and early-American periods. Rick Crawford, former research archivist, at the San Diego Historical Society and assistant director of the California Room at the San Diego Public Library, doubled as both photo editor and text reader. His subtle comments prompted me to rewrite and reconsider every chapter.

Thanks also go to Mr. and Mrs. William R. Dick for their generous permission to use their painting of San Diego by Maurice Braun on the dust jacket. Ruth Dick is the daughter of Joseph E. Dryer, who founded the "Heaven on Earth Club" in the 1930s to boost San Diego during the Depression.

A number of people read portions of the book and offered many suggestions. They included *Union-Tribune* editor Karin Winner, former assistant managing editor Rick Levinson, associate editor Neil Morgan, Homes editor Carl Larsen, features copy editor Susan Dudley, assistant metro editor Irene Jackson and, especially, arts critic Welton Jones; former *San Diego Union* architecture critic Kay Kaiser, and former Sunday *Union* editor Al JaCoby; Indian-era researcher Richard Carrico, San Diego Presidio archaeologist Jack Williams, former San Diego Historical Society curator Lucinda Eddy, architect Wayne Donaldson, downtown redevelopment public information director Donna Alm, former mayoral aide Mike Madigan and Newschool of Architecture Dean Mike Stepner.

The end notes detail the sources I consulted for each chapter. I want to acknowledge especially the seven-volume history of San Diego by the late-*San Diego Union* editor Richard Pourade. Pourade worked from the early-1960s into the late-'70s to compile a consistently informative narrative, richly illustrated and documented with many excerpts from first-hand sources. Every San Diego history writer should start with Pourade and then explore avenues he opened up. One other invaluable source was the two-volume *San Diego Trivia* collection of questions and answers put together by San Diego librarian Evelyn Kooperman. These thick, entertaining paperbacks were never far from my desk as I sought to check facts and dates reported by others. Short of a city encyclopedia, Kooperman's Q&A's is the next best thing.

Of course, it was Charles and Lori Parks at Heritage Media Corporation who put their trust in me to put this history together. For the opportunity to research and write about my own hometown and to see it turned into a beautifully published work for others to enjoy, I am very grateful.

Lastly, I want to thank my wife Carol and two children, Charlie and Cookie, for their love and support as this project went from conception to completion. I could not have done it without them.

Roger M. Showley
San Diego, *July 1999*

PROLOGUE

The exact date of man's first arrival in San Diego is unknown. But anthropologists believe humans first settled in the area as early as 20,000 years ago along the coast and 12,000 years ago in the desert. The earliest cultural group, dated around 7500 B.C, is referred to as the San Dieguito Paleo-Indian, which researcher Malcolm Rogers described in 1929 as a "scraper-maker culture." The Rogers site is above the San Dieguito River east of Rancho Santa Fe.

The second culture was the La Jollan, dating from about 6,000 B.C., and taking its name from an archaeological site at La Jolla Shores. During the La Jollan period, the local climate became drier and hotter. Populations moved away from the spreading desert regions in southeastern California and Baja California. Scholars believe some La Jollans moved inland to find food replacements for the shellfish that declined when bays and lagoons receded. Just as in modern times, some people preferred the coast and others preferred the dry, desert inland. During the first millennium A.D., the La Jollans, joined by the in-migrating Yumans, learned to gather acorns and grind them into flour, from which they made a healthy mush. Archaeologists have found evidence of ceramics, cremations, pictographs, stone tools, clay-lined hearths and elaborate stone walls, some built for defense, others for irrigation.

Yuman and Shoshonean groups moved into the area and gradually assimilated the La Jollans. By 1000, the tribes had formed into five major groups: the Luiseño in North County; Cahuilla in the far northeast, east of Mount Palomar; Cupeño in a small region around Warner's Springs; Ipai or Northern Diegueño, generally from the San Dieguito River Valley to Mission Valley; and the Ipai or Kumeyaay from Mission Valley to Ensenada. The eastern limit was approximately around the Salton Sea and Salt Hills in Imperial County, and in Mexico, the Cocopa Mountains.

By the time of the Spanish conquest, the local Indian population stood at roughly 18,000-20,000 within the county's present-day borders. The Baja California total was about 12,000. They lived in 85-90 villages or *rancherías*, with up to 200 per settlement. But these were more akin to seasonal campsites than villages in the modern sense. Homes were as simple as a pole framework covered with thatch, grass and earth. Around lagoons and sloughs, they might have been rectangular, sand-covered houses and in the desert, palm-leaf thatch on four poles. Mountain-dwelling Indians occupied caves or huts roofed with bark or pine slabs.

Paradise Discovered: Before the Europeans

Major Native American settlements
Courtesy Richard Carrico

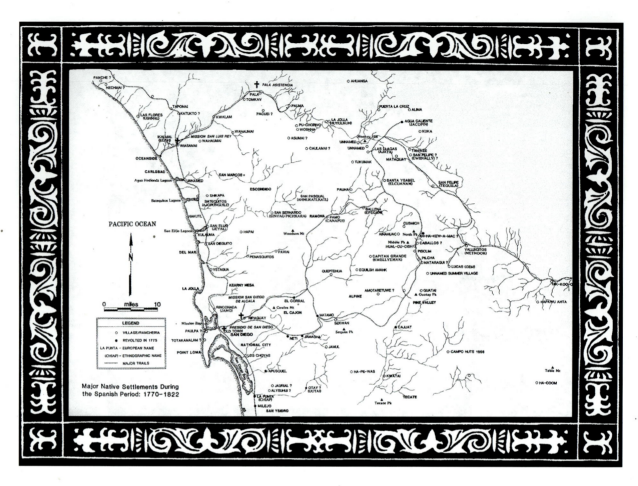

Politically, each band was autonomous. The chief's position was passed on to the eldest son or brother and, rarely, the widow. Within general geographic boundaries, families and individuals owned what they made or obtained, but upon death, everything was burned rather than inherited. Katharine Luomala described the typical Tipai-Ipai annual cycle in *The Handbook of North American Indians*: "A band's seasonal travel was vertical, following the ripening of major plants from coast and canyon floor to higher mountain slopes. Two or three families would arrive at a campsite, joined later by others, to gather, process and cache seasonal vegetal food."

In the coastal zone, men and children wore little or nothing; women donned a two-piece or single apron. Sandals of agave leaves served as shoes and robes of rabbit skin, bark or buckskin were added in the winter. The Indians wore their hair long and pierced their noses and ears with bones, pendants or sticks. Men smoked wild tobacco using a clay pipe. Mockingbirds and roadrunners were caged as pets and a small aboriginal dog, now extinct, was trained for hunting.

The Tipais and Ipais traded salt, dried seafood and dried greens with Yumans at the mouth of the Colorado River but did not generally adopt Yuman agricultural techniques. Instead, the San Diego-Tijuana Indians gathered acorns from at least six species of oaks, collected fresh fruits and vegetables and hunted and fished.

The environmental setting

The region's form took shape about 65 million years ago when volcanic activity died down and Southern California came to rest in its present spot on the west side of the San Andreas fault and the Gulf of California. However, the area is far from geologically stable. The coastline continues to recede; minor earthquakes frequently cause moments of terror.

Prior to European settlement, San Diego's landscape and environment were quite different. There were a few trees and rivers that flowed freely, unhindered by dams. At the end of the last ice age, when the water level was much lower than today, the Indians could probably walk across the shallow bay to the distant shoreline to fish. By around 1000 A.D., the present shape of the region was set.

This 4,200-square-mile county, plus the 612-square-mile Tijuana municipality in Baja California, is neither homogenous nor distinctive, as geographer Philip R. Pryde has stated. The area is large enough to represent four separate landscapes, varied enough, to permit surfing in the morning and skiing in the afternoon.

First, there is the coastline punctuated by bays, lagoons, estuaries and beaches. Then comes a series of canyons, slashing across the mesas, helping to define distinctive neighborhoods. Beyond the hills and valleys are the Laguna Mountains, the highest being 6,533-foot Hot Springs Peak, northeast of Warner Springs. Finally, comes the Anza-Borrego Desert, a wasteland of few people, striking beauty, California's largest state park.

South of the Mexican-American border, the geography and settlement patterns are similar. Indeed, the San Diego-Tijuana region shares the same air basin, watershed and weather. However, without a harbor, most Tijuanans live not along the oceanfront but along the Tijuana River, in the foothills and on the mesas. The Tijuana River Valley, which spans the international boundary, features 400-foot bluffs on the Mexican side and a saltwater estuary on the American. Until Rodríguez Dam was completed in 1937 and a concrete channel installed in the 1970s, the river posed a constant flooding threat.

Lacking excess economic resources, Tijuana did not beautify itself with lush public parks or private

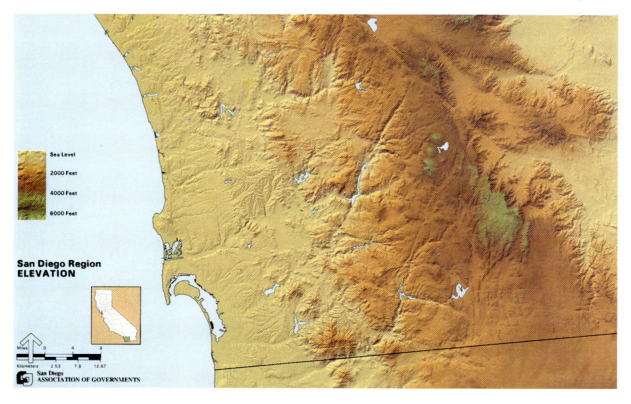

San Diego Region ELEVATION

A California fisherman, depicted in George Shelvock's 1726 publication, *Voyage Around the World*. Courtesy The Huntington Library

throughout the county before urbanization supplanted many orchards. Avocados remain a valuable cash crop, as do cut flowers. The poinsettia plant, a Christmas flower introduced in Encinitas in the 1920s is the most well-known San Diego floral export.

The county is large enough to encompass five natural vegetation communities that flourish comfortably within its borders: coastal sage scrub, chaparral, oak and pine, pinyon-juniper and desert scrub. From the Spanish period forward, nearly 200 species have been introduced locally, from the eucalyptus and queen palm to the flowers, fruit trees and shrubs available at every nursery. Through natural and human interventions, 154 other species also have been identified as rare or endangered. The most celebrated is the Torrey pine, protected at Torrey Pines State Park south of Del Mar and known to exist in only one other spot, Santa Rosa Island off Santa Barbara.

The local wildlife retain a tentative foothold in urbanized San Diego. The city dweller still comes across a family of opossum, skunk, raccoon and deer. Off the coast, an estimated 27,000 California gray whales, once on the verge of extinction, provide an annual treat, fluking and spouting as they migrate between Alaska and the Gulf of California. Seventeen other species have been classified as rare, endangered or threatened; federal and state authorities have identified 25 other potential candidates.

front-yard lawns. In typical Spanish and Mexican tradition, the wealthiest people tend to live near the center of town and the poorest live in *colonias* or squatter settlements in the canyons and on distant mesas.

Weather conditions vary greatly from one end of the region to another. It can be 70 degrees and overcast in Point Loma while it's 105 degrees in Borrego. Within the same climatic zone, conditions can change markedly from sunrise to noon to dusk. Rainfall varies widely, from an average of 10.4 inches downtown to 40 inches in the mountains and 3 inches in the desert.

The soil conditions have made parts of the region ideal for agriculture. Lemon Grove isn't just a lovely name. Citrus once grew abundantly there and

Was San Diego a paradise before the Europeans arrived? To the local residents, it probably was. The natives had abundant food, suitable shelter and sufficient clothing in a location generally unthreatened by outsiders. But in a subsistence economy, they had little time to develop written language and the arts. By modern standards, it was not an easy life. Once the Spaniards arrived, the natives' fortunes tumbled, their culture collapsed and their population nearly vanished. From that standpoint, paradise was lost to the people who first called this area their home.

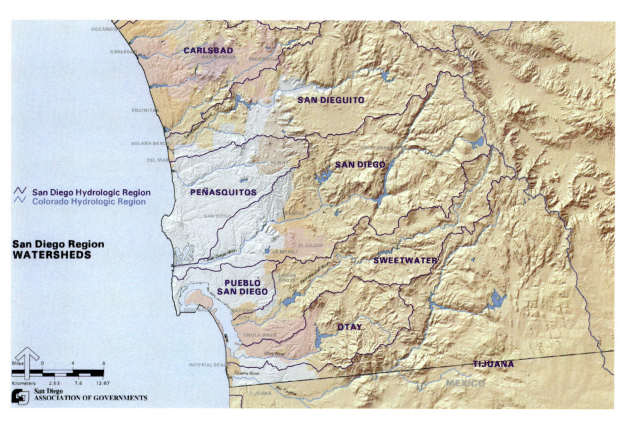

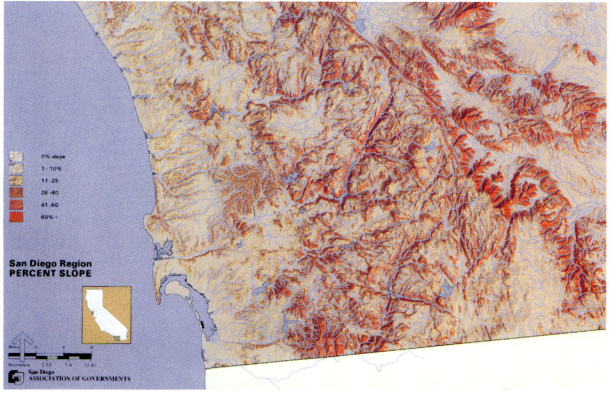

ONE

CHAPTER ONE

"Mission Dam" on the San Diego River, was California's first water project. Built with native American labor between 1813 and 1816, the dam diverted water into a flume system which connected to Mission San Diego de Alcalá six miles downstream. A National Historic Landmark, the masonry dam survives today as a centerpiece to Mission Trails Regional Park.
Courtesy San Diego Historical Society

EXPLORERS AND EXPLOITERS

"*California*" *was a* well-known place in Europe, even before Europeans discovered it. It first appeared in a popular 1508 romance, *Sergas de Esplandián,* by Garci Ordóñez de Montalvo. It tells the story of a pagan siege of Constantinople, featuring Esplandián and Queen Calafia of the island of California. ("California" may be derived from the Greek for "beautiful bird," Arabic for "large province" or French from *Song of Roland*, in which one line reads "*e cil de Califerne*" — and those of Californe — perhaps meaning "caliph's domain.) Ordóñez wrote:

> Know ye that at the right hand of the Indies there is an island named California, very close to that part of the Terrestrial Paradise, which was inhabited by black women, without a single man among them, and they lived in the manner of Amazons. They were robust of body, with strong and passionate hearts and great virtues. The island itself is one of the wildest in the world on account of the bold and craggy rocks. Their weapons were all made of gold... The island everywhere abounds with gold and precious stones, and upon it no other metal was found. They lived in caves well excavated. They had many ships with which they sailed to other coasts to make forays, and the men whom they took as prisoners they killed.

One can imagine a few literate officers retelling Ordóñez' tales to bored soldiers and sailors as they crossed the Atlantic on their way to a new life in America. The visions of gold, beautiful women and fantastic civilizations became real as they encountered the Aztecs, Incas and other exotic native American cultures.

It is uncertain when California became the recognized name of this new territory. Fortún Jiménez reached Baja California in 1533-34, but no records survived his voyage to determine if he named the area "California." Hernando Cortés arrived in 1535 and called his landing spot at La Paz "Santa Cruz." By the time Cabrillo sailed in 1542, according to the summary of his log, "California" was already the commonly accepted name for the peninsula and the lands beyond.

CABRILLO: EUROPEAN DISCOVERER OF SAN DIEGO

Juan Rodríguez Cabrillo, San Diego's celebrated discoverer, is said to have come from Portugal. But researchers have been unable to confirm his birthplace. He usually signed his name Juan Rodríguez and in 1617, his

1542-1835

(Photo on page 18) This 1935 photograph documents the ruins of the Royal Presidio, located below today's Serra Museum. *Courtesy San Diego Historical Society*

"They lived in the manner of Amazons." The image of the Amazon, such as Queen Calafia, was often published as an emblem of the New World. From Cesare Ripa's *Iconologia* (1630). *Courtesy Huntington Library*

Aztec capital of Tenochtitlán, Cortés assigned Cabrillo to caulk 13 small boats needed to cross Lake Texcoco. All the ingredients necessary were present except animal fat. "As a substitute," said the official chronicle, "they used human fat from the hostile Indians they had killed, of whom there were a great number." Following a four-month siege, the Aztecs surrendered.

Over the next 20 years, Cabrillo became rich in Guatemala. But his fortunes began to change, when his former commander, Pedro de Alvarado, now governor of Guatemala, had him build a trading fleet to sail for the Spice Islands (Indonesia). Alvarado was killed in an accident while quelling an Indian uprising and the grand expedition to Asia was suspended. Back home, Cabrillo narrowly escaped the devastating effects of an earthquake on September 10, 1541. He is thought to be the same Juan Rodríguez who wrote an eyewitness account of the disaster. This first piece of journalistic writing published in the New World was circulated throughout Europe.

grandson, Gerónimo Cabrillo de Aldana, testified ambiguously, "My paternal grandfather, Juan Rodríguez Cabrillo, came from the kingdoms of Spain in company with Pánfilio de Narváez." Harry Kelsey concluded in his 1986 biography of Cabrillo that most evidence points to Cabrillo's birthplace as being in Spain, possibly in Cuellar, near Valladolid, about 1498.

Cabrillo first appears in Spanish records as one of 1,400 soldiers dispatched from Cuba in April 1520 to rein in Cortés. The conquistador was moving to conquer the Aztec empire and take control. Cortés surprised the Cuban forces one stormy night, badly wounded the commander and won over several hundred soldiers, including Cabrillo, then a 22-year-old captain of the bowmen. To take the

Following the earthquake, Viceroy Antonio de Mendoza commissioned Cabrillo to explore the upper coast of California and beyond. His assignment was to find the "Strait of Anián," the supposed navigable link between the Atlantic and Pacific. His ships: *San Salvador, La Victoria* and *San Miguel*.

Cabrillo's log of his voyage has never been found. But a summary of his log, a compilation of the original log and accounts by others in his party, sketches out the journey. The account begins: "On the 27th day of June 1542, there sailed from the port of Navidad Juan Rodríguez to explore the coast of New Spain."

By September 23, the party observed "very beautiful valleys and groves, with land plain and rugged, but they saw no Indians." They passed the uninhabited Islas Desiertas or the desert islands, later named the Coronado Islands, and, standing 12 miles offshore, saw "on land great smokes. It appears to be good land, with great valleys, and inland there are high mountains." This was the area south of the present international border around Tijuana.

"On Thursday [September 28] they went about six leagues [about 24 miles] north-northwest along the coast and found *un puerto cerrado y muy bueno* [a very good enclosed port], to which they gave the name of San Miguel [both name of one of Cabrillo's vessels and the saint whose feast day fell on Friday, the 29th]…

"After anchoring in it, they went ashore, where there were people. Of these, three waited, and all the others ran away. To these three they gave some gifts, and the Indians told them by signs that people like the Spaniards had passed inland; they showed much fear. At night, the Spaniards left the ships in a small boat to land and to fish. There happened to be Indians there, and they began to shoot with their arrows, and they wounded three men. The next day in the morning, they went with the boat further into the port, which was large, and caught two boys who understood nothing, not even by signs, and they gave them shirts and soon sent them away.

"The day after that, in the morning, three large Indians came to the ships, and by signs told how inland there walked men like the Spaniards, bearded and dressed and armed like the ones on the ships, and they showed that they had crossbows, and made gestures with their right arm as if they were spearing. They went running as if they were on a horse, and showed that they killed many of the Indian natives, and for that reason they were afraid.

"These people were well proportioned and large. They went around covered with the furs of animals. While in port, a very large storm passed, but because the port was so good they felt nothing… This was the first real storm they had undergone, and they stayed in the port until the following Tuesday [October 3]."

Cabrillo continued up the California coast into November, before turning back to winter in the Channel Islands off Santa Barbara. On or about Christmas Eve, Cabrillo injured his arm or leg while trying to rescue his men from attacking Indians. His injury did not heal and he died January 3, 1543, on the island called Capitana (probably Santa Catalina). His burial site has never been found.

Bartolomé Ferrer assumed command and sailed as far north as Point Arena before turning back. Pausing at San Diego from March 11 to 17, 1543, he arrived back in Navidad April 14. Cabrillo's family spent the next 70 years trying to recoup the debts owed them by Viceroy Mendoza. But by then, his pioneering voyage had been largely forgotten.

The Long Interlude

Rather than build on Cabrillo's discoveries, Spain concentrated on establishing an annual trading venture to the Philippines. Spanish galleons traded Mexican silver for spices, silks and other Asian riches. Occasionally, the galleons were intercepted by English, Dutch and French pirates.

Sixty years after Cabrillo, Sebastián Vizcaíno became the second Spanish explorer to explore California. Born in 1548, possibly in the Extremadura region of Spain, Vizcaíno arrived in the New World in 1583. Volunteering to explore the California coast, he was instructed to locate a safe harbor for the returning galleons. The 200-man expedition sailed in three vessels: *San Diego, Santo Tomás* and *Tres Reyes* (three kings).

The flotilla left Acapulco May 5, 1602, with crowds cheering and artillery firing salutes. On Sunday, November 10, Vizcaíno arrived at a port "which must be the best to be found in all the South Sea, protected on all sides and having good anchorage." This was what he called San Diego two days later. Vizcaíno carried charts and descriptions of the coast dating to Cabrillo's time

Juan Rodríguez Cabrillo, sailing for the flag of Spain, entered San Diego Bay in 1542 and christened the "closed and very good port" San Miguel. A commemorative stamp was issued in 1992. *Courtesy San Diego Historical Society*

JUAN RODRIGUEZ CABRILLO.

but could not match them against his observations. He therefore renamed most of the places Cabrillo had earlier passed by, including San Miguel. "A hut was built and mass said in celebration of the feast of Señor Diego [November 12]," Vizcaíno reported.

Why "San Diego?" Besides being the name of his flagship and notable feast day, San Diego de Alcalá de Henares was a popular saint in Vizcaíno's time. The illiterate, 15th century, Franciscan friar was born in San Nicolás del Puerto, about 50 miles northeast of Seville. In 1456 he joined a Franciscan convent in Alcalá de Henares, also near Seville, where he died in 1463. He was known widely for his concern for the poor and sick. But Rome took no action toward his canonization.

In 1562, Spanish King Philip II's son, Carlos, fell into a coma. Diego's remains were transferred to the prince's room and Carlos awoke the next day claiming he had seen Diego in his dreams. For the next 16 years, Philip lobbied for Diego's sainthood with four popes until Sixtus V granted the request in gratitude for Philip's campaign against English Queen Elizabeth I.

The canonization ceremony took place on July 2, 1588, as Philip's armada set sail for the ill-fated invasion of England. In April 1589, Philip led festivities in Alcalá de Henares, an event that drew thousands of pilgrims. "For the moment, the canonization was the most important event in Spain," said Thomas E. Case, Spanish professor at San Diego State University, "and helped smooth over the disastrous outcome of the armada and the failed enterprise against England."

Fourteen years later, Vizcaíno had this to say about the rediscovered and renamed port of San Diego:

> It has very good wood and water, many fish of all kinds, many of which we caught with seine and hooks. On the land there is much game, such as rabbits, hares, deer, very large quail, royal ducks, thrushes and many other birds… The country surrounding the port was very fertile and near the beach there are very fine meadows. The general [Vizcaíno] and Father Antonio [de la Ascensión] with other soldiers made a turn around the bay and looked over the country. They were pleased to see its fertility and good character, but what gave them the greatest pleasure was the extensiveness, capacity and security of the port, its good depth and its many fish.

About 100 Indians greeted the Spaniards and a few approached them peaceably. Vizcaíno distributed token gifts and received skins and other presents from the Indians, who waved farewell when Vizcaíno pulled up anchor after 10 days and set sail November 20. The expedition continued north past Mendocino until winter forced them to turn back in January 1603, and they returned to Acapulco two months later. Along the way, they discovered Monterey Bay. He gave it such a glowing report — "the best port that could be desired" — that it, rather than San Diego, became a prime objective of future explorations. (He missed San Francisco Bay entirely.) Instead of acting on Vizcaíno's recommendation to colonize Monterey, the new viceroy sent him on a new voyage of discovery, and nothing more was done about California for the rest of the 17th century.

Knowing that California could easily be taken by a foreign power, the Spanish crown found an economical means to exert control over the remote province. In 1697, the Jesuits were authorized to establish a series of missions in Baja California. The converted Indians would presumably defend the territory and spare Spain the cost of colonization and military occupation. Over the next 70 years the Jesuits established 23 missions, stretching from Loreto to within 100 miles of the present Mexican-American border. They established trails, explored the peninsula, cultivated the land and built an irrigation system.

But fear of the Jesuits' growing power in Europe prompted several monarchs and the pope to expel the priests and suppress the order. In 1767, newly named California Governor Gaspar de Portolá sent them out of Baja California. The Franciscans arrived to take over in April. They were led by Junípero Serra.

Father Junípero Serra

Miguel José Serra was born November 24, 1713, in Petra on Mallorca, one of the Balearic Islands in the Mediterranean. At 17, he joined the Franciscan order and took the name Junípero, one of the lay brothers of St. Francis. Ordained in 1739, he taught philosophy for 10 years until he emigrated to New Spain. From 1749 to 1768 he served in various posts before accepting the presidency of the California missions with the opportunity to extend the Jesuits' Baja California chain north into Alta (upper) California.

This expansion was the brainchild of José de Gálvez. Designated *visitador-general*, a post carrying extraordinary powers, he set out to increase the

José de Gálvez (1720-87), visitador-general of New Spain
Courtesy San Diego Historical Society

The revered "father" of the missions, Junípero Serra, founded the first mission in Alta California on Presido Hill, on July 16, 1769, considered to be the founding date of San Diego. Courtesy San Diego Historical Society

royal revenues from New Spain, particularly from California. The plans were already in motion when the Spanish ambassador in Russia warned Madrid that Empress Catherine II (the Great) was planning to expand her North American settlements to California. Gálvez dispatched five parties by sea and land toward San Diego. The *San Antonio* arrived April 11, the *San Carlos* April 29, but the *San José,* dispatched June 16, was lost at sea. The first group by land arrived in San Diego on May 14. It included Father Juan Crespi, a student of Serra's from Mallorca. Six weeks later, Governor Gaspar de Portolá came, accompanied by Father Serra. This is how Serra described the journey and San Diego in his first dispatch dated July 3, 1769:

"The missions in the regions which we have seen will all thrive very well, because there is good land and sufficient water. On the road hither and for great distances back, there are no rocks or thorns; but there are hills, indeed, very high and continuous, though composed only of earth. Some roads are good, others are bad; more, however, are of the latter kind, though it is no matter of importance. About halfway or earlier from where we started, we began to encounter many arroyos and ravines overgrown with

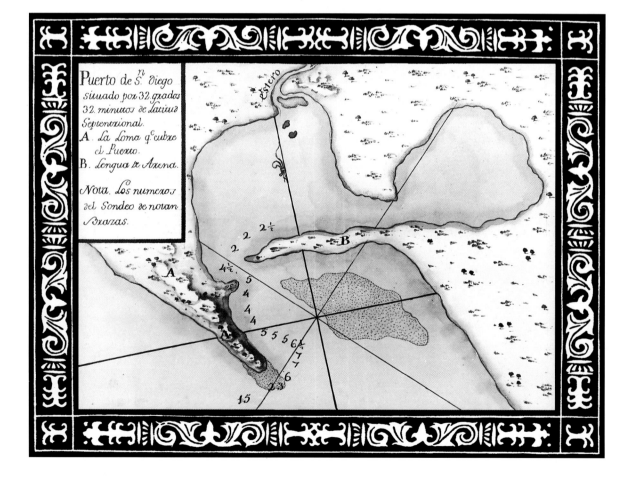

Map of the port of San Diego, drawn around 1170 by Vincente Vila, captain of the Serra-Portolá supply ship, San Carlos. Courtesy San Diego Historical Society

This early image of California Native Americans was published in 1726 in George Shelvocke's *Voyage Around the World. Courtesy The Huntington Library*

poplar trees. There are pretty and large wild vines; in some places they are loaded down with grapes. In various arroyos along the road and in the place where we are now, besides wild grape vines, there are various roses of Castile. In fine, it is a good country, very much different from the land of old [Baja] California…

"The natives are exceedingly numerous, and all people of this coast of the South Sea [Pacific Ocean] along which we came from the Ensenada at Todos Santos… live well on various seeds and on fish which they catch from rafts made of tules and formed like canoes, with which they venture far out on the sea. The Indians are very friendly. All the males, men as well as boys, go naked. The women and girls are decently covered as far as the breast. In that manner they would approach us on the road as well as in the camps. They would treat us with such confidence and ease as though they had known us all their lives. When we wished to give them something to eat, they would say they did not want that, but clothing. Only for things of this kind would they barter their fish with the soldiers and muleteers."

With many men sick and stocks at a minimum, Portolá dispatched the *San Antonio* back to San Blás and on July 14, led a company of 63 on a march north to Monterey. He did not return to San Diego until late-January 1770.

Serra chose the morning of Sunday, July 16, 1769, as the day for carrying out his principal duty, founding the first mission in Alta California. He celebrated mass adjacent to the soldiers' campsite halfway up Presidio Hill. This date is celebrated annually as the founding day of the city of San Diego.

Unfortunately for the little party, the Indians proved increasingly threatening. Within a month, Indians attacked, but were repelled without resorting to firearms. Then on August 15, while the soldiers were watering their horses, a much larger group of 20 Kumeyaay attacked, killing Serra's servant, José

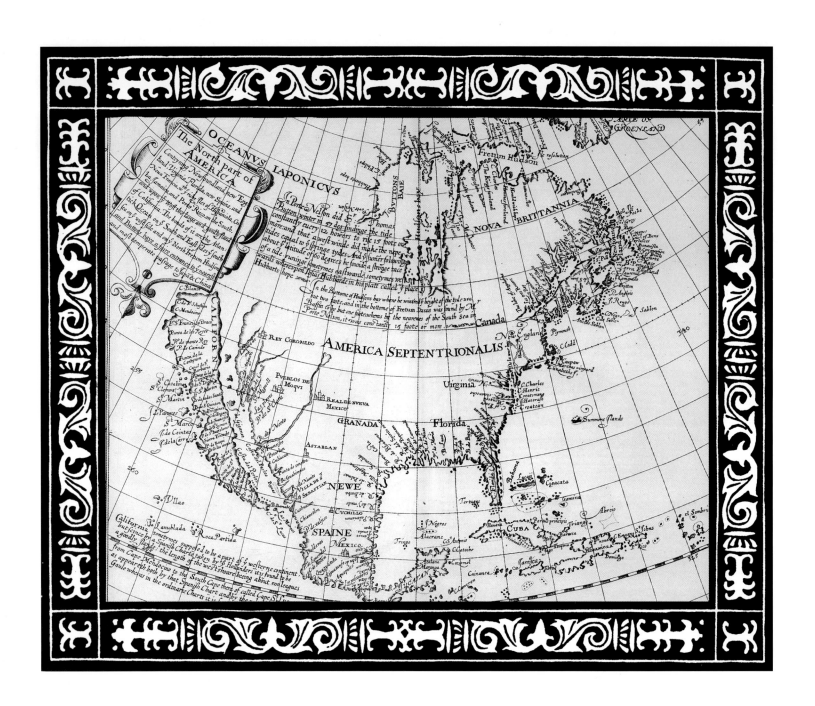

María Vergerano, and wounding three others. The soldiers rushed back and killed five Indians.

In 1770, Serra moved to Monterey and Father Luís Jayme took over in San Diego. By March 1771, a few Indians agreed to enter the mission as neophytes. There were only about 23 non-natives at the presidio-mission compound and they eked out a bare existence dependent on infrequent visits by the supply ships. In October 1772, the Franciscans officially relinquished control over Baja California to the Dominican order; the dividing line was set a few miles south of the present international border. In 1773, Serra won support for establishing more missions in Alta California and for moving the San Diego Mission six miles east of the presidio. Serra commented in his 1775 report, "This place is much more suitable for a population on account of the facility of obtaining the necessary water and on account of the vicinity of good land for cultivation. The place is called Nipaguay."

To the Indians, mission life resembled more of a paternalistic dictatorship than an idyllic brotherhood. Living in an enclosed compound, they depended on agricultural production, a radical shift from hunting and gathering and moving from place to place as the season warranted. In some years, such as 1805-6, deaths far outnumbered baptisms. The natives had no natural immunity to European diseases, especially measles and smallpox, and when an epidemic struck, the Indians succumbed quickly. The rotational living pattern spread the diseases to the villages, far from the Spaniards' settlement, decimating the indigenous population.

Frustrated by the missionaries' growing domination and alarmed by reports of rape by Spanish soldiers, about 800 Indians from at least 15 villages set fire to the mission buildings on the night of November 4-5, 1775, and killed the blacksmith, carpenter and Father Jayme, who became the first martyr in Alta California. Father Vicente Fuster wrote a riveting eyewitness account three weeks later:

"The first thing they did was to circle the ranchería, then the mission, from the four sides; then they pillaged the church of its precious articles, and after that they set fire to it. Next came the guardhouse and building where Father Luís [Jayme] had his quarters. I slept in the storehouse or granary, which was the last place they set afire. Amid the yelling and discharges of the guns, half-asleep, I made my way out of the building, hardly knowing what it was all about. Since I had to cross over to the other side, God kindly kept watch over me. I made a dash for it and got there safely. Then I asked the soldiers, 'What is this all about?' Hardly were the words out of my mouth than I saw on all sides around me so many arrows that you could not possibly count them. The only thing I did was to

(Opposite page) In 1625, English mathematician Henry Briggs published this map showing California as an island. The myth, perpetuated widely in English maps of the period, would not be disproved until the land travels of Jesuit priest, Father Eusebio Kino, in 1701. From *Hakluytus posthumus or Purchas his Pilgrimes* (1625). *Courtesy San Diego Historical Society*

San Diego de Alcalá Henares or St. Dídacus, the namesake of San Diego. *Courtesy San Diego Historical Society*

Sebastián Vizcaíno entered San Diego Bay on November 10, 1602. Unaware that he had found Cabrillo's "San Miguel," Vizcaíno named the port in honor of San Diego de Alcalá. *Courtesy San Diego Historical Society*

drop my cloak and stand flat against the wall of the guardhouse, and use the mantle as a cover so that no arrows might hit me. And this, thanks be to God, is what I succeeded in doing. There we were surrounded on all sides by flames."

The Indians could have finished off the mission, but at dawn they retreated. No further attack came, and by the end of the month, word was sent to Monterey of the incident. Serra reacted in joy rather than sorrow: "The blood of the martyrs is the seed of the church... Thanks be to God, that land is already irrigated; now the conversion of the Diegueños will succeed." An exhaustive investigation by Governor Fernando de Rivera y Moncada followed. Juan Bautista de Anza, who had been exploring a new land route from New Spain to California, arrived in San Diego with reinforcements in January. More troops came by sea. "By this time the Indians believed the Spaniards were coming almost from the skies to punish them," wrote historian Charles Chapman, "and they became afraid. There was no longer any thought of revolt; indeed, the position of the Spaniards was strengthened by the failure of the San Diego outbreak, for the Indians felt from this time forth that it was impossible to throw out their conquerors." However, a more recent historian, San Diegan Richard Carrico, believes that in the Indian eyes, the insurrection was an unqualified success. The chief priest, Luís Jayme, had been killed, the religious objects had been removed and a cleansing fire had swept through the mission property.

Father Fermín Francisco de Lasuén, who had been assigned to oversee the new mission at San Juan Capistrano, was diverted to San Diego to rebuild the mission into a more defensible structure. An adobe building was completed by December 1776. Elsewhere, unrest continued between Spaniard and Indian.

Father Serra died at age 70, August 29, 1784, at the Monterey mission in Carmel. In 15 years in California, he had established nine missions; his successor, Father Lasuén, added nine more in the next 18 years, including one at San Luís Rey in 1798.

PRESIDIO LIFE

Constructed of wood and adobe, the royal presidio of San Diego exists no more, its remains mere mounds of dirt covered by grass lawns at Presidio Park overlooking Interstate 5 and Old Town State Historic Park. In comparison to other Spanish-era sites on which modern buildings have been erected, the undisturbed presidio grounds are a potential treasure trove. Over the years, various excavations have endeavored to uncover the archaeological record left during nearly 70 years of occupation from 1769 to 1835. Several maps have been found to guide the investigations. Computer technology also enables researchers to piece together the possible design of the many buildings that occupied the presidio grounds.

Contrary to legend, it wasn't Serra but expedition engineer Miguel Constansó who selected the site for the presidio. It was located near the Kumeyaay village of Cosoy, a settlement that occupied several locations within a mile or two of Presidio Hill. After the 1775 attack on the relocated mission, a 300-foot defensive wall on each side was built around the presidio. Within the walls were the commandant's house, homes for married soldiers, settlers and a post chaplain, a chapel, warehouses, barracks and a guardhouse-gatehouse. In 1782, outer yards were added along with a new outer wall.

Spanish soldiers farmed the flat land in present-day Old Town on plots given as compensation for their service. By 1818, the presidio was falling into disrepair, its maintenance hampered by the lack of funds and cessation of supply deliveries from Mexico, then in a state of rebellion against Spain. Beginning in the 1820s, when the presidio population soared from about 200 to nearly 500, soldiers and their families sought extra living space by erecting permanent homes in the Old Town area.

It's worth noting that while this was a Spanish outpost, the majority of residents were not natives of Spain or perhaps not even of European extraction. They included Filipinos, Chinese, Indians from India, African-Hispanics and American Indians. By 1835, the presidio was all but abandoned. As Old Town residents salvaged building materials, the adobe structure melted away into lumps of mud, burying artifacts that would be unearthed a century later.

In 1781, the presidio was the headquarters for a district that included most of Southern California, stretching north to Santa Monica and the San Bernardino Mountains, east to the Colorado River and south about 50 miles to the boundary between Franciscan and Dominican California. But the whole region was lightly defended and represented a tempting target for foreign powers. That became clear in late-1793, when British navigator George Vancouver sailed into San Diego Bay, leading the first non-Spanish ships known to anchor in port. Based on his observations during a 10-day stay, Vancouver described the presidio settlement as "dreary and lonesome" surrounded by "barren uncultivated country." He wrote:

The death of Father Luís Jayme on the night of November 4, 1775, is depicted in this woodcut from Zephyrin Engelhardt's *San Diego Mission*.

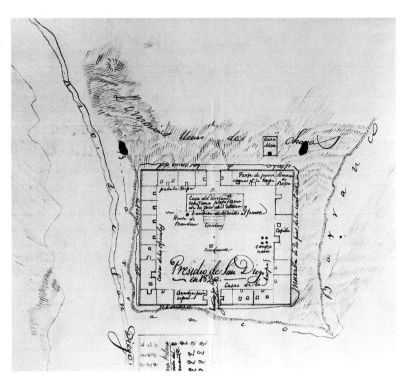

This map of the royal presidio of San Diego, dated about 1820, was discovered in 1982 by a researcher, Rev. Harry Morrison, in the Edward Vischer Papers at the Bancroft Library, Berkeley, California. *Courtesy The Bancroft Library*

"The Spaniards in their missions and presidios, being the two principal distinctions of Spanish inhabitants, lead a confined, and in most respects a very indolent life; the religious part of the society within a cloister, the military in barracks. The last mentioned order do nothing, in the strictest sense of the expression; for they neither till, sow nor reap, but wholly depend upon the labor of the inhabitants of the missions and pueblos for their subsistence, and the common necessities of life...

"With little difficulty San Diego might also be rendered a place of considerable strength, by establishing a small force at the entrance of the port; where, at this time, there were neither works, guns, houses nor other habitations nearer than the presidio, which is at the distance of at least five miles from the port, and where they have only three small pieces of brass cannon.

"Such is the condition of this country as it respects its internal security, and external defense; but why such an extent of territory should have been thus subjugated, and after all the expense and labor that has been bestowed upon its colonization turned to no account whatever, is a mystery in the science of state policy not easily to be explained."

In the wake of Vancouver's trip, the Spanish authorities completed Fort Guijarros (Ballast Point) in 1797 to serve as a defense post at the mouth of the bay for the next 40 years. It remains another archaeological site of great interest and receives special protection from the Navy, which occupies the southern end of Point Loma and encompasses the old fort.

"BATTLE OF SAN DIEGO BAY"

Trade, not military threats, unnerved Spanish California. Officially, San Diego was barred to foreigners. But lacking sufficient supplies, the locals winked at this ban and found ways to skirt official sanctions. In August 1800, the first American ship, the 104-ton Boston brigantine *Betsy* sailed into port. Captain Charles Winship claimed a need for wood and water. But the local commandant suspected illicit trade. The 240-ton *Enterprise* arrived shortly thereafter and was required to anchor about three miles from the harbor and transfer provisions by small boat. In 1803 the 180-ton *Alexander* anchored in port and was discovered to be carrying nearly 500 contraband otter furs. Then came the *Lelia Byrd*.

The 175-ton brigantine was owned by two Salem, Massachusetts, traders, William Shaler and Richard J. Cleveland. They sailed into San Diego hoping to buy 1,600 otter skins. But the commandant of the presidio, Lieutenant Manuel Rodríguez, posted guards on board and gave permission for the Americans to purchase provisions only. On the night of March 21, 1803, two skiffs left the ship to obtain otter skins from willing Spanish soldiers. One returned while the other was captured, its three sailors bound and left on the beach. The next morning,

Cleveland and four other men rescued the prisoners and prepared to depart. The wind was light and the *Lelia Byrd* sailed slowly past Fort Guijarros as shots were fired from the fort's six nine-pound cannons. After 45 minutes of receiving discharges from shore, Cleveland ordered fire returned. "At the first broadside, (we) saw numbers, probably of those who came to see the fun, scampering away up the hill at the back of the fort," Cleveland reported. "Our second broadside seemed to have caused the complete abandonment of their guns, as none were fired afterwards."

In what San Diego historian Richard F. Pourade called the "golden age of the California missions," the Mission San Diego developed into a relatively prosperous estate. The San Diego mission district counted 6,000 head of cattle and 7,000 sheep. There were vineyards, citrus orchards and olive trees. It also was the headquarters of a religious district encompassing the missions of San Diego, San Luís Rey, San Gabriel, San Juan Capistrano, San Luís Obispo and the Dominican mission of San Miguel 55 miles below San Diego in Baja California. There also were four sub-missions or *asistencias* serving outlying Indian populations: San Antonio de Pala (1810) on the upper San Luís Rey River; San Ysidro (1818) north of the Tijuana River; Santa Ysabel (circa 1820) outside Julian; and Las Flores (1823) on the present-day Camp Pendleton Marine Corps base.

In response to a drought, work began in 1807 on California's first aqueduct and dam. The original waterworks included a 244-foot-long dam, 13 feet thick and 13 feet high. The aqueduct ran six miles down to the mission fields. The first three miles were lined in tile. The rest consisted of a dirt ditch just above the bed of the San Diego River. The dam is still visible at Mission Trails Regional Park.

Outside the lands controlled by the mission, the military maintained a grazing ranch at Rancho del Rey (Rancho de la Nación during the Mexican period and National City in the American era). El Cajon Valley was an agricultural center, and cattle and sheep grazed at what are today Warner's Ranch, Rancho Bernardo, Ramona, San Pasqual Valley and Poway.

INDEPENDENT MEXICO

In 1810, as Napoleon was occupying Spain, Mexican nationalist Miguel Hidalgo y Costilla uttered the "grito [cry] de independencia." The supply ships no longer made their annual runs from San Blas and the soldiers went unpaid. After receiving letters reporting the outbreak of revolution in 1811, the San Diego commandant moved to strengthen the port defenses at Fort Guijarros and the presidio. But California remained largely uninvolved in events in Mexico, and the locals generally remained loyal to the crown.

The closest California came to direct involvement in the war of independence was a French intervention in 1818 led by Captain Hippolyte de Bouchard. He commanded two ships carrying 366

Lelia Byrd and the "Battle of San Diego Bay," 1803.
Painting by Jerry MacMullen Courtesy San Diego Maritime Museum

A section of the aqueduct below Mission Dam, photographed in 1929. The tile aqueduct hugged the walls of the Mission Gorge on its way to the mission.
Courtesy San Diego Historical Society

men, including several American privateers. Sailing from the independent kingdom of Hawaii, Bouchard appeared off Monterey and sacked the town around the mission at San Juan Capistrano. Santiago Argüello led 30 men from San Diego to San Juan Capistrano's defense but was unable to stop the Frenchman, who sailed away without threatening San Diego.

Mexico won its independence from Spain on September 21, 1821, but word did not reach California until the following spring. The official handover of power was accomplished April 11, 1822, by means of an oath administered to officials in Monterey; José María Estudillo, acting commandant of the presidio, represented San Diego. At day's end, guns were fired, music played and fireworks exploded. A comparable ceremony occurred in San Diego nine days later. To select California's deputy to the new Mexican *Cortés* or congress, five electors were chosen to represent the presidial districts plus one from the Los Angeles pueblo. The mission Indians also were entitled to a voice in naming the local representative. San Diego's elector was Ignacio Lopez, who represented both the presidio and local missions.

About this time, the estimated 250 soldiers and their families within the presidio compound began moving into adobe homes built at the foot of Presidio Hill. Commandant Francisco María Ruíz built the first known adobe outside the presidio in 1821. (It was restored in the 1920s to serve as the golf shop for the Presidio Hills Golf Course; it is California Registered Historical Landmark 74.) Ruíz's long service was rewarded when he received the first rancho land grant, Santa María de Los Peñasquitos, from California Governor Luís Argüello in 1823.

Other presidio residents also set up farms and orchards, but those who planted crops along the San Diego River lost everything in 1821 when a disastrous flood filled the banks from north to south. This 1821 flood may have been the first warning that, despite light rainfall, floods could strike periodically. It also was this flood that shifted the course of the San Diego River, causing it to empty into San Diego Bay rather than False (Mission) Bay. The subsequent silting threatened to make the bay unnavigable until levees were built in the 1850s to shift the river back to within its original banks.

Trade and Yankees

With the change of flags, outside trade opened up for California and San Diego. Between 1820 and 1827, at least 17 ships — British, American, French and Russian — stopped in port to pick up cowhides for transport to Boston and shoemaking factories. One of these vessels was *Le Héroes*, captained by Auguste Bernard Duhuat-Cilly. He praised the harbor as "without doubt the best in all California, and much preferable for the safety of vessels to the immense harbor at San Francisco, whose great extent leaves it too much exposed to winds and waves." As for the San Diego presidio and Old Town settlement of adobe houses, Duhaut-Cilly had a different view:

> A sad place is the presidio of San Diego, the saddest of all that we had visited in California, except San Pedro. It is built on the slope of an arid hill and has no regular form. It is a shapeless mass of houses, all the more gloomy because of the dark color of the bricks of which they are rudely constructed. Under the presidio on a sandy plain are seen 30 or 40 scattered houses of poor appearance and a few gardens badly cultivated.

The first American to reach San Diego overland was a mountain man, Jedediah S. Smith. Leaving northern Utah in August 1826, he arrived in San Diego in December. Suspicious of all foreigners, Governor José María Echeandía (1825-31) considered Smith a spy and expelled him on the American vessel *Courier*. The next American visitor, James O. Pattie, arrived in March 1828 after a five-month trek through the southwest desert. Pattie, Pattie's father, Sylvester, and six others were thrown into the presidio jail for up to eight months . The elder Pattie died in prison, while the younger Pattie was released after promising to vaccinate Californians against smallpox up and down the coast.

Missions Secularized

The closing of this era in San Diego history coincides with the secularization of the missions. As early as 1813, the Spanish Cortés had passed a law that after 10 years in existence, the missions must be closed. The religious functions were to be taken over by parish priests and the mission lands were to revert to Indian control. But California authorities did not hear of this law until 1821 and by then, the Spanish era was ending. Even if they wanted to obey the law, there were no priests to replace the Franciscan friars.

The mission represented the most prosperous economic unit in San Diego, its agricultural output sustaining the presidio and many residents. Once Mexico gained control, it began taxing the missions and Echeandía adopted a policy in 1826 that effectively freed the Indians from maintaining any allegiance to the missions. In August 1833, the Mexican government ordered secularization to proceed. San Diego's mission was transferred September 20, 1834, to the control of a commissioner, Juan José Rocha and San Luis Rey was turned over to Captain Pablo de la Portilla. Their lands and goods were divided according to law and San Diego gained self-governing pueblo status as of January 1, 1835.

Opinions differ with time and perspective on the role the missions played in San Diego and California history from 1769 to 1835. They provided an inexpensive means for Spain to extend its control over its distant province. They brought Christianity to native peoples and the benefits of civilization, at least from the European point of view. Along with the presidios and pueblos, they formed the basis for most of California's modern-day cities and towns. El Camino Real, the royal road, was the first state "highway." And the architectural style of the missions ultimately was the inspiration for California's enduring love-affair with Spanish Colonial building designs. The red-tile roofs, arcades, patios, white stucco walls and indoor-outdoor lifestyles all owe their origins to mission design and construction methods.

The downside was that the Spanish soldiers and friars introduced European diseases that wiped out about half the native California population of about 300,000 in 75 years. The missionaries succeeded in teaching only a few of the Indians to support themselves through modern agricultural techniques. The conversion from local beliefs to Christianity, while a lasting religion for many, suppressed, if not crushed, the native culture. A people that had occupied the land for thousands of years lost their foothold almost overnight. But the Spanish and Mexican conquerors did not retain control for long. They were about to be swept aside by American traders, settlers, soldiers and adventurers.

This romanticized image of Presidio Hill depicts the "Burial of Mr. Pattie," showing James Pattie at the grave of his father, Sylvester, surrounded by richly dressed soldiers with fanciful castle walls and turrets in the background. The picture was published in *The Personal Narrative of James O. Pattie of Kentucky* in 1833.

TWO

CHAPTER TWO

Guajome, home of the late Col. Cave J. Couts, 4 miles east of the Mission San Luis Rey. Courtesy San Diego Historical Society

PARADISE UNDER NEW MANAGEMENT

Richard Henry Dana Jr. put San Diego on the map for many Americans. Until 1840, the west coast was a fuzzy, faraway province of Spain, then Mexico. But in his very successful memoir, *Two Years Before the Mast*, Dana painted a vivid mental picture of California as seen and lived through the eyes of a Harvard junior classman in 1834-36. Together with an epilogue covering his return 24 years later, the book has remained in print ever since. It represents a fascinating look at life at sea — the floggings, boredom, excitement and adventure of it all. The 20 chapters dealing with California gave the first popular, detailed description of towns, missions and ranchos.

Dana was born August 1, 1815 to Ruth and Richard Henry Dana Sr. When Mrs. Dana died in 1822, her husband, a lawyer, was left with four young children. Richard Jr., then not quite 7, was a "little, rosy-faced, sturdy boy," who endured the strict, punishment-heavy grammar school typical of the 1820s, according to Oliver Wendell Holmes. Entering Harvard in July 1831, he excelled in mathematics but was suspended for six months when his class rebelled over a minor incident. He completed his sophomore year and was entering his junior year in 1833 when he contracted measles. His eyes were so weakened that he could not read a printed page without pain. He left school after a few months and resolved to go to sea, hoping the marine air and physical activity would restore his health.

"I undertook this journey because it was difficult to get any other that would be long enough, at that time, and because California was represented to be a very healthy coast, with a fine climate, and plenty of hard work for the sailors," Dana wrote. (This may be the first time a visitor to California commented on its climate and health-restoring qualities.) Two weeks after his 19th birthday in August 1834, Dana shipped aboard the 87-foot, 181-ton brig *Pilgrim* from Boston. Arriving off San Diego in mid-March 1835, he wrote:

"We sailed leisurely down the coast [from San Pedro] before a light fair wind, keeping the land well aboard, and saw two other missions, looking like blocks of white plaster, shining in the distance; one of which, situated on the top of a high hill, was San Juan Capistrano, under which vessels sometimes come to anchor in the summer season, and take off hides. At sunset on the second day we had a large and well-wooded headland [Point Loma] directly before us, behind which lay the little harbor of San Diego. We were becalmed off this point all night; but the next morning, which was Saturday, the 14th of March, having a good breeze, we stood round the point, and, hauling out

1835-1867

As a 20-year-old seaman, Richard Henry Dana Jr. (1815-82) spent the summer of 1835 curing hides at the port of San Diego. Dana gave only mixed reviews to the region and its people, though he would allow, "for landing and taking hides, San Diego is decidedly the best place in California." Dana's published memoir, *Two Years Before the Mast*, introduced California and San Diego to the nation.
Courtesy San Diego Historical Society

(Photo on page 36) "The Battle of San Diego Bay." In March 1803, the brig *Lelia Byrd* traded cannon fire with Fort Guijarros as it slowly sailed out of the bay. *Oil by Jerry MacMullen. Courtesy San Diego Maritime Museum*

wind, brought the little harbor, which is rather the outlet of a small river, right before us. Everyone was desirous to get a view of the new place. A chain of high hills, beginning at the point (which was on our larboard [port] hand coming in) protecting the harbor on the north and west, and ran off into the interior, as far as the eye could reach. On the other sides the land was low and green, but without trees. The entrance is so narrow as to admit but one vessel at a time, the current swift, and the channel runs so near to a low stony point that the ship's sides appeared almost to touch it.

"There was no town in sight, but on the smooth sand beach, abreast, and within a cable's length of which three vessels lay moored, were four large houses, built of rough boards and looking like the great barns in which ice is stored on the borders of the large ponds near Boston, with piles of hides standing round them, and men in red shirts and large straw hats walking in and out of the doors. These were the hide houses."

The hide trade between Boston and California began in 1822 with the arrival of the *Sachem* under Captain Henry Gyzelaar. Driven by the need for cheap leather, merchants worked out arrangements to collect hides up and down the coast and to transport them to storage houses in San Diego, the first one of which was built in 1829 just north of Fort Guijarros (Ballast Point) at a place called La Playa. Cattle were slaughtered between July and October, their carcasses often left to rot, with the best 200 pounds salvaged for drying. The hides were soaked in vats of brine for up to four days, spread on the beach to dry, hung on ropes and beaten to remove dust and sand. A typical ship carried between 25,000 and 50,000 hides; ultimately, about 5 million hides were exported from California until the mid-1840s. The *Pilgrim's* assignment was to transport hides from other stops in California to San Diego, where they were cured before shipment back to Boston.

These "California banknotes" were traded for clothes, farming equipment, kitchen utensils, coffee, tea and other foreign foodstuffs — in other words, virtually everything needed in industry-poor California. In addition to hides, between 75 and 100 pounds of beef fat per animal was rendered into tallow and cooled to 500- to 1,000-pound blocks. As many as 125,000 tons of tallow was exported from California, much of it to Peru for making candles.

It was now Sunday and Dana and a buddy named Simpson spent their free day on horseback:

"The first place we went to was the old ruinous presidio, which stands on a rising ground near the village, which it overlooks. It is built in the form of an open square, like all the other presidios, and was in a most ruinous state, with the exception of one side, in which the commandant lived, with his family. There they had only two guns, one of which was spiked, and the other had no carriage.

"Twelve half-clothed and half-starved-looking fellows composed the garrison; and they, it was said, had not a musket apiece. The small settlement lay directly below the fort, composed of about 40 dark brown-looking huts, or houses, and three or four larger ones whitewashed, which belonged to the *gente de razon* [civilized people]. This town is not more than half as large as Monterey or Santa Barbara, and has little or no business.

"From the presidio we rode off in the direction of the mission, which we were told was three miles distant. The country was rather sandy, and there was nothing for miles which could be called a tree, but the grass grew green and rank; there were many bushes and thickets, and the soil is said to be good. After a pleasant ride of a couple of miles, we saw the white walls of the mission, and, fording a small stream, we came directly before it ... Coming into the village [of Old Town after lunch at the mission], we found things looking very lively. The Indians, who always have a holiday on Sunday, were engaged at playing a kind of running game of ball on a level piece of ground near the houses. The old ones sat down in a ring, looking on, while the young ones — men, boys and girls — were chasing the ball and throwing it with all their might."

On Monday, Dana got down to business, unloading 3,500 hides and depositing them in the warehouse reserved for the *Pilgrim's* parent shipping company. After nearly two weeks, the ship sailed off to San Pedro and Santa Barbara. On its return to San Diego in early-May, Dana volunteered to stay behind for the next four months to cure the hides. This gave him time to learn the language, history and local customs. He called the provincial government "an arbitrary democracy" and the system of justice hardly more than "will and fear."

Dana was not impressed with San Diegans' industriousness:

"The men are thriftless, proud, extravagant and very much given to gaming; and the women have but little education, and a good deal of beauty, and their morality, of course, is none of the best; yet the instances of infidelity are much less frequent than one would at first suppose." Of the poor Indians, very little care is taken. The priests, indeed at the missions, are said to keep them very strictly, and some rules are usually made by the alcaldes [mayors] to punish their misconduct; yet it all amounts to but little.

A scene from the California hide trade of the 1830s. From *Touring Topics*, September 1931. *Painting by Carl Oscar Berg*

"Such are the people who inhabit a country embracing four or five hundred miles of seacoast, with several good harbors, with fine forests in the north; the waters filled with fish and the plains covered with thousands of herds of cattle; blessed with a climate, than which there can be no better in the world; free from all manner of diseases, whether epidemic or endemic; and with a soil in which corn yields from 70-to 80-fold. In the hands of an enterprising people, what a country this might be, we are ready to say. Yet how long would a people remain so, in such a country? The Americans (as those from the United States are called) and Englishmen, who are fast filling up the principal towns, and getting the trade into their hands, are indeed more industrious and effective than the Mexicans; yet their children are brought up Mexicans in most respects, and if the 'California fever' [laziness] spares the first generation, it is likely to attack the second."

In September 1835, Dana joined the crew of the *Alert*, which sailed to San Pedro and Santa Barbara and returned to San Diego several times before finally heading back, fully loaded with hides and other cargo, to Boston on May 8, 1836.

Cattle as King

In Dana's San Diego, the cattle rancher was king. Mexican independence led to loosened trade regulations in California and the demand for hides gave value to the growing herds of mission cattle. In turn, the land on which the cattle grazed became valuable, and that prompted the rise of the Mexican land grant. From 1769 to 1798, the Mission San Diego herd grew to about 10,000 head and peaked at about 30,000 by 1830; the cattle grazed over some 1,500 square miles. The increase was facilitated by a wetter-than-normal climate and minimal slaughter among mission herds.

Theoretically, Spanish California was designed to develop in two directions. First, the pueblos were to be outposts for Spanish civilians and retired soldiers. Second, the missions were to hold the surrounding lands in trust for the Indians until they became "civilized" and could regain ownership. But after more than 60 years of mission work the Indians never experienced such a devolution of power. The San Diego pueblo also did not develop as intended. To reduce pressure on the lightly populated Mission San Diego to produce food for the presidio, retired soldiers generally were required to move to Los Angeles to farm. This shift partly explains Los Angeles' rapid growth over San Diego during the Spanish and Mexican periods — a relationship that has never changed.

As Mexico began its drive for independence in 1810, payments stopped for the San Diego presidio's soldiers. Understandably, they sought compensation in the form of California land, especially the rich farmlands controlled by the missions. Initially, only the king could grant land to individuals and pueblos. In 1786, the provincial governor received power to grant private tracts of up to three square leagues outside the pueblos and mission holdings. (A square league was equal to 4,439 acres.) It was during the Mexican period from 1822 to 1846 that most land grants were made. Grantees merely had to supply a rough map or *diseño* and written description in the application for a rancho. The U.S. Board of Land Commissioners and subsequent court rulings ultimately confirmed 33 land grants totaling 606,771 acres (948 square miles) in San Diego. They ranged from the 133,441-acre Santa Margarita y Las Flores to the 28.4-acre Cañada de los Coches.

By the time the United States seized California in 1846, many of the original grants had been transferred to other parties. Grantees and their successors had to wait many years until they knew if their holdings were secure. The final rulings did not come until 1876. It was at that time that President Ulysses S. Grant set aside other lands as the area's first Indian reservations. The January 7, 1876, executive order authorized reservations at Portrero, Cahuilla, Capitán Grande, Santa Ysabel (including Mesa Grande), Pala, Agua Caliente, Sycuan, Maja and Cosmet.

Other grants and squatter ranchos that were never confirmed by U.S. authorities fell into other hands over the years. This was partly due to the unsettled conditions in San Diego's back country, where Indians frequently threatened the sparsely populated and undefended ranchos into the 1830s. Owners often vacated their lands and returned to Old Town. In the summer of 1839, for example, about 300 Indians began attacking ranches near Otay Ranch, prompting the ranch's owner, Santiago Argüello to order his Belgian-born employee Agustin Janssens to flee. "I refused to go until I could collect and take with me whatever I could move," Janssens said in his memoirs. "What I was unable to take I gave to various poor neighbors."

In 1823, Francisco María Ruíz received the first Mexican land grant in San Diego, Rancho de los Peñasquitos. Ruíz was the longest serving presidio commandant in various periods from 1806 to 1827. He received one square league in a long-narrow strip along Peñasquitos Canyon 20 miles north of Old Town. It was later enlarged to two square leagues in 1834 and confirmed in 1867 at 8,486 acres. Like many rancheros, Ruíz lived in town, visiting his ranch periodically. His adobe ranch house has been restored in Los Peñasquitos Canyon Preserve. In 1837, two years before his death at age 85, he transferred ownership to his grandnephew, Francisco María Alvarado.

Days of the Dons

Looking back a century later, San Diego historian Richard F. Pourade painted an idyllic view of the rancho period, roughly 1830-1860: "The warm sun of California lighted the flowering of a pastoral scene that would leave its magic and legends for generations yet to come. For 400 miles, from San Diego to Monterey, California became a vast, unfenced grazing ground. Silver ornaments from Mexico grew heavier on trappings of the horses which the landed dons rode through the seas of wild mustard which drowned the hills in blazing yellow. They built rambling houses and yet maintained their homes in the towns, and all doors were open to every visitor."

William Heath Davis in his *Seventy-Five Years in California* described a society of idle wealth: "They wore long vests, with filigree buttons of gold or silver, while those of more ordinary means had them of brass... Their spurs were inlaid with gold and silver, and the straps of the spurs worked with silver and gold thread. When thus mounted and fully equipped, these men presented a magnificent appearance, especially on the feast days of the saints, which were celebrated at the missions. Then they were arrayed in their finest and most costly habiliments."

But records clearly show that the "days of the dons" were enjoyed by only a small elite with

Don Juan Bandini (1800-1859), shown here with his daughter Margarita in 1856, came to California from his native Peru in 1822. In San Diego he was a prominent ranchero, political leader and supporter of the U.S. occupation of California. *Courtesy San Diego Historical Society*

Cave Johnson Couts (1821-1874), shown here (fifth from left) with family and friends at Rancho Guajome in the 1860s. Couts was a Tennessee-born West Pointer, who came to California as a lieutenant of Dragoons in the U.S.-Mexican War. Resigning from the army, he married Ysidora Bandini, the daughter of Don Juan Bandini, and presided over Guajome, a wedding gift from his brother-in-law, the rich Los Angeleño, Abel Stearns.
Courtesy San Diego Historical Society

names like Carrillo, Estudillo, Bandini, Pico and Argüello. This landed gentry operated within a very small population of no more than 800, not counting the Indians who dwelled beyond the mission, pueblo and presidio properties. Residents from Spain or descendants of Spaniards were far outnumbered by immigrants with Asian, African and mixed blood. The pre-American period has been mythologized and sanitized to such an extent that the truth of what San Diego looked like before 1850 represents something of a shock, not resembling at all the lushly landscaped, immaculately maintained reconstruction at Old Town San Diego State Historic Park.

For a more authentic view, see Rancho Guajome in Oceanside, a county-owned historic site restored in the 1990s. Physically, the 12,000-square-foot ranch house is impressive: 22-inch adobe walls and massive redwood beams; space for a blacksmith's shop, bakery, chapel and guest or servants' quarters. While urban development encroached on the original land grant, the setting is rural enough to give visitors an idea of how isolated ranch life was 150 years ago. In 1845 Pío Pico, the last of the Mexican governors of California, granted 2,219-acre Rancho Guajome to two former Indian residents of nearby Mission San Luís Rey. Shortly afterwards, Abel Stearns, a wealthy Los Angeles rancher and merchant, bought the property for $550. Stearns, who had married his San Diego partner Juan Lorenzo Bandini's daughter, Arcadia, in 1841, used Guajome for cattle grazing.

In 1851, Stearns gave Guajome to Arcadia's sister, Ysidora, when she married U.S. Army Lieutenant Cave Johnson Couts. Born in Tennessee in 1821 and a graduate of West Point in 1843, Couts was the military escort to the boundary-setting commission that was established to survey the dividing line between the United States and Mexico following the Mexican-American War. He also oversaw the preparation of the first city subdivision map and gave Old Town its street names (Juan Street honors his father-in-law); represented San Diego in the 1849 state constitutional convention; helped suppress an Indian revolt in 1851; and served in numerous local offices. His uncle, Cave Johnson, was President James K. Polk's postmaster general who authorized the first prepaid and self-adhesive postage stamps.

An engineer, Couts quickly took charge of his rancho, designing the building to incorporate both traditional Spanish-Mexican and American features. Largely completed by 1855, the adobe-brick house's beams and framing were of clear redwood lumber from San Francisco. Couts turned from cattle ranching to farming and was one of the first San Diegans to plant orange trees. El Camino Real passed by Rancho Guajome, and the Couts home played host to numerous visitors, including President Abraham Lincoln's Secretary of State William Seward. Historian Hubert Howe Bancroft stopped by in 1874 as he researched his multivolume California history project. Weddings took place in the courtyard, and Couts stocked wine and champagne in the cellar beneath the chapel for the numerous fiestas and dinner parties. Overcoming early financial setbacks, Couts accumulated about

20,000 acres in real estate holdings, including the neighboring Rancho Buena Vista and Rancho Los Vallecitos de San Marcos.

After Couts' death in 1874, his widow Ysidora remained in residence at Guajome until her death in 1897. Her legendary graciousness escaped her in 1882, when Helen Hunt Jackson, a special U.S. commissioner, came to investigate Indian living conditions. Jackson was locked in her room until her departure by train. Her subsequent novel, *Ramona*, generated a heightened sympathy for American Indians. By then, most Indians had retreated from the coast and resumed their semi-nomadic existence. Nevertheless, disease wiped out most of the population in the second half of the 19th century.

Self-Government, Briefly

Although San Diego was the first place in California settled by the Spaniards, it grew so slowly that presidio commandants remained in charge of civil and military affairs. Finally, on February 22, 1833, six residents petitioned Governor José Figueroa to end military rule and create a self-governing pueblo in recognition of the Old Town settlement outside the presidio. The petitioners complained about capricious judgments by the commandant, Santiago Argüello: "In this port one has to submit himself, his fate, fortune and perhaps existence, to the caprice of a military judge, who being able to misuse his power, it is always easy for him to evade any complaint which they might want to make of his conduct… and there is no other formula than the imperious words of 'I command it.'" On May 4, 1834, Figueroa declared that San Diego's non-Indian population of 432 was large enough to qualify for pueblo status.

There would be an *ayuntamiento* or town council, composed of an *alcalde* or mayor and two *regidores* or aldermen and a *síndico procurador* or city attorney. At an election December 18, 1834, 13 electors were chosen to select the first four local officials to serve one-year terms. Three days later, the electors picked Juan María Osuna as alcalde, Juan Bautista Alvarado and Juan María Marron as aldermen and, as city attorney, Henry D. Fitch, a former American sea captain. José Mier y Terán was named secretary at $20 per month. The officials took office officially January 1, 1835. However, in 1837, a move to centralize authority throughout Mexico required pueblos with fewer than 1,000 residents to be governed by appointed *jueces de paz* (justices of the peace). Lacking the sufficient number, San Diego lost its self-governing status after only three years.

San Diego's lack of growth was reflected in the observations recorded by Alfred Robinson on his visit in 1840: "Here everything was prostrated — the presidio ruined, the mission depopulated, the town almost deserted and its few inhabitants miserably poor. It had changed. From being once the life of and the most important place in California, it was now become the gloomiest and the most desolate."

These local political developments occurred against a backdrop of increasing tension between northern and Southern California and between California and Mexico City. San Diegans were at the forefront of a revolt in 1831 against Colonel Manuel Victoria, who was appointed to succeed Governor José María Echeandía. Victoria countermanded Echeandía's secularization of the missions, thus thwarting private efforts to seize the mission properties for personal gain. Victoria also drew opposition for his refusal to convene the territorial *diputación* (assembly) and his capricious administration of justice. Led by

Henry Delano Fitch (1799-1849) came to California from Massachusetts in 1826 as a sea captain. In San Diego he became the town's most successful merchant and political leader. *Courtesy San Diego Historical Society*

San Diegans José Antonio Carrillo, Pío Pico and Juan Bandini, 150 men defeated Victoria and his force of 30 at Los Angeles on December 5, 1831.

Echeandía became provisional governor for the south and his former secretary, Agustín Zamorano, provisional governor for the north. This arrangement lasted until José Figueroa took over on January 5, 1833. In 1836-37, the northerners revolted against Figueroa's successor, Colonel Mariano Chico, and chose as governor Juan Bautista de Alvarado (not the same Alvarado as the San Diegan of the same name). Alvarado favored Alta California's independence from Mexico, or at least until local control could be ensured. San Diegans now favored continued ties to Mexico and gained support from the rest of Southern California. Within a few months, Alvarado abandoned his ambitions for independence and the revolt ended.

Pío Pico, Alta Califonia's last Mexican governor, (1801-94) governed the province for 16 months, surrendering his office to American control in July 1846. *Courtesy San Diego Historical Society*

Mexican-American War

These internal struggles were soon overshadowed by American designs on California. The U.S. had long coveted the Pacific province. President Thomas Jefferson envisioned an American empire stretching from the Atlantic and Pacific. His acquisition of the Louisiana territory in 1803 represented the first step toward achieving what later was referred to as the young nation's "manifest destiny."

In 1822, the first U.S. ambassador to Mexico, Joel R. Poinsett (who introduced the poinsettia plant to American horticulturists), proposed transferring Texas, New Mexico, California and other northern Mexican territory to the U.S. Seven years later, President Andrew Jackson offered to buy Texas alone for $5 million and in 1835 to acquire northern California above the 37th parallel, roughly north of Santa Cruz.

When Texas declared its independence from Mexico in 1836, Jackson urged the new republic the next year to claim California and its ports. In 1841, the Texas legislature endorsed annexing both Alta and Baja California along with the northern half of Mexico; Texas President Sam Houston vetoed the bill as inexpedient but still favored a greater Texas extending to the Pacific, from the tip of Baja California to the Columbia River.

In 1842, U.S. President John Tyler suggested trading California for Mexico's outstanding debt of about $3.25 million. U.S. Commodore Thomas ap Catesby Jones prematurely seized California on October 19, 1842, when he arrived in Monterey Bay aboard the *Cyane*. He believed war had broken out with Mexico or that Mexico had ceded California to Britain to satisfy a debt of £15 million. He dispatched Captain James Armstrong, commanding the *United States*, to demand the surrender of Alta and Baja California. Two days later, when he realized that neither event had occurred, Jones lowered the Stars and Stripes, withdrew his 150 seamen and ended the 30-hour occupation.

Meanwhile in San Diego, *Alert* Captain W.D. Phelps heard that Mexican troops were headed his way to seize American property and cargo. He had loaded half his cargo on board by the time he received word that Jones' "war" was over. There were Congressional investigations and apologies delivered all around. But as historian Hubert Howe Bancroft later observed, "It confirmed what it had never occurred to anybody to doubt, that California was an easy prey for any nation that had only Mexicans to contend with."

The Mexican-American War of 1846-48 broke out after Congress annexed Texas in March 1846. In California, American residents proclaimed the "Bear

Flag Republic" in Sonoma on June 14 (it lasted until July 7). On July 29, Captain Samuel F. DuPont sailed the *Cyane* into San Diego Bay and two officers proceeded to Old Town Plaza, where they raised the Stars and Stripes. Lieutenant John C. Frémont led his 165 "American Arabs of the West" cavalry battalion off the ship and, on August 8, left town to secure the rest of Southern California. When the *Cyane* also departed, San Diego was left virtually undefended.

Defeat of American troops outside Los Angeles in September opened up a chance for the Mexican Californios to retake the province for Mexico. They bested General Stephen Watts Kearny and his Army of the West at the Battle of San Pasqual on December 6, 1846, where American casualties numbered 22 dead and 18 wounded. The Californios suffered less than a dozen casualties and no deaths. Wrote assistant staff surgeon John S. Griffin, "This was an

General Stephen Watts Kearny (1794-1848) ably led the Army of the West to California in 1846, then lost nearly half his cavalrymen at the Battle of San Pasqual. *Courtesy Hans von Sachsen-Altenburg*

On July 29, 1846, the troops of John C. Frémont left the USS *Cyane* to secure the port of San Diego. *Painting by Carlton T. Chapman in 1913. Courtesy Joseph E. Jessop Collection, San Diego Maritime Museum*

A sketch by Army Lieutenant William H. Emory describes the bloody actions of December 6, 1846. *Courtesy San Diego Historical Society*

action where decidedly more courage than conduct was showed." Kearny and his surviving men retreated to "Mule Hill" (so-named because of the meals they made of their pack animals), just east of present-day Interstate 15 at Bear Valley Parkway overlooking Lake Hodges. But Kearny escaped utter defeat when the victors did not pursue Kearny's force. Alerted by Kit Carson in San Diego, Commodore Robert F. Stockton sent reinforcements to aid Kearny. The Battle of San Pasqual was the United States' worst setback in the war. But within a month, California was securely in U.S. hands after the surrender of Los Angeles and the signing of the Treaty of Cahuenga on January 13, 1847.

In American history, the war has been overshadowed by the Civil War of 1861-65. What is interesting in hindsight and of particular application to contemporary California is the antipathy and disdain many Americans held for Mexicans at the time. Blatantly racist statements appeared in the American press, including this in 1845 from John O'Sullivan, editor of *United States Magazine and Democratic Review*, who coined the term "manifest destiny":

"The Spanish-Indian-American populations of Mexico, Central America and South America afford the only receptacle capable of absorbing that [African-American] race whenever we shall be prepared to slough it off — to emancipate it from slavery, and (simultaneously necessary) to remove it from the midst of our own... Imbecile and distracted, [the] Mexican can never exert any real government authority over such a country [California]. The impotence of the one and the distance of the other must make the relation one of virtual independence... The Anglo-Saxon foot is already on its borders. Already the advance guard of the irresistible army of the Anglo-Saxon emigration has begun to pour down upon it, armed with the plough and the rifle, and marking its trail with schools and colleges, courts and representative halls, mills and meetinghouses."

In his message to Congress December 7, 1847, President James K. Polk defended his policy on California and Mexico in a similar tone: "It is manifest to all who have observed the actual condition of the Mexican government, for some years past and at present, that if these provinces should be retained by her she could not long continue to hold and govern them. Mexico is too feeble a power to govern these provinces, lying as they do at a distance of more than 1,000 miles from her capital; and if attempted to be retained by her they would constitute but for a short time even nominally a part of her dominions."

This dismissive view of Mexico persisted for many years after the war. In his 1908 *History of San Diego*, William E. Smythe said this about the Mexico's loss of its California province: "The soldiers and statesmen of Mexico, in their rule of a quarter of a century, had added practically nothing to the accomplishment of their Spanish predecessors. To a very large extent, they had squandered their time and energies in petty squabbles over personal rivalries...If commerce prospered to some extent under their rule, the fact was chiefly due to the enterprise of outsiders rather than to that of the Mexicans."

New Border, New Regime

Under the treaty of Guadalupe Hidalgo, signed February 2, 1848, Mexico ceded California and the rest of the Southwest to the United States, 1.2 million square miles, in exchange for $15 million. Although American negotiators had sought to acquire Baja California as well, the Mexican side resisted and the southern line was established "from a point on the coast of the Pacific Ocean one marine league [3.45 miles] due south of the southernmost point of the port of San Diego to the middle of the Rio Gila, where it unites with the Colorado." (The Spanish and Mexican boundary between Alta and Baja California had been somewhat farther south between Tijuana and Rosarito Beach.) This arbitrary dividing line split the Tijuana River Valley between the two countries. Its location continues to complicate environmental and law enforcement problems across the border today.

It didn't take long for Old Town San Diego to Americanize. The 350-member Mormon Battalion, which had left Council Bluffs, Iowa, in July 1846 to help secure California, arrived in San Diego on January 29, 1847, after a 2,000-mile march. Some 78 members camped in town for about six months under Captain Jesse D. Hunter (whose wife soon

San Diego in 1846, as sketched by Lt. William Emory. This is the earliest known drawing of San Diego, made just after American occupation. *Courtesy San Diego Historical Society*

delivered a child, Diego, apparently the first American citizen born in San Diego). "I think I whitewashed all San Diego," said battalion member Henry G. Boyle in his diary. "We did their blacksmithing, put up a bakery, made and repaired carts, and, in fine, did all we could to benefit ourselves as well as the citizens. We never had any trouble with [Mexican] Californians or Indians, nor they with us." They also burned some town records as fuel. To commemorate the Mormons' contributions, a bronze statue grouping was later placed in Presidio Park and the Mormon Battalion Memorial visitor center opened on Juan Street in 1972.

Although California gold had been found periodically during the Spanish and Mexican period, John Marshall's discovery on January 24, 1848, at

Sutter's Mill on the American River was the one that set off a huge rush of immigrants from around the world to California. Many passed through San Diego. "Men are deserting and going to the gold mines!" wrote San Diegan Cave Couts in his diary in December 1848. "If the government manages it properly, or luckily, it will be the richest nation on earth; if unluckily, California will prove an ulcer that will follow her to her long unhappy home. We will make our fortunes! Not a doubt of it! All is cut and dried!"

The Gold Rush brought so many people to California that Congress quickly granted statehood on September 9, 1850, an action that not only saved California from territorial status but also figured in saving the Union for another decade via the famous Compromise of 1850 that balanced the interests of slave and free states. Mexican Californians prominently participated in writing the state's constitution but they were outnumbered by American nationals.

The provisional legislature divided the state into 28 counties on February 2, 1850, with San Diego County containing 37,400 square miles, nearly 10 times its present size. At the April 1, 1850, county election, 137 votes were cast for county officers. A Court of Sessions was in charge until the Board of Supervisors was established in 1853. Agoston Haraszthy, a native of Hungary, was elected sheriff, but he later won greater fame for propagating wine grapes in the Napa Valley.

The Legislature also granted a charter to the newly incorporated city of San Diego and the June 16, 1850, election made Joshua H. Bean (brother of the famous frontier Judge Roy Bean) mayor. After only two years, the charter was revoked when the city went bankrupt; an elected board of trustees ruled for nearly 40 years, its actions requiring ratification by the Legislature.

In the interim period between Mexican rule and the city's incorporation, William Heath Davis attempted the first settlement on the bay. Encouraged by boundary surveyor Andrew B. Gray, Davis, a San Francisco merchant who had visited San Diego a number of times since his youth, bought 160 acres of pueblo land on March 18, 1850, for $2,304. The property was located south and west of today's intersection of Broadway and Front Street. Davis and his associates called their endeavor "New San Diego" and secured a new army barracks at what is now North Harbor Drive and Kettner Boulevard. Davis built a $60,000 warehouse and a 600-foot L-shaped wharf and planned the settlement around a public square, named for Spanish explorer Juan Pantoja, who had first charted San Diego Bay in 1782.

Davis imported several prefabricated houses from Portland, Maine, and supported the opening of two hotels, Pantoja House and the Hermitage. (In 1984, one of Davis' houses became the Gaslamp Quarter museum at Fourth and Island avenues.) But in 1851, a fire in San Francisco cost Davis $700,000 in losses and he reduced his activities in San Diego. In 1853 the wharf was damaged by a steamer and never repaired; soldiers burned the remains during the winter of 1861-62. Davis sued the government for damages but it took until 1885 before he accepted a token settlement of $6,000. "New Town" was a

William Heath Davis (1822-1909), a highly successful San Francisco merchant and landowner, tried and failed to build a city on the bay. What Davis called "New San Diego" became better known as "Davis' Folly."
Courtesy San Diego Historical Society

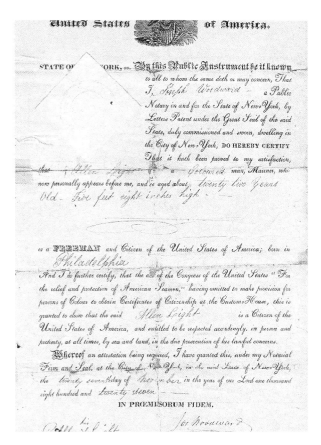

town no more. A second subdivision, 687-acre Middletown, a narrow strip between Old Town and New Town, was sold on May 27, 1850, to another syndicate, but it, too, failed to prosper for many years.

Real estate speculation took a back seat to the area's last major Indian revolt, which began at Jonathan Warner's ranch November 27, 1851. It was prompted by the county's attempt to collect taxes from Indian tribes. But the revolt failed and its leader, Antonio Garra, was executed by firing squad January 17, 1852.

Although the harborside city did not succeed, a U.S. coastal survey in 1851 warned that San Diego's promise as a thriving port was threatened by continued silting of San Diego Bay. In January 1853, Lieutenant George H. Derby of the U.S. Topographical Engineers arrived to build a dike to divert the San Diego River back into its old channel that emptied into False (Mission) Bay. The dike failed in 1855 and permanent flood control was not achieved for another 20 years. Derby achieved greater fame writing as the humorist John Phoenix in the *San Diego Herald,* the city's first newspaper which began publication May 29, 1851. (It ceased publication in 1860.) In another improvement following the American takeover, the Point Loma lighthouse was put into service in November 1855. Located several hundred feet above sea level, it was subjected to heavy fog and eventually was replaced in 1891 by a lighthouse at a lower level.

A port would be next to useless without a rail link east. The United States negotiated the 30,000-square-mile Gadsden Purchase with Mexico in 1853 to secure the Gila River Valley as part of a proposed southern rail route. And the next year, San Diegans incorporated the San Diego & Gila, Southern Pacific & Atlantic Railroad Company to promote the concept. Engineer Charles H. Poole surveyed a 200-mile route to Yuma, but the Civil War put the southern rail route on hold and it would be another 30 years before a direct link east was made.

"Sailor protection papers," shown here, identified Allen B. Light, an African-American mariner, as a freeman. The document was discovered in the adobe walls of Casa de Machado in Old Town in 1946. In the 1850s, Light operated a restaurant and saloon known as the San Diego House. *Courtesy San Diego Historical Society*

Army lieutenant, engineer and humorist George Horatio Derby (1823-61) came to San Diego in 1853, assigned the task of building a dike to rechannel the waters of the San Diego River. In a brief stint as editor of the *San Diego Herald*, the witty Derby adopted the pseudonym of John Phoenix and changed the paper's party alliance from Democrat to Whig. *Courtesy San Diego Historical Society*

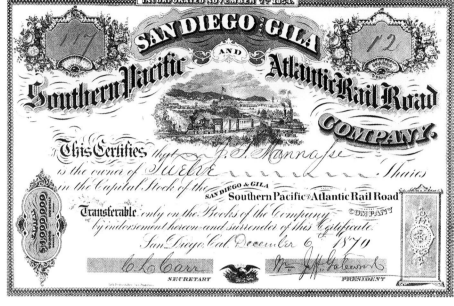

Worthless stock certificates were the legacy of the failed San Diego & Gila, Southern Pacific & Atlantic Railroad Company. *Courtesy San Diego Historical Society*

Louis Rose (1807-1886) namesake of Rose Canyon, Roseville, and other local landmarks was a Prussia-born Jew who came to San Diego in 1850, and quickly established himself as a land-owner and town builder. *Courtesy San Diego Historical Society*

San Diego's primary land-based communication line was an overland stage route, begun in 1857. The so-called "Jackass Mail" route, operated by James Birch, George H. Giddings and R.E. Doyle, featured 87 stops between San Diego and El Paso, Texas; the roundtrip fare was $400. Each passenger was advised to "provide himself with a Sharps' rifle, 100 cartridges, a navy-sized Colt's revolver and two pound balls, a belt and holster, knife and sheath; a pair of thick boots and woolen overshirts, a wide-awake hat, a cheap sack coat, a soldier's overcoat, one pair of blankets in summer and two in winter; a piece of India rubber cloth for blankets; a pair of thick drawers, and three or four towels. Such money as he takes should be in silver or gold." Competition from the Butterfield Great Overland Stage Line prompted the earlier line to close in 1861.

San Diego was populated not only by former Mexican citizens and European-Americans but also some African-Americans. Two of them, Allen B. Light and Richard Freeman, were partners in the San Diego House, an 1841 adobe on the south side of the Old Town plaza that they converted in 1847 to a store and bar. Light, who had deserted from Dana's ship, worked for the Mexican government to control otter poaching; his nickname was "Black Steward." Freeman served at one point as town sheriff.

Also indicative of the diversity of Old Town's small population (U.S. Census in 1850: 650 city, 798 county, not counting the Indian population) was Louis Rose, a German Jew. Within five months of his arrival in 1850, he obtained 80 acres between Old Town and La Playa (plus 260 acres added by 1856) and founded Roseville. He donated five acres in 1862 in the 2900-block of Fordham Street in the Midway area as the first Jewish cemetery and built a brickyard in Las Yeguas (Rose) Canyon. His other occupations included retailer, butcher, hotel owner, tanner and mattress manufacturer; he also served as city trustee, school board member and postmaster.

Also prominent among the newcomers after the American takeover was Thomas Whaley of New York. In 1851-52 he opened two stores, clearing $18,600 by 1853. In 1856 he built San Diego's first all-brick building as his residence and store. The county later rented it as a courthouse and in the 1950s the Historic Shrine Foundation bought and restored the Whaley House, operating it as a house museum.

One other colorful figure of the 1850s was William Walker, a Tennessee physician who in 1854 was reported to be in Tijuana attempting to win support for creating a slave state in Baja California. He was acquitted in San Francisco of violating American neutrality laws, but his intervention (referred to as "filibustering") dashed U.S. hopes for acquiring Baja California as part of the Gadsden Purchase. Instead the Mexican government began laying plans to populate the peninsula to ward off any further American designs on its territory.

With all the changes wrought by the American conquest, San Diego had hardly changed in the view of an old familiar figure. Richard Henry Dana, now aged 44, was conducting a round-the-world tour and visited San Diego in August 1859. "It certainly has not grown," he wrote in a new edition of his *Two Years Before the Mast*. "It is, like Santa Barbara, a Mexican town." He described the Mission San Diego's buildings as "unused and ruinous" and the mission's gardens as "only wild cactuses, willows and a few olive trees."

Instead of a hide and tallow trade, Dana found that San Diego's main industry was now whaling. The *San Diego Herald*, in its first mention of a whaling station at La Playa in February 1859, reported five whales yielding 150 barrels of oil worth $2,000. "If some means could be devised to prevent the whales from sinking," the *Herald* said, "three or four parties could do a good business during the season, by catching whales within 10 miles of the entrance to the harbor."

San Diego voted Whig in its first presidential election in 1852 and Democratic in the next four. It was a stronghold of Southern sympathies, especially after the South lost the Civil War. One story illustrates

Thomas Whaley (1823-1890) with his wife, Anna DeLaunay, and children. A successful merchant and civic leader, Whaley built Southern California's first two-story brick house, a building preserved today in Old Town San Diego. *Courtesy San Diego Historical Society*

Ephraim W. Morse (1823-1906) came to California as a Gold Rush 49er. Failing to strike it rich in the gold fields, Morse came to San Diego as a storekeeper where he prospered in business and local politics. *Courtesy San Diego Historical Society*

(Opposite page) This photograph taken in about 1867 by John Henfield is believed to be the earliest photograph of Old Town San Diego. *Courtesy San Diego Historical Society*

In 1865, a San Diego school teacher, Mary Chase Walker, scandalized the community and risked her job by sharing dinner with an African-American girl. The situation was resolved when she resigned to marry a school trustee, Ephraim W. Morse. *Courtesy San Diego Historical Society*

the temper of the times. Mary C. Walker, a native of New England, was recruited in 1865 to fill a teaching vacancy in Old Town. A few weeks after her arrival on July 5, she invited an African-American woman to dinner at Franklin House in Old Town. The rest of the restaurant cleared out, parents removed their children from her classes and there were immediate calls for her dismissal. "The Yankee school ma'am did not understand things clearly," historian William E. Smythe wrote more than 50 years later, "and made the matter worse by some unguarded remarks comparing the complexion of certain of the protesting Californians with that of her guest."

One school trustee was for her dismissal, as he could not justify spending tax funds operating an empty schoolhouse. Another trustee said he would rather throw the school funds in the bay "before I would dismiss the teacher to please these Copperheads." The third trustee, Ephraim W. Morse, settled the matter. Morse, a widower, had fallen in love with Walker and she resigned her job to become Mrs. Morse.

California did not figure significantly in the outcome of the Civil War, other than to cast a solid vote (except in San Diego) for Lincoln. San Diegans were preoccupied by drought, floods, earthquake, economic depression and a smallpox epidemic among Indians. Wrote A.A. Polhamus, editor of the *Wilmington Journal* after his 1865 visit:

"We found it [Old Town] as quiet as a village graveyard, and the appearance of many of the houses conveys the impression that they are sepulchers for the dead rather than for the living. San Diego was at one time much larger than it is now — between 300 and 400 inhabitants, four stores, three hotels, one church, one school with 53 pupils. The county contains 13,000 square miles yet has but one town, San Diego, one church, one school, no newspaper."

In the mid-19th century, San Diego saw great change and no change. The politics had switched from Mexican to American but the city's prospects appeared no more promising in 1865 than they did in 1835. San Francisco was booming as the state's financial and cultural capital. Los Angeles was the undisputed capital of the south. San Diegans, hanging on in dusty, flea-bitten Old Town were moping about, beset by naysayers and ne'er-do-wells. Into this backwater stepped a man who would change everything: Alonzo Erastus Horton.

THREE

CHAPTER THREE

"View from Shirley and DeWitt's Addition," oil on canvas by Frank L. Heath, 1888. This painting shows the western end of Mission Valley, looking southwest from the site of present-day University of San Diego. Presidio Hill can be seen on the left with Old Town below, and Point Loma in the distance separating San Diego Bay and False Bay (Mission Bay).
Courtesy San Diego Historical Society

Heaven on Earth: The Horton Period

The post-Civil War era of San Diego history belongs to Alonzo E. Horton. Others envisioned what San Diego could be. Horton acted to make his vision come true. Alonzo Erastus Horton was born in Union, Connecticut, on October 13, 1813, when James Madison was president and Napoleon Bonaparte ruled much of Europe. Alonzo, one of seven children born to Erastus and Tryphena Burleigh Horton, left home on the eve of his 21st birthday for Oswego, New York, then Milwaukee, where he traded in land and cattle. Widowed in 1846, he founded Hortonville, 20 miles from Oshkosh, Wisconsin, then moved to California, where he earned a fortune, not in gold but ice. He cut 312 tons of ice in El Dorado County and transported it to the mining towns. After several other ventures, he pulled up stakes in San Francisco and moved to San Diego. Many years later, he told an interviewer how a chance lecture in March 1867 changed his life and that of his adopted city:

"One night a friend said to me, 'There is going to be a big meeting tonight and it might be interesting for you to attend.' 'What is to be the subject of the talk?' I asked. 'It will be on the subject of what ports of the Pacific Coast will make great cities.' So I went, and the speaker commenced at Seattle and said it was going to be a big city; and then he came on down to San Francisco, which he said would be one of the biggest cities in California. Then he kept on down along the coast until he came to San Diego, and he said that San Diego was one of the healthiest places in the world, and that it had one of the best harbors in the world; that there was no better harbor.

"I could not sleep that night for thinking about San Diego, and at two o'clock in the morning I got up and looked on a map to see where San Diego was, and then went back to bed satisfied. In the morning I said to my wife, 'I am going to sell my goods and go to San Diego and build a city.' She said I talked like a wild man, that I could not dispose of my goods in six months. But I commenced that morning and made a large sale that day. The second day it was the same and I had to hire more helpers. By the third day I had five men hired, and in these three days I had sold out all my stock. It was not an auction sale, but just a run of business which seemed providential. Then my wife said she would not oppose me any longer, for she had always noticed when it was right for me to do anything, it always went right in my favor; and as this had gone that way, she believed it was right for me to do so."

1867-1909

"Alonzo E. Horton," c. 1885. This portrait of the "Father of New San Diego" by William Thurston Black was considered by contemporaries as being "beyond criticism, both as regards to likeness to the original and artistic workmanship." *Courtesy San Diego Historical Society*

(Photo on page 56) "View from the Dickinson House," c. 1890. This watercolor by Carl Christian Zeus views San Diego from the third story of the home Col. William Green Dickinson, manager of the San Diego Land and Town Company and a partner in the National City and Otay Railroad. The Coronado Islands, Hotel del Coronado and the Point Loma lighthouse can be seen in the distance. *Courtesy San Diego Historical Society*

Alonzo Horton and his wife Sarah Wilson Babe Horton. *Courtesy San Diego Historical Society*

(Far right) Bill of sale for Horton's purchase of city lands. *Courtesy San Diego Historical Society*

Horton booked passage on the Pacific mail steamer and arrived April 15, 1867. Landing at the foot of D Street (Broadway), Horton hiked a few blocks eastward. "There was nothing there but sagebrush then. I thought San Diego must be a heaven-on-earth, if it was all as fine as that; it seemed to me the best spot for building city I ever saw."

33 Cents an Acre

In Old Town, Horton told Ephraim W. Morse, the local agent for Wells Fargo, that San Diego would be better situated on the bay: "I have been nearly all over the United States and that is the prettiest place for a city I ever saw." To buy public land, required an auction and Horton paid the $10 cost of holding a special election to replace the board of trustees, whose terms had expired. With Morse, a newly elected trustee, acting as auctioneer on May 10, Horton paid $265 for 800 acres in five pueblo lots encompassing most of present-day downtown north to Upas Street. Even at 33 cents per acre, the locals shook their heads at what they considered Horton's foolishness. "That land has lain there for a million years, and nobody has built a city on it yet," said Judge D.A. Hollister. "Yes," replied Horton, "and it would lay there a million years longer without any city being built on it, if it depended upon you to do it."

Horton split his time over the next 18 months between San Francisco and San Diego, promoting

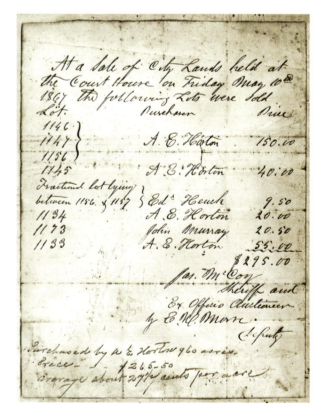

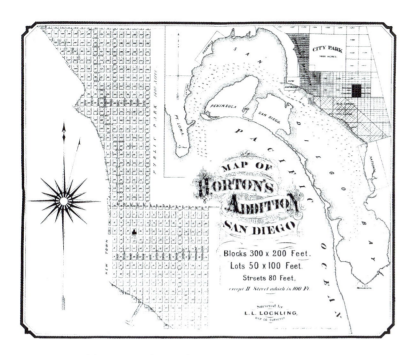

The final survey of Horton's Addition by L.L. Lockling, deputy county surveyor. *Courtesy San Diego Historical Society*

"Horton's Addition" as the real estate opportunity of the moment. He divided the land into blocks of 200 by 300 feet containing 12 50-by-100-foot lots and no alleys, ensuring a plentiful supply of desirable corner lots. He numbered the streets starting at the boundary of his holdings; thus, First Avenue is not at the water's edge but inland nine city blocks. Alphabetical streets started at the edge of City (later Balboa) Park and proceeded south, while to the north, the streets were named for trees and flowers in alphabetical order from Ash to Upas. When the Hortons moved permanently to San Diego in November 1868, the pace of development accelerated. He completed a $45,000 wharf at the foot of Fifth Avenue the next year and on January 1, 1870, led ground-breaking ceremonies for his biggest venture to date, a $150,000, 100-room hotel, Horton House, at Fourth and D (site of the U.S. Grant Hotel today). Opened October 10, 1870, it had all the luxuries available in San Francisco. "I assert," said one writer, "that the Horton House has done more for San Diego than all other improvements combined." The first clerk was a 20-year-old newcomer from Fort Atkinson, Wisconsin, George W. Marston, who would succeed Horton as San Diego's No. 1 citizen 30 years later.

Horton traded lots for services, donated land to churches and paid to whitewash the south- and west-facing sides of buildings to improve the city's appearance for visitors arriving by sea. He supported the *San Diego Weekly Bulletin*, founded in 1869 as the official New Town newspaper, until *The San Diego Union*, founded in 1868, moved from Old Town in 1870. It was also in 1870 that Horton joined others in founding the San Diego Chamber of Commerce, the Bank of San Diego and the Horton Library Association.

The "palatial" Horton House contained 100 rooms, all carpeted, lit with gas, and richly furnished with marble table tops and washstands. The rooms were even connected to the hotel office by a bell — a novelty in its day. *Courtesy San Diego Historical Society*

Chapter Three

One other effort Horton led was the creation of Balboa Park. On one of his trips to San Diego in 1868 prior to his permanent move, he joined Morse in selecting two 160-acre pueblo lots as the proposed site for a permanent city park. With so much vacant land available, the pair boldly recommended that the Board of Trustees reserve an even larger tract and 1,400 acres were selected at the edge of Horton's property. San Diego (population, less than 2,000) was only the second American municipality to lay out such a large piece of centrally located land as permanent, open space parkland; the first was New York (population, 700,000 in 1850) which had established Central Park just 10 years earlier. It is all the more remarkable that San Diego protected the park for more than 40 years before major improvements were ready to commence.

JULIAN GOLD RUSH

While Old Towners looked in dismay at Horton's success in New Town (and denied him a seat on the Board of Trustees in 1869),

On October 8, 1868, the first issue of *The San Diego Union* appeared as San Diego's first newspaper in nearly 20 years. *Courtesy San Diego Historical Society*

(Opposite page) Horton Bank at 3rd and D (Broadway), built in 1873. *Courtesy San Diego Historical Society*

The offices of *The San Diego Union* at 933 Fourth Street in 1897. *Courtesy San Diego Historical Society*

The Old Town Plaza, c. 1872. The Cosmopolitan Hotel (center) is better known today as the restaurant, Casa de Bandini. *Courtesy San Diego Historical Society*

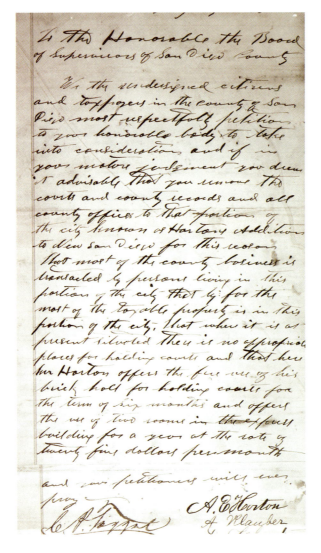

In 1870, petitioners to the San Diego County Board of Supervisors formally requested the move of city offices from Old Town to New Town. *Courtesy San Diego Historical Society*

both communities met a mutual rival in the town of Julian. Frederick Coleman, an African-American who built and operated toll roads, discovered gold in the winter of 1869-70 along what was later named Coleman Creek. Other discoveries soon followed, and by March, hundreds of San Diegans and newcomers rushed to the hills. "These people here are positively wild," the *Union* wrote. "Such a thing as sober thought is unknown… All night long, the ferocious prospectors make the hills resound with their stories of the day's adventures." By year's end, it was apparent that the Julian gold was plentiful but difficult to extract and the gold rush was short lived. In later years, Julian and its environs became known as a rich source of semi-precious stones.

Back in San Diego, the rivalry between Old and New Town finally culminated in the transfer of the county seat to Horton's development. The transfer occurred on the night of April 3, 1871, when county records were removed from the Whaley House, packed onto express wagons and unloaded at the Express Building at Sixth and G in New Town. Eleven days later, the name of the post office in New Town was changed from South San Diego to San Diego. The final blow to Old Town came April 20, 1872, when fire destroyed several buildings. With the dedication three months later of a permanent courthouse at Front and D, Horton's dream of building a new city had become a reality. The future was downtown; the past, as represented by Old Town, slowly faded away into history and legend.

Pining for a Railroad

One dream remained unfulfilled: rail service to San Diego. One of Horton's first acts after making his first investment in San Diego was to interest Civil War General William S. Rosecrans, an incorporator of the Southern Pacific Railroad, in considering terminating a transcontinental line at San Diego. "Horton, this is the best route for a railroad through the mountains that I have ever seen in California," Rosecrans said after a trip to Jacumba Pass. The general returned in 1869 with a group of railroad investors and reiterated his view that San Diego would become a West Coast rail terminus. But no construction commenced. National City founders Frank and Warren Kimball also failed in their attempt to join with Mexican-American War hero John C. Frémont and his Memphis & El Paso line to build to San Diego.

The most promising venture was led by Colonel Thomas A. Scott, president of the Pennsylvania Railroad and organizer of the Texas & Pacific Railroad. When Scott arrived in San Diego in August 1872, the locals pulled out all the stops. Entertained at Horton House, Scott received generous subsidies of land and cash previously promised other railroad ventures. In his speech to more than 1,000 San Diegans waiting in the rain, Scott said:

> I say to you now that we are ready to commence work here at your town, but we expect you to do your share in the enterprise and help us all you can... Your harbor... is more than capacious enough to accommodate the immense amount of trade that will gather at the gateway for the East to be distributed throughout the United States by the trains of the Texas & Pacific Railroad.

Main street in the gold rush town of Julian in the mid-1870s. *Courtesy San Diego Historical Society*

Fifth Street in 1876, looking south to the bay and Horton's Wharf. *Courtesy San Diego Historical Society*

Optimistically, the *Union* editorialized: "Hard times come again no more. In San Diego henceforth, our course is onward without check or hindrance." When Scott left town, the "Scott Boom" broke out. Horton was jubilant. In a letter to a friend in New York, he wrote, "We expect to have a large and beautiful city here, and a railroad running from it through Arizona and Texas to the Atlantic coast, within five years, the building of which will probably be commenced this year."

However, early in 1873 as construction began, it became clear that the route to San Diego would not be so direct; engineers preferred a line through the San Gorgonio Pass east of Los Angeles. In September, a stock market crash on Wall Street unnerved French bankers who reneged on their promise to buy Scott's rail bonds for his railroad. Construction stopped immediately. The population, which had grown from 2,300 to 5,000 from 1870 to 1873, fell back to 1,500. Horton sold his wharf, mortgaged his hotel and faced mounting taxes. One observer described him as "busted and [holding] property nearly worthless."

In the Doldrums

As depression descended across the country, San Diego faced the fact that Los Angeles would be the terminus of any transcontinental railroad to Southern California. Charles Crocker, one of the "Big Four" railroad barons of the Southern Pacific, declared, "You will never live long enough to see a railroad laid to the Bay of San Diego, nor one laid in the state by a transcontinental railroad which we do not lay… I have my foot on the neck of San Diego and I'm going to keep it there."

Others saw San Diego's future not in railroads or heavy industry but in tourism. The great scientist Louis Agassiz happened to be in San Diego the same day in 1872 that Scott was promising railroads. In an impromptu speech Agassiz said, "I have seen many parts of the world and have made some study of this subject. It is the question of climate — of your latitude — that I refer to. You have a great capital in your climate. It will be worth millions to you. This is one of the favored spots of the earth, and people will come to you from all quarters to live in your genial and healthful climate, a climate that has no equal."

The Stonewall Mine, near Julian, yielded over $900,000 in gold ore in the 1880s.
Courtesy San Diego Historical Society

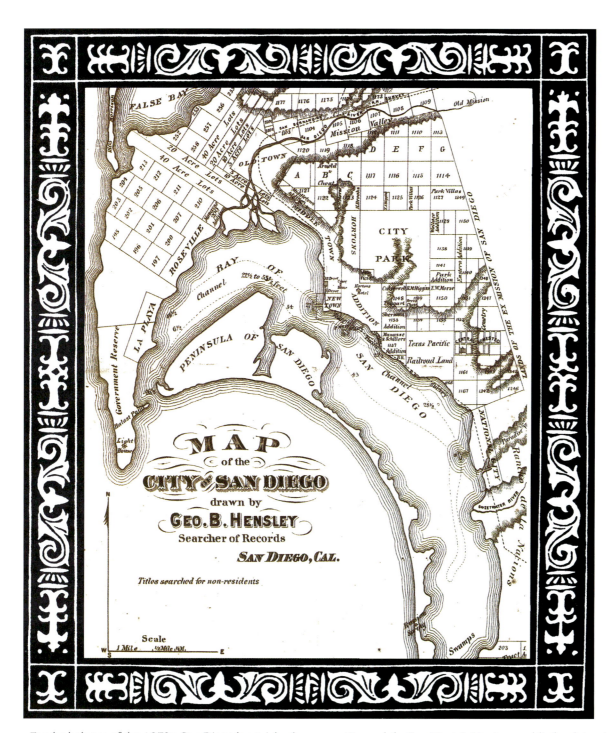

The map of the City of San Diego, by George B. Hensley, 1873. *Courtesy San Diego Historical Society*

For the balance of the 1870s, San Diego languished in the doldrums. Horton leased his prized Horton House to a series of short-term operators but the mortgage was finally foreclosed in 1881. However, he maintained hope that San Diego would prosper again. He visited San Francisco regularly and in 1876 went east one more time to urge Scott to restart his railroad.

Meanwhile, San Diego's Mexican public-land grant of 1835 was confirmed in 1874, when the federal government approved a map defining the extent of the city's pueblo lots. The eastern boundary roughly followed the route of today's Interstate 805; North Island and Coronado fell within the city limits.

Other court action was required to determine whether or not the bayfront tidelands belonged to

Lakeside and Cuyamaca near San Diego. *Courtesy San Diego Historical Society*

(Far right) A typical apple orchard in Julian, near San Diego. *Courtesy San Diego Historical Society*

Street scene, El Cajon *Courtesy San Diego Historical Society*

the city or the state. To press its case for local control, the Board of Trustees promised five miles of tidelands between San Diego and National City to City Attorney Charles P. Taggart and Los Angeles attorney and railroad promoter Volney E. Howard if they could win the case. Taggart and Howard also figured in an attempt to undo the 1868 reservation of City Park and to subdivide most of it for development. The courts refused to privatize the tidelands and the Legislature, acting in response to a last-minute citizens' petition, preserved the park for public use.

San Diegans marked time by developing more than 3,000 farms and hundreds of businesses and civic institutions. There were apples in Julian, strawberries in National City, grapes and walnuts in El Cajon and 20,000 beehives in various locations producing upwards of 90 tons of honey. More than 150,000 sheep produced nearly 1 million pounds of wool. At Ballast Point, a lively whaling industry produced as much as 55,000 gallons of whale oil one year.

To protect the harbor from further siltation, Captain George A. Johnson and Howard Schuyler won an $80,000, federally funded contract to build a 7,735-foot levee that would divert the San Diego River back into its channel emptying in False (Mission) Bay. They blasted out 5,000 cubic yards of dirt and rocks from Presidio Hill for the dike, employing about 150 workers, half white, half

Athletes from the San Diego Turnverein, c. 1898.
Courtesy San Diego Historical Society

Chinese. Lieutenant John Weede of the Army Corps of Engineers assured San Diegans that the dike would hold: "(It will be) stronger by far than those which have for years guided the mighty waters of the Mississippi, the Rhine, the Po and the Adige…" he said.

Melting Pot

San Diego was, indeed, a multiethnic melting pot, drawn from immigrants all over the world. Chinese began living in San Diego in the 1870s, dominating the fishing industry and living west of the Gaslamp Quarter around Third and Island avenues. Anti-Chinese feelings prompted Sheriff Joseph Coyne and local leaders to organize the Committee on Public Safety and seek the army's aid to prevent riots. "The Chinese may not be, in any considerable number, a desirable element of the population," the *Union* editorialized in 1877. "But those that are here are under the protection of the laws and must not be molested…

Here in San Diego we do not mean to permit hoodlumism and rioting."

Germans also became a prominent ethnic minority. Charles P. Gerichten, leased the Horton House in 1879, advertising it as a "Deutsches Gasthaus," where rooms rented for $1.50 per day and $8 per week. San Diego's

Baseball team in 1871. George Marston is fourth from the left in the back row.
Courtesy San Diego Historical Society

As New Town grew, many native Americans continued to live in squalid rancherías on the outskirts of town. This photograph was taken around 1874. *Courtesy San Diego Historical Society*

The future businessman George Marston at age 17. *George White Marston: A Family Chronicle.*

George Marston's first store, at Fifth and F. *Courtesy San Diego Historical Society*

small Jewish community held its first formal worship services for 18 members at Marcus Schiller's home in Old Town in 1872. Temple Beth Israel was incorporated in 1888 and the synagogue opened the next year at Second and Beech. Meanwhile, San Diego's oldest community, the Indians, hung on in town, living at several camps including one at Eighth and Date. "At night, their chanting could be heard for miles, especially if there had been a death amongst them," historian Elizabeth MacPhail wrote.

For fun, San Diegans cheered on the baseball rivalry of the Young Americans and the Golden Eagles. Horse races took place at a track in Mission Valley. The San Diego Philharmonic Society, organized in 1872, performed at Horton's Hall in "the best musical performance ever presented to the citizens of this town," an enthusiastic critic said. The hall also served as the town's principal legitimate theater, outfitted with three sets of scenery (indoors, marine view and woodlands). When the circus came to town, tents were pitched on the Bancroft Block (B, C, Third and Fourth). Sportsmen fished in False (Mission) Bay and hunted rabbits and quail on the undeveloped Peninsula of San Diego (Coronado).

In counterpoint to New Town's abundance of saloons, an active temperance movement sprang up. The "Band of Hope" encouraged a "just say no" attitude toward liquor by young people. The "Band of Mercy" promoted kindness to animals.

GEORGE W. MARSTON

As Horton's fortunes and influence waned, those of George W. Marston grew. After leaving Horton House, he and his partner Charles Hamilton clerked for storekeeper Joseph Nash for five years before buying him out for $10,000. In 1878, they split up the business, Hamilton concentrating on groceries and Marston on dry goods. The two became related when they married two of the Gunn sisters. The Marston Company became San Diego's leading independent department store. "We do not want to be enchained; let us be just Marston's, not The Universal Mercantile Consolidated Aggregation," he said at the 1928 golden anniversary of the business. "We want to jog on in the good old San Diego style for 50 years more." Marston figured in the founding of many local institutions, from the YMCA and the San Diego Public Library to the San Diego Historical Society.

THE BOOM OF THE '80S

The 1880s, in the words of historian Richard F. Pourade, was "the most gaudy, wicked and exciting [time] in San Diego's history." It all began with a final push for a rail line. In June 1879, National City's Frank Kimball went east once again to meet with the railroad barons. In July 1880, he won support from the Atchison, Tokepa & Santa Fe and the Atlantic & Pacific to complete a new transcontinental route. San Diego could have its line in exchange for 17,000 acres in National City and San Diego, 485 prime lots and $25,000 in cash. The railroads formed the San Diego Land & Town Co. to take the land and oversee development. The California Southern Railroad was chartered in October 1880 and 182 miles of track were completed by August 1882 from National City to Colton. Legal action was required to permit the California Southern to cross the Southern Pacific and link up with the Santa Fe at San Bernardino.

The first San Diego train arrived at San Bernardino September 13, 1883, its locomotive decorated with flowers, stalks of corn and round squash. Unfortunately, the railroad engineers ignored advice from long-time residents in routing the tracks along the Temecula Canyon creek bed. Heavy storms in February 1884 washed 30 miles of roadbed away from Oceanside to Temecula. The route was shifted to the coast and continued from San Bernardino to Waterman Junction (Barstow). The last spike was driven November 9, 1885, and the first train bound for the east left San Diego November 15; five days later, the first west-bound train arrived in San Diego and National City. It was a rainy welcome for 60 passengers aboard two coaches and a mail and baggage car. But there was a brass band on hand and a fireworks display.

"The completion of this line, establishing a fourth great highway between oceans in the United States, is an event whose importance, not alone to this city, but to the state and coast, cannot be overestimated," said an invitation to a grand celebration at Leach's Opera House. "The people of San Diego, with persistent energy and steadfast faith, have for a long period of years, looked forward to the day that is now so close at hand. They will cordially greet you at their jubilee."

San Diegans were not ready for the onslaught that followed the opening of the new rail line. A rate war between the Santa Fe and Southern Pacific broke out and the one-way fare from Missouri to California dropped from $125 to $1 on March 6, 1887. The city's population soared from 2,637 in 1880 to about 40,000 in 1887. The city directory swelled with new entries. Real estate promoters subdivided land into imaginary towns. San Diego's natural bay and unparalleled climate became the mantra for drawing immigrants during the great boom. The city's top physician, Peter C. Remondino, a native of Turin, Italy, compared Southern California to the Mediterranean and writer Charles Dudley Warner carried the analogy further with his book, *Our Italy*. Theodore S. Van Dyke, a hunter, engineer, farmer

Frank A. Kimball in 1897 *Courtesy San Diego Historical Society*

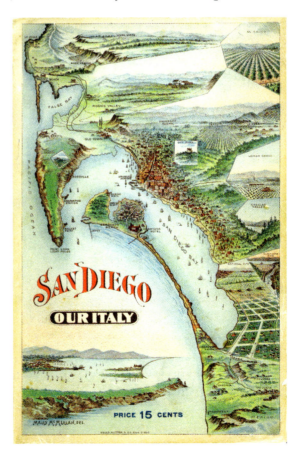

In 1895, the San Diego Chamber of Commerce praised the region's Mediterranean virtues in this brochure containing "Information for the Capitalist, Home Seeker, Tourist and Invalid." Boosters of the era frequently compared the Southern California climate to that of Italy—calling San Diego the "Naples" of America. *Courtesy San Diego Historical Society*

Chapter Three

Fifth Street during the "Boom," 1887. New city services included horse-drawn streetcars and carbon arc street lights (background, center). *Courtesy San Diego Historical Society*

and talented writer living in San Diego, assessed the appeal this way:

It was plain that they were in fact buying comfort, immunity from snow and slush, from piercing winds and sleet-clad streets, from sultry days and sleepless nights, from thunder storms, cyclones, malaria, mosquitoes and bedbugs. All of which, in plain language, means that they were buying climate, a business that has been going on now for 15 years [1872-1887] and reached a stage of progress which the world has never seen before and of which no wisdom can foresee the end... New stores, hotels and dwellings are arising on every hand from the center to the farthest outskirts in more bewildering numbers than before, and people are pouring in at double the rate they did but six months ago. It is now impossible to keep track of its progress. No one seems any longer to know or care who is putting up the big buildings, and it is becoming difficult to find a familiar face in the crowd or at the hotels.

When the "boomers" arrived, they found a very rough and undeveloped town. Streets were unpaved. Homes and workplaces were unavailable. Many people slept in tents while waiting for their for their investments to escalate. "Scarcely a San Diego capitalist invested a dollar in outside property during the boom," wrote A. A. Bynon in the December 1889 issue of *The Golden Era* magazine. "It was our eastern men who were willing to risk their money in wild-cat schemes and paper towns, and hundreds of them have since folded their tents and returned to their homes wiser if not richer men."

Most of the historic buildings in the Gaslamp Quarter date from the boom years and many were restored in another boom time a century later. The crowning jewel was the new, $120,000 county courthouse, designed in Italian Renaissance style by San Francisco architects Comstock & Trotsche. It was topped by zinc statues of Presidents Washington, Lincoln, Grant and Garfield. "Justice," located at the top of the dome, was restored and put on display in the Museum of San Diego History in Balboa Park in the 1980s. A series of

San Diego County Courthouse at D (Broadway) and Front Street in 1889, *Courtesy San Diego Historical Society*

stained-glass windows depicting state seals were salvaged when the courthouse was demolished in the 1950s and installed in the Hall of Justice in 1996.

Another key public building was San Diego High School, opened in 1882 as an all-grade institution and named for Joseph Russ, a Northern Californian who donated the lumber for the $18,430 building. The city's Union Depot, a small but elegant Victorian railroad station, opened in 1886 at the foot of D Street (replaced in 1915 by the twin-domed Santa Fe Depot). The boom was not restricted to Horton's Addition. Speculators laid out a dozen or more subdivisions and towns all over the county. They sold lots through exuberant advertising and at colorful outdoor events and erected grand hotels. Carlsbad, Oceanside, Del Mar, La Jolla, Escondido, Lakeside, Pacific Beach and Ocean Beach were just a few of the communities that originated in the boom times and managed to survive through the subsequent bust to grow at various rates in the 20th century.

Crown Jewel in Coronado

The most successful venture was Coronado. Originally located within the city limits of San Diego, the peninsula was purchased for $110,000 in December 1885 by a syndicate headed by Indiana railroad promoter Elisha S. Babcock and Chicago piano manufacturer H.L. Story. They changed the name from "Peninsula of San Diego" to Coronado (within view of the nearby, Mexican-owned Coronado Islands). Then they hired two Evansville, Indiana, brothers as architects, James W. and Merritt Reid, to design a grand hotel. At a grand auction on November 13, 1886, $1 million worth of lots was sold to some of the 6,000 buyers on hand. With the proceeds, they established a ferry system, water service and the Coronado Gas & Electric Co. The only thing Coronado was not supposed to have was saloons and liquor stores. The hotel would hold a monopoly on booze on the "Enchanted Isle."

But just as the $1 million, 399-room hotel was nearing its grand opening February 19, 1888, it was evident to many San Diegans that the boom was over. Real estate sales had slowed, speculation evaporated and the Santa Fe, which had taken over the California Southern, moved its repair yards and offices up north, signaling the end to San Diego as the railroad's west coast terminus. "The bottom had dropped out of the big boom," Thomas J. Hayes recalled. "From whence the boom came I do not know, and I have never been able to learn to my complete satisfaction. It stopped more suddenly by far than it came. It

Hotel del Coronado
Courtesy San Diego Historical Society

Coronado developer Elisha S. Babcock (1849-1900) *Courtesy San Diego Historical Society* reversed motion and went down like a chunk of sawed-off wood."

The population plummeted from 40,000 to 16,000 within a few months, property assessments dropped from $40 million to $25 million by 1890. Several of the grand suburban hotels were mysteriously destroyed by fire. In Coronado, John D. Spreckels from San Francisco took control of Babcock & Story's hotel and land company. It would be 20 years before San Diego exceeded its boom-time size.

After the Bust

The boom — and its aftermath — brought many colorful characters to San Diego County, from frontier lawman Wyatt Earp and musician (and mystic) Jesse Shepard to English actress Lily Langtry, Buffalo "Wild Bill" Cody and John Philip Sousa. Ulysses S. Grant Jr., the president's son, moved to San Diego in 1892 and his children's governess, Anna Held, built a small cottage in La Jolla that grew into an artists' mecca known as the "Green Dragon Colony." Visitors included Polish actress Helen Modjeska, who performed at the Fisher Opera House. The Hotel del Coronado became a popular winter vacation spot for many notables, including L. Frank Baum, who had gained famed as the author of *The Wonderful Wizard of Oz* (1900). Baum completed three of his Oz stories in Coronado and his 1911 non-Oz book, *The Sea Fairies*, drew on the surroundings of La Jolla Cove.

San Diego gained a powerful literary leader when James Harrison "Harr" Wagner moved his *Golden Era* magazine from northern California to San Diego in 1887. Mark Twain had been one of its contributors. Now it carried poetry by Rose Hartwick Thorpe, who at 16 had written the famous poem, "Curfew Must Not Ring Tonight." She won a contest sponsored by the magazine to rename False Bay by suggesting "Mission Bay." In the August 1888 issue, she wrote:

> Beyond the bay the city lies
> White-walled beneath the azure skies,
> So far remote, no sounds of it
> Across the peaceful waters flit —
> Fair Mission Bay
> Now blue, now gray,
> Now flushed by sunset's afterglow.

Two figures of great significance in the development of San Diego's physical form arrived during this time. The first was Kate O. Sessions, who was hired as principal of the Russ School in 1884. After only three months she was demoted to assistant principal and quit the following year to go into the nursery business. Her interest in exotic tropical plants and determination to make San Diego beautiful through landscaping earned her the title

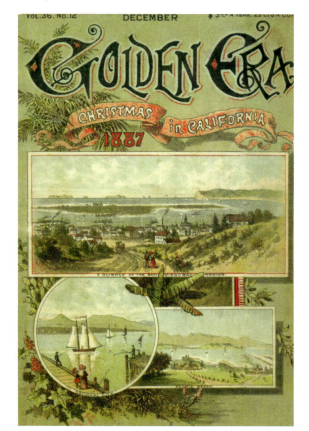

In the wake of the 1887 bust, San Diego was filled with "For Sale" signs at locations like this on 4th Street.
Courtesy San Diego Historical Society

Golden Era magazine
Courtesy San Diego Historical Society

"Mother of Balboa Park." She died in 1940.

The second pacesetter, architect Irving J. Gill, came to San Diego from Chicago in 1893, having worked on that year's World's Columbian Exposition. He designed George W. Marston's house, now a historic museum, and Horton Plaza park and fountain, but by 1910, was shifting from the Craftsman style of design to something more modern and futuristic. He experimented in tilt-up concrete construction and promoted economical design for working class families. Ahead of his time, his achieved new fame and admiration only in the last quarter of the 20th century.

The boom prompted the need for more water and San Diego's first major waterworks, the San Diego Flume, opened on Washington's birthday in 1889. A delegation of VIPs, led by Governor Robert W. Waterman, rode flat-bottomed boats along a portion of the 35-mile wooden aqueduct that transported fresh water from Lake Cuyamaca to just west of El Cajon. Pipes carried the water the remaining distance to downtown. Horton served as vice chairman of ceremonies, but when an air bubble prevented the water from reaching the grandstand set up at Fifth and Ivy, officials tapped the old water supply. Tasters were fooled into thinking the "mountain water" was far superior! It's worth noting that Waterman was the only San

(Far left)
Kate Sessions (1857-1940)
Courtesy San Diego Historical Society

Irving J. Gill (1870-1936)
Courtesy San Diego Historical Society

The first U.S. president to visit San Diego was Benjamin Harrison (center), shown here in the city with his wife in April 1892. *Courtesy San Diego Historical Society*

Diegan to serve as governor of California (1887-1891) until former Mayor and later U.S. Senator Pete Wilson was elected in 1990.

During the 1890s, San Diego's population stagnated at around 16,000. (Los Angeles numbered 50,000.) The Wall Street panic of 1893 led to further bank failures and the Kimballs of National City went bankrupt in 1896. To raise cash, Horton sold his last major asset, Horton Plaza park facing Horton House. The city agreed to pay $10,000 in $100 monthly installments. Officials believed the old man, then 80, would never live to receive the final payoff. But Horton, newly married to 46-year-old Lydia Maria Knapp, cashed his last payment in April 1903.

Coronadans did not like paying taxes to San Diego and voted in 1891 to form their own municipality. Three other cities were incorporated by then: National City (1887), Escondido and Oceanside (both 1888). South of the border, Tijuana gained municipality status in 1889 and it gradually became a tourist attraction.

Festivals and Book Learning

To cheer things up, the city celebrated the 350th anniversary of Cabrillo's discovery of the bay in September 1892, an event that signaled renewed interest in San Diego's Hispanic past. To gain national attention, the Chamber of Commerce raised $2,200 to support local efforts to exhibit products at the World's Columbian Exposition in Chicago in 1893. Fallbrook sent ostriches and high school students sent shells and bottle specimens. There was a palm tree, planted from a seed carried by Junipero Serra, and a pyramid of raisins garnished with plates of lemons and bottles of oil.

Three key educational institutions were founded in San Diego at the turn of the century. In 1897, the legislature approved a new State Normal School, a two-year teacher's training college, which moved into permanent quarters in Normal Heights in 1899 (the site today of the San Diego Unified School District's education center). The Normal School evolved into San Diego State University.

Next came the Universal Brotherhood and Theosophical Society. Katharine A. Tingley bought 132 acres in Point Loma in 1896 and laid the cornerstone in 1897 for the School for the Revival of the Lost Mysteries of Antiquity. The 50-building "Homestead" or "Adyar" compound also included the International Lotus Home, the Aryan Memorial Temple and the first Greek-style theater built in the United States. After she died in 1929, the school continued for a few more years before closing in 1942. California Western University (later, U.S. International University) subsequently occupied the site, followed by Point Loma Nazarene College.

(Opposite page, top) The dedication of the San Diego flume, on February 22, 1889. Gov. Robert W. Waterman, first seated man on right. *Courtesy San Diego Historical Society*

(Opposite page, bottom) The 35-mile flume used 315 trestles to cross canyons and creeks. The 1,800-foot Los Coches Creek trestle, shown here, was the largest. *Courtesy San Diego Historical Society*

Katherine Augustus Tingley (1847-1929). *Courtesy San Diego Historical Society*

The "Homestead" (left) and the "Temple" (right), the main buildings of the Theosophical Society at Point Loma. *Courtesy San Diego Historical Society*

Elected at age 29 in 1893, William H. "Billy" Carlson was the youngest person ever to serve as San Diego mayor. *Courtesy San Diego Historical Society*

(Opposite page) John D. Spreckels (1853-1926) *Courtesy San Diego Historical Society*

The University of California got its start in San Diego, when UC Berkeley zoology professor William E. Ritter honeymooned in the area in 1891 and told the Chamber of Commerce, "There can be no doubt that a laboratory capable of great things for biological science might be built at San Diego." With support from Ellen Browning Scripps, Ritter set up a laboratory in La Jolla in 1903 that became part of the university in 1912. Scripps Institution of Oceanography served as the nucleus for the University of California at San Diego in the early-1960s.

Home Rule

Politically, San Diego finally regained self-rule and replaced its board of trustees in 1889 with a two-house legislature: a nine-member board of alderman, elected at large, and an 18-member board of delegates, two from each ward. The first mayor elected since 1852 was Douglas Gunn, former owner of the *Union*. The most colorful mayor was William H. "Billy" Carlson, elected at age 28 in 1893. He had promoted Ocean Beach during the boom and now, in the mayor's seat, set out to get San Diego a direct rail line to the east via Mexico. He disappeared with $5,000 in donations and resurfaced in Mexico City claiming he had negotiated a franchise agreement for such a line. His San Diego & Arizona Railroad did not materialize, at least on his watch. Carlson won reelection 1895 but placed fifth in 1897.

On New Year's Day, 1901, the *Union's* annual review edition was full of hope for the new century. Wrote Mayor Edwin M. Capps:

"With the immediate natural resources at her command and her strategical position for commerce, the city of San Diego crosses the threshold of the 20th century with most brilliant prospects for the future… Such are a few of the many advantages that San Diego possesses and before the 20th century has fully dawned, she will have merited the title the "Metropolis of the Southwest."

San Diego's future lay in the hands of a small group of wealthy businessmen, who sometimes quarreled over how "their" town should progress. John D. Spreckels, son of the "sugar king" who controlled Hawaii's sugar crop, moved permanently to San Diego after the San Francisco earthquake in 1906. He owned *The Union*, Hotel del Coronado and much land and industry. E.W. Scripps ran the rival San Diego *Sun* and the rest of his chain of newspapers from his ranch in rural Miramar. His sister, Ellen Brown Scripps, devoted herself to charitable work. George W. Marston retired from day-to-day running of his department store and engaged in a wide range of civic matters.

The City Directory listed 606 businesses in 1901, including 11 blacksmiths, 15 Chinese laundries, 34 contractors and 10 hay and grain dealers. Growth had been slow (the 1900 census gave the city's population as 17,700, the county's as 39,578, barely more than in 1890), but 55 real estate agents remained in business. As for the native peoples, they were largely forgotten. Horton's wife Lydia wrote in *The Union*, "The Indians, a dying race, bitten by civilization, will soon disappear into the limbo of the past."

San Diego City Hall, at Fifth and G, lasted from 1900 to 1938. *Courtesy San Diego Historical Society*

San Diego's first public library building opened in 1902, it was the first library west of the Mississippi to be funded by Andrew Carnegie. *Courtesy San Diego Historical Society*

The decade saw the transfer of city hall to a former bank building at Fifth and G. The council was reduced to nine then five members with each assuming a particular role as a commissioner. Progressives attempted to gain control of the council and reduce the influence of big business and bossism. In 1906, San Diego was the first city in California to add the initiative, referendum and recall to a municipal charter.

In 1902, the city's first public library building opened. It was made possible by a $60,000 grant sought by Lydia Horton from Andrew Carnegie, his first to any community west of the Mississippi. The location on only a half-block between Eighth and Ninth on E was to plague the library the entire century because of the lack of expansion space. As Marston wrote *The Union,* "What I regret to see is the disposition to look for the cheapest possible place rather than the best."

This year also saw the first major effort to begin improvements to City Park (renamed Balboa Park in 1910). Marston joined the chamber's park improvement committee and underwrote the $10,000 cost for a master plan by Samuel Parsons Jr., president of the American Society of Landscape Architects and consulting architect for New York City's park system. The plan for the Sixth Avenue side of the park was ready in the spring of 1903 and exhibited at Marston's department store windows. About 2,500 school children celebrated Arbor Day in 1904 by participating in a mass tree planting.

In 1905, Horton stood by to watch his grand Horton House crumble to the ground to make way for the $1 million U.S. Grant Hotel, promoted by the late president's son. Accounts reflect that Horton was not sad but heartened by the changes afoot in his town. Spreckels announced at the end 1906 his plans to build the San Diego & Arizona Railway line to Yuma, a true link to the east. The $6 million venture eventually cost three times as much and was not completed for 13 years. By then, the automobile was gaining prominence and voters were readily approving road-building bonds to support this new, fast, personal mode of transportation. Spreckels received state chauffeur's license Badge Number 1 for his White Steamer.

In November 1907, Imperial Valley voters approved their secession from San Diego County. San Diego politicians' seeming disinterest in the distant valley no doubt prompted the farmers and landowners to go it alone. (In 1998, they joined forces in a precedent-setting agreement to secure San Diego' water supply and boost income for valley farmers and landowners.) Thus, San

Diego County assumed its present size and borders.

The county also sought a new future in welcoming the April 1908 arrival of President Theodore Roosevelt's Great White Fleet on a round-the-world cruise. Sixteen thousand sailors descended on downtown San Diego streets with money to burn. The event added impetus to the local drive to pursue federal defense dollars big-time in the years ahead. The military-municipal partnership did not come cost-free. On July 21, 1905, the gunboat *Bennington* exploded in the harbor, killing 60 crewmen and injuring 46. An obelisk to the victims' memory was dedicated at Fort Rosecrans National Cemetery in January 1908.

The new century, with all its promise, brought death to several 19th century greats. Ephraim W. Morse, the man who befriended Horton and joined in his quest to relocate the center of town and set aside Balboa Park, died January 17, 1906. Father Antonio Ubach, the Catholic priest who arrived in San Diego in 1866 and befriended and defended the Indians, died March 26, 1907. Then on Thursday, January 7, 1909, Alonzo Horton, friend to all San Diegans (excepting a few Southern Democrats), died at Agnew Sanitarium at Fifth and Beech, aged 95. His doctor said Horton had asked to be taken to the roof garden, where he surveyed his city and hoped to see it grow to 100,000 population. The next day, *The Union* editorialized that Horton "built deeply and well for the city that was to come." An estimated 8,000 people paid their respects on Saturday before the 2 p.m. service at the Elks Hall. In his eulogy, John B. Osborne said, "He was a plain, typical American western pioneer, with a true vision and optimism infinite."

At the Horton Plaza park fountain, dedicated in 1910, Horton is pictured along with Cabrillo and Serra in bas relief. Nearby is a bronze plaque, donated in 1939 by the San Diego Historical Society and moved from the County Administration Center to the newly restored park in 1985. It reads: "Memorial to Alonzo E. Horton, 1813-1909: Founder of the modern city of San Diego, 1867; first in civic vision; first in heroic adventure; first in courage and determination. Here he founded the city of his dreams. Therefore we call him Father Horton."

Horton did not live to see San Diego grow as big as he imagined it would be. Six days before his death, he may have been too sick to read *The Union's* January 1, 1909, issue. If he had, he would have seen a possible vision of the future.

Tree planting in a barren Balboa Park on Arbor Day, March 17, 1905. *Courtesy San Diego Historical Society*

Alonzo E. Horton, shortly before his death in 1909. *Courtesy San Diego Historical Society*

Chapter Three

Timeout: The Nolen Plan

San Diego and its leaders often engaged in full-blown boosterism, when it came to promoting the city's assets and potential. But when outsiders were asked to assess the possibilities, they offered practical advice in how to transform a stagnant, backwater coastal village into a thriving port city. The first, fully developed vision was offered by Cambridge, Massachusetts, landscape architect and planner John Nolen, whose work was completed in the summer of 1908 and published in *The San Diego Union*'s January 1, 1909, annual edition.

San Diego — A Comprehensive Plan for Its Improvement grew out of a proposal in 1905 by architect William S. Hebbard to build a civic center around an enlarged Horton Plaza. The concept was in line with the budding City Beautiful movement to inject "art" or beauty into civic projects with the addition of sculpture, grand buildings, pleasant parks and open space.

Samuel Parsons' 1905 plan for developing Balboa Park had outlined the best means for turning the 1,400-acre undeveloped park into a verdant retreat for the city. The San Diego Chamber of Commerce took the lead in going from park planning to city planning. On behalf of the chamber's Civic Improvement Committee, George W. Marston consulted the American City Planning League and brought Nolen (and paid $10,000 of his expenses) to San Diego in 1906 to look things over. He even took Nolen on an outing to Pine Hills near Julian in a car driven by young developer Ed Fletcher. Nolen was in the forefront of professional city planning and many of his concepts for San Diego were repeated in the many other plans he wrote for other cities over the next 30 years.

The Nolen Plan was never officially adopted by the city, but many of the principles and elements inspired the area's development pattern throughout the 20th century. In particular, Nolen urged San Diego to make something of the bayfront by segregating industrial uses at the south end and promoting recreational and tourist uses at the north. He coupled that with a proposal to link the bay with Balboa Park. Although the Bay-Park Link has yet to be carried out, the bay and park have been developed somewhat along the lines Nolen had in mind.

In conclusion, Nolen urged San Diegans to make the necessary investment to achieve civic greatness: "The funds necessary for these improvements, while large, need not be excessive; they must be provided largely by bond issues, giving future generations the opportunity to share in the creation as well as the enjoyment of a more convenient, prosperous and attractive city. After all, the greatest benefits will be theirs. Such expenditures are really investments, and the dividends steadily increase."

What follows are key excerpts from the 1908 Nolen Plan. (Ellipses have been deleted for readability.) The full text is available at the San Diego Public Library and bears re-reading by elected officials, city planners and interested citizens. No statement of San Diego's potential has ever been so inspiring as Nolen's. Twenty-first century San Diego would do well to read Nolen and to improve and enlarge on his challenge, still relevant after 90 years.

San Diego Comprehensive Plan For Improvement
Prefatory Note

San Diego has developed much like other places in this country. But today it is far ahead of most cities of its class in its recognition of the mistakes of the past and in its appreciation of the opportunities of the present.

[It is not] expected that all these plans will be carried out at once — some must wait for years. Primarily, they are intended to awaken and form public opinion, and to present the general ideas which should regulate and control the improvement of the city, ideas which, it is believed, may be safely endorsed by the Civic Improvement Committee [of the Chamber of Commerce] in its present public-spirited movement.

San Diego has the location and the physical foundation in general for an important, perhaps a great city. Its people are awake to its needs, and are resolved to meet them. It stands, therefore, upon the threshold of a truly sound and far-reaching development; for, when to superb natural advantages and human enterprise are added a sound public policy and a comprehensive plan of action, who can doubt the outcome?

John Nolen, Cambridge, Massachusetts
September 1908.

I. Some General Considerations

San Diego is indeed unique. Even in Southern California its situation, climate and scenery make it stand out in permanent attractiveness beyond all other communities. Its resources as a city are in many respects unmatched. The bay on which it directly fronts is one of the safest and most beautiful harbors in the world, a landlocked body of water more than a score of square miles in area, with a channel deep enough to take the largest ships. From the bay the land rises gently to the north and east, and on the slopes thus formed the city has been built. Not only the bay, but every type of scenery, beach and promontory, mesa and canyon, unite in never-ending variety to form a city that is strikingly individual in character and of great beauty.

The climate defies description. Dry, fresh, equable, wholly without extremes of heat or cold, it is a factor that must constantly be taken into account in estimating the future or providing for it. Bright, balmy, invigorating weather invites one outdoors more hours of the day and more days in the year than in any other part of the country. Health is almost guaranteed. A disinterested visitor has remarked that, "if nervous prostration is wanted, it must be brought here, and it cannot be relied on to continue long."

Not only the bay, but every type of scenery, beach and promontory, mesa and canyon, unite in never-ending variety to form a city that is strikingly individual in character and of great beauty.

The scenery is varied and exquisitely beautiful. The great, broad, quiet mesas, the picturesque canyons, the bold line of distant mountains, the wide hard ocean beaches, the great bay, its beauty crowned by the islands of Coronado, the caves and coves of La Jolla, the unique Torrey Pines, the lovely Mission Valley, these are but some of the features of the landscape that should be looked upon as precious assets to be preserved and enhanced. And then the "back country" — hospitable to every sort of

Ed Fletcher, George Marston, and John Nolen touring San Diego's back country, 1907.
Courtesy San Diego Historical Society

tree, shrub, root, grain and flower — is an inexhaustible source of commercial and aesthetic wealth.

Notwithstanding its advantages of situation, climate and scenery, San Diego is today neither interesting nor beautiful. Its city plan is not thoughtful, but, on the contrary, ignorant and wasteful. It has no wide and impressive business streets, practically no open spaces in the heart of the city, no worthy sculpture. Aside from the big undeveloped City Park [Balboa Park], it has no pleasure grounds, no large, well-arranged playgrounds. It has no public buildings excellent in design and location. It has done little or nothing to secure for its people the benefits of any of its great natural resources, nor to provide those concomitants without which natural resources are so often valueless.

Fortunately, the public-spirited men and women of San Diego are preparing to act in time. They realize in general what the city lacks, what it needs, and the opportunity and responsibility of the present generation. The problem, therefore, resolves itself into a call for a sympathetic study of the city as it is, a reasonable estimate of its future and a service of art and skill that will not only provide that degree of convenience and beauty that must soon be regarded as indispensable to city life, but will also recognize in the form of its provision the peculiar opportunity for joy, for health, for prosperity, that life in Southern California, more especially in San Diego, offers to all.

To beautify a city means to make it perfect — perfect as a city, complete in serving a city's purposes. San Diego is potentially many-sided. The plans to improve and adorn San Diego must therefore take many things into account. They must be broad, and, considering the promise of the city, liberal and courageous. In this connection how difficult it is to bring before the people of a city a vision of what 50 years' growth, even 25, will make not only possible, but necessary.

The application of the foregoing to a growing city is obvious. Action must be taken while it is still relatively easy, or it will certainly be costly and

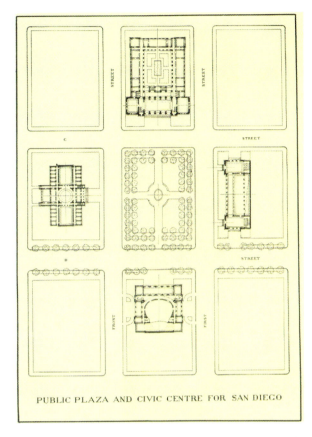

The proposed plaza is in the center, above it is City Hall, to the left is the courthouse. The post office is to the right and below it is the Opera House. *From John Nolen's book, San Diego, A Comprehensive Plan for Its Improvement*

probably inadequate. The present, therefore, is a most propitious time to consider in a frank, clear-headed and comprehensive manner the future of San Diego. As never before, it seems now to have the opportunity to lay firm hold of its heritage.

II. The Replanning of San Diego

There are four general principles of landscape design which are peculiarly applicable to city planning. They are:

1. To conform, so far as possible, to the topography;
2. To use places for what they are naturally most fit;
3. To conserve, develop and utilize all natural resources, aesthetic as well as commercial;
4. To aim to secure beauty by organic arrangement rather than by mere embellishment.

It is too late to make a plan for San Diego based simply upon a thoughtful recognition of the

Timeout: The Nolen Plan

topography, and a skillful consideration of the normal needs of city life and the special needs of San Diego. But it is not the intention of this report to rehearse nor dwell upon the mistakes of the past. And happily it is still within the power of the people of San Diego to make their city convenient, attractive and beautiful.

Each generation has spent too much time in lamenting the errors of the past, and has given too little attention to the opportunities of the present. San Diego's opportunity is so open, so apparent, and relatively easy, that it seems unnecessary to point further the application. Every phase of civic improvement is still within its reach. This is its real formative era. The present city is but the nucleus of the future city, and the citizens of today have an opportunity to rise to the call of a great and fine constructive period.

III. A Public Plaza and Civic Center

The present generation has also a rare opportunity to secure for San Diego a beautiful and permanent grouping of its public buildings. Therefore, I definitely recommend the following:

1. The purchase of the block, approximately 200 by 260 feet, extending from D [Broadway] to C streets and from Front to First streets, and its development as a public plaza;
2. The purchase of the blocks from D to E and C to B, and portions of other adjoining blocks as indicated on the plan;
3. The grouping around this plaza, Spanish fashion, of the three public buildings under consideration, the city hall, the courthouse, the federal building, also the proposed Academy of Music and perhaps the Chamber of Commerce building.

IV. The Great Bayfront

The plan looks to the development of commercial facilities, wharves, docks and piers south of E Street, extending farther and farther as business demands, and pleasure facilities of a simple order north of E Street. The foot of D Street [Broadway] would be emphasized by the development of a Bay Plaza 300 feet by 500 feet, but the main development of recreation and artistic interests would center at the foot of Date and Elm streets, nearer the residential sections and the big City Park. North of Date Street the line of the bayfront might properly be a graceful swinging curve, similar in character to that of Rio de Janeiro.

The Paseo: The people of San Diego would do well if they recognize today the two great central recreation features of the city, now and always, are the City Park of 1,400 acres, and the bayfront, and that the value of both will be increased many-fold if

Proposed civic center around a new plaza at Front and D (Broadway). *Courtesy San Diego Public Library*

"The Bay-Front," San Diego, perspective sketch shows the proposed railroad and water approaches, the Esplanade, the Art and Pleasure Centre at the foot of Date Street, and the Paseo connecting the bay with City Park (Balboa Park). *From John Nolen's book, San Diego, A Comprehensive Plan for Its Improvement*

a suitable connecting link, parkway or boulevard, can be developed, bringing them into direct and pleasant relation. Here, on this hillside [along a dozen blocks between Date and Elm streets east to the park entrance], at comparatively small expense, can be developed what I have called, after the custom in Spanish and Spanish-American cities, "The Paseo," a pleasant promenade, an airing place, a formal and dignified approach to the big central park, free from railroad grade crossings.

At the waterfront the Paseo would spread out to a width of 1,200 feet, and in this perfectly splendid situation, commanding the grandeur of San Diego's most characteristic scenery, the people could establish the proposed casino, art museum and aquarium, surrounding them with the lovely parks and gardens, which only the climatic conditions of Southern California make possible.

The union stations: There would appear to be advantages in having two stations, one north and the other south of D Street, the former for the Santa Fe Railroad, the latter for the San Diego & Arizona Railroad, thus lessening the travel across D Street itself. The vision of this new San Diego from the bay, with the mountains of Southern California and Mexico, noble in outline and rich in color, in the background, is enough to move the most sluggish to action.

V. Small Open Spaces

Each school, each ward, each residence district in San Diego, by nature a play city, should have its playground; and the time to provide them is now before real estate values are prohibitive and before land of suitable character is monopolized for private purposes. The possession of play areas is a necessity of city life, and by obtaining them now San Diego can avoid the heavy penalty of procrastination which New York and other cities have had to pay.

VI. Streets and Boulevards

If any citizen of San Diego wishes to see the street problem in aggravated form, a form in which it will soon appear in San Diego, let him go to Los Angeles and stand at the corner of Fifth and Spring streets or Fifth and Main streets, or go to other sections of that remarkable city. The problem there is already acute, and yet the provision has been much more ample in San Diego. The inadequate width of business streets is but one of San Diego's mistakes in street-making. The most glaring and serious, of course, is the attempt to implant a rectangular system, almost unrelieved by diagonals on so irregular a topography.

In planning for street trees in San Diego, the designer has a peculiar problem. He must aim to dress the street and relieve its barrenness, but avoid shading the houses. Even the sidewalk should not

The vision of this new San Diego from the bay, with the mountains of Southern California and Mexico, noble in outline and rich in color, in the background, is enough to move the most sluggish to action.

be densely shaded unless there remains a choice between a sunny and shaded one. For in San Diego there are few days in the year and few hours in the day, the resident soon learns, when the sun is not more welcome than shade.

Few cities in the United States have a more romantic history and situation than San Diego, and it is to be regretted that they have not expressed themselves in the street names. Southern California is full of color, of picturesqueness, of character, and it is a pity not to embody these qualities in the names that designate the public streets and avenues of the city. No method of honoring those to whom honor is due is more available, more appropriate, more enduring.

VII. A System of Parks

A system of parks is unquestionably demanded. Such a system can be secured more easily than in any other city that I know of. It should include characteristic, inexpensive, almost ready-made parks in every part of the city, and form a unique series of pleasure-grounds. The attractions from which to select are so great that choice is embarrassing:

1. Of course, the nucleus of the new park system would be the City [Balboa] Park and the people are to be congratulated on its possession. It is a magnificent tract of typical California country, especially satisfying in canyon scenery.

2. The improved bayfront would virtually be a park, and it illustrates what is true of many of the proposed parks for San Diego — little more is needed than a viewpoint, a foreground to a picture. Nature herself will supply the picture, and maintain it without cost. The Bayfront Boulevard [Harbor Drive] can with profit be extended all the way to Point Loma, and north and west of Date Street it will probably be possible to fill in a much wider strip.

3. A physical feature of value, the beauty of which it is impossible to overestimate, is Point Loma. The United States government owns and occupies the end of the promontory [Cabrillo National Monument and Fort Rosecrans], but the city should not rely entirely upon the national government's reservation. It should itself possess at least enough land on Point Loma to command at all times the marvelous view that can be enjoyed from there.

4. If only one beach were secured, probably the sand pit south of Pacific Beach [Mission Beach] would be best; but I recommend that the park system include, if possible a number of beaches.

5. La Jolla is practically a village within the city of San Diego, and it is one of the most romantic and alluring spots on the coast. Fortunately, the city now controls a well-located piece of property at La Jolla [Cove]. It needs but to add slightly to it, and give the park a unified treatment.

6. Soledad Mountain is practically a part of La Jolla. It is a natural site for a park.

7. A view of Mission Valley — broad and restful, with the foothills at one end and the bay at the other — is one of the landscape features that the proposed park system should unquestionably

include. The beautifully situated old mission itself, the first established in California, is a landmark of historic interest that should be preserved at any cost.

8. In Old Town, near and including Fort Stockton [Presidio Park], the city owns property which simply needs completing to form another center in this wonderful park system.

9. The final feature, the Torrey Pines, would form a unique addition to the park system, one that the city could not on any account afford to omit.

Connect this system of parks by the boulevards and parkways already planned, develop it naturally, simply, harmoniously, and then confidently invite comparison with it of any park system in the world. It would not be expensive to acquire, to construct, to maintain; it would not be extensive in acreage; but because of the range and grandeur of the natural scenery that it embraces and commands, and because of the rich vegetation and the succession of fine days, month after month, that San Diego's climate guarantees, it would surpass in recreative value any provision that the people of a modern city have yet succeeded in making. It would give to the citizen health, joy and more abundant life, and to the city itself wealth and enduring fame.

VIII. Summary

These recommendations may appear to present a heavy task for a city the size of San Diego; yet, after careful consideration and a comparison with the programs and achievements of other cities, I believe the proposed undertakings are all of a reasonable nature. When they are looked at from the point of view of 25 years hence, so far as that can be brought before the imagination, they will in many respects be considered inadequate. No city regrets its acquisition of parks, but many cities regret their failure to act in time.

While San Diego has not yet a large population, it is steadily growing, and there isn't a citizen without

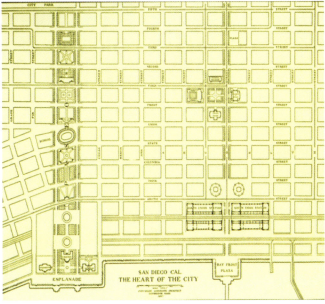

From John Nolen's book, San Diego, A Comprehensive Plan for Its Improvement

faith in its future. That faith must now express itself in action, for it is well known that public improvements requiring the acquisition of large property must precede population; otherwise they are impossible. A comprehensive and practicable plan is under consideration. It will take months to work it out even on paper, and years to execute it. But now is the time to adopt a policy and actually begin work on a far-reaching scheme the result of which, I believe, will surpass our fondest dreams.

But the success of the proposed work will depend not so much upon money as upon forethought, system, wise planning and public-spirited enterprise. Finally, let me say that with suitable approaches by land and water, a broad esplanade on the bayfront, a fine plaza in the heart of the city, a dignified yet simple treatment of D Street [Broadway], a liberal and impressive grouping of public buildings in ample grounds, a series of carefully designed playgrounds, a great system of parks well connected by boulevards — all this with its God-given scenery and climate — San Diego will be able to point with pride to its priceless public possessions, and feel sure that by timely action it has secured to its citizens forever a glorious heritage and advantages of inestimable worth.

FOUR

CHAPTER FOUR

Elaborate gardens were a highlight of the 1915 Exposition. This postcard shows the fountain and gardens fronting the Botanical Gardens
Courtesy San Diego Historical Society

FAIRS, WARS, SMOKESTACKS AND GERANIUMS

John Nolen's challenge to San Diego was bold and comprehensive but politically impractical at a time when San Diego was desperate for growth and development. In the decades ahead, Nolen's ideas would be implemented to varying degrees. However, the immediate priority in the years leading up to World War I was not building a civic center or bay-to-park pleasureland link. Rather, it was industrial development along the Embarcadero and tourist promotion in Balboa Park.

San Diego's tidelands were owned and controlled by the state, as stipulated in the original pueblo grant and terms and conditions for California's entry into the Union. In 1911, reformist Governor Hiram Johnson signed legislation that offered to turn over local control of the tidelands if San Diego would appropriate $1 million within one year for improvements. City Engineer Edwin Capps, a once and future mayor (1899-1901, 1915-17), proposed a commercial pier at the foot of Broadway (called D Street until 1913) along with filling in the tidelands, west of what is today Pacific Highway, for industrial use. This plan flew in the face of Nolen's proposal to devote that section of the bayfront for recreational and cultural uses. "It will be a great commercial mistake, as well as a bad check to the Nolen plans, to build wharves and warehouses for heavy shipping at D Street and northward," wrote merchant George W. Marston, the leading defender of the Nolen Plan.

The San Diego Civic Association, a coalition of environmental and neighborhood-oriented groups, urged that the Nolen Plan be followed or, at least, that the location of the pier be left unspecified in the November 14, 1911, vote on the tidelands development bonds. Nolen returned to San Diego in October and told 300 supporters that Capps' plan was a "grave mistake." But the voters agreed with Capps and overwhelmingly approved the filling of the bayfront and construction of Broadway Pier. It would take another 75 years before the Broadway-north waterfront would rid itself of industrial uses and begin to resemble what Nolen had envisioned.

"Let's Put on a Fair"

Tourist development had been a civic objective from Horton's time forward. G. Aubrey Davidson, a local Santa Fe railroad executive during the boom, championed the biggest tourist promotion of all — but one with far grander goals. Returning from Los Angeles to San Diego in 1907 to found the Southern Trust and Savings Bank, Davidson soon was elected president of the Chamber

1909-1945

Mayor Edwin Capps
Courtesy San Diego Historical Society

(Far right) G. Aubrey Davidson
Courtesy San Diego Historical Society

(Photo on page 90) Alcazar Gardens at Balboa Park with the California Tower in the background. *Courtesy San Diego Historical Society*

The construction of Broadway Pier, 1913. *Courtesy San Diego Historical Society*

of Commerce. At a July 9, 1909, meeting, he proposed that San Diego, "becalmed in the doldrums of its despair," capitalize on its location as the first American port of call for ships that would soon be passing through the Panama Canal. His idea: a world's fair, the "Panama-California Exposition." Clearly, Davidson and other fair promoters did not have in mind tourism as an end in itself. They saw the fair as a means for achieving something else — steady population growth coupled with industrial development. It boggled San Diegans' minds that Los Angeles might capture the developing shipping business along the west coast at a manmade harbor at San Pedro. Thus, what was immediately christened the Panama-California Exposition was intended as a giant public-relations campaign to publicize San Diego. Years later, Davidson explained why he thought it was the thing to do:

"[Our] situation at the time did not look promising for much port business with freight or passenger vessels. An occasional naval vessel came into the harbor and a small coaling station was located on Point Loma. We had the world's most beautiful bay, but very little was being done with it. On the other hand, we were the smallest city ever to propose a world's fair. Money would be needed with which to finance it, and the action of the voters toward our bond issue had not been encouraging, but I felt something must be done to get our city on the map and advertise it to the rest of the world. I

knew we had something here that no other city had, and that all that was necessary was for the people to know about it."

After considering various locations, the fair was sited in City Park, renamed Balboa Park in October 1910, apparently at the suggestion of Harriet Phillips of the San Diego Club and Pioneer Society. The name underscored the San Diego-Panama connection because it was near the Panama Canal site in 1513 that Spanish conquistador Vasco Nuñez de Balboa discovered the Pacific. Departing from the classical architectural themes common at other expositions, fair directors selected the Spanish Colonial style proposed by New York architect Bertram G. Goodhue; San Diego architect Irving J. Gill, the expo's first design director, had favored a simpler Mission Revival style. Also jettisoned was the naturalistic landscaping plan recommended in 1902 by consulting landscape architect Samuel Parsons Jr. of New York City and favored by the expo landscape architects, the Olmsted Brothers of Brookline, Massachusetts. Directors thought a tropical, Mediterranean palette of exotic plantings would be more impressive to visitors. Disagreeing over site, style and landscaping, Gill and the Olmsteds resigned; Marston, their chief defender, was on an extended trip to Europe and had no early involvement in exposition planning.

The civic good was not the only priority of fair backers. John D. Spreckels, owner of the San Diego Electric Railway Co. (as well as *The San Diego Union*, *Tribune* and numerous other holdings), seems to have prevailed upon the expo directors to shift the site to the park's central mesa. The public explanation was that the new site would offer more space for exhibitors; the private reason was Spreckels' desire to extend his streetcar system through the park and toward North Park and University Heights. He and other fair directors had real estate interests that stood to benefit from this move. Research indicates that Spreckels withheld his $100,000 pledge to the exposition until he got his way.

Whatever the backroom deals, the public enthusiastically supported the exposition, voting $1 million in bonds in August 1910 by a 7-1 margin and an additional $850,000 by an even wider margin in 1913. The state of California appropriated $250,000 for the California Building (including the 200-foot California Tower), Spreckels gave $100,000 for the

Where the Cabrillo Freeway (163) now crosses under Cabrillo Bridge, exposition builders constructed a large pond. *Courtesy San Diego Historical Society*

The Cabrillo Bridge was the first multi-arched, cantilever-type bridge in California. *Courtesy San Diego Historical Society*

Chapter Four

Lavish color brochures accompanied the publicity for the Panama-California Exposition. *Courtesy San Diego Historical Society*

(Far right) The official seal of the Panama-California Exposition. *Courtesy San Diego Historical Society*

organ pavilion and Frank P. Allen, director of works, who had managed Seattle's 1909 Alaska-Yukon Pacific Exposition, spent $225,000 on the Cabrillo Bridge, spanning today's State Route 163, as the ceremonial entrance to the fairgrounds.

San Diego had hoped for some of the $5 million earmarked in Washington to celebrate the canal's opening. But San Francisco, more than 10 times San Diego's size, offered a more politically attractive use for the money in promoting its own fair, the Panama-Pacific International Exposition. Republican President William Howard Taft, who needed San Francisco's support in his 1912 reelection bid, saw to it that federal subsidies and foreign representation only went to that city. "To hell with Congress; San Diego has raised $3 million on her own; we won't fight over the lousy $5 million," said D.C. Collier, one of San Diego's biggest fair boosters. "We'll have our own fair." As it turned out, Taft lost California to third-party candidate and former President Theodore Roosevelt. San Diego County went for the winner, Democrat Woodrow Wilson.

Construction rapidly transformed the dry, featureless mesa and canyons into a veritable garden, framing a magical city of beautiful pleasure palaces. To mark the opening on New Year's Eve in 1914, President Wilson pushed a button in the White House, turning on the lights.

In its two-year run the Panama-California Exposition attracted more than 3.7 million people. Receipts topped expenses by $34,000. (The 9 1/2-month San Francisco fair attracted 18.9 million people and netted $2.4 million.) VIPs to the fair included former Presidents Roosevelt and Taft, future President Franklin D. Roosevelt, Thomas Edison and Henry Ford. Seven states and 28 of the state's 58 counties were represented at what was more a regional than a world's fair.

San Diego broke new ground, in both its architectural and landscaping approach. It was the first such expo to operate year-round. Exhibits showed how things worked or were made, not just what products looked like upon completion. For example, Lipton Tea Company set up a working tea plantation. An electrical substation showed how the exposition grounds were lighted at night and visitors could visit a model mine shaft. In addition, there was an elaborate exhibit on the Mayans, organized by the Smithsonian Institution's Ales Hrdlicka.

Opening day of the Panama-California Exposition, 1915. *Courtesy San Diego Historical Society*

(Opposite page) The opening of the Panama Canal was celebrated in the annual issue of *The San Diego Union*. *Courtesy San Diego Historical Society*

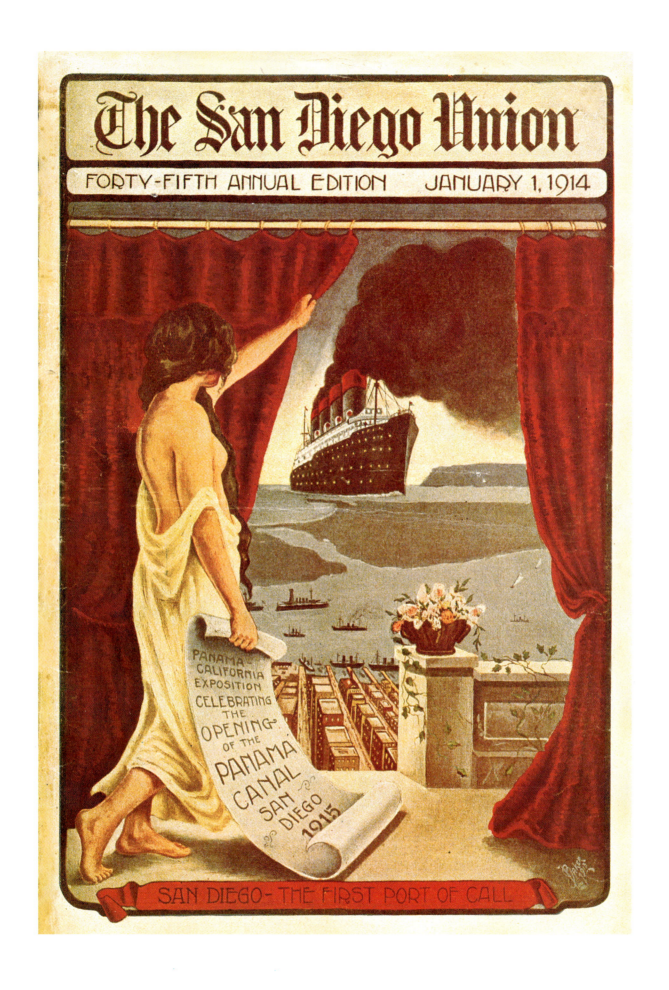

The lily pond of the 1915 exposition featured a balustraded bridge which separated the "Laguna" in two. *Courtesy San Diego Historical Society*

Sweetwater Dam, January 30, 1916 *Courtesy San Diego Historical Society*

(Far right) "The rainmaker," Charles Hatfield, in the field. *Courtesy San Diego Historical Society*

The exposition also included the standard fun zone, known as "The Isthmus," with attractions like a mock opium den, 6,000-foot roller coaster, ostrich farm and working movie studio. *The Liberator* starring Douglas Fairbanks was filmed in the Plaza de Panama in December 1916. A "War of the Worlds" shows depicted the destruction of New York City in the year 2000 by invading Asians and Africans. At the north end of The Isthmus was the 10-acre Indian Village, trading post and "Painted Desert" built by the Atchison, Topeka & Santa Fe Railway and staffed by 300 Indians from Arizona and New Mexico in native dress.

Prospects for a glorious second year were temporarily forgotten as San Diego County experienced its worst flood on record. The Morena Reservoir was dangerously low and the city hired Charles M. Hatfield, the "moisture accelerator," to fill the reservoir, 60 miles east of town. Hatfield, who had begun experimenting with chemicals in 1902 on his father's ranch near Oceanside, built a 20-foot tower and mixed a secret rain-inducing brew. On January 14, 1916, it began raining. The newly opened Agua Caliente Race Track in Tijuana suspended operations. Exposition events were rescheduled. The Lower Otay and Sweetwater dams gave way, bridges went out and train tracks were washed away. Hatfield appeared at City Hall February 5 and demanded his $10,000 payment. The city attorney noted that the contract had not actually been signed and Hatfield filed suit at year's end. The city agreed to pay but only if Hatfield assumed responsibility for $3.5 million in damage claims against the city. He gave his up quest and his suit was not dismissed until 1938. (Burt Lancaster starred in the 1956 movie, "The Rainmaker," but the author of the original Broadway play, N. Richard Nash, claimed there was no connection between his character and Hatfield.)

The exposition, renamed the Panama-California *International* Exposition, was rededicated March 18, 1916, and attendance rose rapidly as visitors came to see exhibits transferred from the San Francisco fair, including those from Canada, France, the Netherlands and Switzerland. New attractions included an ice-skating rink, alligator farm, "Elizabeth the Lilliputian" and a Shakespearean festival performed by 500 school children. The New York Symphony Orchestra under Walter Damrosch performed at the organ pavilion and operatic contralto Ernestine Schumann-Heink, who had opened the exposition while living part-time in San Diego, closed out the fair singing "Auld Lang Syne" as a fireworks display spelled out "World Peace —1917" at midnight December 31. As exhibits closed down from January to March, the exposition continued in a reduced fashion.

Most world's fairs leave few physical remnants behind and architect Bertram Goodhue strongly recommended that all the temporary buildings be immediately razed and replaced by gardens as originally intended. But San Diegans had fallen in love with their dream city and objected to plans to demolish most of the buildings. New uses were found for them and out of those makeshift operations grew many of San Diego's key cultural institutions, including the Museum of Man, San Diego Museum of Art and the San Diego Zoo.

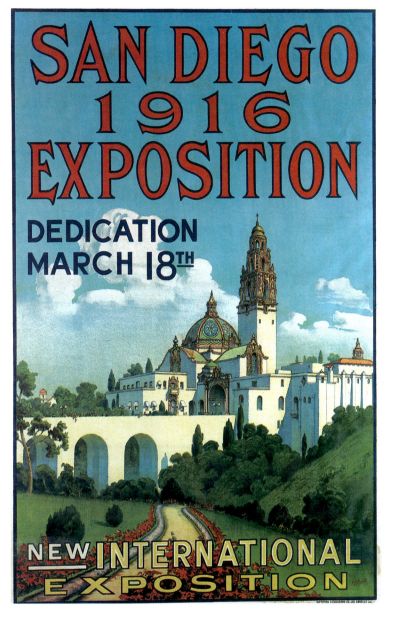

With the success of the 1915 exposition, the fair was extended another year and renamed the Panama-California International Exposition. *Courtesy San Diego Historical Society*

The fair also spurred other developments as its promoters had hoped. The U.S. Grant Hotel, along with a redesigned Horton Plaza, opened in 1910. Glenn Curtiss founded a flying school in 1911 at North Island. The Spreckels Theatre opened in 1912. The new, Mission Revival-styled Santa Fe Depot replaced the Victorian railway station in 1915. Tijuana, seeking to capitalize on the thousands of visitors, opened a racetrack in 1916, and San Diego leaders worked to gain a more dependable water supply and transportation network for automobiles.

Chapter Four

U.S. Grant Hotel, c. 1910
Courtesy San Diego Historical Society

Tensions and Turmoil

The period also saw rising tensions in counterpoint to the upbeat atmosphere for tourists. The outbreak of revolution in Mexico prompted the arrival in Tijuana in May 1911 of radicals led by exiles Ricardo and Enrique Flores Magón. The Magonistas occupied the city until Mexican federal troops liberated it June 22. Members of the International Workers of the World, familiarly known as the "Wobblies," participated in the Magonista revolt and anarchist Emma Goldman arrived in town to help recruit volunteers. Many radicals remained in San Diego into 1912, campaigning for workers' rights and free speech on the streets of downtown San Diego. The City Council passed an ordinance banning speeches on street corners and vigilante groups began to take matters into their own hands. On May 14, police hustled Goldman and her party to the train station and the riots ended.

Six months later, police and health inspectors conducted a raid on the Stingaree (the south section of today's Gaslamp Quarter) and arrested 138 prostitutes. Appearing before a judge, they were given the choice to reform or leave town. Two promised to be good and the rest said they'd leave for Los Angeles. However, most bought roundtrip tickets and in a few days were spotted back in San Diego, setting up house in Mission Hills, along El Cajon Boulevard or in other neighborhoods. As the police had warned, vice now would be more difficult to control because it had spread throughout the city.

As these disturbances indicated, the first few years of the 20th century were hardly the "good old days." The College Woman's Club in its March 1914 *Pathfinders Social Survey of San Diego* declared that the city suffered "from an undeveloped state of social consciousness and unconcern of many of its citizens for the needs of the whole." The milk supply was unsafe due to lax regulation. Mexican residents crowded into old houses and "unsanitary shacks." Less than half the students at San Diego High School received diplomas; nearly half the boys worked from four to 40 hours per week. "The harbor is a cesspool," the women said, because untreated sewage flowed directly into the bay. Half the 85 infants who died in 1913 might have survived if sanitary conditions had been better. And so, it is not surprising that the worldwide influenza epidemic that broke out in September 1918 struck 5,040 of 70,000 residents, killed 366 and prompted the closing of schools, movie theaters and other nonessential places of public assembly. People were required to wear gauze masks in public and urged to exercise in fresh air and take drives into the mountains. The emergency passed early in the new year.

San Diego firemen turned water hoses on Wobblie demonstrators, 1912. *Courtesy San Diego Historical Society*

Smokestacks Versus Geraniums

Like public health and social policy, political development and civic enlightenment fell somewhat short of expectations. For all the talk of a modern, forward-thinking, progressive San Diego, voters twice rejected its leading citizen, George W. Marston, in the mayor's races of 1913 and 1917. The second campaign featured the slogan "Smokestacks versus Geraniums," a phrase that neatly summarized competing forces throughout San Diego's modern history. Was this to be a traditional city, tied to heavy (and polluting) industry or one in which economic growth and development would be tempered by a concern for maintaining environmental quality?

A campaign newspaper ridiculed the "geranium" camp in the 1917 mayoral campaign. *Courtesy San Diego Historical Society*

Proudly proclaiming himself the "smokestacks" candidate was banker and all-round promoter Louis J. Wilde. He held out the prospect of job growth, which had not surged ahead as exposition proponents had expected. His campaign song stated Wilde's priorities best:

> San Diego needs a mayor who will bring prosperity,
> Who will help to build up factories in this city by the sea.
> Oh, we love to have the tourists come, in our sunshine to bask,
> But we need some smokestacks:
> Give us work: a chance is all we ask.
> Yes, we, too, enjoy the flowers in this climate without par,
> But a steady job that pays us well, we need that more by far,
> For our children want to go to school as well clad as the rest.
> Let's elect a man, 'who knows the game:'
> Trust him to do his best.

Marston believed in business, of course, but found himself tagged by Wilde as "Geranium George" for favoring planning and civic beauty. Marston ineffectively fought back with reasoned speeches rather than catchy sound-bites:

"I stand most emphatically for the kind of manufacturing and business that fits in with our natural conditions, has the largest promise of profit and therefore of permanence. Such industries, for instance, as ship building, marine ways, fisheries, the gathering of kelp and other sea products. Factories for the canning of fruit, vegetables and fish are based upon our natural resources. I favor and will work for establishment of cotton factories and packing plants that will give a market to the farmers of Imperial [Valley], give freight to the San Diego and Arizona Railway and add greatly to the payroll of San Diego."

Wilde defeated Marston April 3, 1917, on a vote of 12,818 to 9,167. As Marston wrote John Nolen afterwards, "The forces of commercialism and rapid superficial growth defeated the people who stood for more conservative methods of building the city." Despite Wilde's preelection promises, no new smokestacks industries arrived during his four years in office and he moved to Los Angeles in 1921 where he died three years later. Marston lived another 29 years, adding one accomplishment after another for the civic good.

The candidate for "smokestacks," Louis J. Wilde (left), defeated "Geranium George" Marston in the 1917 mayoral race. *Courtesy San Diego Historical Society*

Sprawling Camp Kearny was a major San Diego Army base during World War I. *Courtesy San Diego Historical Society*

Congressman William Kettner
Courtesy San Diego Historical Society

Navy Town, U.S.A.

From the 1890s onward, San Diegans had seen merit in boosting their harbor as a home to the Navy. The 1908 visit of Teddy Roosevelt's Great White Fleet only served to whet the locals' appetite for a permanent presence. But it was the election of Democrat William Kettner to Congress in 1912 that made possible the growth of the military's presence.

Kettner, an insurance agent, was a Chamber of Commerce director who was recruited to run so San Diego could have its own representative in Washington. The fact that he served during the Democratic administrations of Woodrow Wilson only increased his clout. "I'm sorry he is not a good old-fashioned Republican, as I am," said Spreckels at a homecoming reception in October 1913. "However, for a Democrat he comes nearer to being a Republican than anyone I know."

Working deftly behind the scenes, Kettner garnered support from Southern congressmen, slipped through minor appropriations for modest public works and outfoxed the ambitions of San Francisco Bay area and Los Angeles. By the time he retired in 1921, "the million-dollar congressman" had secured what was to become the North Island Naval Air Station, Marine Corps Recruit Depot, Naval Training Center, Naval Hospital, Miramar Marine Corps Air Station, Naval Supply Depot (now the Broadway Complex) and the Naval Station San Diego at 32nd Street. Illinois Representative Fred Britten said of his San Diego colleague, "He has hypnotized not only the [House military affairs] committee but Congress and that is the reason that he does so well for San Diego." After he died in 1930 at age 65, Arctic Street was renamed Kettner Boulevard in his honor. Kettner paved the way for his successors to carry on his work. For example, Kettner befriended Franklin D. Roosevelt, Wilson's assistant secretary of the navy who visited San Diego during the exposition and later awarded many grants to San Diego when he became president. As historian Roger W. Lotchin wrote in 1992:

"From the very beginning, San Diego leaders had a precise notion of what a city should be and an equally exact idea of how the Navy could be used to help them create it. The partnership of the city and the sword was a very comfortable one, in part because the Navy provided a means to achieve industrial development while not sacrificing the famous quality of life in the city. That alliance eventually focused vast forces of military development on the San Diego area, thereby tying the fate of urbanization to defense.

"Nonetheless, the Border City was not simply a product of the exigencies of the modern nation state. In the future, the city would become ever more reliant upon such outside influences and would never again possess the kind of freedom it had enjoyed in 1913."

World War I

Three days after Wilde beat Marston, Congress declared war on Germany. The two rivals shook hands at a patriotic dinner April 6, 1917, at the U.S. Grant Hotel, where plans were announced to offer Balboa Park buildings and grounds. The Park Commission formalized the deal May 4 and city staff spent $30,000 to convert the buildings east of the Plaza de Panama to handle 5,000 recruits and their training needs. A tent hospital established near Plaza de Balboa became the precursor to the Balboa Naval Hospital completed in 1922. The U.S.

Parade in 1917 *Courtesy San Diego Historical Society*

government also condemned 1,233 acres of North Island for Army and Navy use, paying Spreckels $6.1 million in 1921.

The Army established a temporary base, Camp Kearny, on 3,254 acres within the city and 9,466 acres on adjacent unincorporated area of what was then referred to as Linda Vista. This later became the Miramar Naval (then, Marine Corps) Air Station. In June 1919, Congress authorized the San Francisco Naval Training Station's relocation to San Diego, after the Chamber of Commerce raised $290,000 to buy 214 acres of Loma Portal land and city tidelands. (Eighty years later, the Naval Training Center reverted to city ownership in the wake of post-Cold War defense downsizing.) In all, World War I resulted in $19 million in construction of military establishments in San Diego County. California historian Kevin Starr, declaring that "San Diego had joined the Navy," observed:

> Like all negotiated settlements, joining the Navy had its tradeoffs… San Diego had always been a city that sustained within itself an anti-urban impulse, a city that

On November 15, 1919, John D. Spreckels drove the "golden spike," completing the San Diego & Arizona Railway. *Courtesy San Diego Historical Society*

> wanted to be urban and suburban-pastoral at one and the same moment. Transforming itself into a military theme park, San Diego found a Progressive middle way between the untrammeled capitalism of Los Angeles and the restrictive estheticism that was even then relegating Santa Barbara to the permanent status of a semi-resort. Selective, socially structured through rank and protocol, the Navy brought an idealized industrial presence to San Diego.

John D. Spreckels *Courtesy San Diego Historical Society*

One project that proceeded throughout the war was Spreckels' San Diego & Arizona Railway. The U.S. Railway Administration seized the unfinished line in December 1917 and halted all construction. In Washington, Spreckels successfully appealed the following May for work to resume. The war was long over by the time Spreckels drove the last spike November 15, 1919. It had cost him $18 million for 139.8 miles between San Diego and Seeley. The first through-train arrived in San Diego at 3:40 p.m., December 1. "Here comes San Diego's first real smokestack," Mayor Wilde crowed. It had taken more than 50 years for San Diego to get its own rail connection to the east.

Postwar Prosperity and Growth

World War I ended in November 1918 and with peace came renewed interest in the automobile. A believer in the new mode of transportation was Ed Fletcher, whose far-flung suburban developments depended on a modern road system to succeed. He headed the chamber's highway committee and participated in numerous road races to demonstrate practical routes within and beyond the county. He had the backing of powerful business interests. Spreckels, Scripps and sporting goods magnate A.G. Spalding served on a road commission in 1908 and approved a 1,250-mile county road system costing $2 million. Fletcher's cousin, Austin B. Fletcher, Massachusetts' chief engineer, was hired as county highway engineer to oversee the work. But efficient transportation was not universally welcomed. At a meeting in Julian, farmers heard that the time to transport hay to San Diego could be cut from two days to four hours by means of roads and trucks. "Mr. Scripps," one farmer asked the publisher, "if the trucks bring in the hay, who in hell is going to eat it?" Julian voted against the road bonds but they passed anyway.

Setting the tone for the carefree, post-war period, Edward, Prince of Wales, visited San Diego in 1920 and was entertained at a lavish banquet at the Hotel del Coronado, at which Mayor Wilde's daughter Lucille made her debut. It is almost certain that Edward did not meet his future wife, Wallis Warfield Spencer, at this time. The then-wife of Navy Lieutenant Earl W. Spencer was visiting friends in Monterey and missed the prince's visit. Sixteen years later, as Edward VIII, he abdicated the British throne to marry "the woman I love" and together they became the celebrated Duke and Duchess of Windsor.

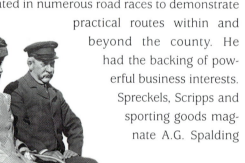

Sporting goods magnate A. G. Spalding and his wife in perhaps the first auto in San Diego, 1905. *Courtesy San Diego Historical Society*

The U.S.-Mexico border at San Ysidro, 1925. *Courtesy San Diego Historical Society*

The Roaring Twenties got a pickup from the easy access to alcoholic beverages in Tijuana, whose nightclubs were not covered by U.S. prohibition laws. The stars motored down from Hollywood and the border city's sordid reputation for rampant vice took firm hold in this period.

Ironically, the lax lifestyles were balanced by a renewal in proper city planning, which Mayor Wilde had left dormant. San Diego was among the first municipalities in California to create a planning commission and adopt zoning ordinances. Individual developers imposed their own special restrictions. For example, the 15-block, 66-acre community of Kensington Park, which opened for sale in 1910 far from the city center, pledged to offer homes that could never "be conveyed, transferred or demised to a person other than one of the white or Caucasian race." There were strict setbacks and limited uses (no apartments, duplexes, hotels or commercial buildings) allowed over the 16-year term of the deed restrictions.

In an indication that San Diego's Latin roots were worth celebrating, later additions to Kensington Park specified architectural designs patterned after the Panama-California Spanish Colonial styles. Local architect Richard Requa reviewed house plans for their adherence to what he dubbed "Southern California Style." The red-tile roof, indoor-outdoor bungalow layout and complementary landscaping remained popular through many changes in fashion for the rest of the century.

The "Southern California Style" achieved its greatest elaboration in Rancho Santa Fe. The rural subdivision was built on railroad property which had been planted with eucalyptus trees in the mistaken belief that the fast-growing Australian native would produce good railroad ties. The Santa

Hilldale Road running east to Marlborough Drive, Kensington Heights, 1929. *Courtesy San Diego Historical Society*

Chapter Four

Fe Land Improvement Co. hired Requa's firm in 1922 to master-plan the ranch and Requa turned it over to his associate, architect Lilian Rice. She designed many of the homes and commercial structures, paying close attention to details, such as wrought-iron and wood grilles, door latches and lanterns. The American Institute of Architects gave Rice, one of the few women working in the architectural profession, its honor award. Incidentally, it was at this time that serious restoration began on the Mission San Diego de Alcalá. Marston was president of the San Diego Mission Restoration Commission, founded in 1914, and major work ultimately costing $76,000 was carried out between 1919 and 1931.

A Second Nolen Plan

In 1921, reformer and planning-minded John L. Bacon, publisher of the *Independent* newspaper, succeeded Wilde and backed Marston's proposal to bring Nolen back to update the 1908 city plan. Nolen declared that San Diego still had the capacity to shape its destiny via good planning and urban design:

> Without doubt San Diego should be a more distinctive city in its physical development. Its topography, its climate, its purposes are all different from the average American city. Not to be distinctive is an advantage lost, and some things in San Diego cannot now be changed. The question is, what can be done to recover lost ground and lead toward a more distinctive San Diego for the future? Careful development based on the character of the site of San Diego, the peculiar merits of the climate and the possibility of a different quality of life in Southern California, remains to be considered later in the proposals.

Among Nolen's key recommendations in 1926 were: (1) a civic center on the filled-in tidelands; (2) waterfront developments, including marinas, anchorages, Harbor Drive and a municipal airport; (3) a parkway system extending across Mission Valley, through Mission Bay, up the coast and through several canyons and river valleys; (4) parks and recreational centers at Mission Bay, La Jolla Shores, Pacific Beach, Ocean Beach and Silver Strand, Torrey Pines Mesa and around water reservoirs and dams; (5) playgrounds, libraries and schools grouped together in neighborhood centers;

Mission San Diego de Alcalá in ruin, c. 1900. *Courtesy San Diego Historical Society*

(6) historic preservation in Old Town and Presidio Park; (7) a second entrance to San Diego Bay; and (8) comprehensive zoning and regional planning.

Unlike the first plan, the second Nolen Plan was immediately embraced by civic leaders. About 1,000 people attended a public presentation in February 1926. Will Rogers, speaking at an American Legion event, urged San Diegans to action: "Now you have a real plan prepared by Nolen. Don't let any prominent citizen get up and talk you out of it." The City Council approved the plan March 8 and it remained in effect for 40 years. The Nolen Plan prompted other long-range planning efforts. In 1930, the city adopted a major street plan that formed the basis for the freeways built 30 years later. In 1938, a $35.5 million capital improvement program was completed. It contemplated the construction of 21 parks, 50 water projects and 151 highway intersections. "The necessity of spending by plan needs no explanation; it is required," said Planning Director Glenn A. Rick. "San Diego, like other progressive modern cities, realizes that government spending is a business — the public's business."

Besides the new city plan, Nolen prepared a new master plan for Balboa Park, constantly threatened by various nonpark encroachments. Already, San Diego High School, Roosevelt Junior High School and the Naval Hospital occupied prime park property and the exposition buildings (or their replacements) remained where gardens had originally been intended to be planted after the 1915-16 fair. Marston successfully led the campaign to oppose the ever-popular San Diego Zoo. In 1925, the voters rejected by a 3,847-6,088 vote a proposal to create a zoological commission that would no longer be subject to the Board of Park Commissioners. In a letter to the editor, Marston wrote:

"Balboa Park is primarily a park, to be cherished as a place of natural beauty. Although it is one of the largest parks in the country the time is coming when the building of hospitals and school houses, or even

San Diego State Teachers College, c. 1927 *Courtesy San Diego Historical Society*

libraries and museums, must cease, or else we shall have a city there instead of a park."

The most serious threat to the park came in 1926, when a mayor's committee recommended 125 acres of the park's northeast section be set aside as a new home for San Diego State Teachers College. The institution at Normal Street had grown to more than 1,000 students as a result of its expansion to four-year status in 1921, and the state legislature offered to build a new campus if the city would provide free land and purchase the Normal School site. But opponents successfully defended retention of parkland as open space. The election went against the college by a vote of 6,561 in favor, 15,560 opposed. Two years later, 85 percent approved an alternate on Montezuma Mesa. This proposal envisioned a Spanish-style campus surrounded by a planned community of golf courses, polo fields and single-family homes on one-acre lots. The ambitious real estate venture faltered but San Diego State got its new home, designed by W.K. Daniels and projected to cost $7.5 million over 10 years. The first classes opened in February 1931.

A new home also was found in San Diego for one of the last of the "tall ships." The *Euterpe*, a 205-foot-long, iron-hulled sailing ship built in England in 1863 to transport immigrants to New Zealand, had been retired by the Alaska Packers Association in 1923. A group of San Diegans rescued the renamed *Star of India* in 1927, hoping she could be used as a

floating aquarium by the San Diego Zoo. and brought to San Diego in 1927. Visitors paid 25 cents for a look, but an aquarium was never built and the ship was nearly ruined through neglect during World War II. The San Diego Maritime Museum took charge from the Zoo in 1958 and restoration was well along by the *Star's* 100th birthday in 1963.

Throughout the first decades of the 20th century, San Diego's water supply system grew to match the booming population. Prompted by the disastrous 1916 Hatfield flood, Ed Fletcher, Phil Swing, William G. Henshaw, James A. Murray and others helped build and promote dams, aqueducts and an eventual link to the Colorado River to secure San Diego's access to water. Not only residents but agriculture and industry depended on it; naturally, land owners and developers were in the forefront of water development. "Water is king," Fletcher wrote, "and the basis of all value in this county is water." Said Shelley J. Higgins, city attorney in the 1920s: "If we are going to live here, we must have water. We pay whatever it costs to put it in our pipes. When we reach the limit of our ability to pay, we reach our limit of existence."

San Diego: Air Capital of the West

The 1920s brought forth a smokestack industry that Wilde would have embraced. The area had long appealed to airplane enthusiasts, dating back to John J. Montgomery's experiments with gliders on Otay Mesa in 1883. He claimed credit for the first controlled wing flight but the Wright Brothers got all the fame in 1903.

Waldo Waterman, 15-year-old son of a former governor, launched a glider from Albatross and Maple streets, flying 125 feet down a hill. But his lasting contribution came in 1910 at the First American International Aviation Meet in Los Angeles, where he volunteered to help Glenn A. Curtiss, then America's most famous flyer who owned Curtiss Aeroplane Company in Hammondsport, New York. Waterman told Curtiss about the ideal flight conditions in San Diego and Curtiss arranged to lease then-vacant North Island from Spreckels at $1 per year. He established a Navy flight school in 1911 and trained numerous pilots who would return to San Diego permanently. Clyde C. Pangborn opened Pangborn Aircraft Company in 1920, charging $10 for 15-minute rides. He also performed self-described "air devil" feats, including boarding a plane on a rope from a moving passenger car.

More serious was *T. Claude Ryan*, who organized Ryan Airlines in 1925 with partner B. Franklin Mahoney. They launched the first regularly scheduled air passenger service in the United States — year-round, 90-minute flights between San Diego and Los Angeles. A Chamber of Commerce aviation committee already was at work developing plans for a municipal airfield. It picked a bayside site in 1924, which John Nolen included in his 1926 city plan.

The next year, San Diego gained worldwide fame when Charles A. Lindbergh contracted to have his *Spirit of St. Louis* built by Ryan Aeronautical Company in San Diego. The 25-year-old airmail carrier was in St. Louis trying to arrange for financing for his entry into the $25,000 sweepstakes to be the first person to fly solo and nonstop from New York to Paris. He read about Ryan's M-1 *Ryan Brougham* and on February 28, 1927, signed a $16,580 contract. While Lindbergh mapped his route at the downtown public library, Ryan crews raced to meet a 60-day deadline. He took off from North Island for New York on May 9 and for Paris on May 20, arriving 33 hours 29 minutes later. Lindbergh returned a hero to San Diego September 21, addressing a record crowd at Balboa Stadium. His popularity carried over into the November 22

Glenn Curtiss on San Diego Bay, 1911 *Courtesy San Diego Historical Society*

(Opposite page) *Star of India* in San Diego harbor, c. 1930. *Courtesy San Diego Maritime Museum*

Pioneers of American aviation, Reuben H. Fleet and George H. Prudden in 1928
Courtesy San Diego Historical Society

Charles Lindbergh (second from left) in 1927
Courtesy San Diego Historical Society

election, when voters approved $65,000 in airport bonds by an 80 percent margin. As the chamber president said the day after the election, "The fact that every precinct in the city gave a majority for Lindbergh Field clearly demonstrates that aviation and the aircraft industry are of universal appeal and that all classes of citizens recognize their potentialities."

Two major aerospace companies resulted from the election. First was George H. Prudden who formed Prudden-San Diego Airplane Co. Edmund T. Price reorganized the company and in 1929 it became Solar Aircraft Co. Then came Major Reuben H. Fleet. He was familiar with San Diego, having patrolled the border following the Mexican Revolution in 1911. He learned to fly at Rockwell Field on North Island in 1917 and in 1929, offered to buy Lindbergh Field for $1 million or build his factories around Mission Bay. Neither effort was approved. But T.C. Macaulay, Fleet's old flight instructor and now manager of the Chamber of Commerce, sent Fleet monthly reports on San Diego's advantages as an airplane manufacturing base. The lobbying paid off when Fleet's board at Consolidated Aircraft Co. (later renamed Convair) in Buffalo, New York, voted May 29, 1933, to move to San Diego to take advantage of the mild climate. "Needless to say," wrote historian Roger W. Lotchin, "the major's arrival at the border city was no simple outcome of geography, economic determinism, climate or culture. San Diego worked hard to acquire Consolidated and did so by providing everything that the manufacturer would need, right down to an old-boy Army Air Corps pal, who as Chamber of Commerce president [actually manager] could make the offer." The Convair-San Diego love affair lasted nearly 60 years.

A Second Exposition

Fleet's arrival in San Diego came none too soon. The Depression had settled upon the land and the locals desperately needed jobs. San Diego benefited from lucrative and frequent Navy construction contracts and federal public-works grants. Major projects completed in the 1930s included the County Administration Center and Harbor Drive; the Del Mar racetrack, Aztec Bowl and Greek Theater at San Diego State; a city hall, jail, and fire station in Escondido; a San Diego Police

Department headquarters on Market Street; a reptile house at the San Diego Zoo; and numerous road, brush-clearing and park projects. In all, San Diego County agencies received an estimated $20 million for more than 1,000 federal relief projects.

Federal subsidies also made possible a second fair in Balboa Park, the California Pacific International Exposition in 1935-36. It was the brainchild of Frank Drugan, former field representative of the Scripps-Howard newspaper chain. He had seen Chicago's Century of Progress Exposition in 1933-34 and proposed moving exhibits to San Diego.

Restoration work already was under way on the 1915 exposition buildings when the architect on that work, Richard Requa, took over management of architecture and design on the much more ambitious undertaking. Requa proposed to complement the Spanish Colonial design of the Prado area with pre-Columbian designs for new and permanent buildings to be placed southwest of the Prado in the Palisades area. Design and construction proceeded at a frantic pace from September 1934 to opening day, May 29, 1935. Ford Motor Co. built what is today's San Diego Aerospace Museum. Standard Oil Company of California built the 108-foot "Tower of the Sun" in Pan-American Plaza facing the Ford Building. The Old Globe Theatre, Spanish Village and a reconfigured House of Hospitality were built for the fair and remained afterwards.

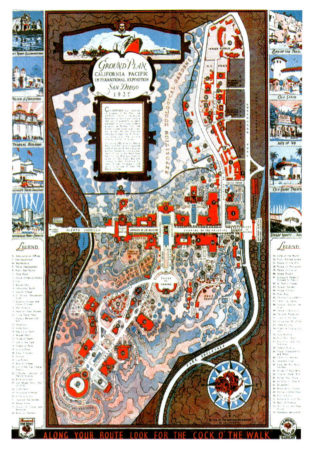

California Pacific International Exposition map, 1935 *Courtesy San Diego Historical Society*

A full range of events included concerts sponsored by Henry and Edsel Ford in the Ford (now Starlight) Bowl. "The Midway" fun zone offered a scale model city and farm, staffed by 100 "little people;" Ripley's Believe It or Not; Gold Gulch, a western frontier town in the Pepper Grove; the Mickey Mouse Circus; and the "Days of '49 Stockade." Elsewhere in the park were the Zoro Gardens nudist colony and Indian Village, peopled by 150 Native Americans. Prominent visitors included President Roosevelt, former President Herbert Hoover and evangelist Aimee Semple McPherson, who spoke to overflow crowds twice at the Spreckels Organ Pavilion. Mae West quipped upon her arrival: "I'm sorry I didn't know the fleet was coming in tomorrow as I certainly would have come down then. I'm very patriotic that

Ocean-going log raft headed for the Benson Lumber Company, c. 1908. *Courtesy San Diego Historical Society*

way." Sally Rand, the fan and bubble dancer performed four times daily in April 1936. The first season closed November 11,1935, and the second ran from February 12 to September 9,1936. Total attendance was 7.2 million.

Once the exposition closed, the debate reopened on what Balboa Park should be. Banker Joseph W. Sefton Jr. was in the minority in favoring demolition of the fair buildings: "Had we torn out the 1915 exposition buildings and landscaped the park, we would have a beautiful place there now and not a long row of ramshackle firetraps… One of these days a fire will sweep them all anyhow." Researcher Richard Amero, after combing through scrapbooks and newspapers chronicling both fairs, concluded the California-Pacific did not equal the Panama-California in architectural legacy or economic spin-offs. But he cited some intangible benefits: "It gave San Diego widespread publicity. It offered visitors enjoyment, culture and hope. The exposition helped to instill confidence in people beset by economic difficulties. For those who were young at the time, the exposition was the time of their lives."

A SECOND WAR

With the arrival of Consolidated Aircraft, San Diego soon took on the pace and appearance of a factory town bent on preparing for war. Contracts flowed to the company and employment climbed to 3,000 by the end of 1936. Ryan Aeronautical Co. received orders for all-metal biplanes and Solar Aircraft Co. built exhaust manifolds. The War Department deepened the bay and Lindbergh Field was expanded. By 1939, Consolidated began producing attack bombers for the Army Air Corps. At the outbreak of war in Europe, San Diego had eight military establishments encompassing 634 buildings spread across 4,000 acres and representing an investment of $51 million. In September 1940, Consolidated employed 9,000 workers on $132 million in backlogged contracts. Solar Aircraft Co. had 700 employees and $3 million in orders. Fred H. Rohr left Ryan and established an aircraft components parts factory in Chula Vista.

The 1940 census pegged San Diego's population at 203,341 and the county's at 289,348. The rise in factory orders was adding 1,500 families per week and three national magazines noted the strain on the community. In July 1941, the *Saturday Evening Post* termed the rapid growth a "boom blitz." Author Frank J. Taylor followed Mayor Percy Benbough around town, describing the nightmare that accompanied the war buildup. "Today, San Diego is a rip-snorting Little Detroit," Taylor wrote, "booming with defense industry." In Mission Valley there were auto trailers connected to temporary gas meters. "In a city noted for its homes and gardens, these mobile slums presented an incongruous site," Taylor wrote. Benbough told him, "Last year we wouldn't allow that sort of thing. Now, what can we do? These people have to sleep somewhere."

Also in July 1941, *Life* magazine ran its own report, "Boom Town: San Diego." The six-page spread said San Diego was the nation's fastest growing city: "Until a year ago people walked leisurely

Famed fan dancer Sally Rand was a big hit at the 1936 exposition. *Courtesy San Diego Historical Society*

down Broadway, drove quietly through Balboa Park. Now they stride hurriedly, drive like mad." The magazine has this advice: "What San Diego must do is to ensure good working and living conditions for its new masses of workingmen. Beyond that it must supply inexpensive entertainment for these workers and for soldiers and sailors who walk its streets."

The third national report on San Diego appeared in the January 1942 *National Geographic*. An advertisement preceding the 35-page account glossed over the war clouds gathering in the fall when the publication was completed and introduced readers to "Defense City No. 1." "Right now San Diego is especially beautiful and especially exciting," the ad read. It was accompanied by pictures of women in bathing suits, women riding horses in the mountains and a boy and his dog fishing at the beach. "Dark-painted men of war slip in and out of the harbor, cruising air squadrons cross the sky, anti-aircraft searchlights sweep the night. You'll have a ringside seat for the greatest drama of our time! Come!"

Entitled "San Diego Can't Believe It," the magazine article by Frederick Simplich captured the mood of a city in transition:

> Down in the southwest nook of the United States there hums, hammers, booms and whistles one of the world's most crowded, most astonished cities. I mean San Diego, "where California began." Today her once quiet, sunshiny air is full of dust, smoke, steam, zooming planes and the roar of gunfire. Without taking thought, she sees cubits added to her stature. Transformed, she is, by the fury of men making ready to fight... To shelter this ever-growing industrial army, government scrapes down hills, lays miles of streets and water pipes, installs big sewage disposal plants, and builds not only rows and rows of houses, but whole new suburbs, complete with markets, movie houses, playgrounds, grassy lawns and shrubbery.

The largest "new suburb" was Linda Vista on the north side of Mission Valley. Opened in May 1941, it eventually grew to 4,846 dwelling units housing about 16,000 residents. Called a "planning disaster" by one researcher, the public housing project was isolated from the rest of the city and lacked many amenities and conveniences its residents should have expected. At first there were no sidewalks, parks, schools, landscaping, shopping facilities or public transit. A congressional committee found that local officials' concerns and warnings had been ignored in the rush to build the homes.

This advertisement in the January 1942 issue of *National Geographic* promoted America's "Defense City No.1" as the ideal tourist destination.

In 1940, the Linda Vista Federal Housing Project sprang up on 1,240 acres on a plateau north of Mission Valley. *Courtesy San Diego Historical Society*

City Manager Walter W. Cooper told a congressional panel in 1943 that "unexampled growth" was playing havoc with city services. "The war has revolutionized the economy of San Diego," he said. Fire Chief John E. Parrish lacked sufficient firefighters to protect the new suburbs. City schools Superintendent Will C. Crawford said federal officials were uncooperative in helping provide school facilities for tens of thousands of new children, whose parents, living in federal defense housing, paid no property taxes. Police Chief Clifford Peterson said his cops spent more time directing traffic than combating crime.

Elsewhere in San Diego, rents escalated and some landlords rented out the same bed to two or three people who slept in shifts depending upon their defense plant work schedules. Testimony revealed that 75 to 85 percent of rentals barred children, a problem for many of the workers who had brought their families with them when they relocated to jobs in San Diego.

Racial minority groups were confined to a few concentrated areas of town by virtue of exclusive real estate covenants that, until a 1948 U.S. Supreme Court decision, allowed the sale or rental of homes only to whites. Even 25 years after the war, minorities were concentrated in those same unrestricted neighborhoods southeast of downtown and in Linda Vista, where federal housing rules barred discrimination.

At an air show in October 1941, Howard "Skippy" Smith demonstrated the aviation parachute before thousands of San Diegans. Smith would soon become a San Diego defense contractor, founding and managing the Pacific Parachute Company. *Courtesy San Diego Historical Society*

Employers also refused to hire non-whites, despite President Roosevelt's Executive Order 8802 banning discrimination. Labor unions generally continued their prewar lockouts to minority members. The San Diego City Council attempted to broaden opportunities. In December 1935 it was the first municipality nationally to adopt an ordinance prohibiting the display of racially discriminating signs in public places. However, no more than 5,200 blacks were employed in local industries and often, their jobs were janitorial only. One exception was the Pacific Parachute Company, founded by Howard "Skippy" Smith, an African-American who gained backing from actor Eddie Anderson ("Rochester" on the Jack Benny radio program). The company hired many women, both black and white, who had not been able to find other work. The San Diego Race Relations Society, led by Dennis V. Allen, championed the cause of Hispanics as well as blacks. Many residents became domestics and, from 1942 to

1947, farm workers under the U.S. "bracero" program to import guest field workers.

Nothing matched the treatment of Japanese-Americans, who in April 1942 were rounded up and, by presidential order, sent to concentration camps away from the coast. Typical of the hysteria was a *San Diego Union* editorial: "The Japs, regardless of citizenship status, are up to no good… If we continue to coddle them because we are afraid we might jeopardize their 'rights,' we probably will get precisely what such an addleheaded policy deserves." Many of the more than 1,900 San Diegans affected spent the war years in desolate Poston, Arizona. "It seems that we are going further and further away from San Diego, but I hope to be back soon," wrote Louis Ogawa to city librarian Clara Breed, who sent letters and library books to the internees throughout the war. San Diego's post-war Japanese population did not regain its prewar size of 2,200 until 1950.

On Sunday morning, December 7, 1941, San Diego's naval radio receivers at Fort Rosecrans on Point Loma picked up the first news flashed from Hawaii of the Japanese attack on Pearl Harbor. By midafternoon, all batteries at the fort were ready to defend the city. There was genuine fear that the Japanese might launch a surprise attack on the lightly defended coastline. Documents uncovered many years later indicated such a plan had been prepared in Tokyo. The Japanese had sent nine subs to the west coast with plans to shell coastal installations simultaneously on Christmas Day. The Japanese submarine I-10 arrived off San Diego at mid-month but the attack was called off at the last minute. A second sub, the I-17, arrived off the coast February 19, 1942, and proceeded to Goleta, north of Santa Barbara, where it shelled oil refineries.

On land, the War Department strung wire netting coated with chicken feathers over Consolidated's airplane factory. Lindbergh Field was camouflaged to resemble a typical subdivision. The 200-man, all-black 77th Smoke Generator Company, based at Fort Rosecrans, stood ready to ignite 3,000 15-gallon, oil-filled smudge pots that would hide the plant with 700 yards of black carbon smoke from enemy bombsights. In May 1942,

At the Pacific Highway plant of Consolidated Aircraft, up to 45,000 workers were employed building B-24 Liberator bombers and PBY Catalina flying boats. *Courtesy San Diego Historical Society*

Consolidated Aircraft, April 15, 1943 *Courtesy San Diego Historical Society*

rumors of a Japanese attack prompted the shipment of 350,000 gas masks to San Diego and the launching of barrage balloons.

The rugged and lightly defended Mexican border presented an easy overland route for potential saboteurs; up to 20,000 troops patrolled the border from San Diego to Calexico. At Campo, the army established 7,107-acre Camp Lockett. On horseback rode the 10th Cavalry Regiment; it included all-black Army units known as the "Buffalo Soldiers," dating back to post-Civil War Indians campaigns. These African-Americans were virtually stranded in Campo until the railroad agreed to add a black-only passenger car to its service. Later in the war, Camp Lockett became a prisoner-of-war camp and hospital for 300 Italians and 125 Germans.

Balboa Park was turned over to the Navy and part of it was named Camp Kidd in honor of Rear Admiral Isaac C. Kidd, who died at Pearl Harbor. The buildings and grounds became an extension of Balboa Naval Hospital. Six hundred nurses moved into the House of Hospitality. More than 3,500 men occupied barracks and hospital beds in various park buildings. To make room, institutions stored their exhibits on site, in private homes or in museums around the country. Only the San Diego Zoo remained in operation and open to the public.

VJ Day, August 14, 1945, Horton Plaza *Courtesy San Diego Historical Society*

In 1942 the Marine Corps condemned the 121,400-acre Rancho Santa Margarita y las Flores north of Oceanside and named it Camp Pendleton after Marine Major General Joseph Pendleton who championed San Diego as a military base during World War I. The price tag: $4.1 million. The other bases that developed during the war included Brown Field in South Bay; Gillespie Field in El Cajon; the Naval Amphibious Base on Coronado's Silver Strand; Ream Field in Imperial Beach; Camp Elliott east of Miramar; Camp Callan and Camp Matthews on Torrey Pines Mesa; and an auxiliary landing field near Del Mar. A $2 million pier was added south of Broadway Pier downtown, along with many buildings at the adjacent Naval Supply Center. The biggest physical change occurred at North Island, where the shallow tidelands area known as Spanish Bight were filled in to provide more space for aircraft maintenance and ship operations.

San Diego's city population swelled to nearly 400,000 civilians and military, requiring emergency public works and service improvements. Facing an imminent water shortage, San Diego rapidly moved to build an aqueduct to connect to the Colorado River. Under gas rationing, people depended on public transit, which carried four times the number of passengers of prewar levels. Cafes and theaters never closed. The Pacific Ballroom downtown and the Mission Ballroom at Belmont Park in Mission Beach booked the big bands. More than 8 million servicemen and women visited the Armed Services YMCA on Broadway in 1944 alone. The strains of war took their toll on local leaders. Mayor Percy Benbough, 58, died unexpectedly in November 1942. The next year, Reuben Fleet, chafing under confiscatory wartime taxes, sold Consolidated Aircraft to Vultee Aircraft Inc., receiving $11 million in return. The new company, Consolidated Vultee, shortened its name to Convair.

For all the crush of people and rush of business, wartime San Diego coped surprisingly well, according to historian Gerald N. Nash:

Few other urban areas experienced as large an increase of people — measured in percentages — as San Diego. Yet, despite stresses, living conditions in San Diego between 1940 and 1945 reflected fewer strains that those in most other congested war manufacturing centers. In spheres such as housing, transportation and education, conditions were more favorable than elsewhere. No doubt the mild climate and the availability of land and open

Two servicemen sharing in the joy of the war's end. *Courtesy San Diego Historical Society*

(Opposite page)
The fall of Japan, headlined in San Diego newspapers. *Courtesy San Diego Historical Society*

Downtown San Diego along Broadway on VJ Day *Courtesy San Diego Historical Society*

spaces in the San Diego vicinity eased the burden of absorbing several hundred thousand newcomers. The prominent role played by the United States Navy in the municipal affairs of San Diego also contributed to the maintenance of order, particularly of the transient population of servicemen and women. Thus, although the war brought a doubling of population in the area, San Diego weathered the shock with amazing resilience.

Then at 4 p.m. Tuesday, August 14, 1945, it was all over. President Harry S. Truman announced that Japan had surrendered. A relieved city poured into the streets, honking car horns, jamming the USO's snack bars, setting off firecrackers, getting drunk. Harold Keen, writing for the *Tribune-Sun*, described the scene: "Sailors, soldiers and Marines — tens of thousands of them — jammed the sidewalks, overflowed into the streets, shouted 'Chicago, here I come!' and 'I'm going home,' smothered women passers-by with kisses, performed strange antics that for V-J Day [Victory over Japan] seemed the thing to do."

Private Charles Moelter, based on Camp Pendleton, climbed a 50-foot palm tree at Horton Plaza and planted the Stars and Stripes on the topmost frond and scrambled back down into the arms of the cheering onlookers. "Women and girls fought for the privilege of kissing him and begged his autograph," The *Union* reported. Others jumped into the Horton Plaza fountain in a spontaneous show of joy."

From 1909 to 1945, San Diego had changed remarkably, transforming itself from a laid-back seaside tourist resort town into a bustling Navy outpost, aerospace manufacturing center and growing metropolis on a dynamic international border. A distinctive identity had developed and San Diego became generally known throughout the nation, largely because of the numbers of military and wartime industrial workers who passed through during World War II. While leadership was tightly held in a few hands, women and minorities occasionally gained prominence. But at war's end, the fundamental question remained the same: Could San Diego develop industrially without sacrificing its natural setting?

FIVE

CHAPTER FIVE

"Sketch Map of Proposed Development, Mission Bay Recreational Area."
This early vision of Mission Bay was published by Frye & Smith Ltd.
The more whimsical features of the plan never passed the design stage.
Courtesy San Diego Historical Society

GROWING PAINS

Five and a half months before Japan surrendered, San Diego received its marching orders for the postwar period. Commissioned by the Chamber of the Commerce, a $350,000 report by Philadelphia consultants Day & Zimmerman foresaw many of the challenges and opportunities:

> If San Diego is to retain its wartime growth, years of action and cooperation will be required by industry and business. Manufacturing will have to decide upon their peacetime products and marketing procedures and arrange to convert production facilities as quickly as possible. Only by all the related elements working together, with the realization that the economy of San Diego cannot be dependent upon the activities of a particular industry group, can employment be provided for the greatly increased labor force.

In five leather-bound volumes of 1,345 pages, Day & Zimmerman studied 88 products and services suitable in the 1940s and beyond, from fountain pens and hats to garter belts and burial caskets. One intriguing idea was toy manufacturing. The Baby Boom had not yet commenced, but the researchers rightly predicted that an upsurge in youngsters would require an increase in playthings. San Diego could tout itself as the "southern headquarters" for Santa Claus and combine toy manufacturing with playgrounds in a "toy town." "The colorful environment of San Diego offers an extraordinary setting for such an enterprise... This project could be planned to ultimately include a miniature city — a veritable fairyland to attract tourists and delight and entertain the young folk." Another opportunity lay in sporting goods, the company said. "With war ended, motoring, traveling and shorter and fewer workdays will become more popular than ever — conditions which stimulate sports, games and outdoor activities."

Anticipating future trade opportunities around the Pacific Rim, Day & Zimmerman recommended San Diego entrepreneurs build television, radio and drug factories and automobile assembly plants. Public warehouses could serve as an "incubator for industry and trade." Port, rail and airport facilities could be expanded, they said, and excess military bases converted to civilian uses. International trade held great promise, especially in "America's largest prewar Pacific market." And Mexico, San Diego's leading source of imports and destination for exports, should remain a top priority of business development; San Diego and Tijuana officials were advised to work together.

1945-1978

The Palomar Observatory, May 1957 *Courtesy San Diego Historical Society*

(Photo on page 120) A world fair dream that never happened: the 1953 "World Progress Exposition." *Courtesy San Diego Historical Society*

HIGH TECHNOLOGY, HIGHER EDUCATION

Basic research and education were barely mentioned in a report devoted to material production. But San Diego's opportunities gradually expanded in that direction, highlighted by four great research institutions: Palomar Observatory, General Atomics, UCSD and Salk Institute.

First came the Palomar Observatory in 1948. The dream of George Ellery Hale, the project to build a 200-inch reflecting mirror for the world's largest telescope received backing in 1928 from the Rockefeller Foundation. The site on Palomar Mountain was chosen in 1934 and the observatory building was finished four years later. Because it lacked high priority during the war, it took 10 more years for the California Institute of Technology at Pasadena to complete the project. In astronomy circles, Palomar conferred world-class status on San Diego.

The second great leap came in atomic energy. General Dynamics, which acquired Convair in 1954, was planning a $40 million Atlas missile production plant on Kearny Mesa and its chairman, John Jay Hopkins, wanted to get in on the growing industry of atomic energy research. Nuclear physicist Frederic de Hoffman, president of GenDyn's General Atomics Inc., toured possible sites with City Manager O.M. Campbell and picked Torrey Pines Mesa, reportedly because he could see Palomar Observatory from the site. Hopkins broke ground in 1956 on a $10 million research center on more than 300 acres in Torrey Pines Mesa, granted by voters. "There will be discoveries here that will amaze the world," he promised. The company, now operating at GA Technologies, specialized in research for nuclear power plants, research reactors and nuclear fusion energy. De Hoffmann was credited with spinning off 50 scientific companies in the La Jolla-Torrey Pines area.

The third and most far-reaching step was the move to expand Scripps Institution of Oceanography into a general campus of the University of California. San Diego had sought a larger UC presence in 1924, when the Board of Regents was looking for a Southern California campus; Los Angeles won that contest. Now, Hopkins' atomic facility prompted a new look at San Diego and led to a state Assembly resolution in 1955 sponsored by local legislator Sheridan Hegland. The San Diego City Council, Chamber of Commerce and other groups added their support. Scripps Institution director Roger Revelle at first conceived a graduate School of Science and Engineering along the lines of CalTech. He outlined his thoughts in an address to Princeton University alumni in December 1958:

Building a university, it seems to us, is just the opposite from building a house. It must be done from the top down and not the bottom up — from the inside out, not from the outside in...

"Another of our basic premises has been that we must, insofar as possible, desegregate the sciences and the humanities and social sciences. This is not only intellectually desirable, but socially imperative, because of the profound effect of technology and scientific discovery upon all aspects of our modern society."

It soon became evident that the budding Baby Boom generation would need more colleges to attend and a San Diego campus of 27,500 students attending 12 interdependent colleges by 1995 was eventually adopted as the goal. Several sites were considered, including the northeast corner of Balboa Park. But prompted by a suggestion from *Union-Tribune* publisher James Copley, campus planners settled on city pueblo lands on Torrey Pines Mesa. By a 4-1 margin, city voters approved the transfer of 450 acres to the university in November 1958. In 1964, when the first undergraduates enrolled, the Marine Corps' Camp Matthews, a 545-acre weapons-training facility, was added.

The fourth major research center founded after the war was spearheaded by Jonas Salk, whose polio vaccine had cured the disease. Armed with a $20 million grant from the National Science Foundation and support from the March of Dimes, Salk considered a number of sites for his Salk Institute for Biological Research. San Diego Mayor Charles Dail, who had had polio, enticed Salk to San Diego in 1960 with the offer of 70 acres of pueblo land just west of the UCSD site. General Atomics' de Hoffmann became Salk's president in 1969. Equal to the research work conducted at Salk was the architectural masterpiece created for the institute by architect Louis Kahn. The stark concrete, temple-like complex, completed in 1967, has drawn architectural students from around the world ever since.

The settings for two new postwar, private higher education institutions also deserve notice. The Roman Catholic Diocese opened its University of San Diego in 1952 on the western edge of Linda Vista. Bishop Charles F. Buddy had selected the site in 1937 and later settled on building in the Spanish Renaissance style. Balboa College, located in downtown San Diego, became California Western University in 1952 and relocated to the old Theosophical Society grounds on Point Loma. Also worth mentioning is the postwar rise of the community college system, which developed many programs to prepare high school graduates for the job market. Meanwhile, San Diego State College expanded far beyond its initial teacher-training mission and became the leading higher education institution in the region into the 1970s. It won its long-sought status as a university in 1972 and acquired its present name, San Diego State University, in 1974. Enrollment skyrocketed above 30,000 before declining to a more manageable level.

The Salk Institute at La Jolla is famed for its architecture as well as its success as a biological research center. *Courtesy San Diego Historical Society*

After the housing shortages of World War II, homeowners rushed to buy in new housing developments such as Clairemont. *Courtesy San Diego Historical Society*

The opening of the San Diego Public Library at Eighth and E, 1954. *Courtesy San Diego Historical Society*

GROWTH BEGETS GROWTH

At war's end, San Diego's population stood at 362,000, the county's at 635,000, compared to 202,341 and 289,348, respectively, in 1940. Returning veterans replaced departing defense workers, and the demand for peacetime goods and services forestalled a depression that many had feared. To relieve the housing shortage, Camp Callan barracks were dismantled and the construction materials sold for reuse elsewhere in town. There had been a long hiatus in home building, from about 1930 to 1945, and, taking their cue from William Levitt in New York's Long Island, builders soon adopted the assembly-line approach to development.

By 1954, *San Diego Magazine*'s Joe Keffler wrote, "No wonder San Diego's business leaders are optimistic. There's nothing wrong with San Diego, they are convinced, that new and diversified industry and a few thousand more homes won't fix." The concept of growth management, growth control and environmental protection was clearly not at the forefront, at least among the elected officials and power elite.

Although the new houses all seemed to look alike, some housing tracts did offer some diversity in siting and design. Carlos Tavares and Louis Burgener began building their 3,500-home project in Clairemont in 1951, generally following the land form around the canyons and mesas overlooking Mission Bay and Tecolote Canyon. Tavares' widow Claire (the "Claire" in Clairemont) recalled, "Everything had to be done quickly... He wanted families to afford Clairemont. He gave schools to the school board at cost, churches at cost and sometimes he built them himself. He tried to do something nice for everyone." Project architect Harold N. Abrams, a Hollywood set designer, also designed Clairemont Square shopping center. By 1957, the community's population reached 38,000.

Clairemont and other postwar communities were made possible by a vast expansion of freeways, first detailed in the 1930 city streets and highway plan. A $3 billion, 10-year state highway improvement program inaugurated California's commitment to freeway building — years before the federal government created a national program. The first San Diego freeway, U.S. Highway 395 (later redesignated State Route 163), cut through Balboa Park beneath the Cabrillo Bridge. Authorized by voters in 1941, it was completed in 1948. The lushly landscaped thoroughfare demonstrated how beauty could coexist with traffic. And yet, no other freeway in San Diego County was ever as beautifully laid out. Over the years, citizens have fought back repeated attempts to widen the freeway at the expense of the trees in the generous median.

The rise in automobile use and its spread to new suburban tracts inevitably impacted the ability of the city's streetcar system to keep up with demand. Buses were added to serve new routes and in 1949 the last streetcars were removed from service. Commuter rail service did not return for another 32 years.

Airplanes began making inroads into rail service for inter-city transportation. As early as 1943, the Civil Aeronautics Administration pronounced Lindbergh Field inadequate for long-term needs. In 1947, the Navy approved a 50-year, $1-a-year lease of Miramar Naval Air Station for municipal use. But two years later, the military decided it might need Miramar for national defense and canceled the lease in 1953. It also vetoed the use of Montgomery Field and North Island as alternatives to Lindbergh. And so, the city began upgrading Lindbergh with an expanded terminal, repeatedly putting off the designation of a long-term replacement.

As vital to San Diego's growth as transportation was its need for water. San Diego's wartime population exceeded projections not expected to be reached until 1970, and officials realized they needed to tap the Colorado River. In 1946, voters approved the San Diego County Water Authority's membership in the Metropolitan Water District as well as a $2 million bond issue for internal water line improvements within the county. Colorado River water began flowing to San Diego at the end of 1947, just in time to avert rationing.

Proper sewage treatment would have to wait a dozen more years. City voters refused to approve a $16 million bond issue in 1954. By the time they endorsed a primary sewage treatment plant at Point Loma in 1960, the cost had soared to $51 million. It was designed to serve the entire south half of the county. A connection was also added at federal expense to process Tijuana sewage that otherwise would have contaminated the Tijuana River, whose last few miles lie in the U.S.

New schools were needed to serve the accelerating Baby Boom that lasted from 1946 to 1964. The first boomer kindergartners began attending classes in 1951. By the time the last boomer graduated from high school in 1983, San Diego County public school enrollment had tripled from 97,600 to 309,700. Voters regularly granted two-thirds approval for general-obligation bond issues in this pre-taxpayer-revolt era.

The city library system also reflected the growth and expansion of service. In 1945 no new branches had been constructed in 20 years; instead there was a string of 26 small, temporary branches in rented quarters and schools. With the addition of a bookmobile in 1948, the total was cut to 13 branches and four stations. By 1978, 23 new branches were built and several others were either opened in temporary space, annexed from the county or enlarged.

The Central Library needed the most attention, since it had long outgrown the 1902 Carnegie building on E Street. Numerous bond measures and alternative funding methods had failed to win voter or city manager approval. Finally, a 70 percent vote in 1949 authorized a $2 million 144,624-square-foot replacement for the 28,000-square-foot Carnegie. "It seemed impossible, incredible," city librarian Clara E. Breed later wrote. "When we finally gave up and went home, we were exhausted and still too

By 1964, developers had won their hard-fought battle to site a shopping center in the heart of Mission Valley. The decline of San Diego's downtown shopping district soon followed. *Courtesy San Diego Historical Society*

unbelieving to celebrate." The library opened in 1954 and attracted widespread interest from librarians and planners from many other cities.

The library's construction represented the end of a dream to group public buildings in a planned, orderly manner east of the Civic Center along Cedar Street toward Balboa Park, as urged by John Nolen in 1926 and endorsed in the Day & Zimmerman report. On the April 15, 1947, ballot, voters were asked if they preferred to group the buildings at Sixth and Laurel on Balboa Park land or along Cedar Street. Both options were soundly defeated. Bonds for a library, courthouse and juvenile center lost in 1948 and Cedar Street Mall lost a third time in 1949. Opponents played up the loss of property from the tax rolls and bickering on the City Council presented a confusing message to the public. With the economic outlook somewhat clouded, this may not have been the ideal time to promote visionary thinking.

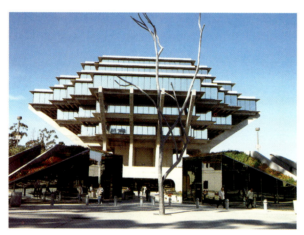

Geisel Library
Courtesy University of California, San Diego

From that time on, the various public facilities were scattered throughout the city and county. The school headquarters ended up at the old Normal School site in University Heights. The San Diego County Courthouse replaced the 1889 edifice on Broadway. The state built a stand-alone office building on Front Street and performing arts and convention facilities did not come until the mid-1960s.

The 1950s witnessed many notable decisions that set San Diego's direction for decades to come. In land use, arguably the most significant was the City Council's unanimous vote in June 1958 to rezone Mission Valley for commercial use to suit May Company's plans for a regional shopping center. Planning Director Harry Haelsig, who succeeded Glenn Rick, had developed an alternate vision that would have established the valley as a recreational greenbelt leading to Mission Bay. James Britton II, architecture critic for *San Diego Magazine* and *The San Diego Union* from 1950 to 1983, carried on a nonstop harangue to embarrass, scold and browbeat officials. But his and other voices were not heeded. "San Diego's public well-being, as I see it, would not be served by allowing a distinctive geographic asset like Mission Valley to be blotted out for the convenience of merchandisers," Britton argued. The debate pitted seemingly self-interested downtown property owners and merchants against consumers and big-thinking national department store chains and shopping center developers.

"If we are not given the privilege and the right to come to your city and locate in Mission Valley," warned May Company director Walter Brunmark, "we will not come here. That is a final statement." Dependent on sales-tax revenue, council members surely did not want the May company building in adjacent La Mesa or other revenue-hungry municipalities.

At the final council hearing, downtown jeweler Arthur Jessop argued for proper planning aimed at tourists, not shoppers: "Now San Diego by nature offers the finest spot in the United States for tourists. And tourism is our largest non-governmental business. We have got one area left [Mission Valley] that can be developed logically and beautifully for this... And should a decision be made before considering these consequences, we may as well tattoo on the council walls right here, 'Thus died planning in San Diego.'"

The council's vote guaranteed continued growth in the city's tax base, at least in Mission Valley. What it didn't realize was that as valley values grew, downtown's shrank. And it took another 25 years to reverse the trend and get the central business district's retail tax base growing again. As for the environmental impact, the valley saw asphalt parking lots supplant dairy farms, shopping instead of fishing.

Fun in the Sun

Postwar San Diego was not only concerned with consumerism and industrialization. Farsighted civic leaders anticipated the growing need to provide for growing leisure-time activities. In the spring of 1945, San Diego city voters wisely agreed and by a 4-1 margin approved a $2 million bond issue to turn the mudflats of Mission Bay into the nation's largest aquatic urban park.

The idea had been simmering from the beginning of the century. County horticulturist George P. Hall asked the Chamber of Commerce in 1902, "Why not make this the center for intense amusements and embellishments?" He spoke of "water sidewalks" and "floating bridges," gondolas and "myriads of dazzling lights." A tent city was erected in North Mission Beach in 1914 and John D. Spreckels' Mission Beach Amusement Center opened in 1925, including Luna Park (later Belmont Park) and its "Giant Dipper" roller coaster. Architect Lilian Rice designed the ZLAC Rowing Club building in 1932 to serve women's recreational needs on the bay. John Nolen endorsed the development of the bay as a park in his 1926 city plan and city Planning Director Glenn Rick worked on the project from 1929 until his retirement in 1955.

Drawing on ideas from a multi-state tour of waterfront developments in 1944, Rick developed a plan for combining commercial improvements, such as hotels, marinas and public amenities, including beaches, parks and bike paths. This public-private approach promised to generate enough funds to maintain a park four times the size of Balboa Park. As Rick recalled in his memoirs:

"Sketches of the proposed development called attention to the fact that it would be a year-round recreational center, second to none; that it would provide employment for many; that it would yield substantial revenues. The project publicity provided for 'picnic grounds, safe swimming areas, yacht basins for large and small boats, an aquarium, amusement center, sailboat course, marine stadium, wildlife preserves, bath houses, rowing course, riding stables and bridle paths, airfield, hydroplane area, golf course, ballpark, power boat course and other

City Planning Director Glenn Rick, the creator of Mission Bay Park *Courtesy San Diego Historical Society*

facilities.' Because it would take a two-thirds vote to pass, everything possible was listed and the more things mentioned, the more it would appeal to everyone, even though $2 million could not do it all."

Fifty years ago, the alternative vision of a natural wildlife habitat, favored by the Department of the Interior and sportsmen, held little attraction. Only a 46-acre corner of the bay remained in its natural state. The rest underwent private development, valued at $344 million in the 1990s, and millions more in publicly-financed improvements. The San Diego River was channelized at its western end to stop siltation of the bay. From 1947 to 1961, 25 million cubic yards of dredged material was used to create a series of islands, sandy beaches and building sites. The public got its first official view of the park at the September 1949 "Fiesta Bahia." *San Diego Magazine* predicted Mission Bay would be "the nation's greatest aquatic park," attracting tourists, whose spending had doubled from $23 million before the war to $48 million in 1949. Predictions proved right: It's been one big, continuous party ever since, from Over-the-Line Tournaments and corporate picnics to bocce ball games and family barbecues.

Many of the tourists — and locals — head for Sea World. The San Diego Aquarium Society urged the city in 1954 to build an "oceanarium" and five years later, a request was issued for parties interested in leasing Mission Bay property for a marine park. George Millay, who originally wanted to build an underwater cocktail lounge at his Long Beach restaurant, The Reef, joined with three fraternity brothers in 1961 to build a rival to Marineland in Palos Verdes. Opened in 1964, the 22-acre, $1.5 million venture drew 415,000 visitors the first year and topped 1 million in 1967 after adding the Shamu killer-whale show. The founders went public with a stock offering the next year, opened new parks in Ohio and Florida, joint-ventured the Magic Mountain theme park in Ventura County and sold out to publishing house Harcourt Brace Jovanovich in 1976. Anheuser-Busch, the beer-and-theme-park giant, took charge in the 1990s. As UCSD professor Susan G. Davis wrote in her 1997 study, *Spectacular Nature: Corporate Culture and the Sea World Experience:*

"If the centerpiece of San Diego's multidecade tourism expansion was Mission Bay, from the beginning Sea World was its jewel… Sea World served the Mission Bay complex as its key attraction, a showplace to divert and occupy the conventioneers and vacationers in the new hotels and motels, while also appealing to the local audience and their guests. The theme park was the bay's largest concession; along with the zoo, the beaches and Old Town, it provided convention planners, travel agents and guidebooks with a way to speak to tourists about San Diego as a cluster of family attractions."

Prewar memories of the Balboa Park expositions prompted some to advocate new fairs and expositions. There was to have been a fair in the park in 1942, an "American Way of Life" celebration in the park and Mission Bay in 1955, a "Festival of the Lively Arts" in Balboa Park in 1957 and a "California World's Fair" in 1967-68. The only events of this kind to occur were "Fiesta del Pacifico," a two-week pageant held annually from 1956 through 1959, and a loosely organized San Diego Bicentennial celebration in 1969. By the end of this period, world's fairs elsewhere were costing billions and losing millions. San Diego was unlikely ever to hold such an event again.

THE 1960S: A DECADE OF SHIFTING SIGNS

By 1960, San Diego had gotten over its postwar jitters and decided to compete with its rival cities for commerce, industry and tourism. But a shadow fell over the city as General Dynamics failed to gain customers for its Convair 880 jet aircraft. The August 1959 peak aircraft industry employment of 56,400 had slumped to 47,600 by the following June. Housing starts had dropped from an annual rate of 32,422 in May 1960 to 20,000 in August.

Time magazine offered the worst-possible swipe to San Diego's pride. In its August 17, 1962, issue, a glowing account of "Boom Town" Atlanta was paired with one on "Bust Town?" San Diego:

"The yacht basins are crowded with boats; sumptuous motels for sybaritic tourists are rising outside town. But beneath the clamor and the glitter, San Diego — the city that brashly bet heavily on the aircraft industry and cleaned up for nearly 13 years — is in missile-age trouble.

"The 'tinbenders' — local jargon for semiskilled aircraft workers — are packing up in droves and leaving the housing developments that sprawled around the city during the past few years. Tied to one industry, San Diego's officials are struggling to lure new employment sources in the city. Says state labor analyst Arthur McCarty: 'We have all the facilities, all of the personnel and all of the money needed to retrain these workers. There is only one real problem: What do we train them to do?'

"In downtown San Diego, a parking-lot operator who last year was regularly netting $800 a month declared last week: 'Hell, business is so dead I won't take home more than $130 this month. Friend of mine offered me a deal, and I think I'm going to fold this thing up and go in with him.' The friend's deal: an outfit to handle merchandise from San Diego firms that go bankrupt."

But the national media were declaring San Diego dead a bit early. Overcoming years of voter reticence, the city, with support from the downtown planning group San Diegans Incorporated, found a way to build a new civic center downtown without going to the ballot. Financed largely from loans from the city employee retirement system, the $15 million Community Concourse (later named in Mayor Charles Dail's honor) encompassed a new city hall, civic theater, convention hall and parking garage.

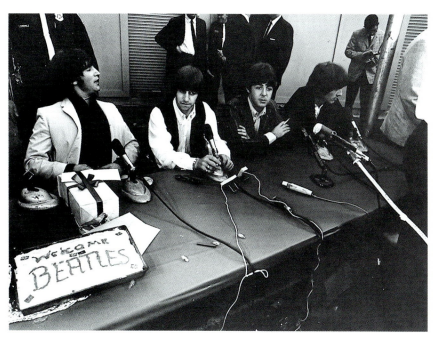

A San Diego press conference with the Beatles, August 28, 1965. *Courtesy San Diego Historical Society*

A private office building fronting on a car-free plaza dominated by a huge fountain ("Bow Wave" by Malcolm Leland) and wide steps suitable for people-watching was later added. The design, the result of many compromises and cost cutbacks, was roundly criticized as sterile, cheap and uninviting. The site plan, dependent on closing Second Avenue and C Street, disrupted the downtown grid pattern and traffic flows. Starting in the 1980s, citizen groups developed various fix-it plans. But the act of creation demonstrated that San Diego could overcome obstacles when it so desired. In 1963, the National Municipal League designated San Diego an "All-American City" in recognition of the concourse effort.

With Frank Curran in the mayor's job, Don L. Nay heading the newly created San Diego Unified Port District and the UCSD campus well under construction, the sullen '60s turned into something more upbeat. The mood was captured by a spontaneous prank in April 1963, when Windansea surfers surreptitiously installed a 6-foot statue of "Hot Curl" on the beach. City crews removed it six days later but public support prompted its replacement in July. Although vandals beheaded the "spindly legged, baggy-bermuda'd" surfer dude within a few days, this nod to San Diego's relaxed lifestyle made it into the movie "Muscle Beach Party" and onto a painting at The Spot restaurant in La Jolla.

Other San Diego trademarks of this era: Hang 10 T-shirts, Jack-in-the-Box hamburgers and WD-40, the wonder lubricant for every do-it-yourselfer. ("WD-40" was the shorthand name for the substance used in the 40th water displacement experiment in 1952 by the three chemists at Rocket Chemical Company. They were seeking a rust-resisting, rust-removing product for the aerospace industry.) The era's top pop music group, the Beatles, performed before 18,000 adoring fans at Balboa Stadium August 28, 1965. *San Diego Union* staff writer Carol Olten, who reviewed the show, recalled it 20 years later as "a cool August night filled with pandemonium."

"I arrived at the stadium early — very early — that August evening as the sun's last shadow spread over the field and already-filling bleachers. Chaos immediately was apparent. Securities forces were tossing out noisy gatecrashers… The first song of their 35-minute set was a good rocker, "She's Your Woman," featuring [Paul] McCartney bouncing across the stage like a woundup Buster Brown… The concert seemed to be over in an instant. The Beatles disappeared into a luxury van and were given a police escort from the stadium."

Chapter Five

Construction of San Diego Stadium in Mission Valley, 1966. Courtesy San Diego Historical Society

From 1961 to 1966, Balboa Stadium hosted the San Diego Chargers. Courtesy San Diego Historical Society

Lane Field on Pacific Highway was home to the Pacific Coast League Padres until 1957. Courtesy San Diego Historical Society

Sportstown

Balboa Stadium also was the venue for another form of fun, professional football. Barron Hilton, son of hotel owner Conrad Hilton, had moved his Chargers team from Los Angeles in 1961 at the behest of Dr. Albert Anderson, chairing the Chamber of Commerce's sports committee. *San Diego Union* and *Evening Tribune* sports editors Jack Murphy and Gene Gregston and many others thought San Diego business and growth could profit from regular mentions in sports columns, especially on snowy days of the American Football League's fall schedule. The Chargers moved to San Diego Stadium [later, Jack Murphy, now Qualcomm Stadium] in 1967, two years after city voters gave overwhelming approval for a $27.5 million stadium in Mission Valley.

San Diego financier C. Arnholt Smith, who had moved the minor-league Padres baseball team from its 1930s Lane Field downtown to Westgate Park in Mission Valley in 1957, landed a National League expansion franchise in 1968 and the major-league Padres began playing at the stadium in 1969. Westgate Park was demolished to make way for the Fashion Valley shopping center.

The third sports endeavor was Robert Breitbard's leasing of city-owned land in the Midway area (site of World War II housing) on which to build the $6.5 million International Sports Arena in 1966. It was intended as the home for professional basketball, hockey and indoor soccer games, but as teams came and went, it became the venue of choice for many rock concerts, circus stops and ice skating shows.

A renewed appreciation of San Diego's architectural heritage appeared in the 1960s. Bea Evenson, a housewife who shamed the port district in 1965 into building Spanish Landing park along North Harbor Drive, founded the Committee of 100 (since grown to several thousand members) in 1967 to preserve and promote the Spanish Colonial architecture of the exposition buildings in Balboa Park. The group's first victory came with the 1968 voter approval of bonds to replace the Food and Beverage Building with the Casa del Prado at the eastern end of El Prado.

SAVE THE PAST

In 1969, another group of architectural enthusiasts banded together to save threatened Victorian homes on the northern edge of downtown. The Save Our Heritage Organisation (SOHO) assumed a stop-the-bulldozers stance on many a preservationist battle in subsequent decades. Citizens Coordinate for Century 3, the brainchild of architect Lloyd Ruocco in 1959, championed reasoned city planning, stepping in when necessary to fight senseless freeway expansions and waterfront view blockages — battles that often were lost. The earliest visions of what the red-light district south of Broadway could be appeared in a remarkable fold-out spread in the March 1968 *San Diego Magazine*. Graphic designer Robert Hostick and writer Roberta Ridgley detailed how Alonzo Horton-era buildings could be spruced up and adapted to appeal to new generations. Their vision of the "Stingaree" became the inspiration for what was to grow into the thriving Gaslamp Quarter.

Architect Lloyd Ruocco, 1959, founder of what became Citizens Coordinate for Century 3. *Courtesy San Diego Historical Society*

The city and many other municipalities passed historic site preservation ordinances and the county created a home for displaced Victorians at Heritage Park in Old Town. The state took charge of Old Town after San Diego's 1969 bicentennial celebration and reconstructed some of the buildings lost between 1820 and 1872. The popular Bazaar del Mundo restaurant and retail complex within the state park was developed at this time. San Diego's most historic landmark, the Hotel del Coronado, changed hands during this period, becoming the property of a group of investors headed by M. Larry Lawrence. He spent millions to preserve and expand the facility before his death in 1997.

The mid-1960s opened an age of rebellion on many fronts, from civil rights to Vietnam to direct-action democracy. Television newsman Harold Keen, writing monthly in *San Diego Magazine*, captured many of the cross-currents. There was the battle over the San Diego-Coronado Bay Bridge, viewed by cynics as a political payoff by Governor Edmund G. "Pat" Brown to Lawrence and other San Diego Democrats. Another struggle ensued over the lease of the Del Mar Racetrack. La Jollans fought over height restrictions in La Jolla Shores and Mission Valley hoteliers unsuccessfully mounted a referendum to block the transient occupancy tax on hotel guests. Keen also took note of the new powers in town, "young Turks," personified by businessmen Robert O. Peterson and Richard T. Silberman who had taken over control of the venerable First National Bank. (The Bank of Tokyo later bought the bank, merged it with Union Bank and used the latter's name).

Preservation activist Bea Evenson, standing before an early success, the restored Casa del Prado, 1970. *Courtesy San Diego Historical Society*

Chapter Five

(Right and opposite page) The "Harlem of the West," the Creole Palace thrived for nearly four decades in the Hotel Douglas at Second Avenue and Market Street. *Courtesy San Diego Historical Society*

BLACK AWAKENINGS

At a time when San Diego was barely taking note of the multiracial diversity beginning to appear in schools, neighborhoods and the workplace, Keen reported a discontent in the African-American community. Such straight talk may have figured in helping San Diego avoid much of the racial violence that rocked other cities in the second half of the decade. In July 1963, Keen wrote: "In the segregated southeast neighborhoods that some Negro leaders bitterly refer to as San Diego's 'ghetto,' there are stirrings through the whole fabric of black society. Mississippi and Alabama have struck sparks even among the hitherto inarticulate, the torpid, the resigned. The militants have become more aggressive, the moderates more demanding. The atmosphere is heady with anticipation of major developments in the civil rights struggle."

San Diego's postwar black community faced widespread discrimination. Jack Kimbrough, the area's first African-American dentist, recalled warnings by neighbors against his establishment of a practice in Golden Hill because of real estate covenants barring sales or rentals to nonwhites. In 1948, he joined in a sit-in at the Grant Grill in the U.S. Grant Hotel, where minorities were refused service. San Diego State students helped serve as witnesses and local restaurants were fined $300 each for violating federal and state laws. "This is the way we got the witnesses," Kimbrough said. "So we had quite a few suits against the smaller restaurants all over town here. And we won all of them except one."

In a celebrated trial in 1947, Coronado resident Elizabeth Ingalls was convicted of having held her black maid, Dora L. Jones, as a virtual slave for 37 years. Ingalls held Jones accountable for the breakup of her first marriage, refused to pay her and forced her to spend the night in a car when the family went on vacation. Ingalls' grown daughters testified against her, leading her to denounce one as a Communist and the other a Nazi.

With most public places barred to blacks, one of the few outlets for enjoyment was the Creole Palace, the "Harlem of the West," in the Hotel Douglas, which had opened in 1924 at Second Avenue and Market Street. The Mills Brothers, Paul Robeson, Duke Ellington and other greats were booked at the nightclub in the 1940s and '50s by Fro Brigham, a long-time jazz musician and bandleader. "There wasn't another place like it," he said in a 1989 interview. "People came from L.A. just to visit the Creole Palace." The hotel was demolished in 1985 to make way for the Market Street Square apartment building.

Building trades also were largely barred to blacks. It took a special program by the U.S. Small Business Administration and the Urban League to help Daniel Dykes and Fred J. Lopez win a demolition contract in 1972 for the $47 million federal courthouse and office complex on Broadway. "We tried for two years to go into business for ourselves but the biggest problem was always the money," Lopez said in an interview. "It takes cash for the bonds, insurance, permits and equipment needed in the business."

Education was promoted among San Diego's minorities as their pathway to success. But opportunities remained limited. "If you were young and black, chances are if you wanted to work you couldn't and no one outside your home really cared about you or your future. If you didn't get a driving push from home, you just didn't get it," said Joseph Vinson, a 1956 graduate of Lincoln High School where black enrollment stood at about 20 percent in 1951 and rose to 82 percent by 1976.

Until the late-1960s, only about 100 African-Americans attended San Diego State. Pat Blevins-Murray, who attended SDSU along with her six brothers and sisters, recalled in 1991 that she was a pioneer in the growth of minority representation in higher education. "We brought the [black] community to San Diego State," she said. However, fellow alumnus Wayman Johnson said the reception was not pleasant. "It was an environment that many blacks felt was hostile. "All of a sudden, a lot of blacks were at a conservative, white campus."

RIGHT AND LEFT THREATS

Meanwhile at City Hall, things were in utter disarray. On the one hand were the professional city managers and planners, technocrats trained with an engineer's eye for efficiency and cost savings, combined with a "Government Knows Best" attitude left over from the days of the New Deal and World War II. On the other hand were conservative property-rights, anti-government advocates, often allied with business interests. A small band led by Martin J. Montroy and backed

by Mission Valley land interests (principally, Charles Brown of Atlas Hotels Inc., developer of the Town & Country Hotel) mounted one initiative drive after another. Their goals included dumping the strong city manager system; loosening land-use and zoning controls; thwarting redevelopment, urban renewal and long-range planning; and sidetracking any thought of promoting racial integration of housing.

In November 1961, former City Manager O.W. Campbell warned, "Current local demagoguery and confusion can destroy San Diego's fantastic potential for future growth. You must make it to the next decade or you are forever a town at the end of the railroad line." In 1963, as retiring two-term Mayor Charles Dail watched 13 candidates vie to replace him, he thundered against Montroy's Jobs and Growth Association ballot proposal, which would have politicized the Planning Commission: "This measure is being forced on us by councilmen lined up with Mission Valley. There has been a lot of appeasement on this council regarding Jobs & Growth. There has been a lot of kowtowing to Mission Valley… The political maneuvering is all the more reason for us to retain independent planning as it exists today in San Diego."

There was continued rough talk over San Diego's urban directions, as city planners struggled to craft a new general plan to replace Nolen's 1926 guidelines. "The greatest potential for corruption in city government is in planning and zoning," Dail warned. "These functions should be independent of the city manager to avoid pressures that can be put on a single individual. Any attempt to emasculate our present planning organization should be resisted. Our Planning Department resists chiselers and land promoters, those who want to gain big windfall profits in rezoning and it helps those who deserve rezoning."

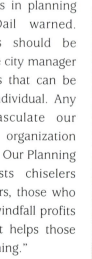

UCSD Marxist professor Herbert Marcuse *Courtesy San Diego Historical Society*

Voters rejected the latest version of the anti-planning Jobs and Growth Association initiative. But Planning Director Harry Haelsig had enough. On his last day, he was not spared the wrath of nitpicking council members over a straightforward presentation of plans by the San Diego Zoo to build its Wild Animal Park in San Pasqual Valley. Incoming Director James Fairman from Riverside lectured the Planning Commission, privately calling it the worst he had ever seen for playing "hanky panky with the City Council." He was quoted as saying, "You should start thinking about what planning means to this city's future." In admiration, Chairman Earl Pridemore replied, "You got a lot of guts, Fairman."

There were two more hurdles for planning to overcome. The first general plan developed by a 196-member citizens advisory committee lost in 1965. Shortened and weakened, a revised plan in 1967 was forced onto the ballot as a result of Montroy's opposition. He and other antagonists read into the document references to open housing and racially integrated neighborhoods. "If you want something typically Marxian, this is it," he told the Serra Mesa Republican Women's Club. But the plan won voter approval, guaranteeing strong city planning for the next 25 years.

The presence at UCSD of philosophy professor Herbert Marcuse — a real Marxist, neo-Marxist, actually — touched off a furious battle between town and gown that epitomized the splits developing in the 1960s. Chancellor William J. McGill faced reappointing Marcuse in the 1968-69 academic year over the strong objections of San Diego conservatives. The same year, chronicled in McGill's *The Year of the Monkey,* featured a battle over the appearance of Black Panther Eldridge Cleaver; Marine Corps recruiters; the redirection of a proposed new undergraduate college from a history-based curriculum to one dealing with racial minorities; and numerous other clashes.

This all occurred against a backdrop of the 1968 assassinations of Martin Luther King Jr. and Robert F. Kennedy, a presidential election and escalation in the Vietnam War. The summer witnessed a time-out from tension for the first landing on the moon in July 1969. But it all started up again in the fall, culminating in sit-ins, shut-downs and one suicide-protest on Revelle Plaza as colleges around the country reacted to the Ohio National Guard's shootings of students at Kent State University.

At San Diego State, the ouster of several fraternities for failure to desegregate was followed by similar anti-war and student-activist incidents. The most contentious year was 1972, when economics instructor Peter Bohmer was fired for his activist stance and classroom comments, such as this one quoted by one student, "Only communists and radicals get A's in this class." The Movimiento Estudiantil Chicano de Aztlán (MEChA) (Chicano Student Movement of Aztlán) led a sit-in at the Administration Building and a bomb injured Laurence Jackson in a student dormitory.

Looking back on this period in 1982, UCSD's McGill, who later served as president of Columbia University before returning to San Diego, wrote:

"Students felt that they were in the majority and also in the right. The impression needed no skeptical testing; it was overpowering. Any opposition was immediately defined as evil. How many times in those days did I hear the singsong chant, 'We are the people — we are the people — we are the people'?

"But as I have tried to suggest, there was something beyond this unsophisticated moral righteousness in the protest activity of the 1960s. Students also needed to portray themselves as victims of society.

"Discussions in those days were nearly always characterized by what seemed to me to be a diminished quality of thought. Adversarial habits of thinking, coupled with assumptions of moral rectitude, led protest groups to assert views that I considered virtually paranoid. Whenever I would say this and ask them to apply higher standards of proof to their own beliefs, they would laugh derisively. Proof was unnecessary.

"It is not a new observation, but the impact of such intense emotional commitment, unaccompanied by genuine critical skepticism, was almost chilling. It shows once more how thin the veneer of our civilization is."

In March 1972, marchers from the United Farm Workers protested plans to bring the Republican Convention to San Diego. *Courtesy San Diego Historical Society*

ENVIRONMENTAL AWAKENING

What McGill and much of the rest of San Diego and society in general were experiencing in the late-'60s was the extremes of the Generation Gap. Don't trust anyone over 30. Make love, not war. The counter-culture flowered in Ocean Beach, where hippies and surfers lived side-by-side and anti-Vietnam War activists battled periodic police crackdowns. The local Chicano community revolted in 1970 against plans for development beneath the San Diego-Coronado Bay Bridge and successfully created their own development, Chicano Park, marked by colorful murals on the bridge's concrete pillars.

Violence was replaced by a rising tide of environmentalism, begun officially with Earth Day on April 22, 1970. This wasn't just a student movement. All Americans seemed caught up in a concern about controlling pollution, population and, in San Diego, unfettered growth. There were reports of a 52,000-person "new town" proposed in Rancho de los Peñasquitos, another of 16,500 in Carmel Valley east of Del Mar. Clairemont and Kensington residents moved to save canyons from development. Solana Beach successfully fought off a bluff-top hotel, only to see condos rising on the same land. Rural Julian was worried about a proposal to turn a 950-acre cattle ranch into a subdivision of 1,650 homes on urban-sized lots. Department store

executive George A. Scott appealed to the City Council: "We ask this council to put your concern for rights of people ahead of your concern for rights in property. Only in this way may we justly retain the title 'All-American City, a city in motion.'" Ted "Dr. Seuss" Geisel, San Diego's most famous author, illustrated the December 1972 cover of *San Diego Magazine* with a grim drawing of dense, featureless-looking houses and a lonely tree. His plea: "Leave Something Green." The local debate was a variation on "smokestacks versus geraniums" of so many years earlier.

Political Scandal

The political order also was undergoing fundamental change. On October 8, 1970, Mayor Frank Curran, a state assemblyman, two county supervisors, four council members and the president of C. Arnholt Smith's Yellow Cab Company were indicted on bribery and conspiracy charges arising out of a 22 percent rate hike granted in 1967. Curran was tried and acquitted, Councilman Allen Hitch pleaded guilty to a misdemeanor and was fined $750 and the others were either acquitted or the charges were dropped for lack of evidence.

This was not the end of political scandal in San Diego, but Harold Keen, writing in December 1970, believed a new standard of behavior was at hand: "Purged are the cronyism, the country club attitude, the casualness of gift-giving and receiving. More than lip service will be paid codes of ethics. Great caution will be exercised in dealing with matters of public concern. An era has ended and in the new atmosphere at City Hall, it is likely that with or without changes in the [city] charter, the relationship between the mayor, council and city manager will be redirected toward greater assertion of power by the elected representatives."

There was no one more powerful at the time than C. Arnholt Smith. A high school dropout from Walla Walla, Washington, Smith began as a bank teller at the Bank of Italy (later Bank of America) and secured control of San Diego's one-office U.S. National Bank in 1933. He used it as a base to amass a fortune on the order of John D. Spreckels' of a half-century earlier. In addition to the taxi cab company, his interests included real estate (Westgate Hotel, San Luis Rey Downs near Oceanside, Kona Kai Club); tuna boats and canneries; fresh produce; Air California airline; and the San Diego Padres (which he bought for $300,000 in 1955 and sold for $12.5 million to McDonald's restaurant magnate Ray Kroc in 1974). A lifelong republican, Smith served on the state Highway Commission in the 1940s, championing the modernization of U.S. Highway 101 along the coast (supplanted later by Interstate 5) and U.S. 395 (State Route 163 and Interstate 15) through Balboa Park. He was a personal friend of Richard Nixon and kingmaker at San Diego City Hall. A supporter of many charities, he was named "Mr. San Diego" in 1961 by the Grant Club.

But in 1969 his empire began coming apart with a sensational story in the *Wall Street Journal*, titled, "Self-Dealing Tycoon." The Securities and Exchange Commission and IRS launched investigations into possible fraud involving Smith and on October 18, 1973, the U.S. comptroller of the currency declared Smith's U.S. National Bank insolvent. With 62 branches and $932 million in assets, it was the largest bank failure in U.S. history. Smith was

(Opposite page) The December 1972 cover of *San Diego Magazine* by "Dr. Seuss." *Courtesy San Diego Magazine*

"Mr. San Diego," C. Arnhold Smith, would end his career fighting federal charges of bank fraud. *Courtesy San Diego Historical Society*

The rapid growth of the Mira Mesa housing development prompted Mayor Pete Wilson's managed growth policies in the early 1970s. Courtesy San Diego Historical Society

indicted on 25 counts of manipulating $170 million in bank funds and in 1979 was convicted of grand theft in the embezzlement of $8.9 million. He served an eight-month term in 1984-85 and died in 1996 at age 97.

The Wilson era

The taxi cab scandal destroyed Mayor Curran's hopes for a third term and paved the way for a new political age dominated by Pete Wilson. Wilson a young Assemblyman originally from Illinois, gained the support of an enlightened business establishment. Wilson pointedly refused all donations from Smith and his associates. Advocating a platform of managed growth, Wilson won handily, and in his inaugural speech December 6, 1971, he laid out his future vision:

"San Diego will not and should not remain static. That is not possible for a dynamic community. But we must see to it that the 'City in Motion' gives direction to its motion. We must plan now for tomorrow. Our planning must integrate social, economic and political — as well as physical factors... Fortunately it's not yet too late. We still have time to do it right — though we frankly need better tools to control development. As the nation's fifth largest city in land area, San Diego has space to do it right; not space to burn, but space to use wisely, with the greatest care...

"San Diego in the '70s can be a spectacular success story. It can be a city of open space and equal opportunity; a city free from visual blight and free from the frustration of jammed freeways; a city wise enough to see that its economic health coincides with its environmental health; a city with jobs for all which provide purpose and satisfaction as well as bread upon the table; a city whose citizens can be secure in their homes and parks and streets, with leisure to enjoy the tonic of sun and sand, of pure air and water, or the diverse educational and cultural fare that only a great city can offer. This would be a success story.

"San Diego can and must be this city in the '70s. To my colleagues [on the City Council] I say that we must be unanimous in our determinations to assure that San Diego is that city — America's finest city."

Mayor Pete Wilson at the groundbreaking ceremonies for the restoration of San Diego's historic Gaslamp Quarter. Courtesy San Diego Historical Society

One of Wilson's favorite targets during his 1971 campaign was Mira Mesa, a distant suburb in the early stages of development. Hundreds of residents were moving into the 10,700-acre community north of the Miramar Naval Air Station. But public services were nowhere in sight. It was Linda Vista, 1941-42, all over again. Schools were in trailers and unoccupied homes. Dirt lots doubled as playgrounds. Access to and from the outside was limited. Wilson quickly took charge by ousting a majority of the Planning Commission, urging the city manager's office to take immediate remedial steps and telling the International Conference of Building Officials' state chapter in February 1972, "The burden is on the government to see that this does not happen again."

Wilson championed a strategy dubbed "Pay as you grow," under which new growth paid for itself, and sought to discourage leapfrog development by redirecting growth to the inner city and older suburbs. Developed by Kansas City land-use attorney Robert Freilich, Wilson's growth-management plan divided the city into tiers, with fees charged to developers in new communities; existing property taxes would be set aside to improve old communities. This strategy was first established as council policy and then institutionalized in the city's 1979 Progress Guide and General Plan. Under threat of a building moratorium, Mira Mesa builders agreed to pay $700 per student to fund schools and speed up other improvements.

Before Wilson could set his reforms in place, he faced one major embarrassment. The Republican National Committee, at President Richard Nixon's urging, had selected San Diego as the site of his nominating convention for 1972 — despite the clear absence of adequate convention facilities and luxury hotels. Mayor Curran, a Democrat, had gone along with the president's wishes but muttered, "We need this like a hole in the head," knowing that San Diego's summer tourist season needed no additional business from conventioneers.

Best laid plans began to unravel early in Wilson's term, when it came to light that International Telephone & Telegraph, owner of the new Sheraton Hotel on Harbor Island, had made a $400,000 pledge to the host committee and that the Nixon Administration had shortly thereafter reached a favorable ruling in an anti-trust case involving ITT. Anti-war demonstrators began announcing plans for massive demonstrations during the convention. Peter Graham, who took over the Sports Arena from its original developer, was making expensive demands in exchange for use of his facility as the main convention venue.

In April, the Republican National Committee announced that it was pulling out of San Diego and moving the convention to Miami Beach in August, the site of the Democrats' conclave scheduled for July. Wilson considered the pullout a major insult to San Diego's pride; he also stood to lose his moment in the national spotlight. But he turned the disaster around locally by organizing "America's Finest City Week" to coincide with the GOP convention. The weeklong festival has been held at the same time ever since.

Evening Tribune columnist Neil Morgan, mirroring the general civic reaction to the Republican pullout, titled his 1972 profile of the city "San Diego: The Unconventional City":

> San Diego is growing up without the brashness of Los Angeles or the narcissism of San Francisco. It offers climate and freedom. It is the oldest but in some ways the newest city of California. It seems to have the best chance for becoming the city of tomorrow, augmenting the amenities of the good life with firm cultural roots and a highly selective base of commerce. The civic character of Los Angeles and San Francisco is already set; San Diego's is only now developing.

Aerial view of Rancho Peñasquitos, 1972 *Courtesy San Diego Historical Society*

San Diego's famed "swimsuit optional" zone — Black's Beach along the shoreline of La Jolla. *Courtesy San Diego Historical Society*

(Opposite page) The construction of the Coronado Bay Bridge in 1969. *Courtesy San Diego Historical Society*

LAIDBACK LIFESTYLES

Like the rest of the nation, San Diego adopted new lifestyle modes and mores in the 1970s. Residents played racquetball in warehouse-like buildings; rollerskated on the Mission Beach boardwalk; danced the disco in nightclubs where disc-jockeys rather than live bands picked the tunes; attended movies at multiplex cinemas; and suffered through gas shortages during the energy crises of 1973-74 and 1979-80.

San Diego added its own touch in the "me decade." In 1974, the City Council designated a "swimsuit optional" zone at Black's Beach north of Scripps Institution of Oceanography; an initiative brought the highly publicized nude beach to an official end in 1977, but officials did not strictly enforce the dress code. Cancer victims streamed to Tijuana pharmacies and cancer centers to buy Laetrile, an FDA-banned drug. Ted Giannoulis donned a chicken costume in 1974 and became radio station KGB's mascot, later serving the same role for the San Diego Padres. The new owner of the Padres, McDonald's restaurant king Ray Kroc, participated in antics of his own when at the April 9, 1974, opening game, he grabbed the microphone and shouted, "I've never seen such stupid ballplaying in my life." Sol Price's Fed-Mart stores gained loyal shoppers for deep discounts, followed by his even more popular, membership-only Price Club (now Costco) warehouses.

San Diego gained an unsavory reputation as a popular hangout for people suspected of cavorting with the Mafia. The scandal-ridden Teamsters Union Pension Fund invested in a billion dollars worth of land and projects in San Diego. La Jolla financier Allen R. Glick, owner of a Las Vegas casino was investigated several times, particularly after the mysterious 1975 murder of one of his business associates, Hillcrest resident Tamara Rand. The local FBI office increased its organized crime squad from three to 15.

DEMOGRAPHIC SHIFTS

San Diego's demographic character began taking on a new look in 1970s with the growth of the Mexican-American and African-American populations and the arrival of Southeast Asian refugees.

"The Death of Tio Taco," a Harold Keen report in *San Diego Magazine* in August 1970, recounted the rising influence of artists, growing popularity of bilingual education and activism of college students in the Hispanic community. "We have a beautiful system in this country," said Don Romero Grady, the first Chicano member of the San Diego Grand Jury, "but it has left some minority groups out. Mexicans have been told their place is in the fields or in common-labor jobs. They want to become good citizens, to improve themselves and to belong to the system." Soon, Peter Chacon became a state assemblyman and Jess Haro a city councilman, the

first Hispanics elected locally to such offices in more than 100 years.

San Diego's African-American community also grew in size and influence in the 1970s. Leon Williams, appointed in 1969 to the City Council, was elected in 1971, 1975 and 1979 before moving on to the Board of Supervisors. He was followed by William Jones, Wes Pratt and George Stevens, all of whom lobbied hard for improved city services and facilities in older inner-city neighborhoods. In education, the most significant development in this period was a desegregation lawsuit filed in 1967 on behalf of Kari Carlin and other students against the San Diego Unified School District. A judge's ruling in 1978 led to a voluntary busing program that relied on developing special programs at "magnet schools" in minority-dominated schools to attract nonminority students. Judicial review of the program did not end until 1998.

A third major ethnic group, Vietnamese and other Southeast Asians, suddenly appeared in San Diego in the wake of the evacuation of American personnel from Saigon in April 1975. More than 50,400 refugees began arriving in April at temporary quarters in Camp Pendleton, where they remained until they found permanent homes locally and throughout the country. The camp closed in November.

"I remember it was early May when we got here," De Tran told *Union-Tribune* reporter Pat Flynn 20 years later. "It was extremely cold, especially at night. We had just come from a tropical place. I remember everyone had on these Army jackets that really ill-fitted us." Residents in the temporary city included former South Vietnam Presidents Nguyen Cao Ky and Nguyen Van Thieu. Instead of relocating, many refugees settled in San Diego, first in East San Diego, then in Linda Vista and Mira Mesa and gradually in many parts of the county.

More than 30 years after the end of the World War II, San Diego showed new confidence, driven not by mindless boosterism but by a new elite of political, business and academic leaders. The

An arson fire destroyed San Diego's famed Old Globe Theatre in Balboa Park on March 8, 1978. *Courtesy The San Diego Union-Tribune*

The last moments of PSA's Flight 182, September 25, 1978. Hans Wendt, a photographer for the San Diego County Public Information Office had just finished an assignment in the area when he heard an explosion in the sky.
With no time to focus, Wendt raised his camera and took this photograph.
Courtesy Hans E. Wendt

"sleepy Navy town" was now a big city, with all the trappings and pitfalls that come with urban growth. The ferries stopped running across San Diego Bay when the San Diego-Coronado Bay Bridge opened in 1969; the view was better and the trip faster, but the romance was gone.

The era's growing pains were particularly painful in 1978, a year when tragedy and setback were never far from the news. In February, arson destroyed Balboa Park's Electric Building, home to the San Diego Aerospace Museum and its priceless collection of vintage air craft and archives. In March, arson struck again, this time at the Old Globe Theatre. It took four years to replace both buildings. In June, Pete Wilson made a poor showing in the gubernatorial primary, illustrating once again that San Diego was not yet a proper springboard for statewide office. The same election saw passage of Proposition 13, the property-tax-cutting initiative that lowered tax bills but played havoc with municipal finances. The measure, incidentally, disrupted San Diego's carefully constructed growth-management funding plan by halting the flow of taxes to inner-city revitalization. In September came the nation's worst civilian plane crash to date, when a Pacific Southwest Airlines jet collided with a private plane over North Park, killing 144 persons.

What was San Diego's future to be? Was this natural paradise, finetuned by man, permanent or temporary? Two professors from opposite coasts sketched out a compelling new vision of an environmentally oriented, different kind of urbanism. Like John Nolen at the beginning of the century, Kevin Lynch from the Massachusetts Institute of Technology and Donald Appleyard from the University of California at Berkeley presented an alternative to ponder. Their work was entitled *Temporary Paradise?*

Chapter Five

Timeout: Temporary Paradise?

San Diego needed a new vision of its future by the 1970s. John Nolen's plans written early in the century sketched out several options, some of which were fulfilled. But by now, new priorities required new thinking. Environmental protection, growth management, urban revitalization and grassroots public participation had gained new prominence. Also on the minds of many was the need to develop closer connections between San Diego and Tijuana.

Hamilton Marston, grandson of George W. Marston, and was active in the Chamber of Commerce and San Diegans Incorporated, said later that the focus on downtown's needs, the future of the airport and other projects required a broader focus. He and his aunt Mary Marston offered the city $10,000 to hire one or more outside consultants to perform what came to be called a "reconnaissance" of the San Diego landscape and what the potential might be. "The conditions were that the plan would be the property of the city and the city would give wide distribution to it," Marston recalled. But the document was to be considered a guide rather than a legal plan or policy. "What we were attempting to do was add to the intelligence of the area."

The prime visionary hired was Kevin Lynch, a noted urbanologist from the Massachusetts Institute of Technology, located in Cambridge, where Nolen, too, had been based. Lynch brought along as a colleague Donald Appleyard from the University of California, Berkeley. Together they spent much of 1974 visiting San Diego, polling citizens and working with a 15-member resource panel. They completed their work September 15, 1974, and 25,000 copies in newsprint were published and distributed citywide.

The City Council accepted the report without adopting it as official policy. But over the years, many of its provisions made their way into community plans, ordinances and policies. Twenty-five years after its release, long after the authors had died (Appleyard in 1982, Lynch in 1984), major recommendations continued to resonate with policy makers. For example, Mayor Susan Golding's proposal for a "Bay-to-Bay Link" between San Diego and Mission bays echoed a similar proposal in Temporary Paradise?

The title of the report signifies the tenuous nature of San Diego's destiny, the question mark underscoring Lynch and Appleyard's concern that San Diego might cease being a paradise unless the right course of action was taken. What follows are excerpts from key passages in the study.

Ellipses have been deleted for readability.

San Diego: Perfecting Paradise

Prefatory Letter to Planning Director James Goff

We hope that publication of the main report will stimulate that popular discussion and backing which is absolutely essential if San Diego is to conserve and enhance its magnificent site. We are under no illusion that our rapid analysis, and our many recommendations, will all be found adequate or acceptable. Our advantage has been that we could take a fresh view of the region as a whole. Our hope is that our ideas will be useful material for the public debate, and the extended action, in which San Diego must engage in the years to come.

In Brief

This is an illustrated discussion of the landscape of San Diego, made by two newcomers. The city's magnificent site, for which its citizens have such strong affection, is still intact but may be losing its best qualities. In this report we analyze these qualities the history of the regional landscape, its meaning to its people and how it stands today.

We make many suggestions about saving the valleys and the canyons, restoring the bay, rebuilding the neighborhoods and major centers. We recommend slowing down and redirecting growth to the present urban areas, and thence along the coast. We suggest ways of doing it that will conserve water, energy and the land, while making the landscape more humane. We discuss airports, highways, better transit systems, walkways and cycle trails. We try to show that Tijuana as an integral part of the San Diego landscape, must be managed by strong joint action.

The situation of the region is chancy (when are human affairs not so?) But San Diego has a very possible future in which its splendid assets have been conserved, and its amenities shared more equitably among all its people. The city should take thought for the long-term quality of its environment. We suggest a way to do that and end up with a few questions and basic principles.

We hope San Diegans will find this report provocative, will agree and disagree with it, and will make their feelings known. Most of all, we hope San Diego takes charge of its future.

Where the Region Stands Today

This is a special landscape, yet much of its development is a faithful copy of U.S. models. Freeways, arterial streets, airports, industries, shopping centers, the downtown renewal area — they all look familiar. The new suburbs are quite the same, if more closely built and barren. At first glance this is a standard American city, still new and clean, without trees, rather dried up, dropped onto a big landscape.

But the fine climate and the dramatic site are not yet destroyed. Large open areas remain: underused military and industrial lands, numerous airports, flood plains, steep slopes, discontinuous urbanization, farms, wastelands waiting for development. San Diego is not yet committed, not yet seriously congested.

Los Angeles was not unlike much of San Diego a half-century ago [1920s]: treeless, scattered, and-semi-rural. Much of the new growth in San Diego's North County is occurring to accommodate commuters to Orange and Riverside counties. The two metropolitan regions are beginning to merge, flanking Camp Pendleton. It may seem inevitable that Los Angeles and San Diego will one day be a single urbanized region.

Still, if San Diego cannot hope for Los Angeles' great size, it can easily imitate it in other ways: spread out its dry suburbs, channel its streams, fill its valleys and lagoons, choke its roads and darken its air, sharpen the social gradient, harden the border. Could we then rename it San Diego de Los Angeles?

San Diego will grow and change, but the city is already here and will continue to be a major determinant of quality. A careful look at what should be saved in the existing city is our first task. Conservation of the natural setting is surely an urgent priority, and the finer parts of the city can also be preserved. As in any city that has grown fast, mistakes have been made and the public environment is all too often simply the leftover space between.

slower compact growth along northern coastal shore

Mission Bay completed and linked to San Diego Bay

Mission Valley a new recreation center

new residential communities around the head of the Bay

offshore floating communities

public recreation and residential uses supplant industrial and military uses of the Bay

Tijuana River Valley as a recreation and cultural resource for San Diego and Tijuana

The Seacoast

In people's minds the ocean shore is the most important asset of the city, as evidenced in our interview and tourist literature... This is the basic question: how much of the shore should be accessible to whom, and by what means? For our part, we believe that the ocean shore should be the possession of all those who live in the region. Shore communities should not have exclusive rights, nor should tourist accommodations be able to appropriate special frontages. The diversity of beach character and diversity of access should be maintained... Maintain the mix of income and type in the present coastal communities, and give a greater number of people — of all incomes — the chance to live near the sea.

Keep private development back from the water's edge — whenever possible, private land should be at least 100 yards back of the beach or shore and set well behind the brow of the bluff. In many places it should be set farther back. Forward of that line, the land should be given to water-related public recreation, or occasionally leased to moderately priced commercial recreation open to the general public.

continued on page 148

THE VALLEYS AND CANYONS

The valleys and canyons are San Diego's priceless asset… It is of great importance that San Diego now, at the last moment, preserve all the remaining undeveloped valleys and canyons. Keep the building up on the expansive flats above. Protect the valley sides and rims, as well as the floor, so that the rural character of the valley is preserved, even within the city, and erosion and flood damage is prevented.

No more highways, not even transit lines, should be carried along these green fingers, however reasonable that may look at first glance… Parts of the valleys should be ecological preserves, others campgrounds and wild lands for children to explore… A complex trail system — for walking, cycling and horseback riding — should be developed along these natural valleys.

Productive activities related to water would add to the "liveliness and meaning of the Bay" and remind people of the " historic use of the waterfront" in San Diego.
From Temporary Paradise?

(Map on page 146) "A birds-eye view of the San Diego/Tijuana region as it might become." Lynch and Appleyard suggested the international region could become a vital meeting point of two living cultures.
From Temporary Paradise?

Lindbergh Field and the Marine Corps Depot, together with the cluttered growth just north of them, would furnish another 2,000 acres in a strategic location through which waterways might run to relink the bays. None of these moves will be easy, and many will take a long time, but returning the bay to San Diego will maintain the inner city as a prime place to live and ease the pressure for suburban growth.

Existing Communities

Maintain the existing residential character — Make a community survey to identify and then conserve the streets, landmarks and areas that have a sense of place or history. Develop guidelines to keep new development in character, in regard to such things as height, bulk and setback, use, open space, parking, landscaping, roofs, walls materials, windows, balconies and detail.

Protect the residential areas from through traffic. Bring more open space into use. Improve the conditions for walking and cycling. Improve the surroundings of schools, libraries, churches and community facilities. Improve the pedestrian environment in the commercial strip. Increase the traffic capacity of the arterials.

Planting alone could raise the quality of San Diego's arterials far above their present mediocre level. Streets need not be lined with trees on the standard model. Problems of maintenance and the use of water set limits to this. But there could be frequent oases of lush planting, not located for visual reasons alone, but where they also serve to shade pedestrians. It is striking to the observer how few plants San Diego has along its major streets.

Make the beaches accessible without destroying the local communities behind them — major transportation and parking should be kept well back of the beach, with free transit forward and frequent foot access... Encourage housing of mixed price and type to locate along the shore... Control the height and bulk of shorefront development — tall buildings and massive beachfront walls block the view and impair access.

In the long term, remove all uses from the shore which are not water-related, and are not residence or recreation — much of the shorefront industry, military and transport is there for historic reasons, and not because they use the water today. The people of San Diego will lay increasing emphasis on access to their bay, and these uses hedge them out. Some, like the airfields, are noisy and dangerous. In the long run, large-scale industry can be dispersed to inland locations or removed to Camp Pendleton or other locations.

Vast areas of land by the bay could thus be opened up for residence and recreation — some 2,500 acres and six miles of beach in North Island alone (which is sufficient for a population of 100,000 to 150,000, at moderate densities).

Signs can be more lively, more informative and yet less cluttered... Signing is a necessary art and can create character and sparkle, instead of simply assaulting the eye... Lights and graphics can enliven the scene... Coordinated management can bring people out to use the street.

The major centers

Establishing a comfortable connection [from the downtown business district to the bay] will not be easy. Moreover, any further structures like the Royal Inn [Holiday Inn on the Bay at Harbor Drive and Ash Street] will disrupt the clustered image of downtown and destroy its outward views. Centre City renewal will have to be handled with care.

Mission Valley is the second "downtown" of the region and its future appears gloomy. It presents a fragmented and uninspiring image... Yet this is the very place where people from all over the region could meet in an environment befitting the grandeur of the valley... The north-facing slopes of the valley are still untouched, and could be saved. The center of the valley is still miraculously open; the creek [San Diego River] flows unseen. This area could take on the relaxed and delightful character of the Tivoli Gardens in Copenhagen... Mission Valley is a landscape disaster, yet few disasters are beyond all repair. It is only that repair demands money, time and effort.

Growth: Where? Of What Kind?

Slow down the inland suburban growth, but do not try to stop it. Extend public services gradually, on a phased basis, and not automatically, on the request of developers. Tie the pace of development strictly to that extension of service so that all public services (schools, utilities, roads, fire protection) are budgeted and provided before houses are complete.

Encourage smaller, less homogeneous development... Fundamentally, this means a change in the way the land development business is organized, which will come harder. Could there be public ways of encouraging small builders and community enterprises?

Use a more appropriate form of settlement, based perhaps on the Mediterranean prototype, which developed in this type of landscape. What is wanted is much more compact site planning, narrow (even shaded) streets, the use of roofs, interior courts and small intensive gardens in place of lawns and yards.

"Increase the traffic capacity of the arterials..." the report urged, as it suggested enhancing pedestrian flow and adding special bicycle and bus lanes.
From Temporary Paradise?

Respect the land. Keep the valleys and canyons, and their rims, out of development, using public purchase, and flood plain and hillside zoning with real teeth in them.

Save water and energy. Concentrate the use of water and recycle it to the canyons. Develop solar energy inland (and wind energy on the coast?). Minimize the use of the automobile, by dispersing employment and services to local areas... Perhaps it may even in time become necessary to ration, or to sell, a temporary right to park a car in a local area... New suburbs should be designed so that they can adapt quickly to a low-energy, low-water regime.

Timeout: Temporary Paradise?

But the policies we have outlined for regulating suburban growth could be extremely dangerous, if no alternate location for growth were provided. San Diego cannot stop migrants at her borders, nor forcibly reduce its birthrate. A check in suburban growth alone will simply raise the price of housing and confine moderate income families to a shrinking, inadequate, inner-city stock of houses. If there were acceptable ways of controlling the mix of house prices and rents, to prevent discrimination against the less affluent, or of directly supplying low-cost housing, then growth could be more severely controlled without loss of equity. As it is, a suburban slowdown must be accompanied by the encouragement of new growth in present urban areas... Any "densification" should follow certain rules:

It should be by the consent of the local community, a consent gained in return for public investment and services... Its rate and character should not destroy existing community character... Public improvements should focus on the present urban areas, and not on the open land north of Mission Valley, as is presently the case... Suburban restraint and the revitalization of the existing city must go hand in hand.

How To Get About

In many parts, San Diego's freeway system is magnificent. It was put in place largely prior to development, and is still today not badly congested, except in certain locations and at certain times... The freeways clearly cannot be replaced or relocated. But they need repair.

The city should pay attention to its highway landscape. Cluster vegetation, use native plants. Use highway detail in nonstandard ways. Coloring the pavement and the guardrails in dark green, blues and browns could do much to relieve the sense of glare and heat. Accommodate other uses, other modes of travel. Incorporate the freeway into the community landscape where feasible.

San Diego is an auto city, but it is beginning to see the costs of its narrow transportation base. Air pollution is an immediate problem... Congestion is not yet as acute as in other cities, but the gasoline crisis [of 1973-74] hinted at the uncertainties of depending on cars... But it will take a massive effort to get people out of their automobiles, a two-pronged strategy of damping the growth of auto facilities, while speeding that of other modes.

The remainder of the freeway program should be delayed [a drawing of South County shows the elimination of State Routes 52, 125 and 54]. The bus is the fundamental unit of a public transportation system, but people will be attracted to them, and away from cars, only if the frequency, character and location of service is much improved. Fixed rail transit, now under serious consideration in San Diego, can offer a fast, comfortable trip. Cycle trails in the valleys and canyons have already been proposed. Dispersing workplaces into residential districts may make it feasible to walk to work. Airports should be separated from residential areas. It may be that some site well inland would be the best of all, but of all the three places examined, consolidation with the Tijuana airport at the border is clearly to be preferred.

The Mexican Connection

San Diego thinks of itself as a border town, but in reality it is part of the functioning metropolitan region of San Diego/Tijuana. Tijuana, with its estimated 400,000 people, is almost one-quarter of the total regional population today. It is one of the most rapidly growing cities in the world — perhaps 6 or 7 percent per year, although there is no sure information. At these current estimated rates, Tijuana will have a population of 1.4 million by 1990 and

Downtown retail outlets in the 1970s best served shoppers who used the automobile. Lynch and Appleyard suggested improving the pedestrian environment for shopping by adding shade, arcades and wider sidewalks to create a human atmosphere. *From Temporary Paradise?*

will be as large as San Diego in 40 years [2014].

It is Tijuana that makes San Diego truly unique among the great U.S. cities. Vitality comes from the interchange between two cultures when they communicate with each other.

The U.S. conquest of California in 1847 imposed an artificial boundary, which not only cut heedlessly through a local landscape, but separated the port of San Diego from its natural region of Baja California and the lower Colorado. San Diego became a remote U.S. border town, instead of a regional center. But once again now, if cooperation proves possible, San Diego/Tijuana, already a single metropolis, could become the center of an international region… The key actions that are needed are economic, social and political ones. Stable, equitable regional institutions must be built up. But actions in the environment might help to lead off and might alleviate some present problems. For example:

Establish an international airport on the Otay Mesa to provide a major focus for growth. Keep the lower Tijuana River Valley open for joint use. Build bicultural institutions on the mesas above the river valley. Let the new center of Tijuana become the major southern subcenter of the San Diego/Tijuana region. Joint action [should be taken] to protect the natural setting. International studies are needed of the two populations, the two economies, the social changes.

What The Region Could Become

Dreams have some use. They give us hope, but they also move us to act. Can one dream about a region as large and as complicated as San Diego/Tijuana? We think so. There are dreams for the future region that one might realistically work for.

•San Diego de Baja California: San Diego/Tijuana could be the center of a large international region, a vital meeting point of two living cultures. The metropolis would share its water, its energy, its landscape, its culture, its economy. The border would be converted into a zone of confluence.

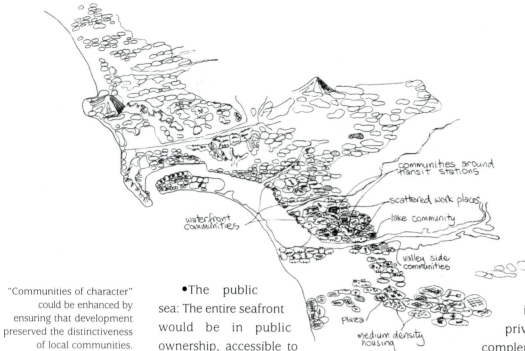

"Communities of character" could be enhanced by ensuring that development preserved the distinctiveness of local communities. From Temporary Paradise?

• The public sea: The entire seafront would be in public ownership, accessible to everyone by all modes of transport.

• The coastal band: The great majority of San Diegans live in a compact, low-rise urban band along the store, a band rarely more than two or three miles deep, except where it projects along the present chain of communities out towards El Cajon or has moved up the Tijuana Valley. There are two principle centers in the region: San Diego Centre City/Mission Valley and the new Tijuana/San Ysidro focus. The former is unfortunately broken into two parts — the old center and the lower Mission Valley — but each part is connected to its bay and to the other part through the new water-threaded settlement where Lindbergh Field used to be.

• Communities of character: The growth of the older areas has been fitted to community character, and based on local advice, so that the distinctiveness of the local communities has been preserved. Fine existing buildings have been saved, and the new ones fit with them in intricate and interesting ways. Public reinvestment and private rehabilitation are continuous and complementary. There are many small parks, the canyons are open and green, the sea not far.

• The inland kingdom: Inland of the coast the land is much more lightly occupied. No more than 20 percent of the region's population live here. They occupy low, dense communities of modest size and mixed income, many of them new, but which have grown only slowly. They are separated by large tracts of open land, used for farming, recreation, heavy industry, the collection of solar energy, military reservations or airports. Traces of the earlier Indian and Spanish occupation have been preserved. One senses the connection to the land and its history, to the mountains behind, the sea before, and the sun and stars above.

• Traveling light: People go to work by cycle, bus and ferry, and some can do it on foot. Since work weeks are flexible, there are no tense commuting peaks, nor any frantic weekend race. Cycles are easy to rent. Rail transit is for longer trips up and down the urban band. Light aircraft and dirigibles go from center to center. Automobiles are for trips out of the city, or for the handicapped, or for special deliveries or emergencies. The arteries and freeways give as much space to buses and bicycles as they do to cars. Traveling has become a pleasure, a way of enjoying the region, and no one is confined.

Why have things Gone Wrong?

Many people might agree with us that this would be a desirable future. But it will never happen unless we understand how the city is actually built, and thus how it might be built differently.

A few issues, a few principles

In conclusion, we see four questions that seek an answer:

1. Will San Diego and Tijuana continue as border towns, each at the end of its nation's line of development, and each dependent on an exotic and uncertain economy? Or can they realize their role as a bicultural metropolis, the center of a great natural region, safely sustained by the resources of that region?

2. Will San Diego grow as an extension of Los Angeles, and in that city's image, or can it find a new form, adapted to its own site and climate, a form which conserves water, air and energy, and supports the well-being of its people?

3. Will the region make sure that its amenities are available to all its people, regardless of nationality or income, or will present inequities continue to grow at the regional scale?

4. How can this region organize itself to conserve and enhance the quality of its environment, without losing touch with the local people in whose name that quality is being conserved?

In the course of discussing those questions, we have presented many suggestions and possibilities. Our ideas can be reduced to just a few principles:

1. Begin now to manage the environmental quality of the whole region in a coherent, effective way.

2. Save the shorelines, bays, valleys and mountains and restore them to everyone.

3. Retard suburban development, and change its form to one better adapted to the site.

4. Redirect growth to the existing urban neighborhoods. Restore and enhance the special character of each one. Shift public investment to those existing localities and increase the measure of local control.

5. Reduce dependence on the automobile and encourage all forms of nonpolluting lightweight transportation.

6. Reach across the border. Treat San Diego/Tijuana as one unified metropolis.

7. Flatten the north-south social gradient, and exploit the east-west natural one.

8. Conserve water, conserve energy, conserve the land.

six

Beyond Irving Gill's famed fountain, bare land awaits development as the new Horton Plaza. Office buildings, movie theaters and historic sites have been razed. New construction began in 1983. *Courtesy San Diego Historical Society*

CHAPTER SIX

Retooling for the 21st Century

The final years of the 20th century featured a rerun of many of the issues of previous decades. A constant theme featured a tug-of-war between the suburbs and the central city. Meanwhile, there was new attention directed at Tijuana and its interaction with San Diego. Similar connections with Imperial Valley, Orange County and the "Inland Empire" of Riverside and San Bernardino counties also tended to break down San Diego's historic isolation from the rest of Southern California. North County and South Bay developed their own identities, while East County and rural areas tried to hold back urbanization. Economically, San Diego was forced to transfer its reliance from defense industries and military spending to the new fields of biomedical research, telecommunications and computers. As the region moved to close the book on the 1900s, it was seeking its destiny in a newly fashioned combination of both smokestacks and geraniums.

Downtown: The Core Recovers

The revitalization of Centre City into a thriving, modern downtown became a top priority at century's end, one made necessary when the City Council opted in 1958 to open Mission Valley to commercial development. The first rescue effort resulted seven years later in the completion of the Charles C. Dail Community Concourse with the new City Administration Building, Civic Theater, Golden Hall convention facility and parking garage. To the east was the expansion of City College. In between, along B Street, rose a series of high-rise office buildings.

But as San Diego celebrated its bicentennial in 1969, these improvements proved insufficient to reverse the downtown decline. The symbol for this failure was Horton Plaza park, Alonzo Horton's one-time resting place for guests at his Horton House hotel. "South of Broadway," where sailors had partied during World War II, became a shorthand phrase to describe the panhandlers, rundown buildings and bawdy uses on lower Fifth Avenue, western Broadway and along the waterfront. A call to improve the restrooms beneath the park broadened into a general discussion about bolder measures.

To oversee the redevelopment job, the City Council formed the Centre City Development Corporation (CCDC) in 1975. This quasi-public body with a board appointed by the mayor and confirmed by the council had the day-to-day responsibility to negotiate with developers and oversee spending the "tax

1978-2000

The site of the future Horton Plaza in 1980. Balboa Theater remains surrounded by cleared land. *Courtesy The San Diego Union-Tribune*

(Photo on page 156) The "Bow Wave" sculpture on the wide steps of the Centre City Plaza office building in the Charles C. Dail Community Concourse. The Concourse, the first major downtown redevelopment effort, was completed in 1965. In the background is the city-owned parking structure. *Courtesy San Diego Convention Center Corporation*

The construction of anchor store Nordstrom in 1984. *Courtesy The San Diego Union-Tribune*

Ernest W. Hahn, a Los Angeles-based retail developer, outbid three competitors in 1974 to build a million-square-foot shopping center and signed a development agreement in 1977. One of the runners-up was James Rouse, who popularized the "festival marketplace" mall in Boston, Baltimore and other downtowns. "In terms of timing, for downtown it was about a hair's breadth between the nick of time and too late," wrote Beth Coffelt in *San Diego Magazine* in April 1974. Hahn argued that new downtown retail would fail unless the city enlarged its vision to include new mass transit, housing, a convention center and Gaslamp Quarter cleanup. In a May 16, 1974, letter to the City Council, Hahn said a comprehensive plan was "critical to the proper redevelopment in downtown San Diego."

In 1976, two additional redevelopment projects were adopted, the Marina residential zone, south and west of Horton Plaza, and the Columbia, generally north of Broadway and west of Union Street, for office buildings and a convention center. The Gaslamp Quarter, a 16 1/2-block historic district along Fifth Avenue, became an official redevelopment project in 1982 and in 1992, the balance of downtown was brought into the redevelopment program: Little Italy (Middletown) along India Street; East Village (Centre City East) east of Gaslamp; Cortez Hill around the historic El Cortez Hotel; and the central business district (excluding a few newly completed high-rise office towers and hotels).

But revitalization of the city's heart did not proceed smoothly. The energy crises of 1973 and 1979 threw the nation, and San Diego, into recession. The state taxpayers' revolt that resulted in the passage of Proposition 13 in June 1978 destroyed the financing plan for Hahn's Horton Plaza shopping center. Hahn faced problems attracting key department stores to

increment" — the new property taxes flowing from new construction and rehabilitation in the redevelopment zone.

CCDC's first job was implementing the first redevelopment project, Horton Plaza. In 1972, in one of his early acts as mayor, Pete Wilson unveiled the 15-block Horton Plaza Redevelopment Project to spur improvement south of Broadway. The plan incorporated a new federal courthouse, hotels, housing, office buildings and, above all, a retail center. The key site became available with the decision by the Union-Tribune Publishing Company to relocate its newspaper plant to Mission Valley, leaving room for a high-rise office building just west of the plaza (and generating new property taxes to support redevelopment budgets).

anchor his project. Planners and preservationists also criticized his design that required the razing of several historic sites and replacing them with a fortress-like, suburban-style mall.

"This project stands on what you would call a hairline, as it relates to the practicality of the project," Hahn said in July 1979. Two years later, he sold his company for a reported $270 million to the Canadian conglomerate Trizec but reaffirmed his intention to build Horton Plaza. "Horton Plaza, if we get it built in the way we want to build it," he said, "is going to be one of the most exciting projects I personally have been involved in and I think one of the most exciting projects in the United States."

It took another four years before the $140 million center was completed. The city's investment totaled more than $40 million. By then, the design was utterly different from the original 1974 proposal. Los Angeles architect Jon Jerde created a Post-Modern interpretation of an Italian hill town, where level upon multicolored level of shops and restaurants greeted the visitor. It was a shopping center like no other and it received national attention from opening day on August 9, 1985.

New York Times architecture critic Paul Goldberger offered a rather backhanded compliment in his review seven months after the opening:

"There is a bit of Disneyland inside every shopping mall, struggling to get out. In Horton Plaza in the center of downtown San Diego, the struggle is over: Disneyland has burst through with a vengeance... It is wildly exuberant, a kind of Southern California fantasy of a European street. It even has an abstract version of the cathedral in Siena as a focal point on the main plaza... This city has desperately needed a town square, and now it has one. It is probably the right kind of square for San Diego, not threatening the priorities of Southern California too strongly. In it, one can pretend to be in a city while living a suburban life."

Confounding many critics, Horton Plaza succeeded beyond its developer's expectations, becoming a popular tourist and conventioneer draw. Its makeup changed over the years, replacing one of the original department stores with a theme restaurant, for example, and in 1998, it was sold along with other local Hahn shopping centers to Westfield. But Ernie's Hahn's imprint remained intact; a plaque in his honor is located near the entrance to the parking garage at Fourth Avenue and F Street.

Housing, the second component of downtown development, proved no less of a struggle. The city's first new residential projects were two high-rise, federally subsidized (and architecturally bland) senior-citizen apartment buildings, Horton House and Lion's Manor, which opened in 1979-80. The

The grand opening of Horton Plaza, August 9, 1985. This view looks north on Third Avenue, renamed Broadway Circle for the portion that fronts the project. The obelisk is located in the stairway entrance to the Lyceum Theater. *Courtesy The San Diego Union-Tribune*

Chapter Six

San Diego: Perfecting Paradise

first unsubsidized housing, Park Row and Marina Park, opened in 1982 around historic Pantoja Park, the center of William Heath Davis' aborted New Town effort of 1850. The low-scale condominiums appealed to residents unaccustomed to urban high-rise living. But their timing could not have been more inopportune. Interest rates had skyrocketed to 16 percent, and few urban pioneers by then could afford to buy without subsidized loans. The two projects eventually sold out, but their developers, Pardee Construction Company and Shapell Housing, abandoned plans to build out the rest of the Marina housing program. In 1985, a third housing project, the 27-story Meridian condominiums, introduced million-dollar living units, valets and Manhattan-style accommodations. But sales were exceedingly slow and a planned-for twin tower was abandoned. Block-by-block development meant that the Marina would not be completed until after 2000. Other housing was promoted in Little Italy, Cortez Hill and East Village.

The third downtown priority, a convention center, also encountered some turbulence on the way to completion. CCDC planners had envisioned a four-block center just east of the Santa Fe Depot. But its $224 million cost prompted a citizen's referendum and the city's first-ever mail-in ballot election in May 1981. The project was defeated and debate ensued over an alternative that might meet with voter approval. Eventually, the San Diego Unified Port District agreed to pay in cash what ultimately cost $161 million (plus some $30 million in lawsuit-related costs) to build the convention center on the old Navy Field property along Harbor Drive. Voters approved the deal in 1983 and the building, designed by Canadian architect Arthur Erickson, opened in 1989. Its most distinctive features were architectural and financial: the sail-like covering on the rooftop terrace and the debt-free financing provided by the port. This is where the 1996 Republican presidential nominating convention was held. In June 1998, voters approved a $216 million expansion to double the size to about 500,000 square feet of exhibit space. A proposed third phase to bring the total to 1 million square feet is projected to be built someday across Harbor Drive.

The Gaslamp Quarter, so popular today as a lively restaurant and shopping mecca, was anything but appealing in 1974, when area property owners formed the Gaslamp Quarter Association to promote restoration of the heart of Alonzo Horton's downtown. The first new attraction, which opened that year, was the Old Spaghetti Factory restaurant located in the 1897 McKenzie, Flint and Winsby Building at the southeast corner of Fifth Avenue and K Street. In subsequent years, the city spent more than $8 million throughout the 16 1/2-block nationally recognized historic district on public improvements, including new sidewalks, landscaping, signs and gaslamp-styled streetlight fixtures. An old-fashioned

(Opposite page) San Diego, host of the 1996 Republican National Convention, lit up the sky with "the largest pyrotechnics display west of the Mississippi," August 10, 1996. *Courtesy The San Diego Union-Tribune*

Fourth Avenue and G Street and the exterior of the Golden West Hotel, a residential hotel that was spared when Horton Plaza was built. It lies across the street from the Gaslamp Quarter. *Photo by Robert A. Eplett*

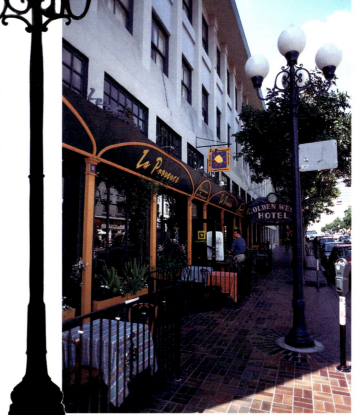

San Diego Marriott and Marina (left) and San Diego Convention Center were both completed in the 1980s on the site of the former Navy Field recreation facility. Harbor Drive was relocated upland from the bayfront to make extra room for this redevelopment by the San Diego Unified Port District.
Photo by Robert A. Eplett

One of the more striking office buildings completed downtown in the 1980s was the Emerald-Shapery Center on Broadway, featuring towers of varying heights. A hotel is located on the Broadway frontage and an office tower on the C Street side. The property was developed by San Diegan Sandor Shapery.
Photo by Robert A. Eplett

trolley along Fifth Avenue also was considered but never constructed.

Some Gaslamp property owners failed to improve their properties, and CCDC fought a years-long struggle to rid the district of adult bookstores, X-rated movie theaters and decrepit residential hotels. Retailers and restaurateurs came and went, the victims of overoptimism that Horton Plaza, the convention center and other improvements were just around the corner. The historic district finally hit its stride in the 1990s when Starbucks, Urban Outfitters, Hard Rock Cafe and other national chains opened outlets that a few years earlier would only have been feasible inside Horton Plaza. With the success came renewed debate between preservationists and developers, local merchants and outsiders, over the "soul" of the Gaslamp.

Office buildings and hotels left the greatest visual impact on the downtown skyline after 25 years of redevelopment. The total square footage of speculative office space rose from about 4 million to 10 million square feet from 1980 to 1990, as more than a dozen projects rose along B Street and Broadway. Downtown hotel rooms doubled from 3,000 to 6,000 over the same period. One particularly interesting development was the $143.5 million Symphony Towers. Opened in April 1989, the two-tower project spanned the old Fox Theater building at Seventh Avenue and B Street. The San Diego Symphony Orchestra Association bought the theater from the developer and renamed it Copley Symphony

Hall in honor of *Union-Tribune* publisher and major donor Helen Copley. A multistory parking garage was built over the theater to connect the 33-story office building on the south to the 207-room Marriott Suites hotel on the north. At the top of the office building was the newly reconstituted University Club, a commercial venture that replaced a nonprofit organization of the same name that dated back to the turn of the century.

As impressive as these towers of steel and glass were to locals and visitors, many ended in financial disaster for the original developers. Typical was the One America Plaza project that opened in 1991 at Kettner Boulevard and Broadway. Built on the site of the historic Tower Bowl with its distinctive Art Deco sign, the block was where a Hyatt Regency hotel was slated, linked to the planned convention center. When the convention center site shifted to the waterfront, banker Gordon Luce of Great American Bank (formerly San Diego Federal Savings & Loan Association) planned a $200 million, 33-story building designed by Chicago architect Helmut Jahn. But when Great American, along with many financial institutions, failed in the wake of the savings-and-loan collapses of the late-1980s, Luce's Japanese partners, Shimizu Land Corporation, completed the project. It was the last of downtown's high-rise offices for at least a decade.

After 20 years of redevelopment, downtown had seen $1.6 billion of private investment, supported by $266 million of public spending; $229 million of property taxes collected; 4,427 condominiums and apartments constructed (including 1,761 for low-income renters); 3,696 hotel rooms built; 5.7 million square feet of retail and office space finished and 5,465 permanent jobs created as of mid-1998.

One agency that did not endure many economic or political obstacles downtown was the San Diego Unified Port District. Controlling the valuable waterfront tidelands, the port excelled in the art of real estate development. It began with Seaport Village, a specialty shopping center that opened in 1980 on the site of the old San Diego-Coronado ferry terminus. Then came the convention center and hotel developments on the old Navy Field recreation grounds at the foot of Fifth Avenue; redevelopment of B Street Pier into a cruise ship terminal; beautification of G Street Mole and Harbor Drive; and finally a $240 million expansion of Lindbergh Field terminals, parking and access. The port was widely criticized for ignoring sound urban design principles and giving short shrift to public opinion. But competing demands on its once-hefty reserves by other port district cities began forcing a more conciliatory tone at century's end. More development was mapped out for the North Embarcadero area from G Street to Laurel Street, and discussions commenced over converting the 10th Avenue Marine Terminal to hotel and retail uses.

Rounding out the downtown success story was the creation of the San Diego Trolley. Championed by state Senator James R. Mills, the reintroduction of streetcar service, abandoned in 1949, was made possible by two events: a state constitutional amendment allowing gas taxes to be used for fixed-rail transit and Hurricane Kathleen in 1976, which caused major damage to the San Diego & Arizona

The San Diego Trolley's service began in 1981, returning streetcar service to the city for the first time since 1949. The original line, linking downtown with the Mexican border, has been joined by routes to Santee, Mission Valley and along the San Diego bayfront, past the convention center.
Photo by Robert A. Eplett

(Right and below) A new main library? Architect Robert Wellington Quigley designed a 300,000-square-foot library for downtown San Diego that featured a trellis-like dome covering a top-floor reading room. Its initial location was to have been directly east of the Santa Fe Depot, shown here in the model in the lower right-hand corner. The tallest building shown in the model represents the existing One America Plaza office building.
Courtesy Rob Wellington Quigley, FAIA

Eastern line owned by Southern Pacific Railway. The Metropolitan Transit Development Board (MTDB), formed in 1975 to build light-rail or streetcar service in the south half of the county, bought Southern Pacific's 108-mile line for a mere $18.1 million in 1979. Two years later, MTDB opened the first San Diego Trolley line — an $18 million, 15.9-mile route from the Santa Fe Depot to the San Ysidro border crossing. Critics dubbed it the "Tijuana Trolley," but that cute but misleading moniker soon disappeared from general use.

The on-time, under-budget construction and favorable fare-box return prompted many other cities to build similar systems. "If it pays off," said MTDB Vice Chairwoman (and later Mayor) Maureen O'Connor, "it is going to be the cheapest built system in the United States and the cheapest run system in the United States." MTDB later extended service along the waterfront to the convention center, eastward toward Santee and north to Old Town and Mission Valley. Future routes are planned north to UCSD and east past San Diego State University.

There was a price to pay for progress. Gaslamp, the Marina district and other parts of downtown had remained intact largely because interim, low-cost uses had taken hold during the middle decades of the century. Into once posh hotels moved hundreds of low-income residents, who paid perhaps $100 per month for a one-room apartment. When redevelopment arrived, many moved to other low-cost housing or found quarters in a new version of the old residential hotel. The city won national attention for its single-room-occupancy ordinance that superseded traditional zoning rules. San Diego adopted a building code that allowed hotel-like living units in a form not constructed for 50 years. In addition, the city encouraged live-work loft spaces in former warehouses and industrial buildings. Traditional zoning separates workplaces from residences on the theory that noxious fumes and noise are not conducive to home life. But in the post-industrial society, many computer-based jobs are perfectly compatible with residential land uses. These reforms, along with the construction of new shelters, did not solve the endemic homeless problem that all major cities suffered from the 1970s forward. But they offered new choices to people who were down on their luck or had minimal resources.

Art, music and drama thrived downtown as new developments gained new admirers of the urban lifestyle. The Museum of Contemporary Art, San Diego, opened a gallery in One America Plaza and the Children's Museum relocated from University Towne Centre to a former warehouse at the foot of Front Street. An annual "Art Walk" festival highlighted the work in downtown art galleries. "Street Scene" grew from a modest jazz festival to a multi-stage musical extravaganza in the Gaslamp Quarter each September.

Theater groups often survived on less than a shoestring as playwrights and performers took over empty lofts, warehouses and forlorn theaters. At one time, a "Theater Square" of historic stage theaters and movie houses was promoted as an alternative to Horton Plaza shopping center. As a compromise, the city built the two-stage Lyceum Theater, operated by the San Diego Repertory Theater, in the basement of the mall. Its name was derived from the 1913 stage theater on F Street that was bulldozed to make way for a Horton Plaza garage. At century's end, the fate of the historic Balboa, California, Fox (Copley Symphony Hall) and Spreckels theaters rested on the hope that downtown's growing popularity as the region's premier entertainment center would attract more live music, dance and dramatic productions. While opera and theater thrived, the 1995 bankruptcy of the San Diego Symphony and its 1998 shaky revival illustrated how fragile the performing arts remained in a city with so many choices for spending leisure time.

Despite the turnaround represented by Horton Plaza, the convention center and the many new office, hotel and residential projects, downtown's future was far from secure at century's end. Numerous parcels of land remained underutilized as parking lots. Ambitious development plans remained unfulfilled in the wake of major changes in real estate lending and tenant preferences. Two such stalled plans were developed by the Navy for its Broadway Complex and Catellus Development for its Santa Fe Depot property. Both would add millions of square feet of offices, hundreds of hotel rooms and splendid high-rise apartment or condo towers — if only the demand so warranted.

Similarly, public projects have proceeded fitfully as funding dried up in the wake of Proposition 13. The city's Central Library is perhaps, pitifully, the most public priority yet to be realized. The 1954 building on E Street quickly outgrew its three-story facility and a replacement was proposed as part of Horton Plaza. When that stalled, the city considered a joint-use development with an office builder on the existing site, but economics killed that plan. Then came a plan to rebuild on the site of a closed Sears store in Hillcrest, a move that prompted downtown interests to successfully lobby the City Council to commit to remaining in Centre City. Mayor Maureen O'Connor proposed building a "storybook" library on port tidelands at the foot of Broadway. But the port district did not cooperate and the idea died with O'Connor's departure from office in 1992. Mayor Susan Golding toyed with a variety of solutions before backing the purchase of a block east of the Santa Fe Depot. Local architect Rob Wellington Quigley and a team of associated architects designed a 300,000-square-foot building, twice the size of the old library. But rising costs (from $62 million to as much as $118 million) and design issues threw that plan into doubt. Most library supporters turned their attention to improving neighborhood branch libraries.

Ted Giannoulis played the KGB Chicken (later, the San Diego Chicken) at Padres and Chargers games. The unofficial team mascot, representing radio station KGB, cavorted for crowds at San Diego Jack Murphy (later Qualcomm) Stadium. *Courtesy Union-Tribune Publishing Co.*

This artist's rendering shows an early plan for the proposed 42,000-seat Padres Ballpark planned for the area east of the Gaslamp Quarter. It would be located near the expanded convention center and surrounded by new housing, offices and hotels.
Courtesy San Diego Padres

This pin, produced in the fall of 1997, was designed to boost the wishes of Chula Vista officials who offered bayfront location for a new Padres ballpark. The site selection committee, appointed by San Diego Mayor Susan Golding, recommended a downtown San Diego location instead.

The apparent stall in downtown's redevelopment came to an abrupt end in 1998, when city voters overwhelmingly approved two major public works projects: a $216 million addition to the San Diego Convention Center and a $411 million ballpark for the Padres in the East Village (Centre City East) area adjacent to the Gaslamp Quarter. The convention center had already proven its worth in attracting hotel development and more tourist and convention business. The ballpark was marketed to voters as a catalyst for jump-starting revitalization beyond the central business district. Even Main Library supporters spoke of locating their facility near the ballpark, alongside new residences, offices, hotels, shops and other developments. Besides the convention center expansion and the ballpark, approximately $3 billion in dozens of projects were poised to be started or completed by the time the Padres were scheduled to move from Qualcomm Stadium in Mission Valley in 2002. Chula Vista wooed the Padres in 1997, but San Diego downtown won the sweepstakes. The November 1998 ballpark vote seemed to settle once and for all the question: do San Diegans want a vibrant downtown? By a 60 percent margin they said they did.

Mission Valley Makeover

While downtown struggled to revitalize, Mission Valley prospered. Mission Valley Center, opened in 1961, was followed by San Diego (renamed Jack Murphy, then Qualcomm) Stadium in 1967 and Fashion Valley in 1969. Car dealerships, movie theaters, condominiums, themed restaurants, hotels and office towers filled up the 2,400-acre valley. Served by the region's three main freeways, this became the unofficial urban center of San Diego for 30 years.

But as planners and long-time residents had warned, urban development in a river valley poses problems. In the 1970s and '80s, severe storms periodically flooded the valley, causing some businesses to evacuate. Plans had been prepared by the U.S. Army Corps of Engineers to build a concrete channel to contain the river. But environmentalists fought the plan and Mayor Pete Wilson killed it.

In the 1980s, a $29 million private alternative — the First San Diego River Improvement Project (acronym FSDRIP, pronounced "fiz-drip") — aimed at taming a stretch of the river. The riverbed was deepened, natural habitat restored and 261 acres of riverbanks reclaimed for more development. Completed in 1989, the project stretches from State Route 163 to Qualcomm Way. It made possible construction of Hazard Center (a retail redevelopment on the former Hazard brickyard), Park in the Valley (another retail center) and several condominium complexes.

Grander visions evaporated with the onset of the recession in 1991. Most prominent was the Riverwalk commercial-residential project on the Stardust Country Club golf course, west of Fashion Valley. Chevron Land Development Company had proposed a massive complex of high-rise office and residential towers lining an extension of the FSDRIP natural channel. Ultimately, only the golf course was reengineered; it reopened in 1998. Similarly, Atlas Hotels proposed and then scuttled a major enlargement of its Town & Country Hotel.

After the recession, major expansions and renovations went forward at Fashion Valley and Mission Valley Center. Just west of the stadium, H.G. Fenton Materials and CalMat Properties Company mapped plans for turning their rock and gravel mining pits into building sites for housing, offices and shopping. And tying the valley together was a $120 million extension of the San Diego Trolley, which opened in time for the January 1998 Super Bowl XXXII at Qualcomm Stadium.

Mission Valley may never become the verdant gateway to Mission Bay Park that city planners had sketched out in the 1950s. But a series of community plans has called for humanizing the valley by limiting traffic, upgrading signage and landscaping and installing neighborhood-level services, such as a school, branch library and recreational facilities. There are periodic calls for locating regional facilities, such as the new main library, in the valley. But downtown now generally gets the lion's share of such public investments. In Mission Valley, private enterprise and initiative still remain in the driver's seat.

University City — Edge City

The original 1959 community plan for the 11,000 acres around the University of California campus on Torrey Pines Mesa envisioned a largely single-family-home and apartment complex to serve the projected 25,000 students, 2,100 faculty, 7,500 staff and 14,000 other residents. But by the 1980s, UCSD was but one component of a much more diverse community. University Towne Centre, developed by Ernest W. Hahn Inc., opened in 1977 as a typical regional shopping center. Hahn also figured in the construction of the Plaza at La Jolla Village high-rise office complex north of UTC.

The character of the UCSD campus also developed differently from what Roger Revelle envisioned in the 1950s. The plan to build 12 colleges of 2,200 students each by 1995 stalled with the pullback of state funding for higher education. Instead, UCSD construction proceeded fitfully, dependent on grants, donations and creative financing. By century's end, there were only five colleges and an enrollment of less than 20,000. North of the campus, Torrey Pines Road was lined with corporate headquarters and biomedical research-and-development firms. In nearby Sorrento Mesa and Sorrento Hills, computer and telecommunications companies appeared, many owing their existence to research at UCSD. In 1997, the campus counted at least 124 local companies, employing 15,000 and earning $2 billion revenues, that were based on UCSD technology or founded by faculty, alumni or staff. Qualcomm Corporation, a leading developer of wireless telephones, is a standout example of UCSD's spinoff potential.

Tijuana: San Diego's Bridge to the Pacific Rim

As San Diego disdained polluting heavy manufacturing, Tijuana welcomed it. For decades, the border town was hardly more than an small, insignificant appendage to San Diego. In 1950 its population of 65,000 was barely one tenth of San Diego's 557,000. It was the bawdy side of the region, where teenagers, sailors and tourists ventured for a few hours of food, drink and sport.

Amid rolling hills, the rapidly growing Tijuana now rivals San Diego in size.

Workers at Orbis Technologies assemble circuit boards at a maquiladora plant in Tijuana. *Courtesy San Diego Historical Society*

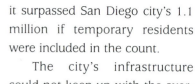

But in the 1970s, all this began to change. First, there was a major redevelopment project, the channelization of the Tijuana River beginning in 1972. In the place of squatter camps (periodically destroyed by flood) came shopping centers, high-rise offices, a cultural center and major thoroughfares. Next came the oil boom, when skyrocketing prices boosted Mexico's oil income and foreign loans. Then followed several economic crises, when oil prices collapsed. When the peso lost much of its value, investors from Europe, Asia and the United States discovered the economic benefit of low-wage manufacturing a few miles from the American market.

The vehicle for this new investment was the *maquiladora*, a "twin-plant" factory involving the production of parts elsewhere and their assembly in Mexico. First authorized in 1965, the industry employed as many as 60,000 people or 29 percent of the local work force in 1990 and accounted for $500 million of foreign exchange earnings that year. Some 12 million of the 22 million television sets sold in the United States were assembled in Tijuana maquiladoras by 1998. The attraction was bottom-line driven: Tijuana factory workers received only about $1.50 per hour, including benefits, less than a tenth of that earned by many union workers with comparable jobs in the U.S. The implementation of the North American Free Trade Agreement in 1994, followed by another sizable peso devaluation, increased even more Mexico's attractiveness to foreign investment.

New job opportunities drew new residents, many from the interior of Mexico, where unemployment was high and wages were even lower. Even the film industry discovered Tijuana and northern Baja California; the 1997 hit movie, "Titanic," was mostly filmed south of Rosarito Beach. The Tijuana municipality population rose to an official 747,400 in 1990 and, by some estimates, it surpassed San Diego city's 1.1 million if temporary residents were included in the count.

The city's infrastructure could not keep up with the average annual growth rate of 3.8 percent from 1970 to 1990. Only 68 percent of the homes were connected to running water. Less than two-thirds had access to sewer service. Much of the excess sewage flowed untreated into the Tijuana River and emptied into the ocean on the American side, fouling local beaches.

Thousands of squatters live in dozens of shanty towns, many constructed of discarded building materials and concrete block. Many of these makeshift homes sit on unstable hillsides subject to severe erosion during winter storms. Many roads are unpaved, public transportation is rudimentary and parks and educational establishment remain far below what such a large population required. Roberto A. Sanchez, professor at the Colegio de la Frontera Norte (College of the Northern Frontier), observed in a 1993 essay: "Tijuana is now going through a process of historic transition. Its possibilities for balanced growth and the search for future development are threatened by a wide variety of economic, social, physical and environmental problems generated by the constant imbalances in its urban growth."

Many efforts have been launched to draw San Diego and Tijuana closer together. Lucy Killea (a future City Council member and state legislator) ran the Fronteras 1976 educational program during the American Bicentennial celebration to boost understanding across the border. In the 1980s and '90s, San Diego Dialogue, a UCSD-sponsored coalition of San Diego and Tijuana academics, business and civic leaders, concentrated on binational issues. Special cooperative agreements between police and fire agencies, public utilities and higher-education institutions mirrored growing connections in numerous businesses, from electronics to real estate. Various arts and sports events also contributed to a growing common vision. The Population Crisis Committee included San Diego-Tijuana in its 1991 list of the world's 100 largest metropolitan areas and one of only four international cities. "San Diego would not have been in the study if it weren't for Tijuana," said Richard Forstall, a social demographer who worked on the report.

Looking to the future, it will take billions of dollars and much greater official cooperation, along with wider social and economic interaction, to transform San Diego-Tijuana into a region of influence and power. Perhaps a joint international project, such as hosting the 2020 summer Olympics, would speed up the necessary development of institutional and interpersonal relationships. Writing in *La Frontera: The United States Border with Mexico*, Alan Weisman said in 1986, "This frontera is the border between the present and the future: Along it, its people must eventually create a newer world."

Suburban Growth, South, East and North

From the 1880s, San Diego's hinterlands and coastal enclaves developed slowly while the city of San Diego attracted most of the growth in population and jobs. But beginning in the 1970s, the balance shifted. The regional freeway system made it possible for residents to live in Chula Vista and commute to Rancho Bernardo.

South Bay: The growth of Tijuana spurred growth across the border in Otay Mesa and San Ysidro. A vast high-tech industrial park was planned in Otay Mesa around a new border crossing that opened in 1985. For a time, there was talk of building a binational airport, TwinPorts, with one runway in Tijuana and the other at Brown Field. But public sentiment never coalesced around the idea in San Diego and Mexican officials balked at backing an idea from which they saw little economic benefit. A building moratorium was lifted and housing projects went forward in the late-1990s. Meanwhile, the 1981 opening of the San Diego Trolley line inaugurated an efficient connection for tourists heading toward the border and Mexicans heading for shopping and employment in San Diego. However, periodic peso devaluations disrupted the economic bustle.

In Chula Vista, development proceeded in the eastern part of the city after Interstate 805 was completed. One of the first master-planned communities, EastLake, was built around a manmade lagoon. Another, Otay Ranch, was made possible by the sale of thousands of acres around Otay Lakes to the Baldwin Co. in 1988. Recession stalled the project and Baldwin went bankrupt. The first homes were not offered for sale until 1999. In between, the area by the lakes became the home in 1995 of the ARCO Olympic Training Center, a $65 million, 154-acre hangout for America's hopeful athletes. A site was reserved nearby for a University of California campus, but there was no commitment by decade's end to build there. Three other attractions that opened late in this period made Chula Vista the entertainment and recreational capital of South Bay: the 10,000-square-foot Nature Interpretive Center on the waterfront; $17 million Whitewater Canyon water-slide park; and $20 million, 20,000-seat Coors Amphitheatre.

The Visitors Center at the ARCO Olympic Training Center. The new training facility overlooks Otay Lakes in Chula Vista and is adjacent to the Otay Ranch new-town project that offered its first homes for sale in 1999. *Courtesy Olympic ARCO Visitors Center*

Chapter Six

Attempting to stop pollution from the mouth of the Tijuana River, Imperial Beach Mayor Brian Bilbray directs a tractor to dam the river and stem the flow of raw sewage into the ocean, June 19, 1980.
Courtesy The San Diego Union-Tribune

In nearby National City, the period's biggest event was the opening in 1983 of Plaza Bonita shopping center. Developed by May Stores, it was the first freeway-oriented regional shopping center serving the South Bay. Some downtown San Diego redevelopment planners feared the project would draw business away from Horton Plaza when it opened. But the two coexisted in a healthy competition. National City also gained a reputation for interest in preserving and honoring its past. Its "Brick Row" group of Victorian homes on the 900-block of A Street was carefully restored. And local officials backed plans to turn the long-abandoned California Southern railroad depot into a railroad museum. It is thought to be the nation's oldest transcontinental railroad terminal.

Imperial Beach gained fame in 1980, when Mayor (and later, Congressman) Brian Bilbray personally steered a tractor along the Tijuana Riverbed to halt the flow of untreated sewage into the ocean and onto the city's vulnerable beaches. Federal and state authorities ordered Bilbray to desist from violating environmental protection laws and the sewage flowed out to sea and onto Imperial Beach sand once again. Even the opening of a new sewage treatment plant in 1998 was not expected to solve the problem. The small city had other problems, such as a low tax base and relatively little commercial development, that kept it from sharing substantially in the good fortune of its neighbors. Without the long-dreamed-of second entrance to San Diego Bay, Imperial Beach had to rely on its own resources to revitalize and rebuild its neighborhoods.

In prosperous Coronado, residents maintained an uneasy relationship with their biggest local businesses, tourism and the Navy. Several expansions of the Hotel del Coronado, under owner M. Larry Lawrence, prompted grumbling over compromising a national historic site. After his death in 1997, while serving as ambassador to Switzerland, the hotel was sold twice. Its latest owners promised to proceed slowly and with local support on any major changes to the landmark.

Construction of two major rival hotels, Le Meridien (now operated by Marriott) and Loewes Coronado Bay Resort, did not elicit nearly as much concern as the completion of the 10 Coronado Shores condominium towers on the site of the former Tent City grounds south of the Hotel del. The last tower was completed before the state's 1972 coastal protection laws banned such structures so close to the beach. As for the Navy's presence, the homeporting of three nuclear-powered aircraft carriers worried some residents about increased traffic across the San Diego-Coronado Bay Bridge, especially if the $1 toll were eliminated or reduced and more traffic flowed into town.

East County: Suburban development first inched its way in this direction as freeways stretched to El Cajon and beyond. Parkway Plaza, developed by Ernest W. Hahn Inc. in 1972, doomed traditional retail centers in El Cajon and other nearby communities, just as Mission Valley Center had done to downtown San Diego.

Each community responded with its own effort at redevelopment and revitalization. La Mesa opted for a beautification drive in its business district. El Cajon welcomed the construction of a county government regional center and performing arts center. Santee incorporated in 1980 and attempted to develop a new urban center. The extension of the San Diego Trolley eastward to Santee gave residents a convenient alternative to congested freeway commuting. The community's economic development and tourist strategy emphasized affordable living in a fog-free environment near the mountains.

However, most rural communities remained unincorporated and witnessed the spread of tract home and estate-lot developments. Alpine felt the brunt of growth in higher air pollution. Borrego Springs developed into a golfing mecca and winter resort community. Rancho San Diego became one of the largest unincorporated developments along State Route 94. And Barona, Sycuan and Viejas Indian bands set up gaming operations on their reservations. San Diegans joined the rest of the state in November 1998 to approve an Indian-sponsored pro-gambling initiative and the local bands used some of their winnings to support civic causes in town.

North County: Growth accelerated north of Mission Valley along the major freeway arteries.

The Hotel del Coronado is the most popular and venerated hotel in the San Diego region. It underwent substantial expansion and restoration in the 1970s and '80s when M. Larry Lawrence was the owner. The new owners plan further expansion.
Photo by Robert A. Eplett

Chapter Six

Rancho Bernardo was the first of the leapfrog developments in inland North County. It began as an unthreatening retirement community in 1962, attracting families in greater numbers in the '70s and '80s. Poway incorporated in 1980 as a defensive move against rapid growth. It was surrounded by such San Diego city developments as Scripps Ranch to the south, Rancho Peñasquitos and Sabre Springs to the west and Carmel Mountain Ranch to the north.

Legoland California is San Diego's latest tourist attraction. It opened in March 1999 in Carlsbad as the first of the Danish toymaker's theme parks outside Europe.
Photo by Robert A. Eplett

The other North County cities pursued separate strategies for both encouraging and managing growth. Oceanside adopted a strict growth control measure in 1987 that took five years to win court approval. Meanwhile, the city tried to diversify its economy beyond its reliance on business with the nearby Camp Pendleton Marine base. Its population growth was partly fueled by workers in Orange County seeking affordable housing.

San Marcos successfully wooed the California State University and Colleges system to open its 20th campus within its boundaries. Championed by state legislator William Craven, the campus grew from a satellite unit of San Diego State into its own institution that opened on a 305-acre site in 1990. Escondido built the $75 million, 12-acre California Center for the Performing Arts in 1994, hoping to use culture as a civic booster for quality growth and development. Vista sought to attract big-box retail outlets and to preserve its place as the North County headquarters for county courts and other regional services.

Along the coast, Carlsbad succeeded in phasing growth — at the cost of boosting housing prices — while expanding its tourist business. La Costa Spa and Resort, a Teamsters development in the 1960s (and the subject of an unsuccessful 1981-82 libel suit against *Penthouse* magazine for its 1975 article on the project), was joined by a $200 million Four Seasons hotel in 1997 in the Aviara master planned community north of Batiquitos Lagoon. The city's biggest coup was to land Legoland California, the Danish toy company's third theme park for young children and its first in the United States. Final authorization in 1994 came during the recession when Carlsbad voters were in no mood to veto a potential economic generator. Lego, opened in 1999, was but the latest feather in Carlsbad's cap. The city already was a major manufacturing and marketing center for sporting goods (principally golf equipment) and computer software development. It also was home to the Gemological Society of America.

Several communities that made up the unincorporated area known as San Dieguito banded together in 1986 to form the city of Encinitas. But by then, there was little left to plan. Neighboring Solana Beach incorporated the same year, while Rancho Santa Fe opted out of cityhood, preferring to remain governed by its 1927 covenant, a restrictive set of development standards that protected millionaires on their multi-acre avocado and citrus estates.

The development battle that crystallized many of the issues of the latter-20th century in San Diego County was the fight between the cities of Del Mar and San Diego over North City West. Later renamed

Carmel Valley, the 4,300-acre project east of Del Mar began taking shape in the 1970s under the direction of Pardee Construction and the Baldwin companies. Del Mar, which had incorporated in 1959 to avoid annexation to San Diego, had only 5,000 residents. Its boundary did not extend east of what was to be Interstate 5, and that property was annexed by San Diego and masterplanned for development in the years following the opening of UCSD.

Some of the county's most expensive tract homes were built in Carmel Valley and the first sales went rapidly. Buyers liked the local school districts and proximity to the coast. But as Del Mar had feared, the added population clogged the freeways and crowded the beaches. During the Del Mar Fair and horse racing season, the area becomes a nightmarish bottleneck.

"I don't think anybody's angry at the people who are moving in," said Del Mar Mayor Rosalind Lorwin in 1984 at the time of the first move-ins. "When you meet people on the street, you don't know where they live. The realities of living in North County are that the area within five or 10 years is going to be extremely impacted — the beaches are already impacted. Traffic is going to be unbearable — there are going to be 20,000 car trips more per day than now. It's not their fault. The city (of San Diego) should have taken all that into consideration before it allowed this development."

This pervasive suburban sprawl from the mid-1970s onward was broadly condemned as "Los Angelization," the transformation of San Diego into a mirror image of its nemesis to the north. There was even a short-lived organization formed called "PLAN" — Prevent Los Angelization Now. Commuting times lengthened, home prices soared and stratification of society along economic and racial lines intensified. The future appeared no better. Workers in Orange County began buying homes in Carlsbad and Oceanside, where prices were relatively reasonable, and commuting north to jobs in Irvine, Costa Mesa and Mission Viejo. Workers in San Diego County began shopping for homes in Temecula and other parts of southern Riverside County and commuting south to jobs in Escondido, Kearny Mesa and downtown San Diego. To relieve

Poster for "Orchids and Onions" awards program, 1988. Since the 1970s, local architects and other design professionals have applauded the good (orchids) and chastised the bad (onions) in local building, planning, landscape and graphic design work. *Courtesy American Institute of Architects, San Diego chapter*

some of the sprawl, three major open space systems were approved as greenbelt buffers: San Dieguito River Valley between Del Mar and the mountains; Mission Trails Regional Park from Mission Gorge to Santee; and Otay River Valley Regional Park from San Diego Bay to Otay Ranch.

Along the San Diego-Tijuana border, commuting patterns went both directions. Managers and skilled workers, both American and foreign-born, lived in Chula Vista, Coronado and San Diego and crossed the border to oversee workers in the hundreds of maquiladora factories. Mexican nationals retained homes in Tijuana and commuted north for better paying jobs in San Diego hotels, restaurants, construction and agriculture. By 2020, these commuting patterns can only get worse. San Diego County's population is expected to grow by 1 million residents, or nearly 30 percent, and Tijuana's size could grow even faster. Regional forecasters warn that suburban land is running out to accommodate these new residents.

Back to the City

While the suburbs exploded, the inner-city neighborhoods within San Diego changed but not often for the better. As an unexpected consequence of Mayor Pete Wilson's growth-management policies, development accelerated in some communities where hefty developer fees were not collected. The theory had been that the existing infrastructure was sufficient to handle the growth envisioned in the underlying zoning. In practice, generations-old sewer and water lines, schools, parks, streets and other public improvements needed repair or replacement.

But under 1978's Proposition 13, property taxes collected from the old neighborhoods remained relatively static. (The state initiative set a 1 percent tax rate cap on assessed valuations, which were allowed to grow by a maximum 2 percent annually until a resale triggered a new assessment.) Since tax revenue did not rise with the rate of inflation, maintenance lagged and local governments generally chose to fund programs rather than capital improvements. Consequently, libraries were kept open but libraries deteriorated and their collections aged. Recreation programs continued but parks went to seed.

In North Park and surrounding neighborhoods, whole blocks of single-family homes were replaced by six-unit apartment complexes — "six-packs" they were called, characterized by inadequate parking, minimal landscaping and marginal architectural and design treatment. In Barrio Logan, Golden Hill, Encanto, Emerald Hills and other neighborhoods southeast of downtown and toward the National City, La Mesa and Lemon Grove city limits, absentee landlords let their properties deteriorate and city inspectors grew lax in their enforcement of building codes. Even in highly desirable coastal communities from La Jolla to Point Loma, density increased. Streets became congested and the public grumbled.

All this was analyzed in a series of reports prepared after Roger Hedgecock succeeded Mayor Pete Wilson, who resigned in early-1983 to assume his seat in the U.S. Senate. A task force found in 1984 that only half the growth had occurred as expected in the new suburbs compared to nine times the expected growth rate in the older neighborhoods. The pricetag to fix the backlog of maintenance and repairs exceeded $1 billion and the conventional wisdom held that the voters would neither agree to undo the bad effects of Proposition 13 nor vote to increase taxes.

Ballot-box planning took over, as slow-growth advocates mounted a series of initiatives and referendums to rein in development. The first measure to pass, a citizens initiative in 1985, overturned one project (La Jolla Valley) and required voter approval of any future shifts out of the urban reserve. In 1987, the San Diego City Council adopted an 18-month interim development ordinance to allow only 8,000 homes annually within city limits, several thousand fewer than authorized in 1986. In 1988, five growth measures appeared on the ballot. Two pertained to the city of San Diego and two to the unincorporated area of the county; the environmental and slow-growth advocates sponsored one version and the elected officials another. Similar measures were placed on other municipal ballots in the county and around the state, a reflection of the widespread frustration with growth and its consequences. All four local measures failed but a fifth, sponsored by the Board of Supervisors, passed. It mandated that a regional growth strategy plan be prepared by the San Diego Association of Governments.

The growth battles petered out suddenly, when the housing boom ended in 1990 and the nation fell into recession. California and San Diego had previously weathered downturns better than the rest of the country. But this time, California suffered more than most other states. The collapse of the Soviet Union in 1989, the Persian Gulf War in 1991 and fires, floods, earthquakes, riots and other calamities hamstrung the state government in its efforts to boost the economy. The wild overbuilding of the 1980s also left a huge development surplus that took years to absorb. In San Diego, post-Cold War defense cutbacks prompted the closing in the mid-1990s of the 70-year-old Naval Training Center. A 500-acre redevelopment plan envisions new homes, hotels, workspace and parks to be undertaken by a private developer.

By 1998, construction of housing, hotels, office buildings and industrial parks was on the rise once again. San Diegans who had left the county for work elsewhere began returning and shortages ensued. Voters rejected several growth-control measures and approved a series of school bonds, including a record $1.5 billion measure for the San Diego Unified School District. They previously approved a tax increase to build more roads and trolley lines and narrowly supported a similar tax for courts and jails, although the latter was successfully challenged in court. A majority of county voters twice approved a temporary sales tax increase to benefit branch libraries. But a two-thirds margin was required for passage, and local library systems immediately sought alternate funding options. The city of San Diego considered tapping the money it was due from a national tobacco lawsuit settlement. It appeared that San Diego would keep busy in the 21st century repairing and replacing the public infrastructure built in the 19th and 20th.

Bright Spots at Century's End

The 1980s and '90s witnessed some exciting times. Queen Elizabeth II made a royal pilgrimage (in the rain) through California in 1983 and helped dedicate the rebuilt Old Globe Theatre, which won a Tony as best regional theater of 1984. The La Jolla

England's Queen Elizabeth visited in 1983 to dedicate the new Old Globe Theatre in Balboa Park, and it was remembered by many as an "international incident." San Diego City Councilman Bill Cleator, who was acting mayor, innocently "touched" Her Majesty as he was trying to steer her in a particular direction during an event. Cleator later lost his bid to be mayor, but he did not blame the royal incident for his loss. *Courtesy San Diego Historical Society.*

Playhouse reopened in the Mandell Weiss theater at UCSD in 1982 and also won wide acclaim for provocative and Broadway-bound productions. The San Diego Repertory Theater matured at its new home in the Lyceum Theater complex that opened in 1986 beneath Horton Plaza shopping center. Lamb's Players Theater moved from National City to the restored Spreckels Theater in Coronado. A wide variety of hole-in-the-wall and community-based theater companies performed throughout the county.

Mayor Maureen O'Connor organized the 1989 Soviet Arts Festival, featuring an eye-popping display of Fabergé eggs. The San Diego Museum of Art hosted a series of blockbuster exhibitions, from Frank Lloyd Wright architectural models to Dr.

Seuss drawings. The perennially cash-plagued San Diego Symphony missed all or part of several seasons, declared bankruptcy in 1995 and sprang back to life in 1998. The popular Starlight Musical Theater (San Diego Civic Light Opera) struggled to maintain its summer season of musical productions (under the Lindbergh Field flight path) at the former Ford Bowl in Balboa Park. Meanwhile, the San Diego Opera thrived and former symphony conductor David Atherton founded an annual "Mainly Mozart Festival" in the Spreckels Theater downtown.

Other cultural institutions seemed to gain new energy at century's end, marked by the opening of new or expanded facilities and museums. The San Diego Historical Society opened a museum and archives in Balboa Park's rebuilt Electric Building (renamed Casa de Balboa), which also contains the Museum of Photographic Arts and San Diego Model Railroad. The San Diego Automotive Museum occupied the former Conference Building in the park's Palisades area; nearby, the San Diego Hall of Champions Sports Museum moved into the refurbished Federal Building. The Museum of Man expanded into the neighboring Administration Building; the Reuben H. Fleet Science Center completed a major expansion; and the San Diego Natural History Museum began a $20 million north wing. The Mingei International Museum moved from University Towne Centre to the park's reconstructed House of Charm, and the La Jolla Museum of Contemporary Art dropped "La Jolla" from its name and opened a satellite museum downtown. It also remodeled and enlarged its La Jolla facility in the former home of Ellen Browning Scripps, designed by Irving J. Gill. Escondido opened the *California Center for the Performing Arts*, which includes theater and exhibition space, and smaller communities developed a wide variety of cultural attractions, from historic houses to performance spaces. Tijuana developed its own Centro Cultural, complete with concert hall and museum.

Under an ambitious master plan approved in 1989, Balboa Park witnessed major improvements, particularly the reconstruction of the House of Charm and House of Hospitality. A new activity center was constructed on the site of one of the old Balboa Naval Hospital buildings. The San Diego Zoo embarked on its own rebuilding and upgrading program, reorganizing its collections into climatic zones and hoping to expand into its Park Boulevard parking lot. The zoo continued developing its Wild Animal Park in San Pasqual Valley, and twice arranged displays of giant pandas from China. For all these improvements, the park suffered a major blow when the Navy insisted on rebuilding its giant Balboa Hospital in the park in

The San Diego Padres win the 1998 National League Championship.
Courtesy San Diego Padres

1981 rather than in Murphy Canyon or Helix Heights. The new hospital represented an even bigger visual intrusion into Florida Canyon than before, its design not at all compatible with the Spanish Colonial expo buildings nearby. The park also suffered from highly publicized murders and crime waves before city officials instigated a police patrol on foot, bicycle and horseback. With park improvements came more visitors, and more traffic. Better circulation and parking remains a challenge for the early-21st century to solve.

In sports, the San Diego Padres made it to the World Series for the first time in 1984 and again in 1998. The Chargers went to the Super Bowl in 1996. Both teams changed ownership during this period and became embroiled in heated debates over facility needs. The Chargers signed a new lease that called for expansion of their stadium to 71,000 seats. But the $78 million cost prompted a year-long debate in 1997, settled only by an $18 million investment by Qualcomm Corporation, whose name replaced San Diego and Jack Murphy. The "Murph" became the "Q" in local parlance. The Padres' lease at the stadium was due to expire after the 1999 season and the team's new owner, John Moores, and president, Larry Lucchino, campaigned hard for a home downtown, where the minor-league Padres had first played six decades earlier.

Plans also were drafted to demolish the Sports Arena in the Midway area and replace it east of the Gaslamp Quarter. But without a major-league basketball or hockey franchise, the $60 million project was shelved. Instead, the arena owners refurbished the facility and planned a cinema-restaurant entertainment addition nearby.

Local sailor Dennis Conner won back the America's Cup yachting championship in 1987 and the San Diego Yacht Club defended the cup three times before losing it to New Zealand in 1995. Other homegrown sports heroes during this period included Olympic diver Greg Louganis, basketball player Bill Walton (Boston Celtics), football running back Marcus Allen (Los Angeles/Oakland Raiders) and baseball pitcher David Wells (New York Yankees). Local favorites included the Padres' Tony Gwynn and Chargers' Junior Seau.

As in any era, the 1970s, '80s and '90s in San Diego saw plenty of sex scandals, financial frauds, natural disasters, sensational murder trials and goofy events. They consumed the public's attention for days, sometimes months. But in hindsight, their historical significance dwindled to mere footnotes in the bigger picture.

San Diego Mayor Susan Golding. *Courtesy Office of the Mayor, City of San Diego.*

On November 3, 1998, San Diego voters overwhelmingly approved local Proposition C, giving a green light to downtown redevelopment and construction of a new ballpark.

Chapter Six

In the 1990s, suburbanization has continued unabated in San Diego.
Photo by Robert A. Eplett

An Agenda for the New Millennium

Mayor Susan Golding, elected to replace Maureen O'Connor in 1992 and reelected in 1996, identified three sectors as important to the city's future — trade, tourism, technology — and introduced a new slogan to replace the 1972 shopworn boast, America's Finest City: "San Diego: The First Great City of the 21st Century." She outlined her vision in her December 1992 inaugural address:

"Many decades ago, America's first great cities were made up of vibrant, self-reliant, closely knit neighborhoods. But as these cities grew and freeways cut through them and the buildings became larger and taller, they lost their neighborhood quality.

"As people lost their sense of community, they also lost their sense of identity and hope... This must not — and will not — be the future of San Diego. We need to begin building a city of urban villages — a city where people identify with their block and their neighbors as much as they do with the city center.

"I promise you this: I will meet my commitment to you — to lead, to build the coalitions that will make our city government work, to add neighborhood police and to help restore neighborhood pride. But I ask, too, for your commitment today to do your part — to clean up your neighborhoods, to volunteer in your schools, to spend time with the children, the elderly, the sick, the homeless and those afflicted with AIDS — the people who need your help the most.

"We can work to encourage private businesses to provide day care for working parents — and we will. We can expand our park and recreation activities, our after-school programs and other alternatives to gangs and drug-dealing — and we will. But most important, we can take back our streets and neighborhoods so that our children once again can grow up in safety — and we will. My friends, this is my pledge to you tonight. We will make San Diego the first great city of the 21st century. A city that is good for business. A city that is environmentally sound. A city of self-reliance. And a city where all children — and all people — can succeed."

Conservative San Diego, shaking off the problems of the recessionary, post-Cold War '90s, seemed ready to tackle a long list of public and private priorities at the turn of the century. There was a growing can-do- spirit, tempered by watchful environmental and taxpayer groups. Blessed by its admirable climate and undeveloped hinterland, San Diego still aspires to greatness, attracting men and women both from within and outside its borders to turn dreams into realities.

And yet, oddball characters still turn up as they did a century ago, getting involved in bizarre incidents that can gain worldwide attention. In 1997 alone:

- Heaven's Gate cult members committed mass suicide in Rancho Santa Fe;
- Hillcrest resident Andrew Cunanan killed himself after murdering fashion designer Gianni Versace in Miami;

- Hotel del Coronado owner M. Larry Lawrence, President Clinton's ambassador to Switzerland, was exhumed from Arlington National Cemetery after his bogus military record outraged veterans and embarrassed his family and the White House; and,
- 270 Michigan school children contracted Hepatitis A after eating frozen strawberries illegally imported into the United States and shipped from an Otay Mesa frozen storage plant.

The same year, San Diego won praise for adopting the Multiple Species Conservation Program to coordinate habitat preservation on a vast regional scale. A UCSD chemist, Michael Sailor, used baked silicon to demonstrate a possible new lighting source. Astronomers at Mount Palomar discovered two moons orbiting Uranus.

And so, this paradise is not yet perfect, not quite "heaven on earth" or the finest or greatest American city. In 1908, John Nolen sketched a vision for San Diego that he said could be realized, despite mistakes made already. Many more mistakes have occurred in the last 90 years, but there have been many more successes. San Diego's future now, as then, can be bright "not so much [dependent] upon money, as upon forethought, system, wise planning and public-spirited enterprise."

Just as Nolen's to-do list of civic priorities for San Diego was never fulfilled, today's lengthy wish-list includes many projects that will never be accomplished. But history shows that San Diego can achieve the seemingly impossible. It has turned a desert into a lush landscape; held fairs, festivals and sporting events with worldwide appeal; helped defend the nation and cure disease; advanced the arts and contributed to popular culture.

In the 21st century, in Nolen's words, "San Diego will be able to point with pride to its priceless public possessions and feel sure that by timely action it has secured to its citizens forever a glorious heritage and advantages of inestimable worth."

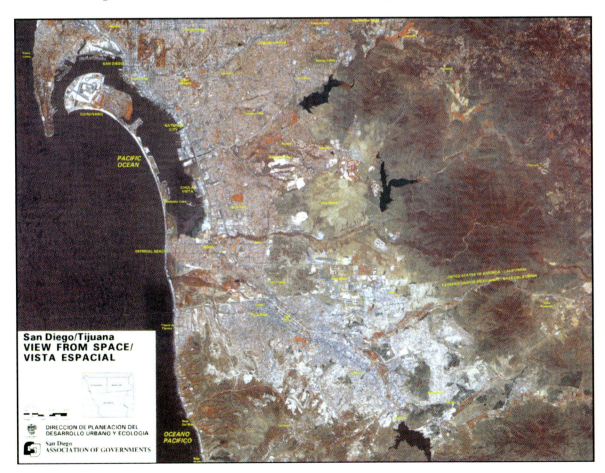

Courtesy San Diego Historical Society

Partners in San Diego
table of contents

Building a Greater San Diego *182*

Business and Finance *222*

Entertainment *232*

Manufacturing & Distribution *244*

Marketplace *272*

Networks *322*

Professions *340*

Quality of Life *368*

Technology *406*

Real estate and construction industries shape tomorrow's skyline while providing working and living space for San Diego area residents.

Partners in
BUILDING

Building a Greater *san diego*

The EastLake Company LLC	184
San Diego Historic Properties	188
Bannister Steel, Inc.	192
California Closets	194
Collins Plumbing, Inc.	196
D.A. Whitacre Construction, Inc.	198
Dewhurst & Associates	200
Kenai Construction Co., Inc.	202
Newland Communities	204
Reno Contracting	206
T&B Planning Consultants	208
Techbilt Companies	210
Warren West, Inc.	212
Architect Milford Wayne Donaldson, FAIA	214
C&B Steel	215
Casper Company	216
Center Glass Company	217
Erreca's Inc.	218
J.P. Witherow Roofing Co.	219
Steigerwald-Dougherty Inc., General Building Contractors	220
Tower Glass Inc.	221

The EastLake Company, LLC

Residents enjoy a Summer Sounds concert at Chula Vista Community Park. The park, which opened in July 1994, comprises 13 acres and is adjacent to EastLake High School.
© Dalia De La O

Families enjoy the swim lagoon at EastLake Shores, which also features a sandy beach, boat launching and fishing facilities and a walking trail.

Years from now, when history records the contributions of The EastLake Company to San Diego County, it will undoubtedly make reference to its land preservation efforts and technological innovation.

EastLake is a master-planned community in the city of Chula Vista, east of Interstate 805, south of Bonita and west of Otay Lakes Reservoir. When the $2 billion development is completed, EastLake is expected to have approximately 8,900 dwelling units and a population of about 22,000. The EastLake Company oversees all development within the community, which is located on both sides of Telegraph Canyon Road. It is also responsible for the backbone infrastructure and facility planning. The company markets land to home builders and commercial, industrial and retail users. Upon completion, EastLake will feature a wide variety of housing options, commercial, industrial and office uses, as well as recreational facilities including parks, lakes, trails and new schools. And more than 1,100 of the anticipated 3,200 acres, or one-third, is slated to comprise just parks, recreation and open space. That's only fitting considering the rich history and tradition of the land.

Once the site of Rancho Janal, a sprawling 4,436-acre ranch, the history of EastLake property can be traced back to the Mexican-American War. When the war ended in 1846, California became a U.S. territory, which created some problems for ranch owners in substantiating their rights to the land grants given to them by Mexican governors. As a result, it wasn't until 1872 that Señor Don Jose Antonio Estudillo received the property title to the Janal grant. Some three years earlier a San Diego County surveyor had created a stage route from San Diego to Yuma, Arizona, that passed right through Rancho Janal. By the turn of the century, Rancho Janal had become the site for both the upper and lower Otay dams and reservoir. Today, EastLake's eastern boundary provides three miles of magnificent view frontage along the picturesque upper and lower Otay Lakes. There is also a national wilderness preserve to the east of the lakes that offers an equally stunning scenic, open-space backdrop. One historical footnote: the dams were built by innovator E.S. Babcock, the mastermind behind the construction of the world-famous Hotel del Coronado in 1888.

Centuries have passed and the owners of this land in eastern Chula Vista have changed, but the respect for its natural surroundings, fortunately, has not. Since creating its community master plan in 1979, The EastLake Company has enhanced the sheer beauty of the majestic area by incorporating the natural lakes and vistas into its community with the addition of walking and jogging trails. "With the name EastLake there has always been the vision of water within all of our neighborhoods," said EastLake President/Chief Executive Officer

William T. Ostrem. "In addition to water features in our neighborhoods, we've pioneered the use of reclaimed water and low-flow water devices as well as composting and recycling."

"We're a master-plan developer, not a home builder," Ostrem added. "Being the first master-planned community within Chula Vista, we set the pace for what a master plan is." The initial phase of the EastLake master-planned community was built over a six-year period, which began in 1985. This phase included the first two residential neighborhoods, EastLake Hills and EastLake Shores, and the first phase of the EastLake Business Center. Initial residential sales started in April 1986 with the last of the 1,823 units being sold in June 1990.

The EastLake plan focuses heavily on the creation and development of open space, parks and recreational facilities to support and enhance the surrounding landscape and to provide gathering spots for neighbors. For instance, EastLake's residential neighborhoods are centered on activity areas such as parks, which are interconnected by a user-friendly system of pedestrian and bike pathways and trails. Additionally, the design of homes' front porches and yards are a key point of the EastLake development philosophy, created so that a casual stroll down the neighborhood streets on a Sunday afternoon includes interaction with neighbors. What's more, a community trail system, which began with the EastLake Hills neighborhood, will eventually connect all of the residential neighborhoods of EastLake when the 25-year development program is finished. Meandering walkways and special landscaping will designate the trail system. Pedestrian travel will be further favored by natural paths, rather than concrete or asphalt trails, and the Salt Creek Corridor will become a recreational area with park-like zones creating peaceful and serene hideaways. *San Diego Home/Garden Lifestyles Magazine* recognized this tremendous attention to detail and emphasis on quality living when it named The EastLake Company recipient of the first editor's choice "Designs for Living Award" in its February 1996 issue. Prior to breaking ground, EastLake's development plans were also endorsed by both the Sierra Club and the Chula Vista Chamber of Commerce.

Each of EastLake's residential communities is in a unique class. Home options cover the entire

An aerial view shows EastLake Country Club, Country Club Park and EastLake Greens homes. The 4.5-acre park offers residents access to five tennis courts, a junior Olympic-sized swimming pool and a community room that is used by residents for large social gatherings.

spectrum, from 1,300-square-foot bungalow-style residences to a 7,500-square-foot luxury address along a picturesque rolling hill. Most striking is that each EastLake community maintains its own identity and charm. For example, EastLake Hills features Country French- and English-style living, offering numerous amenities such as the EastLake Swim and Tennis Club, a private 2.8-acre park with a junior Olympic-size swimming pool, spa, children's play area, picnic area and lighted tennis courts. Meanwhile, at EastLake Shores, life's a beach as a plentiful and pristine 15-acre man-made lake covers the landscape. The lake features a sandy beach, boat-launching and fishing facilities and a walking trail around the lake. EastLake Shores homes display Mediterranean- and Cape Cod-style architecture.

In the fall of 1989, The EastLake Company upped the ante on its unique approach to design when construction began on the third residential neighborhood, EastLake Greens, which opened in February 1991. The first residents moved into EastLake Greens in July 1991. EastLake Greens not only features five spacious separate parks, it is also home to a 160-acre, 18-hole championship-caliber golf course designed by Ted Robinson. Enhanced by a wealth of lakes, EastLake Country Club officially opened for public play on June 22, 1991, wasting very little time in establishing itself as a big favorite among San Diego County's dedicated golfing set. As for the homes,

Dolphin Beach in EastLake Greens, shown in this aerial photo, debuted in the summer of 1997, just in time for those dog days of summer.

Augusta Place, named after the historic and prestigious professional golf tournament, is an exclusive gated community in EastLake Greens that offers expansive views of the plush golf course. Twenty-three additional enclaves of homes round out the residential mix in EastLake Greens. Designed for the active Southern California lifestyle, EastLake Greens also features a swim lagoon, better known as Dolphin Beach, which debuted in the summer of 1997. The 4,900-square-foot swimming pool with sandy beach access is located in Dolphin Beach Park, which includes a bronze fountain sculpture of three dolphins entitled "Synchronicity" created by the renowned marine artist, Wyland. EastLake Greens' first neighborhood park, Augusta Park, opened in 1991. The 4.5-acre Country Club Park opened in July 1994, offers residents access to five tennis courts, a junior Olympic-size swimming pool and a community room that is used by residents for large social gatherings.

But perhaps the crown jewel of EastLake Greens is EastLake High School. Opening its doors to students on September 8, 1992, the public school was completed in the fall of 1994. Situated on a sprawling college-like campus, the school teaches students in grades nine to 12 on a year-round calendar. Eastlake High School was granted the prestigious California Distinguished School Award in 1999. Upon build out, EastLake will also have four elementary schools and a middle school. While retirees and empty nesters enjoy living and playing at EastLake, roughly 60 percent of the homeowners have school-age children. In 1995, EastLake established the EastLake Educational Foundation to ensure full support of current and future academic programs during those times when a typical public school budget may not. The results of the foundation have included an observatory at EastLake High School and support of technology programs at all EastLake public schools. This support will extend to the other schools upon build out. After-school programs have also been available at EastLake schools since inception and "vacation camps" are another popular form of extracurricular activity. EastLake's churches also offer day-care and after-school programs.

Tying in 21st-century technology and innovation with quality public education is a major component of EastLake development philosophy. All of EastLake's schools are computer-equipped, offering students access to the Internet, the World Wide Web and the world beyond EastLake. In 1996, EastLake made history by becoming the first master-planned community in San Diego County to launch an Intranet service for its homeowners and businesses. On the Intranet's bulletin board, EastLake parents can inquire about a baby sitter for the night from their personal computer at work while EastLake children of all ages can seek event listings for the neighborhood park or check out the final scores of local soccer and baseball games. In

Students work inside the CAD CAM lab at EastLake High School. Opening its doors to students on September 8, 1992, the school teaches students in grades nine to 12 on a year-round calendar.

 San Diego: Perfecting Paradise

January 1999, EastLake took its innovative philosophy one step further when it debuted its "EastLake Adopt an Olympian" program, which enables EastLake school children to interact over the Internet with athletes from EastLake's U.S. Olympic Training Center. "The innovation mentality has always been part of the vision," Ostrem explained. "Technology is a common ingredient and continues to be a part of our innovations."

Fostering lasting community relationships is another important facet of EastLake's long-term goals and objectives. The EastLake Company provided 150 acres of its land to the United States Olympic Committee, with groundbreaking for Phase I of the training center occurring in June 1990. The country's first warm-weather Olympic Training Center, and third overall, officially opened on June 10, 1995. With the close proximity of the training center, EastLake residents and business owners never have to look far for inspiration. That attitude also symbolizes the Exercise the Dream Program, which enables elementary school children to participate in clinics and learn Olympic principals from resident athletes in training at the Olympic Training Center. The program, sponsored by The EastLake Company, the Chula Vista Elementary School District and the Olympic Training Center, began in 1995.

A number of social and community-oriented activities are held year-round throughout EastLake. One of the most popular annual events is the Summer Concerts in the Park, which premiered in 1995 at the Chula Vista Community Park in EastLake. The $1.8 million park comprises 13 acres and is adjacent to EastLake High School. The park, which opened in July 1994, is one of three community parks within the EastLake master plan. EastLake also hosts an annual Easter egg hunt, Fourth of July fireworks show and a benefit bicycle tour, all supported by resident homeowners. "We consider ourselves a community where people take pride in ownership," said Ostrem. A $3 million professional performing arts center and a $1.9 million library and media center, as well as EastLake Village Center neighborhood shopping and the EastLake Business Center, also call EastLake home.

The South County area of San Diego and specifically Chula Vista will remain one of the few local growth areas where a significant number of homes can be purchased in a variety of price ranges, from modest to upscale to exclusive. Additionally, Chula Vista has the broadest spectrum of potential housing demand. The EastLake Company has met this demand from its beginning and continues this tradition with its final residential neighborhoods of EsatLake Trails, EastLake Vistas and EastLake Woods.

The eastern boundary of EastLake consists of three miles of view frontage along the upper and lower Otay Lakes.

It took three years for The EastLake Company to complete its original development proposal, believing that collaboration with city leaders was vital for the project's success. By paying close attention to detail and building with a conscience, EastLake has developed a spirited people-friendly neighborhood, and made a significant mark on San Diego County in the 20th century. It's a mark that will likely continue far into the 21st century. "Our residents have voted EastLake the Best New Home Community in San Diego repeatedly in a countywide poll," Ostrem commented. "It's gratifying that they're proud and show it."

San Diego Historic Properties

The father-daughter team of Leon Herrick and Cathy Herrick-Anderson, co-founders of San Diego Historic Properties, established in 1983, has been instrumental in restoring more historic properties in San Diego's famous Gaslamp Quarter than any other single group. Since first buying an old run-down, mixed-use building in the Gaslamp Quarter in 1984, Herrick and Herrick-Anderson

Gaslamp Quarter Hotel

have subsequently purchased and fully restored nine other buildings. They include the Louis Bank of Commerce Building, Gaslamp Quarter Hotel, Llewelyn Building, Cole-Block Building, Dustin-Arms Hotel, Buckner Hotel, La Pension Building, Reed-Pauley Building, Wilsonian Hotel, and Old City Hall Building.

Herrick and Herrick-Anderson feel an enormous sense of accomplishment and pride that comes from completing the accurate historic restoration of a building that is more than 100 years old. In a sense, they are also providing an important archeological service to San Diego as they have unearthed a treasure trove of historical relics over the years.

Both father and daughter have brought a unique set of skills to their business. For 25 years, Herrick had individually owned and acted as managing partner of numerous projects involving investment in real estate property, raw land held for development, apartment buildings, residential hotels, commercial and historic properties. He was also president of Health Practice Management, a medical management-consulting firm based in San Diego.

Herrick-Anderson served for a number of years as a consultant and venture capitalist to other groups wanting to purchase Gaslamp Quarter properties. She also founded SBW Network, an organization of women entrepreneurs with businesses located in the Gaslamp District. She continues to be involved with various civic organizations in San Diego, including the Gaslamp Quarter Foundation and the San Diego Historic Society. She was even toasted — at age 30 — as the "Grande Dame" of the Historic District as part of San Diego Magazine's "89 People to Watch in '89."

Father and daughter's keen love of history and historic preservation is reflected in each property they buy and restore. The detail work done for each individual project is impressive — it has included replicating finely carved Victorian cornices, restoring long-inactive birdcage elevators, recasting original metal stanchions, stripping and refinishing century-old banisters, balustrades, picture rails, window and door frame escutcheons, and replicating etched and leaded glass.

San Diego Historic Properties has also garnered numerous public rewards for its restored properties such as San Diego's Alonzo Horton Award, the Founding Pioneer's Award and the California State First Place Award for Historic Preservation (for the Louis Bank of Commerce Building).

Herrick refers to the Gaslamp Quarter as the real "Field of Dreams." The area is now home to one of the best-preserved collections of Victorian buildings in the United States. But it wasn't always a tourist attraction. Herrick likes to remind people that the Gaslamp Quarter has actually undergone two major redevelopments during its long history. The first immigrant settlers from the East Coast arrived in San Diego in 1850. Their attempts to set up businesses on land that became the Gaslamp didn't take root and they moved a few miles up the road to the area now known as Old Town. The area sat dormant for more than 40 years until Alonzo Horton bought up 800 downtown acres in 1867.

The second attempt at settlement caught hold. Following his stints as marshall in Abilene and Dodge City, Wyatt Earp opened a gambling hall and several taverns between Third and Sixth avenues and from H Street to the wharf. In addition to housing a substantial Chinese population, the area also became well known as a thriving red-light district. Famed Madam Ida Bailey ran a profitable brothel from her Canary Cottage on the south side of H Street (now Market Street). Madam Ida used to parade her women through the district on slow nights and was a constant target of the establishment. Under heavy pressure from the town ladies, known as the Puritan Leaguers, a police captain was suborned into raiding the Canary Cottage one night in June 1897. Unfortunately, two of the leading lights of San Diego — the mayor and chief of police — were regulars and were paying a visit to the brothel that evening. They managed to scramble out the rear windows, out of sight of the crowd that had followed the paddy wagon!

Madam Cora, another well-known local fixture, ran a brothel in the upper floors of the Louis Bank of Commerce Building, which at that time was known as the Golden Poppy whorehouse. Herrick said Cora started out as a turbaned fortune-teller but found greater returns from her high-class "house." Her unique system provided some 20-odd individual rooms, wall papered in pastel colors to match the attire of their occupants. A customer, upon entry at the street-level door, paid for his visit and received a colored marble token to deliver upstairs to his chosen lady.

During the first two decades of the 20th century, the Gaslamp Quarter served as the thriving commercial heart of San Diego, until it began a 40-year slide during the Great Depression. After World War II, housing demands by returning soldiers led to the creation of suburbs and urban downtown areas in most big cities, including San Diego, giving way to suburban shopping centers and convenience stores. By the late 1950s and early 1960s, the Gaslamp Quarter sank into a sad state of disrepair. Many of the buildings were boarded up and deserted by their owners. The Rescue Mission on Fifth Avenue became the busiest "business" in the area, and street people staked out building entrances, alcoves and trash enclosures to bed down for the night.

The second resurrection of the Gaslamp Quarter began in 1976, when the city adopted the Gaslamp Quarter Revitalization Plan. A year later, the area formerly known as the Stingaree District became the state's only nationally certified first historic district. One of the early tasks under the plan was to install electrified lamps throughout the 38-acre, 16-block district reminiscent of turn-of-the-century street lighting. The widening and brick

(Left and following page) Old City Hall

paving of the district's sidewalks shortly followed this. The combined effect permanently stamped the name "Gaslamp" to the area.

In 1979, after spending more than $33 million to buy up six blocks just below Broadway, the San Diego City Council sold the property to mall developer Ernest Hahn for $1 million, who in turn agreed to build a mall which, in 1985, opened as Horton Plaza. But Herrick said despite the success of Horton Plaza, which was grossing more than $95 million annually (this included the stores, restaurants and movie theaters), the nearby Gaslamp remained a risky district. Designated a National Historic District in 1981, the Gaslamp was still heavily populated by pornography patrons and there was a lot of squalor.

But in 1989, things began to turn around. The San Diego Convention Center opened just a few hundred yards from the southern portion of the Gaslamp. Coupled with substantial tax incentives and loan programs made available to developers and property owners, as enticements to historically rehabilitate these buildings, the Gaslamp was reborn again.

Herrick said the tax incentives that have benefited his company and others have included a 25 percent tax credit on all monies spent for the rehabilitation of the buildings, up to a 30 percent tax deduction for the donation of facade easements on the buildings, and a 19-year straight-line depreciation schedule instead of the customary 30 to 40 years. The federal government also provided low-interest rehab loans from the Department of Housing and Urban Development and encouraged banks to loan to the developers at lower rates and at higher loan-to-value levels to satisfy Community Reinvestment Act credit requirements. There are guaranteed loans from the Small Business Administration to qualified tenants. Lastly, the Historic Building Code, adopted after 1977, provides flexible interpretations of codes for structural, seismic, fire safety and occupancy ratings of rehabilitated historic buildings.

As a result of these tax incentives, the Gaslamp Quarter now contains the largest collection of turn-of-the-century commercial and mixed-use buildings in San Diego. Many investors in these historic preservation properties have realized tax savings of two to four times their cash investment in the first year.

While tomes could be written about each of the properties that San Diego Historic Properties has purchased and restored, the Louis Bank of Commerce Building certainly has one of the most colorful histories. Herrick said it was originally constructed in 1888 by Isidor Louis, who was born in the Polish city of Lessen in 1836. Louis came to San Diego in 1879 and opened a boot shop on Fifth, between G and H streets. Five years later he had also opened an oyster bar and ice cream store. When the railroad finally came in 1885 it sparked a real estate boom. The town swelled from 5,000 to 35,000 in only two years and the population influx created a need for more banks, office space and living quarters.

Louis and his partners began erecting a four-story building on the lot he had originally purchased from Alonzo Horton. When finished in 1888, it was the tallest building in San Diego. The Victorian-style structure had twin mansard roof towers, each topped by an eagle with spread wings. The front was cut from granite with large bay windows. Other intricate design details included an ornate cornice, elaborate wood detailing, and bas-relief in cast terra cotta. Louis maintained a real estate office in the building and he and his family resided on the fourth floor. There were also 33 office spaces rented to tenants of all occupations — a bookseller, jeweler, watchmaker, optician, and other real estate agent-speculator and investment firms. In fact, one of Louis' tenants, Isaac Davidson, a Lithuanian immigrant, later became a banker and built the St. James Hotel in 1912, located directly behind Louis' building on Sixth Avenue.

Today, the handsome interior has been restored to its fine finished banisters and wood paneling. The original brick walls extend all the way up to the stairs from the second floor, where the bank teller windows are still located, to the fourth floor, which still has a large skylight spanning the length of the ceiling.

Isidor Louis died in 1895. He had transformed himself from a poor Eastern European immigrant into a respected and popular entrepreneur that became a pillar of the community and an important part of San Diego's early history. If he were around today, he would be proud to see how his building, and the entire Gaslamp Quarter, has fared. The Louis Bank of Commerce Building's tenants are similar to those of yesteryear with a few exceptions — they include lawyers, investment advisors, talent managers, real estate agents and designer jewelers.

San Diego Historic Properties has played a significant role in restoring the Gaslamp Quarter. Property values in the area doubled between 1995 and 1998 and property taxes from the parcels have added millions of dollars to the city's coffers. What used to be one of the more unsavory areas of the city after dark has become one of the most popular tourist draws. There are now scores of top-quality Italian and other ethnic restaurants, nightclubs, coffeehouses and numerous retail stores.

And what does the future portend for the Gaslamp Quarter? San Diego Historic Properties will purchase and restore more buildings in the district and take a lead role in recommending innovative ways to further increase business and attract tourists. These include removing all parking along Fifth Avenue except for emergency vehicles, creating a gazebo at Fifth and E Avenues, cobblestone streets, outside carousels and more outdoor jazz cafes.

Companies such as San Diego Historic Properties have helped architecture, entertainment and history to intersect in ways the city's founding fathers could never have imagined. But if they could take a stroll around the Gaslamp Quarter, they would be pleased.

Wilsonian Hotel

Louis Bank of Commerce Building

Bannister Steel, Inc.

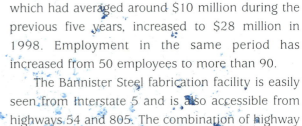

Many businesses have originated in cramped quarters - some perhaps more cramped than others. Ralph Bannister, founder of Bannister Steel, Inc., may have faced some limitations in the confines of his 5-by-13-foot office when he started doing business in 1947, but he utilized the advantages it offered over permanent workplaces boasting more square footage. Bannister's office was on wheels, a well-worn pickup truck, which provided transportation to the job sites as well as storage for materials and his major piece of equipment, a portable welder. Ralph Bannister built Bannister Steel into what is now the oldest and largest steel fabricator in the San Diego area, located on seven acres in National City, California.

Ralph Bannister's death in 1995 brought about changes in the ownership of Bannister Steel, Inc., when six key employees, each with their own individual area of expertise in the industry, formed a partnership and purchased the company. Ted Rossin, president; John Achuff, chief financial officer; Jeff Clinkscales, general manager; Arnold Baumgartner, purchasing agent; Ron Bowers, shop superintendent; and Guadalupe Nunez, shop foreman, led the new management of the company.

During the next three years, revenues of the company, which had averaged around $10 million during the previous five years, increased to $28 million in 1998. Employment in the same period has increased from 50 employees to more than 90.

The Bannister Steel fabrication facility is easily seen from Interstate 5 and is also accessible from highways 54 and 805. The combination of highway accessibility with a direct rail service into the plant gives Bannister Steel a significant advantage over its competition in both receiving raw materials as well as delivering the finished product. The plant fabricates on average more than 1,500 tons of raw steel per month.

"We sure move quite a lot of steel through this shop," says Ron Bowers. It's his job, with his 80 shop employees, to see that the materials are absolutely correct when loaded for delivery to the job sites. It is this dedication to quality that has built Bannister Steel's stellar reputation in the local construction industry. Bannister Steel's commitment to its customers is a quality product at a fair price and always on schedule.

"The company doesn't come up to the job site two days before the delivery of steel and start giving excuses as to why the steel is not there," Jeff Clinkscales explains. "When the customer wants the steel on their job site and they're ready for it, it's there. Dependability is very important to us and our customers. Our customers know that they can depend on us. It's not just words — it's reality."

Bannister Steel has been involved in the construction of several high-profile buildings and facilities in the San Diego area that stand as eye-catching evidence of the company's impressive capabilities. Some of Bannister's most notable projects include the downtown Horton Plaza shopping center and

Horton Plaza, located in downtown San Diego, was one of Bannister Steel's first major projects.

the grandstands at the Del Mar Racetrack. Other significant projects include the Hahn Towers in the Golden Triangle, five San Diego trolley bridges located from downtown San Diego to the Mexican border, the new airport tower at Lindbergh Field, and numerous buildings for Qualcomm and others in the burgeoning high-tech industries.

Bannister Steel markets the whole Southern California area and has delivered as far north as Santa Barbara and as far east as Palm Springs. Although it does significant business in Los Angeles and Orange counties, Bannister Steel employees prefer to hang their hard hats in their hometown of San Diego. Ted Rossin, president of Bannister Steel says, "It's great to drive around San Diego and see all the buildings we have had a major role in the construction of."

Employees of the company are equally committed to supporting a cause close to the heart of the late Ralph Bannister, who funded the construction of the Bannister Family House at the University of California at San Diego Medical Center. This eight-unit apartment building became a reality when he donated over $2 million to build the project. The house provides a home away from home for families undergoing long-term care at the Center. The nonmedical atmosphere of the house provides a retreat from the stress of keeping constant bedside vigils at the hospital. Families have a chance to meet other families in similar situations and develop a network of support with each other. Families pay what they can afford even if it's a few dollars. Bannister understood the immense stress involved for families, having lost both his beloved wife and daughter to cancer. The house was Bannister's dream come true and will always be the main charity of Bannister Steel. The company helps sponsor an annual golf tournament from which about $50,000 goes directly to the house to fund its operating expenses. Ted Rossin and John Achuff are on the board of directors for the house. "It's a great place to visit and the house means so much for so many people," Rossin says.

On October 15, 1998, Schuff Steel of Phoenix, Arizona, purchased Bannister Steel, Inc., with the intent that current management would continue controlling operations for at least five years. Schuff Steel, a publicly-owned company, is the largest steel fabricator in the country and produces steel for projects worldwide. Bannister Steel is the fifth major company they have acquired in the last year, and they now have combined revenues of over $260 million. All of the acquired companies are key regional areas where Schuff anticipates continued economic growth. The acquisition of Bannister Steel gives it ownership of a dominant market player in the Southern California area. With the backing of Schuff Steel, Bannister Steel looks forward to continued growth and playing an important role in the San Diego construction industry in the 21st century.

Qualcomm building "L," one of Bannister Steel's projects, before completion

(Far left) Constructing the Del Mar Racetrack grandstands presented Bannister Steel with its biggest challenge to date. The project called for 6,000 tons of steel.

The Hahn Towers, located at University Town Center, are among the many high-profile facilities built by Bannister Steel.

California Closets

More than 20 years ago, Neil Balter and Mike DeHart installed a floor-to-ceiling rack of shelves and a second pole in the closet of a close friend. The high school buddies returned to their makeshift office of a beat-up van and carport and went on their way in search of more odd jobs. Within a few weeks the dynamic duo had remodeled every closet within a two-block perimeter of their friend's home — and California Closets was born.

Now offering a full range of home storage solutions, California Closets was quick to change with the times. The tool belt was traded in for a compressor and nail gun, and the company began looking at other areas of the home to remodel. It soon saw the opportunity to expand and began franchising in 1981.

"Nobody else was revamping closets at the time," says DeHart, now president of San Diego's California Closets. "We were beginning an entirely new industry and our products were continuing to grow in popularity."

After spending time traveling the country training new franchise owners on the varied aspects of operating a California Closets franchise, DeHart swapped his suitcase for a franchise of his own. When he opened San Diego's California Closets in 1982, it was the ninth franchise. The company is now the fastest growing and most profitable franchise in the $500 million installed closet industry with more than 150 outlets worldwide including Singapore, Brazil, New Zealand and Saudi Arabia.

While California Closets as a corporation has seen some substantial growth over the years, DeHart and his franchise have also come a long way. What began as a two-man show — DeHart and a closet installer — with revenues of less than $350,000, has grown into a staff of 32 that posted $3 million in revenues in 1998, and estimates $3.5 million for 1999. In addition, DeHart says the number of projects completed by San Diego's California Closets has increased 35 to 40 percent a year for the past two years and predicts the same far into the next millennium.

He added that California Closets manufactures all of its own products in San Diego. DeHart is emphatic about keeping every aspect of his company within arm's reach. "We build our products, sell our products and service our customers with people we have carefully trained," he explains. "Professional work starts with choosing the best people and constantly evaluating their work for quality control. It may be basic, but it works."

The San Diego franchise, a runner-up for Franchise of the Year in 1997, prides itself on the quality of its product and its impressive employee retention. A sure sign of a pleasant working environment, at least 50 percent of DeHart's employees have been with the company for more than eight years.

"I have always felt the better I treat my employees, the better they will treat me and the better they will treat the customer," says DeHart. "When a customer is treated well and a great product is produced, that customer is more likely to tell a friend or family member."

More than half of DeHart's business comes from customers referring their friends, family and neighbors. "From the very beginning, I recognized that identifying a client's specific needs was everything," recalls DeHart. "When we create a system that's perfectly suited to our customer, we have truly made a difference in their everyday life. They are more organized, they have a place for everything and they are happier."

California Closets has produced and installed closets for San Diego residents from all walks of life.

Mike DeHart, president of San Diego's California Closets, strongly believes the greatest key to his successful franchise has been a dedication to customer service and satisfaction.

Bus drivers, schoolteachers, firemen and local celebrities like KFMB's Jeff and Jerr and Channel 10's Carol LeBeau, have all been satisfied customers.

"Every client's design starts with a designer visiting their home and discussing their needs and wants. They find out what that person is looking to achieve: more hanging space, more shelving space, drawers? Or is it more room for sports equipment? Each house is different and everybody wants something different."

DeHart added that home office systems in particular have flourished in the past few years, as some 44 million people are now estimated to work from their homes. Garage systems and custom pantry and utility systems have also increased in popularity.

"The industry has become much more personalized and, in response, we have really expanded our product line. People have become more sophisticated, wanting raised panel drawers and glass doors in front of wardrobes."

DeHart strongly believes the greatest key to his successful franchise has been a dedication to customer service and satisfaction. Voted No. 1 in customer service in 1995 by California Closets' customers — and ranking within the top four franchises nominated for the Customer Satisfaction Award for the past five years — the San Diego franchise is well known within the worldwide chain for its commitment to both its clients and its staff.

"The most rewarding part of the Customer Satisfaction Award is that it is based entirely on customer votes," DeHart explains. "All of our customers get a survey card that they fill out and send to our corporate office. That information is entered and then the cards are sent back to us. This way, we learn from our customers which aspects of our work please them most. It's all about making the customer ecstatic and achieving their goals."

He added that he has always enjoyed being a franchise owner because, as they say, two heads are better than one. "Instead of just Mike DeHart creating

California Closets can revamp closets to look like this one, offering more room for shelves, drawers, hanging space — whatever the client needs.

San Diego's California Closets has created home office systems for everyone from bus drivers to schoolteachers to local celebrities.

new ways to improve the company, we have more than 100 other franchise owners coming up with unique ideas. We have access to new product lines, unique products and larger suppliers. Our corporate office also has a large research and development office, as well as a substantial marketing department."

For years, the corporation, which has helped organize the lives of Oprah Winfrey, Bob Villa and Katie Couric, has offered unique and innovative products. In 1999, California Closets will launch its newest product, a high-end Italian line that suits the most discerning customer's taste.

Since its inception in 1978, San Francisco-based California Closets has opened its doors to the world. As the dominant player in the custom storage industry, the company posted $100 million in sales in 1998, and predicts $140 million by the year 2000.

Collins Plumbing, Inc.

Collins Plumbing has been a solid performer in the San Diego area since 1979. The company has been a major player in the building of San Diego and in keeping it on the cutting edge of technology. Specializing in new construction, Collins Plumbing has installed plumbing systems in schools, military bases, hotels, motels, supermarkets, hospitals, shopping centers and amphitheaters. Projects have ranged from subterranean parking to the designing and building of high-rise construction as well as renovation projects.

Collins Plumbing became a leader in its field because of the guidance and business acuity of its owner. Richard Collins is one of those rare people who knew exactly what he wanted for a career at a young age. He wanted to have his own business. To prepare, he took accounting and business classes in high school and continued his business education throughout his four years of military duty.

After leaving the Navy in 1973, Richard Collins took a class in pipe fitting. What he didn't realize was that the class prepared pipe fitters for working on ships, not commercial or residential plumbing. Since the defense industry and shipyards were strong employers in San Diego at that time, he went ahead and continued the class.

After completing his training, he started to work with Campbell's Shipyard as a journeyman pipe fitter while taking business law and business management courses at night. When Campbell's Shipyard workers went on strike, Collins went to work for a residential plumbing repair company. A neighbor on his block, the owner of a plumbing firm specializing in new construction, eventually convinced Collins to start working for him.

By 1979, Richard Collins had the experience he needed to start his own business, Collins Plumbing. Though San Diego was suffering from a significant construction recession, Collins took advantage of the lack of business to establish his firm and its credibility. Applying years of classes and a good business sense, he networked to develop the contacts that would ensure the future of his business. He proved his company's skills, its ability to finish a job on time and on budget, and won the reputation for dealing with employees, developers and contractors squarely.

Collins continued to apply solid business management techniques as he developed his company. When the mid-80s construction boom hit, Collins Plumbing was ready to go. His organizational skills made the difference and his "small" business grew quickly. His customer list includes people in both the private and public sector — general contractors, sewer and water municipalities, and the city, state and federal governments.

Public projects Collins Plumbing has done include the San Diego County Emergency Communications Center, the Point Loma and South Bay Waste Water Treatment Plants, the Camp Pendleton

Collins Plumbing was the design/build plumbing contractor for the 20,000-seat Coors Amphitheatre.

Plaque presented to Richard Collins from the Associated Builders and Contractors as the San Diego Member of the Year 1997.

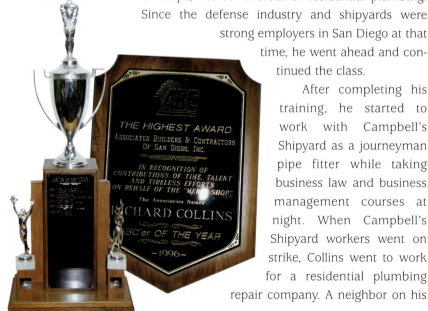

Physical Fitness Center, Miramar Cogeneration Plant and the Fleet Tactical Support OT3.

The Reuben H. Fleet Science Center, Qualcomm, the Hall of Champions, Target, the Viejas Retail Outlets and Harbour Lights Resort are part of a vast number of private clients on the Collins Plumbing list. The company has also been involved in the designing, building and installation for a number of clients including the Sony Warehouse, Clairemont Town Square Police Service, and Coors Amphitheatre in Chula Vista, which it completed in 51 short days.

Modern technology has helped Collins Plumbing computerize not only cost accounting and job estimates, but also space design. In 1997, the company expanded its business to include plumbing design. Using a CAD program, senior designers can interface with architects and contractors as Collins Plumbing designs the plumbing for a facility so that it meets or exceeds code and need expectations. The company's extensive experience gives it the insight to find creative solutions to meet capacity needs. An example of Collins Plumbing's design concepts is the Coors Amphitheatre. In order to accommodate needs and cut down on wait lines for the women's restrooms, Collins Plumbing installed five-station circular wash sinks in the center of the room, freeing up the wall space for more stalls.

Part of Collins Plumbing's success is due to the expertise of its workers. The company is highly active in the trade, keeping abreast of the changes in the industry in order to maintain an extremely competitive edge. Richard Collins strongly believes in providing ongoing training as well as training to improve skills. New employees are encouraged to participate in a paid, four-year program that teaches them the skills needed to become journeymen. Of all the companies in San Diego that qualify to offer such a program, less than 10 percent take advantage of this industry-run program or pay for employees to continue their education. "This is a good investment in the future of Collins Plumbing," said Richard Collins. "We're not here just for the immediate profit, we're here for the long, continued service of Collins Plumbing."

Collins is so committed to making continuing education available to those in the construction industry that he serves on both the advisory committees for the Regional Occupational Project (ROP) and the Associated Builders and Contractors (ABC) Journeyman Training Program and has been the chairman of the education committee for the Plumbing, Heating, Cooling, Contractors Association (PHCC). Collins has also been the past president of the executive board of PHCC, the chairman of the apprentice board for ABC and has received numerous industry awards over the years. Two additional honors he received were the prestigious Above and Beyond Award and the ABC'er of the Year Award presented in 1997.

The Viejas Casino and Outlet Center was completed by Collins Plumbing in 1998.

Collins Plumbing holds a C-36 license and is DBE/SMBE-certified (American-Indian) through CalTrans. Collins is a certified member of the Tallige Cherokee Nation.

Richard Collins' goal "to build a safe, high-quality project in a timely and cost-effective manner" has won him acclaim within the construction community and the loyalty of his customers. The professionalism of this company's dedicated employees and the expertise of its highly qualified team keeps Collins Plumbing in the forefront of an industry that is building the San Diego of tomorrow.

D.A. Whitacre Construction, Inc.

The construction industry in San Diego has taken several major hits since the mid-70s. D. A. Whitacre Construction not only survived those recessions but came out of them even stronger than before. The credit goes to its founder, Donald A. Whitacre, and his ability to predict future needs within his industry. Today his company is involved in many of the major construction and renovation projects in the San Diego area and throughout the western United States including shopping centers, hotels, restaurants, industrial complexes and entertainment centers.

The team behind the success of D.A. Whitacre Construction (left to right) Vicki, Don and Bill Whitacre

A native of San Diego, Whitacre became interested in the construction industry while in high school. In 1972, after completing a year of college, he moved to Telluride, Colorado, where he became an apprentice on construction sites. While there he had the opportunity to learn firsthand not just one trade but ground-up, turnkey construction. After returning to San Diego three years later, Whitacre signed up with an overseas contractor, Holmes and Narver, for a construction project in Antarctica supporting the National Science Foundation. During his eight-month tour, Whitacre's crew worked at the McMurdo Station, the South Pole Station and on the Ross Ice Shelf. They built new research structures and maintained existing sites including the geodesic dome at the South Pole Station.

It was on this tour that he decided to get his contractor's license. Upon returning in 1978, Whitacre opened a one-man operation. It was a challenging time to start any business due to the oil embargo and gas rationing that was prevalent during the Carter years. Whitacre resorted to doing almost anything in the residential arena. Eventually he focused on large custom homes. His crews poured the concrete foundation, laid the masonry and framed the structures.

The company entered the commercial market in 1981 when a superintendent for Douglas Allred Co., a commercial developer in San Diego, hired him to do the miscellaneous carpentry for several of its commercial projects. With that jump-start and with the return of a healthy economic environment, D.A. Whitacre Construction expanded and grew. Although his company continued to frame houses, its specialty became commercial framing.

By 1984, D.A. Whitacre Construction had grown from a one-person operation to more than 25 employees. Whitacre incorporated and his brother, Bill Whitacre, became the company's vice president. Don's wife, Vicki, took over as corporate secretary. Vicki has been an important part of the business since they first put together bids and prepared payroll on the family coffee table in their home.

Bill had started with the company while in high school when he worked part time for his brother during the summer. After securing a business degree from San Diego State University, Bill had gone on to work as an apprentice real estate appraiser in Los Angeles. In 1984, Bill joined his brother's business full time and has since concentrated on its field operations. Together, they became power players in the commercial building field. By 1990 D.A. Whitacre Construction employed more than 100 framers. The company moved out of Don

Whitacre's residence and into the El Cajon location it built and still occupies.

Then in the 90s the recession and cessation of the defense industry in San Diego hit the construction industry hard. Since Whitacre started the business in a recession, he had a unique insight on survival. Instead of laying off his employees and closing the doors when work became scarce, he continued to keep his core workers on the payroll. The company accepted whatever new construction, remodel or reconstruction job it could find — work not typically performed by the company in the regular market.

His loyalty to his workers paid off. When the construction industry began to grow again, starting in 1995, and jobs were plentiful, his workers stayed with D.A. Whitacre Construction, Inc. In fact, some of the crew have been with his company for more than 18 years! This strong core of highly experienced workers gave him the edge his business needed for rapid growth.

By late 1998, D.A. Whitacre Construction had developed enough business to support more than 250 framers and welders and an office staff of 15. Specializing in commercial construction, Whitacre's business focused on commercial wood framing, roof structures and mezzanine decks for tilt-up buildings. They also framed shopping centers, medical buildings, retail centers, auto centers and dealerships, warehouses, hotels, multistory office buildings, restaurants, schools and churches. Business increased dramatically. In 1998 the company completed close to 200 projects.

D.A. Whitacre Construction's project list is as varied as it is long. The company has worked on SeaWorld's Shamu Close Up, Wild Arctic, which won a "Build America Award," the Dolphin Interaction Program and Shipwreck Rapids. The Kona Kai Hotel, Mission Bay Hilton, Fashion Valley and Mission Valley Shopping Center redevelopments and the ARCO Olympic Training Center in Otay Mesa were projects in which D.A. Whitacre participated. Other projects include Qualcomm buildings and the San Diego State University library that also won a "Build

The ARCO Olympic Training Center in Otay Mesa

America Award." D.A. Whitacre Construction has worked with the best of San Diego's general contractors.

D.A. Whitacre is already preparing for the future. As wood prices fluctuate, the construction industry is finding new ways to keep construction prices reasonable. Advances in construction technology include the tilt-up building construction technique that now incorporates steel along with wood in roof structures and metal decks. D.A. Whitacre Construction provides ongoing training to its workers in the latest framing techniques and safety programs in order to stay on the cutting edge of this industry.

With an eye toward the aesthetic balanced with the expertise that more than 20 years in the construction industry brings, D.A. Whitacre Construction continues to be an integral part of the growth and development of San Diego. The company has weathered construction depressions, major changes within the industry and strong competition. It's a safe bet to say that D.A. Whitacre Construction is as solid as the structures that it frames.

D.A. Whitacre Construction has worked on a number of projects for SeaWorld California including Wild Arctic, which won a "Build America Award," and Shipwreck Rapids.

Dewhurst & Associates
Established 1929

A little after the turn of the century, Ernest W. Dewhurst left England where he had owned a construction company in a small maritime village east of Brighton. Arriving in the United States, he sought a place that would remind him of his former home and the seaside settlement of La Jolla, just north of San Diego, was just what he was looking for. In 1929, Dewhurst established the forerunner of what today is La Jolla's oldest and largest building and design firm.

When Ernest Dewhurst opened shop in his adopted country, he selected a site on Girard Avenue in the heart of La Jolla's "industrial district." In today's La Jolla, the very notion of an industrial anything is anathema to the character of the area, but in the 1930s a lumberyard sprawled where Vons is today. A variety of other building supply and service establishments surrounded the lumberyard to support the construction of the new homes and businesses that were sprouting up all over the hills and shorelines of La Jolla. It was the perfect place and the perfect time for a determined general contractor.

From the beginning, the Dewhurst firm worked with highly regarded architects, including Lilian J. Rice and Tom Shepherd. The many La Jolla and Rancho Santa Fe homes resulting from these collaborations remain a testament to craftsmanship and understated elegance. Besides private homes, the Dewhursts built a number of the original buildings that comprised the heart of La Jolla's commercial area. The best-known example still in use today is the Athenaeum, the exquisite music and arts library on Wall Street.

In the 1940s Ernest Dewhurst's son, Walter, joined the firm and when the founder retired in the late 1950s, Walter took over the reins. During this period the company, renamed Dewhurst & Sons, ventured into real estate in addition to its core competencies of new construction and remodeling. Walter Dewhurst became an influential member of the San Diego Planning Commission where he was instrumental in the city's development of Mission Bay. It was during this era that the Dewhurst company erected one of the most visible landmarks in all of San Diego, the cross atop Mount Soledad.

By the mid-1970s Walter's sons started working in the business and when Walter retired, they shouldered the day-to-day running of what is now named Dewhurst & Associates. The company is still located on Girard Avenue, though the area is no longer an "industrial" zone. Though the firm has grown to 50 employees with over eight million dollars in annual revenues and a satellite office in Rancho Santa Fe, it still retains the intimacy of a family business. Walter's son, Don Dewhurst, is at the helm and several of the fourth generation of Dewhursts work as project managers and administrators. They include two of Don's sons, Dave and Doug, and one of his daughters, Donna.

A visitor to the offices of Dewhurst & Associates will discover that the entire facility — architectural

All Hallows Catholic Church, Mount Soledad, completely remodeled by Dewhurst & Associates

department, administration center and custom kitchen display — is a living showroom. Open ceilings reveal construction methods, duct layout and conduits routing. A plethora of moldings, doors, windows and wall treatments presents a melange of the materials, techniques, finishes and design options available from the Dewhurst spectrum.

A modern company with the full capability of melding the traditions of fine home design with the best building technologies, Dewhurst & Associates specializes in high-end custom home construction and renovation. Most of their work is in La Jolla and Rancho Santa Fe, but they have also constructed distinctive residences in other parts of San Diego, Arizona and as far away as the Cayman Islands. In addition to new homes, the company also builds custom interiors for the finest residential structures, including more than 60 interiors at the distinguished Meridian in downtown San Diego.

While residential structures account for the greatest portion of the company's construction and design projects, Dewhurst & Associates has also left its distinctive mark on civic, commercial and church buildings. In a recently completed, high-profile remodeling of All Hallows Catholic Church on Mount Soledad, the company strengthened the entire structure with caissons up to 60 feet deep before replacing the deteriorating concrete floor and renovating the interior. Other non-residential projects completed by Dewhurst in La Jolla include remodeling Warwick's Book Store, Stella Maris Academy, Mary Star of the Sea Chapel and Hall, the La Jolla Historical Society offices and numerous shops in the village.

The firm, not content to rest on its laurels, is engaged in a constant process of growth and improvement. Recently, the company added to their line of interior possibilities the consummate artistry of custom kitchens by Wm Ohs. These designs feature Tuscany, French Country, English Manor and other styles from times-past. With the addition of Wm Ohs kitchens, Dewhurst & Associates continues a tradition of using the most advanced materials and methods to create a residence reminiscent of antique construction.

A magnificent Dewhurst kitchen

Homes built by Dewhurst & Associates have been featured in *South Coast Style, Remodeling, San Diego Home and Garden*, and many other publications. The company's custom construction has received both national and local acclaim including being awarded "Small Business of the Month" for June 1995 by the San Diego Chamber of Commerce.

The firm specializes in accommodating the sophisticated, knowledgeable customer. To serve such a clientele with cohesion and integrity, Dewhurst's on-staff architects and draftsmen design specifically for the company's own artisans and construction teams. This reflects their guiding precept which is, as stated by Don Dewhurst, "to cut the cloth to fit the pattern for the client. At this rarified level of the construction industry, clients are not shopping around. They come to Dewhurst & Associates because they know what they want, and that is the finest home or remodel they can procure."

An entryway to a Mediterranean-style home

Kenai Construction Co., Inc.

From the smooth concrete platforms of the Santa Fe Train Depot in downtown San Diego to the masterfully engineered stairway that gracefully descends down a cliff to Solana Beach, Kenai Construction Co., Inc. has left an indelible mark on nearly every corner of the county. With a solid foundation built from quality service and knowledgeable staff, the firm is responsible for the creation and upgrading of numerous building projects throughout California and western Arizona.

President Gary W. Dulgar and Executive Vice President Donald McIntosh established the company in 1989, just when the construction industry was about to wither through the recession of the early 90s. In hindsight, Dulgar admits it was an extremely lean period for new projects. But the men earnestly promoted their services to public and private enterprises and began securing several lucrative bids, including one from Ochs Oil Distribution Center in Vista.

The Ochs project was a six-month job that involved building a bulk oil distribution facility complete with new offices, underground tanks for petroleum storage, and fuel islands for a pumping station in Vista. As with many other projects that followed, Kenai entered the venture under a "design/build" plan, which meant teaming up with an outside architectural firm to assist with the overall design and construction. Today, the company works with about 30 different architects in order to provide more clients with a complete service package. It's an approach that leading construction companies throughout the world have begun offering.

Kenai immediately started out as a corporation and was initially based in an 1,800-square-foot office in Mira Mesa. At the time, Dulgar's and McIntosh's wives helped streamline administrative operations while the two men fused together their management and craftsmen skills. Dulgar holds a degree in architecture and McIntosh earned his degree in civil engineering. Before launching the business, both had also gained considerable training at the nationally known Hensel Phelps Construction Company. Their combined experience enabled them to form a construction company of superior strength and reputation.

In 1996, Kenai purchased an 8,000-square-foot building in Miramar to accommodate an expanding staff that helped facilitate a steady stream of new contracts. From its modest beginnings, the company grew to 20 salaried employees, plus nearly 50 carpenters, laborers and finishers. The move into larger office space clearly signaled the success of Kenai's sharp marketing efforts and the end of a debilitating recession for the construction industry.

Dulgar and McIntosh quickly established themselves through several construction projects that brought vital improvements to popular institutions within San Diego County. Included in the list is a series of nearly 100 different jobs for the University of California at San Diego. For instance, Kenai provided seismic upgrading for about 10 of the university's older buildings, each of which required different upgrade schemes to better secure their foundations.

For San Diego State University, Kenai built a two-story tower with an elevator that transports students

High tides and rugged cliffs presented Kenai crews with challenging conditions when building this masterfully engineered stairway in Solana Beach.

from a lower parking lot onto higher campus ground. The structure also includes a pedestrian bridge that stretches across a canyon to provide easy access for students.

The Salk Institute, another well-known establishment in San Diego, hired Kenai to make renovations to its laboratory and office spaces. As one of San Diego's modern architectural wonders and important research facilities, Dulgar and his crew needed to make the upgrades without altering the basic structure of the building.

Kenai's proven track record for creating edifices and making structural improvements amid environmentally sensitive areas has steadily set it apart from other construction companies. In 1995, for example, Kenai began work for the city of Solana Beach on a concrete and heavy timber stairway which zigzags down a rugged seaside cliff to the sandy beach floor. A major portion of the work took place below sea level in the tide zone for casting and placing concrete caissons. And much of the drilling was done by hand because of the lack of access for a standard drill-rig.

The thick concrete columns supporting the stairs and several landings are anchored firmly in steep slopes that were once inaccessible to pedestrians. Dulgar admits the job was among the company's toughest in terms of special features and rough landscape conditions.

Soon after, San Diego's Centre City Development Corporation learned of Kenai's impressive reputation and strength of services for a federally funded expansion project of the Santa Fe Rail Depot. It was a design/bid/build proposal that included the expansion of track platforms over a two-block area in downtown San Diego. Walkways, passenger shelters, custom lighting and ticket dispensers were all part of the eight-month improvement process, which has resulted in more efficient rail service for San Diegans today.

Kenai prides itself on repeat business from clients who are looking for something other than average, low-cost construction services. No two projects are ever alike. Banks, hospitals, golf resorts and recreation parks such as SeaWorld have all called upon Kenai to meet their growing needs.

The company exceeds basic standards in customer service by providing clients with in-depth evaluations for how projects are handled. Dulgar relies on the good will, support and respect of all subcontractors and suppliers — and gives the same in return. Employees are offered growth opportunities while stockholders generally enjoy a return on their investment of 20 percent after taxes. The company is also committed to meeting contract schedules in a timely manner and maintaining close, personal customer relationships from the drawing of a contract to the completion of a project.

Dulgar and McIntosh named their company after Alaska's Kenai Peninsula, where they periodically take fishing and camping trips. A large wall map of Alaska even hangs in the company's conference room, which aptly reflects the team's proficiency for tackling new adventures in their less-bucolic Southern California work environment. Having fun during the construction process and providing safe working conditions are among a long set of priorities that make Kenai Construction a perfect fit for San Diego's commercial and civic builders.

New concrete platforms walkways and outdoor seating at the Santa Fe Depot Courtyard have greatly improved the station's functionality and visual appeal.

Newland Communities

The 1,100-acre community of Bernardo Heights features distinctive architecture and an 18-hole championship golf course.

Family-filled houses close to shopping and schools, sun-drenched parks, hiking trails and swimming pools symbolize San Diego's master-planned community lifestyle. For more than 30 years, Newland Communities has successfully completed major master-planned community projects that have shaped the character of the region, creating desirable living and working environments while preserving natural habitats and open space.

The sophisticated and environmentally sensitive developments Newland has created in San Diego are characteristic of the high-quality, master-planned communities the company has designed and established nationwide. With a strong emphasis on the Sunbelt, Newland has developed 30 distinctive communities in seven states, each designed to reflect the specific requirements of their regions. The company has developed more than 50,000 acres that now contain 225,000 homes and 12 golf courses as well as 650 acres of commercial property on which millions of square feet of retail, office and industrial development have been completed. Projects have ranged in size up to 8,000 acres and produced more than $5 billion in revenue.

Today, Newland fulfills the dual roles of master-planned community developer and advisor to pension funds and other institutional partners on the acquisition and development of residential communities. In both of these roles, the company has been consistently profitable throughout the ups and downs of the real estate development cycles of the last three decades.

A Builder of San Diego Communities

San Diego County has been one of California's fastest-growing regions, with tens of thousands of new residents arriving or being born each year. The area's impressive economic growth and clean, diversified industrial base, combined with a desirable

climate and lifestyle, have been powerful catalysts to population growth.

At the same time, as the demand for housing has risen, San Diego has been more sensitive to the impacts of growth than many other regions. "Slow growth" and "no growth" political movements have endeavored to prevent urban sprawl and have been an important force in shaping the community. In response to these pressures, successful developers such as Newland have adopted an approach that includes strict rules for land use, cooperation with regulatory agencies and local communities in obtaining plan approvals, and a strong environmental sensitivity. Unlike many tract home subdivisions constructed in the region, Newland's master plans have placed a high priority on open space, plant and animal species preservation, and creating opportunities for the year-round enjoyment of recreation.

For three decades, Newland and its affiliates have been involved with San Diego planned development. The company's San Diego division has been responsible for nine projects that encompass 16,000 acres. Their most well-known and influential projects include:

Bernardo Heights, a 1,100-acre community located in Rancho Bernardo on the Interstate 15 inland corridor. Originally envisioned as a retirement community, the area attracted thousands of upwardly mobile families who were drawn by an excellent master plan located on rolling foothills, distinctive architecture, good schools and a large number of amenities, including an 18-hole championship golf course.

North University City, known as The Golden Triangle, which is framed by the triangle formed by Interstate 5 to the west, Interstate 805 to the east and state route 52 to the south. The 1,100-acre area is truly a city in itself, featuring high-rise office buildings, hotels, restaurants, luxury apartments and condominiums, all clustered around the University Towne Centre regional mall.

Rancho Peñasquitos, an 8,000-acre community located 15 miles from downtown San Diego on the I-15 corridor. With views of mountains to the east and the Pacific Ocean to the west, Rancho Peñasquitos is a vibrant and picturesque area that is popular with middle-income families. In creating this community, Newland dedicated 3,000 acres of open space now known as the Los Peñasquitos Canyon Preserve, one of the city's most prized natural resources.

Sorrento Hills, which includes Torrey Reserve and Torrey Hills, a 600-acre community at the confluence of Interstates 5 and 805, close to La Jolla, Del Mar and Rancho Santa Fe. With unparalleled views, the community combines low-rise, campus-like commercial spaces with single-family and multifamily housing that serves the people and companies involved with the University of California at San Diego and the booming high-technology industry that surrounds it.

As Newland created these ground-breaking communities, the company took special care to improve the lifestyles of their residents. Lot sizes and housing were designed to be affordable for the average home buyer. Extensive landscaping and amenities such as hiking trails, bike paths, parks, swimming pools, recreation centers and golf courses were included in Newland's community plan design. In several cases, significant open space was preserved. Newland has also made contributions of land and funding for the construction of libraries and YMCAs. The company's well-orchestrated planning and expert execution have set standards for managed growth in the region.

A National Community Developer

Founded in San Diego, Newland has become one of the largest master-planned community developers in the United States. Under the leadership of Robert McLeod, LaDonna Monsees and Derek Thomas, Newland has expanded nationally, drawing on a portfolio of skills that it honed in the building of San Diego.

As it moves into the third millennium, geographic diversification and a focus on the Sunbelt will remain essential to the company's strategy. Newland has

North University City or "The Golden Triangle" has become a city in itself, featuring high-rise office buildings, hotels, restaurants, luxury apartments and condominiums.

development operations in eight states, including California, Oregon, Washington, Arizona, Texas, Florida, Georgia and North Carolina. Newland Communities will soon be opening in the cities of Raleigh, Charlotte, Atlanta, Houston, Phoenix, Orlando and Tampa.

Newland will continue to create high-quality, high-value communities that enhance the lifestyles of its residents. Newland understands that a community must provide a positive living environment now, and for many generations to come. The communities Newland has created uphold the highest standards of building a greater San Diego.

Reno Contracting

Matt Reno established his contracting firm during the depths of a recessionary slump in 1993, the same way any one of his distinctive, gleaming projects are completed throughout San Diego

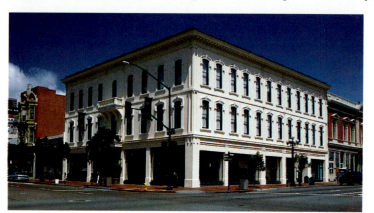

Reno used state-of-the-art construction techniques to help preserve tradition in its renovation of the historic Z Gallerie building in San Diego's Gaslamp Quarter.
© Bill Robinson

County: from the ground up, with precise attention to detail, and by doing everything right.

Today, Reno Contracting is well-known for shaping the landscape of corporate San Diego in the most literal sense possible — through the construction of more than 50 high-profile projects including office buildings, shopping centers, and manufacturing and warehouse facilities. If high-tech and biotechnology industries best represent the commercial face of America's Finest City, then Reno could be considered one of its most accomplished makeup artisans. That's because Reno not only succeeded in overcoming initial economic obstacles, but so excelled in the precise, unforgiving building form known as concrete tilt-up construction that it has helped architects transform a previously generic and overlooked building style into the more sophisticated, intricate form seen today.

"It's a matter of balancing the user's appetite for embellishment, the architect's desire for critical recognition and the developer's financial constraints," says Reno. "My job is to juggle all those factors and satisfy everyone's expectations."

Perhaps Reno is able to satisfy both aesthetic and budgetary bottom lines because of the many hats he has worn in the industry. His first hats, naturally, were of the hard variety. As a teenager growing up in Los Angeles, Reno swept floors, toted lumber and ran to the hardware store after school for a custom home building company owned by his best friend's father. He dug ditches as a summer laborer in the early 70s, a decidedly unattractive job if it wasn't for the memory of working at Bob Dylan's house during his senior year. While seeing the likes of Diana Ross and Kenny Rogers on a property that had American Indian tepees and a commune-style atmosphere might seem an unlikely start to a career in building corporate headquarters, in Reno's case it was merely an apt metaphor for someone who isn't afraid to buck a trend in the conviction of a personal vision and the satisfaction of a job done right.

Or, as Matt Reno puts it, "You need to figure out what you want to be, and then be the best at it."

This philosophy would help Reno in several ways. Whether it was earning his bachelor's degree in business administration from the University of San Diego while he worked as an apprentice and then journeyman carpenter, or taking a pay cut when he decided to trade in his blue collar for a white one, Reno's eye was always trained on the long-term goal of finding his contractor's niche and then simply doing it better than anyone else.

Reno's $40,000 salary was nearly halved in 1982 when the young man gave up his tool belt to become an estimator with Trepte Construction Company in San Diego. Four years later, he joined Ninteman Construction and became senior estimator with an eye toward succeeding Dean Ninteman. However, when Ninteman sold his firm three years later, Reno realized that if he wanted to achieve his goals he would have to take a more proactive approach.

After agreeing to stay one more year "and a day," Reno bought into MQ Construction, Inc., one of the largest firms erecting concrete tilt-ups in San Diego at the time. The date was April Fool's Day, 1989, a detail Reno notes wryly when he recalls how it took more than six months to square away the company's accounting and streamline its operations.

"My wife affectionately called me 'the hatchet man,'" Reno says. "I let go every person there except three — and those three are still working with me to this day."

As president of MQ during the recessionary slump of the early 90s, Reno oversaw the company's work in building concrete tilt-ups, a process in which exterior walls are cast on the slabs in sections and then put into place with a large crane. He also felt that when the economy turned around there would be an opportunity for a new midsized company that could fill a void created by competitors who had grown too large for the tilt-up niche and were developing interests outside San Diego.

So in 1993, Reno parted amicably with partner Pete Minegar and founded Reno Contracting. The recession was in full swing but his goals were not based on revenue, per se.

"I only want to get as big as I have to in order to service the people that I want to do business with," he says. "I never wanted to get big for the sake of getting big. My feeling has always been that if you're the best you'll always have all the work you need."

By catering to the private sector in a city which was successful in attracting high-tech companies, Reno experienced such steady growth that by the time the economy began turning around in 1995, it was common knowledge that Reno Contracting was the leading expert on constructing concrete tilt-up projects in San Diego. The company built $5 million in projects its first year, roughly doubling that total each successive year. Including backlogged projects, Reno expects to construct approximately $105 million in new projects in 1999. Today, the firm has more recent corporate "build-to-suit" projects completed and under construction than virtually any contractor in San Diego.

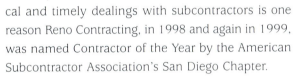

However, true to Reno's vision, growth has not cost the company its higher values. Reno, which has finished every project ahead of schedule, operates without a marketing department, as well as most of the middle management found on the payrolls of other firms. Almost all of its business comes from repeat clients, and its ethical and timely dealings with subcontractors is one reason Reno Contracting, in 1998 and again in 1999, was named Contractor of the Year by the American Subcontractor Association's San Diego Chapter.

While Reno is too attached to each of his projects to single out any particular one, the $10 million, 142,000-square-foot Intuit corporate headquarters in San Diego stands as an especially proud achievement, since it was more than double the size of Reno's previous largest job.

There is little doubt that as San Diego continues to fulfill its promise as a high-tech industrial nexus, Reno Contracting will be there to help build that vision from its very foundation.

In terms of size and technical achievement, construction of the $10 million, 142,000-square-foot Intuit corporate headquarters in San Diego was a particularly significant project for Reno.
© Bill Robinson

T&B Planning Consultants

A journey of a thousand miles begins with a single step. If that first step, however, is just a few degrees off course, the traveler can end up miles from the intended destination.

Successful land development is no exception to this rule. Miscalculations in the beginning of a project can result in huge errors only discovered later, when correcting them is very costly and difficult. The use of an expert land planner from the outset is crucial. Vibrant communities result from a planning consultant's high-quality front-end work.

One premier planning firm esteemed for its high quality is T&B Planning Consultants. The firm, founded in 1974 by Lou Turrini and Bob Brink, originally designed and processed the land where many San Diego area residents now live, work, play and shop. Many of T&B's early designs have become vital San Diego communities and institutions. Cottonwood and the design for Penasquitos Regional Park arose from T&B efforts, as did the design for a portion of the University of San Diego campus. T&B also designed and processed large portions of Rancho de Los Penasquitos and the job creation centers located in Sorrento Valley known originally as Pacific Corporate Center and Lusk Business Park. Today, T&B is the lead design, documentation and processing firm for new communities such as Torrey Hills, the Villages of La Costa and Encinitas Ranch.

T&B serves all of Southern California — as well as other areas in the United States — from offices in San Diego and Santa Ana. The nationally renowned company is recognized for its multi-disciplinary approach to planning, design and environmental analysis. As a pure planning firm, T&B provides a wide range of services related to producing "developable" projects. These services include design, site evaluation, master planning, land planning, "urban-infill" and "transit-oriented" design, planning and environmental documentation and processing.

The firm's five owner/principals — Doug Boyd, Barry Burnell, James Greco, Firouz Ghaboussi and Russ Garcia — draw on more than 95 years of combined professional experience. Their varied but complementary backgrounds make the company stronger as a whole. All five have worked as a team at T&B for most of their planning careers, bringing a unique continuity to the firm's vision and creative energy. This enduring relationship enhances the ability of these talented professionals to tap all of their experiences effectively. Through their efforts, T&B's projects are consistently accepted by approving agencies, communities and the marketplace.

While widely acclaimed for its role as a traditional planning consultant, T&B's aesthetic and physical design elements make it truly distinctive. The firm has been praised for wedding the architect's creativity with the engineer's practicality: T&B creates appealing designs that work.

For a plan to work today, it must be more than functional. Environmental and community issues often have a major influence on project design. Because of its experience, creativity and dedication to research, T&B can anticipate problems and design plans that mitigate many of these concerns. The T&B approach transforms potential physical and

T&B Principals — (seated left to right) James Greco, Doug Boyd, Barry Burnell, (standing left to right) Firouz Ghaboussi and Russ Garcia — draw on complimentary yet varied talents and more than 95 years of combined experience.

environmental obstacles into opportunities to preserve resources while promoting efficient and economically feasible design.

Torrey Hills, originally Sorrento Hills, demonstrates this approach. Confronted with inefficient and costly existing entitlement, T&B provided a dramatic design solution and creative entitlement documentation. T&B's design creates a new mixed-use community that meets or exceeds the City of San Diego's and the developers' high design standards while drastically reducing grading quantities and preserving all the developable area. Another example is T&B's superlative design for The Greens, a 660-acre portion of the Villages of La Costa. A three-party agreement among the federal government, the City of Carlsbad and the predecessor to the Bank of America, established a massive habitat conservation area that required a sensitive and creative redesign. T&B, retained by B.of A., created a distinctive design that respects the new conservation area and Carlsbad's strict design standards. T&B is also preparing the environmental impact report for the Villages of La Costa, as it did for Sorrento Hills.

T&B has also demonstrated unsurpassed expertise in its ability to fashion plans that aid and enhance the eventual transformation of large tracts of land from their current use. Owners of entities such as dairy farms, landfills and mining quarries have had the vision to recognize that their current or planned uses, though often long-term, will not be maintained permanently. They have retained T&B to design the initial use so that it not only efficiently yields current resources but will also facilitate the site's future conversion and development to generate the highest environmental and monetary value.

An example of T&B's virtuosity in such planning, Rio Vista West was a winner of the prestigious Gold Nugget Merit Award. It was designed and processed for CalMat Properties Company in San Diego to replace a 95-acre Mission Valley resource extraction operation. This mixed-use, transit-oriented project features residential products, a much-needed power center, an office complex, a transit hub, and a series of public places that provide passive and active

open space amenities for residents and employees. The City of San Diego has recognized T&B's innovative approach by designating another similar project, the Carroll Canyon Master Plan, as a "Transit-Oriented Design" (TOD) demonstration project.

These award winning projects and the company's superb national reputation have resulted in T&B being retained by an impressive list of diverse clients. Among those in San Diego who have sought out the company's expertise include Brookfield Homes, Centex, Genstar, Kaufman & Broad, McMillin Homes, Pardee Construction Company, Shea Homes, Standard Pacific, and Western Pacific Housing.

T&B has performed varied services for many diverse clients, both large and small. It has done master planning for such atypical sites as cemeteries, high schools, landfills and dairies. Private landowners, who have long maintained large pieces of family-owned land, have trusted T&B's pure planning talents, singleness of purpose and tradition of excellence to inform them and help them make the best decisions on current and future use of their land.

Personal attention is a T&B hallmark. The company has carefully controlled its growth to continue to allow one of the firm's principals to personally direct each project.

T&B's devotion to quality, efficiency and creativity has helped ensure the successful planning, design and entitlement of over 100,000 acres of land. The company's well-conceived and dedicated approach has left its countless clients happy that they chose to take the first step of their land development journey with T&B Planning Consultants.

Gold Nugget Merit Award winner Rio Vista West includes theaters, shopping, offices and town homes focused on a central commons and a transit stop for the San Diego Trolley.

Techbilt Companies

Pictured at Techbilt's Emerald Cove La Jolla subdivision, with Crystal Bay in the background: Founder Paul Tchang (second from right), with (from left) Doug Woods, director of construction, Jenny Tchang Frost, director of marketing, and Ted Tchang, vice president of finance and industrial projects.

Paul Tchang embodies the quintessential American success story — the immigrant who triumphs over seemingly impossible odds to start a new life and a new business, in this case, a thriving real estate enterprise. Today, the Techbilt Companies are the oldest family-owned companies building homes in San Diego. Since 1956, Techbilt has built over 10,000 homes, from modest entry-level dwellings to lavish million-dollar-plus showcases in communities throughout Los Angeles and San Diego counties. During its proud history, Techbilt has never veered from its original philosophy of service, quality and integrity.

The United States was in turmoil when Tchang disembarked at Boston Harbor on December 6, 1941. A 17-year-old struggling to master English, his third language, Tchang had journeyed from China to study mechanical engineering at the Massachusetts Institute of Technology (MIT). Pearl Harbor was bombed the following day and the United States entered World War II. As a result, Tchang's study grants from the Chinese government were withdrawn and he found himself without a place to live because the U.S. Army had taken over the dormitories at MIT. However, he was able to continue his schooling thanks to funds made available from the U.S. State Department reparation fund from China for the Boxer Rebellion. Not only was his tuition paid, he also received the princely sum of $70 a month for food, rent and books. Thus began Paul Tchang's enduring love affair with America, the country he calls "the greatest in the world."

In the ensuing years, Tchang earned his bachelor's and master's degrees from MIT and a master's degree in business administration from Harvard Business School. After receiving his citizenship in 1955, he began his own construction company in Stamford, Connecticut, where he experienced the frustration of being an outsider. Harsh winters led to his decision to move to Palmdale, California, to build tract homes. However, the young entrepreneur soon realized this fledgling firm was no match for the more established Los Angeles builders, who began purchasing huge portions of raw land, so he headed south to San Diego.

In 1956, Techbilt purchased its first piece of undeveloped land in San Diego in Linda Vista. An environment of discrimination persisted in the 1950s. The Chinese Exclusion Act prevented any Chinese person or Chinese-owned company from purchasing land. Although the act was rescinded in 1951, it was still tied to the title of the Linda Vista property. Told to ignore the exclusion, Techbilt constructed its first 100-unit housing development, offering entry-level VA/FHA homes starting at $11,000. Tchang is proud to have been able to provide the community with affordable, quality housing when the demand was great and starter homes were in short supply. Techbilt continued to create attractive neighborhoods in Kearny Mesa, Clairemont, University City and Pacific Beach. Tchang was a hands-on developer and in the earlier years, served as project superintendent to ensure quality control.

His subcontractors quickly learned he was a stickler for detail, a trait he vows will continue as long as Techbilt is in business.

In 1964, Techbilt expanded into La Jolla with single-family detached view homes beginning at $25,000, a price some thought to be too high at the time.

In 1966, a joint venture between Techbilt and Ted Gildred Sr.'s Lomas Santa Fe, Inc. resulted in the creation of Lomas Santa Fe Golf Course in Solana Beach and approximately 1,000 homes in the Lomas Santa Fe community built in the late 1960s and 1970s.

In 1969, Techbilt acquired 300 acres in La Jolla on the southern slopes of Mount Soledad. The company already owned approximately 170 acres to the north and south. Many of San Diego's most prominent builders shunned the property, deeming it too risky to develop a tract-type community in La Jolla, a strictly custom home enclave. La Jolla Alta is now a prestigious community complete with elegant luxury homes, recreation centers, tennis courts, swimming pools and approximately 100 acres of open space.

Over the years, Techbilt's residential communities have garnered a host of local, regional and national awards.

Techbilt also diversified into the industrial market, beginning with the 180-acre Carlsbad Oaks industrial park in Carlsbad in the 1980s and expanding into Poway in the 1990s, where it continues to sell lots and build industrial facilities at Tech Business Center and Poway Corporate Center.

A number of factors have contributed to Techbilt's success and longevity. First and foremost, are the executives who are guided by the company's philosophy of service, quality and integrity: Jenny Tchang Frost, who oversees sales and marketing; Ted Tchang, in charge of finance and Techbilt's industrial projects; Doug Woods, construction manager and general administration; and Jim O'Hara, controller. Another factor contributing to Techbilt's success is its uncommon loyalty to its employees and subcontractors; that loyalty is returned. Some Techbilt employees have been with the company over 20 years and some subcontractors are in their second generation of continued involvement with Techbilt.

Quality and integrity are hallmarks of Techbilt — quality in the products and services it offers and integrity in its dealings with customers, subcontractors, government agencies and the public.

Normally a reticent man, Paul Tchang glows with enthusiasm when he speaks of his gratitude toward his beloved America and the opportunities it has afforded him and his family. He is proud to have had a positive impact on the San Diego housing market by providing quality developments. As further evidence of his good citizenship, Mr. Tchang participates in the Rotary Club of San Diego and has served on many boards, including Scripps Memorial Hospital, the Museum of Man, the Francis Parker School and the Housing Commission. He has given back to the industry by his service to the California Building Industry Association (CBIA) where he has earned a lifetime directorship and the San Diego BIA, which recognized his 25 years of service with the coveted Lee Hubbard Award.

Crystal Bay La Jolla homes sell for over $1 million today.

Warren West, Inc.

If Tim Warren's sister hadn't picked a cold day in Ohio to get married in San Diego, Warren West Construction, which specializes in earth moving for commercial and residential builders, might have turned out to be Warren East.

Warren was born in Springfield, Ohio, and grew up working in his father's construction business. By 16, he was a skilled equipment operator. In the cold Ohio winters, he had to learn to operate the equipment with one hand so he could warm the other hand in his pocket.

In 1985, his parents flew to San Diego for his sister's wedding. Soon after the wedding, his father phoned Warren, who told him the chill factor at Port Columbus Airport in Ohio was minus 71 degrees. His father replied that in San Diego, it was in the 70s and a beautiful day for the beach. Not long afterward, Warren became a San Diego resident.

He arrived in town with $300 and owed $10,000 to the Internal Revenue Service. After becoming more financially secure, he started Warren West Construction in 1988. His office was a spare bedroom. Although the construction business had been booming when Warren arrived in San Diego in 1985, by 1988 it was slowing down. The company's early years were full of struggle. The years 1989 through 1992 were tough ones for construction in San Diego and, for a time, Warren went into partnership to stay afloat.

Warren West continued to grow, however, despite the really hard years of the early 1990s. In its best year — 1997 — gross sales increased 330 percent from the previous year. The company continues to grow through repeat customers and word-of-mouth; it didn't start advertising until 1998.

Over the years, Warren West has moved its headquarters from Mission Valley to Lakeside and increased its full-time work force from three to 18. A desk drawer full of letters from satisfied customers attests that Warren West is filling a need in San Diego.

The company specializes in earthwork and excavation, such as site development for commercial and residential customers. These range from high-end residential builders to a surfer's custom beach

Tim Warren, founder and president of Warren West Construction Inc.

Warren West saved a sliding slope and the home above in Oceanside: (left) strengthening and stabilizing the slope; (center) repairs to slope completed; and (right) finished landscaping on repaired slope.

house. In 1995, when local construction was booming, Warren found he had to compete for available trucks and material movers, so he added a trucking division to his company and hired his own drivers.

Warren attributes much of the company's success to his field personnel, some of whom have been with him since the company started. He likes their positive attitude and willingness to learn new skills. His people in the field go out of their way to meet the needs of the neighborhoods and communities where they happen to be working.

For example, customers appreciate Warren West's concern for the environment and its experience in dealing with hazardous materials found in soil or groundwater. Because so much of San Diego's open country has been "built out," construction projects often begin with demolishing old structures. Many of these sites contain such hazards as unexploded bombs (on former military sites), lead paint, ground chemicals, asbestos and other toxins.

Field crews are trained in handling these hazardous materials, as well as certified in first aid, CPR and other emergency procedures. In addition, crew members are certified by manufacturers of new construction materials in the proper ways to install or retrofit such products.

Another key to success is the reputation Warren West has built with other contractors in the area. They trust the company to perform precise operations that might be outside their specialized knowledge. Some of these company owners have guided Tim Warren from his beginnings in San Diego and acted as his mentors.

He credits Bob Tyner, owner of American Asphalt, with helping him get his business off the ground by offering subcontracting jobs. Tyner has shown Warren the value of marketing and a positive attitude and has become a close friend as well.

Another long-time supporter has been Enniss Enterprises, where the entire Enniss family has inspired Warren with their ethics of hard work and family values. "Reid and Delpha Enniss treated me like family and reminded me of the values my dad

Soil erosion threatened a washout road in Fallbrook: (top) repairs begin with concrete supports and (bottom) end with a raised roadway and stabilized slope.

had taught me," Warren says. These mentors have taught Warren such success essentials as (1) never give up trying to achieve your goals and (2) keep everyone on your team working as a team.

Larry and Dan Hunter, owners of Hunter Construction, also encouraged Warren's early efforts and convinced him that the only thing he lacked to achieve all his goals was faith in himself.

Through hard work and a commitment to high standards, Warren West Construction has grown from just an idea knocking around in a young man's mind to a viable company that anticipates the challenges of the new millennium. Skies are still sunny and the beach still beckons in San Diego as Warren continues to form deep bonds with his new home.

"It's been exciting being part of the growth of such a wonderful city with such a rich heritage," Warren says. "I am fortunate to be a part of the experience and be able to add my own personal history to the larger story of San Diego."

Architect Milford Wayne Donaldson, FAIA

Since its founding in 1978, Architect Milford Wayne Donaldson, FAIA has established itself as one of the leading preservation architecture firms in the western United States. Founder and President Wayne Donaldson, FAIA began working with historic buildings when the idea of preservation was still a new concept, opening his office in the Gaslamp Quarter, the historic heart of San Diego. Donaldson and his team of architects, conservators and historians have been instrumental in preserving, restoring and reconstructing hundreds of buildings throughout the Western states, with an emphasis in California.

House of Hospitality, Balboa Park, San Diego
©1998 Ed Gohlich Photography

Architect Milford Wayne Donaldson, FAIA has extensive experience in almost every variation of building type, scale and use. Diversity is the hallmark of Architect MWD's work. The firm has more than 20 years of technical know-how as well as a comprehensive knowledge of codes and how they relate to historic buildings, especially the Secretary of the Interior's Standards for Treatment of Historic Properties, the State Historical Building Code and the Americans with Disabilities Act.

Whether the project requires museum-quality historic restoration, seismic stabilization, complete reconstruction, adaptive reuse, a master plan or simply a report of existing conditions and space planning, Architect MWD can fill each client's needs in an expert and professional manner. Donaldson is also a licensed general contractor, giving him real-world expertise for assisting clients during the construction phase and making sure that the project is completed on time and on budget.

Architect Milford Wayne Donaldson, FAIA has been involved in over 300 historic projects in San Diego County including the House of Hospitality, Horton Grand Hotel, Vallecito Stage Coach Station, Leo Carrillo Ranch, Carlsbad Santa Fe Depot, Citrus Soap Factory, Guajome Ranch, National City Depot, Chollas Heights Community Center, Old Town Transit Center, Organ Pavilion lighting restoration and San Diego Aerospace Museum expansion.

Architect Milford Wayne Donaldson, FAIA has won numerous awards for preservation and design, including a Special Award for Excellence in Historic Preservation, an Honor Award from the American Institute of Architects California Council, 1998 National Trust for Historic Preservation Award and several State of California Governor's Historic Preservation Awards.

Leo Carrillo Ranch, Carlsbad

C&B Steel

In 1970 C&B Steel opened its doors for business. Twenty-eight years later, the company successfully completed the largest steel-framed building ever attempted by a local steel contractor, the eight-passenger gate expansion of the west terminal of Lindbergh Field. The $75 million project used almost 5,000 tons of structural, earthquake-resistant steel and took 10 months for C&B Steel to fabricate and erect, on time and within budget.

Owner John McMahon was one of the original owners of C&B Steel, and within one year of business, he became the sole owner. While serving an apprenticeship to the steel trade in Dublin, Ireland, McMahon attended engineering school at the College of Technology in Dublin. John and his wife, Vera, left Ireland in 1964 so he could take a position in South Africa. They spent two years there before moving to Central Africa where they spent another two years before deciding to come to the United States.

When C&B Steel began business it was a small, miscellaneous steel-fabricating company. By the mid-80s it was bidding jobs up to $1 million and by the late 80s, it was up to $5 million contracts. While John was building the business to this size, Vera did all the accounting and managed the office, all while working out of the home and raising three children. John did all the bidding and supervised the fabrication, welding and installations.

One of John's biggest thrills in business was when his son, Derek, graduated from San Diego State University and decided to join him in the business. Kevin, his other son, graduated from Santa Clara University, and some years later he also decided to join his father.

Some of the San Diego County projects completed successfully by C&B Steel, besides the airport project, include Eastlake High School, the Centrifuge/Biosolids project, El Centro High School, the Price Center at the University of California at San Diego, the Otay Mesa Kaiser Permanente facility, the Callaway golf facility and the Calexico port of entry. Some of C&B Steel's out-of-town projects include the Squadron Operations facility at Travis Air Force Base, the Procter & Gamble Co-Generation Plant in Sacramento, Riverside High School and the UPS cargo facility in Los Angeles.

The Eisenhower Hospital addition in Rancho Mirage, the seven-story Seaview Corporation Center in Sorrento Valley, the science facility at the University of Redlands and the Mark V. Water Operating Facility at the Naval Air Station on North Island will also be C&B Steel projects.

The expansion of the west terminal of Lindbergh Field was the largest steel structure ever completed by a local steel contractor.

C&B Steel continues to build its business and reputation on integrity and trust. Today it is clearly a big player in the steel construction industry, throughout California, especially since the Lindbergh Field job. The company's new location in Otay Mesa will allow for additional expansion and the ability to bid on even bigger jobs. With the demand for high-quality, earthquake-resistant, steel-framed buildings, C&B Steel will undoubtedly play an important role in the growth of San Diego and California.

Casper Company

Some of the historical buildings Casper Company has worked on include the House of Hospitality in Balboa Park.

From Balboa Park to the Gaslamp Quarter, Casper Company has been called upon to perform delicate interior demolition and modification to some of San Diego's historical buildings and high-rises. Many of the buildings in Balboa Park, from the Reuben H. Fleet Space Theater to the House of Hospitality, were remodeled with the assistance of Casper Company. "One of the most difficult aspects of working on a historical landmark is maintaining the integrity of the historical structure while demolishing and modifying the interior to make way for building improvements," says Roger Casper.

Specializing in concrete demolition, modification, and wrecking, Casper Company was established in 1984 by Roger Casper with only three employees and three saw trucks. After struggling through the recession of 1987, Casper Company witnessed an explosion in growth and now boasts more than 130 employees and annual gross sales of more than $10 million. Roger Casper, owner and president, Bill Haithcock, vice president, and Ken Ringer, chief estimator, bring nearly 60 years of combined experience to this enterprising company.

One of Casper Company's standout sites was the renovation and beautification of La Jolla Village Square. The crew performed partial demolition of the mall to create what now resides on Villa La Jolla Drive; what was once a useless piece of property is now a viable piece of real estate. "One of the things I enjoy most about what we do is the pride we take knowing we're cleaning up San Diego," says Ken Ringer. Casper Company has also assisted in the demolition and remodeling of many buildings in the Gaslamp Quarter. In 1998 Casper Company worked on the old downtown San Diego Trust and Savings building on Broadway to remodel the interior and make way for a new Host Marriott Hotel.

Casper Company takes pride in the fact that they have a safety record that is second to none. It maintains a full-time staff safety inspector, a chief dispatcher to monitor its specialized fleet of trucks and heavy equipment, all of which are radio dispatched, and full-time supervisors present on all medium-to-large job sites.

Casper Company is a member of the Associated General Contractors Association (AGC), Engineering General Contractors Association (EGC) and the San Diego Chamber of Commerce (SDCC). It has demonstrated a continued commitment to its community relations efforts in San Diego through its participation and contribution to associations and many local charities including Habitat for Humanity, Boys and Girls Clubs, YMCA, various local churches and St. Vincent De Paul.

Casper Company has expanded its market reach to include Las Vegas, Nevada, and Phoenix, Arizona. The San Diego office is located in Spring Valley on one acre of land, housing 30 trucks and specialized equipment. As a full-service concrete cutting and demolition organization, Casper Company plans on continued growth and development to keep pace with the progress of these three cities for years to come.

Center Glass Company

Visiting Center Glass Company's modest headquarters in La Mesa, one might not guess that it has installed not only glass but also leading-edge construction materials for some of the largest and best-known buildings in San Diego. Many have won architectural design awards.

In fact, during its 35 years of existence, Center Glass has installed more glass in San Diego than any other company, says Jackson R. Witte, managing partner and CEO. The company appears each year on *Glass Magazine's* list of America's Top 50 Glazing Contractors.

Many of the most spectacular, glass-facade buildings San Diegans drive by every day are Center Glass projects. To name only a few, they include: Terminal 2 at Lindbergh Field, Children's Hospital in Kearny Mesa, Symphony Towers in downtown, UCSD Inpatient Towers in Hillcrest, the NCR building in Rancho Bernardo, and the San Diego Chargers' training facility in Mission Valley.

Center Glass Company was founded in 1963 by Jackson's father, Fred R. Witte, only a few blocks away from its current site on El Cajon Boulevard. At first, Center Glass bid on small jobs and scrambled for capital, like most start-up ventures. In the 1970s, however, the company jumped into a higher-profile position.

Center Glass found its niche as a small company that could deliver on big projects. Annual earnings for 1998 were $16 million.

Especially satisfying, says Jackson Witte, is working with talented people on exciting architectural designs that often use the latest in construction materials. For example, most people don't get excited over a new city jail. But the new San Diego County Central Jail is a 12-story, $84 million structure that opened in 1998 to rave reviews. Center Glass was the glazing subcontractor on the state-of-the-art building.

Center Glass has a fabrication facility in Spring Valley and high-profile clients in Hawaii, such as the 47-story Hawaiki Tower condominiums. But its office remains in La Mesa, home to Witte and his partners: Gary J. Vincent, president; and Ron A. Leaverton, vice president. All three started at the bottom with the company.

Center's policy of promoting its best people from the field into management has led to an unusually stable and dedicated workforce, numbering more than 100. Center Glass supports such local organizations as Handicapped Children of America, the Special Olympics, the Foundation for Disabled Firefighters, Grossmont Family YMCA, Vietnam Veterans Program, youth sports and many others.

Jackson Witte has built Center Glass Co., started by his father, Fred, into a $16 million enterprise.

(Above) Witte's partners, Gary Vincent and Ron Leaverton, started with him more than 25 years ago as field apprentices at Center Glass.

The San Diego County Central Jail, built in 1998, uses glass extensively to enhance its downtown facade. Center Glass was the glazier subcontractor.

Erreca's Inc.

Most people don't consider losing a job a good thing. However, when M.H. Golden Construction's owner pushed Charlie Erreca out the door in 1955 after years with the company, Erreca knew that he had been given a priceless gift. For six months prior, he had been working during the day for Golden and at night with his father, Joseph Erreca, with whom he had started a water truck business. Both a friend and employer, Golden

The city of Vista proclaimed Erreca's Inc. "1998 Contractor of the Year" for its redesign and widening of Vista Village Drive.

wanted to encourage the father/son team. With the understanding that if the new business didn't work out Erreca could have his job back, he handed the young entrepreneur his walking papers. Over the years, Golden Construction became one of Erreca's best customers.

It was a good time to start the business due to the amount of road construction being done in San Diego. By 1960, the company had 25 water trucks in service. However, by the mid-70s, it became apparent to both Errecas that in order for their company to continue to exist, they had to adapt to the changing world around them. In fact, it is that willingness to metamorphose that has given the company the ability to prosper in the ever-changing economic and construction environment of San Diego.

Erreca's new direction was inspired by the company's own need. In 1975, it had acquired a number of bulldozers, loaders and backhoes that it rented out to other construction companies. While regrading and improving Erreca's own site with this equipment, the father/son team realized that they enjoyed this type of work. They both got contractor's licenses in 1978 and began tackling earthwork and underground utility jobs. By 1985, the company had become one of the main excavation, demolition and grading contractors in San Diego.

Today, Erreca's builds roads, highways, retaining walls and other diverse jobs. It also has in-house divisions that specialize in bridges, underground utility work (sewer, water and storm pipes), excavation and grading. About 40 percent of the work the company does is in the public sector, including portions of Highways 54, 125, 78 and 52. It also enclosed the U-shaped Qualcomm Stadium into a bowl, created an emergency water storage structure for the Veteran's Administration Hospital in San Diego, worked on the sewage treatment plant in Miramar and various projects at California State University, San Marcos. In the private sector, the company has contracted with Pardee, Shea Homes, McMillin, Fieldstone, Pacific Bay Homes, Standard Pacific, Presley Homes, Westbrook Development, Morrow Development and Kaufman & Broad to prepare building sites for construction.

Erreca's is truly a family business, with third generation Scott Erreca now sharing the helm with his sister Charmaine Bridwell working in the office. He shares his father's excitement and enthusiasm for the challenges Erreca's will face as San Diego changes and grows.

"A company can only survive by moving up or down with the times," philosophized Charlie Erreca, now senior owner. "We're still in business after the early 90s. Many companies haven't been as fortunate as we have."

J.P. Witherow Roofing Co.

James P. Witherow was born and raised in Philadelphia, Pennsylvania. In the late 1920s, he moved to San Diego at the urging of his older sister who sold him on the opportunities that San Diego had to offer. Arriving in San Diego, Witherow secured employment with a local painting and roofing contractor as a salesperson. In 1935, unable to get a pay raise, Witherow quit his job. With start-up capital provided by a loan from his father-in-law, the J.P. Witherow Roofing Company was born. It has since flourished in the expanding San Diego community for more than 64 years.

From the beginning, Witherow knew success in the roofing business meant servicing the military as well as the commercial and residential customer. During World War II, nearly 90 percent of Witherow Roofing's focus was in support of the war effort — from defense housing in National City, Chula Vista and Camp Consair to Ryan Aircraft Company, Rohr Aircraft Company, Consolidated Aircraft Corporation and many defense-related projects. Today, Witherow Roofing continues to service the military with projects at Miramar Marine Air Station, Marine Corps Recruit Depot and Camp Pendleton.

Witherow Roofing participates in many high-profile commercial projects. During the 1990s, the company installed roofing systems on the Del Mar Racetrack Grandstand, Museum of Contemporary Art, the 1998 Lindbergh Field terminal expansion, the Civic Center, Thornton Hospital, the Viejas Casino and the 1999 San Diego Convention Center expansion. Each year also brings extensive work for various San Diego County school districts.

Witherow Roofing nurtures its commitment to the residential customer as well. The company regularly receives requests from past customers whose original roofs were installed by Witherow Roofing 30 or 40 years ago. Many times the customer is amazed when told that their original contract is still on file.

Witherow Roofing also strives to be sensitive to the needs of the community. The company has contributed time and materials to the San Diego Central Animal Shelter, the American Red Cross, Mercy Hospital and to Tijuana flood victims.

When Witherow passed away in 1986, Richard and Barbara, Witherow's children, purchased the company from the founder's estate. Although they do not know the total number of roofing systems the company has installed, it is interesting to note that in 1973 their father reported that the rapid development of San Diego had led to the installation of 50,000 roofs by his company.

Witherow Roofing received recognition in 1994 from the San Diego Better Business Bureau for being a member in good standing for more than 40 years. In 1995, *Roofing, Siding and Insulation* national magazine named the company "Roofing Contractor of the Year."

Employees have been Witherow Roofing's biggest assets. Richard and Barbara exhibited this in 1998, when four individuals were recognized for more than 30 years of service with the company.

J.P. Witherow Roofing Company continues today as the oldest and one of the most respected family-owned and operated roofing contractors in San Diego.

Founder James P. Witherow

The dedicated team behind the success enjoyed by the J.P. Witherow Roofing Co.

Steigerwald-Dougherty Inc., General Building Contractors

If quality and integrity are traits to seek when selecting a contractor, it's no wonder the team of Steigerwald-Dougherty, General Building Contractors, is successful. The list of long-term clients, who represent repeat business and referrals, is confirmation of the company's commitment to its values. And the striking, bright blue structure in the design district of Solana Beach that houses the partner's office is a testament to their talents.

David Steigerwald and Patrick Dougherty met in 1980 while working together on several projects, including the remodeling of The Fish Market in Del Mar. Recognizing their similar values and goals, they formed a partnership in 1984 and incorporated in 1985.

This San Malo, Oceanside, residence displays timeless craftsmanship.

Doing what it takes to satisfy clients, by listening to and meeting customers' needs, has earned Steigerwald-Dougherty respect and an outstanding reputation. These contractors have remodeled the same house for three or four different owners, have built homes for two generations of the same family, and have even completed four or five projects for the same client. Staying in touch with clients through all phases of construction enables them to make the experience enjoyable for everyone.

Versatility is what sets Steigerwald and Dougherty apart from other general contractors. Although they build both residential and commercial structures, their operation also includes the J.D.S. division, as well as a remodeling division, S-D Home Care, which handles smaller to midrange jobs, as well as repairs and maintenance.

Steigerwald and Dougherty perform a wide variety of tasks. From project scheduling and coordination to securing new business and delivering bids, they oversee every project. They work closely in every project with their staff to problem solve and conduct periodic quality control checks. Staying closely in touch is paramount and they make maximum use of technology to maintain optimum communication.

Supporting these two dedicated men is a highly skilled team of supervisors, office staff and subcontractors. Many of the employees have been with the company over five years, some over 15; and long-term relationships have been established with reputable subcontractors who share similar values. Steigerwald-Dougherty employees have always maintained a close family environment, even through the toughest of times.

Beyond the intrinsic rewards of appreciating their own creations, Steigerwald and Dougherty have been rewarded by the design community. In 1992 they won the *San Diego Home & Garden* House of the Year award for a home they built in La Jolla, and the company received the Lillian Rice award for a commercial project in Rancho Santa Fe.

The partners' creations can be viewed throughout Southern California, each house unique in appearance yet consistent in quality of craftsmanship. They are especially proud of building the downtown Fish Market Restaurant which, at 20,000 square feet, is one of the largest and most successful restaurants in San Diego.

Steigerwald and Dougherty plan to continue doing what they do best: listening to their customers and providing them with the highest quality materials, workmanship, and service. These are the hallmarks of Steigerwald-Dougherty, Inc.

Tower Glass Inc.

Since its inception in 1989, Tower Glass Inc. has grown to become one of San Diego County's largest and most competitive glazing contractors. Founders Barry and Evelyn Swaim have expanded the company from a small glass shop into one of the top 30 glazing contractors in the nation (as ranked by *Glass Magazine*, 1997 and 1998). The Associated General Contractors named Tower Glass the Specialty Contractor of the Year for 1998.

The management staff of Tower Glass brings over 150 years of glazing experience to its clients. Working closely with contractors, architects and owners of commercial and industrial projects, Tower Glass offers extensive knowledge of glass, aluminum and a wide variety of construction materials. This enables Tower Glass to provide information ranging from ultraviolet resistance to thermal transfer to sound attenuation, for project-specific performance levels. Its expertise secures for the customer cost-saving options while retaining aesthetic and design objectives.

Based in East County, Tower Glass engineers, fabricates and installs a wide range of standard materials, including storefronts, all types of glass, composite, aluminum and porcelain panels, window walls and curtain walls. It specializes, however, in meeting the challenges of a custom design, including canopies, sunscreens, handrails, grilles, trelliswork, skylights and many other custom fabrications.

The company continues to increase its diversity of large, demanding projects. Tower Glass installed 70,000 square feet of high-performance glass and aluminum for the new terminal at San Diego International Airport, Lindbergh Field. This required working closely with the artist to provide and install custom-designed art glass. One of its largest projects to date is the Veterans Administration Hospital in Sepulveda, California, involving 85,000 square feet of canopies, translucent skylights, composite panels, curtain wall and a window wall system with operable blinds contained in the glass.

San Diego International Airport expansion
Ed Gohlich Photography

Other projects include the Salk Institute in La Jolla, the Ontario Convention Center, the 10-story Uniden Research & Development Center in Sorrento Valley, the seven office buildings at Torrey Reserve and the 13-story San Diego Hall of Justice. Current projects include the Seaview Office Building, the Kaiser Permanente facility in Chula Vista, GEICO Insurance headquarters in Poway, and newly underway, the expansion of the San Diego Convention Center.

Tower Glass Inc. expanded during the recession of the early 90s and is committed to continued growth and prosperity. The company strives to be a source of pride and stability for its employees and to continue to provide its clients with the "craftsmanship of yesterday and the technology for tomorrow."

San Diego Hall of Justice
Photo by Wes Thompson

Investment banking and securities brokerage, insurance and diversified holding companies provide a financial foundation for a host of San Diego companies.

Partners in BUSINE

San Diego Business & Finance

American Security Mortgage	224
Arrowhead Group of Companies	226
DEFT Companies, Inc.	228
San Diego County Credit Union	230

PATRON: LA JOLLA SAVERS/HOME INVESTORS & LOAN

American Security Mortgage
A Division of U.S. Mortgage Bankers Corp.

John Olbrich, founder of American Security Mortgage, learned a lesson early in life that led him to carve out the niche that distinguishes his company. Fresh out of college, Olbrich bought his first house. Thinking he was clever, he paid all closing costs and extra points to secure a lower loan rate. He gambled on the rate being stable long enough to earn back his up-front costs. When rates dropped even lower a year later, John learned that important lesson, the one that has earned his business overwhelming success: don't pay closing costs if you don't have to.

American Security Mortgage pioneered and pursued the path of providing no-cost loans — no title, escrow or appraisal fees to the buyer. The mortgage company pays all closing costs out of its commissions, yet still offers the lowest loan rates on the market. This irresistible offer coupled with ultimate service epitomizes American Security Mortgage.

Olbrich launched American Security Mortgage in 1991 after working as a mortgage broker for several years. He began the company with the goal of providing high quality personal home loans with top quality service. His motivation derived from hearing disturbing tales clients told of "bait and switch" tactics. Brokers promised one loan rate, the client signed on, and the final papers indicated a higher rate — too late for the client to back out.

Since the majority of its clients are referrals, American Security Mortgage is committed to long-term relationships. Integrity, honesty and good old-fashioned service are the key ingredients that promise customer loyalty. Finding the best loan rates available rounds out the winning recipe. Current and previous clients are apprised of industry news and changes through a monthly newsletter, which maintains a vital connection between service provider and clientele. American Security remembers its customers even after the loan is made and business is concluded, by being available to answer questions and concerns as well as sending cards for special events and holidays. Prospective patrons are supplied with a list of references of satisfied previous loan recipients, a testament to American Security Mortgage's confidence and success.

"We listen to our customers," says Olbrich. "We find out what the customer wants and look for the product that best fits their needs." Through the use of extensive computer technology, the mortgage company does online research, investigating more than 100,000 loan programs until the right match is found for the client. "This affords us access to the lowest rates in the nation and gives us an edge," Olbrich says. Once the loan is secured, American Security opens title and escrow and walks the client through the ensuing process. If the customer does not want a no-cost loan, Olbrich and his loan officers offer other choices, explaining all available options.

With more than 20 employees, including loan officers, processors, coordinators and administrators, a client is always assured support. Olbrich rarely leaves the office, believing it is essential to be available for his customers when they need him. While he manages his staff, Olbrich also manages a

John Olbrich started American Security Mortgage to provide premium home loans with superior service.

full load of clients. Not surprisingly, his loan production in 1998 placed him in the top 1 percent of mortgage brokers in the nation, with his personal loan volume (not including loan production of his loan officers) approaching $91.5 million.

Computer technology, while a boon to American Security by offering research that was heretofore unavailable, is also fraught with perils for the consumer. As mortgage applications become available online, people are taking advantage of what they believe to be a shortcut and the lowest loan rates. Loan applicants often find, however, that these mortgages have hidden costs that they are not equipped to decipher, and that the loan rates are sometimes changed upon approval. American Security Mortgage generates loans with rates that are comparable to if not lower than computer-generated mortgages and affords the bonus of full personal services at no extra cost.

Customers enjoy this hand-holding in the comfortable and gracious offices lodged in a Victorian mansion of historical significance, built in 1906 for John Forward, mayor of San Diego. Olbrich purchased the building in the Bankers Hill area of San Diego in 1998 and restored it to its original splendor. During the Christmas holidays, the house is illuminated with thousands of lights. Rooftop reindeer, as well as a live Santa who distributes candy canes to neighborhood children, add to the festivities. The employees at American Security attempt to answer as many letters as possible from the many that get dropped in Santa's mailbox on the front lawn. The celebration, which has attracted media attention, will grow annually with additional lights and activities.

American Security also reaches out to the community through its sponsorship of a variety of causes, including the YWCA Battered Women's Shelter and the Leukemia Society. Olbrich is an active supporter of a San Diego Unified School District board member, who advocates educational improvements. Olbrich additionally serves on the board of directors for a local business that manufactures high-security dispensing machines. When he joined on, this public company was floundering. Through strategic planning and hands-on management, he and the others involved helped expand the business to successful national and international status.

Olbrich has continued to expand American Security Mortgage as well, even as mortgage rates have ridden the seesaw of real estate trends. In 1990, fixed rates were in the high 9 percent range. The next year the rates dropped and the market saw an explosion of new mortgage lenders. Then in 1994, when the rates again topped 9 percent, many of these upstart companies went out of business. American Security not only survived, but saw a surge in business that year and has grown consistently since. It did not jump in to make a quick profit when the rates dropped. Its goal was initially and has always been to serve its customers. Through its pledge to this goal and its ability to secure the best loans and the lowest rates available, American Security Mortgage is poised to ride the inevitable economic waves.

The 1906 Victorian mansion that houses the offices of American Security Mortgage

Arrowhead Group of Companies

(Above) Pat Kilkenny, chairman and CEO
Photo by Thom Mudrick

(Right) *Photo by Angelo Ecija*

The success of true entrepreneurs is often tested by their ability to be flexible — to change with time and to provide customers with new, innovative products that meet their evolving needs. Patrick Kilkenny, chairman and CEO of Arrowhead Group of Companies, fulfills this mission and has built a company where the members feel that flexibility and investment in people and technology fulfill the needs of insurance buyers. Daily, it dispels the myth of the cold and aloof insurance organization and instead, is viewed as a respected and professional insurance friend.

Arrowhead employs more than 300 people, writing more than $310 million in premium dollars. Its headquarters are located in downtown San Diego on Broadway in the Emerald Plaza.

Focused on product development, marketing and building new relationships, the Arrowhead Group

continues to distinguish itself as a leader in the property and casualty insurance industry. It is guided not only by the desire to be the lowest-cost provider of quality insurance and related products and services, but also by its commitment to the highest standards of excellence to its customers and employees.

One of the largest privately held general agencies in the United States specializing in nonstandard auto insurance, Arrowhead also markets a wide variety of other programs, including: homeowners, commercial auto, motorcycle, private passenger auto, artisan contractors, apartment, dwelling fire, mobile home, professional liability, workers' compensation and general & subcontractors insurance, to name a few.

And while Arrowhead thrives today, its success did not come overnight. Like many businesses, Arrowhead grew and evolved from a vision and the dedication of many people. Arrowhead General Insurance Agency was formed in 1983 by Classified Financial Corporation to create a general agency which would produce nonstandard personal automobile insurance in Southern California. Classified hired insurance industry veteran Kilkenny, an avid sports buff and a quick-thinking, insightful competitor, to lead its operation.

In 1984, Arrowhead's premium volume was close to $2 million; by 1998, that figure had increased by more than 1500%. The company has grown to an impressive level, however the path during the first decade and a half was not always easy. Like all growing companies, Arrowhead had its obstacles; the major one was defining its position in the industry.

Despite Arrowhead's lack of certificate of authority, capital and surplus, the company existed thanks to its close relationships with its reinsurers. With its unique ideas, a professional nimbleness, and its good sense of timing, Arrowhead used the capital brought to the table by the reinsurers to take on the risk — and reinsurers welcomed this approach because they saw profit being derived from their investment.

In 1985, Kilkenny, seeing the potential for expansion and profit, purchased what at the time was the fledgling Arrowhead General Insurance Agency. His hope was to take this infant organization and develop it into a recognizable general agency that would extend its boundaries beyond Southern California. Not having the Arrowhead name on the insurance policies nor the clout of a typical insurance enterprise, Kilkenny realized that his organization had to be not only innovative but creatively different. He then set out to establish a new breed of insurance company.

The first step was to build the organization from a distinct base, nonstandard personal auto insurance. The high-risk driver needed insurance protection; after all, it is the law in all 50 states. The standard carriers did not want to touch these "bad" drivers, so Kilkenny and Arrowhead stepped in.

As the years passed, even with the success of the various nonstandard personal auto products, Kilkenny realized that a one-product company would not make for continued growth and success. Thus began a Specialty Products division of Arrowhead to market multiple products in numerous states using various distribution systems.

Realizing that natural disasters in California frightened away the majority of homeowners insurance companies, Arrowhead began to offer an affordable homeowners product for Californians. Arrowhead also decided to write mobile home, motorcycle, apartment, commercial auto, artisan contractors, workers compensation, general contractors and subcontractors insurance programs.

Kilkenny also had the foresight to closely link Arrowhead with independent agents who contract business. At the same time, the company retained its own retail arm, Insurance Express.

Arrowhead has made a continuous commitment to give something back to the community that supports the company. It is a frequent and regular contributor to St. Vincent de Paul charitable activities in San Diego, donates to local YMCAs and hosts several blood drives each year for the American Red Cross. Arrowhead also sponsors food drives to benefit other local agencies assisting the homeless.

During the past 16 years, key employees have also had the opportunity to acquire approximately one-third of the shares in Arrowhead. When the additional profit centers were established, equity positions for division presidents were also created. Further, a profit-sharing system has been set up to include all of Arrowhead's tenured employees.

As for the future, Kilkenny's plans revolve around both product and geographic expansion. The Specialty division will see an increase in homeowners insurance from coast to coast. It will also offer a new homeowners product for coastal properties in the East Coast and Gulf states. Often unable to find reasonable insurance due to fears of hurricane and windstorm claims by large carriers, these consumers will now have peace of mind through Arrowhead's insurance protection.

Arrowhead also hopes to fill the void placed on California consumers who cannot obtain earthquake insurance coverage. Recognizing that the economy of insurance is now on more of a global scale, Kilkenny also plans to work with more multi-national companies and serve consumers worldwide. He will also expand Internet access for the review and purchase of Arrowhead products.

In fall of 1998, Arrowhead collaborated with longtime partner Clarendon National Insurance Company to become an insurer. This partnership created Sorrento Insurance, which, under the Arrowhead Group of Companies, will provide consumers with another option for automobile insurance and possibly other programs in the future.

Arrowhead's innovation will continue to take on many forms, from products to sales to distribution. With Kilkenny's guidance, Arrowhead will develop and engage in new opportunities in order to grow and serve its customers even further.

Corporate headquarters at Emerald Plaza
Photo by Thom Mudrick

Partners In San Diego

DEFT Companies, Inc.

"The only thing that counts in today's business is a strong financial answer," states Joseph F. Dau, CEO of DEFT Companies, Inc. "Businesses always are asking, 'Where can we find the funds?'"

Since 1981, DEFT Companies, Inc., part of the Nevada Investment Trust, has secured millions of dollars in funding for businesses in San Diego and throughout the United States. Its areas of expertise include business project financing, major business loans, direct equipment leasing and debt financing syndication.

DEFT Companies was founded by businessman and financier, Joseph F. Dau, a longtime San Diego resident and businessman. Dau was born in Chicago and studied business, finance and law at several colleges and universities in the midwest. A man ahead of his time, he is credited with the invention and market introduction of "Rovafone," the world's first cordless telephone.

(Below and opposite page) DEFT Companies has secured millions of dollars in funds for San Diego businesses to purchase or lease equipment including machine tools, manufacturing systems, computer systems, embroidery machines, injection molding machines, printing equipment and commercial vehicles.

Dau has been involved in raising money for companies all of his life. DEFT Companies' philosophy, "the harder you work, the luckier you get," comes from his own business background. In business, Dau was always willing to take the financial liability and risk but demanded that those working with him achieve results. His experience taught him that people who develop and believe in business goals turn them into realities.

DEFT custom tailors financial transactions; all loan requests are approved on an individual basis. Backed by a team of highly experienced financial professionals including financiers, bankers, business developers, and specialists in equipment manufacturing and leasing as well as the most advanced data processing system in the leasing industry, DEFT Companies is becoming one of the largest finance and leasing companies based in California. Its Web pages have brought business from throughout the world.

Project Financing

DEFT Companies has established fluid relationships with major financial intermediaries, private-placement investor pools, institutional-fund providers and conventional-lending institutions. DEFT Companies also acts as a primary lending institution. Its specialists carefully review submitted projected business plans and evaluate the possibility of sourcing low-cost financing. If the financing is accepted, lines-of-approach are then discussed to induce financiers or lenders. In some circumstances, DEFT Companies will extend its industry-specific support team to help the customer's long-term relationships with investors, on which the project's success depends.

Equipment Financing And Leasing

DEFT Companies believes that in most circumstances, leasing equipment makes smart financial sense. Profits come from equipment use, not equipment ownership, therefore leasing preserves capital. With equipment leasing there are minimum up-front outlays; this protects bank credit lines for income producing needs such as salaries and production inventory. In many cases, leases are 100 percent tax-deductible and can protect the user from obsolescence of equipment such as computers and manufacturing equipment. As a private lending company, DEFT Companies is able to customize lease payment plans to meet specific clients' needs, even taking into account seasonal "slow periods."

The type of equipment that DEFT Companies has helped to finance spans a broad range. It includes rail cars, MRI systems, medical research equipment, electronic manufacturing systems, water purification equipment, computer systems, machine tools, trucks, tractor trailers, embroidery machines, injection molding machines, printing equipment and major manufacturing equipment.

CIRCO…CSFX®

A division of DEFT Companies, CIRCO is the world's leading manufacturer and lessor of specialty lined liquid hazardous chemical containers: rail tank cars, oceangoing ISO Inter-modal containers and tank trailers. Its Web site has pages of information for world users of the lined liquid containers.

The CIRCO division of DEFT is always concerned with the danger of a hazardous chemical spill due to manufacture defects: a pinhole in a tank lining, a poorly welded seam or improper lining inspections. Although there have been hazardous spills from other types of liquid containers, CIRCO, due to its high inspection qualities, has yet to have a spill accident due to a fault from its lined containers. CIRCO…CSFX® has researched and developed a highly qualified lined tank container that can withstand the impact, high temperature, internal pressures, vigorous cleaning and corrosive chemicals to which lined tanks are exposed.

CIRCO-CSFX®'s Operating Lease Programs allow the customer to use a specially-lined rail tank car, tank trailer, or ISO Inter-modal container for as long as is necessary without the high cost of purchasing the equipment or period inspections. Since these containers receive heavy abuse, the operating lease service assures a higher degree of safety in transporting potentially dangerous chemicals.

Recently, the holding company of DEFT Companies, Nevada Investment Trust, gave birth to a third company, The Mort Grp, a full service mortgage and real estate company providing funds and marketing for both residential and commercial mortgages and equity loans. This mortgage company is headed up by experienced personnel who secure property loans nationwide. The addition of The Mort Grp gives DEFT Companies a greater lending spectrum.

DEFT Companies has opened offices throughout the United States and found that having its offices centrally located in San Diego is the best of all worlds. DEFT Companies' future is indeed bright. In 1998 the company processed over $200 million in transactions, asset-based loans and leases.

DEFT Companies' upcoming plans include increased railcar, hazardous liquid container leasing and manufacturing with additional commercial/ manufacturing loans and leases. The yearly funding of DEFT Companies will soon reach the billion-dollar mark.

DEFT Companies is in the business of finding funds for companies to use in development, expansion, and operating capital. There are thousands of companies today that owe their existence and success to DEFT Companies. As such, DEFT Companies plays an integral part in the growth of San Diego.

San Diego County Credit Union

San Diego County Credit Union is a billion-dollar financial institution whose heritage is steeped in a long line of members and their families. It is the largest locally owned credit union in San Diego County and ranks first in assets on a county-wide scale.

Unlike banks or savings and loans organizations, San Diego County Credit Union (SDCCU) is a not-for-profit institution that is wholly owned and operated by its members. It was founded in 1938 by a handful of local government employees who were frustrated over their inability to obtain loans from traditional banking systems.

The group originally named itself the San Diego County Employees' Credit Union. Its purpose was to provide peers and colleagues with small loans and basic deposit accounts. Decades later, however, the organization opened its doors to entities outside of local government, giving more San Diegans a new alternative in banking. By the early 1970s the credit union modified its name to reflect a much broader membership and wider range of services.

Since then, San Diegans have taken pride and comfort in the organization's affordable loans, higher dividend rates and free banking services. There are no stockholders, which means gains are returned entirely to the membership in the form of superior dividend rates, innovative home banking services and convenient branch locations.

Over a half-century ago, SDCCU operated from only a single office on Mildred Street in Linda Vista. That structure is part of a growing 16-branch network serving 120,000 members throughout greater San Diego County as of mid-1999. Much of the organization's success stems from SDCCU's ability to balance growth with myriad of new services it frequently introduces.

The institution, now headquartered in Sorrento Mesa, consists of a volunteer board of directors and an executive staff that includes a president/CEO and five executive vice presidents. In total, SDCCU employs more than 400 people, each of whom carries the torch for providing unparalleled, personalized service for serving their members' financial needs. The credit union today offers everything from insured savings and money market accounts to automobile loans and leasing, individual retirement accounts and even free financial counseling.

The organization constantly examines ways to make its services even more affordable while tailoring the operation to better suit the needs of its members. Regular checking accounts are free with direct deposit; electronic home banking services are complimentary; and most credit cards carry no annual fees. Additionally, each branch office is fully staffed and in mid-1999 there were more than 170 automated teller machines in key locations throughout the county.

SDCCU's established presence and credibility have attracted a kind of community loyalty that other companies rarely achieve. For instance, SDCCU's checking account market share is one of the highest within the western region of the United States. In the third quarter of 1999, about 65 percent of the membership had checking accounts with SDCCU, and nearly 45 percent of the membership enjoyed competitive interest rates on the Visa credit cards SDCCU offers.

A group of SDCCU employees makes time for a quick photo before taking part in a paint and landscape project for the United Way's Hands-On San Diego program.

The ease with which individuals and companies manage their finances through SDCCU has also netted high scores from reader polls and member surveys. In 1996, it was rated No.1 for service leadership among credit unions nationwide by *Callahan's Credit Union Report*. In 1997, it was voted No. 1 in service by *The San Diego Union-Tribune*. It also retained the top rating in assets among other credit unions in the *1998-99 San Diego Business Journal's "Book of Lists."*

Through frequent surveys, SDCCU management discovered that three-quarters of the membership considered SDCCU to be their primary financial institution. Equally impressive is that 96 percent of its members consistently report being "very satisfied" to "satisfied" with the credit union's overall services and products.

Growth and popularity, however, came steadily in its first 40 years. With the mid-1970s came a legion of new biotech firms, major hospitals and large organizations, which raised SDCCU's asset level. The membership also came to include San Diego County and its growing municipalities, such as Santee, Poway, Del Mar, Carlsbad and Encinitas.

By the 1990s, under the direction of President and CEO Rod Calvao, SDCCU began experiencing its most dramatic growth, moving from $300 million in assets to over $1 billion. Global companies like Science Applications International Corporation and QUALCOMM, for example, began choosing SDCCU as their primary banking source for their employees as did scores of individuals from San Diego's expanding population.

The technological boom that occurred at SDCCU in the late 1980s made it particularly easy for new members to conduct business with the credit union. In 1986 it introduced TouchTone Teller service, which allows members to use their telephones to make transactions.

The greatest strides in home banking were made shortly afterward when SDCCU expanded onto the Internet. In keeping with national competition, the organization offers free, user-friendly banking services via an interactive Web site. Members can make payments, inquire about their account balances, view their transaction histories or track stock investments directly from their personal computers.

The credit union pays close attention to its members' needs and to the community at large, combining monetary support with team participation for numerous charitable events. For instance, as a regular sponsor of the United Way's Hands-On San Diego program, dozens of SDCCU employees turn out each year with paintbrushes and shovels to help beautify community centers or landscape little league baseball fields. SDCCU is also a major sponsor of the annual Multiple Sclerosis Walk, which typically draws hundreds of SDCCU employees and their families in helping to raise money or work the event.

The community spirit at SDCCU extends generously to other popular events and organizations such as the Holiday Bowl, the Make-A-Wish Foundation and various chambers of commerce.

San Diego County Credit Union has become a financial cornerstone for an area that is defined by its diverse population and continual growth. The prestigious standard it sets in alternative banking remains unsurpassed. Like with many past generations it has served, the credit union is helping today's members build their futures with even greater confidence and financial security. It is a model organization that remains strongly etched in San Diego's economic portrait.

The Encinitas branch pictured here is among the growing number of SDCCU sites located throughout the county. Each varies in architectural design.

As a center for entertainment, culture and spectator sports, San Diego attracts international visitors and provides year-round leisure activities.

Partners in
ENTERT

San Diego ENTERTAINMENT

Fireworks & Stage FX America, Inc.	234
San Diego Film Commission	236
San Diego Hall of Champions	240
Balloon Flights, LLC	242
San Diego Sports Arena	243

Fireworks & Stage FX America, Inc.

As the lights go down an expectant murmur moves through the stands. All eyes turn toward the blackened sky. The music begins and pink, gold and red flowers of fire burst in the air. It's show time! And no one puts on a better show than Fireworks America.

Fireworks America is unique in the fireworks industry. Started by an investment group of pyrotechnicians, the company has received international recognition for its precision, outstanding visual effects, innovative show design and artistry in presenting some of the finest fireworks and pyrotechnic displays ever seen. At Fireworks America people make the difference. Its goal is a simple one: provide the best people with the best products to produce the best show for its clients.

The choreography of an outdoor fireworks display, like a dance performance, involves the careful arrangement of fireworks to enhance and heighten the mood and beat of the music. A good show designer uses light and sound to manipulate emotion. Fireworks America's artists draw on their extensive experience with audio systems, computer-firing systems, and knowledge of the characteristic effects of

thousands of aerial shells and pyrotechnic devices to create breathtaking, inspiring and exciting shows.

Show design actually begins with the creation of a soundtrack. The music is digitally edited into a seamless whole. Once completed, the designer visualizes fireworks shells and effects that will complement the mood and flow of the music. Then the actual firing commands are digitally recorded on the same soundtrack to ensure precision in the sky. The end result is that the shells explode in the air in time with the music, painting the sky with color as the show builds to an emotional climax.

Evidence of the company's excellence is found in its client list and events that include the KGB

Skyshow, SeaWorld California, the San Diego Padres, Six Flags Magic Mountain, Paramount's Great America in Santa Clara, Thunderboats on the Bay and the San Diego Symphony. Each year, Fireworks America performs over 2,000 indoor and outdoor shows nationally and internationally.

Fireworks America is equally renowned for its indoor and proximate (theatrical) pyrotechnics and special effects. The company has done thousands of weddings, promotional meetings, conventions, stage shows, musical productions, major concert tours, movies, television productions and professional sporting events. Known as an innovator in the field, it is constantly developing new techniques and trying new ideas for the best effects possible.

Fireworks America is dedicated not only to presenting a high-quality show but also to the safety of its workers and viewers. The company has an outstanding safety record and conducts annual training seminars to upgrade its employees' technical and product knowledge, safety skills and to provide hands-on experience. Fireworks America also holds training seminars for fire service personnel to assist them in regulating the industry.

Its commitment to the community is evident in the numerous school and charity events in which Fireworks America participates. One of the charities close to the company's heart is the San Diego Burn Institute and the work it does in educating the public on the dangers of setting off fireworks at home.

The people at Fireworks America are passionate about their work. It's hard to believe that anyone loves a good fireworks display more than they do. One of the pyrotechnicians summed it up. "I feel like the director of a stage production when I do a show. The fireworks are the performers and they create magic in the sky."

San Diego Film Commission

San Diego is camera-ready and film-friendly thanks to the enthusiastic efforts of the San Diego Film Commission. This nonprofit economic development program, established in 1976, is solely responsible for attracting and servicing companies that produce television series and made-for-TV movies, feature films, commercials, documentaries, corporate films, music videos and print advertising in the city of San Diego, the San Diego Unified Port District and San Diego County.

The genesis of the film commission dates back to 1974 when the producers of the television show,

Russian "sleeper" spies take a suspenseful ride on the San Diego trolley with FBI man Roy Parmenter, played by Sidney Poitier. Columbia Pictures' taut drama of espionage and family honor, *Little Nikita,* was filmed on location in San Diego in 1987 and directed by Richard Benjamin.

"Harry O," chose San Diego in which to film the series. After meeting many challenges in getting the necessary permits and finding it overly difficult and expensive, the producers returned to Los Angeles to film. Closing down Broadway, for example, required that the police, fire department, streets division, property department and city attorney's office be contacted and permits be obtained, which proved time-consuming and costly. In addition, there was no Screen Actors Guild office in San Diego, so extras had to come from Los Angeles, thereby generating additional costs.

Several San Diegans who had been connected to "Harry O," and other local film industry business professionals, expressed their concern about losing the production and appealed to Mayor Pete Wilson. The group had the brainchild of creating an office that would be a one-stop shop to issue permits and be a central clearinghouse, making San Diego a welcome alternative to Hollywood. After two years in the making, the San Diego Film Commission became a reality. It was housed in the offices of the San Diego Chamber of Commerce and remained there until 1997 when, with the assistance and support of Mayor Susan Golding, it moved to its own location and became an independent, nonprofit California corporation.

Although financed by the government, the commission is sanctioned by the International Association of Film Commissions and has its own board of directors and bylaws. It began with a budget of $70,000 and one employee, and by 1998 a staff of eight had a budget of more than $800,000. Funded by the transient occupancy tax from hotels, approximately 90 percent of the budget comes from the city of San Diego, while the county and port districts contribute the rest. For every dollar supplied by the city, however, the commission's efforts bring back $98 in economic returns. In 1998 the commission tracked $77 million that had been spent by crews in San Diego as a result of all film production. Strong government and community support has empowered the film commission to fulfill its mission: to market, attract, facilitate and permit film, video and print production.

Having a film commission to entice production companies and troubleshoot their operations while in San Diego has more than direct financial impact on the city. San Diego benefits by increased exposure that, in turn, boosts tourism. Often film companies make improvements that can leave private homes or public locations in a better condition than they were before. Jobs are created for local actors and others associated with the industry, while businesses such as hotels and restaurants enjoy free advertising and extra business.

The San Diego Film Commission has been a trendsetter for other film commissions, as evidenced by being the first to have a billboard on Sunset Boulevard in Hollywood advertising the San Diego region as a filming destination. As one of the first film commissions in the world, the San Diego Film Commission is highly successful in an extremely competitive field. In 1998 San Diego ranked third in television production behind New York and Los Angeles, and second in California behind Hollywood for all film production.

San Diego is attractive to film companies for three principal reasons: the location is versatile — with its zoos, beaches, mountains and desert, San Diego can look like any number of places ranging from Hawaii to Florida (13 of the 17 worldwide climate zones exist in San Diego); cooperation between government and community is simplified since the commission handles all permits; and the filming costs are competitive because the commission works diligently to give the producers what they want and still meet production budgets. For example, with more than 1,000 San Diego SAG members, producers do not have to hire actors and crews from Los Angeles, thus saving travel and hotel expenses.

Cathy Anderson, film commissioner and CEO, is the dynamo who has significantly built the film production market in San Diego. Having received both her bachelor's degree in theater arts and her master's degree in telecommunications and film at San Diego State University, Anderson joined the commission in 1986 with 15 years of experience producing, directing and acting. After expanding the print advertising division, she put her energy into television. She is credited with streamlining the permitting system, which was a primary factor in drawing more production business to San Diego.

When Anderson heard that Stu Segall Productions was looking for a location to film a new prime-time series, "Silk Stalkings," she did her homework and drew the show to San Diego, beating out the company's first choice of Florida. Since 1990, Stu Segall has also used San Diego to film "Renegade," "Push," "Pensacola," "Vanishing Son" and several made-for-TV movies. Over an eight-year period, he has brought more than $600 million into the local economy.

The television division of the film commission continues to grow and has seen the productions of many series including "Simon & Simon," "One West Waikiki," "Nightman," and "Unsolved Mysteries," and the made-for-TV movies, "The Tiger Woods Story," "1,000 Men and a Baby" and "What Love Sees."

Although not yet as lucrative as television production, several feature-film companies have shot all or part of their movies in the San Diego region, including *Top Gun, Jurassic Park: The Lost World, True Lies, K-9* and *The Hunt for Red October.* Independent, low-budget films also account for steady filming,

A stunt scene from the 1995 feature film, *Ripper Man,* shot on location in San Diego by Tanglewood Productions, starring Michael Norris, directed by Aaron Norris

Reunited at the Hotel Del Coronado for the 25th anniversary of the release of the 1959 classic film, *Some Like It Hot,* are director Billy Wilder and stars Tony Curtis and Jack Lemmon.

Director Richard Rush is shown here on location at the La Jolla Cove for *The Stunt Man*, his one-of-a-kind drama/suspense/ romance about a mysterious fugitive who becomes a stunt man for a flamboyant director. *The Stunt Man* was filmed in 1980 for 20th Century Fox, starring Peter O'Toole, Steve Railsback and Barbara Hershey.

while commercials such as those featuring Nike, IBM, Taylor Made Golf, Chrysler and Snapple products regularly employ San Diego as a production location.

Anderson and her staff are on call 24 hours a day and have a diverse set of duties. "What makes this business so complex is that we have several customers: the film customer (the client), the government customer (the supporter), the community customer and the free-lancer. We have a different pitch for each customer," Anderson says, "and we have to keep them all happy."

Inviting production companies to shoot in San Diego is the initial phase of the commission's responsibilities. After a location manager chooses San Diego, the commission works directly with the visiting company to facilitate its production. At any one time there may be hundreds of projects shooting, and the film commission attempts to be involved in as many as possible.

In order to solicit business, the commission staff reads *The Hollywood Reporter* and *Daily Variety* to keep abreast of the entertainment industry and find out what's in development. Additionally, the commission conducts a national advertising campaign in these same publications and others to attract new business, using slogans like "Hollywood ought to sneak a peek in their own backyard." Participation in the film industry trade shows "Location Expo" and "ShowBiz Expo" offer additional exposure for San Diego as a filming destination. Staff members from the commission have attended several film festivals, such as Sundance and Cannes, which gain the commission increased visibility, new contacts and film projects.

Anderson and her staff are thorough when investigating what producers are looking for and determining how to meet their needs. Sometimes a package with photos of opportune locations and costs are sent to location managers and producers, resulting in several discussions. When a company does decide to shoot in San Diego, the film commission schedules a round-table meeting for everyone connected with the production. The script is broken down to anticipate and address all permit needs and any potential problems. Safety, liability and community issues are investigated and resolved. Representatives from the sheriff's department, the California Highway Patrol (CHP), and the police and fire departments may be present along with the director, production manager, location manager, special-effects person and anyone else concerned. The round-table process has proven to be an efficient and concise way to liaison all parties impacted by the filming and to issue all permits at one time.

Once a project is in production, the commission may be called upon to address a multitude of challenges and crises and to negotiate solutions to everyone's satisfaction. On one occasion, when a script called for an actor to jump from the Coronado Bridge, the commission worked with all jurisdictions associated with the bridge — the city of San Diego, the city of Coronado, Caltrans, the CHP, the Harbor Police, the Coast Guard and the FAA. If a company wants to film on either side of the Mexican border, the commission can assist with locations, work permits, passports and customs requirements.

The commission produces several publications that assist in the filming process. Two booklets instruct homeowners in how to present their property if they have an interest in offering their home as a location. Another invaluable publication is the annual *Film &Video Resource Guide*, which lists a wide range of locations suitable for filming, as well as more than 1,500 listings of qualified local crews, services and products connected to the film and video industry. The guide is given out to every film inquiry and at trade shows, and it is also sold at community bookstores. In addition, the commission maintains a library displaying more than 30,000 pictures of San Diego regional locations that can be sent to producers looking for specific sites.

In November 1998, the San Diego Film Commission hosted its first annual awards banquet, "Behind the Screens." Created to reward and showcase many of those who have enabled the commission to operate successfully, the formal event was set up like a Hollywood movie set. Those honored included sheriff and police representatives, an Oceanside councilwoman and Four Square Productions, a San Diego film production company.

The San Diego Film Commission enjoys offering opportunities to students from San Diego college and university film and telecommunications departments to gain real-world experience. The interns answer phones, scout, visit sets, prepare packages for customers, read and break down scripts, paste up location pictures and answer letters. The students often get jobs as a result of their internships. The film commission offers scholarships to film students and participates in career days at San Diego schools that show an interest in the entertainment industry. In 1997 the commission donated scholarship money to the National Academy of Television Arts and Sciences for aspiring young filmmakers. Occasionally the commission hosts movie screenings and wrap parties to benefit various charities.

In 1998 the San Diego Regional Film Advisory Council was formed by the film commission. It consists of a panel of community leaders from incorporated and unincorporated areas with the goal of attracting film production to all areas of San Diego County. The commission's intention in creating the council was to educate community leaders on the advantages of having film production in their communities; to advise them of the needs of the film industry; and to encourage the different communities to work together to create a countywide, uniform permit procedure that would allow filmmakers to shoot at any location in any jurisdiction with the same permit and procedure.

Through its ambitious accomplishments, the San Diego Film Commission continues to strengthen the San Diego economy by creating jobs, stimulating spending, supporting the local production community and showcasing San Diego as the ideal filming destination. Its outstanding achievements and continued growth during its more than two decades of operation are convincing more and more filmmakers to consider San Diego as their next location destination and to make the San Diego Film Commission their first call.

An on-set action shot from Stu Seagall Productions' episodic television series, "Silk Stalkings," originally starring Rob Estes as Chris Lorenzo and Mitzi Kapture as Rita Lee Lance, two homicide detectives with a sense of style who solve high-profile crimes of passion
Photo by Chris Canole

San Diego Hall of Champions

The San Diego Hall of Champions moved into its new home in the renovated Federal Building in Balboa Park in 1999. *Illustration by David Gerken*

The San Diego Hall of Champions is more than a treasure trove of sports memorabilia; it is a place where stirring stories come to life and the special place sports occupies in our society comes to light. It is more than a museum of athletic accomplishments; it is a reflection of a community, its heritage and values. It is more than a pantheon of hometown heroes; it is a living monument to people with dreams and the drive, dedication and determination to make them come true. The role models celebrated here are not only professional athletes and coaches, but stars who went on to distinguish themselves in other walks of life.

The mission of the Hall of Champions is "to promote, recognize and preserve athletic achievement for the purpose of inspiring individuals of all ages to reach their full potential." True to that goal, it is both a sports museum and an active outreach organization. For more than half a century, it has honored champions and encouraged participation and the pursuit of excellence. Now housed in the renovated Federal Building, its third home among the museums and other cultural attractions in Balboa Park, the Hall celebrates the individuals, teams, moments and memories that have made sports an integral part of life in San Diego. Its exhibits and events are intended to entertain and educate, tell uplifting stories, stimulate active imaginations and teach lifetime lessons.

What grew into the Hall of Champions began as the Breitbard Athletic Foundation in 1946. Bob Breitbard, who graduated from Hoover High School with Baseball Hall of Famer Ted Williams in 1937 and from San Diego State in 1941, coached at both schools and then joined his three brothers (Ed, Will and Al) after World War II in what had been their father's business, California Linen and Laundry Supply. In making the difficult decision to leave coaching, which he loved, Bob enlisted his brothers' support for a foundation that would honor local athletes. Breitbard remained a pillar of the San Diego community — he built the Sports Arena, owned the Gulls of the Western Hockey League and the Rockets of the National Basketball Association, served as a longtime and influential board member of the Greater San Diego Sports Association (now the San Diego International Sports Council) and many other organizations, and mentored countless other civic leaders. All the while, he kept emphasizing the core values and expanding the vision and good works of the foundation and later the Hall of Champions.

Baseball Hall of Famer Ted Williams (left) and Hall of Champions Founder/President Emeritus Bob Breitbard were classmates at Hoover High School, class of 1937, and have remained close friends ever since. *Photo by Thom Vollenweider*

Star of the Month awards were bestowed, beginning in September 1946. Starting in 1948, Stars of the Year were selected from among the Stars of the Month. In 1953, the Breitbard Hall of Fame was established to honor San Diego athletes, amateur and professional, for their career accomplishments. It became the centerpiece of the Hall of Champions and the prestigious local honor for San Diego athletes.

In 1959, Breitbard arranged for space in Balboa Park and established the Hall of Champions as a nonprofit sports museum. He had begun collecting artifacts to commemorate the achievements of local athletes: a bat Ted Williams used to hit .406 in 1941, a racket Maureen Connolly used to win Wimbledon, legendary boxing champion Archie Moore's gloves and robe from a light-heavyweight title fight and the bathing suit Florence Chadwick wore while swimming the English Channel. "I wanted to put them someplace where the whole community could see and enjoy them," Breitbard said.

The first Hall of Champions opened January 10, 1961. In 1983, an enlarged and improved edition was relocated to the Casa de Balboa. In 1999, the Hall nearly tripled in size, moving to a magnificent new home in the renovated Federal Building. With 70,000 square feet on three levels, the Hall now has architecture and exhibits to match the soaring spirit of the champions it celebrates. It was designed not just to showcase artifacts, but to highlight the compelling sagas, human qualities and enduring dramas of the people and events that helped make San Diego, as *Sports Illustrated* once called it, "Sports Town, USA."

The Federal Building, a designated San Diego Historical Site, was built in 1935 for the California Pacific International Exposition and housed the exhibits of the federal government. The exterior, decorated in a Mayan motif based on the ancient Palace of Governors at Uxmal, was painstakingly preserved in the renovation. Used for many years as a single-story gymnasium for badminton, table tennis, volleyball and other activities, the building was the training home of the Olympic medal-winning U.S. Men's and Women's Volleyball teams from 1981 through 1996.

The current Hall of Champions was designed to feature interactive exhibits and dynamic displays. The spectacular center court and other flexible, functional spaces increased the Hall's opportunities to host topical touring and temporary exhibits that examine current events as well as historical milestones, and to extend the community outreach of the organization with clinics, sports-themed expositions and special events. The Stephen & Mary Birch Education and Resource Center has expanded the Hall's archival, research and outreach capabilities.

In the image of its founder, Bob Breitbard, the Hall of Champions is really a tribute to the traits that define winners, on and off the playing field, and the value of sports. It is about the unity and identity that champions bring to a community, the magic moments and shared memories they create and the lessons they instill.

San Diego Padres relief pitcher Trevor Hoffman
Photo by Kent Horner

Former Football star Marcus Allen
Photo by Kent Horner

Partners In San Diego

Balloon Flights, LLC

Over 200 years ago in September 1783, a sheep, a duck and a rooster had the dubious honor of being the first creatures to travel in a hot air balloon. In Paris two months later, two French noblemen became the first humans to travel by balloon. The flight lasted 22 minutes, drifting over the rooftops of Paris before landing in a vineyard. Legend has it that the noblemen had to placate irate local farmers with champagne — a tradition that has become part of the ballooning experience.

Ballooning came to North America in January 1793 when Jean-Pierre Blanchard piloted a balloon over Philadelphia. Ballooning went on to play a part in the Civil War, when both sides used hydrogen balloons for airborne reconnaissance.

Since that time, ballooning has made its way into the realm of adventure and fun via modern-day enthusiasts who began flying in Nebraska during the 1960s. Ballooning caught on in the next decade, becoming the hobby of choice for many young adventurers. Del Mar proved to have some of the best wind and weather conditions in the country, meaning that balloonists were able to fly in the late afternoon, as well as enjoying the more usual early morning flights. With their quiet, majestic silhouettes, hot air balloons enjoy a mystique of their own.

By 1979, hot air ballooning in Del Mar had developed into a small cottage-type industry. But the 1980s saw a shift to more commercially run enterprises. By 1988-89 there were as many as 11 companies flying in the area.

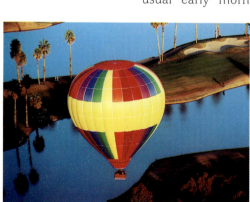

Balloon Flights, LLC started flying in early 1997. Established by seasoned Del Mar balloon pilots, the company flies four balloons. Each balloon is able to carry between eight and 14 people, and because of the nearly ideal weather conditions in San Diego, the balloons have been able to fly an average of 310-320 days per year.

The pilots are in the business because they love what they do. Phil Simpson, head of the company and the executive manager, loves to fly and is one of the senior pilots. Frank Reed, chief pilot with Balloon Flights, LLC has been flying for 19 years and plans to continue for quite some time. He started his flying days in Alaska and has flown over 3,000 flights and 30,000 people so far. All pilots and balloons are FAA tested and regulated.

Balloons are usually thought of as being peaceful and passive, but the experience of hot air ballooning is one of exhilaration and fun. Often seen as a once-in-a-lifetime experience, people give gifts of balloon flights to each other for birthdays, graduations, and of course, weddings. The average balloon flight is 45-50 minutes. There is, however, a story about a vertigo-stricken groom who asked that the balloon be let down as soon as the wedding vows were exchanged. Total flight time was a record 12 minutes. But it is something he will never forget, for which Balloon Flights, LLC aims. All flights are followed by a champagne celebration picnic on the ground while the crew packs everything up.

An "atmosphere" business, ballooning adds an ambience to the whole San Diego area. As subtle as the sound of the sea and the beauty of the sunsets, hot air balloons over Del Mar are an integral part of the visual legacy of San Diego. It is a tradition that Balloon Flights, LLC takes pride in continuing.

San Diego Sports Arena

The official attendance was 11,692 on November 17, 1966, when the San Diego Gulls of the Western Hockey League won their home opener, four goals to one. Their victims were the Seattle Totems and the result was particularly nice since, locally, professional ice hockey had been absent for 16 years. However, in deference to the old sports cliches, winning wasn't "everything" nor was it "the only thing." That night, beyond the box score, the people of San Diego realized a greater, more enduring sports achievement: the birth of the 14,500-seat San Diego International Sports Arena.

The $6.4 million, state-of-the-art facility rested on 38 acres of the underdeveloped Midway-Frontier area. Five acres were devoted to the structure itself, while the remaining 33 housed the 4,500-car parking lot. The visionary behind the Sports Arena was local native Robert Breitbard, a football hero at Hoover High and San Diego State University, who cemented his legend by founding the popular Hall of Champions in Balboa Park in 1961.

Breitbard's mission and purpose was to bring professional sports and entertainment to a state-of-the-art, multiuse venue. This plan proved successful as the Gulls, the original tenant of the Sports Arena, later shared the facility with the Rockets of the National Basketball Association (who relocated to Houston), the San Diego Clippers, the 10-time Major Indoor Soccer League champion San Diego Sockers and teams in the old American Basketball Association as well as the current San Diego Gulls of the West Coast Hockey League. All of these franchises provided memorable sports moments at the building, but none topped the individual accomplishment of local boxer Ken Norton. In 1973, before a capacity crowd, the underdog Norton defeated Muhammad Ali by split-decision to become world champion of boxing. It was an upset for the ages, made shocking by the rare sight of Ali's swollen face and broken jaw.

Each year the building relies on its reputation for excellent sight lines, flexible configurations and its central location in San Diego to attract an average of more than 170 events. Additionally, a 1997 interior and exterior renovation, along with plans to add retail and development to the site, make the arena an attractive destination for promoters, teams and performers.

San Diegans have attended a range of shows and concerts including the 1999 $1.4 million grossing

San Diego's Place for Entertainment

Andrea Bocelli concert, the musical brilliance of Luciano Pavarotti and Garth Brooks, the family fun of the Ringling Bros. and Barnum & Bailey Circus and the Harlem Globetrotters, and the brash outrageousness of monster-truck rallies and professional wrestling. Amphitheater-type concerts and Kobey's Swap Meets are also major attractions that management added to keep the facility visible and active.

Staying an active and vital part of the community is a strength of the Sports Arena. Evolution has been kind, as it has gone from a one-tenant venue to "San Diego's Place for Entertainment." Though the word "international" is gone from the area signage, the Sports Arena is San Diego County's pre-eminent large-scale, all-purpose facility.

In addition to providing an astounding variety of goods for individuals and industry, manufacturing and distribution companies provide employment for San Diego area residents.

Partners in
MANU

San Diego Manufacturing & Distribution

John Lenore Company	246
Logret Import and Export Company	250
BF Goodrich Aerospace/Aerostructures Group	252
RPM Material Handling Co.	254
Deering Banjo Company	256
Pacific Sportswear Co., Inc.	258
Palomar Mountain Spring Water	260
Solar Turbines Incorporated	262
Flag Crafters, Inc.	264
Taylor Guitars	265
Babe's, Inc	266
Central Meat & Provision Company	267
Daily Marine	268
Plastic Display Products	270
Rhino Linings USA, Inc.	271

PATRON: FABRICATION TECHNOLOGIES INDUSTRIES, INC.

John Lenore Company

"*In this country* you can be whatever you want to be. If you want to work hard enough. The John Lenore Company was founded and endures on that principle." The engraving under the large photograph of Lenore's grandparents in the reception room goes on to say, "Taught by Pietra and Antonio de Chiazza, maternal grandparents of John P. Lenore."

John Lenore took that belief to heart at a young age. With a talent for predicting consumer trends, strong creative instincts, a gift for innovative niche marketing ideas, and the courage to stand behind his convictions, Lenore has become one of the most influential beverage distributors in California.

Lenore was born in Wheeling, West Virginia, to a family that had nothing but hope. His mother was widowed at the age of 21, at the height of the Depression, so his Sicilian grandparents helped to raise Lenore and his three siblings. It was a staunch Democrat, Union and Catholic family; their beliefs made him strong and self-sufficient. During World War II, at the age of 14, Lenore joined a section gang on the Baltimore & Ohio Railroad to support himself. He worked summers and weekends during the school year putting in rails, ties and working in the tunnels. Even at this young age he demonstrated the determination and perseverance that would contribute so greatly to his success by breaking the record for the number of ties spiked in one day — 135. Despite the hard times in the country and his life, John Lenore developed and maintained a tremendous desire to succeed. Hard work would not stand in his way.

In high school he won a football scholarship to Manlius School, a military prep school in upstate New York. They played college freshman and J.V. teams and were undefeated for the two years he played with them. Lenore was in the starting lineup of every game, playing both offense and defense. He graduated in two years and went back to West Virginia where he met his wife, Dorothy. After five months the two teenagers married. They celebrated their 50th anniversary in 1998. Lenore attended West Liberty College working full time in a coal mine at night while taking a full schedule of classes during the day. By the end of the school year the Lenores had saved $300. They packed their little car and moved to California in 1950 in search of opportunities not available in a small community.

In California he enrolled at Pasadena City College where he again attended classes while working full-time, this time as a turret lathe operator. His daughter was born in September 1950. At

Today, three generations of Lenores are proud that Snapple is part of the foundation and future of the John Lenore Company. Pictured from left to right are: John Lenore, son Jamie, grandson Geoffrey Tobias, and son Jay.

These seven men, including John Lenore, purchased Theodore Hamm Brewing Company in 1973. It was sold to the Olympia Brewing Company one and a half years later.

school, a teacher took a special interest in him and guided him into a sales career — though he would have preferred to be a football coach. It was through this experience that Lenore found his passion and the key to his future career.

His first sales and marketing job was at Pacific Indoor Advertising Company. After a year, Lenore was offered a position with Bromar Market Specialties, now the biggest food brokerage in the world. While there, he helped to introduce a line of beverages called "Party Pak." He did so well at Bromar Market Specialties that Dr. Pepper, the parent company, offered him a job. For the next two and a half years, he moved through the ranks of Dr. Pepper, doing an outstanding job both in sales and merchandising.

Eventually Lenore was offered an opportunity for advancement at Dr. Pepper, but on the east coast. Lenore turned it down, preferring to stay in California. Instead, he did some career research, and, after much consideration, chose the brewing industry as his lifetime career. Lenore applied at three brewing companies: Lucky Lager Brewing Company, Theodore Hamm Brewing Company and the Joseph Schlitz Brewing Company. They all offered him a job, and Lenore chose the Theodore Hamm Brewing Company in which to build his future.

He started as a merchandiser in the Western Division. After five months the company promoted him to merchandising supervisor responsible for three states, then district manager, and finally western regional sales manager. In 1966, after nine years with the company, Lenore decided to start his own company, the John Lenore Company, in San Diego. This was a change in focus for Lenore because he had wanted to become president of a brewery. However, the chance to raise his family and live in San Diego overcame his other career ambitions.

Lenore started with leased trucks and borrowed money. His parents also helped by taking out a loan on their home. The Hamm Brewing Company agreed to let him put his inventory in bond, a way they had of helping new distributors. Within the year, he had done so well that he was able to buy up the leases and go on regular terms with the brewing company. Lenore worked long hours not only as the owner and sales manager, but also pitching in as a loader, warehouseman and driver. He did it all and his distributorship grew rapidly. Lenore's marketing talents and abilities opened doors and created

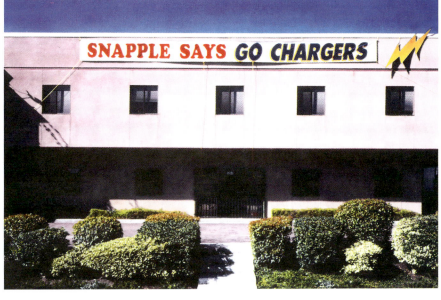

Shown is the current location of the John Lenore Company. The family will always be grateful for the three men who came from New York and gave them Snapple.

long-term business relationships that helped the business grow.

In 1969 his company moved into its current location just outside of Golden Hills, and he started to buy other brands and distributorships — Falstaff, Regal, Colt 45, Schlitz, Burgie, and Lucky Lager, which were major brands in the 60s and 70s. The John Lenore Company became the first major distributor that represented multiple major brands simultaneously. At first, the brewers didn't believe he could fairly represent each brand. Lenore dis-

John and Dorothy Lenore breed, raise and show American Saddlebred horses in Kentucky to show on the Kentucky circuit. Lenore is on the board of trustees for the American Saddlebred Horse Association and president of the American Saddlebred Horse Museum at the Horse Park in Lexington, Kentucky.

agreed. He recognized and proved that multiple brand marketing could be accomplished with sound planning.

To increase business Lenore designed niche marketing programs for specialty and imported beers. For instance, he believed that Old Town merchants would do well to feature Mexican imported beers. At that time, the late 60s, they primarily carried the same American beers many other San Diego bars and restaurants served. To illustrate his point Lenore would typically approach a restaurant owner with a line like "Can I have a hamburger, please?" The restaurateur usually responded, "We don't have hamburgers, sir, this is a Mexican restaurant." "You're right," Lenore agreed. "Then why don't you carry Mexican beers?"

This one creative idea was indicative of the kind of work for which Lenore's company became known. His ingenuity in visualizing niche penetration benefited all. As Lenore's business grew he directly increased the sales potential of the retailers and the brands he represented. The next four years were ones of intense growth as the John Lenore Company developed and pioneered many of the beer imports in San Diego. Lenore held sacred ideals such as honor, respect and abiding by all of his agreements. Because of these values and his honesty in dealing with people, his respect among beer companies and distributors grew.

Lenore's marketing abilities and hard work helped him to develop brands like Hamms, Schlitz, Colt 45, Burgie, Moosehead, Dos Equis, Guinness, Bass, St. Pauli Girl, Old Milwaukee and many others. He lost Hamms after Olympia, who purchased the brewery, canceled the entire Hamms' distributor network in California including Lenore, who had been part owner and on the board. It was a roadblock but not a detour.

Lenore went on to design gift packages of all kinds including the "24 Beers of the World" which sold through Price Club/Costco for many years. According to Lenore, "I had to be creative because God did not give me Bud, Miller or Coors. I was the guy who had to create, innovate and make something out of nothing!" In the late 60s, he had sold Meister Brau Lite, which ultimately was purchased by the Miller Brewing Company. They renamed it Miller Lite and the beer became part of the foundation of the modern Miller Brewing Company.

In the middle to late 1980s, after the fair trade law was rescinded in California, it became apparent to Lenore that the distributing process in the beer industry was about to change. In 1989 Lenore took a significant offer for his entire beer distribution company in San Diego County and began to focus on other areas in which his company could expand.

He spent a significant amount of time developing his portfolio and applying new marketing concepts through the Logret Import and Export Company, a subsidiary of the John Lenore Company. Logret was originally a Hispanic company which sold a full portfolio of beers, wines and spirits. As part of the Lenore Company, it has become a significant factor in the domestic and imported beer business throughout California and still maintains its Hispanic portfolio.

Lenore also became interested in new-age, non-alcoholic beverages. He began to research that market in order to build a new John Lenore Company, one that would focus on beverages other than beer. New-age beverages had arrived in San Diego!

One day, three wonderful men from New York came to see Lenore, having heard of his interest in new-age beverages. They were the owners of a then relatively unknown product called Snapple. They asked Lenore to become the Snapple distributor in San Diego County and assist with marketing. At the time they had a small distributor in San Diego who was having a great deal of difficulty and had not made much progress. Lenore made sure the other distributor was treated fairly by Snapple, then bought his inventory and truck and gave him a job. One and a half years later, in 1992, Snapple ran its first television ad, and sales skyrocketed.

Today the John Lenore Company is known coast-to-coast as one of the foremost pioneers of a full new-age beverage portfolio. He introduced, pioneered and owns part of SoBe, a nutraceutically enriched beverage line of teas and juice drinks. It has become one of the most successful start-up beverage companies in recent times. With Lenore assisting as a major distributor in the United States, helping to develop marketing strategies and convince other distributors around the country that SoBe was for real, the beverage went from $0-$200 million in value in just two years.

Lenore has also introduced and pioneered many other beverage innovations, which have also become part of this new category of beverages. Products the John Lenore Company represents besides Snapple and SoBe include Sparkletts, America's Best Coffee, National Beverage Line, Coffee House USA, Langers — a nutraceutically enriched juice line, Hansen's Functionals, and Stewarts Root Beer. There are a number of others still under development that Lenore has agreed to consult with and pioneer.

A strong believer in family, John Lenore is as dedicated to the youth of San Diego as he is to his business. His company sponsors various youth programs, sports teams and contributes regularly to charities that encourage strong family values. He firmly believes that the breakup of families today has created a tremendous need for the sharing of wisdom by grandparents and seniors, which he experienced as a child. With that in mind, Lenore, along with his wife, Dorothy, is establishing a "Grandparent for a Day" program, and will support it with a foundation. The kids who live in Golden Hills and the orphans of Mexico are of special interest to him.

"I feel privileged to have had so many great employees supporting our efforts over the years," John Lenore went on to say. "Bill Stevenson at the John Lenore Company and a great team at Logret. Jose Mazaira, Phil Alexander Sr., Phil Alexander Jr., Dave Pergl, Tom Slamer, Ray Campos, and my two sons Jay and Jamie — these people have been my partners. They have helped to make the John Lenore Company and Logret Import and Export the success stories they are today."

Perhaps no other company in San Diego has affected our drinking habits like the John Lenore Company. Single-handedly he has introduced dozens of imported and domestic beers to the area, as well as provided the people of San Diego with many healthy alternative beverages choices. John Lenore has definitely proven that success can be achieved with hard work, integrity, and initiative.

Antonio and Pietra de Chiazza, John Lenore's grandparents

Logret Import and Export Company
a subsidiary of the John Lenore Company

At the Center for Brewing Studies in Sonoma, California, internationally renowned brewing consultant Dr. Joseph Owades and a panel of beer experts did an archival research and comparative beer tasting on various brew styles from throughout the world — foreign, domestic and micro — to determine which, in their opinion, were the best in the world. The panel looked for the most appealing characteristics in brew head, color, aroma, taste and aftertaste.

Logret then commissioned Dr. Owades and his staff to create 12 formulas that represented the "best of the best." The resulting collection of brews is available throughout California, Arizona and Nevada and ultimately will be found throughout the United States. Each brew is presented in a specially designed, molded bottle with a full-color, detailed, collector-quality label. The project took three years to complete, but today The Twelve Greatest Brews of the World is a highlight in the John Lenore-Logret story.

John Lenore became involved in the Logret Import and Export Company in 1981 when he was looking for a way to diversify interests and expand his business portfolio beyond San Diego County. A small shell of a company in downtown Los Angeles owned by Jose Mazaira, Logret Import and Export specialized in distributing beer, wine and spirits to the Hispanic market throughout California. Lenore saw the company as an opportunity to distribute specialty lines and implement the privilege label program he created with Russ Cleary, CEO of the Heileman Brewing Company.

Lenore also saw the Logret Import and Export Company as a way to market to chain stores in California and try some innovative marketing approaches to expand business. Traditionally, beer is distributed by major beer distributors, sold and delivered by their sales people and trucks. Smaller brands — those that don't have the resources and advertising budgets of the large brewing companies — typically haven't been able to compete.

Lenore approached some of these smaller brewing companies and their distributors and purchased the right to distribute their brands throughout California. He then implemented a privilege label program in which each chain store would get a different brand, one with a historical equity and value that could be developed. The privilege label system grew into a multimillion-plus case program very quickly. The store owners liked the idea of exclusivity and the brewers benefited as well. The Heidelberg Brand, for example, saw immediate success, going from zero cases in one chain to 300,000 cases almost overnight. Then the Weideman Brand was put in another chain, and Blatz in another, etc. It has proven to be a major point of expansion for the second-level brewers and also a great deal for the consumer.

Logret Import and Export also developed an alternative distributing system for beer. With this system, stores can buy in truckloads and warehouse the beer in their own distribution centers. They then can send it out to their stores with other food products. The stores save money by self-distributing, allowing them to sell the beer as a value program by taking advantage of their highly developed delivery systems. It's a great deal for the retailers, the second-level brewers, Logret and, most importantly, the blue-collar consumer.

Logret Import and Export, with the cooperation of the Heileman Brewing Company recreated a new appearance and marketing approach for this company. It has since become a fixture in the state of California.

In 1991, Lenore negotiated for Logret to purchase the California distribution rights for Pabst Blue Ribbon, one of the four original national premium beers in the United States. With his creative instincts for sales and distribution, and by using Logret's alternative distributing system, Pabst annual sales in California increased from 5,000 barrels to more than 250,000 in less than two years (a barrel of beer equals 13.77 cases of 24 12-oz. cans or bottles). Lenore also developed the Henry Weinhard brand, Mickeys Malt and many others.

Recently, Logret was appointed the Prime Importer for San Miguel beer in California, Arizona and Nevada. The company will utilize its alternative distributing system for the chain retailers and also establish a correlating complete Direct Store Delivery (D.S.D.) system of independent distributors throughout the state of California. This will help to develop the smaller wholesalers in the state, giving new brands an opportunity to use the Logret system, its benefits, and still have a D.S.D. program with complete distribution in every market. This is a historic first as each system will be managed by Logret.

In 1993, a few of the major distributors raised some questions about Logret's alternative distribution system in the legislature. Lenore then went to the legislature to protect both his and the chains' right to sell beer on a direct warehouse basis. Lenore spent seven months in Sacramento with other friends of consumers such as Common Cause and Consumers Union. The chains also joined in with Lenore's efforts to fight off an attempt to legislate him out of business. Logret's coalition won the fight and today Lenore's company is an established and accepted entity in beer distribution in California.

Selling beers made by others is only part of the Logret Import and Export business. Lenore has not only created the Twelve Greatest Brews of the World but also designed a beer line inspired by the American Colonial period — Jeremiah James. As with the Twelve Greatest Brews, Lenore focused a great deal of time on capturing the feeling and the experience associated with the ales and stouts of that era, as well as the immigrants who brought the recipes here from Europe.

Another malt beverage under development by Lenore is John Henry, a beautiful drinking experience in a specially molded bottle. John Lenore also owns an equity interest in the Gluek Brewery, in central Minnesota, and is helping them develop an outstanding portfolio of brands that will hit the market in 1999. Logret will distribute and manage the brands in California, Arizona and Nevada. As with The Twelve Greatest Brews of the World, all of the malt beverages Lenore develops are of high quality, with specially molded bottles and designer labels that highlight the feelings and experience associated with the beverage and past periods of history.

Clearly, this John Lenore company is in the pioneering forefront of the beverage distributing industry. Lenore's gift for niche marketing, creative instincts and dedication to quality products will quench the thirst of beer drinkers for many years to come. It will be his legacy.

Logret conducted a worldwide search for the best brews. The company then recreated the recipes, designed the bottles and bottled the brews in this exciting package.

BFGoodrich Aerospace/ Aerostructures Group

BFGoodrich Aerospace/Aerostructures Group — the name sounds like a hot new company full of bright engineers and worker-geniuses busy inventing and assembling amazingly smart, durable and effective components for spacecraft and aircraft. With a name like that, this company must have

At BFG, as at other defense plants, "Rosie the Riveter" was essential in meeting production quotas during World War II.

The headquarters and the company's largest manufacturing facility located in Chula Vista, California, employs 2,500.

enlightened, state-of-the-art management principles designed to bring out the best in people. And in fact, all of this is accurate except for one thing: this thoroughly modern company is 60 years old.

As the terrible events of World War II were about to reach across the seas and pull the United States into the conflict, a sheet metal mechanic at Ryan Aeronautical Company named Fred Rohr started his own aircraft company in a garage near the southern limits of San Diego. In 1940 the new company acquired a three-story building that still stands at Eighth Avenue and J Street in San Diego's wholesale district. There, in response to President Roosevelt's plea for a 10-fold increase in the production of war material, Rohr Aircraft began its climb to the top rank of military subcontractors by building engine-related components and structures with unprecedented speed. Winning contracts to build power packages for B-24 Liberator and Hudson A-28 bombers, Rohr Aircraft moved to 10 acres of land on the shore of lower San Diego Bay. The original 10-acre site in Chula Vista is part of the 142-acre site that the company occupies today.

When the war ended, Rohr changed its focus from military aircraft to the design and manufacture of power packages and other parts for the emerging commercial aircraft industry. The company also tested other waters, including the manufacture of commuter train cars for the Bay Area Rapid Transit system, but Rohr found its greatest success in commercial aircraft components. By the 1980s, Rohr-built components were found in 90 percent of the world's commercial airliners (the most significant exception being aircraft built in the former U.S.S.R.).

On December 22, 1997, Rohr, Inc. entered a new era when the firm merged with the BFGoodrich family of companies. As one of four BFGoodrich Aerospace business groups, Rohr maintains its personnel and unique set of capabilities. It even uses the name Rohr for many purposes, but today the company operates as BFGoodrich Aerospace/ Aerostructures Group, or BFG/AG.

Today, BFG/AG is a world leader in the design, integration and manufacture of aircraft engine nacelle systems for large commercial and military aircraft. A nacelle is the aerodynamic structure surrounding an aircraft engine, including the inlet, fan cowl, thrust reverser, exhaust cone and nozzle. The company also designs and makes pylons, the structures that attach propulsion systems to the aircraft wings or fuselage. BFG/AG not only designs and builds nacelles and pylons, it also integrates these components with the engine and the aircraft, and supplies support services for its customers around the world.

BFG/AG's primary customers are the manufacturers of commercial airframes and engines, including all three of the world's major manufacturers of commercial airframes, Boeing, Airbus and the Douglas Products Division of Boeing, as well as the major jet engine manufacturers, including General Electric, Rolls-Royce, Pratt & Whitney, CFM International and International Aero Engines.

With vast experience in creating advanced aerostructures, it was inevitable that BFG/AG would find a niche in the aerospace business — BFG/AG also designs, manufactures, integrates and supports specialized aerostructures for tactical military aircraft, satellites and space vehicles. In the tradition of Rohr's beginnings as a military contractor, BFG/AG makes components for the F-15, F-22, AV-8B Harrier and other tactical military aircraft.

BFG/AG's involvement with satellites and launch vehicles dates back to the Titan rocket. Currently the company is one of the primary contractors for the X-33, the fully functional smaller version of the next generation of space shuttles known as the VentureStar™. The first of what is officially known as a single stage to orbit vehicle, the X-33 is a rocket-powered, wedge-shaped spacecraft that will not only land like a conventional airplane but will also take off like one. A primarily commercial venture, this new spacecraft will greatly reduce the costs of placing satellites and people into orbit compared to the current space shuttles. With the first launch of the X-33 planned for January 2000, the new spacecraft's metallic and composite aeroshell and thermal protection system is nearing completion.

Leading-edge products like liquid-interface diffusion-bonded titanium structures, ultralight metallic thermal protection systems and high-temperature brazed metallic acoustic components would be impossible without BFG/AG's leading-edge management and human resources practices. Company-wide policies focus on the positive aspects of the workplace and employee empowerment. BFG/AG gets the best from its 4,800 employees (2,500 in Chula Vista) by treating them with dignity and providing plenty of opportunities for maximizing their involvement and advancement.

Always a bold innovator of management and productivity practices, today the company is an industry leader in lean manufacturing and concurrent product development. The simultaneous involvement of every key discipline through the use of multifunction teams has cut flow time from concept to service-ready product by 50 percent, maintained ISO 9000 certification and reduced waste.

BFG/AG's Chula Vista facility is located directly adjacent to the environmentally sensitive Sweetwater Estuary Preserve. With coyotes, rabbits and a great variety of bird and sea life literally outside the plant doors, BFG/AG has become very proactive about environmental issues. Special programs focus on not creating toxic waste in the first place, but where toxic materials must be used, the company's respect for the environment has led to careful recycling and disposal procedures.

It has been a long way from Fred Rohr's sheet-metal work for the engine cowling on Charles Lindbergh's Spirit of St. Louis to BFG/AG's VentureStar space vehicle, but the spirit of innovation and tenacity that was present at the start still drives this San Diego born-and-bred company.

Employee working on nacelle component.

BFG designs and manufactures engine systems that are required for complete propulsion systems.

BFG designed and manufactures the X-33 prototype vehicle's thermal protection system, which covers virtually the entire exterior of the vehicle.

RPM Material Handling Co.

When Clarklift of San Diego, Inc. entered the San Diego marketplace in 1960, Otay Mesa was nothing but a vacant, wind-swept plain. Yet with neighboring Mexico a growing international market, its landscape has distinctly changed.

RPM Material Handling Co., A Division of Clarklift of San Diego, Inc. has been one of Otay Mesa's major contributors and strongest supporters since 1992. That is when the company — founded in 1960 — officially switched mesas, moving from Clairemont Mesa to a 2.2 acre lot in Otay Mesa. Located on Avenida Costa Norte in Otay Mesa, RPM Material

From left to right: The Clarklift family — Peter Otis, vice president of sales; Mike Grady, vice president of operations; Anne Otis, matriarch; and Rick Otis, president

Handling Co. lies just two miles from the Otay border crossing and a stone's-throw away from the U.S./Mexican border. The company has long been one of the major forklift truck distributors in San Diego and Imperial Counties for Southern and Baja California. It specializes in the sale, service, replacement parts and rental/leasing of forklift truck equipment. It is also the authorized distributor of some of the industry's leading brands, namely Clark, Nissan, Kalmar AC, Drexel, Barrett and most recently, Linde forklift trucks. The company, which has offices in Otay Mesa, El Centro and eastern Tijuana, Mexico, considers itself a one-stop shopping source for all types of material handling equipment, industrial storage racking and shelving, among other products.

The history of RPM Material Handling Co. can be traced back to December 1960 when Charles Myers Industrial Trucks was formed. A branch of the Robert Braun Company and the first distributor of Clark Forklifts in Southern California, Myers incorporated as a stand-alone distributor of Clark Forklift trucks and also sold new and used forklifts in San Diego and Imperial Counties. Myers sold his business in 1979 to Gerald Macchia, who then changed the company's name to Clarklift of San Diego, Inc. Then in September 1982, Harry J. Otis and family purchased Clarklift of San Diego, Inc. from Macchia. Otis, who worked for Clark Equipment at the factory level, long desired to run his own operation. Otis also wanted to have a business that he could pass on to his two sons, Harry ("Rick") and Peter. In his first year of ownership in 1982, Otis's company employed 27 people and posted sales of $3.6 million.

When Otis died in April 1986, his son Rick took over as the company's president and chief executive officer. One year later, Rick became majority stockholder of Clarklift of San Diego, Inc. while Otis's other son, Peter, became vice president, responsible for overseeing the company's sales efforts. In 1989, the company opened a 7,000-square-foot branch office on a one-acre lot in El Centro in Imperial County, moving from a smaller leased facility on Imperial Avenue. But the biggest event in 1989 was when Clarklift of San Diego, Inc. formed a Mexican subsidiary company, Servicios a Equipos Para Manejo de Materiales S.A. DE C.V. (SEMMSA). The effort provided the company a legal platform to conduct business in Mexico with the ability to invoice in dollars or pesos. By 1997, SEMMSA's operations volume was 17 percent of the company's total service, parts and rental revenues. Also in 1989, Clarklift of San Diego, Inc. received national recognition from the factory by earning its Dealer of Distinction Award for being the highest-performing distributor. A Dealer of Excellence Award was won again in 1998.

"We've been fortunate to be successful with our business," says Rick. "We've had some really good people work here. San Diego has gone through a nice transformation from a sleepy little military town to a regional manufacturing town with Maquiladora businesses south of the border that are very influential in our growth."

The company began to move its operations from its Clairemont Mesa Boulevard offices to its new Otay Mesa facility in 1990. The transition was completed two years later in 1992, the same year Mike Grady joined Clarklift of San Diego, Inc. as vice president.

Grady focused the company in the service area as it became a more customer-oriented business. The increase in service business was appropriate considering the company's move to Otay Mesa now made it truly a regional company with Mexico.

In 1994, the company's employees participated in a naming contest and selected RPM Material Handling Co. as the company's new name. The letters RPM were chosen to symbolize the first letter in the first name of the company's top three executives — Rick, Peter and Mike. The company had another reason to celebrate that year when it became Nissan's exclusive distributor of forklift trucks in San Diego and Imperial Counties. In December 1998, RPM celebrated once more when it was chosen to be the exclusive distributor of Nissan Forklift in the state of Sonora, Mexico.

Since relocating to Otay Mesa in 1992, the company has played an integral role in improving the Otay Mesa community. Rick served as president of the Otay Mesa Chamber of Commerce for two years as well as on the board and executive committee as chair of the transportation committee. Rick has also been actively involved in the chamber's work on border transportation issues. RPM worked with the Otay Mesa community to push for the widening of Otay Mesa Road as well as the improvements of state Route 905 and 125. Mike Grady has helped San Diego's Welfare-to-Work program, both with Episcopal Services and Maximus. Rick has also served as chapter chairman of the Young Presidents' Organization, Las Californias Chapter. At the Borderview YMCA, Rick has served on the board of directors, helping with fundraising efforts. Additionally, Rick has also been a board member of San Diego Dialogue, serving on its prosperity planning board. The purpose of San Diego Dialogue is to improve the business and social relationships between the United States and Mexico.

Rick added that RPM will continue to advocate for a regional San Diego Air Commerce Center on 350 acres of vacant land at neighboring Brown Field in Otay Mesa. Rick envisions that by 2010 there could very well be a shortage of landing slots for air cargo at Lindbergh Field, subsequently creating business for Brown Field, Otay Mesa and neighboring Mexico. In the future, RPM expects to take advantage of its close proximity to the border. As the North American Free Trade Agreement between the United States and Mexico blossoms, more Mexican companies must modernize and partner with other companies with resources. Steady growth is projected in the market for many years to come, and RPM intends to be a major player.

The first Tructractor was built to haul materials between various departments of Esra Clark's axle plant. Visitors to the plant were impressed with the practicality of this truck and asked Clark to build trucks for them.

Deering Banjo Company
The Great American Banjo Company

In the early 1970s, a group of college-aged artisans working in San Diego's East County banded together to form a cooperative guild which they named "The American Dream." Their chosen name was no less than a prophecy of what their lives would become. The American Dream spawned a number of builders of fine musical instruments, several of whom endured and prospered. Foremost among them were Greg and Janet Deering and the team of Bob Taylor and Kurt Listug. While Bob and Kurt went on to create Taylor Guitars, Greg and Janet founded the Deering Banjo Company.

Greg and Janet Deering are lifelong residents of San Diego. Both of their parents, Pat and Gene Deering and Nancy and Hugo Miller, moved to the city after World War II where Gene and Hugo worked as aerospace engineers. Growing up in the Clairemont area of San Diego, Greg and Janet met as teenagers and discovered that they shared an interest in woodworking and artisanship. They both began working with wood under the tutelage of their fathers. Janet's father began teaching her at the tender age of 12 when she helped him build an addition to the family home. Greg learned from his father to appreciate the characteristics of wood by first crafting models with little more than sandpaper and hand tools before he was ever allowed to touch a power tool.

Majoring in industrial arts and music at San Diego State University while working at The American Dream, Greg wanted a better banjo but could not afford it. He found a book written by Earl Scruggs describing how to build a banjo and, using his woodworking skills, he crafted his first banjo. He played his new instrument around town with his band, "Deering, Learned and Prim, Prim." Greg and Janet found that they shared the dream of building something so fine that it would last for generations. After marrying and starting their family, the Deerings set about turning their dream into reality by creating Deering Banjo Company.

During Deering Banjo's first 15 years, Greg and Janet created banjos in their home, using their garage as a workshop and spraying the finishes by their chicken coop. They eventually moved to a succession of small shops in Spring Valley and Lemon Grove. As they slowly built Deering Banjos into a company known for quality instruments and always delivering what they promised, their dream was repeatedly challenged by growing pains. From starting with only the money they made from selling Greg's first banjo, his personal instrument, they mortgaged their home to acquire the dies for special banjo parts. To save money, Greg visited aerospace salvage yards to get materials which he fabricated into the parts they needed. The growing company involved the entire family as the Deering grandparents helped with baby-sitting and the Millers helped as they could.

By the late 1980s, the Deerings knew they had a great line of banjos with realistic prices and top-notch quality, but sales were relatively flat. Up until that point, Greg and Janet had survived lean times with a shared commitment to persevere "no matter what." Then they made a fundamental change in their approach, going from the reactive "don't quit" to the proactive "let's do everything we can to prosper." From this new attitude came the notion of bringing banjo music to more people. They identified two problems that were limiting overall banjo sales. First, most people saw the banjo as a bluegrass and Dixieland instrument unsuitable for other genres of music. Second, there was no easy-to-play, relatively inexpensive, beginner's banjo on the market.

To address the first problem, the limited venues for banjo music, the Deerings began to study the market. They discovered that guitar players were often mystified by the four- and five-string tuning of traditional banjos, so in 1985 Deering tackled this problem. Greg solved the construction issues that had caused the muddy sound of earlier six-string banjos to create a beautiful-sounding six-string played just like a guitar. The company also designed and patented the first electric banjo that actually worked (previous attempts had been plagued with feedback problems). With the electric banjo, the six-string and eventually an ethereal-sounding 12-string, the Deerings and other pioneers undertook a fruitful campaign to expand the banjo's popularity into country/western, rock, jazz and other musical formats.

As to the second problem, the lack of a good beginner's instrument, the Deerings designed and introduced the Goodtime banjo in 1996. The Goodtime is a full-size, rugged, easy-to-play banjo that sounds better and costs less than imported banjos. It is built to be exactly what Greg wanted when he was first learning to play the instrument.

Today, Deering Banjo Company employs 20 skilled workers. Shipping more than 200 banjos each month from the company's shop in the San Diego suburb of Lemon Grove to domestic and overseas customers, Deering surpassed Gibson in 1997 to become the largest banjo manufacturing specialist in the world. The many bluegrass and Dixieland musicians who play Deering banjos have been joined by growing numbers of rock, jazz and country/western musicians. Traditional players of Deering banjos like Roy Clark, John Hartford, Wayne Newton, Herb Pedersen (Laurel Canyon Ramblers), Steve Cooley (Dillards), Steve Simpson (Banjomania) and George Grove (Kingston Trio) are pleased and sometimes surprised to find banjos showing up in bands like Los Lobos, Violent Femmes, Counting Crows, Smashing Pumpkins and others, as well as in the hands of Rod Stewart, Bela Fleck, Jeff Cook (Alabama), Jimmy Olander (Diamond Rio), John Sebastian, Emily Erwin (The Dixie Chicks), Gerry Beckley (America) and Joe Satriani.

One of the reasons for the success of the Deering Banjo Company is that Greg, Janet and their team of artisans are able to provide the banjo player with a wide choice of standard and custom models to create the special tone to fit any style of music. A perfectly balanced tone derives from the tone ring, the heart of any banjo. Deering developed a unique alloy of virgin bell bronze that they sand cast in the way church bells have been made for centuries. The casting is then machined to a tolerance of two-thousandths of an inch to create a perfect tone.

The Deerings believe that banjos make the world a better place to live. According to Janet, most people can learn to play banjo pretty well in just a year, making it easy for an aspiring picker to join Steve Martin in saying, "You just can't be sad when you're playing the banjo."

Partners In San Diego

Pacific Sportswear Co., Inc.

Pacific Sportswear President and Class of 2000®, Inc. Co-founder Rich Soergel stands next to one of his collector cars, a 1982 Ferrari 308 GTSi, overlooking beautiful downtown San Diego.

San Diego's coming of age as a city on the leading edge of technology and innovation is personified in Pacific Sportswear Co, Inc., an enterprise with garage roots that has grown to nothing less than fashion gatekeeper of the future.

As a custom manufacturer of private-label headwear, patch and apparel programs, Pacific Sportswear has consistently leveraged high-tech advances to break down design barriers. Whether assembling hats with glow-in-the-dark threads, designing metallic and reflective patches, creating 3-D looks for its apparel line or patenting a one-of-a-kind hat with removable logos, the company has made it a practice to anticipate trends and forge new ones.

Founder and President Rich Soergel grew up in Saratoga, California, where family expectations led him to pre-dental studies at San Jose State University. A change of heart soon changed his life. After one year, he switched his focus to business and enrolled at San Diego State University in 1979. His eventual degree in marketing gave him the tools to begin transforming entrepreneurial dreams into reality.

In 1983, Soergel purchased a hat and patch mail-order business for $5,406 — an amount he can recall to the dollar, along with every square foot of inventory, hat pressing equipment and customer records. He achieved $74,000 in sales the first year and then sold the business for $15,000. He then started Pacific Sportswear from scratch in 1984, operating the business out of a 150-square-foot office space in El Cajon.

It wasn't long before his company became known for what Soergel describes as "extreme quality, critical delivery and pure innovation." Even his business cards, affixed with embroidered or glossy 3-D patches, distinguish themselves with characteristic singularity. Serving three main markets — custom

private label programs, promotional markets and licensed wholesale brands — Pacific Sportswear, since 1989, has operated out of its 6,000-square-foot location in the Mission Valley section of San Diego.

Advancing technology, a willingness to take a risk and a sixth sense attuned to trends just over the horizon have kept Pacific Sportswear's staff of 12 busy implementing Soergel's visions. In 1986, Soergel introduced the low crown, six-panel baseball cap to the activewear business and developed cost-effective private-label headwear programs for clients such as Stussy, Calvin Klein, Hard Rock, Warner Bros., M&M's, Billabong, Harley Davidson and many others. Three years later, he created and trademarked LaserCut™ patches, which became a cost-saving alternative to direct-embroidery.

As one of the five founding shareholders of the World Pog Federation, a company started by Alan Rypinsky of Armor-All fame, Rich was responsible for marketing and merchandising the accessories that were sold when the little cardboard milk caps known as "Pogs" became a hugely popular game for kids.

In 1989, Soergel invented and patented one of his most notable products — MagiCap®...The

Collectible Logo Cap. MagiCap® is a hat constructed with a poly/cotton, hook-and-loop fabric that allows one to easily remove and replace logos onto a cap. The unprecedented design not only has caught the attention of corporations such as KFC, Nabisco, McDonald's, Disney and Chevron, who are interested in promoting their own products, but also earned Soergel one of his three MOTI awards, a prestigious industry citation. He has helped design, manufacture and market other new products such as the Twist Away Tray, an inexpensive, reusable bib and lap tray that drivers can use to protect their clothing from fast food spills.

It was perhaps appropriate that Soergel's fashion-forward talents would help put a stamp on one of the most ballyhooed events of our lifetime — the advent of a new century and millennium. In 1991, a friend of Soergel's, Ody Demetriadi, first hatched the idea of trademarking and patenting the phrase "Class of 2000®" for the purpose of marketing an exclusive line of apparel and merchandise. It was up to Soergel and several partners to officially protect their brainchild. They applied for a U.S. Patent in 1994 and received it with Reg. No. 2,018,220 on November 19, 1996 and started Class Of 2000®, Inc.— another numeric milestone Soergel will never fail to recall instantly.

Of course, receiving a federal trademark was only the start for Soergel and Pacific Sportswear, which is one of 55 licensed companies marketing and selling Class of 2000® merchandise. Creating a line of more than 160 products and apparel for an estimated market of more than 100 million people was next, as well as finding the appropriate sales channels. Their patented phrase has been called "America's No. 1 millennium brand" and sales estimates go as high as $200 million.

And yet, when asked which technological advances have been most instrumental in Pacific Sportswear's growth, Soergel credits "the ability to anticipate trends, twist the familiar and remain innovative" as the top three aids to success. With the advent of e-mail, faster modem speeds and the Internet, turnaround time on manufacturing orders was dramatically reduced. What once took weeks now transpires in days, if not hours. It's now possible to go from design board to overseas manufacturer to product-in-hand in as little as five days.

Sometimes, the unexpected has even become a hurdle for Soergel. In the mid-90s, he developed a line of apparel called "Fault Line." The devastating Los Angeles earthquake in 1995 suddenly rendered the phrase inappropriate and unmarketable, and he abandoned the project.

Pacific Sportswear's sensitivity to the community's needs, of course, take place outside of marketing concerns. Soergel is a member of the board of directors of the Copley Family YMCA in San Diego. He is also co-chair of the KSWB Copley Family YMCA Golf Classic. In 1991 and 1992, he sponsored a race car in the Racers Against Drugs, street stock division, at the El Cajon Speedway and continues to donate money and merchandise to many worthwhile causes in San Diego and throughout the country. Soergel's hobbies include jet skiing, running, attending collector car auctions, boating and playing the piano after a full day's work schedule.

Whether it's community involvement or trademarked inventiveness, Pacific Sportswear Company will be defining fashion trends well into the future with continuous ingenuity and foresight — truly the quiet force in cutting-edge technology in the headwear and accessory market.

Pacific Sportswear's array of quality custom products include private-label, premium and retail headwear (including the Class of 2000® brand), emblems, lapel pins, a countdown clock and MagiCap® . . . The Collectible Logo Cap.

Hard-working employees who help implement Pacific Sportswear's fashion-forward designs enjoy a break in front of their embroidery machines.

Palomar Mountain Spring Water

High in the pristine, pine-covered mountains of northern San Diego County in the Cleveland National Forest lie acres of protected springs of the purest mountain water. In 1985, Richard and Judy Einer, owners of 160 acres of Palomar Mountain land that included 19 fresh springs, decided to fulfill a dream. They recognized a need to bring the pure natural drinking water of their springs directly to homes and businesses in San Diego County. Their unique idea involved filling 60-gallon tanks and delivering them to their customers. Conveniently providing fresh spring water directly to the kitchen, bathroom and refrigerator would eliminate the difficulties with the traditional yet cumbersome five-gallon bottles.

Richard partnered with a Dutch couple, Ludolf (Dolf) and Cornelia Scherpbier, and Palomar Mountain Spring Water (PMSW) was founded. In the beginning, word-of-mouth was the only form of advertising. As a matter of fact, employees referred to the bulk water service as "San Diego's best kept secret." No one else in San Diego offered this service, so it was relatively unknown.

In addition to the 60-gallon tanks, Palomar produced half-gallon, one-gallon, and 2.5-gallon bottles for the retail market and in 1989, smaller sizes were added. By 1996, the company's growth necessitated the opening of a bottling plant in Corona, Riverside County, which employs 50 to 60 people and operates around the clock. The bulk water service and corporate offices are located in Escondido, in northern San Diego County, where 15 to 20 employees work in sales, service, administration and delivery. Richard had retired in 1994 and turned the company over to Dolf. Other members of the Einer family have worked in the business including Richard and Judy's son and son-in-law. Several employees have been with the company since inception.

Palomar's water is derived from 100 percent natural sources. Snow-fed ancient springs filter water for years to a depth of 300 feet before the water flows to the surface. After being collected in stainless steel tankers, it is treated with ultraviolet light and passed through various natural filters to catch any sediment. The water that is bottled must go through an ozonation process to preserve its shelf life. PMSW meets all Food and Drug Administration standards and goes to whatever lengths necessary to create a high-quality product. One taste offers unmistakable proof of this.

Most people associate bottled-water service with five-gallon bottles. PMSW has just recently entered that market, in addition to offering the unique bulk water and the popular personal-sized bottles. These have made their way into retail outlets (Ralphs, Vons, Albertsons, Smart & Final and Costco) and local television and radio studios as well as the World-Famous San Diego Zoo, Wild Animal Park and SeaWorld. PMSW customizes bottles with private labels for a variety of businesses including Vons, Albertsons, and La Costa Resort and Spa.

Palomar Mountain Spring Water comes in a variety of convenient sizes.

Always looking for opportunities to support the community that has supported them, PMSW is immersed in community events. It supplies water to the Escondido Fire Department for special events like burn seminars. Bottles of water are also donated to many sporting events, including triathlons and bikeathons. Most activities occurring on Palomar Mountain, such as children's camps and sporting events, have bottles of the fresh water there. A year of bulk service has been used as an auction item for charity events hosted for a variety of causes such as the Children's Hospital Burn Center.

PMSW was the official sponsor and only water provider of the SuperFest pre-Super Bowl XXXII game festivities in San Diego. The water has been supplied to the San Diego Padres' dugout and the San Diego Chargers' locker room. Free drinking water is available at many Convention Center and Sports Arena events. PMSW provides water for the California Center for the Arts in Escondido, Coors Amphitheatre in Chula Vista, chambers of commerce around the county and the California Department of Forestry. Water has been sent to victims of El Niño in Mexico and to Los Angeles during the riots and earthquake. "We're ready for any natural disaster. Our bulk water service is perfect for this," explained Pam Crane, residential sales representative.

Customers in Southern California, Nevada and Arizona as well as Mexico and parts of the Orient enjoy Palomar's delicious water. The Japanese selected PMSW because they liked the color of the logo on the bottle. Although the bulk business accounted for only 10 percent of its overall business in 1998, Palomar took an aggressive stand to jumpstart the growth of that portion of the business with a media campaign in prime time television, radio and newspapers. The 30-second commercials and ads are aimed at increasing awareness and educating the public about the conveniences of bulk water service.

The company is poised for continued growth and expansion, yet it still considers PMSW a grassroots operation. The staff is committed to the success of the business. The employees believe in the product and work together as a team. They also socialize outside of work. They see the results of their efforts in the letters and calls they receive from children and adults telling them how much they like the product and how good the water tastes.

Palomar Mountain Spring Water is San Diego's homegrown water and customer loyalty is strong. A monthly newsletter sent to bulk water customers educates, entertains and keeps the company connected to its customers. Going above and beyond, listening to the customers' needs and being there when bottled water can help is what Palomar is about. People can even drive up to the springs on beautiful Palomar Mountain to fill their bottles directly from the source that has served and will continue to serve millions around the world.

Bulk Home Delivery Service: From 60-gallon drum to kitchen tap

Solar Turbines Incorporated

Solar Turbines Incorporated has a long, colorful past in the fabric of San Diego's history. What began as a small, humble aviation company in the late 1920s has grown into a Fortune 500 company manufacturing gas turbine engines that are shipped to almost every country in the world. And what began as a dream of a few men in the "Air Capital of the West" has evolved into a conglomeration of employees who manufacture some of the world's finest turbomachinery systems, helping others around the planet recognize their dreams by meeting the world's ever-increasing energy needs.

The 1920s were turbulent years in the United States. Memories of World War I were vivid, jazz was flourishing, prohibition was in effect and the economy was booming. Industries that had been in their infancy early in the century were struggling into adolescence. One such industry, aviation, gravitated to Southern California. San Diego attracted aviators like Charles Lindbergh, who took off from North Island's Rockwell Field to begin his legendary trans-Atlantic flight on May 10, 1927. San Diego's burgeoning aviation industry also lured a man named George Henry Prudden, who started an aviation company called Prudden-San Diego Airplane Company with seven local investors and $60,000.

The new company was located on leased tidelands property in a former fish cannery adjacent to the Ryan Aircraft Company owned by B.F. Mahoney, where the Spirit of St. Louis had been built for Charles Lindbergh. This is the site of Solar Turbines' Harbor Drive facility today. In 1928, the Mahoney organization moved to St. Louis, leaving Prudden as the only San Diego aircraft manufacturer for several years.

In August 1928, the company began work on an aircraft, the TM-1, with a tri-motor and two outboard engines slung beneath the wing struts. Another aircraft, the MS-1, was also under development. Unfortunately for this fledgling company, selling airplanes and borrowing money weren't viable options as the country headed straight into the Great Depression.

Knowing that it could not subsist on aircraft alone, the company, renamed Solar Aircraft Company Ltd., began designing manifolds from leftover stainless steel. Solar made its first manifold sale to the Navy's Bureau of Aeronautics at the end of 1930, and it slowly became a new business opportunity for a company with just six people on a sporadic payroll. Fortunately, by the end of 1934, Solar went international and celebrated its first year of earning a profit. Airplane manifolds continued to be a dominant part of Solar's business throughout the next decade as World War II broke out in Europe. Solar began fabricating manifolds, cowlings, flame dampers, tail pipes and shrouds in late 1938 and by 1939, the company was in full three-shift operation with sales topping $500,000.

By 1944, Solar exhaust manifolds were on most of the nation's war planes and the company had grown to 12 sales offices and three plants, manufacturing, among other things, heat exchangers, jet exhaust thrust recovery systems and welding flux. At the height of World War II, 5,000 people were employed at this young, San Diego-based company and Solar continued to make significant contributions to the war effort on many fronts. But when victory in Europe and the Pacific came in August 1945, Solar once again had to diversify its products and services to meet a whole new marketplace. To keep its 850 employees working, Solar developed a line of

The Solar Turbines Incorporated corporate headquarters is situated on the "entryway" to America's most beautiful city between Lindbergh Field and downtown San Diego on the edge of San Diego Bay.

products that included caskets, midget-race-car bodies, film processing machines, coffee brewers, Popsicle trays and even kitchen sinks.

In 1946, Solar employee Paul Pitt was asked to establish a design team to create a gas turbine engine. It was this engine that would revolutionize Solar's future. Solar's initial involvement in gas turbines was with the military for power generation. In 1959, Solar's first commercial sale of a 400-hp turbine to the Texas Eastern Pipeline company opened up a whole new market for Solar — the oil and gas industry. The development of the gas compressor further enhanced Solar's product line and made Solar gas turbines an attractive investment for oil and gas companies throughout the world. Through continued research, development and just plain hard work, Solar employees have created a product line known worldwide by oil and gas giants like Shell, Chevron, Exxon and Mobil. These oil and gas customers continue to make up a major segment of Solar's market to this day.

Throughout the 1960s and 70s, Solar's gas turbine industry continued to grow and expand. In 1974, a new, modern manufacturing plant was started on Solar-owned land in Kearny Mesa. By the end of the 1970s, Solar had once again become internationally known for its turbomachinery packages installed worldwide, parts and overhaul depots positioned to support these installations, and a growing reputation for being the world's leader in industrial turbomachinery products.

In the early 1980s, Solar Turbines Incorporated became a wholly owned subsidiary of Caterpillar Inc. As the oil and gas industry prices took a downturn, Solar looked to another market to continue to build its business — industrial power generation. In 1985, U.S. legislation made it attractive for companies with generation equipment to sell electrical power to the utilities. This co-generation arrangement created an expanded market for Solar's generator packages and became a market that continues to be a large part of Solar's overall business equation to this day.

During the 1990s, several new gas turbine packages were developed including the 10,000-hp Taurus, 18,000-hp Titan 130 and the Mercury 50, utilized for distributed power generation. Solar's wide range of products expanded its operations on every continent, with 40 offices and more than 6,000 employees throughout the world. In 1998, Solar built a new maquiladora facility in Tijuana, took over a new manufacturing plant in National City and renewed their lease with the San Diego Port Authority until 2020 — ensuring that Solar Turbines Incorporated would remain at their Harbor Drive location well into the new millennium. Also in 1998, Solar Turbines was the first San Diego-based company to win the coveted Malcolm Baldrige National Quality Award for recognition of achievements in quality and business excellence.

Solar continues to manufacture the world's leading midrange industrial gas turbines and turbomachinery systems. At the core of its business is its new product development that delineates Solar Turbines from an international roster of competitors. With over a billion dollars in sales and a bright future, Solar promises to be a part of the San Diego community well into the 21st century.

This is Solar's 1938 manifold line in full swing. Solar manufactured a specially designed manifold, at Howard Hughes' request, which was on the plane that took him around the world in 91 hours and 14 minutes — a world record in July 1938.

Flag Crafters, Inc.

"Quality people making quality products" is more than a motto at Flag Crafters. It is Flag Crafters' employees gathered around television sets during World Cup soccer matches, World Series games, NBA All-Star weekends, NHL and NCCA Championships and more than 10 Superbowls and enjoying the beauty and pageantry of their work along with millions of fans all over the world. It is their quality work and dedication to on-time delivery to every customer, every day, that gives these employees, the company and its loyal customers such great satisfaction.

Since 1981, Flag Crafters' employees have been making custom-designed flags and banners of all sizes. They do so with a detailed craftsmanship that rivals the hallowed tradition of flagmaking that has endured for centuries. Blending Old World, hands-on skills with modern state-of-the-art equipment and knowledge has brought Flag Crafters national acclaim.

Flag Crafters selects only the highest quality materials and processes to produce high performance flags and banners, durable table drapes and eye-catching street banners. These products have the fine stitching and strength needed for indoor or outdoor events. Besides constructing the banners, Flag Crafters's graphics department also assists clients with refining ideas and creating the images for imprinting. Today, hundreds of companies throughout the world contract with Flag Crafters. In fact, these companies come back year after year for their custom flag, banner and sewn, printed or appliquéd decorations.

Whether it is a four-color process, dye-sublimation, screen printing, appliqué or embroidery on a broad range of fabrics from nylon and satin to vinyl or sunbrella and more, Flag Crafters provides the best value and the best on-time delivery in the industry. That is why Flag Crafters has never lost a major customer since its inception — a record the company is very proud of and committed to preserve.

Flag Crafters is especially proud of its long-term association with Rotary International, one of the largest and oldest service organizations in the world, now serving in more than 183 countries. Flag Crafters has been a licensee for Rotary for more than 10 years and its founder, Bob Crowe, has been a member of Rotary since 1986.

Flag Crafters' new Web site is a great resource for ideas and has brought the company worldwide attention.

Flags, street banners and table drapes are a powerful way to promote an event, add festivity and get attention. With a talent that breeds tradition, Flag Crafters has definitely gotten ours.

Flag Crafters makes a complete line of banners, table drapes, flags and promotional products for Rotary International, Kiwanis and Lions Clubs, as well as other organizations.

Street banners, screen printed on canvas and vinyl

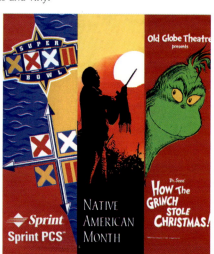

Taylor Guitars

Bob Taylor was just a kid who wanted a guitar. Kurt Listug was a music junkie just trying to avoid the rat race.

So begins the story of Taylor Guitars, a rags-to-riches tale with more ups and downs than your typical country song.

Today, as one of the world's premier makers of high-end acoustic guitars, Taylor Guitars stands as an overnight success story more than 25 years in the making. By combining Old World craftsmanship with state-of-the-art computer technology, it has forever changed the way guitars are made. Its roster of worldwide musicians who swear by the quality and beauty of their instruments reads like a who's who of popular music: Jewel, Bonnie Raitt, Garth Brooks, R.E.M., Jackson Browne, and Neil Young, to name just a few.

If it wasn't appropriate symbolism that Taylor Guitars was founded in 1974 through the purchase of a small guitar shop in Lemon Grove named the American Dream, then at least it was a fitting start. As self-professed dreamers who naively believed that making guitars as good as industry giants Martin and Gibson would come naturally, 19-year-old Taylor and 21-year-old Listug didn't realize they were headed for a long and winding road when they bought the shop in which they worked.

Taylor was a self-admitted wood shop nerd who was too ignorant to know that you weren't supposed to file down the standard fat and clunky guitar neck until it was slim and felt good. But his first customers were immediate converts. He wasn't skilled enough to make a dovetail joint, so he simply bolted the neck onto the body — considered blasphemous at the time but offering the benefit of easy removal. Later, after 15 years of hand-carving necks, Taylor utilized a computerized machine to perform the job more accurately. He then had to fend off complaints that his guitars were no longer "hand-made," even though today such methods are considered standard and Taylor guitars remain a triumph of aesthetics and beauty.

Acceptance didn't come easily. For years, the company floundered at a plateau of making about 10 guitars a week, and several times it nearly went out of business. But Taylor and Listug gradually learned how to keep overhead costs down while increasing productivity and making technical refinements. In 1984, when the popularity of synthesized music threatened to relegate the acoustic guitar to coffee house oblivion, Taylor created a guitar for Prince. The purple-stained Taylor guitar Prince played in his "Purple Rain" and "Live Aid" videos helped create a demand for Taylors, and may have aided in the eventual re-emergence of the acoustic guitar. It wasn't long before famous and unknown musicians alike began clamoring for all the available Taylors.

Today, the company turns out about 150 guitars daily at its two facilities in El Cajon, California, grossing nearly $25 million in 1998 with its 250 employees, 700-plus nationwide dealers, and 64 international distributors in 32 countries. Taylor Guitars is the only American acoustic guitar maker of the 20th century to successfully make the quantum leap from small shop to major manufacturer while remaining owned and operated by its founders. Not bad for a couple of guitar shop kids whose real achievement resounds in the wordless appeal and exquisite sound of their elegant instruments.

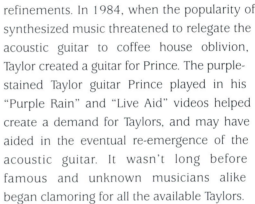

This beautiful model 914-C six-string acoustic guitar is just one of 150 instruments produced daily at the Taylor Guitars factory in El Cajon.

Babe's, Inc.

The mention of Loida Stillwell's National City-based company, Babe's, Inc., might raise eyebrows and pique curiosities. However, the moniker has nothing to do with the medical uniforms she manufactures. Instead, it pays tribute to her beloved Pomeranian who disappeared in 1992, shortly after the company opened. The gesture exemplifies Loida's ideology — tempering decisions with her heart and intelligence, a technique that serves her well, personally and professionally.

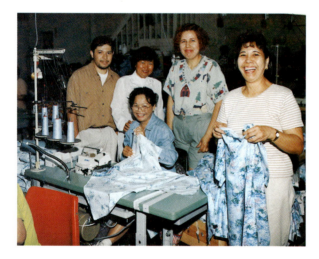

A "worker-friendly" atmosphere is enjoyed by Esteban Villa, Loida Stillwell (Babe's, Inc., owner), Patricia Tamayo, Minerva Marquez and Thuay Chandara.

Loida Stillwell, founder and president of Babe's, Inc., moved to the San Diego area in 1986 and became a bookkeeper for a uniform manufacturer. She realized the business's potential and felt she could provide overworked employees with a more enriching professional environment. Her sewing background, however, was limited to sewing a few skirts and her bank account was modest. She prayed for divine assistance and promised the Lord she would take care of her employees if he would provide her the means to do so.

Unexpected opportunities allowed her to work with a mentor who helped broaden her business knowledge. Soon, with three reliable employees, a working space and Loida's last unemployment check, Babe's, Inc. became a reality. The San Diego business world seemed friendly, but a slow market and the theft of her machinery during her first year of business made her journey difficult. Each time a door closed, Loida says, "the Lord opened a window for me."

Currently, Babe's, Inc.'s almost 90 employees produce colorful scrubs-style uniforms worn by San Diego's medical personnel. High production levels at Babe's, sometimes up to 5,000 scrubs daily, ask a lot from workers, but complaints are few. The worker-friendly atmosphere is ever-present, especially for young parents. The mother of two, she understands parental stress and she frequently adjusts employees' schedules for baby-sitter problems, illnesses, and school functions.

Loida enjoys giving recognition for dedicated job performance, awarding "Service Pins" and sponsoring family-oriented company functions. She is proud to be a Chamber of Commerce member and Babe's success allows her to share her blessings with the community, through generous donations to Outreach For Christ, an organization which offers food, shelter and counseling to San Diego's homeless.

Loida is considering creating a line of affordable school uniforms, which would help local parents defray clothing costs. Babe's would make a higher profit margin if Loida opted to buy advanced automated machinery, but in doing so she would have to let some employees go. Loida would rather give her employees overtime instead. Little wonder that the employee turnover is almost nonexistent and regard for Loida remains high.

Loida continues to direct credit for Babe's, Inc.'s success to a higher power. "I don't want to be selfish," Loida says. "I want to try to help others and try to help them do their best because then nothing is impossible. The Lord knows I'm doing my best."

Central Meat & Provision Company

San Diegans who dine at the city's finest resorts and restaurants will appreciate the professional expertise of Central Meat & Provision Company, even if they don't recognize the name. One of the area's most respected wholesalers, Central Meat has been offering discriminating chefs consistently high quality for nearly a century.

The history of this family-owned business with a dedication to its customers begins in 1912 when Charles Kuhlken founded Central Meat Company. After gaining knowledge and experience working in meat departments of local Piggly-Wiggly markets, Charles opened his own neighborhood butcher shop on 18th and C streets in San Diego. He was determined to provide the highest-quality products at fair prices — and never stint on personal attention to each customer.

When Ed Kuhlken succeeded his father as president of Central Meat in 1937, he changed the company's direction from retail to wholesale. Within 10 years, Central Meat was the leading wholesaler of quality beef in San Diego. Ed expanded the plant and incorporated such technological advances as vacuum packaging and temperature-controlled processing.

But quality alone hasn't made Central Meat the leader it was then and is today. Personal relationships take top priority. The Kuhlkens are proud and pleased when their efforts result in customer growth

Central Meat & Provision's staff and storefront at 18th and C streets
c. early 1900s

and success. Generations of Kuhlkens have been doing business with generations of San Diegan resort owners and restaurateurs.

When Bob Kuhlken joined the company in 1965, he expanded Central Meat's line of products to include veal, lamb, pork, fish and shellfish. Yet, he continued to carefully age the beefsteaks while at the same time offering customers the convenience of precut, portion-controlled steaks that are easy to store and ready to grill.

Carrying on the family tradition of quality and personal service paid off handsomely. Bob increased the company's business by 500 percent and in 1976, became its third-generation owner. Today, his son, John, has joined Central Meat with new ideas of his own.

Bob wants his customers to feel that Central Meat is more than a provider — it's a partner, making sure diners return again and again. By ordering Central's precut steaks of consistent portions, for example, restaurateurs can more easily price out their menus, ensure accurate inventory and save the expense of training and supervising meat cutters.

Today's team of professionals at Central Meat cannot afford the leisurely pace of 1912. They work long hours, always trying to improve on what they do, to keep their competitive edge and satisfy the discriminating tastes of a world-class city.

Interior view with old-fashioned scales and meat hung high on hooks
c. early 1900s

Daily Marine

San Diego, a major Pacific coast seaport, owes part of its early prosperity and development to the fishing and boating industries. Even today, these industries play a vital role in the economy of the area. Servicing the boats that call San Diego home as well as those that cruise past its shores has become the focus of a number of small businesses, including Daily Marine.

Founded in 1970 by George and Virginia Daily, Daily Marine provided a vital product to the boating industry from the beginning. The amount of time boats can spend at sea depends primarily on two factors: the amount of fuel and usable water on board. Seawater conversion equipment allows commercial fishing boats to stay out longer and thus, bring larger loads of fish to market. In fact, this equipment may extend the amount of time a boat can stay out by several weeks.

Daily Marine became the only Beaird Industries Maxim® Evaporators distributor in California. At first, George and Virginia operated out of their garage with tuna boats as their main business. Their client base grew quickly due to word-of-mouth referrals and they were able to hire their first employee, Wes Myers. Toward the end of 1970, the Dailys decided to retire and sold him their flourishing business.

Myers moved the business to its present location on Shelter Island in 1971. Evaporators remained the focus of the business. The evaporator uses heat from engine jacket water to distill freshwater from seawater.

Since the evaporator is under a vacuum, seawater will boil into vapor at a low temperature (about 125 degrees Fahrenheit). The vapor, when condensed, is distilled water. Thus, engine jacket is used as a cost-free source of heat for providing freshwater for drinking, bathing, washing and cooking.

Today, in addition to evaporators, Daily Marine makes its own line of reverse-osmosis watermakers. Seawater under pressure is passed through a semipermeable membrane. Salt does not pass, only freshwater can. These reverse-osmosis watermakers are used by both commercial vessels and cruising yachts. A water filtration/ultraviolet sterilization system is also provided to purify freshwater taken onboard at foreign ports.

Daily Marine's client list includes the U.S. Coast Guard, the San Diego sportfishing fleet, the G Street tuna fleet, the purse seiner fleet and cruising yachts up and down the West Coast. In fact, it's not unusual for recreational craft to stop in San Diego at the beginning of cruising season and have Daily Marine service their equipment before heading into international waters.

For more than 28 years, the company has been dedicated to providing quality products and service. Daily Marine is a vital part of the boating and fishing communities up and down the Pacific coast as well as into Mexico.

The evaporator uses heat from engine jacket water to distill fresh water from sea water. Since the evaporator is under a vacuum, sea water will boil into vapor at a low temperature (about 125°f). The vapor when condensed is distilled water. Thus, engine jacket is used as a cost-free source of heat for providing fresh water for drinking, bathing, washing and cooking.

Photo by Robert A. Eplett

Plastic Display Products

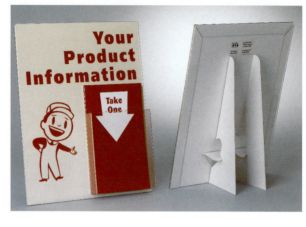

People have seen these products everywhere but probably looked right through them. That's because they're clear, plastic display products used to hold everything from sales literature and price tags to advertising signs and products.

Plastic Display Products (PDP) was born when Ray Biernacki, Jr. decided to start a business and asked his father for help. The senior Biernacki had been a sales representative for a plastics manufacturer and saw a need in the marketplace for low-cost, functional, durable display products. In 1982, the dining room of the Biernacki home became the laboratory where father and son tested new ideas to create lower cost, versatile, vinyl products. Ray Jr.'s father-in-law, Harold Wilmoth, a retired aerospace engineer, pitched in by designing machines that manufacture most of PDP's products.

The products PDP produces and distributes are unique because they are manufactured with a virtually unbreakable vinyl that can be preformed or scored, shipped flat and then formed into the desired shape upon receipt by the client. The vinyl doesn't shatter and is thinner than acrylic, which has been traditionally used for displaying marketing materials. A low-cost alternative to acrylic, the vinyl stands up just as well. The flat materials also cost the client less since the material doesn't need to go through the extra process of being molded with heat into permanent shapes.

PDP products can be seen in most grocery stores holding signs for product identification, in greeting card stores where the vinyl has been formed into card racks, and anywhere promotional literature is displayed. Warehouses use the products for shelf signage, while manufacturers of consumables like wine and film, order special displays to feature their products. PDP can also imprint directly onto the plastic, such as literature holders and menu displays, to provide product advertising or restocking information. A 1995 consumer buying habits study conducted by POPAI (Point of Purchase Advertising Institute) indicated that 70 percent of buying decisions are made in the store. Therefore, stores know that point-of-purchase plays a tremendous role in affecting what a consumer purchases.

Ray Jr. now focuses on his favorite aspects of the business — product design, research and development. In 1995 he handed the company reins to his daughter, Theresa Franchimone. Since then, Theresa has been steering PDP toward increased growth. Theresa will frequently travel to a customer's location to offer on-site consultation to determine how to best fill a client's particular requirement. One-on-one customer service has been a key factor in PDP's continued growth.

Twenty-five employees, and up to 100 at busier times, manufacture a variety of products that are customized to each client's needs and are distributed around the globe. "We're primarily in the United States, Canada and Mexico, but our distributors have been opening overseas markets," says Theresa, company president. "Our future plans include increased participation in the global marketplace and continuing to provide customers with products that fit their specific needs."

(Right) Literature Holders

(Below) Product Merchandisers

Rhino Linings USA, Inc.

Russell Lewis founded Rhino Linings in 1988 after immigrating to the United States from South Africa. At that time, he didn't just start a company, he spawned an industry; one that would offer an exciting, new alternative to standard, drop-in truck bed liners.

Sprayed-on polyurethane technology had been developed in South Africa to protect mining equipment from highly corrosive elements. A visionary and successful entrepreneur, Lewis recognized that this same process had limitless potential, especially in the automotive, trucking, military and construction industries. His belief in this new product was so strong that he invested his own money and opened the first Rhino Linings dealership. Today, Rhino Linings has hundreds of dealerships in more than 45 countries around the world and is a recognized global leader in sprayed-on polyurethane linings.

Until Lewis opened shop, truck owners could only protect their beds with drop-in liners. Unfortunately, these did not provide an industrial-strength, airtight and watertight seal, prevent rust or corrosion or insulate against noise or road vibration. Sprayed-on polyurethane not only deals with these problems but will not crack, split or warp, provides a maintenance-free, easy-to-clean contour surface and tenaciously adheres to virtually any substrate — steel, aluminum, rubber, fiberglass, wood and even concrete. It can be sprayed to any desired thickness and in varying textures. The lining cures to a 100 percent solid in just seconds and forms a seal that resists abrasion, corrosion, impact and chemicals, even under temperature extremes. It is a solvent-free, environmentally friendly product with no volatile organic compounds (VOCs) or chlorofluorocarbons (CFCs).

"Tuff Stuff," Rhino Linings unique polyurethane surface, can also be used by owners of marine vessels, trailers, RVs, Jeeps and horse transports as well as by the commercial industry.

Its uses are virtually limitless. Rhino Linings' products have been used for protective coverings on waste and recycling bins, consumer goods, above and underground storage units, splash wells, roofing and in garbage and refuse management. The company's research and development department is highly instrumental in helping Rhino Linings stay a global leader in the industry it helped to found.

Rhino Linings is equally dedicated to the community. The company is a strong supporter of the Black Rhino Foundation as well as numerous other organizations that help endangered species. Recently, Rhino Linings developed a literacy program that will be offered nationwide through the company's local dealerships. This program will help teachers to stimulate reading interest in the classroom.

It takes courage to take on a Goliath like the automobile manufacturers and the company's growth, product acceptance and popularity has been dramatic. There are few today who can say they gave birth to a new industry. Russell Lewis and Rhino Linings not only did just that, but gave the public access to a new, affordable, tough, industrial-grade protective lining that will impact truck usage forever.

Jeep® with black Tuff Stuff® polyurethane lining

Rhino Linings adds value and durability to any high-wear surface.

Retail establishments, service industries and leisure/convention facilities offer an impressive variety of choices for San Diego residents and visitors.

Partners in MARKE

San Diego
TPLACE

Seaport Village 274	San Diego Refrigerated Services 306
Bazaar Del Mundo 280	Sky's the Limit Muralist Co. 308
Promus Hotels 284	Stanley Steemer 310
Anthony's Fish Grotto 288	Baja Duty Free 312
Warwick's 289	Bernardo Winery 313
The Bedroom Superstore 290	Coles Carpets 314
Jakob Gerhardt 292	Deer Park Winery & Auto Museum 315
Josh Mitchell Photography 294	Dutch Growers Nurseries, Ltd. 316
Karl Strauss Breweries 296	El Indio Mexican Restaurant 317
"King" Stahlman Bail Bonds 298	Orfila Vineyards & Winery 319
La Valencia Hotel 300	Peaches en Regalia 320
Rancho Valencia Resort 302	San Diego Catering Concepts 321
San Diego Office Interiors 304	

PATRON: SOUTHERN CALIFORNIA DISCOUNT TIRE CO.

Seaport Village

It's difficult to imagine a time developers would hesitate to become involved in any project connected to the Seaport Village area. That was the case in the mid-1970s, when the U.S. Navy vacated the property surrounding the old San Diego Ferry Landing. The San Diego Port District assumed ownership of the scenic waterfront property, but no list of enthusiastic tenants materialized. The Gaslamp Quarter had yet to become a reality and, with the

The San Diego Pier Cafe provides diners with fine food and one of the most exquisite bay views in town.

exception of the Westgate Hotel, downtown San Diego offered little to entice locals or tourists. Those making the trek were mostly interested in the entertainment provided by the peep shows, massage parlors and topless bars that lined the side streets. Prostitutes and con men made up the unofficial welcoming committee for the throngs of young servicemen eager for some excitement, legal or not. Alcohol and vice-related violations abounded and police officers working the area seldom experienced a slow night.

City officials knew they had a problem but were not sure where to begin. Initial talks of a downtown redevelopment plan seemed like wishful thinking. Many felt the problems plaguing the downtown area were beyond repair, but the late businessman M.B. Taubman was not among them.

Taubman, one of the three principals involved in developing Seaport Village, saw the diamond in the rough. Daughter Anne Taubman, now president of Seaport Village, remembers her father's enthusiasm during her first tour around the construction site. She says, "People could see it was fabulous property but everyone thought they were crazy because this area was not surrounded by a very nice part of town. It was really kind of seedy."

Business partners Bryant Morris and Sheldon Pollack, a general contractor, also shared in M.B. Taubman's vision of transforming the 14 acres of available seafront property, located at Kettner Boulevard and Harbor Drive, into one of San Diego's most inviting attractions. Prior to breaking ground, the group invested almost four years in perfecting the detailed proposal required by the San Diego Unified Port District. Port District officials liked what they saw and granted their approval, allowing Seaport Village to lead the way in the first phase of a comprehensive downtown and waterfront development program.

The matter of financing presented another sizeable challenge and again, investors did not rush in with checkbooks in hand. This reluctance stemmed largely from the bank's constraint requiring the shopping village to be 100 percent leased before any financing would be granted. This formidable restriction fed the appetites of naysayers who harbored doubts about the success of downtown redevelopment. Many in the business community doubted if the project would ever truly begin, and one important question lingered in those same minds: Would shoppers venture downtown to shop when they could drive to a mall closer to home?

A number of investors felt the answer was no, but a flood of savvy shopkeepers said yes and the tenant requirement was met with no problem. Many in the business community (those not blessed with M.B. Taubman's keen sense of vision) continued to harbor doubts about Seaport Village's ability to stay afloat financially, regardless of how unique and inviting the shops promised to be. Everyone involved with the project knew from the onset they were taking a calculated risk, but the treasure at the end of this particular rainbow seemed worth the gamble.

The transformation of the seafront property involved more than following basic blueprints. M.B. Taubman and his partners knew they did not want Seaport Village to fall into the shopping mall category. They wanted Seaport Village to possess a certain charm and character that would provide its visitors with more than just the opportunity to purchase quality gift items or dine in a good restaurant. They felt compelled to provide visitors with an atmosphere that would delight shoppers of all ages and they wisely turned to design consultant Raymond E. Wallace for guidance.

Wallace, owner of Special Productions of Palos Verdes, had already exhibited his talents and established a name for himself with previous projects that warranted considerable attention in various locales, such as Ports O'Call Village in San Pedro, Fisherman's Wharf in Marina del Rey, Cedar Point Amusement Park in Ohio, and the shops and marine effects in Disneyland. His task centered on Taubman's desire to incorporate three distinctive plazas within Seaport Village: one with the feel of Old Monterey; another with the look of Victorian San Francisco; and the third with the ambiance of traditional Mexico. The main challenge called for an array of specific components that could merge in a natural way, while complementing and enhancing the visual and sensory experience for the Seaport Village visitor.

Those overseeing the development believed the key for achieving this goal depended on the sense of authenticity presented by the village's surroundings. This aim sent Seaport Village representatives on a dedicated search throughout the United States and Mexico to gather artifacts, furnishings and fixtures for the complex. The shopping list included old-fashioned planters, benches, turn posts, street lamps and porches. New plaster walls within the complex had to become "aged" before their time through sandblasting and the magic of special techniques used by "authenticators" from Disneyland. Washed aggregate, along with other rustic pavement treatments, gave pathways the look of 100-year-old roads while

Architectural historians and critics have declared Seaport Village "the most successfully knit large-scale urban design since the great exposition of 1915 in Balboa Park."

Seaport Village's most popular attraction, the authentically restored Broadway Flying Horses Carousel (c. 1890), draws more than 400,000 riders each year.

Spanish tile and walls, artistically chipped to show adobe, added to the illusion of being transported to another time and place. A Victorian clock tower and a Northern Pacific-style lighthouse lent to the quaintness as they took their places among assorted arched rooftops over vertical columns, rounding out the meld of distinctive styles.

Seaport Village officially opened its doors for business in June 1980 and Vice President and General Manager Ann Lane, who joined the company four months into the project, recalls, "From the first year, we exceeded any projections that had been made. People couldn't wait to get in and see the little jewel that had formerly been fenced, inaccessible land."

San Diego was no stranger to malls and impressive department stores, but most San Diegans had never experienced a shopping area geared to cater to their aesthetic senses. The influx of consumer-friendly megamalls has continued over the past 20 years and has presented some competition, but the same magic that first lured curious visitors to Seaport Village continues to entice shoppers and browsers back with its incomparable charm.

Visitors can choose from four miles of village pathways to stroll upon and savor the sensory feast offered by the sight of seagulls gliding overhead and the sound of gentle waves breaking along the quarter-mile slate boardwalk along the San Diego harbor. The transition from each distinctive plaza — Old Monterey, Victorian San Francisco and traditional Mexico — is made seamless by the blend of subtle colors and distinctive designs of the 73 specialty shops within the 90,000 square feet of the village. Equally as individual are the wares found in each store. There is something to appeal to the most discriminating shopper, whether it's a window full of deep sea coral frozen in a delicate bouquet, a willowy kite waving in the ocean breeze or a stained-glass sun catcher reflecting the glint of admiration in a passerby's eye. A visitor's willpower is also put to the test by the scents of gourmet coffees, freshly baked cookies and an array of aromas wafting from the village's four fine dining restaurants and 13 quick eateries.

Seaport Village was the first specialty retail center to incorporate entertainment on the grounds and it is a concept others in the retail business have enthusiastically embraced. Visitors to the village enjoy a wide range of entertainers ranging from street performers, face painters, clowns, jugglers, caricature and portrait artists, all regularly on hand to enrich one's visit. For those in the mood to sit back and enjoy some melodies, the sounds of jazz, country, acoustic arrangements, blues, brass and other types of music fill the air at different times during the week.

Programs for children are always a top priority at Seaport Village with programs such as the "Top Hat Party" and the "Young Audiences Showcase" being among the crowd favorites. "Top Hat" features Kazoo the Seaport Mime, portrayed by Jerry Hager, who has been performing at the village since it opened in 1980. He also amuses audiences with his "Kazoo's Kids Show," a weekly presentation featuring comedy, magic, puppetry and mime.

"Young Audiences" features one showcase performance for children each month. These free presentations and special appearances by members of the San Diego Symphony, La Jolla Playhouse and the San Diego Opera introduce the world of arts to children who may not be exposed to it elsewhere.

Seaport Village's most popular attraction, the renowned Broadway Flying Horses Carousel, delights children of all ages with its rich music from the 52-key, 175-pipe Gebruder Bruder Waldkirch Band Organ (Germany, 1914) and the carousel's turn-of-the-century hand-carved beauty. This magnificent specimen of craftsmanship dates back to 1890 and originally operated at Coney Island. In March of 1980, the entire carousel was shipped in pieces from Sandusky, Ohio's, Cedarpoint Amusement Park to Seaport Village. Extensive repair efforts were employed to strip the numerous layers of "park paint" to reach the base poplar wood. Months of gluing, clamping, sanding, sealing and painstakingly detailed painting followed, but the efforts resulted in a work of art that draws more than 400,000 riders each year.

Although the carousel is a frequently photographed "member" of many bridal parties, it has impressive competition as a perfect background from the village's shimmering bayfront view and the profusion of plants and flowers residing in rustic carts and barrels nestled alongside the meandering pathways. Four times each year, gardeners undertake the daunting task of revitalizing this flowery wonderland through color-planting, which keeps the grounds bursting with healthy, picture-perfect gardens. The resident painter also faces nonstop work to keep signs and building exteriors in prime condition.

Lane feels fortunate to have these dedicated workers and she points out, "Attrition is usually a problem in retail but we have lots of people who have been here over 10 years, which is especially unusual for janitorial and maintenance staff. Personnel is your biggest expense but it's one of your biggest assets."

Although only minutes from downtown San Diego, visitors to Seaport Village can step back in time to explore this turn-of-the-century-style shopping, dining and entertainment complex.

Seaport Village also employs its own security staff, but the park itself is under the jurisdiction of the Harbor Police since it is the Port of San Diego's property. The San Diego Police Department handles the surrounding area and all work well together. The village prides itself for its reputation as being a safe place, day or night. No soliciting or passing out of leaflets is allowed on the property and shoppers do not have to worry about dodging skateboarders or bicyclists. Security is alerted if someone looks like he's going to cause a problem and the potential troublemaker is tactfully but promptly escorted out. Given the caliber of Seaport Village's visitors, this is a rare occurrence.

No official count has been kept of the number of people to stroll the grounds, but it is estimated to be in the millions with many of the visitors taking advantage of the connecting boardwalk from the neighboring Hyatt Regency Hotel and the Marriott Hotel and Marina. A sizeable part of the crowd filters in from the nearby San Diego Convention Center, always bustling with business. Large crowds also flock to Seaport Village to view the twinkling flotilla of sailboats, powerboats and yachts that glide by in the harbor's annual Christmas Parade of Lights. Fireworks fans fill the village when glittering displays light up the summer nights. Crowds frequently overflow into the adjacent eight-acre Embarcadero Marina Park, which provides visitors access to 22 acres of village and parkland.

Because of its pristine setting and invigorating sea breezes, Seaport Village often serves as a meeting site for groups holding charity events like walkathons and races. The village's marketing department offers whatever assistance it can to ensure a well-attended and memorable event. Community support remains important to those on the executive staff. President Anne Taubman explains, "We all love San Diego and we love the community, so we feel it's very important to participate in whatever we can to help make San Diego a better place."

Numerous plaques and awards on display in the corporate offices, located within the village, serve as a reminder that commitment to doing one's best does matter. Each token of recognition is valued, but Seaport Village is particularly proud of the Helping Hands award from the Travelers Aid Association, which was awarded for special services rendered by an employee to a visitor in grave need of assistance. Other meaningful recognition has come from the International Council

One million visitors a year enjoy Seaport Village's unique shops and incomparable charm.

of Shopping Centers in the form of the Maxi Award, an honor bestowed for the village's involvement in organizing or sponsoring charitable or special events that affect the community.

Praise is one commodity that has never been in short order for this bayfront attraction, and accolades continue to pour in from the tourist industry, government officials and the millions of visitors who appreciate its beauty and uniqueness. Architectural historians and critics have declared Seaport Village "the most successfully knit large-scale urban design in San Diego since the great exposition of 1915 in Balboa Park." *Sunset* magazine called it, "The most approachable waterfront on the West Coast" and "one of America's most entertaining waterfronts." *Los Angeles Magazine* listed San Diego as its No. 1 getaway and Seaport Village as its first attraction: "The state's most enjoyable waterfront complex."

Expansion remains a goal for Seaport Village planners, but they must face more obstacles than when they began in the 1970s, as Lane explains. "Twenty years ago you didn't have a coastal commission, you didn't have downtown residents and you didn't have environmentalists. It was a totally different world for developers. Now, there are a lot of very specific hurdles one must overcome in the development process on Port of San Diego land — and they are spelled out in great detail."

Expansion plans include additional retail stores, a large public park, entertainment areas, restaurants, arcades and office space. Besides expansions to Seaport Village and Embarcadero Marina Park North, plans have been discussed to add a second hotel tower to the Hyatt Regency Hotel, adjacent to the village.

Once again, finding tenants to set up shop will not be a problem since the village maintains a long list of vendors who want to conduct business within the walls of this shopping Shangri-La. Seaport Village has always been 100 percent occupied — a rare statistic since the retail industry norm is a 5 percent vacancy rate. According to Lane, "We have a lot of people beating on the door to get in, but not too many beating on the door to get out."

Anne Taubman believes her father's initial philosophy on specialty retail remains alive and says, "If you walk around the village today, you'll primarily see mom-and-pop-type operations and very few chain operators. We don't like the term 'shopping center' applied to us. We want it to be a unique experience for people so we search hard to find more unique concepts to populate our stores."

Anne intends to keep her father's dream flourishing and this includes keeping a close eye on the merchandise offered by village shops. "We're a family-oriented operation and we don't allow inappropriate merchandise to be sold. We're very hands-on and involved with our tenants, and we have an open-door policy for them to come into the office anytime to talk about this or that. We've encouraged that because none of us would be comfortable in an ivory tower, closed-door, corporate setting. We feel their success is our success."

Seaport Village shoppers can enjoy a peaceful stroll upon four miles of meandering cobblestone pathways which wind past ponds, lakes, fountains and lush, colorful landscaping.

Bazaar Del Mundo

For all its color and pageantry, the history of Bazaar Del Mundo begins with a boarded-up motel and a weed-choked courtyard — and the irrepressible vision of a designer whose creative exuberance drove her to deliver faraway beauty to the hometown she loved.

Few of the six million annual visitors who stroll through the lively collection of boutiques and restaurants in San Diego's historic Old Town would guess that the teeming multicultural enterprise swirling in color and awash in mariachi music once was considered such a white elephant that when the state invited developers to bid on the then run-down site, a grand total of one application was filed. Because if Bazaar Del Mundo now seems like a perfect marriage of historic preservation and commercial development, its history suggests a transformation better explained by determination than destiny.

The signature on that single application belonged to Diane Powers. The year was 1971. A young woman with a love for horses and a talent for design, Powers was learning to trust her creative instincts while running her own business, the Design Center, located then on Fifth Avenue in San Diego. She was also cultivating her passion for Latin American folk art by traveling to Mexico and Central America, places where her love for color, culture and countryside spoke to her like nowhere else.

A visit to the Bazaar Sabado in a town outside Mexico City would soon become the inspiration for Bazaar Del Mundo. What she saw was an old hacienda inhabited by seven artists, each one selling a different craft out of his room. Downstairs, a mariachi played outside a cafe. "I'd love to do something like that sometime," she thought.

Opportunity soon presented itself when the state invited bids for redevelopment of Casa de Pico, a dilapidated motel that time had forgotten. Designed in 1929 by renowned architect Richard Requa, the once-proud building sat in sleepy Old Town as an empty shell in a lifeless courtyard, its paint peeling from years of sun and neglect. Where others saw a virtual ghost town, Powers heard mariachi music. Even though she was the 16th person to

Bazaar Del Mundo, in historic Old Town San Diego, welcomes visitors with a festive explosion of color, brilliant gardens, colorful banners and splashing fountains.

Sights, sounds and flavors from south-of-the-border surround visitors. Every weekend folkloric dancers perform in a swirl of color on the stage in the Bazaar's courtyard and mariachis entertain daily.

A collector's paradise for quality folk art, Artes de Mexico showcases a brilliant and extraordinary selection from the various regions of Mexico.

pick up a bid form, she was the only one to show up in Sacramento with a proposal.

Not many would have guessed that a designer without formal financial or development experience would create the most successful concessionaire in the state park system and nearly single-handedly revitalize Old Town, but that's exactly what she did. With only a three-month deadline to complete her planned renovation, Powers called on her own design skills and the financial backing of former client Richard Silberman to get the job done.

There were many obstacles in the beginning; interested and qualified tenants were unexpectedly hard to find. Not even after she visited virtually every Mexican restaurant in the city was she able to land a single interested restauranteur. Undeterred, she simply operated the first four restaurants herself, as well as 12 out of the 16 retail shops. All told, it took about seven years before Powers bought out her partnership and became sole owner. But like the relentless

Dining alfresco in the colorful patio restaurants is a favorite pastime at the Bazaar. At Casa de Pico, mariachis serenade diners enjoying a courtyard vista and fiesta atmosphere.

Locals flock to the Bazaar's four famous Mexican restaurants, renowned for excellent Mexican cuisine, both traditional and innovative. Attention to every detail in the culinary presentation and the environment contribute to a memorable experience.

bougainvillea that greets visitors who pass underneath the Bazaar's various trellises, success became an inevitable outgrowth of Bazaar Del Mundo's many cultural goods, festive attractions and acclaimed restaurants, all of which still bear the Diane Powers stamp of vision and quality.

The initial mix included specialty shops offering apparel, baskets, books, Mexican folk art, plants and jewelry. Other shops included a toy store, a Mexican bakery, a fruit bazaar, a gallery and a farmer's market. And while the medley has evolved over the years, it remains unusually stable. Perhaps that is because, unlike shopping malls, Bazaar Del Mundo operates under a single, cohesive theme that reflects the cultural richness that Powers has long admired.

The state became an admirer as well. Seeking a second stage of renovation, it asked Powers in 1973 to redevelop the visitors and information center into a restaurant, which today stands as the award-winning Rancho el Nopal. Then, in the early 80s, a third makeover was undertaken in the restoration of the historic hacienda of Juan Bandini, one of only two large adobe homes still standing in Old Town. Built with three-foot-thick walls in 1829 — a full century before the Casa de Pico — the magnificent but long-vacant home became today's acclaimed Casa De Bandini restaurant.

Today, Bazaar Del Mundo thrives amid lush gardens and Early California ambiance with its popular labyrinth of 16 specialty boutiques and four acclaimed international restaurants. Whether its locals who can't wait to introduce

Beautifully restored and now an award-winning restaurant, Casa de Bandini welcomes guests to resplendent courtyard gardens and elegant dining rooms. Originally the one-story 1829 home of prominent Old Town citizen Juan Bandini, the dwelling acquired a second floor in 1869 when it became the Cosmopolitan Hotel.

out-of-town visitors to the aroma of fresh homemade tortillas and the best margaritas in the city, or shoppers delighting in finding everything from gourmet salsas to books on Mexican architecture, Bazaar Del Mundo lives up to its pledge of being "Mexico, this side of the border!" Annual community events, such as the Latin American Festival and Old Town's popular Fiesta Cinco de Mayo, accentuate the Latin experience, along with nearly constant, free folkloric entertainment.

Although mostly known for its distinctively Latin flavor, the Bazaar Del Mundo, literally meaning "marketplace of the world," also takes visitors beyond its south-of-the-border fare with events, exhibits and merchandise from many lands and cultures.

It's an alliance of the exotic that Diane Powers, a believer in the power of travel, wouldn't have any other way. To her, it's not just a collection of stores. It's very nearly who she is, as evidenced by the dazzling, Mexican-styled ensembles she likes to wear not as costumes, but as sincere statements of personal identity. She still owns and supervises 13 of the shops and all four restaurants, as well as a fifth restaurant outside the state park. Her professional accolades include the 1994 Entrepreneur of the Year award by the California Tourism Industry Association, and recognition in 1996 from the California Department of Tourism for Best Multicultural Tourism Program. Powers was also named 1997 Woman Business Owner of the Year by the San Diego Chapter of the National Association of Women Business Owners. Bazaar Del Mundo was rated by *Niche* magazine as one of the nation's top 100 craft retailers and is the fifth largest woman-owned business in San Diego.

As for the future of Old Town, Powers would like to see the adjoining Presidio area linked to the historic district, and Old Town itself beautified and expanded with trees and vegetation. And while she believes San Diego could strengthen its overall architectural image, it could be said that the modern-day mother of Old Town has not only created one of the most popular local destinations for tourists and residents alike, but already has fashioned the embodiment of America's perception of San Diego design.

Promus Hotels

"Promus" means "to serve" in Latin, a definition that needs no translation to tourists, business travelers and residents in San Diego, where the Promus Hotel Corporation operates three Doubletree and two Embassy Suites hotels.

Located just three blocks from the San Diego Convention Center and situated near many tourist attractions such as Seaport Village and Balboa Park, Embassy Suites San Diego Bay is ideally suited for business and leisure travelers alike.

The story behind these five hotels embraces a pair of industry success strategies common in today's competitive corporate landscape: mega-merger leveraging combined with a mom-and-pop touch. Both have helped earn Promus an acclaimed legacy of innovation and service. Whether it is Embassy Suites becoming the first national upscale hotel chain to offer an unconditional satisfaction guarantee, or Doubletree's clever service campaign that greets each guest with a freshly baked chocolate chip cookie, the Promus Hotel Corporation has consistently shown why it is the U.S. lodging industry's third-largest revenue producer and one of the fastest growing hoteliers, opening a new hotel every other day.

Doubletree hotels in San Diego, situated next to popular venues and outdoor sporting options that make America's Finest City such a popular destination for travelers, are located in Mission Valley, Del Mar, and Carmel Highland. Embassy Suites serves guests at its San Diego Bay hotel, and at its La Jolla location.

In 1983, the all-suite hotel was a new concept in the lodging industry. That year, however, marked the beginning of the Embassy Suites hotel chain, which today is credited with launching the upscale, all-suite segment of the hotel industry on a national level. Embassy Suites was founded on the notion of providing guests "Twice the Hotel," the tagline of its well-known, award-winning advertising campaign, and the hotel chain has successfully introduced this concept to travelers around the world.

With 145 hotels across the United States and in international markets, Embassy Suites maintains a commanding presence in the all-suite hotel segment in terms of system size, geographic distribution, brand-name recognition and operating performance. The chain's occupancy and room revenues consistently achieve premiums over industry averages and competitors in the upscale hotel segment.

"The added benefits we offer provide the convenience, hospitality and cost-effectiveness that you don't often find in typical upscale hotels," said Ray Schultz, Promus Hotel Corporation's chairman and chief executive officer. "In a sense, Embassy Suites has reinvented the upscale hotel experience, and our concept appeals to both business travelers and weekend leisure guests."

In 1993, Embassy Suites became the first all-suite, upscale hotel chain to offer its guests an unconditional satisfaction guarantee. The service enables all employees, from housekeeping to the front desk, to enact the policy. The guarantee was introduced after comprehensive research and testing at various Embassy Suites hotels across the country. While less than three-tenths of one percent of annual guests invoke the guarantee, the inventive policy helped change the way the hotel industry operated and how guests viewed hospitality service.

One year later, Embassy Suites, along with other Promus-managed hotel brands, became the first hotel company to distribute hotel information over the Internet, allowing guests to make reservations and inquiries by computer.

The attention to high-tech amenities is part of Embassy Suites' effort to improve productivity for the business client and provide more comfort for leisure travelers. The suites feature a separate living area that can serve as a work space or small meeting room, as well as a mini-kitchen, private bedroom and bathroom. Each suite also includes two remote-controlled televisions, two telephones with voice mail and data ports, a wet bar, coffee maker, refrigerator, microwave oven, iron and ironing board.

Embassy Suites opened its San Diego Bay hotel in July 1988. Located at Harbor Drive and Pacific Highway, across from Seaport Village, the 12-floor, 337-suite hotel is within walking distance from the San Diego Convention Center, as well as the Civic Center, the historic Gaslamp Quarter, Horton Plaza shopping mall and Balboa Park.

As in all Embassy Suites, the hotel offers a central tropical atrium as the setting for its complimentary, cooked-to-order breakfast, and a two-hour manager's reception each evening, with beverages of the guest's choice.

Opened in July 1987, Embassy Suites in La Jolla offers 335 suites and a 12-story tropical atrium with a winding koi pond and is located across the street from the University Towne Centre shopping mall. Nearby attractions include the Scripps Birch Aquarium, Salk Institute, La Jolla Playhouse, La Jolla Cove, and the Torrey Pines Golf Course. Recreational facilities at both of the Embassy Suites in San Diego include an indoor pool, whirlpool, sun deck, redwood sauna and complimentary use of the hotel's fitness center.

Doubletree Hotels Corporation, whose roots can be traced to 1969, formed its present company in 1993 when two strong regional hotel brands, Boston-based Guest Quarters Suite Hotels and Phoenix-based Doubletree Hotels, merged to form a single national organization. In 1995, Doubletree and joint-venture partner, Grupo Propulsa of Mexico, converted properties in Mazatlan and Ixtapa to the Doubletree Hotel brand, the first outside the United States. One year later, Doubletree acquired Red Lion Hotels, giving the company a dominant presence in the Pacific Northwest. Considered one of the nation's largest hotel management companies, Doubletree has more than 250 properties, comprising approximately 58,000 guest rooms and suites in 41 states, Mexico and the Caribbean.

Most Doubletree Hotels are located in major metropolitan areas, close to popular venues, and offer full-service facilities and amenities, including restaurants and lounges, room service, health clubs, business centers, and meeting and banquet space. In competing against other hotel chains such as Hyatt, Marriott, Hilton and Sheraton, consumer surveys have rated Doubletree as the best in the industry, with more than 92 percent of those guests indicating they intend to return.

Today, the Doubletree name signifies upscale

(Far bottom) Embassy Suites, La Jolla

The Doubletree Carmel Highland Resort, situated in a lush green valley with its 6,428-yard golf course and five championship tennis courts, offers guests the quintessential Southern California retreat.

hotels that have a wide following among frequent business and leisure travelers. But when most people think of Doubletree Hotels, the first thing that comes to mind is the hotel chain's hallmark chocolate chip cookie. Upon arrival, guests are treated to a special package of the freshly baked cookies as a creative way of saying, "Welcome."

This delectable service icon played a starring role in the company's $50 million marketing campaign launched in 1997, which helped differentiate Doubletree from its competition. "Our Version

The Doubletree Hotel San Diego-Mission Valley opened in March 1997 and is centrally located near SeaWorld, Balboa Park, Qualcomm Stadium and Old Town. Next door is the 27-hole Riverwalk Golf Course.

of the Sleeping Pill," read one advertisement headline that accompanied a close-up photograph of the famed cookie. Said another: "To You, It's A Cookie; To Us, It's A Mission Statement."

The celebrated cookie first became an integral part of the Doubletree culture in the early 90s, with the hotel chain's longtime tradition of greeting VIPs with the tasty treat. It quickly became synonymous with Doubletree's hospitality, and the welcome gift was expanded to include every Doubletree guest. Today the sweet treat still dominates Doubletree's guest comment cards that rate service and accommodations.

"What began as a way to ensure a memorable guest experience has become one of Doubletree's most effective promotional tools," said Thomas W. Storey, Doubletree sales and marketing executive vice president. "In consumer focus groups, when asked to identify the qualities that make a hotel company unique, Doubletree's chocolate chip cookie was consistently and overwhelmingly praised by participants."

Two of San Diego's Doubletree hotels opened in the summer of 1991 — Del Mar in June, and Carmel Highland in September. The Del Mar Doubletree, located just east of Interstate 5 and close to the Del Mar Racetrack and Torrey Pines State Park, has an attractive Spanish mission-style architecture and offers 220 guest rooms and suites. Each room has a modem hookup on the desk phone; professional meeting space and elegant banquet facilities are available in the La Jolla Ballroom, which opens onto a beautiful patio area.

The Doubletree Carmel Highland Resort is cradled in a lush green valley north of San Diego and has the appearance of the sort of idyllic retreat that many associate with the Southern California recreational culture. The exclusive golf and tennis resort has 173 richly furnished guest rooms and suites, each with a patio or balcony overlooking the golf course, pool or gardens. Guests can enjoy the 6,428-yard golf course as well as five championship tennis courts. The resort also offers more than 11,000 square feet of meeting and banquet space.

The Doubletree Hotel San Diego-Mission Valley opened in March 1997. Located within minutes of SeaWorld, Balboa Park, Qualcomm Stadium and Old Town, and situated next to the 27-hole Riverwalk Golf Course, it features 300 guest rooms and six suites. The hotel also has more than 13,000 square feet of flexible meeting and banquet facilities, including 15 meeting rooms, an executive boardroom, and a spacious ballroom that can accommodate 1,000 people. Most rooms feature built-in public address systems, audiovisual equipment and adjustable lighting.

As one of the world's largest hotel companies, Promus Hotel Corporation's roots can be traced to the formation of Holiday Inns of America, Inc., in April 1954. By the 1980s, Promus had entered gaming and had launched Embassy Suites as well as another new concept — Hampton Inns, which remains a leader in the upper mid-market, limited service segment. In the late 80s, Promus introduced a new extended-stay hotel brand, Homewood Suites, which was ranked first in its category by Business Travel News in 1998.

The Promus Companies, Inc. was launched in February 1990, following the sale of the Holiday Inn hotel brand. In 1995, the Promus Companies split into two separate companies: Promus Hotel Corporation, which included the company's hotel brands; and Harrah's Entertainment, Inc., which included Harrah's casino entertainment brand.

The merger of Doubletree Corporation and Promus Hotel Corporation took place in 1997, a year that hotel industry mergers were not uncommon. The merger, combining Doubletree's strength in hotel management with Promus' strength in franchising and building brands, established the company it is today. These two major players pooled an estimated $2 billion in assets to create a new industry giant with a portfolio of more than 1,300 hotels, approximately 190,000 rooms, about 40,000 employees, and system-wide sales of $5 billion in 1997.

By combining their respective reservation and information systems, purchasing functions, accounting and payroll tasks, and many other corporate operations, the two companies realized an estimated cost savings of $15 to $20 million annually.

"This merger was a defining moment for Promus," said Schultz. "In joining with a quality upscale full-service brand in Doubletree Hotels, as well as its other brands, the combined company is able to offer a full range of quality accommodations to meet the needs of business and leisure travelers in markets throughout the United States."

Aside from pioneering new concepts such as the satisfaction guarantee and reservation access through the Internet, Promus has introduced other innovations. These include the 1996 launch of Club Hotels by Doubletree, the first co-branded concept in the industry. Targeted specifically for the mid-market business traveler, each Club Hotel features a 2,000- to 5,000-square-foot Business Club Room located just off the lobby, which serves as equal parts office, den and cafe.

Promus expanded internationally in 1992 with the opening of the first Embassy Suites in Markham, Ontario, Canada. Hampton Inns quickly followed suit by opening its first property in Niagara Falls, Ontario, Canada, in 1993. The company has subsequently entered the Latin and Central American markets, with properties currently operational in Columbia, Chile, Costa Rica, and throughout Mexico.

Promus continued its diversification in 1994, entering into the vacation ownership industry with the opening of the first Embassy Vacation Resort in Kauai, Hawaii. The first Hampton Inn Vacation Resort opened in 1997.

Plans for future expansion by Promus include continued emphasis on hotel franchising and management. Based on current announced plans by franchisees, the company expects to open a new hotel approximately every two days through the end of the century.

That may sound like an ambitiously frantic pace, but as countless business travelers and tourists can attest, a productive stay at any one of the five Promus hotels in San Diego can be as relaxing as a chocolate chip cookie.

The Doubletree Hotel Del Mar has an attractive Spanish mission-style flavor and is located near the Del Mar Racetrack and some of San Diego's most stunning beaches.

Anthony's Fish Grotto

Catherine Ghio understood that good ingredients made lasting creations. As a mother of three children, she embodied this idea by blending love, a main ingredient, with equal amounts of tenderness and nurturing. "Mama" Ghio, a widow, raised two sons and one daughter. They were each of sound mind and healthy body, thanks to their wonderful mother, and the delicious presence of Ghio's other lasting creations: fish recipes, chowders, sauces, batters and dressings. These too were borne out of love and, of course, "secret" ingredients.

Eventually, family and food found meaning for Ghio beyond simply large household gatherings. In 1946, she combined her favorite creations, and along with her sons Tod and Anthony and her son-in-law Roy Weber, she opened an 18-seat seafood eatery. They called their new business Anthony's Fish Grotto. It earned a respectable $179.19 in the first month of operation, and more money in subsequent months. But while profits were an indicator of success, they could never match the restaurant's true value to future generations of the Ghio family and the San Diego community.

Anthony's Fish Grotto, then and now, features fresh seafood from local waters and from the oceans that Mama Ghio sailed in 1912 to arrive from her native Genova, Italy. The classic culinary delights that she instituted, including Mama's clam chowder and cioppino casserole (halibut, shrimp, scallops and crab meat), remain on the menu and are joined by contemporary grilled specialties and multiregional seafood entrees. This respect for tradition, while still appealing to current customer tastes, is attributable to the third generation of Ghio family ownership — cousins Rick and Craig Ghio, Phil and Beverly Mascari and Pauline Gaus — who have successfully grown Anthony's into a San Diego fixture and nationally recognized leader in casual dining.

Anthony's corporate banner is anchored by the world-class, fine dining of the Star of the Sea on San Diego Bay. Underneath this umbrella is a chain of thriving local Grottos, Anthony's Seafood Deli Mart located within Grottos, and Ghio Seafood Products, Anthony's year-round fish-buying and processing division. The respective synergies derived from these areas result in numerous company awards from respected restaurant industry names, including *Wine Spectator* and Distinguished Restaurants of North America (DiRONA). However, the most important recognition always comes from guests. San Diegans consistently rate the Anthony's restaurants No. 1 in local magazine and newspaper surveys. Similarly, word-of-mouth from travelers has made Anthony's the most requested restaurant at San Diego's visitor and convention information agencies.

Anthony's level of acclaim is not solely the product of a mission, but of a unified corporate vision. Annually, through the service of more than one million dinners, elements of this vision are literally on display for public consumption. Guests will notice that Anthony's is the realization of a company built by passionate, fun and caring people who are committed to excellence.

Founders (left) Anthony and "Mama" Ghio, Roy Weber and Tod Ghio (c. 1946)

Warwick's

Like the town it is an intrinsic part of, Warwick's is a bustle of activity and a place that comfortably blends the Old World and the new. Located in the heart of La Jolla, it offers local customers and tourists alike a comprehensive selection of books, office supplies, gifts and stationery. Here the traditions of exemplary personal service and classic merchandise mix with the modern environment and ever-changing array of products.

When W.T. Warwick founded his paper goods shop in Minnesota in 1896, he sold books, writing paper and writing instruments, as well as wallpaper and anything related to paper. Upon relocating to California in the mid-1930s, Warwick re-established his store in downtown La Jolla. The next generation, Wynn and Louise Warwick (W.T.'s son and daughter-in-law) took over in 1950, expanding and modernizing the shop. Additionally, they introduced new items they discovered while traveling internationally.

In 1964, Wynn and Louise's son, Bob, and his wife, Marian, moved into the ownership position and again remodeled, streamlined and upgraded the stock. Under their management the store grew both in size and prominence, undergoing two expansions and establishing loyal customers all over San Diego County. Bob and Marian retired in 1998 to devote more time to another family tradition, travel. Their daughters, Nancy Warwick and Cathy O'Neill, became the owners of Warwick's and have continued to emphasize the store's traditions of one-on-one personal service and top-quality merchandise.

However, Warwick's is more than a place to buy books, office supplies, gifts and stationery. It's a mecca for social activity. Regular customers expect to run into friends or chat with their favorite longtime store employees, several of whom have been on staff more than 10 years, including the store manager, who has been employed at Warwick's for over 25 years. At least six times a month Warwick's holds special events, ranging from book signings to a variety of craft classes. The monthly calendar is mailed to more than 2,000 people, and 100 can be accommodated at most events. Julia Childs, Colin Powell and Margaret Thatcher are among the authors who have graced Warwick's premises. At a book signing for an author of a book on dogs, even customers' four-legged friends were welcomed and received treats.

Warwick's has been a family-operated business since 1896.

Warwick's cooperative family environment has attracted talented, career-oriented employees, who are encouraged to utilize their areas of expertise. The bookstore manager runs the department with little owner input and feels proud that her contributions are reflected in the store's success. Every staff member is well-trained in his or her product area. The serious book lover knows he or she can get recommendations on books that employees have actually read and discussions are often lengthy. "That's why we have a big staff," Nancy explains, "so we can provide the personalized service we are known for and that customers are missing in big chains or on the Internet."

On any day a new or repeat visitor to Warwick's will find it humming with energy. A vital part of the community, Warwick's remains the place to find great books, unique gifts, good friends and dog biscuits.

The Bedroom Superstore

"Where America buys bedrooms for less and the mattress is always free."

Rob Kelley, vice president of The Bedroom Superstore; Jack Poe, vice president of Poe Advertising; Rick Haux Sr., president; Rick Haux Jr., COO; George Meier, group executive

Perhaps no room in the house more strongly reflects the personality of its owner than the bedroom. The decision of what furniture to purchase is a highly personal and difficult one. Most people only purchase a full bedroom set once or twice during their lifetime and they want to make sure that in 10 years they will love each piece as much as they did on the showroom floor. The people at The Bedroom Superstore understand this. Their "sleep specialists" are experts in the category of bedroom furniture, mattresses and furnishings.

Each of The Bedroom Superstores features an irresistible array of close to 50 bedroom suites, plus youth furniture. This design concept allows each person to experience the furniture and imagine it in their own bedroom. Rather than walking up and down unexciting rows of beds, cabinets and nightstands, customers are invited to wander from gallery to gallery of completely decorated bedroom suites full of sleigh beds, four-poster beds, bunk beds and rich cherry wood, oak, maple and pine chests, dressers and armoires.

The latest styles in bedroom furniture, affordably priced and in complete packages, can be found at The Bedroom Superstore. Customers have been known to return after purchasing their furniture to borrow interior decorating ideas. Each suite is a unique design, dressed with wallpaper or painted walls, lamps, pictures and other accessories. The furniture is of high quality, with a high-end look. In fact, collections often mirror those found in design and home magazines. The furniture is sold both individually and in complete deluxe suites discounted into one low price. With the purchase of a complete four-piece set, the mattress is free.

The Bedroom Superstore is known as a category specialist, a store that focuses on one product grouping only. It also varies from other stores in that it carries complete furniture lines, not just one or two sample styles. It carries the largest selection of bedroom furniture and mattresses of any one store. This makes The Bedroom Superstore important to vendors and gives it the ability to command exclusives, offer the lowest prices and approach manufacturers with critical input on design and style from mattress lines to bedroom furniture.

This unique store has an edge with the customer because its salespeople are bedroom specialists. Within moments of arrival, customers are welcomed by sales associates who assist them through the selection process. The Bedroom Superstore believes that people often are unsure of what bedroom they want because they are unaware of their choices and, as a result, purchase the wrong mattress or furniture.

Sales associates often question customers on lifestyle needs and how the rest of the home is decorated so they can suggest certain collections. Mattress selection is discussed at length — firmness, size, durability and type. The store offers waterbed, air and flotation mattresses as well as a wide range of conventional coil and spring mattresses. Highly trained, The Bedroom Superstore's sales associates are the ultimate professionals in their field. They focus on health problems and sleep needs, not the coil counts or the gauge of the steel in the construction. In recommending specific mattresses, they can help customers avoid back pain and sleeplessness and get the best night's sleep.

The Bedroom Superstore started as Waterbed Emporium in 1977 on Clairemont Mesa Boulevard. From the beginning, it dominated the market. Owner Rick Haux, Sr. advertised "get the best night's sleep on a waterbed" and customers flocked to his door. In 1981 Jack Poe joined the corporation and the company expanded to include a full-service television advertising agency.

A specialist in marketing and advertising, Poe has spent more than 30 years as a copywriter, editor, director and producer of television spots. Consequently, Poe Advertising not only provides the script but also produces and tapes the commercial in its own state-of-the-art digital studio. It researches viewer demographics and then places the spot on the air. Today, it is the largest local television advertising agency in San Diego.

Poe Advertising not only gave the company an additional dimension but gave The Bedroom Superstore control over its own destiny by allowing it to produce and place its own televised ads. In 1983, Waterbed Emporium expanded to the Pacific Northwest and eventually became The Bedroom in 1987.

In 1990 The Bedroom teamed up with a 35-store Phoenix chain, Sun Valley Waterbeds. Then, in 1992, the company consolidated and started to convert its locations to The Bedroom Superstore. Floor space increased to about 12,000 to 15,000 square feet per store, and product lines deepened.

The original marketing concepts of providing quality products at guaranteed lowest prices and always offering the best night's sleep continue. Since the inception of The Bedroom Superstore, its offer of a free mattress foundation with any deluxe-suite purchase has never wavered.

Due to its enormous success and the public acceptance of its stores, the company opened the first America's Sofa Superstore in December 1998, specializing in living room and family room furniture. As with The Bedroom Superstore, the furniture is clustered together in complete design suites allowing customers to see how the ensemble might look in their homes. Plans are to build a strong base of business and then expand into different cities. America's Sofa Superstores also carry sleepers, recliners, leather, reclining sofas, sectionals and all other room accessory pieces. Living room and family room furniture will be sold as a unit suite as well as individually.

Today, The Bedroom Superstore is the largest, most respected retailer of bedroom furniture and mattresses in the western United States. It has 30 retail stores in cities including San Diego, Bakersfield, Fresno, Seattle, Reno, Las Vegas, Phoenix, Tucson, San Francisco, Modesto, Spokane, Denver, Colorado Springs and Salt Lake City. With the opening of more locations of America's Sofa Superstore, the company's goal to become unrivaled in the furniture-sales industry may soon be fulfilled.

The Bedroom Superstore carries one of the largest selections of bedroom furniture and mattresses.

America's Sofa Superstore specializes in living room and family room furniture.

Jakob Gerhardt

Jakob Gerhardt wants to open the eyes of American wine drinkers, which is why the agent always blind-tastes each prospective vintage. As an international brokerage that samples and tests at least 40 wines for every one it decides to recommend to its clientele, it is helping to educate the national drinking public by combining Old World tradition with the practical philosophy of trusting one's own taste buds.

Few industries carry the history and romance of the wine trade. Unfortunately, history doesn't certify reputations, it only creates them, while romance can blur judgment like a third glass of merlot. As humorist James Thurber once put it, "It's a naive wine without any breeding, but I think you'll be amused by its pretension."

Jakob Gerhardt USA, Inc. was founded to dispel such double-talk. Understanding that for many Americans ordering wine can be a haphazard process of impulse and intimidation, it employs an educated sales staff that helps consumers select premium wines and even create custom labels and bottle etchings.

"So often people drink what they think they're supposed to be drinking," says Fonda Hopkins, vice president of Jakob Gerhardt. "What I found was that the public didn't have the knowledge and there was no one to help them. We knew that people wanted to learn; they just needed somebody who cared and would help them. Americans have generally never been very sophisticated about wine, and so they fall prey to lots of inferior products on the market and bulk-produced wines that have very little to do with quality wine-making."

Hopkins teamed with Herbert Leckert in 1991 to change all that. Leckert, a European wine merchant with 30 years of experience, helped establish the brokerage that would become Jakob Gerhardt USA, Inc. The brokerage in 1992 purchased the W.G. Best Company, which gave Hopkins and Leckert the ability to import and sell wines through wholesale and retail outlets. Then the brokerage acquired the rights to use the name of Jakob Gerhardt, one of the largest and most prestigious wine sellers in Europe for nearly 300 years.

With its global reach and crucial name recognition in place, Jakob Gerhardt embarked on its mission to educate the American palate. It opened an office in Orlando, Florida, in 1993, and today operates in San Francisco and from two offices in San Diego. In 1997, it purchased the Las Cerezas winery in Napa, California, giving the brokerage the ability to create for local restaurants their own line of house wines.

Those are mere addresses, however. The true location of Jakob Gerhardt's calling can be found in large and small vineyards around the world, where Gerhardt's representatives seek out the very best-tasting wines regardless of reputation or pedigree.

"Because of climate and geography, less than 5 percent of all wines can be considered great wines," says Hopkins. "We're constantly chasing that elusive 5 percent."

The chase never quite ends. In constantly assessing vintages from the line of 300 to 400 wines

Teaching people to trust their own taste buds is a big part of Jakob Gerhardt's educational focus.

it will carry in any given year, as well as evaluating new discoveries, the brokerage will experience as much as 90 percent annual turnover on its product line. After rigorous blind-tasting, wines do not become part of the Gerhardt line until they then pass muster from independent lab tests, which can uncover hidden additives and reveal a wine's truer character.

It is because of such attention to detail that Gerhardt's customers are aware, for example, that some vineyards may flavor their wines with oak chips in order to force upon their vintage the "oaky" taste that is currently fashionable (hence, profitable) in this country. They learn such insider secrets from any one of Gerhardt's 50 brokers, who are continually educated so they can do more than simply recommend wine to their customers.

"What we want to bring to our clients is that history and experience," says Hopkins. "When they talk to our staff it's as if they visited the winery itself as opposed to just browsing in a store and randomly picking a wine by reading labels. Our business is predicated on personalized service and our ongoing relationships with clients."

Perhaps that is why Jakob Gerhardt's revenues have grown by 35 percent in each of the last three years. Benefiting from an industry that has gone upscale in this country, as well as recent studies that have linked various health benefits with moderate consumption of red wine, the retail division of W.G. Best recorded $8 million in sales in 1998, while its emerging wholesale division notched $1 million. A typical customer buys about four cases of wine per year, and repeat business remains the foundation of the brokerage's success.

Sales to restaurants, corporations and organizations hosting special events represents a growing market for the company. It provides wines for up to 300 restaurants in San Francisco, and in less than a year the brokerage helped more than 50 restaurants in San Diego launch their own wine programs. The brokerage can create for individuals or businesses custom labels and bottle etchings for any occasion with an unusually quick turn-around time. The brokerage is also a visible presence at many community events and charity functions, debunking myths and showing consumers how to follow their own particular taste. During the 1996 Republican National Convention in San Diego, for example, many delegates were skeptical when offered samples of various after-dinner wines at an official function.

"People assumed that all German wines are sweet and initially said, 'No, thanks,'" Hopkins recalls. "But once they were coaxed into trying them, they were amazed. It blew away their preconceived notions. That's the fun of this business."

Future plans for Jakob Gerhardt include establishing a presence in the Los Angeles market and expanding nationwide. The company also plans to open local tasting rooms in which the public can sample wines and enjoy the same sort of wine tour experience that makes Napa Valley such a popular destination among tourists that it allegedly draws more visitors annually than Disneyland.

While the mystique attached to wine in this country may never be replaced by the cultural formality wine enjoys in Europe, it's clear that Jakob Gerhardt will continue to serve as usher and educator to the American palate.

Jakob Gerhardt frequently hosts wine tastings at various community events and charity functions in order to introduce others to the pleasures of wine drinking.

Josh Mitchell Photography

(Right) Cirque du Soleil, Treasure Island, Las Vegas

(Below) Jim Burrows, Universal Studios

(Far bottom) Sidney Kimmel Cancer Center

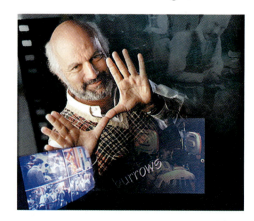

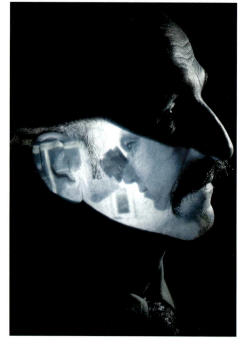

Josh Mitchell drove toward Los Angeles after another busy week of commercial photography in San Diego. He had made the same trip many times before, but the bright lights and chaos on this spring evening in 1997 had nothing to do with Hollywood. Instead, Mitchell, a photographer and image-maker for high-profile companies, advertising agencies and magazines, was stranded in a nonglamorous traffic jam along the I-5 freeway near Mission Viejo. The situation was in stark visual contrast to what energizes him and makes him passionate about his work. It was the antithesis of the enjoyment he had experienced just hours earlier. Realizing this, Mitchell called upon what has served him well in more than 20 years of photography — instinct, ideas and action. He suddenly reversed his course on the freeway and executed what he calls "his least original idea." He happily moved to San Diego.

Mitchell's freeway epiphany struck with the brilliance of a flash bulb. Today, the results of this decision are undeniable. He is an award-winning (*Communication Arts, Graphis, Print*, and *Art Direction* magazines), much sought-after photographer. His creative range is as broad and dynamic as the cliffs of Torrey Pines at sunset (one of his favorite scenes) yet also embraces the smallest, most subtle details. This versatility is one reason for his success. However, proof is always in the pictures: portraits capturing the magic and wonder of Cirque du Soleil or the intelligence and wit of acclaimed television director/producer James Burrows; corporate collateral projecting the enduring innovation and prosperity of Qualcomm, Inc. and Sony North America; and photos for the *Los Angeles Times* and *American Airlines* magazine that add candid visual commentary to socio-conscious and lifestyle-oriented articles.

Mitchell's goal is to create high-impact storytelling images. He recognizes that the audience for a photograph must be moved to feel, understand and respond. These reactions are elicited, on the surface, from his natural talents, but also result from his extensive background research. He studies his clients' business histories, products and services. He also examines their competitors to pinpoint potential areas of differentiation. This preparation is useful because clients are often either uncertain of the visual statement they want, or they present

Mitchell with undeveloped seedlings of ideas: "I need broad outlines," "This must deliver such-and-such message," or "This portrait must show this executive at the top of his field." Mitchell is inquisitive and resourceful enough to interpret and shape these ideas, which brings added value to all of his projects.

Mitchell acknowledges that two areas are fundamental to his craft: design and content. In his own words, design "gets you to look at the photo," while content "keeps you looking at the photo." However, the marriage of these two elements translate to more than merely style and substance. Mitchell is a self-professed specialist in generalities, which means that he actively avoids "trademarking" his style as some photographers do by repeating the same visual techniques. Instead, he favors a fresh approach to every assignment that ensures that clients receive 100 percent creativity. This chameleon-like quality is in part derived from Mitchell's commitment to keeping one foot grounded in the "physical" techniques of traditional photography. The other is planted in the technical world of multimedia technology.

Mitchell's physical technique can use light and multiple angles to produce a spectacular photo of a landscape at Glacier National Park. Or it can result in a distinguished photo of a high-level business executive. If the client chooses, the process can end at that point. However, Mitchell believes that concept drives a great photo, and that concept often arrives when traditional and multimedia elements interact. This might entail creating a customized background or enhancing an image using computers. Or more organically, he might soak a print in coffee to create an original color, or scratch a print with steel wool to create texture.

Ultimately, a simple photo is never enough. Mitchell believes that his clients deserve more than simplicity. Basic interiors or a cloth backdrop will not suffice. The columns of Balboa Park's museums demand more attention, and San Diego's beaches, mountains and desert deserve more than a point-and-shoot. Even amidst such man-made beauty and natural wonders, the client is always the star of a Josh Mitchell production.

(Above) Kajima Construction Company

(Below) Academy Awards, the Real Oscar!

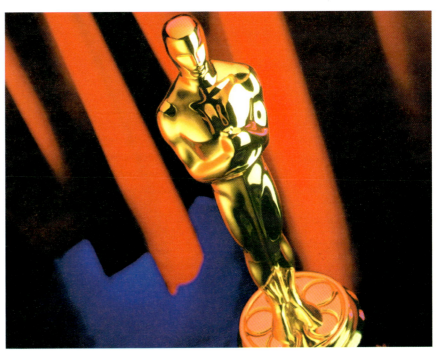

Karl Strauss Breweries

There's nothing better than a frosty mug of cold beer to quench a big thirst on a hot day. Pale ale, amber lager, Pilsener or light, beer is a celebration of life. Indeed, the ingredients of beer are the same as bread — water, grains and yeast. Karl Strauss Breweries, makers of San Diego's Original Local Beer, celebrates life every day, in fact, seven of its beers are made with specific anniversary dates in mind.

Karl Strauss Breweries is the oldest and largest independent microbrewery in Southern California. The company is a living legacy to Master Brewer Karl Strauss who has developed its 32 different varieties of beer, both ales and lagers. Strauss designs the brewery operations and processes, formulates the beers produced and personally trains all brewmasters of the company.

Born in Minden, Germany, Strauss is one of the world's most famous and accomplished Master Brewers. Many claim he has beer in his blood because he was actually born and raised on the premises of his father's small brewery. As a young man, Strauss left Minden to get a degree in malting and brewing at the Technical University of Munich at Weihenstephan which has trained the greatest Master Brewers in the world.

In 1939, Strauss emigrated to the United States and became a brewmaster with the Pabst Brewing Company of Milwaukee. He spent 44 years at Pabst, eventually working his way up to vice president of production and brewmaster for all of Pabst's brewing operations, responsible for more than 17 million barrels of beer per year. Karl Strauss retired from Pabst in 1983 and began consulting internationally for both major and small breweries. He is a past president of the Master Brewers Association of the Americas (MBAA) and co-author of *The Practical Brewer*, the definitive handbook of brewing in America. He is the only person ever to receive both the MBAA's lifetime achievement Award of Honor and the Award of Merit, the two highest honors in the American brewing industry.

The first Karl Strauss brewery and restaurant opened in San Diego on February 2, 1989, in downtown San Diego. It was the first new brewery to open in San Diego in more than 50 years, well ahead of other microbreweries now in the city. Located just a few blocks from the convention center, this award-winning microbrewery is a favorite watering hole for those who live, work or visit the downtown area. Housed in a historical 1920s building, the interior features a wooden, barrel-vaulted ceiling with skylights and historical photos of early San Diego on the walls. A glass wall separates the bar and restaurant so that patrons can watch the brewing process. This downtown brewery actually brews most of the specialty beers for the Karl Strauss company and hosts brewery tours on weekends.

The Feldschlosschen Brewery c. 1900 in Minden, Germany, where Karl Strauss was born. His father, the president of the brewery, is the third man from the left in the second row.

In 1994, Karl Strauss Breweries opened its second restaurant location in the Sorrento Mesa area within the San Diego Tech Center. There's a good reason that this restaurant is closed on Saturdays for private parties, banquets and weddings. Coming in from the parking lot, you cross a wooden bridge into another land. This beautiful restaurant is set amidst five and a half acres of Oriental gardens which include a dramatic waterfall, babbling brook, koi pond, majestic trees and bushes and quiet walking paths. The restaurant is designed to resemble Munich's famous Chinesicher Turm Biergarden, or Chinese Pagoda Beer Garden, which is identified by its tall Chinese pagoda.

Diners can enjoy the serenity and beauty of this location either at tables indoors or outdoors on the tiered decks. The Stargazer Ale, a bold, dry-hopped ale, is made here and named for world-famous artist Alexander Lieberman's large, red, landmark sculpture, "Stargazer," which marks the entrance to San Diego's Tech Center.

The Karl Strauss Brewery & Grill in La Jolla opened its doors in August 1996. It's located just one block from the La Valencia Hotel. This is the only Karl Strauss location featuring La Jolla Hefeweiss. Served with a slice of lemon, this unfiltered, full-grained wheat beer is slightly heavier and more full-flavored than most weizen.

In the fall of 1999, a fourth restaurant will open in Carlsbad. It is located just atop the flower fields, and will offer the same great American cuisine. All of the Karl Strauss restaurant locations feature an award-winning menu. During the month of October, more traditional German dishes are featured in addition to the regular menu. However, for the rest of the year, diners have a wide variety of meal items to choose from including fresh fish of the day, a mixed grill, peppered New York steak, herbed chicken with feta cheese, beer battered fish and chips, pizzas, sandwiches, a sausage sampler, salads and even tortellini with wild mushrooms. The restaurants have won awards from *San Diego Magazine*, The *San Diego Union-Tribune* and the *San Diego Metropolitan* for being the best microbrewery in San Diego as well as the San Diego Restaurant Association's coveted Gold Medallion Award.

The restaurants also feature a wide selection of Karl Strauss handcrafted beers to enjoy. It is the only microbrewery that always has 10 to 12 brews on tap of its own line. A favorite selection is the "Taster 8," a chance to sample a variety of Karl Strauss' own signature lagers and ales and conduct a private beer tasting.

Besides providing beers for its own restaurants, Karl Strauss Breweries distributes its handcrafted, signature beers to more than 350 local bars, restaurants and hotels. In addition to its six San Diego Natives — Karl Strauss Amber Lager, Gaslamp Gold Ale, Karl Strauss Pale Ale, Red Trolley Ale, Karl Strauss Pilsener and Karl Strauss Light — the brewery always has at least four seasonal, specialty beers in production. In 1996, the company purchased a large corporate headquarters and brewery building on Santa Fe Street. This facility produces all the San Diego Natives.

The Karl Strauss Brewery & Grill, downtown San Diego, is a favorite with locals and visitors.

Karl Strauss Breweries participates as a key sponsor in numerous community outreach programs. The brewery also supports various nonprofit groups with food and beverages during fund-raisers.

In his lifetime, Karl Strauss has brewed more than seven billion glasses of beer. From the Blond Bavarian Oktoberfest beer to Karl's Christmas Ale and his signature Karl Strauss Amber Lager and Pale Ale, each glass celebrates the life of one of the world's most talented brewmasters. And isn't it fortunate San Diego is home to his breweries?

"King" Stahlman Bail Bonds

"Let me help you out" has been George "King" Stahlman's motto for over 50 years.

"King" Stahlman Bail Bonds never closes. Bondsmen are available 24 hours a day, seven days a week.

George "King" Stahlman, Sr. is the self-proclaimed king of bail bondsmen in San Diego. His competition might dispute that. What they can't dispute is that his company has grown from a one-person operation in 1952 to the No. 1 bail bonds company in San Diego and a leader in the state of California. He's become an institution in San Diego and as much a part of the city's history as a historical landmark or a founding father.

"Let me help you out," reads "King" Stahlman Bail Bonds' yellow pages ad. "I've been helping people get out of jail for over 50 years ... successfully and with a minimum amount of hassle. If you, a family member or a loved one needs help ... we'll be here. Count on it." These words aren't just a slogan for George Stahlman. They are the heartfelt assurance of a man who has dedicated his entire adult life to helping others.

Being a bail bondsman wasn't the career George Stahlman had planned on. Just after he turned 17, he joined the Navy. World War II broke out a few months later. Part of the Pacific theater, Stahlman was on the destroyer USS Cushing when it was sunk on November 13, 1942. He spent 13 hours in the water off Guadalcanal and then 10 months in and out of hospitals in New Zealand recovering from wounds and malaria. Three years later Stahlman was aboard the USS Lunga Point, an escort carrier supporting the USS Enterprise and Admiral Halsey, when three kamikaze planes hit the vessel during the fight for Iwo Jima.

After the war he moved back to Los Angeles, planning to take classes via the GI Bill. It was during that time his father, a prominent attorney, introduced him to a friend, a bail bondsman. George wanted to work with him part time while attending college. His father was outraged. Finally, George's sister convinced his father to let him try. "He's never finished anything in his life," she said. That was in 1947.

Stahlman stayed with the Los Angeles company for about five years. He left the bail bonds business to work with the Camp Pendleton Fire Department where he stayed for three and a half years. However, while there, he started to write bail bonds again, this time in Oceanside to make some extra money. Eventually, he opened his own company. It was then that the name "King" became a part of his legend. An Oceanside police friend asked one day if the "BBK" in his car license meant "Bail Bond King." Stahlman knew a good slogan when he heard it and the rest, as they say, is history.

By 1960 several other bail bond companies had moved into the North County area. "King" Stahlman relocated his company near the downtown San Diego jail. While most of the area was car dealerships, he found a small office on C Street in the corner of a used car lot. Then in 1963 he moved into his current

office on Union Street. Eventually, he would buy the lot and the building. "King" Stahlman Bail Bonds now has three locations — San Diego, Vista and Chula Vista.

The bail bonds business isn't one that most people would consider a life's career, but it is one in which "King" Stahlman takes great pride. For years, people used to consider the bail bondsman an associate of the underworld, attached to the bootlegging business and backroom deals. Along with statewide and national bail bondsmen associations, Stahlman has spent years and millions of dollars upgrading that image to that of a professional business.

"King" Stahlman Bail Bonds is based on the premise that all people are innocent until proven guilty. His employees write the "insurance bonds" that the court requires to let people out of jail until their trial dates. Usually a fee of 10 percent is paid for the bond. It may not be a glamorous job but it is one used by people in all walks of life. Bondsmen give people opportunities to carry on a normal life while preparing a defense and getting disentangled with the justice system.

George Stahlman has been honored by those within his industry numerous times. He's been president of the Association of Bail Bondsmen three times, in 1962, 1966 and 1996. He was inducted into the U.S. Bail Agents Hall of Fame in 1990 and as of 1998, "King" Stahlman was the oldest active licensed bail bondsman in California. He's also run for political office twice in San Diego. In 1967 he ran for mayor and in 1969 he ran for the board of supervisors. "I was unsuccessful both times but I had a lot of fun during the campaigns."

His face is well-known throughout the San Diego area. In this fiercely competitive business, the "King" knows that name recognition is everything. Most people don't plan to get arrested and during the stress of those first few hours in jail, Stahlman knows that his name must rise through the confusion of the moment. His billboards can be found in every district of the city and he has spent thousands on imprinted matchbooks, logo screened shirts, and bumper stickers and license plate frames that say, "My child was citizen of the month at 'King' Stahlman Bail Bonds."

A firm believer in giving back to society, George Stahlman has donated thousands of dollars to charities including the YMCA, Cancer Society and Alzheimer's research. "I don't like to turn people down," he said. If he thinks it is worthwhile, he finds a way to help.

Working 14 hours a day in his business isn't enough for this active senior citizen. George Stahlman has sponsored rising golf pros for different tours since 1965 when he and two others helped John Jacobs enter the Florida Tour. As a charter member of the Stardust Country Club, El Camino Country Club and La Costa Country Club, he wanted to give rising pros a better opportunity to earn the money they will need as they continue in their careers. In January 1997 he started his own minitour, the "King" Stahlman Royal Golf Tour. His tour gives players more perks than in any other minitour today. Besides earning money for winning, tour participants can also earn bonuses for holes-in-one, breaking a course record, closest to the hole and double eagles.

It's hard to imagine San Diego without a George "King" Stahlman. This colorful character has been instrumental in the development of this city. For someone who "never finished anything," George Stahlman has completed at least three lifetimes of good deeds and has made a difference in the lives of thousands. "King" Stahlman Bail Bonds has more than earned its place in San Diego history.

Early to bed and early to rise, work hard and advertise are words that Stahlman has taken to heart. They're the backbone of his success.

"King" Stahlman has sponsored golf tournaments for rising pros since 1965. His tours and tournaments distribute more money to participants than any other minitour.

La Valencia Hotel

Arriving visitors pass under Mediterranean colonnades. European elegance is highlighted by the Spanish handcrafted mosaic tiles, a handpainted ceiling, the brocaded cloth on the overstuffed sofas and chairs, imported rugs and antique chandeliers. La Valencia's infinite beauty with spectacular ocean views and sunsets over the La Jolla Cove makes the hotel a perfect spot for a romantic getaway, wedding, impressive business retreat or an opportunity to pamper that special someone.

La Valencia Hotel in 1927 prior to the construction of the famous tower added in 1928. *Courtesy San Diego Historical Society — Ticor Collection*

La Valencia and La Jolla grew up together. On December 15, 1926, MacArthur Gorton and Roy B. Wiltsie opened the La Valencia Apartment-Hotel on Prospect Street and Herschel Avenue. It was designed by Reginald Johnson. Tucked in the middle of downtown La Jolla, it overlooked the already-famous La Jolla Cove.

Guests slowly discovered this little gem, and the hotel outgrew its limited size. So, on December 30, 1928, Gorton and Wiltsie added an eight-story building with even more elegant hotel rooms, a lounge with an outside wraparound balcony affording a breathtaking view of the Pacific and a new restaurant. Also added at that time was the distinctive tower with its gold and blue dome. Herbert Mann and Tom Shephard designed the additions.

La Jolla's favorite watering hole, The Whaling Bar (c. 1947), depicting Wing Howard's original murals.

Roy Wiltsie planned another change. He wanted to add more levels extending the hotel down the cliff's slope to the beach, but due to the Depression, he never began construction. They even numbered the lobby the seventh floor, anticipating the addition. When three lower floors were finally added in 1949, they became the fourth, fifth and sixth floors. In the mid-40s, Richard Irwin, who would manage the hotel for the next 40 years, tried to renumber the floors. La Valencia's guests so opposed the plan, the hotel left the floor numbers just the way they were.

From the beginning, La Valencia attracted the wealthy and famous. In the 30s, Garbo and John Gilbert, Ramon Navarro, Charlie Chaplin, Groucho Marx, the Talmadge sisters, Lillian Gish, Mary Pickford and others used La Valencia as the perfect hideaway. After the opening of the La Jolla Playhouse, La Valencia played host to such notables as Gregory Peck, Dorothy McGuire, Mel Ferrer, Louis Jourdan, Charlton Heston, Ginger Rogers and David Niven.

Early on, La Valencia acquired its reputation for graciousness and finesse, something that usually takes many years to establish. Along with the charm established by the decor, excellence in customer service became a standard at La Valencia. Guests received the kind of deferential treatment usually reserved for guests at the most expensive hotels. This endeared La Valencia to the celebrity clientele even more. Even while remaining "anonymous" they could enjoy celebrity treatment.

Many guests began leaving parts of themselves at this home away from home. Most of the furniture and decorations of La Valencia are antiques, some donated by former patrons. Each guest room and suite has its own individual character with a suggestion of the Old World tempered with modern conveniences, as well as its own color scheme and distinctive furniture.

With such a loyal following, changes happened slowly at the La Valencia Hotel, sometimes as a result of world events. During World War II, many of the hotel guests, along with La Jolla residents, manned the gold-domed tower to scan the skies for enemy aircraft. As part of the Civil Defense program, the tower was manned in two-hour shifts for 24 hours a day.

When San Diego underwent major growth at the end of the war, La Valencia became an even more popular vacation spot. The lower three floors (numbered four, five and six) were built in 1949. The Cabrillo Hotel, designed in 1908 by famed architect Irving John Gill, was acquired in 1956 and incorporated as a West Wing to La Valencia, boosting its available rooms to 100.

After the war, Hollywood wrote yet another chapter in La Valencia's story. The La Jolla Playhouse continued to gain fame from 1947-1964 until it became one of the most prestigious summer theaters in the country. Without doubt, it boasted the most celebrity-studded productions. Accommodations at La Valencia became negotiated benefits to celebrities performing at the playhouse.

After World War II, La Valencia added The Whaling Bar with its authentic New Bedford harpoons and lanterns, pewter candle holders, antique wooden shutters, miniature paintings and displays of carved ivory scrimshaw. The bar instantly became the central focus of not just La Valencia guests, but also of La Jolla residents, especially after opening nights at the La Jolla Playhouse. Celebrity cast members and their famous guests waited into the wee hours for the first reviews to hit the stands and to celebrate their achievements.

Devotees of the hotel made their contributions to the Whaling Bar as well. Colonel Billy Mitchell gave the unique barrel clock that hangs behind the bar. Bert Hupp, former president of National Biscuit and Atchison, Topeka and Santa Fe, provided the model of a full-rigged sailing ship.

The Wing Howard murals in the Whaling Bar are world famous. Especially notable is the mural behind the bar called "Whale's Last Stand." Originally, Howard intended to paint a new mural every few months so they were all painted in tempera. However, the same outspoken patrons who refused to allow the hotel to renumber the hotel floors insisted that the original murals remain. Unfortunately, tempera is not as resilient as other paint mediums so, in 1998, a complete renovation of the Whaling Bar included restoring this mural to its original state.

Patrons may dine in The Whaling Bar and Grill, the intimate Skyroom with its breathtaking view of the Pacific Coast or in the Mediterranean Room, known for its excellent European cuisine. Many guests reserve hotel rooms at La Valencia year after year, often planning more than five years in advance.

The "pink lady of La Jolla" has come a long way since its opening in 1926. History has been kind to this most elegant of hotels. La Valencia has brought pride to its owners and to La Jolla, the city that has embraced it with open arms.

The "Pink Lady" as she appears today — La Valencia's patrons can enjoy a panoramic view of the Pacific Ocean.

View from the Garden Suite

Rancho Valencia Resort

Rancho Valencia Resort, nestled amidst the rolling hills of Rancho Santa Fe, offers the ultimate in service and luxury. Built in 1989, Rancho Valencia exudes casual elegance and simple refinement reminiscent of the early California inns. Developer Harry Collins meticulously planned every detail of the resort, from the antique furnishings and hand-painted tile work to the positioning of each suite and the luxuriant landscaping.

Lavish attention to guests' desires is Rancho Valencia's trademark. With only 43 suites and more than 100 employees, guests are assured a level of personalized service not available at larger resorts. More than half the staff have been with Rancho Valencia for more than five years, serving returning and new guests. They not only greet guests by name, but also remember their personal preferences. Each employee is empowered to make guest-related decisions that will guarantee the highest level of service.

Twenty-one secluded Spanish-Mediterranean-style casitas accommodate the 43 elegant suites. All are appointed with fireplaces, wet bars, mini-bars, spacious bathrooms, walk-in closets, open-beam cathedral ceilings and large garden terraces. Each suite has two televisions, a videocassette player, coffee maker, a basket of gourmet snacks, combination safe, terry cloth robes and assortments of bathroom amenities. Guests may select either the cozy Del Mar suite with a combination bedroom/sitting area or the roomier Rancho Santa Fe suite with a separate bedroom and living room. For groups, families, or special events, Rancho Valencia offers The Hacienda, an impressive three-suite adobe estate, complete with swimming pool, Jacuzzi, cabana, central kitchen and secluded grounds.

Executive conferences and corporate meetings are often held at Rancho Valencia, the perfect place to mix business and pleasure. Conference facilities include meeting rooms which accommodate up to 125 attendees and are supported by extensive audiovisual systems. Professional conference coordinators ensure that corporate group events run smoothly and efficiently.

Additionally, with 20,000 square feet of indoor and outdoor banquet space, Rancho Valencia can accommodate events for a variety of party sizes. The 9,000-square-foot regulation Croquet Lawn accommodates up to 500 guests. That same number can easily attend a magical wedding ceremony on the rolling expanse of the Casita Lawn situated on the highest plateau of the grounds. The lush, private garden of The Hacienda provides room for a more intimate event of up to 140 guests. Two bubbling fountains and original Mexican tile make the Sunrise Patio a perfect setting for a 120-guest reception. The Fountain Courtyard, with its towering palm trees, hand-painted tile bar, stunning

Twenty-one secluded Spanish-Mediterranean-style casitas accommodate the 43 elegant suites.

terra-cotta fountain and huge Spanish-style fireplace fits a cocktail party of 400 as easily as an intimate dinner for 30. The colorful, patterned ceramic-tiled Sunrise Room serves up to 30 guests for elegant dining. The generous, tastefully appointed Terrace Room allows 120 guests to enjoy award-winning cuisine. La Sala's two sets of French doors open onto the partially covered, tiled terrace, which affords magnificent views for small groups.

Guests are warmly welcomed in Rancho Valencia's reception area.

Guests at Rancho Valencia can hide out or explore the world around them. Quiet time is enjoyed strolling the beautiful grounds, swimming in the heated pool, relaxing in the Jacuzzis, or being pampered with a full range of body-care treatments. For the more active guest, the fitness room, croquet court, 18 tennis courts and nearby golf courses provide convenient recreation. The award-winning tennis facility offers private lessons with eight available tennis pros, a tennis-ize fitness program, junior tennis, doubles events and a completely outfitted pro shop.

A day at Rancho Valencia begins with the delivery of a preferred newspaper and fresh orange juice squeezed from oranges grown on the dozens of trees decorating the grounds. Impeccable service and award-winning cuisine in the California-Pacific Rim tradition is available year-round to guests as well as the community in the exquisite signature restaurant. Dining is available indoors or alfresco on the tiered terrace.

Numerous awards have been bestowed upon Rancho Valencia Resort, among them *Conde Nast Traveler's* 1999 Gold List, the *Zagat Survey's* No. 1 San Diego Best Overall Hotel in 1998/99, *Tennis Magazine's* 1998 list of Top Ten Tennis Resorts, and *Gourmet Magazine's* 1996 America's Top Table Award. As a member of the world-renowned Relais & Chateaux group of small resorts, Rancho Valencia has international recognition.

Participation in several organizations keeps Rancho Valencia in contact with the community. The resort is a member of the San Diego Convention and Visitors Bureau, and several staff members belong to local civic and trade associations. Various charities receive the benefit of Rancho Valencia's involvement. The Tennis for Tots fund-raiser for homeless babies, sponsored by the American Association of University Women, is held annually at the resort. Rancho Valencia lends its chefs to participate in Mama's Kitchen fund-raisers, events that raise money to provide food for homebound AIDS patients. The annual event the staff anticipates most is hosting nearly 100 homeless children, ages 5 to 17, from St. Vincent De Paul shelters at Christmastime. The staff and their families participate in many of the day's activities including a wild animal show and barbecue. The highlight of the day occurs when Santa arrives by helicopter bringing gifts for the children.

Only 90 miles south of Los Angeles and 30 minutes north of downtown San Diego, Rancho Valencia is close enough for a quick getaway, yet remote enough for a peaceful escape. Whatever luxuries and amenities guests require — whether that entails more 21st-century business amenities beyond the fax machines, dataports and Web TV now available — Rancho Valencia is ready to say "Yes!" Balancing the desire for seclusion with the need to stay connected to the outside, Rancho Valencia offers both with exquisite style.

San Diego Office Interiors

Vincent E. Mudd, CEO and founder

Office of the future

The story behind the creation of San Diego Office Interiors is one of trust, determination and unique vision. It started in the late 1980s when Vince Mudd joined a company called San Diego Office Supply. His job was to head the newly formed San Diego Office Interiors, a division of the parent company dealing in office furniture. With seven years' experience in the industry, it didn't take Vince long to realize that customers wanted him to do more than just sell them a couple of desks. People were looking for a full-service company that could design and set up creative, functional workspaces; places where prospective clients could walk in and see exactly what the company's philosophy and style were all about. Ideally, these would be workplaces that employees would enjoy, where productivity and communication would be improved and OSHA standards would be met.

During a furniture trade show Vince gathered other San Diego Office Interior employees and presented them with a proposition. He wanted to buy San Diego Office Interiors and turn it into an office evaluation, design and creation company. He wanted to know if anyone would support him in his bid. Twelve employees responded positively. Vince took this positive support and, along with encouragement from customers, put together a business plan and started looking for funding.

But it was the early 1990s, and banks were still reeling from the recession. Not one of the seven banks he visited would back him without a substantial capital input from Vince. Finally, Vince found himself talking to the people at The Money Store. The Money Store liked what they saw and loaned Vince Mudd $400,000 in operating capital. Using this money, and mortgaging his house, Vince was able to buy the name and the customer lists of San Diego Office Interiors from its parent company in 1993. It was a scary yet exciting time, as the new company, SDOi, started with no accounts receivable and no inventory. It was in essence a company in name only.

Four months into their first year, Vince had to ask his employees to take a 20 percent pay cut. All but one agreed, and with an esprit de corps that has become their trademark, employees of the fledgling company pulled together, determined to make the company succeed. The payoff was immediate. By the end of the first year of business, not only had everyone had their pay restored, they received a 10 percent increase. Even more gratifying, SDOi was able to pay off the loan to the Money Store and still turn a profit of $38,000. The secret to SDOi's success? Teamwork, quality of service, and a deep, enduring respect for each other and their customers.

What makes SDOi unique? Vince describes the company as a turnkey contract-office-furniture dealership. What this means is that a customer comes to SDOi with an idea or a problem, and the SDOi team of designers, estimators, field service workers and project coordinators work together to come up with a solution. For example, the challenge can be outfitting a reception area to reflect a company's philosophy, or modernizing the company's offices to provide a more competitive, upscale image. Other examples include a large contemporary bank with a brand new facility that needed to blend in with a conservative 60-year-old community, and a government office that needed 600 new workstations designed, planned, manufactured and installed in under nine weeks. SDOi thrives on, and has built its reputation around, these challenges. The company has worked with clients as diverse as the Zoological Society of San Diego, KPBS broadcasting, government agencies, pharmaceutical companies, hospitals and high-tech engineering firms.

San Diego Office Interiors is San Diego's only true full-service commercial design-build office interiors firm. What does this mean? This means SDOi offers a variety of services which include turn-key interior fit out, design and interior planning; construction management; ergonomic furniture planning, procurement and order tracking; certified delivery, installation and repair; and move management services. From furnishing solutions that address the lobby and conference room to advanced answers to open workstations and executive offices, SDOi offers the most complete range of options and solutions. Products range from the better-known modular office workstations to some truly innovative, beautiful design pieces. One of SDOi's more unique specialties is creating fully modular office interiors. Not only is the carpet modular, the floor is raised and the voice and data cabling is modular. With the exception of the fire corridor and the bathrooms, every full-height wall in the building is modular, electrified and easy to reconfigure and relocate.

SDOi delivers the ultimate combination: cost-effective, tax-friendly solutions that save time and money by allowing customers to take control of the interior of their office buildings.

When San Diego companies expand throughout the United States and overseas, SDOi goes with them. Demand has been so great that in 1999 SDOi moved to a new 25,000-square-foot office in Kearny Mesa and opened a branch office in Virginia.

SDOi is proud of its success and is pleased to offer its customers office furnishings of the highest quality. Principal among their offerings is Haworth Inc., the largest manufacturer of ergonomic modular systems furniture and the second largest manufacturer of office furniture in the world. A family-owned company, like SDOi, Haworth has over 150 innovative patents and has introduced among other firsts, modular electrical furniture, ergonomic keyboard trays and modular voice and data cabling systems. SDOi shares its success with the community. Over 80 percent of SDOi employees are involved with charitable organizations, something that Vince Mudd encourages by paying a bonus to any employee who decides to devote his or her time to do volunteer work. The company has made donations of equipment to nonprofit organizations, and has provided furnishings for Big Brothers and Sisters and the San Diego Urban League just to name a few. It is a supporter of KPBS and a firm believer in playing an active role in the community.

A young company, San Diego Office Interiors plans to become an enduring part of the rich and developing history of the city that shares its name.

Hometown bank

A new-look lobby for a business moving forward

Partners In San Diego

San Diego Refrigerated Services

Aerial view of San Diego Refrigerated Services plant at its downtown Imperial Avenue location

On the proposed site of the new San Diego ballpark, along Imperial Avenue between Eighth and Ninth Streets, is a block of history going back to 1890. That year, Thomas Edison designed one of the city's first electrical installations for the fledgling San Diego Ice and Cold Storage, the first company in the area to produce crushed ice for storing freshly grown vegetables. The company also delivered blocks of ice, from 25 to 300 pounds, by horse-drawn truck to local residences.

That company has grown into San Diego Refrigerated Services, with approximately $3 million in annual revenue. Its current owner/operator, Edward F. Plant, has the entire history of the company in his head and has the original 1890 electric meter from San Diego Consolidated Gas & Electric Company sitting on a shelf in his office.

San Diego Ice & Cold Storage was founded in 1890 on the northwest corner of Ninth and Imperial. (Photo taken 1919)

In 1922, the original ice company became California-San Diego Ice and Cold Storage and moved into larger quarters across the street, Plant says. The new structure had 160,000 square feet in which to produce, crush and store ice. The larger space was needed to serve a new customer base: wholesalers in San Diego who were shipping their fresh produce around the United States by railroad. Lettuce, green beans, tomatoes and other perishables were loaded into boxcars, then covered with tons of crushed ice.

"Those boxcars leaked water from one end of the country to another but the railroads opened new markets. At one time San Diego was one of the top vegetable growers in the state," Plant says. The 1922 plant had a large engine room with a 10-foot diameter balance wheel that turned a 17-inch, steel-encased piston to compress ammonia and produce ice.

By 1952, however, refrigeration was taking the place of crushed ice to preserve food. The old engine room was dismantled (Plant has a photo of it on his wall), and the latest in refrigeration equipment was installed. Unfortunately, railroad cars also switched to refrigeration and the enormous trade in crushed ice melted away.

With the railroad business gone, the company looked for new ways to use what was essentially a giant freezer that took up an entire city block. It began to provide cold storage for giant supermarket chains and other businesses. From 1952 to 1987, the company was the sole provider of cold storage for the U.S. Navy (in 1987, the Navy built its own facility).

From 1974 to 1981, the business was taken over by a Los Angeles-based company. When Plant bought it in 1981, primarily as a real estate investment, the business was in a slump. But Plant saw possibilities for new markets and rebuilt the company as San Diego Refrigerated Services.

Today, the company can blast-freeze more than 90,000 tons of fresh fish, fruits and vegetables a year, much of it from Mexico. It annually freezes 7,500 tons of strawberries alone. From a small company that sold crushed ice to local produce markets, San Diego Refrigerated Services has grown into a cold storage provider for foods headed to such world markets as Japan, Australia and Israel as well as major U.S. food processors.

Freshness is the primary concern of San Diego Refrigerated Services. It can blast-freeze up to 400 tons of food daily. The process works by taking produce from the field at 70 to 80 degrees, putting it in drums, then blasting it with air at minus 40 degrees moving at 65 mph. Workers wear such protective suits they resemble astronauts. During the winter, the company processes squid, sardines, octopuses, scallops and sea urchins for markets in China, Japan and the Philippines.

While focused on providing excellent service to its customers, the company strives to serve the community as well — sometimes in unusual ways.

In 1998, SeaWorld made world headlines when it rescued J.J., an ailing whale that the park nursed back to health. "We store all the animal and fish food for SeaWorld, about 40,000 pounds of fish a week," Plant says. "When J.J. was there, food consumption doubled. I was a little sorry to see him released into the ocean again."

Ever wonder what happens when books get soaked after fire hoses and sprinklers put out a fire at a library? San Diego Refrigerated Services has the answer. It has dried books from the Los Angeles County and the University of California, San Diego libraries. The sodden books are shipped to the company and freeze-dried — just like coffee! The moisture is removed and the books are as good as new.

For the Salk Institute, San Diego Refrigerated Services stores a frozen sample of the original polio vaccine developed by Dr. Jonas Salk. For the Scripps Institute, it stores sections of ice from Greenland that enables researchers to study atmospheric conditions going back millions of years.

Plant says that as one of the few owner/operators in the cold-storage business, his company might be called a dinosaur. But he has carved out a special niche that serves San Diego well and has personally contributed to the development of the Gaslamp District and Convention Center. Plant chaired the gala opening of the center on January 19, 1990, with dozens of celebrities and entertainers on hand. "It was my 50th birthday," Plant recalls, "and 3,000 people sang 'Happy Birthday' to me."

If the Padres' new ballpark replaces the Imperial Avenue site of San Diego Refrigerated Services, Plant will move its operations, processing more than one million pounds of product daily, to the company's National City site.

The company also provides cold storage on-site for the Port of San Diego, as well as for a number of local entrepreneurs who outfit small fishing fleets and sell wholesale to world markets. San Diego Refrigerated Services employs 50 to 200 workers (if a ship has come in for unloading). In fact, Plant sees the future of his company in supporting San Diego as the base port of a thriving shipping trade with Asia and beyond.

"Today we're more involved in the shipping business worldwide than ever before," Plant says. "We look forward to continue working with the Port of San Diego and to developing new markets."

San Diego Refrigerated Services' Harborside Building on Terminal Street provides cold storage for the Port of San Diego.

Sky's the Limit Muralist Co.

If it is true, as philosopher Alfred North Whitehead once said, that art flourishes where there is a sense of adventure, then San Diego continues to thrive as a work in progress thanks to the efforts of artists such as Erica Jung, whose creative impulse and sweeping murals have transformed homes and businesses into imaginative dreamscapes.

Whether adorning a child's bedroom wall with animated figures, painstakingly turning a blank wall into a fine art mural, or creating a unique faux finish to strike a chosen theme or mood, Jung provides homeowners and business clients with something their architects and contractors cannot — the missing aesthetic link between a construction worker's blueprints and their own hearts' desires. Jung's talent can rejuvenate interior spaces with imagination and illusion. For her San Diego clients, Jung often executes a variety of trompe l'oeils by painting onto walls anything from arches and bookcases to columns and fireplaces — any of which can create a window overlooking an Italian countryside or turn a wall into a Mediterranean terrace. The three-dimensional effects that are possible are no less persuasive than what she can achieve in a child's room, transforming it, say, into a magical forest or an outer space fantasy.

Jung's business is appropriately called Sky's the Limit; her murals span such a wide range of themes and types that she is hard-pressed to pin down her

Jung re-creates an old Las Vegas scene in this acrylic work.

This 9-by-30-foot mural for a client in Las Vegas depicts a scene from a John Wayne movie.

style with any particular description. She can adapt her style to a particular region or sensibility, which is why she painted so many Western and Southwestern murals for her clients in Las Vegas when she lived there. One executive was such a huge John Wayne fan that he enlisted Jung's talents to create a mural in his office from one of the American hero's movies. Working with a freeze-frame image from the film as a model, she designed a stunning 9-by-30-foot mural in vibrant acrylic color depicting the Duke and his cavalry emerging from a mountain pass.

Sometimes function follows form rather than the other way around. When a travel agency asked Jung to somehow find a way to join two rooms that were sealed off by a polarizing wall, she had six openings cut into the wall that became portholes. Then, she created a surrounding nautical mural that lent a relaxed tropical feeling to the entire work space.

"Each project is a new adventure, an opportunity to give a room something it's never had before," says Jung. "The effect can be amazing. It's always satisfying to see what a difference my work can make — not only in someone's home or business, but in themselves and how they feel."

All of Jung's murals are rendered freehand; most of her work is done on interior walls using acrylic and other water-based paints. Oil paints are used by special request, or whenever needed to create a more convincing effect. Her numerous projects over the last few years have taken anywhere from a few hours to several months to complete. Almost all of her business comes from referrals.

While it was Winston Churchill who said, "We shape our buildings; thereafter they shape us," it's clear that when Erica Jung colors our walls, thereafter they color our lives.

This tranquil outdoor scene was painted for a child's room in San Diego.

The deck of a ship is re-created to set the mood for Sundance Travel.

Various faux finishes were part of the recent expansion at the Africa & Beyond gallery in La Jolla.

Stanley Steemer

Chances are, anyone who lives in San Diego or a neighboring community has seen one of Stanley Steemer's bright yellow carpet cleaning vans in the neighborhood, on the street or parked right in someone's driveway.

(From left to right) Wes Bates, Steve Thompson, Jack Bates

Just how did Stanley Steemer become the "brand name" that is synonymous with carpet cleaning in San Diego? The answer is Steve Thompson, owner of Colt Services, Inc., d.b.a. Stanley Steemer San Diego. Thompson has built Stanley Steemer into San Diego's No. 1 carpet cleaner and the largest carpet cleaning franchise nationwide. Thompson grew up with Stanley Steemer. His stepfather, Jack Bates, was the original founder of Stanley Steemer in 1947. One may wonder why "Steemer" is spelled with two "E's." When the original steam cleaning equipment was operating, it reminded Bates of the old Stanley Steamer steam-powered automobile. He liked the name, so he made it his own with a slight spelling variation to make it unique.

Thompson was introduced to the carpet cleaning business at an early age. As a teenager, he liked to make money, so he would work with his stepfather carrying in the buckets of water and hoses. He learned the business from the "carpeted" ground floor up. Thompson worked in the corporate environment of Stanley Steemer for several years and in the branch operations in various management positions. Stanley Steemer International began its franchise operations in 1972. Although Thompson didn't realize it at the time, the door to his future had just opened.

In 1979 when he was 21, Thompson began operating a Stanley Steemer branch office in San Diego with one truck and one man — himself. With the reputation of Stanley Steemer in his favor and endless hours of hard work, Thompson began to build his dream. In 1982 he incorporated as Colt Services, Inc. d.b.a. Stanley Steemer San Diego and purchased the San Diego franchise. Just as the name "Stanley Steemer" has a story, so does the name "Colt Services." As Thompson was building his business, each day he would give Bates an update. His stepfather would always tell him "It's a chance of a lifetime!" While doodling those words one night, Thompson's corporate name came to him — Chance Of a LifeTime, COLT Services.

The San Diego franchise continued to expand. In 1983, Thompson purchased the El Cajon and Oceanside franchises. Two years later, Stanley Steemer San Diego became the first Stanley Steemer operation to have sales in excess of $1 million.

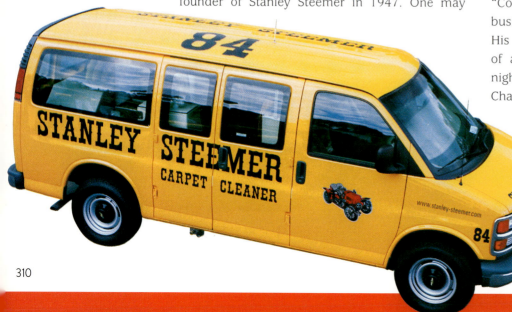

Stanley Steemer San Diego continues to provide the finest service to its customers and supports the community in which it operates. Quality service, fair pricing and ethical business practices are key to its success and outstanding reputation. Thompson realized early on that his franchise had to meet the special needs of his San Diego customers. Not all cities are alike, and the culture of San Diego called for new ideas. Same day service, price quotes by phone, emergency water extraction, 24-hour service, no hidden charges, and guaranteed customer satisfaction are all services provided. While the company has an aggressive marketing program, it still places great value on both the referral of satisfied customers and the loyalty of previous customers.

Employees that share Thompson's vision of "being the best" are a major factor in the success and growth of the company. Stanley Steemer has many long-tenured employees who share their experience and expertise.

A day in the life of a Stanley Steemer carpet cleaner is rather unique in itself. Customers see only a small part of their day. It begins very early to enable the crew to arrive at the first home by 8:00 a.m. Crew members arrive at the base of operations in Mira Mesa at approximately 6:30 a.m., don their red-and-white uniforms, then head out to the exercise area for 15 minutes of stretching and calisthenics. On any given day, one crew may move more than 2,000 pounds of furniture and swoop a few thousand strokes with a 12-pound cleaning wand. The job requires them to be in top physical condition.

Before spending their first day on a truck, crew members receive extensive classroom instruction. Stanley Steemer realizes their carpet cleaning technicians are "invited guests" in the homes and businesses of their customers. As guests, they want to be welcomed back, so they strive for perfection. Carpet and upholstery fabric identification, cleaning methods, spot removal techniques, water extraction procedures, safety, and customer service are but a few of the classroom topics. Their training is extensive, taught by industry experts. Stanley Steemer wants

their customers to rave about their carpet cleaning service. The many thank-you letters and phone calls received each month are a testimony to the outstanding work performed.

With more than 50 equipped vehicles and more than 100 service technicians, crews travel all over San Diego County. Days can be long, so it takes a special individual to ensure that each one is successful and profitable.

As a company, Stanley Steemer is an enjoyable place to work. Picnics, banquets, barbecues and contests are all part of the benefits the employees enjoy. Stanley Steemer isn't just about carpet cleaning, it's about providing a safe and enjoyable work environment for the employees, taking care of their needs and serving the community. It isn't surprising to see Stanley Steemer employees selling newspapers on the street corner for the Children's Hospital Kids News Day or asking for a food donation for the Holiday Food Drive. Two crew members were also recognized for rescuing a child who was accidentally locked in a car on a hot summer's day. The employees are there to serve the community and their contributions continue to be numerous.

The company's bright yellow vans symbolize the dreams, ambitions and visions that have made Stanley Steemer a household name. If Stanley Steemer carpet cleaners are needed, they will be there 24 hours a day, seven days a week. Stanley Steemer is more than just a business — it's a neighbor as well.

Baja Duty Free

Baja Duty Free opened its doors in 1989 at a 1,000-square-foot store in San Ysidro. By 1999 the store had increased in size to 5,500 square feet and another expansion is underway that will almost double the duty-free store to about 10,000 square feet. In 1996, a second Baja Duty Free was opened in Eagle Pass, Texas — that store too has enjoyed tremendous success.

San Ysidro store interior

The secret to Baja Duty Free's success is relatively simple. The retail operation carries top quality duty free brands — major product lines include cigarettes, imported and domestic liquor, fragrances, leather goods, accessories, sunglasses, candies and crystal.

Instrumental in the growth of Baja Duty Free in both San Ysidro and Eagle Pass has been the expertise of parent company Fairn & Swanson, which operates both stores. Fairn & Swanson, established more than 50 years ago, is recognized as the largest duty-free wholesaler and distributor on the West Coast of North America and as one of the leaders in the American duty-free industry. Fairn & Swanson supplies to cruise ships, ship chandlers, foreign military personnel, foreign consulates and United States embassies and consulates overseas.

Fairn & Swanson's annual sales are about $45 million. The company is a wholesaler, retailer, agent and distributor and provides warehousing services. In addition to Baja Duty Free, other companies include the Fairn & Swanson Group (duty-free wholesale, distribution, diplomatic, military); South Seas Distribution (beverages, snacks, tobacco, consumer goods); South Seas Duty Free (duty-free sales, distribution, retail concessions); Spring Rock Brewing (beer and wine sales and marketing); and Cloud Trading (fishing fleets, commercial shipping).

Baja Duty Free also benefits from Fairn & Swanson's relationships with manufacturers not only as an agent but also as a master distributor of the manufacturer's products to other agents and wholesalers worldwide. These services include: extensive experience with bonded and nonbonded merchandise; consolidation of FCL and LCL shipments; worldwide shipping via land, sea or air; in-house freight forwarding and customs brokerage; computerized inventory control and tracking systems; electronic data interchange (EDI) capability for customers and vendors; inventory management; merchandise repacking and manipulation; and marketing and promotional support.

The Fairn & Swanson Group has also expanded its traditional customer relationship with many vendors and has become an exclusive and nonexclusive agent and distributor for many major manufacturers including Allied Lyons, Anheuser Busch, Bacardi, BAT, Bayer, Bristol Myers, Heineken, RJR-Nabisco, Seagram and Unilever. Baja Duty Free can thus offer wholesale business services for Mexican companies.

The rapidly growing potential of the United States/Mexico border has allowed Fairn & Swanson to not only develop its wholesale business, but expand the existing retail facilities. Over the next several years, a number of new Baja Duty Free facilities at other border crossings are slated to open, and they too should prove very popular with customers.

Bernardo Winery

In 1889 Bernardo Winery produced its first barrel of wine at the same location and in many of the same buildings it uses today. Hidden away 20 miles north of San Diego in hilly countryside that was once part of a Spanish land grant, this rustic facility is one of the oldest continuously-operating wineries in Southern California. On the winery's property east of the Rancho Bernardo Inn, some of the vines have been producing for over 100 years.

The locally-grown zinfandel, merlot, cabernet, syrah and muscat grapes that are harvested each September and October, supplemented by chardonnay, riesling and gewürztraminer grapes purchased from other California growers, go into making the 4,000 gallons of wine produced each year by Bernardo Winery.

Bernardo Winery has a long and colorful history. During Prohibition, the winery continued producing but the product line consisted of "medicinal" wine and fresh grape juice that would begin fermenting before the barrel reached the coast. During World War II the winery, under Vincent Rizzo, reduced its wine production to grow vegetables for the soldiers at nearby Camp Elliot, and the winery still grows the Italian fava bean. Not only do grapes and vegetables grow well in this climate, olive trees thrive in the Mediterranean weather. In January and February, the winery's trees are laden with ripe black olives, which each year yield 500-600 gallons of cold-pressed virgin olive oil. After the war, the winery also produced olive oil for the tuna canneries that once thrived in San Diego. When construction of the sprawling Rancho Bernardo community began in the 1960s, Bernardo Winery sold hundreds of olive trees for landscaping the new development.

At one time there were 35 wineries in San Diego County, but only a few, Bernardo among them, have survived. The local wine industry is making a comeback, and today, Bernardo Winery is helping to lead this resurgence through its activities on behalf of the San Diego County Vintner's Association.

Master vintner Ross Rizzo, representing the second generation of Rizzos to own the winery, continues the tradition of making wines in the Old World style. Besides overseeing the winery, he has pioneered a new tradition of social outreach, hosting several annual fund-raising events to benefit the American Cancer Society, the Make-A-Wish Foundation, the local chamber of commerce and other civic groups.

Scattered on the grounds of Bernardo Winery are a dozen one-of-a-kind shops, a restaurant and coffee house. The many antique farm implements and 100-year-old structures from the original winery create an air of authenticity surrounding the wine tasting room and shop. There visitors can purchase not only wines with the Bernardo label, but also savory herbs, spices, rare sauces and dressings, pickles, olives, jams and jellies.

Besides the tasting room, shops and restaurants, the winery offers Western-style barbecues for up to 250 people. A gazebo, bandstand and dance floor provide a serene setting for the many weddings and parties that take place here each year. Every spring and fall, the winery hosts a weekend-long craft fair where 125 small businesses come in and display their wares.

San Diego's Bernardo Winery, operating continuously at the same location since 1889.

Coles Carpets
Since 1947

San Diego homeowners and business owners have turned to Coles Carpets since 1947 for quality floor and window furnishings. In fact, over half the company's business comes from referrals and repeat customers. It's more than reasonable prices that accounts for such incredible customer loyalty. For over three generations, the Coles family has dedicated itself to providing professional customer service, the widest possible selection of fashion-focused floor coverings as well as the most rapid turnover time from purchase to installation in the city. Coles Carpets has three giant showroom/warehouse locations: San Diego, San Marcos and El Cajon.

> **Instead of making selections from small swatches or pictures, Coles Carpets customers are able to see the actual carpet piece that will be installed in their home or business.**

The Coles Carpet story began in Phoenix, Arizona, when Frank Coles started a family home furnishings business. Hubert Coles later joined his father's business after graduating from college. After a stint in the Navy during World War II, he found himself in San Diego, decided to stay and opened "Coles of La Jolla Complete Fine Home Furnishings" in 1947. In 1965, after almost 20 years of business in La Jolla, Hubert moved the business to its current location on West Morena Boulevard in San Diego. Seven years later, his son George entered the business and was soon followed by his siblings—Christine, Jane, and Steve Coles. All the family members are active in the business and George Coles took over as co-owner and president in 1979.

A tour of Coles' Morena location reveals another secret to its success in a highly competitive market — hundreds of rolls of carpets direct from the mills of Georgia and Europe. The city's largest collection of area rugs can also be found there, often exceeding 8500 domestic and hand woven rugs from all over the world including India, China and Nepal. Instead of making selections from small swatches or pictures, Coles Carpets customers are able to see the actual carpet piece that will be installed in their home or business. Should a customer desire, Coles Carpets will custom make a rug to specific pattern and design.

Coles Carpets carries more than just area rugs and carpets. Its showrooms feature full lines of professionally finished hardwood floors, laminates, vinyl and imported floor tiles as well as drapery and custom window treatments. Coles also offers professional carpet cleaning (commercial and residential) and carpet repair. Highly trained and experienced designers assist each customer in making the right buying decision for their needs and budget. Coles Carpets' commitment to customer satisfaction extends beyond carpet wear guarantees. All Coles' products installed by Coles come with a "If you're not satisfied with your floor, we'll replace it" one year satisfaction guarantee (subject to designated terms).

According to George Coles, the company's client list ranges from J. Edgar Hoover and Johnny Weismueller to Jerry Lewis, the San Diego mayor's office and even the Saudi Arabian Navy, which ordered 400 prayer rugs after one of its ships stopped in San Diego. Coles Carpets also replicated the original carpets of the Titanic for that movie. For over half a century, this family-owned business has earned high praise from top interior designers, museums, school districts, restaurants, hotels, and home owners. "And," George Coles said, "we look forward to serving San Diego County for another 50 years."

Deer Park Winery & Auto Museum

In one of San Diego County's hidden valleys in North Escondido are two fabulous vintage products: premium wines and antique cars.

Started in 1979 by Robert and Lila Knapp, Deer Park Winery & Auto Museum was inspired by the family's Deer Park Winery in Napa Valley and a growing family auto collection, both dating to the turn of the century. Deer Park Escondido began producing wine grapes locally in 1979. Until 1998, the estate exclusively produced chardonnay and, at that time, red grapevines were planted to produce the winery's hallmark zinfandel, cabernet sauvignon, petite sirah and merlot.

Clark Knapp, third-generation winegrowing owner and San Diegan, is proud of Deer Park's wine, which is produced in small lots and sold primarily at the winery gift shop and at select restaurants in town. Most of the wines, crafted in the Old World tradition, are barrel-aged for a minimum of 10 months and bottle-aged for at least a year, with many varietals aged up to six years before their first release. Deer Park wines have received numerous awards every vintage year; the colorful labels featuring a vintage car surrounded by grapes have garnered gold-medal design awards as well.

The Deer Park Vintage Vehicle Museum, which surrounds the Escondido vineyard, houses more than 100 automobiles spanning 100 years, in restored and running condition. It is the world's largest collection of convertibles and Americana. Neon car dealership signs, classic garage tools and period advertisements enhance the automobiles as well as thousands of radios, TVs, bicycles, appliances, games, Barbies, Elvis and Marilyn Monroe displays and countless memorabilia from America's century of the auto. Of course, many wine artifacts from the family's early winemaking roots are also on display.

The Deer Park annual harvest festival and picnic celebrates the summer grape and orchard harvests. Every June, the Concours d'Elegance, a showing of rare automobiles is held at Deer Park. Proceeds from the event go to the Red Cross and American Cancer Society. Twice a year winegrowers and guest chefs gather to create Dinner with the Vintner, a five-course gourmet extravaganza specially paired with Deer Park award-winning and rare library wines. Early spring and fall bring the Deer Park Bridal Fair in the Park's picturesque lawns, arbors, orchards, shady oaks, creek bridge and vineyards. And every day, guests enjoy gourmet deli sandwiches, estate sauces, oils and seasonal orchard produce, as well as viewing the many car club and company meets "on-the-green." Whether sampling estate wines or taking an excursion into the past, Deer Park Winery & Auto Museum is a refreshing retreat from the modern world.

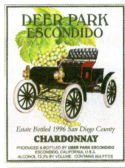

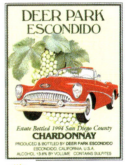

Deer Park Winery's award-winning wine labels

(Top left) The world's largest collection of convertibles at Deer Park Vintage Vehicle Museum

Clark Knapp and Jackie Rinden picnic in the orchard beside a 1903 curved dash Olds.

Dutch Growers Nurseries, Ltd.
Where growing plants is a growing business

The nursery business has coursed through Knoppert blood for seven generations. Pieter Knoppert thought he retired from the family tradition when he left his irrigation company in the Netherlands and moved his family to California in the mid-1970s. However, he couldn't stay away from his heritage for long — the prime growing conditions and inferior quality of plants he encountered in Southern California prompted him to start Dutch Growers Nurseries, Ltd.

Dutch Growers Nurseries, Ltd. in San Marcos

Five acres in San Marcos, where the Knoppert family propagates and sells indoor plants to retail nurseries throughout the Western United States and Canada, attest to the exceptional growth experienced from the humble beginnings in Escondido. A coop house made from plastic piping served as the greenhouse where father and son celebrated their first sale of $45 in 1976. Mrs. Knoppert saved coffee cans to start plant cuttings and deliveries were made in an old, rusty Chrysler New Yorker.

Peter Jr., who now runs the nursery since his father's passing, claims the nursery's success is due in part to specialization and the use of sophisticated technology. By focusing on only 10 to 15 varieties, including ficus, croton petra and spathiphyllum, Dutch Growers can offer the highest quality plants. Custom-mixed soil and computer-controlled lighting and thermostatic control guarantee healthy plant growth. Photocells open and close sun shades as the needs of the plants are determined. Each building has its own unique environment, imitating the plants' native habitats — from arid to tropical climates. State-of-the-art computerized machinery increases production space and efficiency.

Plants thrive in optimum conditions aided by computer technology.

Dutch Growers also opens its doors to educational programs. Several times a year, students from elementary schools to universities tour the nursery for science or agriculture projects. Scripps Research Institute conducts genetic research in a leased portion of the nursery, and professors at several universities work with Peter on crossbreeding and other horticultural experiments.

As one of the highest producing commercial nurseries per-square-foot in California, Knoppert is considering additional acreage and automation. At Dutch Growers Nurseries, Ltd., growing plants is a growing business.

El Indio Mexican Restaurant

Drive down any street in San Diego and there will be at least one fast-food Mexican restaurant. However, in 1940, when the Pesqueira family first opened El Indio, there were no other restaurants of its kind.

From the beginning, El Indio stood out from the other dine-in Mexican restaurants by the quality and authenticity of its food. Originally from Spain and then Sonora, Mexico, the Pesqueira family moved to Calexico, California, in 1901. It was there that Ralph Pesqueira's father, Ralph Sr., got the idea of turning a tortilla shop into a take-out restaurant. When the family moved to San Diego in 1940, they opened their shop on India Street, next to the DeFalco family market.

In this 25-by-75-square-foot location, they sold handmade tortillas, enchiladas, chorizo, beans, rice, taquitos and tamales made by Ralph Jr.'s mother and grandmother. His father is credited with coining the word "taquito," or little taco. It has been the most popular item on the menu since 1940, when they sold three for a quarter.

The Pesqueira family moved to El Indio's current location in 1949. During World War II, Ralph Sr. revolutionized the handmade tortilla business by inventing a tortilla machine. His machine, the first in San Diego, increased production from 30 dozen tortillas daily to more than 30 dozen per hour. El Indio began to provide tortillas for many of the larger Mexican restaurants in town.

Ralph Jr. took over the family business in 1981 after his father passed away. He had grown up behind the counter and long-time customers still greet him as "Sonny." Eva Sanchez Pesqueira, his wife, began El Indio's catering business in 1982. The restaurant now caters hundreds of private parties yearly as well as corporate meetings, lunches and dinners for many of the major companies in San Diego. Presidents Clinton, Reagan and Bush as well as numerous members of congress have had El Indio ship its famous chips, tamales and enchiladas to Washington, D.C., sometimes on less than 24 hours notice. Eva's motto is "we want the hosts to be guests at their own party."

While completely dedicated to El Indio's future, Ralph Jr. is also dedicated to the future of San Diego and the education of its children. He has served as a commissioner for the California Postsecondary Education Commission, a trustee for the California State University system and has advised Governor Davis on education issues. He has also been a member of the board of directors for St. Vincent de Paul (where El Indio provides the annual Thanksgiving breakfast for the homeless), the San Diego Convention and Visitors Bureau and Historical Society, the United Way of San Diego and the Greater San Diego Chamber of Commerce as well as a host of other organizations.

Since 1940, El Indio has been serving San Diego fresh, quality Mexican food based on old family recipes. It's a tribute to the Pesqueira family and a San Diego tradition.

El Indio's founder, Ralph Pesqueira Sr.

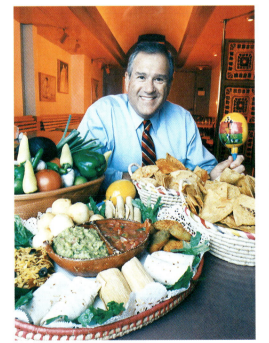

Current owner, Ralph Pesqueira Jr., with many of the foods that made El Indio famous

Orfila Vineyards & Winery

Orfila Vineyards & Winery, located near Escondido, has helped resurrect the art of wine production in San Diego County. In its few years of operation, its wines have won 327 medals, including 43 gold and 110 silver, in worldwide competitions. Its new varieties of Viognier, Syrah and Sangiovese have been favorably reviewed in the *New York Times*, *Wine Spectator* and *Wine Enthusiast* magazines, among others.

One reason that San Diego has become wine country worthy of notice is the work of Orfila's winemaker and general manager, Leon Santoro. He asserts that California's first wine grapes were planted by Padre Junipero Serra in San Diego County in the 1500s. "In the early 20th century, the county had more than 20 wineries and thousands of acres of grapes," Santoro says. "Then, about 50 years ago, Pierce disease destroyed vineyards and later, urban sprawl eliminated many others."

In 1973 two wine entrepreneurs, Mickey Fredman and Charles Froehlich, started the San Pasqual Winery in the San Pasqual Valley Agricultural Preserve, practically next door to the San Diego Wild Animal Park. In 1987 it changed hands and became the Thomas Jaeger Winery.

In 1993 the property was bought by Alejandro Orfila, the former Argentinean ambassador to the United States. A career diplomat, Orfila was born to a third-generation winemaking family in Mendoza, Argentina. He and Santoro make a knowledgeable and successful team.

Santoro also was born into a family of winemakers and chefs in a small town near Rome, Italy. He saw the new enterprise as an opportunity to experiment with grafting more competitive and unusual varieties, such as Orfila's gold-medal-winning Sangiovese and Syrah, onto young Chardonnay vines. The growing list of medals attest that most of his experiments have succeeded. He even has disproved the idea that San Diego is incapable of producing good red wine by creating award-winning vintages.

"I have designed a rainbow of wines to appeal to just about every type of American wine drinker," Santoro says. For serious wine enthusiasts, for example, Orfila offers its Ambassador Reserve Merlot. *South Coast Wine Magazine* stated that "Orfila Merlots and Syrahs best some of the most highly respected names in Napa and Sonoma."

In addition to its San Pasqual location, Orfila Vineyards has an exclusive agreement to grow merlot, chardonnay and Johannisberg Riesling grapes in Fallbook on a 45-acre parcel owned by Tony and Sue Godfrey.

Although Orfila wines are sold extensively in San Diego County and by special order all over the world, many San Diegans do not realize they can visit this local success story for tours of the vineyards, wine-tasting and picnic baskets of cheese, bread and fruit. Many visitors, fascinated with the history and pastoral beauty of the vineyards, become enthusiastic supporters of Orfila's efforts in reviving San Diegan winemaking.

Orfila Vineyards and Winery is located on 32 acres in the San Pasqual Valley Agricultural Preserve. Yellow mustard is grown in winter to enrich the soil and delight the eye.

Leon Santoro (left), winemaker, and Alejandro Orfila, owner, have developed successful new varieties of San Diego-grown wine grapes.

Partners In San Diego

Peaches en Regalia

While living in Aspen, Colorado, in the early 1970s, Patricia Straight relied on her Pinto station wagon to personally deliver handmade garments and fashion accessories to a niche customer base. Her modest origins in retail fashion became the

Ryan Gonzales stands amidst an impressive selection of jackets, slacks, dresses, coats, shirts, ties and unique accessories for both men and women.

foundation for opening a store that would provide the ski resort town with exciting, new choices in men's and women's clothing.

By 1973 the former fashion model and single mother of one decided to combine her experience in sewing and fashion to introduce a small clothing store called Peaches en Regalia. For Patricia, it was what she knew best. The shop was situated in an old Victorian house, located in downtown Aspen. Displayed behind lace-draped windows were ensembles of unique one-of-a-kind men's and women's apparel — most of them sporting labels by popular designers. Armed with a passion for fashion since the age of nine, Patricia earnestly began learning how to achieve business growth.

Searching for the best location near the ski lifts of Aspen Mountain, she moved the store several times. Patricia continued to build a loyal clientele and became an established player in the retail fashion market. Buying trips frequently took her to New York, Milan and Los Angeles, and she eventually employed 25 people.

After 15 years of growth, Patricia felt the change in the Aspen retail market and looked to Southern California, where she was born and raised. With the business ready to expand, she opened a second store in the Del Mar Plaza in 1989. The idyllic setting of a seaside town was exactly what Patricia had in mind to showcase her elegant line of day-to-evening casuals and sportswear.

Patricia received help from her grown son, Ryan Gonzales, who applied his youth and expertise in finance and operations. Together, they made the Del Mar store a San Diego success.

In addition, the company's name, Peaches en Regalia, was annexed with "PR Ltd. For Men" to better emphasize its sophisticated collection of men's sportswear by designers like Jhane Barnes, Mondo, Zanella and Remy. For women, the store became a treasure chest of sought-after designs by Tadashi, Votre Nom, Wayne Rogers, Duna and more.

Ryan, who became vice president, also helped elevate sales through new promotions and marketing techniques. His strategies paved the way for yet another location in San Diego County. In October 1997, the company opened a third store 10 miles up the road at the posh Four Seasons Resort Aviara in Carlsbad. That same year, *San Diego Magazine* voted Peaches en Regalia/PR Ltd. for Men as the third-best specialty store in the county.

Patricia and Ryan meticulously select from a long list of exciting fashions on the marketplace from nearly 200 different designer manufacturers. Broad representations of designer lines, rather than portions of them, is what sets the company apart from customary department stores. Here, the relaxed Southern California look is cleverly integrated with classic international flair to satisfy every shopper with a taste for good style.

San Diego Catering Concepts

In the seaside community of Ocean Beach is a highly professional company dedicated to top quality and service. Located near Sunset Cliffs, San Diego Catering Concepts has become the choice of many corporations and individuals throughout San Diego.

After completing his culinary arts schooling, owner Ken Coley spent the next 12 years working as an apprentice and chef in various landmark hotels and restaurants in Southern California. With a bachelor's degree in business from California Polytechnic Institute, Coley made San Diego Catering Concepts successful from the start, with earnings of a half million dollars in the first three years.

He chose to settle in Ocean Beach because it is small, friendly and easygoing, with a central location to serve all of San Diego and a large potential workforce. Many of Coley's employees are highly trained professionals he's worked with in the past. "Having worked with many hospitality professionals, I only wanted people with a dedication to service and a commitment to quality," he says.

San Diego Catering Concepts has positioned itself to serve the broad market; that demands a variety of quality fresh foods at a reasonable price. Many corporate customers use Coley's services weekly and appreciate the consistent quality and reasonable prices.

Just as important as corporate clients are San Diego Catering Concepts' individual clients. "Your special occasion becomes our special occasion," Coley tells them. Using state-of-the-art equipment and on-site cooking demonstrations, Coley and his staff cater weddings, luaus, tailgate parties and cookouts that allow clients to enjoy their role as worry-free hosts.

The full-service catering company extends its services far beyond the preparation of fine foods. It can assist clients with arranging equipment rentals, floral designs, party decorations and live entertainment. The company is able to offer these services because, over the years, it has established an extensive network with other businesses.

San Diego Catering Concepts is a member of the Greater San Diego Chamber of Commerce, Better Business Bureau, National Association of Catering Executives and Chefs de Cuisine. The company also cosponsors the San Diego Drug Court biannual graduation ceremony, Zoological Society of San Diego events, local food and shelter centers, San Diego Urban League events, Hire-A-Youth Program and the Ocean Beach Restaurant Walk. For the restaurant walk, which raises money for community projects, Catering Concepts puts up a tent in its parking lot and provides hors d'oeuvres to hundreds of neighbors and guests.

Another way the company has introduced itself to the community is through cooking classes for people who want to learn the best way to delight their dinner guests with exciting and unique foods. These classes, held in San Diego Catering Concepts' roomy, well-stocked kitchen, often lead to catering assignments for larger parties.

Coley attributes his success to an adherence to his motto: "Always give them more than they expect." An equally effective motto, describing San Diego Catering Concepts' rich visual display of artful dishes, could be: "First, taste with your eyes — then enjoy!"

(Above) Chef Ken Coley whips up a custom omelet at one of his client's catered events.

San Diego Catering Concepts prides itself on presentation and freshly prepared foods.

San Diego transportation, communications and energy companies keep people, information and power circulating throughout the region.

Partners in NETWO

Photo courtesy of Pacific Messenger Service

Pacific Messenger Service 324

Cloud 9 Shuttle 328

Greitzer Brokers, Inc. 330

Pacific Bell 332

Port of San Diego 334

United Airlines 336

Televideo San Diego 338

Pacific Messenger Service

From messenger boys pedaling bicycles into San Diego's unofficially winked-at red light district in the early 1900s to today's fleet of freeway-ready trucks delivering parcels and shipments throughout Southern California, the history of Pacific Messenger Service reads like a classic chronicle of the American Dream.

It is a story of fortitude and perseverance, how a $200 loan and a pair of bicycles were parlayed into a successful family business that is regarded as the 22nd oldest in San Diego. It is also a parable of tenacity and ingenuity, a business survivor's blueprint on how to prevail against bank failures, corporate competition, government deregulation and creeping technological obsolescence.

Whether it was delivering lunchtime malts to downtown secretaries or transporting a Vietnam veteran home in an empty water heater crate so the soldier could surprise his unsuspecting wife, Pacific Messenger's secret to longevity has remained deceptively simple: "Customers will pay for good service. They won't pay for bad service."

That was the oft-repeated philosophy of Ross Starkey, a Western Union messenger who purchased Pacific Messenger Service on April 1, 1932 from Bernard Hubbard for $200. In order to buy Pacific Messenger, Starkey borrowed the money from Guy Urquhart and Bob Sarkejian, owners of the Indian Motorcycle agency in San Diego. Besides the Pacific Messenger name, he got the sum total of two bicycles. It would turn out to be enough.

Founded in 1908 and operating from its first address of 949 Fourth Avenue, Pacific Messenger learned early how to cater to supply-and-demand realities in San Diego. Its primary business in those

initial years was delivering food, jewelry and clothing to prostitutes and madams who lived in the notorious Stingaree red light district below Market Street. The Stingaree District, which openly flourished for years around the turn of the century with its saloons, gambling halls and parlor houses for lonely sailors and anyone looking for a "good time," enjoyed an unwritten agreement at the time with police. As long as the ladies of the evening stayed below Market Street and did not venture downtown, where their customers' wives might be shocked by them, they were allowed to work, and the general public could pretend they didn't exist. This meant that for more than 20 years, Pacific Messenger bicyclists were needed to pick up and deliver jewelry from Jessop's, clothing from Marston's Department Store, and ice cream sodas and food from Hamilton's grocery store. At meal times, messengers could be seen on their bicycles carrying trays of food into the Stingaree, often from the Minneapolis Cafe at Fifth and F.

However, by the time Ross Starkey purchased Pacific Messenger Service in 1932 and put in two telephones at its 745 Third Avenue location, the Stingaree District had been effectively rehabilitated by authorities and the company was forced to find

An advertising placard from the company's earliest days shows former owner Bernard Hubbard, who founded Pacific Messenger in 1908 and sold the business for $200 to Ross Starkey in 1932.

new avenues for its service. Instead of delivering messages to its market, the market was now delivering a message to Starkey: change with the times or perish. The price of a message in those days was 15 cents; the price of inflexibility meant going out of business. So Pacific Messenger began running messages for advertising agencies, performing deliveries for engraving companies and picked up more commercial business with local firms such as Jessop's and Marston's.

When President Roosevelt closed the nation's banks on April 1, 1933, it was no April Fools' Day joke. The Great Depression was in full swing and the maximum withdrawal allowed during the bank closure period was $10. Even though he was unable to pay his employees, Starkey was able to scrape by until banks reopened a few weeks later.

The addition of motorcycles to its delivery fleet facilitated growth and by the time the nation was drawn into World War II, Pacific Messenger was using up to three trucks to deliver medicine and pharmaceuticals to hospitals. However, the war necessitated more belt-tightening measures when his employees either went into the service or into work for Consolidated Aircraft. Gas rationing also took its toll, allowing the company only 21,000 driving miles when it had been logging 150,000. The company hired girls and elderly men to ride trolley cars to the end of the line, where they would walk packages to their destination.

Rod Starkey remembers being picked up at grammar school each day at 3 p.m. to accompany his father on his remaining deliveries. They would stop at the same store each afternoon for a licorice stick and wouldn't arrive home until 8 p.m. "Those were rough times," he says now.

After the war, Pacific Messenger entered a new era in which delivering parcels became practically 90 percent of its business. Engaging in a friendly, mutually beneficial competition with United Parcel Service, the company picked up business whenever a UPS line haul truck broke down driving from Los Angeles to San Diego. Pacific Messenger would finish the delivery in such cases, but according to Rod Starkey that collaboration ended around 1950 because "they figured if their truck broke down, it was just too bad."

If the increase in parcel business signaled a less colorful era in which panel delivery trucks supplanted the more fanciful bicycle messengers, then holidays during the 1950s and 60s were periodic reminders of the company's more dashing roots. During those years, every florist in town used Pacific Messenger to deliver arrangements all over the city. The sight of 5,000 floral bouquets filling the warehouse was a memorable one every Christmas, Easter and Mother's Day.

Some deliveries left indelible legacies in other ways. In the 1950s, General Motors contracted Pacific Messenger to pick up a donkey in Sorrento Valley and bring it to the El Cortez Hotel for a sales convention. It took four workers to load the animal into a truck. They watched as a sales manager rode the donkey on stage, dismounted, took a microphone and said, "OK, guys, I just got off my ass — now I want you all to get off yours!"

In the early 1970s, a Vietnam soldier on special leave wanted to surprise his wife and hired Pacific Messenger to deliver him to his front door in a sealed box. When workers presented the crate to the woman, she initially protested that she hadn't ordered anything and refused to sign for the delivery. When she finally did, the resulting scene made for a memorable

(Below, top) A group of messengers pose in front of the company's former address of 316 C Street, c. 1935.

(Below, bottom) Ross Starkey in full messenger uniform with a three-wheeled motorcycle, c. 1933

A fleet of trucks and their drivers take a break after a long day of floral deliveries in April 1951.

picture in the next day's newspaper, while Rod Starkey can still remember her joking, "You didn't give me a chance to get my hair done!"

Advancing technology and government deregulation were just two of the forces in the 1980s that would usher Pacific Messenger through yet another crisis of identity. Gone completely were the days when a teenager could earn his summer job income as a bicycle messenger; new realities such as bike thefts had made those days a memory since the mid-60s. And then the advent of the fax machine all but relegated the messenger to just another quaint symbol of a bygone era.

Most serious of all, though, was the deregulation of the parcel delivery business in 1983 by the California Public Utilities Commission. By eliminating minimum rates that could be charged to customers, United Parcel Service was able to offer 10 to 20 percent discounts to some of Pacific Messenger's largest clients. The company simply couldn't compete.

While his father's business philosophy focused on good service, Rod Starkey's credo necessarily hinged on adaptability. "You have to change to stay in business," Starkey says. "And you have to change fast." With its parcel business dwindled by deregulation and messenger service increasingly antiquated by fax, Pacific Messenger was forced to find a new niche. It found two: establishing San Diego's only downtown-based record storage service, and delivering medium-sized shipments known as LTL, or "less than truckload," trucking.

To this day, LTL trucking throughout Southern California accounts for at least half of Pacific Messenger's business. And with its warehouse safely storing some 40,000 boxes of files for legal firms, hospitals and governmental agencies, Pacific Messenger Records Storage, Inc.'s exclusive downtown location means that city clients can have files retrieved and delivered with one phone call and minimal waiting time. Some of its LTL business came in tendering loads for Morley Trucking in Los Angeles. When Morley called Rod Starkey in 1983 to say it was ceasing operations because it was unprofitable, Pacific Messenger took over, giving itself a foothold outside San Diego. Rod Starkey kept five of Morley's 60 trucks, made some necessary and difficult personnel cuts, kept only the most prosperous of Morley's existing accounts and gradually established a profitable presence blanketing Southern California.

Plans for future growth remain wedded to Ross Starkey's simple pledge of good service and the motto that if a job can't be done right it shouldn't be done at all. "As San Diego grows, we'll grow," Rod Starkey says simply. Extending service to Arizona and Northern California will only be carried out if existing standards of good service can be upheld.

Pacific Messenger chooses not to advertise — not unless you count the common sight of its delivery trucks that annually cover two million miles and bear the company's sprightly logo designed in 1932 by Ross Starkey's brother, Len. The logo, a jaunty cartoon figure of a uniformed messenger in an old-fashioned cap, is an apt symbol for a company that utilizes computers only sparingly in favor of the personal touch. The company remains the only parcel delivery business that eschews bar coding on its packages, preferring to directly inform customers exactly who signed for a package and when. It also benefits from the public relations created by a staff of longtime employees whose dedication has forged Pacific Messenger's well-known reputation for personal service and uncanny longevity. Service of three decades or more has not been uncommon at the company. Former and current workers with such long-standing stature include: Dick Cram, Harold Davis, Doug Church, Delbert Green, Mike Kuttich, Don Durbin, Mike Gibbons, Edward Monroy, Salvador Perez, Julio Calderon, Alfredo Saucedo, Frank Modic, Bobby Lawless and Bob Pinegar.

Another factor in the success of this family business was an effective collaboration of father and son. After riding shotgun as a young boy in his father's truck on those long afternoons during the war years, Rod began delivering messages by bicycle in 1950, at the age of 14. Rising in the ranks from truck messenger, route driver and route supervisor, he eventually joined the office in 1959 and became secretary-treasurer when the company incorporated in 1971. Not every son can serve side by side with his father in a business and the secret to the Starkeys' success was a working philosophy of mutual agreement.

"Dad and I had an understanding," Rod says. "In any decision we made about the company, we both had to agree before we instituted it. Sometimes that created a disagreement and we would discuss it back and forth. But we stuck by that policy. And when we both agreed on something, 99 percent of the time it turned out successful."

When Ross Starkey passed away in 1990, it was more than an immeasurable personal loss. Because of the nature of federal inheritance tax laws, the younger Starkey was left with only $10,000 to run the company. The business had suffered a similar crisis in 1974, when Ross' wife Helena died. To this day, Rod Starkey considers the inheritance tax plight the single largest threat the company has faced since 1908. "We can handle the competition," he says, "but the government is the tough one."

Handling competition isn't just something Rod Starkey had to face in the business world. Many of his clients might be surprised to learn that he is a former national champion in badminton. From 1969 to 1971, Starkey was the American Badminton Association's No. 1-ranked singles player. He never lost a match during Thomas Cup play, which is the sport's equivalent to tennis' Davis Cup. He is also a former president of the San Diego County Humane Society and is a trustee for the San Diego Hall of Champions.

Ross and Rod Starkey, c. 1986

Today, Pacific Messenger covers two million miles per year, utilizing about 50 trucks between its Los Angeles and San Diego locations. Proudly located in downtown San Diego since day one, its current address on E Street is the company's 12th location and occupies half a city block. It may not deliver sandwiches and malt shakes to downtown secretaries like it used to, but messenger service still comprises about 10 percent of the company's business. The remaining workload is split between parcel delivery, LTL trucking and record storage. And even though only two original customers remain from its early days — San Diego Hardware and McPherson Leather Corporation — a historic legacy of service throughout a century of change remains Pacific Messenger's most lasting message of all.

Always located in downtown, Pacific Messenger has occupied its current location on E Street in San Diego since 1984.

Cloud 9 Shuttle

John Hawkins, president, and Mike Diehl, vice president of Cloud 9 Shuttle

Like San Diego, Cloud 9 Shuttle came from humble beginnings. The share-ride, ground transportation company faced enormous obstacles in 1994. But armed with a clear vision, the management team embraced San Diego and strove to recreate the company into a profitable entity whose product would match the look, feel and spirit of San Diego. The goal was to successfully provide a reliable, efficient product with excellent customer service while making a positive contribution to the San Diego community so aptly called paradise.

Cloud 9 Shuttle is now San Diego's most popular transportation solution, providing share-ride ground transportation to and from Lindbergh Field as well as general charter transportation service. The Cloud 9 fleet operates door-to-door service 24 hours a day, seven days a week throughout San Diego County. The fleet includes 100 airport vans, a line of luxury Cadillac DeVilles, accessible vehicles and large-capacity motor coaches. The total fleet logs a million miles per month and takes more than a half-million cars off San Diego's roads each year.

Cloud 9 Shuttle's road to success was, and continues to be, very much a San Diego story. To truly understand that story, it's necessary to go back to the beginning. In November 1994, the vision was clear and the goals were set high. The management team, spearheaded by John Hawkins and Mike Diehl, set out to reposition and rename the shuttle company to become San Diego's own, serving not only visitors to the area, but residents as well.

First, the company was renamed Cloud 9 Shuttle because the concept of "cloud 9" truly describes the paradise that is San Diego. Next, Hawkins asked the San Diego Convention and Visitor's Bureau for permission to incorporate elements from the organization's logo into Cloud 9's graphics. It enthusiastically agreed, and Cloud 9 set out to give the company a whole new look and personality that would be consistent with the spirit of San Diego. The vehicles were painted a cheerful white with palm trees and silver clouds. New uniforms were designed for the drivers and a campaign began to make customer service and satisfaction a marquee of the recreated company. Most importantly, out of this new relationship between Cloud 9 and San Diego's tourism industry developed a strategic alliance that was to go far beyond anything either group could have imagined.

Concurrently, another alliance was in the making with local radio stations. Cloud 9 Shuttle set up a media barter alliance that provided outdoor advertising space to radio stations in the form of van signage in exchange for radio time to build awareness of the Cloud 9 product through radio infomercials.

With these two key alliances in place, Cloud 9 went on to develop an enormously successful seven-day ambassador training program for its drivers that focused on providing stellar customer service, a fun narrative on San Diego and a safety record second to none; Cloud 9 calls it "transportainment." The program also includes training in the areas of corporate culture, marketing, sales and routing.

As Cloud 9 Shuttle continued striving to provide its customers with more than they expected, San Diego residents embraced the shuttle company by providing more than half the company's business. Growth took off at a phenomenal rate! It soon became apparent that Cloud 9 had to enter the world of high technology, or growth and operating efficiencies could not be sustained. Once again, Cloud 9's management team set out to take the business to another level by empowering employees with technology.

The first step was to use computer technology in both reservations and dispatching vehicles so that customers would receive better service. Next, cellular technology was used to track the location of every vehicle in the fleet.

Through this creative use of technology, Cloud 9 moved to a modern automated system that was highly integrated throughout the company. One of the hidden values of such a new system was that the technology to accommodate the year 2000 had already been programmed into the new software to ensure uninterrupted, quality transportation service to San Diego County.

Cloud 9's focus on training, technology and safety has resulted in providing San Diego residents outstanding service and turning the shuttle company into a profitable entity. But the principles at Cloud 9 don't stop there. They have continued to work hard to foster alliances and to make a positive contribution to San Diego. To that end, Cloud 9 management joins civic organizations in an active way, working hard to help shape the community. For example, when the Cystic Fibrosis Foundation (CF) sent out a corporate challenge to raise money at its golf event, vice president and CF board member Diehl responded by raising thousands of dollars with his record 247 holes of golf in one day. President Hawkins' huge commitment in time and energy as the chair of San Diego's first annual Fleet Week celebration in 1997 brought vast numbers of people into the area to celebrate and increase awareness of the military's important role in San Diego. On a monthly basis, Cloud 9 furthers its contribution by reserving the signage on 10 percent of its vans to promote positive community involvement through such events as the Mainly Mozart Festival, the San Diego Crew Classic, the Buick Invitational, organizations like the Girl Scouts of America and the county-wide chambers of commerce. Cloud 9 has also partnered with Mothers Against Drunk Drivers and donated the use of its vans on New Year's Eve to provide safe, no-cost transportation home to partygoers.

This world-class city has a world-class company in Cloud 9 Shuttle. The numerous awards the organization has received for its forward thinking, innovative business practices and its civic-minded approach to the transportation business include the San Diego Chamber of Commerce Small Business of the Month Award; the *San Diego Business Journal* Total Excellence in Management (T.E.I.M.) Award; the prestigious Best Practices Award from Arthur Anderson for Technology and Strategic Alliances; the Blue Chip Enterprise Initiative Award; and Bank of America's Most Enterprising Business Award.

The future of Cloud 9 Shuttle is intrinsically tied to the future of San Diego. Wherever transportation goes in the 21st century, Cloud 9 plans to be there in the forefront, helping to meet the transportation needs of the residents of San Diego while serving as an ambassador to the millions of visitors who call this unique part of the world paradise.

Cloud 9 Shuttle team celebrating winning the Best Practices Award from Arthur Anderson for Technology and Strategic Alliances

Greitzer Brokers, Inc.

Understanding the laws and regulations associated with the U.S. Customs Service is a necessity to any company importing or exporting cargo, but handling the process without the assistance of specialists can be tantamount to disaster. With more than half a century in the customs brokerage industry, Greitzer Brokers, Inc. is that specialist. The company serves as a middleman to help a commercial business or individual ship or receive merchandise to and from other countries, file the appropriate paperwork with the Customs Service and pay the required tariffs. Greitzer Brokers offers services such as customs brokerage, air and ocean freight, NAFTA assistance, bonds, electronic communications to track cargo from initial shipping to receipt of merchandise, Total Logistics Cargo (TLC) — its own bonded interstate trucking company — and much more. Greitzer Broker's mission is to work closely with its clients to provide the most efficient, safe and cost-effective brokerage services possible.

Prior to World War II, steamships and trading companies communicated through telegrams or cablegrams delivered by Western Union bicycle messengers. The Teletype systems had to be kept in separate "communication rooms" because of the amount of noise the machines made. Shipping containers had yet to be designed and the only method to load and unload cargo was with ship's tackle, docking cranes and stevedoring gangs. Customs inspectors wore military uniforms and spent most of their time checking on the legitimacy of cargo and collecting duties, which had to be paid in cash or with a cashier's check made out to the "Collector of Customs."

More than fifty years later, customs has come a long way. Changes in the import tariffs, the passing of NAFTA and the modernization of the communication process to include real-time interchange via electronic tracking systems and the World Wide Web have turned this industry into a high-tech enterprise. This requires brokerage firms to not only keep up with the changing regulations, but also with the growth of technology to continually better serve its clientele. As the first border brokers in both San Diego and Imperial Valley to be electronically linked with the Customs Service, giving them on-line access to information for easy monitoring of client shipments, Greitzer Brokers continues to remain a step ahead of its competitors worldwide.

Greitzer Brokers has been ranked one of the top three customs brokers in San Diego by the *San Diego Business Journal*. Licensed by the Department of the Treasury, customs brokers are import specialists who must be thoroughly knowledgeable in tariff schedules, customs regulations and constant changes in the law and administrative regulations. Every shipment entering the United States can require an "official greeting" comprised of more than 500 pages of customs regulations and thousands of tariff items. A good broker must be able to determine proper classifications, dutiable value and be aware of the number of commodities subject to quotas. The broker must be aware of any potential problems involving every entry item represented in the paperwork as well as cargo handling. This includes appraising, exchange rates and regulations concerning calculation of duties. Communication plays

J.T. Greitzer with his daughter, Sandy, at their first office in San Ysidro

an integral part in the entire process as broker operations transcend customs, calling for contact with more than 40 other government agencies — including the Department of Agriculture for food product importation, the Environmental Protection Agency for vehicle emission standards, and the Food and Drug Administration for product safety.

Greitzer Brokers has offices located on Otay Mesa, adjacent to the Customs Service, in Calexico, and in Tijuana, Mexico, near the U.S. Port of Entry. Greitzer Brokers can personally attend to client needs thanks to its close proximity to the Customs Service facilities. For many clients who ship perishable cargo, Greitzer Brokers' dedication to its clients, and the availability of customs brokers seven days a week, are what makes this family-run, binational company a leader in the industry. Greitzer Brokers conducts 75 percent of its business with maquiladoras, and because of its presence in Baja and the passing of NAFTA, it anticipates continued growth and strong relationships with the maquila parent companies for years to come.

J.T. Greitzer, president, entered the import/export field shortly after leaving the army in 1951. By 1955, he had obtained his first broker's license and developed an expertise in petroleum imports. After 25 years in the Los Angeles area, Greitzer developed a large client list and was ready to move his operation to San Diego. On March 16, 1976, he opened his first office in a small, one-room trailer located on a dirt lot in San Ysidro. Through hard work and the dedication of his wife, Ofelia, who has worked with him side by side to grow the business, by Christmas of that year, Greitzer opened two other offices, purchased land to expand his San Diego facility and had 18 employees. In 1977, they set up the first electronic communication system linking Greitzer Brokers to the Customs Service. Greitzer Brokers later became one of the top Automatic Brokers Interface (ABI) filers in the San Diego area.

Since that time, Greitzer Brokers has grown from having one licensed customs broker to four and expanded its San Diego facility to include a 10,000-square-foot building, housing its corporate office and primary warehouse. It has more than a half acre of parking for its own fleet of trucks (TLC) that provides personal, international freight forwarding from the southern tip of Baja to the Canadian border. Although its import specialty is textiles, such as fabric materials and dry goods, Greitzer Brokers ships a variety of products worldwide either via its own transport or through connections worldwide with other customs brokers and international freight forwarders.

Greitzer Brokers has been a family-run business almost since its inception. When Greitzer moved to San Diego with his wife and his two young daughters, Marci and Sandy, he never imagined how closely involved they would become with the company. The girls spent most of their school vacation time "working with dad," and they learned all aspects of the business. Today, Marci is one of the four licensed customs brokers and Sandy is the treasurer for this multimillion-dollar company.

This family business is a leader in the import/export industry, both in San Diego and worldwide. Well-respected by its clients and the Customs Service, Greitzer Brokers fully intends to maintain its status as a progressive, stable, experienced customs broker to service the needs of its clients for at least another 50 years.

Greitzer family —
(left to right) Marci, J.T., Ofelia and Sandy

Pacific Bell

For more than a century, San Diego County residents have relied on Pacific Bell to keep in touch with friends, family and business associates. Yet Pacific Bell is more than a local phone company. It is an advanced telecommunications company, offering a full array of state-of-the-art products and services. The increasing demands and technological advances in this billion-dollar industry have opened the doors for Pacific Bell to provide leading-edge technology and become a major player in almost every aspect of telecommunications.

In 1878, the American Speaking Telephone Company, Pacific Bell's earliest predecessor, established the first telephone exchange in California. Two years later, the company merged with National Bell Telephone Company to form the Pacific Bell Telephone Company. Continued changes in the industry saw the formation of Pacific Telephone and Telegraph Company in 1906, which remained until the 1984 divestiture, when Pacific Telesis Group became the holding company for Pacific Bell. In 1996 Pacific Telesis became part of SBC Communications, Inc., an international telecommunications industry leader.

Rooted in a more than 120-year tradition, Pacific Bell's commitment to its customers and the community is primary. Endeavoring to be a one-stop tele-communications provider, Pacific Bell offers local telephone service, digital wireless phone service, Internet access, voicemail, pagers and high-speed data transmission. It spends more than $300 million a year in San Diego to upgrade and modernize equipment for its residential and commercial customers. In an information-centered society, sophisticated and well-maintained telecommunications networks are as vital to personal communications and economic success as railroads were a century ago.

In the latter half of the 1990s, the telecommunications industry saw unprecedented growth as businesses and consumers alike added additional phone lines for faxes, computers and in-home businesses. The continual splitting of area codes indicates a growth explosion that seems to have no limits. Pacific Bell works diligently adding services and employees as necessary to meet the needs and expectations of customers, creating such innovations as three-way calling, Caller ID, call-return and advanced ways of transmitting voice and data.

In entering the wireless phone market in 1996, Pacific Bell utilized digital technology based on an eight-year proven European model. This aspect of the business has grown at an extraordinary pace since initial start-up. When it became an Internet provider, Pacific Bell implemented advanced technology, which brings subscribers the power of the Internet at unparalleled speeds and is not affected by the number of users.

Its superior ability to provide strategic business solutions and advanced telecommunications networks and services was recognized when Pacific Bell was named as sole prime contractor on a U.S. Navy five-year contract in 1998. The contract requires Pacific Bell to administer services that support voice, video and data transfer among 13 major Naval command centers as well as other officially authorized Department of Defense and federal facilities in San Diego.

Pacific Bell operators keep customers connected. (c.1900)

Pacific Bell's Network Operations Center in San Diego uses state-of-the art technology in providing top notch telecommunications services to customers c.1999

Community involvement is part of Pacific Bell's corporate identity. It donates more than $3 million annually to a variety of San Diego organizations to support its volunteer efforts chiefly in the areas of math and science education and economic development. Pacific Bell's intent is not only to contribute financially, but to be a catalyst for positive change and enhancement of the lifestyle and well-being of the communities in which its employees and customers live and raise their families.

Technicians ensure superior service for Pacific Bell's customers. c. 1999

Pacific Bell's role in its education outreach is its commitment to curriculum, which is achieved by working closely with educators to provide technology that supports what is being taught in the classrooms. Log Onto the Future, a landmark partnership with the Classroom of the Future Foundation and the County Office of Education, brings high-speed data transfer and video conferencing into the classroom and supports a math and science intensive curriculum. The 12 San Diego elementary, middle and high schools involved are linked via high-speed digital lines and allow the students to collaborate on various projects ranging from building a station on Mars to exploring the ethical, political and scientific implications of human cloning.

Another project that matches technology to curriculum is WeatherNet. In partnership with NBC-TV 7/39, Pacific Bell is providing automated weather systems to area schools. Not only is data on local weather available, but an Internet link connects the schools to other systems at schools and science centers around the world. Students in the participating San Diego classrooms study weather, science, math, and geography as well as social studies programs emphasizing reading and writing.

Promotion of supplemental education in science and math in grades kindergarten through 12 serves not only the community directly, but the benefactor indirectly. Pacific Bell sees its future workforce in the students of today and has a vested interest in improving educational opportunities. In addition, the students of today are the technology users of tomorrow and Pacific Bell wants to ensure better consumer knowledge of increasingly sophisticated communications equipment.

To support and assist in the economic development of the region, Pacific Bell works with area chambers of commerce and other business organizations, funding and sponsoring economic development seminars, symposiums, technology expositions and other special programs.

A key factor in the success of implementing many of its community activities can be credited to the Pacific Bell Pioneers, the volunteer arm of the company. Drawing from more than 5,500 active and approximately 5,000 retired employees, the Pioneers donate time and money to civic organizations and causes.

Pacific Bell's sponsorship efforts run the gamut. With the San Diego Padres, it has promoted literacy programs. It supports research on endangered species, having donated millions of dollars to the World-Famous San Diego Zoo and Wild Animal Park. Pacific Bell aided in flood relief after El Nino's crippling storms; it supports the YWCA programs on prevention of domestic violence; it sponsors after school programs; it has installed computer centers in underserved communities; and through the United Way it lends support to more than 30 organizations.

Pacific Bell's early headquarters in San Diego c. 1930

Pacific Bell, a long-time fixture in the San Diego community, may be the oldest phone company, offering a heritage of stability, yet it is also the most advanced. Innovative thinking coupled with state-of-the-art products and a deep commitment to community involvement keeps Pacific Bell in the forefront of telecommunications and corporate leadership.

Port of San Diego

The Port of San Diego was established in 1962 by an act of the state legislature to protect, promote and oversee San Diego Bay's waterfront and maritime property. As the steward of the bay and adjacent tidelands, the Port has jurisdiction of more than 2,500 acres of property and 3,000 acres of water. Operations include San Diego International Airport at Lindbergh Field, two marine terminals, a cruise ship terminal, and more than 600 tenant leases for businesses such as restaurants, hotels, bay and excursion marinas, ship building and repair yards and sportfishing. Sixteen waterfront parks, several wildlife reserves, and a host of attractions such as 10 miles of

The Port of San Diego manages more than 27 miles of waterfront property.

bicycle paths entice and delight millions of local, national and international visitors each year.

The Port operates under the authority of the Board of Port Commissioners. The board is comprised of seven members appointed by their respective city councils from Chula Vista, Coronado, Imperial Beach, National City and San Diego. Each city appoints one commissioner to the board, with the exception of San Diego, which has three.

Real Estate

Since 1962, the Port of San Diego has invested approximately $835 million in public improvements including parks, walkways, landscaped promenades, cargo terminals, airport expansion, San Diego's waterfront convention center and public anchorages. Balancing recreational, environmental and commercial priorities on the tidelands enables the Port to provide the community with enjoyable access to the waterfront at no cost to taxpayers.

The Port oversees hundreds of tenant leases stretched along the waterfront and coordinates the development of the waterfront with the intent of attracting more business and tourist trade to the area.

Most recently, special focus has centered on the prime waterfront areas of the North and South Embarcadero — San Diego's "front porch" — where plans call for expanded convention, park, hotel, shopping and cruise line facilities. The cruise industry in San Diego continues to make strides with increasing numbers of port calls from most major lines.

International attention brought to San Diego's marinas by the America's Cup competition and an increase in recreational boating has spotlighted the America's Cup Harbor on Shelter Island. Plans to revitalize and enhance view corridors, create more public spaces and enliven surrounding buildings and structures are a part of the Port's ongoing redevelopment process in this area.

The South Bay cities of Chula Vista, Coronado, Imperial Beach and National City are also home to revitalization projects. There are plans to build a 250-room hotel on the Chula Vista waterfront, providing a venue for large group meetings and special events. The 1998 purchase of the South Bay Power Plant in Chula Vista allows the Port to consider new development ideas designed to better use the area for residents and visitors alike. Skateboarders and in-line skaters enjoy a new public, pay-per-use recreational facility in Coronado. In the Imperial Beach area, the public will benefit by the expansion and refurbishment of Dunes Park and the Imperial Beach Pier Plaza and the building of a new Safety Center. National City's waterfront renaissance includes the creation of a new marina and commercial retail complex adjoining the marine terminal.

Environment

The Port of San Diego is leading a dynamic effort to coordinate environmental projects that benefit the region's wildlife and bay resources now and in years to come.

A historic move was made in 1998 to preserve San Diego Bay's natural resources by entering into an agreement with the U.S. Fish and Wildlife Service and Western Salt Company to purchase and transfer approximately 1,300 acres of land in the South Bay. This acreage will become the largest wildlife and wetland habitat preserve on the bay.

The Port is active in the Comprehensive Management Plan for the environmental quality of the San Diego Bay along with 30 other agencies and organizations. Other environmental projects include a partnership with the San Diego Zoological Society to help save San Diego Bay's endangered species.

The Airport and Convention Center

Once a vast mudflat, San Diego International Airport at Lindbergh Field is one of the world's busiest single-runway airports, serving more than 15 million passengers annually. Future growth and the ability to support the region's rapidly growing air travel needs continue to be the center of focus for the Port and the airport.

To assist in meeting the region's air transportation needs, the airport completed a $232 million upgrade and improvement project in 1998. The improvements allow 29 passenger and cargo airlines to operate more than 600 flights each day. The next step is a first-ever master planning effort to develop the airport to meet the region's air travel growth needs into the year 2020 and beyond.

More than 15 million passengers arrive or depart from Lindbergh Field each year.

Another project that infuses booming business into the region is the San Diego Convention Center. Built debt-free in 1989 by the Port of San Diego at a cost of $200 million, the Center is one of the largest and most beautiful meeting sites in the nation. The city of San Diego and the Port cooperatively worked to double the size of the facility. Due to be complete in 2001, the expanded facility will pump almost $1 billion annually into the San Diego region.

Maritime Services

Close proximity to the open ocean and uncongested waters make San Diego an excellent location for cargo shipping. Out of the National City Marine Terminal, vehicle imports and exports are the strongest revenue source. Niche cargo operations at the Tenth Avenue Marine Terminal include cottonseed, soda ash, cement, fertilizer, lumber and newsprint.

Since 1962 the Port of San Diego has dramatically changed the face of the waterfront by enhancing tourist attractions, bringing new business and industry to the city, and creating thousands of new jobs, and since 1970, all without cost to taxpayers. With a bold eye toward the future and a solid foot in the present, the Port of San Diego is committed to continued development of San Diego Bay and its tidelands as a highly respected, world-class region.

United Airlines

Since its first biplane soared into the sky in 1926 to deliver the U.S. mail, United Airlines' pioneering efforts have helped to expand commercial aviation and refine airline service. For more than 70 years, United Airlines has built a history of innovation and leadership that includes the world's first flight attendant service in 1930, the first nonstop, coast-to-coast U.S. flight in 1955, and in 1990, the first commercial carrier use of satellite data communications in-flight.

Firmly entrenched in San Diego since 1930, United has been serving the growing travel needs of a growing community. Customer satisfaction is the philosophy that has enabled United Airlines to maintain its position as San Diego's largest full-service airline and to become the world's largest airline, with 2,300 flights each day.

A full range of flight schedules and long-term track records for safety and superior service set United apart from its competitors. United conducts extensive research and ongoing surveys that reveal exactly what its customers want — and United's mission has been to comply. Customers asked for comfort, so United offers ergonomically contoured seats that have adjustable headrests and extendable leg rests, individual wand-mounted reading lights and armrest-mounted controls. Frequent travelers want recognition for their loyalty, so United offers Mileage Plus, which provides a variety of discounts as well as earned miles on international flights with several levels of upgrades. The 1996 renovation of San Diego's Lindbergh Field created extra space for the addition of a fifth gate as well as a private membership club, the Red Carpet Room, which affords added comfort and recognition for frequent business travelers.

In 1994, United Airlines offered stock to its employees, which made it the largest majority employee-owned company in the world. With increased responsibility and control, pilots, machinists, administrators and managers began steering United to greater profitability and customer satisfaction.

United's employees as owners take great pride in their company. If they have suggestions for improvement, they do the necessary research, investigate possible outcomes and draw conclusions: Is this idea cost effective? Will this work? They are given an understanding of corporate goals and strategies as a foundation for decision making and know they are responsible for the effects of their choices. The results are visible in the many employee innovations that have been initiated.

Passengers requested convenience and a hassle-free experience. United's Web site gives fliers the ability to purchase tickets electronically, 24 hours a day. If a customer finds self-ticketing confusing or if a trip is more complex than a single flight, the Web site can be used for research on flight and seat information and airport maps and travel tips. Then ticketing can be completed by a travel agent or at either of United's two San Diego ticket offices. United places a major focus on its largest market segment — business travelers, or "road warriors" as they are affectionately called. In accommodating their expanding needs, for example, United is installing plug-ins onboard its aircraft for laptop computers.

Another employee idea sparked the creation of United Shuttle, which, since 1994, has offered 16 low-cost daily flights from San

With more than 30 daily flights connecting to United Airlines' international gateway at San Francisco International Airport, United Shuttle links San Diego to the world.

Diego to San Francisco. This increased United's service, which in 1998 was roughly 35 daily departures. Sky West, a United affiliate, carries passengers to Los Angeles more than 30 times a day. And up to eight daily flights out of Palomar Airport to Los Angeles afford the North San Diego community local convenience.

Another employee innovation was to improve the deplaning times in certain airports by adding manual stairs to disembark passengers simultaneously from the front and rear doors of the plane. This has been innovated at airports where there is minimal ground activity and has significantly reduced delays due to slow boarding.

To celebrate its 65th anniversary, United flew a 777 into San Diego. This innovative twin engine plane was designed by United in concert with Boeing especially for long distances — the plane can fly from California to Europe without a refueling stop.

Employees of United in San Diego have many opportunities for input and participation, including the Promotion & Community Involvement Team, the Employee Scheduling Team and the On-Time Performance Team. The 10 to 15 members of the promotion team meet monthly to review requests for sponsorship and decide how they want to be involved in the community. United has been a supporter of the San Diego Ballet, the La Jolla Half Marathon and the Toshiba Tennis Classic, among other events. It was an official sponsor of the 1996 Republican National Convention which was held in San Diego.

Every December, United helps make holiday wishes come true for underprivileged children. Working closely with the county of San Diego Social Services Department, approximately 80 children plus their chaperones are taken on a 30-minute "Fantasy Flight" and then treated with a party at the "North Pole." The air freight area is converted for visits with Santa, gift-giving and snacks. United employees coordinate the entire event.

Another community effort of the San Diego employees is their participation in the Welfare to

In San Diego, United employs nearly 300 people. The airline has more than 90,000 employees worldwide.

Work program. United works with local charity organizations to find potential employees from welfare recipients who are then groomed for employment through a job readiness and business skills training program. The chairman of United Airlines is the national chairman for the program, and several of United's San Diego employees were hired through the program.

In addition to its customer surveys, United conducts regular surveys to monitor employee attitudes and from the information gathered, the company can continue to provide an environment that allows employees to be successful and to provide outstanding customer service. This philosophy that focuses on the concerns of airline employees and customers has evolved over time and is paramount to United's success globally as well as locally. For more than half a century United Airlines has been serving the San Diego community and will continue to cater to the changing needs of air travelers.

Televideo San Diego

In today's complicated world, effective communication is critical to the success of a business. With this in mind, many companies have turned meeting rooms into high-tech communication centers that allow for multisite participants. They have replaced low-impact sales presentations using paper graphs and flip charts with exciting, high-quality video presentations that dramatically increase buyer interest. Companies can now integrate workshops by experts with long-distance learning through interactive video to simultaneously educate employees working at multiple sites, thereby saving the cost and time of travel.

Since 1976, Televideo San Diego has developed business solutions to bring these high-tech video advances into company boardrooms, training facilities and offices. For more than 25 years, this minority-owned company has led the independent video dealer industry in studio systems design, turnkey installations, component integration, modular upgrading, end-user training, equipment testing, authorized service repair and systems maintenance.

Televideo San Diego's full-service process starts with trained designers evaluating a company's specific needs for today and the future. The designers get input from company executives and the employees who are directly impacted by new equipment — sales and support staff, media and information system personnel. Televideo San Diego then orders and installs the necessary equipment, sometimes integrating new components to upgrade existing systems. Finally, its technicians test the entire system and provide additional services from end-user training to custom cabinetry.

The concept for Televideo San Diego came as a result of David Stepp's experience in using video to evaluate teachers in the classroom for the Department of Health, Education and Welfare (HEW) program and Linda Stepp's experience in motion picture production. David and Linda began to sell video equipment to businesses and broadcast studios. Their business expanded when they showed companies and organizations in San Diego how video equipment allows for clear, cost-effective, highly productive communication. Children's Hospital, Solar Turbines, the Padres, SAIC and the San Diego Zoological Society were some of the first organizations to utilize video equipment in the boardroom and in educating employees and the public. Other clients include Sea World, the University of California, San Diego, San Diego State University, KUSI, KFMB, KGTV, and Televisa, the largest broadcast station in Mexico.

Televideo San Diego's reputation extends beyond San Diego into the entire video communication industry. Sony has designated the company as its primary partner in the greater San Diego region. Along with the other lines it carries, Televideo San Diego has access to all the broadcast and commercial video equipment its clients may need for high technology applications. Video communication has taken a giant leap into the future with the transition from analog to digital technology. Advances in the industry will continue to change the way companies communicate, store information, educate personnel and conduct business. From basic PCs to 3D graphic workstations to the most sophisticated interactive multi-media training and communication centers, Televideo San Diego can supply the latest solutions. For the best in broadcast, professional and industrial video products, systems and service, Televideo San Diego is the only answer.

Televideo San Diego's owners David and Linda Stepp

Photo by Robert A. Eplett

Various professional companies and firms provide engineering, legal, financial, and business and personal services to greater San Diego.

Partners in
PROFES

ABC Veterinary Hospitals	342
Borton, Petrini & Conron, LLP	344
Broadcast Images, Inc.	346
Center for Leadership Studies	348
Dyson & Dyson Real Estate Associates	350
The Executive Group	352
FAS-EBA Insurance Services	354
Hirsch & Company Consulting Engineers	356
Hovey & Kirby, A.P.C.	358
Luchner Tool Engineering Inc.	360
Urban Systems Associates	362
Falcon West Insurance Brokers	364
Klinedinst, Fliehman & McKillop	365
North County Economic Development Council	366
Southern California Security Services	367

ABC Veterinary Hospitals

A pet tarantula is shedding its skin. A 150-pound potbelly pig has been gored by its brother. These are actual but unusual scenes at ABC Veterinary Hospitals, which began as a mobile veterinary clinic that once covered San Diego County in a 1960

Founder Dr. Jay Shrock checks his patient at the mobile clinic

Ford van. Now it covers the county with five state-of-the-art, full-service hospitals. Low-cost basic pet protection through vaccinations, spaying and neutering, now combined with high-quality advanced care still prevails.

Founder Dr. Jay Shrock believed veterinarians owed the public an affordable protection program for their pets-to keep the animals healthy and avoid unwanted litters. In 1981, Dr. Shrock set up his $950 van as a mobile clinic and traveled throughout the county charging only $10 for basic immunizations.

In response to the demand for more comprehensive veterinary care, Dr. Shrock opened the first ABC Veterinary Hospital in 1983 in Kearny Mesa, his most frequented mobile clinic stop. He opened the second hospital in 1985 in El Cajon, another popular vaccination clinic location, on the site of an old gas station. He looked for veterinarians to work in his hospitals that were not only skilled doctors, but also compassionate and caring people. He maintained the mobile clinic and continued to offer the same low-cost basic pet protection program in his hospitals.

Dr. Shrock spearheaded a major transition in veterinary medicine by giving vaccinations to animals without charging for an office visit in his hospitals, just as he was doing in the mobile clinic. Charging for an office visit every time an animal received vaccinations was common practice for most veterinarians. Ultimately other animal hospitals reversed their policies and began charging true value for vaccinations. The service became more available to everyone because it was now affordable to the general population.

The mobile clinic continued to draw a substantial following in San Marcos. Therefore, Dr. Shrock opened hospital number three at that location in 1989. Dr. Barry Neichin, who was working at the El Cajon hospital, became a partner and was responsible for the San Marcos hospital. In 1992, Dr. Michael Weber came aboard as the third partner and opened the Pacific Beach location, another busy site of the mobile clinic. The fifth hospital in Solana Beach was established in 1997.

The partners believe that if the veterinarian who runs the hospital is an owner, he has a vested interest. He will therefore maintain the same quality standards of the other hospitals, as well as impart his own personality. They see this as the primary difference ABC has over other large corporate practices which are penetrating the market. Each ABC is unique, stamped with the partner's character, while sharing the same philosophy, standards, services and advertising.

Open seven days a week, each hospital's services include low-cost vaccinations as well as low-cost spaying and neutering, which is now done exclusively in the hospitals. For those clients who desire optimal veterinary care for their pet prior to surgery, electrocardiograms, blood chemistry analysis and pain management packages are available. The mobile clinic still operates, though exclusively for vaccinations.

As clients demand more services and expect the same level of care for their animal "family members" as they expect for themselves, technology has afforded ABC Veterinary Hospitals the opportunity to offer exceptional care. The hospitals are equipped with continually updated equipment. Through the new field of telemedicine, outside specialists in fields such as cardiology, orthopedics and radiology can assist in diagnoses.

Being part of a group of hospitals has several advantages: sharing of resources for staff education, employee benefits, administration, advertising and purchasing. Together all five ABC locations employ more than 10 veterinarians and more than 125 ancillary staff, consisting of receptionists, office managers, registered veterinary technicians, veterinary assistants and kennel workers.

The hospitals treat a varied assortment, everything from African cichlid and koi to ferrets and Fennic fox. Rats, birds and snakes are fairly common, while hedgehogs, ducks and goats are the rare exception. After the dreadful Harmony Grove fire, the veterinarians at ABC treated two feline burn victims who were rescued from the trailer of a woman who had housed as many as 30 cats. The hospital bills for "Smoky" and "Inferno" were partially paid by neighbors who collected funds for the two survivors. Another group of neighbors donated money to restore the health of an abandoned dog that was hit by a car the day after its owner died. ABC went a step further and found a new home for the dog.

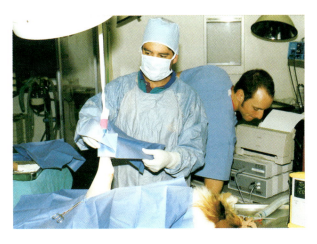

ABC's commitment to provide pets with proper protection and health care extends even to the less fortunate. The hospitals created a memorial fund, which accepts donations from clients and members of the community, to assist people who cannot afford veterinary care. Unwanted or abandoned animals are occasionally boarded in the hospitals and adopted to loving homes. One of the ABC partners raises puppies for Canine Companions for Independence, which trains dogs for the disabled.

ABC takes the same charitable spirit it shows its two and four-legged clients into the San Diego community. The hospitals sponsor football and basketball programs at Mission Bay High School. They annually support city soccer and baseball teams as well. The veterinarians participate in career days at elementary schools and give tours of the hospitals to 4H clubs, Girl Scouts and high school students who may be considering a career in animal medicine. Regional Occupation Program students often perform their externships at the ABC hospitals.

ABC Veterinary Hospital partners Drs. Shrock, Neichin and Weber believe their hospitals are places where science and compassion coexist. They thoroughly enjoy working with the animals; however, they know taking care of the concerns of the owners is also of paramount importance. With state-of-the-art facilities and the caring attitude of the doctors and staff, getting the best care for your pets is as easy as ABC.

Partner Dr. Michael Weber with a cuddly client

Partner Dr. Barry Neichin begins orthopedic surgery

It all began in a 1960 Ford van (lovingly named "Lucille").

Borton, Petrini & Conron, LLP

When Fred Borton established his law firm in Bakersfield in 1899, people often sealed agreements with a handshake. However, as life transitioned from horses and vaudeville shows to automobiles and motion pictures, advancing technology and greater monetary risk brought forth a need for increased legal protection both personally and in the emerging industries. As life became more complicated, so did the laws. Borton, Petrini & Conron, LLP has not only stayed in step with the evolution of law, but has risen as a leader in its field.

Borton, Petrini & Conron's partners include (counter-clockwise from bottom left) Rocky K. Copley, Paul Kissel, Michelle Van Dyke and Thomas J. Stoddard.

Shortly after Borton formed the business, James Petrini joined the firm, and Harry C. Conron became a partner 30 years later. Together, the three original partners formed a strong alliance of legal talent to create a business that would become a leader in defense law. It would become one of California's leading law firms with 13 strategically placed offices throughout California, from Redding to San Diego. This growth, from a small local firm to a well-respected, statewide entity, is the on-going product of expertise, excellent client relationships and dedication to the practice of law.

Having grown along with the state, Borton, Petrini & Conron has developed an effective understanding of California, its people and its law. Throughout the 20th century, the firm's partners have become noted judges and justices within the state's court system. Many of the firm's attorneys have helped to shape California law through precedent-setting cases. It has participated in the evolution of business practice, land use, tax planning, water, employment, public entity, professional liability, environmental and health care law, to name a few.

As a leading litigation firm, Borton, Petrini & Conron provides legal services in a number of fields of law including antitrust, unfair competition, personal injury defense, insurance coverage, bad faith defense, professional defense (medical, accounting, engineering, etc.), product liability, toxic waste litigation, employment discrimination, construction defect, trademark and copyright infringement, appellate litigation, arbitration, alternative dispute resolution (ADR) and tort liability.

Regular communication with clients and effective case management are paramount at Borton, Petrini & Conron. Its system quickly determines which cases can be settled short of trial (95 percent) and finds the most cost-effective, efficient way of accomplishing desirable solutions. The firm takes full advantage of the vast diversity and scope of experience of its attorneys. Each week all new files are reviewed by a team of partners to assess case needs and litigation strategies. Clients are kept current on the status and progress of each phase of the case as well as any issues that may affect the outcome. The firm's 13 offices work in conjunction with each other and are able to coordinate similar cases, thereby avoiding the expense of duplicate research and work. This also gives the attorney an advantage in presenting a more powerful case.

The firm's communication with and service to its clients does not end with the closing of a file. Clients are kept current on the issues that affect business through publications and updates. To this end, the firm publishes the *California Business Counsel* and *California Defense*, magazines that focus on business and tort-related legal matters. They also distribute *Labor and Employment Law Update*, a publication reporting the most recent legal decisions affecting this area of law. Several partners produce industry-specific newsletters, such as *Health Law Update* and *Environmental Update*.

Rocky K. Copley is the managing partner of Borton, Petrini & Conron's San Diego office. With a degree from McGeorge School of Law, Copley is a specialist in cases that deal with product liability, unfair competition, director and officer liability, wrongful termination, insurance bad faith and professional liability. The San Diego regional office specializes in unfair competition, real estate and commercial law, trade secrets and copyright protection, employment litigation, personal injury and corporate law. The attorneys at the firm share a blend of specialized knowledge and diverse experience, a base that results in expert legal representation for every client.

The attorneys at Borton, Petrini & Conron work not only with individuals and companies dealing with litigation issues, but also assist businesses to develop strategies that take into consideration legal restrictions and laws that affect business. By helping them to form better business plans and rewrite contracts, policies and company procedures, the firm can help businesses avoid unnecessary and costly litigation.

Borton, Petrini & Conron recognizes the best way to serve a client is to establish a presence in the community. The attorneys are actively involved in various charitable, community and professional associations. However, the firm also has the advantage of being a multilocation corporation. The regional offices have linked together to create a central legal research facility and expert witness databases that are not available to other law firms. Another advantage to clients is the firm's ability to represent them in more than one location without incurring excessive travel expenses.

The firm hosts a variety of seminars each year for clients and members of the general public. One of its seminars is the annual Bakersfield Business Conference, which features internationally known speakers and entertainers. This conference has received worldwide acclaim and is a multiyear winner of the "Best One-Day Conference in the Nation," awarded by the International Platform Association. Speakers have included former Presidents Ronald Reagan, George Bush, Gerald Ford and Jimmy Carter. Other dignitaries have included former Pakistani Prime Minister Benazir Bhutto, Republican presidential candidate Steve Forbes, Nobel Peace Prize Laureate and former President of the Soviet Union Mikhail Gorbachev, Nobel Peace Prize Laureate and former Prime Minister of Israel Shimon Peres and the Rt. Hon. John Major, former prime minister of Great Britain.

Borton, Petrini & Conron, LLP is celebrating more than 100 years of service to the individuals and businesses of California. While times have changed dramatically since Fred Borton established his office, you will still find a legal practice committed to the community, California, the law and expert legal representation.

The law firm of Borton, Petrini & Conron, LLP is located in Emerald Plaza, one of downtown San Diego's most prestigious addresses.

Broadcast Images, Inc.

The production facility and corporate offices of Broadcast Images, Inc. are located in the Kearny Mesa area of San Diego.

Broadcast Images' Dean Taylor, Jeff Freeman and Jim Holtzman at the Baseball Hall of Fame in Cooperstown, New York, while working on the documentary "Cooperstown: Baseball's Main Street"

To quit a job and venture out on your own is daunting enough. For Jeff Freeman, that wasn't the half of it. During his years as a local TV news, documentary and production photographer, Freeman developed a working relationship with the Zoological Society of San Diego. Traversing brush and savanna in his spare time to document the zoo's international work, Freeman gained a reputation as an extraordinary wildlife photographer and documentarist. So deciding to leave the relative comfort of employment and start a video production company called Broadcast Images was easy. What followed immediately was not.

That first month in 1989 would bring Broadcast Images to the jungles of Papua, New Guinea to shoot a documentary, no small task where the mercury routinely pegs 120 degrees and rain falls six hours each day. More uncomfortable still was the weight of the brand new Betacam — the bulk of company assets at the time — on Freeman's sweaty shoulder. This was not a hospitable place for man or machine, especially a delicate electronic one.

Freeman and crew were traveling with zoo researchers. The objective of the video was to document the scientists' work and tell the story of this remote and isolated island north of Australia. The party visited places on Earth where they thought no one had likely been before. One spot offered the ghostly remains of a B-17 bomber, crashed and permanently snarled in a jungle thicket. Freeman's footage of the wreck poignantly reminds us of the far reaches of World War II. But discovery wasn't the travelers' alone. After shooting a ceremonial dance in a remote village where mirrors were unknown, let alone electricity and television, Freeman played back his footage to the villagers' bewilderment and delight.

The Papua, New Guinea project set the tone for much of Broadcast Images' future. The team of broadcast professionals Freeman put together has documented events all over the world. From China to Costa Rica, Australia to Guyana, New York to Los Angeles and even here at home, Broadcast Images has become known for the ability to work in any environment or circumstance and be ready to go at a moment's notice.

As its name would suggest, Broadcast Images is a regular contributor to the airwaves, be it in the form of a news magazine piece for the likes of ABC's "20/20" or a full-length program for public broadcasting. Do it well and have it by deadline! It's a broadcast discipline this creative shop brings to each of its projects — TV and corporate alike. It boils down to an efficiency in better-quality video production Broadcast Images' competitors are hard-pressed to match. BI ranks in the top third of San Diego's video production companies by revenues and provides everything from production services billed hourly to complete long-form and live television production.

Freeman is joined by a small staff of creative, technical and support personnel with a combined broadcast history of over 100 years. Broadcast Images is a video boutique with an impact far beyond its size and place. ABC News was among the first of Broadcast Images' clients and remains an important one today. National networks from Italy, Australia, Japan and elsewhere call on BI to cover international events such as America's Cup yacht racing and the Academy Awards. BI even produces its own programming. One such program, "Cooperstown: Baseball's Main Street," a half-hour program hosted by Joe Garagiola, was syndicated nationally and is now in the home-video market.

Not everything Broadcast Images does is so widely viewed, of course. When the San Diego Natural History Museum wanted to raise funds for expansion, BI produced a video with location footage, on-camera testimonials and a computer-generated "walking tour" through the proposed site. Although the video was shown to just a handful of potential donors, it raised $12 million for the organization.

Likewise, the San Diego Wild Animal Park was raising funds for a new animal hospital. With over 3,000 exotic animals in its care and inadequate facilities, the park's need was critical. Broadcast Images knew this firsthand. They had been to the park's cramped operating room many times before, documenting groundbreaking procedures: a gorilla appendectomy, setting the malformed leg of a baby rhino and the heroic efforts to save a lead-poisoned California Condor. BI's video wasn't just the centerpiece of the campaign, it was the only promotional material seen by many potential donors. On the strength of the video alone, one donor gave $1.25 million of the $14.6 million total raised for the project.

To tell their stories, nonprofit organizations are increasingly dependent on professionally produced videos. But the stories are like a tree in the woods — without an audience they fall unheard. One way to get the message across cluttered media pathways is the video news release (VNR). Like its print cousin, the VNR tells a succinct, digestible story that news outlets can consume. But where the print release might provide copy and still photos, the VNR provides all the elements for a complete TV news story. Broadcast Images created a VNR for the Girl Scouts about their trip to a center for the homeless. This occurred on a weekend when stations were short-staffed and unable to send crews of their own to this type of event. The story was picked up by San Diego's four major stations and aired on eight newscasts. BI has produced regional and national VNRs for major corporations as well as the smallest nonprofit groups.

The video production business in San Diego County is quite competitive. There were 78 production companies chasing an estimated $30 million of work at last count. BI expects this number to grow considerably in the next decade as the television universe continues to expand, electronic and digital media converge and more companies become media-aware.

Plans call for increased CD-ROM, DVD, HDTV and other digital production services in the near future. But if there is just one thing that defines the company's niche in the video marketplace, it's that broadcast discipline — do it well and have it by deadline!

One of Broadcast Images' edit rooms equipped with Betacam SP, D-2, 3/4," SVHS and computer graphics

Center for Leadership Studies

The best-kept secret in the management training community is nestled in the heart of downtown Escondido. Dr. Paul Hersey, the father of the Situational Leadership Concept, established the Center for Leadership Studies in the mid-1960s. Through the development of his training model, the Center has reached more than 10 million managers in more than 1,000 organizations. The Center offers instruction and training expertise in leadership and management, sales, customer service, team leadership, consulting, research and instrument design (clarifying standards of performance). The Center has a network of professional trainers and consultants across the nation and in more than 26 countries.

The Situational Leadership Model

The Situational Leadership Model focuses on a leader's ability to influence others. The model covers four basic leadership styles: telling, selling, participating and delegating. The key to the model lies in the leader's ability to match the appropriate people to the right tasks and to determine the amount of direction and support needed to meet those objectives. The benefits of Situational Leadership training "take the mystery out of effective leadership, improve workforce commitment and motivation, increase leader and staff probabilities of success, ensure a leader's understanding of the staff's need for direction and support, and invest in the professional development of leaders."

Participants in the classroom training sessions

What distinguishes the model from other training concepts is twofold. To be effective, a leader must earn the right to coach and train his team to complete the tasks set before them and the employees must reciprocate by fulfilling the expectations of the leader through their ability to follow through and their willingness to participate, delegate when necessary and complete the specific objectives as scheduled. Second, and probably more important, the model is designed to teach individuals how to apply it within their specific company settings, tailored to their distinct needs.

Dr. Paul Hersey

Hersey, a behavioral scientist, first published his Situational Leadership Concept in articles in the 1960s. In 1969, he co-wrote a textbook with Ken Blanchard, containing the model. *Management of Organizational Behavior* has been translated into more than 14 languages, has sold more than one million copies and is currently in its eighth edition.

Hersey came to California in the 1970s to work on another book with Blanchard that applied the Situational Leadership Model to parenting. After three months in California, Hersey fell in love with San Diego County and made Escondido not only his home, but headquarters for the Center for Leadership Studies.

When Dr. Ron Campbell, president of the center, first met Hersey, he was at a conference in San Francisco researching leadership management programs to utilize as part of the training curriculum in the Coast Guard. He happened to sit in on a presentation given by Hersey on the Situational Leadership Concept and was surprised at how much the model came alive through Hersey's "real world" examples, all the while preserving the integrity of the model. Because of his love of training and coaching, when Campbell left the Coast Guard, Hersey invited him to work for the Center. More than 15 years have passed since he became a team member and a leader at the

Center, giving Hersey more leisure time to spend with his family and continue his writing.

The Center

The Center doesn't profess to be an expert in the field of leadership training nor does it jump on the latest management training trends. The Center's success is due to the stability and continuity of the model. The clients and their enthusiasm about the concept are what keep the organization strong. The Center doesn't depend on heavy advertising to stay on top of the market; instead, its growth comes from word-of-mouth. As managers and leaders transition to different organizations, they bring the leadership concepts they learned at the Center with them. The Center is proud of the fact that many of its clients have been with them for 10 to 15 years. One of the highlights of the Center is to continue doing business with someone who may be working for their third or fourth company and has brought the model with them into each new organization. The reward is in the continuity of the model. The companies may change, but the leaders keep the model alive as they grow within their careers.

Thanks to the contribution of Hersey, the Center is a living testimony to the Situational Leadership Concept. Even with its significant customer base, the Center has consistently worked to develop its small staff to their full potential through creative use of resources and dedicated coaching. Part of what makes the Center work so well with such a modest staff is the Leadership model and the staff's belief in and adherence to its philosophy.

The Models

The Center for Leadership Studies offers a suite of models attuned to Situational Leadership. Sample in-depth courses include: The Situational Leadership Model, Leveraging Human Performance, Case Studies in Team Leadership and Change, and Hard-hitting, Proven Techniques for Team Leadership. Each model is broken down into modules and follows through with applications for implementation at the clients' organizations and tools for interpreting leadership and team skills. The Center carries a supply of books, videos and tapes to nurture the participants beyond basic training and give them the tools to be effective leaders in any circumstance.

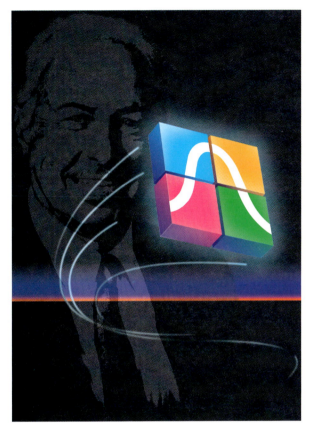

Dr. Paul Hersey, behavioral scientist, and the Situational Leadership® model, the performance tool of more than 10 million managers worldwide

Each training seminar is taught either at the Center or on location via classroom-style instruction. The trainers provide the attendees with the necessary tools to build the leadership skills that gain immediate results. Although career paths and long-term goals are important, assessing present needs is the immediate concern — to get the job done today to serve as the building blocks for tomorrow.

The cornerstone of the training program is to listen, modify, make adjustments and keep current. The Center isn't interested in growing so large or so fast that it loses its perspective. It wants to make winners for today, manage the moment, survive the imitators and earn the right to assist leaders and followers in realizing their full potential.

Dyson & Dyson Real Estate Associates

Bob and Loraine Dyson are dedicated to providing clients with professional and enthusiastic real estate assistance.

(Right and top of opposite page) Dyson & Dyson represents homes of all styles including Spanish, wood and glass, and contemporary.

Most real estate firms market homes — North County-based Dyson & Dyson markets a "lifestyle" with the home being the centerpiece of that lifestyle. For Bob and Loraine Dyson, the husband and wife team who established Dyson & Dyson in 1988, that basic philosophy has enabled them to build San Diego's most successful independent real estate company.

The Dysons are not merely marquee names on buildings and corporate letterhead stationery. They are totally immersed in the operation and complement each other well. Bob is the former chairman and CEO of Red Carpet Corp. of America, one of the nation's largest real estate franchises, and has worked all over the country. Loraine is a local, born and raised in La Jolla. Bob is considered the "brains" of the business; Loraine the "heart" and the marketing/promotional expert. Over her many years in the industry, she has personally viewed thousands of Dyson & Dyson listings. They both rely on a team approach by working closely with Dyson & Dyson agents and clients.

The key to their success has been crafting and molding a quality sales and support team and providing them with an environment reflecting the company's high standard of professionalism. The offices are tastefully decorated — terraced multilevels, interior archways, stone balustrade railings and caps, fountains, fireplaces and a library filled with comfortable furniture — in short, they have a residential look designed to make people feel at home.

The support staff is comprised of more than 50 professionals. An in-house legal department provides on-site accessibility for document review. This saves clients time and money, as any legal problems and unforeseen entanglements during a transaction can be rectified immediately. The company's escrow department insures documentation compliance. It also coordinates all inspections and closing details.

Other services help distinguish Dyson & Dyson. The company has a luxury-leasing program with a separate department devoted exclusively to seasonal or long-term leasing of luxury homes. A fleet of complimentary vehicles (limousines, utility vans and moving vans) is provided to clientele at no cost for property tours, airport transfers, social events and for moving. There are two company aircraft and a helicopter available for regional air travel and aerial photography.

Innovative marketing and advertising is another key to the Dyson & Dyson success story. The company uses a multimedia

approach — full-color, double-page newspaper ads appear regularly in select markets. Professionally designed, full-color ads are placed in lifestyle magazines with editorial formats pinpointing affluent, luxury-home-buying readers. Direct mail is selectively employed to market special-appeal properties. Special interest properties are also advertised on the company's Web site.

Dyson & Dyson uses unconventional advertising media to make an impact on spectators at special venues such as skywriting at the World Series. The company also holds an annual Dyson & Dyson charity golf tournament. Dyson & Dyson utilizes a live-action corporate video to promote and market the company to clients and associates worldwide. In fact, Dyson & Dyson agents use the corporate video to create their own customized videos to market specific properties to potential buyers nationwide and overseas. Lastly, the company airs a television show, "Lifestyles," that showcases their exclusive properties.

Dyson & Dyson's presence during the past decade has been mostly in the coastal communities of Southern California. While the average sales price for Dyson & Dyson properties is about $500,000, the company represents and markets properties from $100,000 to estate properties in the multimillion dollar range. Dyson & Dyson has provided quality service to thousands of satisfied clients, including corporate executives from blue chip firms like Qualcomm and Microsoft.

The Dysons are looking ahead to the future and will adapt their business philosophy to other areas of California. Since 1998, the company has opened six offices in the Palm Springs area that service the upscale residential home market in Indian Wells, La Quinta, Rancho Mirage and Palm Desert. Dyson & Dyson has discovered that its clients enjoy two lifestyles — the desert in the winter, and the cool, coastal area in the summer; the company advertises coastal properties in the desert and desert-based homes to coastal owners.

The combination of skilled agents and support staff and the personal attention of Bob and Loraine Dyson have resulted in a business formula that has served both the company and its clients exceptionally well.

All offices are appointed in taupe and black and have state-of-the-art equipment to assist the award-winning sales force.

The Executive Group

When one San Diego executive realized his company's merger with another might lead to a layoff, he turned to The Executive Group, a career planning and job search firm. He liked working with his current employer but didn't know how to guarantee his future employment or how to climb the corporate ladder in the newly formed company. Not having looked for a job in more than 10 years, he worried about how to attack the current job market, should that be necessary.

"Career management and job searching are universal issues," says Larry Rossi, president of The Executive Group. He knows of what he speaks, having spent more than 25 years in the arenas of finance, banking and business consulting before entering the field of career management. "Often we work with clients at crossroads who are facing the tough decision of which direction should be taken next. Ideally, we'd like to meet with people before a crisis happens, to help them develop a preventative plan. However, we also add this dimension into our consulting while working with a client in the midst of a job search as well." This proactive, rather than reactive, focus is what sets The Executive Group apart from traditional job search firms and ensures the success of its clients.

San Diego's oldest and largest local career management and search firm, The Executive Group was founded in 1989 by Paul Bouzan. A specialist in corporate operations, Bouzan has served as vice president/managing director and chief administrative officer for such firms as The Henley Group, Inc.; Fisher Scientific Group; The Signal Companies, Inc.; and the Garrett/AiResearch Corporation. It was while searching for high-level employees for the newly merged Allied/Signal Company that he realized San Diego lacked an in-depth, local career management firm, one with an intimate knowledge of the workplace and the needs of the region's companies. After interviewing numerous candidates, he also realized that some highly skilled professionals need help in effectively positioning and marketing themselves in San Diego's extremely competitive and complex job market.

Today, clients of The Executive Group benefit from the combined skills of Rossi and CEO Robert Kaplan as well as a staff of highly experienced specialists in the fields of business management, law, finance, industry, science, communications and technology. A former trial attorney, Kaplan has spent over 20 years working in the field of employment and labor law including wrongful termination and discrimination suits and employment contracts. With his local contacts and expertise in human resource management and job sourcing, Kaplan's leadership has expanded the business dramatically. Besides assisting clients in career management, The Executive Group also provides outplacement assistance, has a recruiting department and conducts extensive executive-level searches for client companies.

The Executive Group does more than just help people find jobs. It provides a course that every

For more than a decade, The Executive Group has provided career and workplace information through a weekly radio program.

The Executive Group visionaries — Robert Kaplan and Larry Rossi

student should be required to take in college, the place a career truly begins. The program combines a dynamic job search attack plan along with strategic product marketing techniques that help ensure success. It also answers critical questions that must be asked: What needs to be in a resume? How do I find out who the decision-maker is and how to meet that person? What do I do and say once I'm there? How do I negotiate the best salary and benefit package? How do I position myself to move forward instead of just staying in the same job? Is this job a stepping stone or a dead end? Where do I go now?

The Executive Group professionals work one-on-one with their clients. The first step is to identify career and financial goals and desires. Most individuals have a very limited view of the job market today, so throughout the process, alternate career options are evaluated for potential opportunities. For example, a bank executive might explore other avenues in management, operations, customer service or finance. The analysis also reveals forgotten skills and successes that will better the client's position in the market.

Once career, financial and lifestyle requirements have been established, the next step is to research the market for target industries and companies. The Executive Group uses an exclusive, computerized, corporate research program as well as research briefs of the major companies in San Diego to expose the "hidden" or unpublished job "attack plan" is made, including whom to contact, how and when. These are the keys to a successful job search.

For many people, it is difficult to objectively put together a professional "product" summary, a resume that flows logically and sells a client with an honest yet dynamic presentation. In fact, many resumes focus on the wrong approach and seriously jeopardize the candidate's possibility of being interviewed. The Executive Group designs and provides not only the clients' resumes but also the marketing letters and other supportive material necessary to conduct a successful job search.

Clients practice interviewing techniques and personal appearance strategies with The Executive Group professionals. Videotaped sessions highlight areas to strengthen and provide clients with vital dress rehearsals of actual interviews. Even compensation negotiation is covered in The Executive Group's thorough program, a skill which, once acquired, can be used throughout a successful career. This complete approach to job search is powerful and one that has brought The Executive Group international acclaim.

Because the job market is in a constant state of flux and career management is a lifelong process, The Executive Group professionals maintain ongoing relationships with clients. Since 1994, The Executive Group has hosted a Saturday morning radio program on KPRZ 1012AM called "The Workplace." During this live, public service program, Rossi and Kaplan share general information about job searches and answer listeners' questions. It has become a forum for the frustrations, concerns and successes of San Diego's job seekers.

In 1999, The Executive Group extended its programs to include "Executive Coaching." This exclusive program is a dynamic, fresh approach to business management. It's designed to help executives, already at the helm of a large company, enhance their value to the business and ultimately increase profitability.

The services offered by The Executive Group are the most important investments a person or business can make. To get the most out of one's productive years, to maximize accomplishments and financial compensation, to build for a future both in business and in life, career management is vital. It shouldn't be left to chance.

FAS-EBA Insurance Services

Behind the success of a business is the quality of its employees. An essential element for a company to attract, motivate and retain the highest quality of employees is the quality of its employee benefits package. And behind the success of a premium benefit plan is Financial Advisory Services-Employee Benefit Advisors (FAS-EBA) Insurance Services.

"We are the Nordstrom of insurance brokerage firms," says Founder Thomas P. Freismuth, CLU, ChFC, who in 1986 brought his successful company from Detroit, Michigan, to San Diego. His desire to work for the client rather than the insurance company led him to strike out on his own after affiliating himself with one insurance carrier for several years. His prime motive was and continues to be finding out what the customer wants, locating and providing it for them and maintaining it with superior service.

As an undergraduate at Michigan State University, Freismuth began his company in 1970 selling life and health insurance. He subsequently expanded to include employee benefit and retirement plans. Now one of the largest independent full-service insurance brokerage firms in San Diego, FAS-EBA designs, implements and monitors pension and profit-sharing plans, 401(k)s, employee benefit packages and executive benefit plans. An effective compensation and benefit program must meet employee needs, government regulations and organized labor demands while at the same time contain costs at an acceptable level. FAS-EBA's success in this specialized area of financial services is evidenced by its extensive, satisfied clientele.

Founder and President Thomas P. Freismuth, CLU, ChFC

As corporate America has downsized to maximize profits, human resources departments have decreased personnel. FAS-EBA serves as an extension of a company's staff, filling the need to create and support benefit packages that keep employees happy and employers in compliance with the law. Through its extensive network of insurance contacts and affiliations with major financial organizations, FAS-EBA is able to develop flexible solutions tailored to fit a company's special needs.

Freismuth maintains his original client base in Michigan, has expanded to San Diego and travels with his staff all over the United States serving the needs of clients whose companies average 300 employees. Many clients have opened additional sites, or merged with or been acquired by other companies; therefore FAS-EBA finds itself with customers worldwide. The company successfully serves a global customer base through the use of sophisticated software and 21st-century technology. However, when a customer requests a conference, FAS-EBA readily complies and meets throughout the year with all of its clients.

Several months prior to a policy's anniversary date, pre-renewal strategy sessions are scheduled in order to determine if the client has undergone any changes in its industry, personnel, business plans, growth patterns or philosophy. The client's benefit plans' claim status is reviewed as well, and if necessary, recommendations to improve claims experience are provided. If, for example, several employees had respiratory illnesses, FAS-EBA may suggest setting up smoking-cessation classes. It also encourages employers to advocate preventive health care and to this end creates health fairs for its clients, providing cholesterol testing or ergonomic products. In addition, it may arrange investment and financial planning seminars at its clients' premises to educate employees about their benefits.

By using outside experts, such as financial planners and marketing strategists, Freismuth believes he can expand the services he offers his clients. Beyond the benefit plans, for which his company is paid by insurance company commissions, he expects to provide more fee-based consulting services in the future. While discussing an executive benefit package, for example, Freismuth may find the executive is in need of personal financial planning. In this way his initial client has spawned a new generation of clients with a unique set of needs and problems.

FAS-EBA employees respond to customers' needs and problems with innovative and carefully crafted solutions. If a claim is inappropriately denied, they find a way to get it settled. If a program isn't meeting a client's needs, a new one is designed and implemented, even to the extent of requesting that insurance carriers modify their plans to meet the customer's specifications. When choosing a medical plan, for example, FAS-EBA professionals research available physicians across the spectrum of client locations and confirm that the doctors are taking new patients.

This kind of attention to detail generates grateful clients who are the major source of referrals for new business. "Our clients sell us," Freismuth says. "Everything we do is customized and clients are amazed by the quality of our products and services." Although each client is assigned a team of several FAS-EBA personnel, every employee at the insurance firm is briefed on every client and can personally service most inquiries. "We work together as a team," says Freismuth. "We treat every customer the way we would want to be treated."

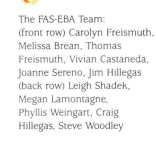

The FAS-EBA Team:
(front row) Carolyn Freismuth, Melissa Brean, Thomas Freismuth, Vivian Castaneda, Joanne Sereno, Jim Hillegas (back row) Leigh Shadek, Megan Lamontagne, Phyllis Weingart, Craig Hillegas, Steve Woodley

FAS-EBA sets high standards for its employees and even hires consultants to determine if a prospective employee is aligned with its values and culture of service. Staff members are all required to attend various trainings on subjects such as customer service and insurance industry regulations. Twice yearly the staff participates in team-building sessions, in which psychologists administer personality assessments and design activities to encourage synergy. As a result of these sessions, FAS-EBA is better equipped to decide which employees work best together and which employees are best assigned to specific clients.

This highly cooperative team also lends its support to a variety of charity events, from raising money for multiple sclerosis and cerebral palsy to sponsoring a family for the holidays in connection with an inner city after-school youth program.

Through its dedication to serving client needs, FAS-EBA is meeting its commitment to offer the best prices and services available. Larger national benefit consulting firms have profits and quotas as their goals. FAS-EBA Insurance Services has customer service as its foremost goal. By listening to and keeping aligned with the business and professional objectives of each client, it has more than met that goal.

Hirsch & Company Consulting Engineers

In 1998, Hirsch & Company began the most comprehensive study of San Diego's wastewater collection pipes ever to be done. More than one million feet will be inspected with the use of a remote-controlled video camera. Mounted on a small tractor, the camera will travel through pipes from La Jolla to Barrio Logan and from Point Loma to the San Diego State University area. A highly trained crew in a mobile video studio will follow the camera tractor foot by foot above ground. As they find problems in the pipeline, such as roots breaking

This 78-inch pipeline was installed as part of the North Mission Valley Interceptor Sewer Project, which was designed to rehabilitate the existing pipeline and increase flow capacity.

through joints or cracks in the lining, they will mark the repairs needed on appropriate maps and add a voice-over on the videotape for further study. The three-year study, when completed, will help San Diego leaders identify immediate needs as well as accurately prioritize future repair needs.

Much of San Diego's infrastructure (water, storm and sewage systems and roads) are more than 50 years old and were not designed to accommodate the current usage. In 1997, an El Niño storm caused a major storm drain in Kearny Mesa to break open and fail. It took more than five months and millions of dollars to repair the damage. Thousands of people were forced to take alternate routes and businesses in the vicinity lost income when customers could not reach their stores. The break brought the importance of San Diego's infrastructure into the limelight.

One company that constantly keeps an eye on San Diego's infrastructure is Hirsch & Company. Founded by Larry Hirsch in 1965, this civil engineering firm has spent the last 30 years working with San Diego to study and rehabilitate the city's infrastructure including water distribution and wastewater collection and drainage. The firm's work has earned it numerous awards and honors as well as the respect of its major clients — the city of San Diego, the county of San Diego, the U.S. Navy and the Zoological Society of San Diego.

The firm received its first major award in 1972 for its design of the water delivery and wastewater systems of the San Diego Wild Animal Park. The Honorable Recognition Award for Environmental and Water Resources Management Planning and Construction Design was presented by the Consulting Engineers Association of California and was one of the top 10 awards given that year. It also served notice to other consulting civil engineers that Hirsch & Company would be a formidable force within the community.

In 1973, the company received the American Society of Civil Engineers' (ASCE) Outstanding Civil Engineering Achievement Award for the first complete industrial waste facility used by the San Diego Metropolitan Sewer System and by the 11th Naval District. Located at North Island Naval Air Station, the system still extracts oily waste, toxic solids and heavy metals, and neutralizes corrosive chemicals from more than 100,000 gallons of wastewater per day.

Hirsch & Company took on the "Clean Up the Mission Bay Project" in 1987. Its team of engineers and surveyors developed a master plan for a storm drain interceptor system which would divert "nuisance," or low flows, from entering the bay. Frequently, low flows contain high amounts of wastes and oils washed from streets into storm drains during the beginning of a storm. Hirsch & Company's dual storm drain system directs low flows into the sanitary sewer that goes to San Diego's wastewater treatment plant. The high flow, cleaner drainage water is diverted into pipes that empty directly into the bay. The total system took almost 10 years to design and construct. Hirsch & Company developed a similar system for the protection of the Pacific Beach/La Jolla Shores area.

The 1990s also saw Hirsch & Company involved in the design of both Phase 1 and 2 of the $35 million North Mission Valley Interceptor Sewer Program. This pipeline collects wastewater flow from most of central San Diego as well as Santee, El Cajon, La Mesa and Alpine. The work done for Phase 1 earned the company an Award of Merit from ASCE in 1992.

Bringing trenchless technology to San Diego, the team used a laser-tracked, remote-operated tunneling and boring machine to install new sewage pipelines for Phase 2. For its innovative approach, Hirsch & Company received the 1997 ASCE Outstanding Civil Engineering Project Award for Wastewater Systems.

This new technology allows engineers to continue working without the usual disruptions to traffic and the surrounding community and also minimizes biological and ecological impact. It was the first time a microtunnel of this scope had been successfully completed in the region. The project also won Hirsch & Company the 1997 Project of the Year — New Construction, given by the North American Society of Trenchless Technology, the highest award presented for trenchless work done in the United States that year.

Besides their daily work, the people at Hirsch & Company keep involved in education outreach programs. Working closely with a local middle school, the company has been participating in "Public Works Week." After discussions about the job of a civil engineer, the staff works with groups of students on their engineering projects to help them improve design and functionality, and to introduce students to the technology available for use in their projects.

The early years of the 21st century promise to be busy ones for the staff of Hirsch & Company. With the retirement of Larry Hirsch, John Harris will manage the firm and foresees continuing the firm's commitment to the city of San Diego and other local public works agencies. The company will be involved in the development of a reclaimed water project from wastewater treatment plants, specifically the one in the Miramar area. The Marine Station in Miramar will be retrofitted to use reclaimed water for landscaping. Also on the agenda is a 72-inch sewer diversion pipeline project in the west end of Mission Valley and work on the Natural History Museum expansion. Finally, once the city's pipeline system has been thoroughly inspected, it's not too hard to believe that this award-winning company will be high on the list of companies that help with the rehabilitative process.

As a civil engineering firm, Hirsch & Company is looking forward to assisting all public works agencies throughout San Diego County to improve, rehabilitate and upsize their infrastructure systems to meet the challenges of the next millennium. Priorities will include better drinking water, conservation through recycled water programs and improved disposal of storm water and wastewater throughout the region. It is work that is vital to the future of the San Diego area and its residents.

Hirsch & Company's team of civil engineers and land surveyors at the site of the $30 million expansion of the Natural History Museum in San Diego

Hovey & Kirby, A.P.C.

Hovey & Kirby, A.P.C. (A Professional Corporation) is a specialty law firm providing legal services in the areas of real property, land use, environmental, commercial, bankruptcy and business law, including transactions, litigation and administrative hearings.

The firm was founded by Dean Kirby and Gregg Hovey in 1992 in response to their clients' needs for a more efficient and responsive approach to the provision of legal services. The three partners — Gregg Hovey, Dean Kirby and Leslie Hovey — have undertaken an entrepreneurial and proactive approach to the practice of law in anticipation of the dramatic changes businesses will experience in the 21st century. Young and forward-looking, the partners view themselves as active participants in the growth of San Diego.

The firm represents a broad spectrum of clients, including financial institutions, title insurers, escrow companies, major real estate owners and developers, homeowner associations, bankruptcy trustees, and other individuals and entities. The firm's size enables it to offer personalized services tailored to its clients' special needs and to establish a close working relationship with them, which the principals of the firm believe is essential to delivering excellence in legal services.

The firm's specialization and investment in technological support enables it to deliver its services promptly, efficiently and at a reasonable price. The firm maintains the highest level of expertise and has been rated by Martindale-Hubbell, Inc. as "a v"— its highest rating. Gregg B. Hovey, M. Leslie Hovey and Dean T. Kirby Jr. are all individually rated "a v" by Martindale-Hubbell.

Hovey & Kirby's approach to the practice of law is to act as if it was a client. A client benefits by having attorneys who have specialized legal knowledge and are familiar with the client's business. By being true partners with its clients, the firm can prevent legal problems and contain legal expenses in transactions and disputes.

In one case, an industrial client with a natural resource mine trucked heavy materials up and down local roads. As the adjacent land became built up with new homes, tensions mounted between the mine owner and the residents. Citizens' groups and local agencies made demands that would have severely curtailed the mine owner's business.

Hovey & Kirby used mediation techniques to avoid litigation fees for its client and to accommodate all the parties involved. The mine owner cut back on the daily number of truck runs. In return, he was allowed to conduct business until the time when

The law firm of Hovey & Kirby is located in Emerald Plaza, one of downtown San Diego's premier addresses.

he voluntarily closed up shop and sold the land to residential developers.

Experienced attorneys using the latest technology allow the firm to be as efficient as possible in serving its clients' needs, and Hovey & Kirby has had a long-term interest in technological innovation. The firm maintains information systems and computer technology that enables it to communicate effectively and directly with its clients around the world. Technological advances have also brought efficiency to the practice of law and enabled all the firm's attorneys to access legal information and communicate with their clients from the convenience of the office, home, or anywhere telephone lines are available.

Even so, the successful practice of law is more than an office, technology and lawyers. The attorneys at Hovey & Kirby believe that the approach each law firm takes to legal problems characterizes the differences between each firm. Hovey & Kirby's approach is to emphasize practical, reasoned advice in an effort to minimize or prevent legal difficulties. When clients are involved in disputes, the firm's primary concern is to achieve a fair, expeditious and economical result.

"Each of our clients has its own business focus, and that business is not litigation or handling legal problems," says Dean Kirby, head of the firm's commercial and creditors' rights practice. "The faster we can return them to what they know how to do best — the running of their

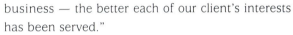

Partners Dean Kirby and Leslie Hovey

business — the better each of our client's interests has been served."

The firm's commitment to remaining small and specialized also enables it to respond quickly to its clients' changing legal needs. It is uncertain as to how law will be practiced 10 years from now, though at Hovey & Kirby, an infrastructure has been developed that will allow immediate change to meet new demands, new needs, and new concerns of its clients.

All three attorneys enjoy practicing law in San Diego and appreciate being a part of the community. They are raising families here, supporting youth athletic programs and serving as board members for museums, trade organizations and community service organizations.

The firm encourages all its associates to contribute both professionally and individually to the local community. It believes it is an attorney's professional responsibility to contribute meaningfully to his or her community. Hovey & Kirby attorneys are pleased to have had the opportunity, both as a firm and as individuals, to make a difference. They are looking forward to remaining a part of this exciting city.

"We enjoy practicing law and helping to shape the future of San Diego," says Kirby. "The fact that we relish living here and participating in the activities San Diego has to offer carries over into the entire attitude of the office and our relationship with our clients."

Partner Greg Hovey enjoys all that San Diego has to offer and believes that carries over into the entire attitude of the office.

Luchner Tool Engineering Inc.

In the years since 1969, when Herman Luchner opened his tool shop in Spring Valley, California, he has guided it through the full spectrum of what a tool and die company can do. At one time or another, Luchner Tool Engineering has designed and built tools that make or handle everything from missiles, munitions, spacecraft hardware and stealth bomber components to consumer products, automotive machinery, mass transit systems and loading equipment.

Today, Luchner Tool Engineering is a complete manufacturing and engineering service and certified tool supplier meeting the advanced technological demands of the aerospace industry. One key to the company's diversified tooling capabilities is the way Mr. Luchner has been careful to staff the business with what he considers to be "30 of the best tool and die craftsmen, designers and administrative personnel to be found anywhere."

Operating from its 23,000-square-foot plant in a Scripps Ranch eucalyptus grove, Luchner Tool Engineering has found success in the international marketplace by providing better prices, on-time delivery and custom tool services using cutting-edge technology. Approximately half of Luchner's business is with foreign companies, a fact reflected in the company's client list, which includes dozens of airlines in Europe, the Middle East, Asia and Latin America as well as the huge European consortium that builds the Airbus jetliners. Domestic customers include numerous U.S. airlines and General Electric, Rohr (now B. F. Goodrich), Solar Turbines, Boeing/Douglas and United Technologies Chemical Systems (Trident-II rocket motor program).

With the decline in military spending in recent years, Luchner Tool Engineering has changed some of its focus toward manufacturing ground support equipment for commercial aircraft, and that has become a leading source of revenue for the company. Whenever mechanics remove one of a jetliner's immense engines, the specialized equipment that supports and moves it is probably made by Luchner Tool Engineering.

The company's tremendous capabilities require a tremendous capital investment in machinery. One glance inside the Luchner shop reveals an astonishing assortment of large and small lathes, electro-discharge cutting machines, mills, jig borers, punch presses, grinders, saws and inspection devices. In temperature- and humidity-controlled rooms around the plant, esoteric computer-controlled machines hum with the precision and complexity of their tasks. Among the company's six electro-discharge cutters is the world's most advanced five-axis wire-cut computer controlled device capable of manipulating work pieces up to 330 pounds and cutting aerospace materials with an accuracy of plus/minus .0002 inch. The machinery in the plant would satisfy a Star Fleet commander, and at any given moment some of the parts being manufactured here may well be destined for a rocket or aircraft engine.

The Scripps Ranch headquarters of Luchner Tool Engineering Inc.

Herman Luchner, the company's founder, is a German immigrant who received his early training in mechanical engineering in the old-world apprenticeship-based way. He immigrated to Canada as a young man and made his way to the United States where he worked in different cities as a tool and die designer and builder. Eventually, Mr. Luchner landed at Rohr Industries and General Dynamics in San Diego where he was a senior engineer. There he noticed that every time he needed special tooling, he had to go to a machine shop in Los Angeles or Orange County. "There simply were not any tool and die shops here capable of doing aerospace-type work. I saw the need, so in 1969 I started the forerunner of this company."

In a classic example of hard work, determination and skill, Mr. Luchner set about building his enterprise by working evenings and weekends while still a full-time employee at General Dynamics. Cash was tight, so using his vacation time, he visited potential vendors and cajoled them into giving him 60 days to pay for the parts he needed instead of the 30 days that was customary in those days. He rented space, hired part-time workers and gradually built his new company into a thriving subcontractor serving the major players in San Diego's booming aerospace industry.

Mr. Luchner describes his formula for success this way: "I was a good engineer and I was fortunate to surround myself with really good people (and they are loyal — the average employee has been with Luchner more than 10 years). I also believe that only practical engineers can come up with the best tooling in the shortest amount of time, so I never hired an engineer who was not well-grounded in the practical side of design. But that wasn't enough to make a company succeed. Fortunately, my uncle had taught me how to juggle money, which gave me an instinct for business, so I became a good manager."

In the spirit of a true Renaissance man, Mr. Luchner not only predesigned much of both of the company's two energy-intensive plant layouts, but he predesigned his Escondido home as well.

Founder and President
Herman Luchner

"Most design takes place on computers now, of course, but I sometimes still close a deal based on my sketch of the way I envision a tool. I try to take the bull by the horns, solve whatever the problem is and do it right now."

Luchner Tool Engineering is different from most other American tooling manufacturers in that this company has not specialized itself into a limited niche market. To survive during the early days, the company took any job and the versatility that came from this policy continues to be a Luchner touchstone. Another unique aspect of this company is that it conducts its business without a single salesperson. This saves on overhead and contributes to keeping Luchner competitive.

Luchner Tool Engineering has received many accolades, including numerous "Subcontractor of the Year" commendations from all the major aerospace companies.

Continuing a tradition of steady growth, Luchner Tool Engineering is planning to almost double the plant area of the Scripps Ranch facility in the near future while continuing equipment upgrades to remain at the forefront of advanced precision tool making. This way, the company will stay faithful to the founder's goal of always providing its worldwide customers with quality tooling at competitive prices on schedule.

Urban Systems Associates

Without a company like Urban Systems Associates, the traffic flow throughout San Diego County would likely become lodged in the kind of gridlock commonly seen in cities like Cairo or Rome. As a leader in transportation planning and traffic engineering, the Kearny Mesa-based company works with major developers to tackle some of the most complex traffic alterations necessary to the future growth of the region.

For example, Urban Systems played a vital role in obtaining numerous development permits for the expansion of Lindbergh Field, which subsequently involved the engineering of construction detours, road widening, striping, signage and traffic signals in the surrounding areas. The end result was an improved road system that conforms to the airport's enhanced design and new terminal.

The company was also involved in an important project that now connects San Diegans to their urban core. Through extensive coordination between local municipalities and the Metropolitan Transit Development Board, Urban Systems provided expert solutions in traffic control both during and after the creation of the San Diego Trolley East County line. In-depth analysis studies were conducted around sustained commercial developments served by the trolley, such as the 440,000-square-foot expansion of Fashion Valley Shopping Center. The mall now incorporates a new bus terminal and elevated trolley station which required meticulous planning due to the flooding that occurs at the site during heavy storms.

President and owner Sandee Witcraft-Schlaefli founded Urban Systems Associates in 1980 after gaining experience as a project coordinator at a large engineering firm. Born in San Diego and raised on a two-acre farm in El Cajon, she grew up in a family of urban entrepreneurs who inspired her to become involved in numerous civic projects such as the USDA food commodities program and job development for Indian reservations. She was also an eligibility worker for Social Services and served on various advisory boards.

As a young child, she immersed herself in daily farm chores and became a junior leader for 4-H. Never one to sit still, she won numerous awards in cooking and sewing competitions at the El Cajon and Del Mar fairs.

During the early 1970s, she studied art and politics in Spain for one year before earning her bachelor's degree in political science at Humbolt State University. By 1983, she had achieved a juris doctorate with an emphasis on land use from Western State University and was the recipient of the American Jurisprudence Award in Property Law.

While attending graduate school, she began the company with a one-room office which quickly became a 10-employee operation for Witcraft-Schlaefli. She used her own money from a childhood savings account to start Urban Systems. The success that followed stemmed from a unique combination of solid business ethics, extensive family involvement and strong experience in environmental management.

Witcraft-Schlaefli, who is bilingual (English and Spanish), specializes in all aspects of development impact feasibility analysis, project implementation and marketing. Nearly 80 percent of her clientele

San Diego Convention Center expansion

are repeat customers from both the private sector and government agencies. Known for her integrity among politicians and community leaders, she is a recipient of the YWCA's Tribute To Women In Industry Award.

Her husband Andrew Schlaefli, an urban transportation engineer, became the first employee when Urban Systems began growing. As principal engineer, he currently works alongside a proficient staff of civil engineers, planning experts and draftsmen. He is a licensed civil and traffic engineer in the states of California and Arizona and was director for the city of San Diego's Transportation Planning Program. He also managed the city's Overall Residential Growth Management Program and was responsible for the management of San Diego's Capital Improvements Program.

Witcraft-Schlaefli's oldest child, Mark Schlaefli, also became a team player in providing graphic design for producing high-quality presentations, project reports and maps. His wife, Erica, later joined the company as an administrative field assistant and proved she had a knack for the business while working on a construction site for Metro Biosolids Center near the Miramar Landfill. In addition, Witcraft-Schlaefli's father, Robert, has helped "count cars" for traffic forecasting studies and offers his expertise in security management for special projects. After the company moved into a larger office, her younger children often helped as well, gaining experience in filing, typing, general organizing and technical computer support. As Witcraft-Schlaefli proudly states, "To talk about this company is to know my family."

With the proliferation of new development, Witcraft-Schlaefli remains committed to enhancing the communities where people live and raise families. She is lauded for her progressive management techniques and honest business practices by developers and community groups alike. She firmly maintains consistency in her staff, choosing not to hire or fire based on particular projects. In addition, the company will decline work if asked to misrepresent information or if it cannot deliver a service on time. Conversely, Witcraft-Schlaefli admits that clients expect the same high standards in return, saying they simply want their projects evaluated fairly and honestly.

Equipped with the latest tools of technology, Urban Systems has successfully remained open and flexible to a host of exciting new projects that were perhaps unforeseeable in its early days. Computers and improved software are now used to forecast traffic in large areas, showing where a street could be widened or whether another road is desirable.

Lindbergh Field expansion with a temporary detour for North Harbor Drive during construction

And the staff must often assess a piece of land for opportunities and constraints long before a project actually begins there.

The company's foresight and skills are reflected in an impressive portfolio listing projects all across San Diego County as well as in neighboring states. A few of the local ones include: Car Country Carlsbad, La Jolla Village Square, Pacific Highlands Ranch, Lusk Industrial Park, National City Marina, California State Prison at San Diego, Otay Ranch, Santee Town Center, Lakeside Navy Housing, Jacumba Valley Ranch plus many more.

In addition to transportation planning and traffic engineering, Urban Systems offers development support services in project management, design approvals, proposal packages, permitting, bid documents, administration, arbitration and mediation. The company's commitment to wholesome development is among the important cornerstones keeping San Diego's landscape accessible and desirable for generations to come.

Falcon West Insurance Brokers

In 1993, after 33 years in the insurance industry working for others, Kurt Woelck opened his own agency, Falcon West Insurance Brokers. Many of his clients over the years had encouraged him to open his own agency-brokerage firm and were delighted when he decided to become self-employed.

Kurt Woelck hadn't expected to have a career in insurance. When he left Germany in 1960 he was 22 years old and had spent a couple of years working in the electronics industry, both in sales and as a technician. However, when he moved to the United States he didn't speak English and that proved a severe disadvantage in finding work in electronics. After much searching, he found a job at National American Insurance in Los Angeles as a stock boy.

Kurt Woelck, owner of Falcon West Insurance Brokers

Over the next eight years, Woelck worked his way through the ranks of the company. He studied English both at school and at work. Eventually he was promoted to file-room supervisor then to personal lines rater-underwriter and eventually to commercial underwriter. A new career had emerged.

Desiring even more challenges, Kurt Woelck took a job at Continental Insurance in 1968 and then two years later, he went to Maryland Casualty. While there, he and his wife requested a move to San Diego, hoping to enjoy its cleaner air and business opportunities. Maryland Casualty transferred him to its San Diego office in 1976 and promoted him to the position of underwriter manager in the property department. When he left the company in 1979 he was a marketing field representative.

In that position Woelck had had the opportunity to get to know many of the independent insurance brokerage firms in San Diego. Several had encouraged him to become a broker. After much consideration, Kurt went to work for Kindler and Laucci, a California brokerage. Over a period of several years the brokerage went through a series of mergers and buyouts. Woelck wanted more stability so he started working for Fiss-Whaley Insurance Agency in 1988 as an independent insurance broker.

When Mr. Whaley retired in 1993, Mr. Fiss wanted to concentrate his efforts on the life and employee benefits segment of the insurance business. At that time Fiss gave Woelck the opportunity to purchase his property and casualty book of business. He seized the opportunity. Since the initials FW had a strong customer identity, Woelck wanted to keep those initials part of his company's new name. Dozens of names were considered until the name Falcon West Insurance Brokers was settled upon. Today, a stunning Amani statue of a falcon in flight graces Kurt Woelck's marble conference table.

Today, Falcon West Insurance Brokers sells all lines of personal and commercial insurance including long-term care coverage which is a fairly new insurance product that has been endorsed and encouraged by the U.S. government due to the ever-increasing longevity of the population. To place insurance coverage for nationwide clients, Falcon West Insurance Brokers is licensed in 27 states.

Finding the right policy for specific needs can be time-consuming and frustrating. Falcon West Insurance Brokers is an independent brokerage and looks forward to helping clients find policies that fit their exact needs, today and for the future.

Klinedinst, Fliehman & McKillop

Klinedinst, Fliehman & McKillop (KF&M) was established in 1983 with one overriding vision: achieving pre-eminence in the Southern California legal community by providing the best value in legal services to its clients and the greatest opportunities to its employees. From its inception, Klinedinst, Fliehman & McKillop has provided high-quality and value-oriented legal services. This approach to client service has continued, enabling the firm and its members to enjoy extraordinary growth and success in an extremely competitive environment.

KF&M's attorneys believe that a clear understanding of each client's business goals is crucial to achieving the best possible outcome for any legal matter. This approach enables KF&M and its clients to work together as a partnership, emphasizing maximum communication between attorneys and clients. In doing so, KF&M attorneys provide their clients with consulting services designed with two purposes in mind: helping clients to achieve their overall business objectives, and ensuring that each client fully understands the legal process and how it may impact the client's "bottom line."

The attorneys have chosen San Diego for their home and career because of the city's diversity, climate and quality of life. These factors have helped to attract the best attorneys from across the country through the firm's national recruiting program. Indeed, in 1998, the firm was recognized by Harcourt Brace & Company as one of "America's Greatest Places to Work with a Law Degree."

Each of the attorneys at Klinedinst, Fliehman & McKillop actively participates in the management and direction of the firm, and views each other as vital to obtaining the firm's goal of becoming "the premier provider of legal services." Since the attorneys at KF&M work in a merit-based and team-spirited atmosphere, they routinely assist each other in achieving their fullest potentials. Lawyers at KF&M introduce their clients to any other attorney in the firm who might be able to make constructive contributions to the matter at hand.

The expert team of attorneys at Klinedinst, Fliehman & McKillop provides high-quality, value-oriented legal services.

During the last five years, the firm has doubled in size, a phenomenal growth rate achieved by providing superior legal representation while maintaining a reputation for ethical practices, professional integrity and civility. Today, Klinedinst, Fliehman & McKillop's clients range from local start-ups to national Fortune 200 companies. Clients include American International Group, Buffets, Inc., Centex Corporation, CNA Insurance, Coca-Cola Enterprises Inc., Fireman's Fund Insurance, Freddie Mac, GTE Mobilnet of San Diego, In-N-Out Burger, National Steel and Shipbuilding Co., San Diego Padres Baseball Club and Washington Mutual. Although KF&M is not formally departmentalized, the firm serves its clients in a variety of primary legal specialties: appellate, banking, bankruptcy, business litigation, corporate, employment and labor, environmental, intellectual property, products liability, professional liability defense, real estate and construction, restaurants and hospitality, securities, transactions and trusts and estates. The firm has also expanded its practice to include international law with an emphasis on Latin America.

North County Economic Development Council

San Diego — North County distinguishes itself with its scenic beauty, economic vitality and welcoming communities. From magnificent coastlines and lush inland valleys, to picturesque mountains and the tranquil desert, newcomers will find virtually unlimited choices in housing, education, employment, culture, recreation and lifestyles.

North County, covering more than half the area of San Diego County, is home to one-third of the county's population and enjoys a reputation of higher than average employment growth, family incomes and civic services. Its public and private schools are often mentioned as being some of the best in the country. One community was featured in the sourcebook 50 Fabulous Places to Raise Your Family, both in 1995 and 1997. The same could be said of most North County communities.

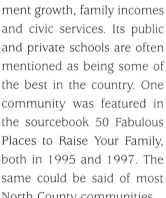

The world famous flower fields of Carlsbad

Coastal North County's beaches are as diverse as the region. The distinctly different communities of Del Mar (home to the famous Del Mar Racetrack and Fairgrounds), Encinitas (with Quail Botanical Gardens), Solana Beach, Carlsbad and Oceanside (with its beautiful harbor and historic mission) all enjoy breathtaking views of the ocean and surf with spectacular sunsets. The area features a wide range of resorts including Aviara and La Costa, aquatic and cultural activities and retail centers. Recently Legoland opened a $130 million children's wonderland near the famous and colorful flower fields in Carlsbad. Camp Pendleton, the world's largest Marine amphibious base, is a major contributor to the economic growth of the region.

Virtually anything can be grown in the Inland Valley areas. Avocado orchards, massive nurseries and strawberry fields abound. The communities of Vista, San Marcos, Fallbrook, Escondido, Rancho Bernardo, Rancho Santa Fe and Poway are known for upscale homes, outstanding medical and education institutions along with award-winning wineries and restaurants, challenging golf courses, equestrian areas, state-of-the-art theater and cultural centers as well as the San Diego Wild Animal Park and California State University, San Marcos. Understandably, this area has also enjoyed significant business growth with more than 1,000 firms recently choosing the area.

The mountain areas to the east are rich in heritage and offer adventure for recreational enthusiasts as well as peaceful communities with romantic getaways. Many enjoy the world renowned Palomar Observatory, the gold-mining town of Julian and beautiful areas surrounding Ramona.

North County's desert area has some of the most dramatic terrain and breathtaking views. Anza-Borrego State Park, the nation's largest state park, beckons with beauty and adventure and also features excellent golf resorts and a limitless supply of clean, fresh air.

The North County Economic Development Council was formed to enhance the economic development activities in the North County region. Its primary goal is to retain and attract quality businesses and create additional, higher-paying jobs. The diversity, innate beauty and welcoming attitude of North County make it a preferred business and visitor destination as well as a place to live. It will be "San Diego's Smart Place to Grow" for years to come.

Southern California Security Services

When Ty Odeh took over Southern California Security Services in 1993, he immediately implemented a fresh style of quality management that transformed the company into a popular and trusted friend of the region. Today the family-run firm offers a diverse range of superior protection services to more than 300 businesses within San Diego County.

Having gained considerable organizational skills in the international marketing arena for Hewlett-Packard, Odeh wanted to apply his talents to a civic enterprise that could make a positive impact on society. The rigors of corporate bureaucracy and excessive traveling eventually prompted him to purchase Southern California Security Services, which was originally founded in 1975 by a previous owner. With administrative support from his wife, Fadiya, and daughter Lenna, he soon expanded the company from 55 employees to nearly 300.

The company is lauded for maintaining high-quality and personalized service to a broad range of clients. Each member of the company's security team, for instance, exceeds the basic requirements necessary for state certification as they are required to undergo additional classroom and on-site training once they are hired. Employees are systematically informed of new changes to security posts, government regulations and general security information.

More importantly, Odeh made it his goal to elevate employee morale through an "open-door" policy that literally allows employees to walk freely into managers' offices to ask questions or discuss projects at any time. With doors rarely closed, the staff enjoys generous employee benefits and a workplace ambience that is far removed from the common corporate structure.

Before purchasing the company, Odeh felt the security industry shouldered a negative stigma that needed revamping. To help restore its reputation, he focused on raising the customer service level to the same high standard he observed at Hewlett-Packard. That meant exercising personal and friendly contacts with his entire client base.

Odeh further enhanced the industry's credibility by developing a strong working relationship with the San Diego Police Department. In doing so, he meets regularly with various divisions to share and discuss important security issues. In addition, he equipped the company vehicles with a cutting-edge technology known as Teletrac, which gives him a firm competitive edge throughout the region.

Teletrac is a modern, satellite-based system that allows supervisors to monitor their entire vehicle fleet for safety and timeliness of response. It is supported by online documentation for easy tracking of events, and has allowed the company to greatly increase its communication and dispatching capabilities. The system provides exact locations of its officers, and can detect the speed and precise locations in which their patrol cars are traveling.

By offering a flexible menu of quality services, such as on-site security officers, mobile patrol and private investigation, the company is able to solve a variety of problems. Odeh attracts clients who are primarily referred to him by past or existing ones. His customers include high-tech companies, automobile dealerships, shopping malls, construction sites, hotels, hospitals and more.

Based in Kearny Mesa, with branch offices in San Marcos and Los Angeles, the company remains one of the fastest-growing security companies in San Diego County. The strong safety net it provides will allow numerous businesses and organizations to further grow and prosper.

One of many well-maintained patrol vehicles equipped with the latest security technology.

Ty Odeh, president of Southern California Security Services

Medical, educational, cultural and religious institutions contribute to the quality of life enjoyed by San Diego residents and visitors to the area.

Partners in QUALI

San Diego
Quality of Life

PharMingen	370
Thomas C. Ackerman Foundation	374
American Specialty Health Plans	376
Brighton Health Alliance	378
David L. Wolf, M.D., F.A.C.S.	380
Gen-Probe	382
Kearny Mesa Convalescent Hospital and Nursing Home	384
Sharp Rees-Stealy Medical Group	386
Thomas Jefferson School of Law	388
Toward Maximum Independence	390
University of Phoenix	392
Digirad Corporation	394
Big Sister League of San Diego	396
Dr. Alan M. Blum, D.C.	397
Coleman College	398
De Anza Bay Resort	399
Dr. Peter K. Hellwig, DDS & Associates	400
Environmental Health Coalition	401
Loma Alta Children's School	402
San Diego Maritime Museum	403
St. Clare's Home	404
Women's History Reclamation Project	405

PharMingen

There is a myriad of magic formulas that people use to describe the success of a business. In the biotechnology industry, success is rare indeed. From its entrepreneurial beginnings to its current position as a wholly owned subsidiary of a Fortune 500 company, PharMingen stands out in the crowd of biotechnology companies in San Diego that are trying to succeed in an increasingly competitive market.

From its humble beginnings, the company has grown to become the preferred partner for life science researchers worldwide. The company provides an unsurpassed breadth of products, systems and expertise in cell analysis for research applications. But to truly understand the success of PharMingen is to understand where the company started and where it is going in the 21st century.

PharMingen was established in 1987 with just three people, occupying 2,000 square feet of laboratory space in Sorrento Valley. Initial funding for the start-up company came from the founders' personal savings and that of their relatives and friends in Taiwan. PharMingen "boot-strapped" its way to profitability in its second year through the hard work of its dedicated employees and the help of some key researchers in the biomedical research industry. To support the rapid growth of the company, additional funding was raised from several strategic partners in Japan. The company also received several Small Business Innovative Research (SBIR) grants from the National Institutes of Health to develop new products.

The company now employs more than 350 employees worldwide. The corporate headquarters is located on an 80,000-square-foot facility, six-acre campus in the prestigious Torrey Pines area. The facility houses all company operations, including product development, manufacturing, and business administration. About 44,000 square feet of office space has been converted to custom designed, state-of-the-art laboratories. The headquarters also contains a lunch and outdoor patio facility, a library and a fully equipped multimedia conference center that enables PharMingen to host seminars and symposia, providing a forum for scientific exchange.

Alongside other strong scientific communities around the country, San Diego is viewed as one of the premier locations in the world for biotechnology and biomedical research and continues to be a hot-bed for biotechnology and pharmaceutical companies such as PharMingen. With the support of local leaders and business groups, the biotechnology community prospers from the availability of a highly educated and talented labor pool as well as the proximity to key collaborators at area scientific institutions and universities. Within minutes from PharMingen are the University of California at San Diego, the Scripps Research Institute, the Salk Institute and numerous biomedical research institutions and companies.

Over the years, PharMingen has taken part in many local community events held by national nonprofit organizations such as the American Cancer Society, American Heart Association, and Leukemia Society of America. Furthermore, PharMingen has joined fellow biotechnology companies in events for local organizations such as BIOCOM, the University of California at San Diego Cancer Center, and the San Diego Chamber of Commerce.

Being a part of the community continues to be a big priority for PharMingen and the City of San Diego has recognized this. For example, in 1996 PharMingen's founder, Ernest Chun-Ming Huang, Ph.D., was awarded the Ernest & Young San Diego Entrepreneur of the Year Award. That same year, he accepted on behalf of PharMingen the San Diego Small Business of the Year award. This recognition not only highlights the success of PharMingen, but also the efforts of the City of San Diego in fostering burgeoning businesses, especially in the biotechnology community.

Since the company's inception, PharMingen has built a diversified technology base and has positioned itself as a major player in such scientific fields as immunology, cell biology/neurosciences and molecular biology.

PharMingen's strategy of rapidly developing cutting-edge products relies heavily on the transfer of technology from universities, research institutes, and pharmaceutical companies worldwide. After the publication of papers using biological reagents (a substance used, as in detecting or measuring a component because of its chemical or biological activity), scientists are inundated with requests for samples and technical assistance by colleagues. Although this system of reagent exchange contributes

to scientific advancement, it can become a burden on researchers.

Therefore, PharMingen facilitates the transfer of technology from this research, develops the technology into products, and scales up production of the reagents according to rigorous quality control standards. As a result, the reagents become commercially available to researchers worldwide. Institutions providing the technology receive royalties from sales and their scientists save valuable time. PharMingen also offers technical service to answer any questions customers might have about the company's reagents and applications.

To serve international customer needs, the company is supported by a network of over 30 offices around the world. International sales account for more than one-third of the company's overall revenues. These offices support direct sales, business development, technical service, application support and marketing.

PharMingen has introduced more than 3,000 products addressing the needs of a broad spectrum of biomedical researchers. PharMingen manufactures monoclonal antibodies and their conjugates, polyclonal antibodies, protein expression systems, and recombinant proteins using advanced bioprocessing techniques. Using these advanced bioprocessing techniques, PharMingen manufactures over 90 percent of its products in San Diego. By focusing on its initial objective to be the premier company in providing quality reagents, applications, technology and service to life science researchers worldwide, PharMingen continues to seek opportunities to meet its customer needs.

PharMingen leverages its technological strengths to produce innovative products by relying on internal product development and technology transfer to drive the product pipeline. To keep pace with rapidly advancing research fronts, PharMingen's scientists are continually developing new products in strategic areas such as cytokines, signal transduction, apoptosis, cell cycle regulation and neurosciences. The company also collaborates with key scientists and institutions around the world, completing hundreds of technology licenses to commercialize reagents.

In May 1997 PharMingen was acquired by Becton Dickinson & Company, a Fortune 500 medical supply company. The acquisition is part of Becton Dickinson's worldwide business strategy to broaden the horizon of health care through the enhancements of systems, software and reagent technology.

A key to the success of the acquisition is the synergy created by the partnership between PharMingen and Becton Dickinson Immunocytometry Systems (BDIS), located in San Jose, California. By joining forces with BDIS, PharMingen has gained access to integrated, advanced instrument systems and applications. BDIS also will utilize PharMingen's ability to quickly launch research products and to facilitate the development and delivery of clinical solutions. PharMingen can also focus on developing and moving applications from the research arena toward clinical acceptance. The partnership also capitalizes on PharMingen's ability to bring research products rapidly to market. Furthermore, PharMingen and BDIS also joined together to form the Custom Technology Team (CTT), a group dedicated to providing custom solutions and technology for biopharmaceutical companies and organizations worldwide.

The resulting global partnership with Becton Dickinson is advantageous in a number of key arenas:

Expanded Product Lines:
1) Faster introduction of important products
2) Broader access to reagents for basic and clinical research
3) More clinical assays and complete systems for diagnosis
4) Continued competitive pricing

Dedicated Sales & Service:
1) Direct sales force and dedicated applications support
2) Accelerated product development and worldwide distribution

Enhanced Customer Support:
1) Workshops and tutorials at key worldwide meetings
2) Customer training programs

Becton Dickinson continues to add to its product portfolio through additional acquisitions. In December 1998 the Lexington, Kentucky-based Transduction Laboratories was acquired by Becton Dickinson through PharMingen. Transduction Laboratories also develops products for biomedical research and is a leader in developing reagents, primarily in the field of signal transduction. By joining forces with PharMingen, Transduction Laboratories will be able to increase its customer base by leveraging Becton Dickinson's worldwide distribution system while continuing rapid commercialization of quality products.

With its strength in providing tools for life science research in immunology, cell biology and molecular biology, Becton Dickinson & Company, PharMingen and Transduction Laboratories stand poised to achieve its goal of helping people live healthy lives through the advancement of scientific discovery.

Thomas C. Ackerman Foundation

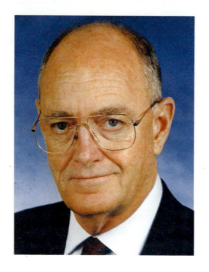

Thomas C. Ackerman

To hear his colleagues and friends tell it, Thomas C. Ackerman loved San Diego. When the lifelong San Diegan died in 1991, he left his entire estate to charity, leading to the creation of the Thomas C. Ackerman Foundation.

Since being established in 1993, the foundation has helped improve the lives of San Diegans in the areas of education, health and human services, the arts and community development. By the end of 1998, the nonprofit organization had awarded more than $3 million in grants.

Ackerman was born in San Diego in December 1927. His father, Thomas Sr., had been a U.S. soldier in World War I, decorated for bravery for fighting in the trenches of Germany and France. Ackerman's mother, Adair Leovy Ackerman, served as a schoolteacher at a one-room schoolhouse called Witch Creek, located between Ramona and Santa Ysabel. It was one of the only back-country schools in the county at the time, and today is the Julian Public Library as well as a historical site. George J. Leovy, Adair's father, moved the family to San Diego from New Orleans, Louisiana, in 1887. George was a lawyer who, in the early 1900s, served as president of the San Diego Bar Association. The Leovys lived in the Christian House in Old Town and also at Red Rest cottage in La Jolla, both of which are today historical landmarks. George Leovy's father, Henry, served as a colonel in the Civil War on the staff of Jefferson Davis.

Ackerman graduated from San Diego High School and in 1950 earned a degree in economics from San Diego State College, graduating first in his class. Ackerman then attended Boalt Hall Law School at the University of California, Berkeley.

While at Boalt Hall, Ackerman served as editor-in-chief of the *California Law Review* and was a member of the Phi Alpha Delta legal fraternity. In 1953, he received his juris doctorate, again graduating first in his class. Ackerman was also invited to join Order of the Coif, a national honor society for top law school graduates. Following graduation, he became an associate with the San Diego firm of Gray, Cary, Ames & Frye in 1953 and became a partner in 1959.

During his career, Ackerman established himself as one of the foremost business lawyers in San Diego, representing such prominent companies and their leaders as Jim Copley of Copley Press and Evan Jones of Ace Parking, as well as Robert Golden of M.H. Golden Construction Company and Frank and Chuck Hope of the Hope architectural firm. Ackerman also represented entrepreneurs Myron Eichen, John Thornton and Robert Sensibaugh, who were pioneers of San Diego's high technology industry. In 1990, Ackerman retired from his active law practice.

"Tom was a great friend and teacher," said foundation President Robert G. Copeland, who worked with Ackerman at Gray, Cary and is now a senior partner at Luce, Forward, Hamilton and Scripps LLP. "Tom spent much of his free time enjoying San Diego: sailing, bicycling, fishing, visiting the museums and touring the back country and Baja."

"He was always proud to be associated with the individuals and businesses that built modern San Diego," Copeland added. "Most importantly, Tom wanted San Diego to be a great city and devoted many volunteer hours to this goal through organizations ranging from his church to the San Diego Taxpayers Association to Big Brothers."

The Ackerman Foundation has awarded more than $800,000 to educational organizations. One of its largest awards was $300,000 for the development of the Author and Marge Hughes Administrative Center at the University of San Diego. The foundation has also awarded $11,000 annually to four San Diego students pursuing post-graduate studies in education through the San Diego Education Fund. Additionally, the foundation awards scholarships to local area college students pursuing studies in the sciences through the Achievement Rewards for College Students. Other education-related grants include the Rolling Readers program, San Diego State University, the University of California, KPBS Radio Reading Service, the Academy of Our Lady of Peace, St. Stephen's Christian School Education Foundation, St. Madeleine Sophie's Center, the Elementary Institute of Science and San Diego City Schools.

The foundation's first major grant of $250,000 was made to the San Diego Child Abuse Prevention Society for the development of the Polinsky Child Care Center. Then in December 1996, the foundation made a $50,000 emergency grant to St. Vincent de Paul for continuation of its homeless meals programs. Other grants have included $50,000 to the Greater San Diego Chamber of Commerce Foundation for its biotechnology internship program and $45,000 to the Second Chance organization for its STRIVE program, a comprehensive training program to help individuals find employment in San Diego. The foundation has awarded more than $500,000 in community development grants over the years.

It has also made grants in excess of $500,000 to various arts organizations. The Mingei International Museum has been the recipient of a multiyear grant while the foundation has also awarded grants to the San Diego Natural History Museum, the Museum of Man, the San Diego Historical Society and the Reuben H. Fleet Science Center. Other arts beneficiaries have included Sledgehammer Theatre, Malashock Dance Company, San Diego Children's Museum and the Museum of Contemporary Art.

In the area of health and human services, the foundation has contributed more than $1 million. Some of the recipients have included Mama's Kitchen, Logan Heights Family Health Center, Fraternity House, Inc., Ladle Fellowship, the San Diego Blood Bank Foundation, San Diego Hospice, Special Delivery San Diego, Pacto Latino Aids Organization and the Vista Hill Foundation. The foundation has also supported numerous other programs, assisting youth, families in crisis, the elderly and the disabled. These beneficiaries have included the Challenge Center, Mercy Hospital, the Helen Woodward Society, Canine Companions and several Boys and Girls Clubs and YMCAs.

Appropriately, the colleagues, clients and friends of Ackerman serve as trustees of the foundation. In addition to Copeland, trustees Kenneth G. Coveney, Richard A. Burt and Christopher C. Calkins worked with Ackerman at his law firm. Trustee Terrence R. Caster, chairman of Caster Family Enterprises, was a longtime client and friend of Ackerman's. Trustee Dr. Author Hughes, served as president of the University of San Diego from 1991 to 1995. Former John Burnham and Company executive and trustee Joanne M. Pastula is an executive with Junior Achievement.

The Thomas C. Ackerman Foundation annually awards more than $500,000 in grants. Today, the foundation continues Ackerman's goal of making San Diego a better place to live.

The board of directors of the Thomas C. Ackerman Foundation: (bottom row, left to right) Joanne Pastula, Robert G. Copeland, Terrence R. Caster (top row, left to right) Kenneth G. Coveney, Richard A. Burt, Author E. Hughes, Christopher C. Calkins
Courtesy Alta Readdy Photography

American Specialty Health Plans

Founder, president and CEO of American Specialty Health Plans, George DeVries

In the ever-changing world of health care, employers and employees alike seek health care benefits that allow for a broader dimension of specialty and complementary managed care. While full-service medical care remains the cornerstone of any health benefits program, American Specialty Health Plans (ASHP) provides more options to patients than ever before — chiropractic, acupuncture and traditional Chinese herbal supplements. By applying managed care systems to these programs, it can offer cost-effective, quality benefits plans within an HMO delivery system. That is the ASHP difference.

The popularity of complementary health therapies such as chiropractic and acupuncture has been growing steadily with consumers. A national research study conducted by Stanford University and ASHP in 1998 showed that complementary alternative medicine is one of the nation's fastest-growing segments of health care. They found that 69 percent of consumers in the United States have used a complementary health therapy in the past year, and 81 percent have used complementary health care within their lifetime. The *New England Journal of Medicine* reported in 1993 that Americans spend upwards of $18 billion annually on "unconventional" medical therapies, a statistic confirmed by a Harvard University study.

ASHP has been led since its inception by San Diego's 1997 Health Sciences Entrepreneur of the Year, George DeVries. Finding himself unemployed due to a company acquisition in 1987, DeVries and two others began to develop the concept for a chiropractic network and management program in California.

"I started out of the second bedroom in our condominium, with just a couple of thousand dollars. My wife worked to support us. For more than two years, I didn't draw a salary," DeVries said. The first year's income was only $26,000, but after the fifth year he posted $1 million in revenues. At first ASHP (then known as American Chiropractic Network/ ACN) provided just administrative services and a network of chiropractic providers that would offer services through California health plans.

In 1992, it became apparent that to move forward within the health plan industry the company would need to become a chiropractic HMO. The two-year application process included filing more than 15,000 pages of documentation with the California Department of Corporations. Due to limited funds, DeVries and his staff had to build the application themselves. In 1994, ASHP (then American Chiropractic Network Health Plan) received its license as a specialized health care service plan for chiropractic, becoming the first licensed plan in the nation. It became the foundation for American Specialty Health Plans, a name the company adopted in 1997.

In 1988, PacifiCare became the first HMO that contracted with ACN. Blue Cross of California followed the next year, with 17 HMOs contracted by 1999, including Aetna/U.S. Healthcare, Blue Shield HMO, CIGNA Health Care, Health Net, Kaiser Foundation Health Plan, Prudential and United Health Care. By 1999, ASHP had more than 1,700 network chiropractors and 600 acupuncture providers participating in the program statewide.

ASHP has become the recognized leader in specialty and complementary managed care. It was granted accreditation by the American Accreditation Health Care Commission, a nonprofit, third party that monitors the quality and service of national health care programs. The company also became the nation's first HMO licensed in acupuncture and traditional Chinese herbal supplements in 1997. ASHP's success can be measured in the growing popularity and acceptance of its plans. As of 1998, ASHP was the largest chiropractic HMO, with more than 3 million Californians enrolled in the plan, and had contracted with nine of California's 10 largest health plans.

Along with the acupuncture benefit program, covered employees may have access to traditional Chinese herbal supplements. ASHP's affiliate, American Specialty Health & Wellness (ASHW), has established a unique, centralized delivery system for these supplements. ASHW warehouses 150 Chinese herbal combinations in its San Diego offices and express mails authorized supplements directly to members.

Another affiliate, American Specialty Health Networks, provides chiropractic and acupuncture networks and managed care services to self-funded employers and insurers. It also provides a discount affinity network program for acupuncture, chiropractic, massage therapy, yoga instructors, personal trainers and fitness clubs.

A new fourth program was introduced by ASHP on the Internet. It allows the general public to order via a Web site and receive by mail high-quality vitamins, minerals and nutritional supplements. The Internet catalog also offers books, newsletters, videos and audiotapes, and other products to enhance health and wellness.

Despite almost overwhelming challenges, ASHP has successfully found a way to blend complementary health care with traditional medicine and managed care. By directly assisting all parts of the triad — the con-

High-quality vitamins, minerals and nutritional supplements can be ordered through ASHP's Internet health and wellness catalog program.

sumer/patient, the health provider and the health plan or employer — ASHP has enabled complementary managed care to be more readily available. In 1987, no California health plans offered a chiropractic benefits rider for employers. As of 1996, with ASHP's impact, almost every major health plan in California offered a chiropractic benefits rider. It is reasonable to predict that in the near future ASHP's complementary managed health care programs will become as commonplace as traditional health care insurance programs are today.

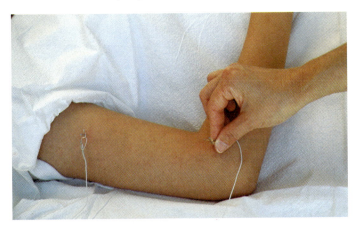

ASHP was the first managed care provider to offer acupuncture care.

Brighton Health Alliance

Brighton Health Alliance has successfully served San Diego County for more than 20 years, managing and operating six skilled nursing and rehabilitation therapy facilities and three residential and Alzheimer's care facilities. All nine facilities offer a full complement of services, geographical locations throughout the greater San Diego and Palm Springs areas, and specializations offering a wide range of programs for patients seeking either a successful transition from hospital to home or permanent, around-the clock care.

Harbor View Chateau

Brighton's co-owners, Berry T. Crow, president, and Carol Van Horst, CFO, combined have more than 50 years of experience in the health care industry. In 1990, they took over the ownership and expanded the operation of this small, independent-based company. Since that time, Brighton has established each facility as its own separate entity, held under the parent corporation, Brighton Health Alliance. This locally owned and operated company believes in a hands-on approach to the management of its facilities. As such, both Mr. Crow and Ms. Van Horst make themselves available and stay involved in the day-to-day events at each of the facilities. With their presence on the individual properties, their close interaction completes the unification of the entire Brighton family as individual staff members, residents and their families have an opportunity to meet the owners and witness firsthand, their commitment and dedication to long-term care (LTC) needs.

It would be difficult to duplicate the pride, enthusiasm and dedication to the LTC business that Brighton Health Alliance maintains. Driving Brighton's success is its belief that the dignity of its residents is the number one priority.

For many people, the concept of long-term care (LTC) is more of an afterthought than a primary consideration of future health care needs. As such, decisions on a LTC facility are usually not planned and are generally made during crisis situations. Brighton Health Alliance strives to make LTC decisions an integral component of the overall integrated, patient-centered care process and offers a personal commitment to excellence with a high level of care.

Brighton's nursing and rehabilitation facilities offer a comprehensive array of therapy programs that include physical, occupational, speech and respiratory.

The facilities include:

• Point Loma Convalescent Hospital, established in 1963 and recognized as a five-star skilled nursing facility, as listed in the 1998-1999 edition of *The Inside Guide to America's Nursing Homes*, specializes in numerous treatment programs including cardiac disability, pain control and Parkinson's disease.

• Brighton Place East in Spring Valley, which offers such services as Alzheimer's care and a state-of-the-art system for monitoring the wandering resident.

• Brighton Place Spring Valley providing programs that include, but are not limited to, hospice care and IV therapy.

• Brighton Place San Diego, which offers a broad range of integrated health care services including social, therapeutic and physical activities for resident participation.

- California Nursing & Rehabilitation of Palm Springs, where residents focus on returning home, offers the finest rehabilitation, skilled nursing, and subacute care in an elegant resort setting.
- Brighton Place La Mesa, tucked away in a beautiful outdoor setting, offers exceptional nursing and rehabilitation care in a smaller, quiet environment.

Its residential facilities include:
- Sun and Sea Manor located on the Silver Strand, which offers specialized programs for individuals with Alzheimer's and related dementia in a safe, protective environment.
- Harbor View Chateau in San Diego, also offers specialized programs for the Alzheimer resident in a secured setting. It is worth the visit to view the stately building and the aesthetic gardens that traverse the entire property.
- Cloisters of the Valley, overlooking scenic Mission Valley, boasts full activity programs and considerate health care from a dedicated staff, in elegant surroundings.

All of the facilities offer personalized support services in a caring, home-like atmosphere. This includes varied social activities, laundry and linen services, beauty and barber shop services, all types of therapy, assistance with transportation, additional personal assistance as required, social get togethers for residents and their families and regularly held religious services. Brighton believes that all its residents should be given the respect and consideration they have earned in a lifetime of living.

Brighton Health Alliance has been credited as a Southern California managed care leader. As such, quality assurance programs are an ongoing process at all nine facilities. Skilled nurses constantly monitor and make recommendations on such issues as resident care, dietary needs and even housekeeping. Teamwork and input is encouraged from all employees and followed up by monthly meetings to discuss present policies and procedures, and compliance and regulatory issues. Recently, physicians and nutritionists from both Japan and Russia toured Brighton's facilities

Point Loma Convalescent

on a fact-finding tour to research LTC. These auspicious visits clearly show that through its many programs and services, Brighton's dedication to the quality of care for its residents is recognized worldwide.

In addition, families of residents play a large role in the Brighton organization. Families are encouraged to visit and take part in many of the activities sponsored by the individual facilities. Families are grateful for the dedication of the staff — as indicated by the hundreds of letters written by family members commenting on the "dedication, love and compassion" of the staff toward the residents — and the willingness to discuss patient advocacy and educate the families on the individualized care and therapy provided to their family members. One resident family member comments, "As time went on, I became more and more convinced that I had done the right thing and that my father was in a place that respected him, cared not just for him, but about him and treated him with the respect and kindness that I can only hope that you and I will encounter in our later years." Other visitors commented on the welcome smiles and greetings they received on each visit, even when visiting at unscheduled times. "All the personnel, down to the cooks, knew my mother as an individual and lovingly cared for her."

Through years of solid management experience, skilled administrative leadership and a firm commitment to excellence, Brighton Health Alliance has developed a unique collection of outstanding facilities serving the LTC needs of San Diegans with quality, ambiance, service and distinction.

David L. Wolf, M.D., F.A.C.S.

David L. Wolf, M.D., F.A.C.S.

The state-of-the-art operating rooms have the latest equipment and are fully accredited by the state of California.

Southern California is noted for many things, including well-known and skilled plastic surgeons. Among San Diego's best and most prominent plastic surgeons is David L. Wolf, M.D. of La Jolla. Dr. Wolf specializes in aesthetic surgery with the natural, no-hint-of-a-facelift look as his trademark.

Plastic surgery (from the Greek word "plasticos" meaning "to mold") covers a broad range of procedures. Both cosmetic and reconstructive surgeries come under the heading of plastic surgery. Cosmetic or aesthetic surgery is indeed a molding or reshaping of the body's normal features, primarily to reverse signs of aging, to remove unwanted fat or to reshape an undesirable area. Ultimately, the goal is to improve appearance and often to increase self-esteem.

Some of the cosmetic procedures Dr. Wolf performs include facelifts, breast enlargement and lifts, liposculpture, laser, nasal surgery and tummy tucks. A portion of this type of surgery is revisional work — that is, to revise another surgeon's work in which the patient did not get the results they expected. Men account for 20 percent of Dr. Wolf's clients, typically coming in for eyelid surgery, liposuction, face and neck lifts and nasal surgery.

Approximately 10 percent of Dr. Wolf's patients have reconstructive surgery performed. These surgeries may include correction of birth defects or problems secondary to accidents or illness, or reconstruction following excision of skin cancer. Throughout his career, Dr. Wolf has volunteered his time in Mexico, Taiwan and Guatemala, performing cleft lip and palate surgeries. He still offers these procedures at no charge to patients without the proper insurance coverage.

Although no surgeon can promise perfection, Dr. Wolf maintains that prospective patients can improve their chances for success by carefully choosing their surgeon. Most of Dr. Wolf's new patients come as referrals, some from as far away as Italy and Japan. Referrals may be obtained from friends and physicians as well as through the telephone or Internet referral service of the American Society of Plastic and Reconstructive Surgeons. According to Dr. Wolf, a surgeon's results improve based on training, experience, skill level and the quality of staff and facilities.

Dr. Wolf's training began at Tulane Medical School, where he obtained his medical degree in 1971. After being a Navy doctor for two years, he went back to Tulane for his general surgery training. From 1978 to 1981, he did his residency in plastic surgery in San Francisco at St. Francis Hospital and University of California San Francisco Medical Center. Dr. Wolf chose plastic surgery as his specialty because it offered the greatest variety and complexity of surgical procedures. He enjoys the artistry involved in well-planned and well-performed cosmetic surgery.

While stationed in San Diego with the Navy in the early 1970s, Dr. Wolf fell in love with this beautiful city and returned in 1981 to open his private

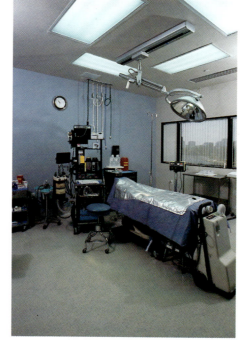

practice in La Jolla. In 1996, he moved into an elegant, efficient 4,000-square-foot office in the Scripps Memorial Hospital La Jolla complex that includes two state-of-the-art, fully accredited outpatient operating rooms. Dr. Wolf has a professional and caring staff which provides reassuring support for the patients. He performs most of his surgeries with his patients under general anesthesia because this has been shown to be the optimum and safest method for most aesthetic procedures. After surgery, the patients either go home with family or a nurse, or to an overnight care facility.

Patients, prospective patients and guests can relax or review books of photographs in the comfortable, tastefully appointed waiting room.

Dr. Wolf spends a great deal of time with prospective patients, as he feels this is the best way to give the patients all the information they need to make intelligent decisions about their surgery. Only with a consultation of adequate length, directness in answering the patient's questions, and examples of the surgeon's work and capabilities, can a prospective patient have confidence in the goals and abilities of their surgeon. In addition, Dr. Wolf's prospective patients can view examples of his work that are similar to their proposed procedures, and they may also interview previous patients who have had similar surgeries.

"I like what I do and take pride in it," Dr. Wolf says. "Patients relate to my warm and personal approach. I explain to them that I am extremely meticulous and very much a perfectionist in surgery." Dr. Wolf reminds patients that while a facelift will not stop aging or the effects of gravity, it will set the clock back significantly, often 10 years or more. This benefit will allow the patient to always look younger as a result of the surgery. Some patients may desire additional surgery after 10 years or so.

Dr. Wolf stands out from others in his crowded field by offering a unique blend of the best possible surgery based on skills and facility, with an unpretentious and caring attitude. His sterling reputation has been built on his commitment to giving his patients fabulous results. His happy patients are walking advertisements for his talents.

Dr. Wolf is very much a part of the city he loves. He has been a trustee of the Rancho Santa Fe Community Center and was involved in the planning of a new center for the children of the community. He has both coached and sponsored a variety of local teams, including baseball and soccer. He is also a sponsor of many local charities such as cancer organizations and the La Jolla Jewish Community Center.

Advances continue to be made in plastic and cosmetic surgery. Facelifts have become more dramatic through the use of both mid-facelifts and deeper lifts. Lasers can give wonderful results with facial resurfacing. Liposuction has improved dramatically with the use of the tumescent technique and smaller cannulas giving experienced surgeons safer and predictably excellent results.

As technology progresses, patients of David L. Wolf, M.D. can rest assured that they are in the hands of a professional who will use technology to their best advantage. When they look in the mirror, they will have Dr. Wolf to thank.

Gen-Probe

The health care environment is changing rapidly — escalating costs, the emergence of managed care and declining government funding have resulted in a price-sensitive market demanding simpler, more automated diagnostic methods. New infectious diseases and microorganisms that are resistant to antibiotics also pose a challenge. Diagnostics will play an even more important role as earlier detection and faster intervention will improve patient health care and help reduce costs. Screening of high-risk population segments for specific diseases, as well as screening the blood supply (using the latest technology to ensure there is an acceptably low risk of transmitting diseases), are also areas of increasing importance to our society.

Since its founding in 1983, San Diego-based Gen-Probe has never forgotten that its ultimate customer is the patient. Gen-Probe, a wholly owned subsidiary of Chugai Pharmaceutical Co., Ltd., a major Japanese pharmaceutical company, has become one of San Diego's premier biotech success stories. The company is internationally recognized as a leader in the development, manufacture and commercialization of genetic probe tests for diagnosing human diseases, including tuberculosis, strep throat, pneumonia, fungal infections and sexually transmitted diseases such as chlamydial infections and gonorrhea. It is currently developing tests that will make our blood supply the safest it has ever been.

Since its first FDA-cleared product in 1985 (a culture confirmation test for Legionnaire's disease), Gen-Probe has developed and marketed more than 40 products. The company sells several product lines including the PACE® 2 System, the ACCUPROBE® System, the ACCUPACE® System, and the GEN-PROBE® AMPLIFIED™ Direct Test System.

Three proprietary technologies form the foundation for Gen-Probe's revolutionary genetic probe tests: 1) Targeting of ribosomal RNA (rRNA), an abundant species of nucleic acid found in all living cells; 2) Hybridization Protection Assay (HPA), an extremely sensitive and convenient means of detecting nucleic acid hybridization; and 3) Transcription-Mediated Ampli-fication (TMA), a process for increasing the number of target nucleic acid sequences to allow detection of even a single nucleic acid molecule.

Gen-Probe has successfully combined these and other technologies, enabling clinical laboratories to obtain test results in hours instead of days or weeks, and with accuracy that has made the Gen-Probe assays the reference standard for many applications.

Over the years, Gen-Probe has achieved a number of industry firsts:

• First company to receive FDA clearance to market a clinical diagnostic test using genetic probe technology;

• First to market a test to detect both chlamydial and gonorrheal infections using one test method and one patient specimen;

• First FDA-approved direct amplified test for the detection of Mycobacterium tuberculosis, which cut the time to diagnose tuberculosis to a few hours, instead of the weeks to months needed by the culture method.

In 2000, the company anticipates placing the first fully automated, high-throughput DNA probe

Gen-Probe's ongoing customer education program includes attending major scientific and professional meetings, sponsoring workshops and symposia, and maintaining active publishing and speaking programs.

instrument system, TIGRIS™. Designed for use with Gen-Probe's amplified tests, the TIGRIS™ system will integrate the sample processing, amplification and detection steps into one instrument and will be able to process 1,000 tests per 12-hour shift, making it especially effective for high-volume testing.

Also key to Gen-Probe's success has been the formation of strategic alliances, collaborative partnerships and global distribution agreements. Gen-Probe was selected by the National Institutes of Health to help meet the government's commitment to ensure that our nation's blood supply is as safe from infection as the latest technology will allow. In 1996, the National Heart, Lung and Blood Institute (NHLBI) awarded Gen-Probe a $7.7 million contract to develop a screening system for HIV and hepatitis C for the nation's blood supply. This test is expected to be placed in blood banks across the country by the end of 1999. In 1997, Gen-Probe signed a cooperation agreement in the field of molecular diagnosis of infectious diseases covering both marketing and scientific areas with bioMerieux, a French diagnostic company recognized as a world leader in microbiology. In July 1998, Gen-Probe formed an alliance with Chiron Corporation to enter the blood bank screening market with a combination assay for HIV and HCV utilizing TMA and the TIGRIS™ system. In October 1998, Gen-Probe received another $4.3 million grant from the NHLBI to develop a nucleic acid amplification test for HIV-2 and hepatitis B (HBV) virus for use in blood screening.

Gen-Probe's sister company, Chugai Biopharmaceuticals, Inc. (CBI) was established in 1995 to conduct basic discovery research and clinical development using state-of-the-art technologies. As a member of Chugai's Pacific Rim Research Network, CBI researchers collaborate with research scientists in Japan, Korea, and Australia and have access to Chugai's extensive toxicology and pharmaceutical development resources in developing novel therapeutics for the global pharmaceutical market. CBI's major area of focus is cardiovascular disease.

CBI's medium-term plan includes building a presence in the North American hospital markets by licensing and developing later-stage products in several therapeutic areas, including cardiovascular diseases and cancer. The company will also pursue tailoring its product portfolio to the needs of managed care. Gen-Probe and CBI expect to collaborate to create disease management programs for specific therapeutic areas.

The company has begun phase 2 clinical trials with a novel GI motility drug, GM-611, for the treatment of nonsurgical gastroparesis and gastroesophageal reflux disease.

And what does the future portend for Gen-Probe? The worldwide DNA probe market is expected to exceed $735 million by 2000. Gen-Probe is poised to capitalize on this market growth. The company's primary focus will remain where it can have the greatest impact on human health: developing and commercializing clinical diagnostics. Over the next five years Gen-Probe will expand its core offerings in the areas of sexually transmitted diseases (STDs) and respiratory diseases. It plans to develop and license new technologies and expand into areas such as cancer diagnosis, blood-virus screening and genetic testing. Research and development, the cornerstones of Gen-Probe's history, will continue to play significant roles in its future growth.

Gen-Probe's success has propelled it to the forefront among San Diego's biotech companies. As it enters the next century, Gen-Probe will continue to lead the way in offering innovative products that provide accurate diagnoses in time to make a difference.

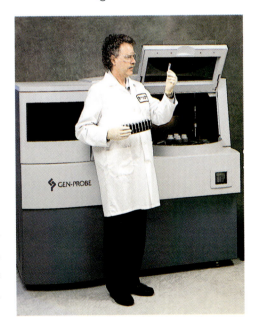

Gen-Probe's scientists are committed to exploring uncharted frontiers in science, developing improved diagnostic tests and targeting new disease areas.

Kearny Mesa Convalescent Hospital and Nursing Home

The Hebbel family has owned and operated Kearny Mesa Convalescent Hospital and Nursing Home (KMCH) since its inception in 1965. Yet the family identity of this warm, attractive facility extends beyond the three generations of Hebbels that still take part in the daily operation. "Family" includes the 98 residents, their families, the staff of more than 100 employees, many volunteers, student trainees and interns.

A family-run business is rare in today's nursing home field and Administrator Richard J. Hebbel believes that's what makes his facility unique. "We're able to provide personalized service to every resident," he says as he strolls the halls greeting everyone by name. He also maintains personal contact with residents' family members and each employee.

The consistency of ownership and low staff turnover provide an atmosphere of quality and security. Many employees have worked at KMCH for more than 20 years. They think of the facility and residents as their own and offer a deep commitment to their jobs and caring service to the residents. This is the kind of assurance people look for when they entrust the care of a loved one to a nursing home.

John and Jeanette Hebbel founded KMCH in 1965 after having built and managed several skilled nursing facilities in the Midwest. Rather than developing a large chain of nursing homes, they moved to San Diego to pursue their dream of building a smaller home where they could make a real difference in the lives of their residents. The senior Hebbels are now semiretired, but John still poses as Santa at Christmas and carves the Thanksgiving turkey, while Jeanette edits the newsletter and coordinates special activities.

Their son, Richard, became administrator in 1971 after graduating with a business degree from Loma Linda University. His wife, Carolyn, serves as office manager while the three Hebbel children, Brian, Jeff and Melinda, work or volunteer in the family business as well.

Kearny Mesa provides individualized care to residents with four primary needs: those with a variety of chronic illnesses, including Alzheimer's Disease, who need to live in an environment where 24-hour skilled care and supervision is available; those needing rehabilitation to recover from illness or injury; those needing short-term skilled services; and the terminally ill in need of hospice care.

Available to all residents are around-the-clock licensed nurses who supervise a full nursing staff capable of providing complete care as needed by the residents; a rehabilitation staff, including physical, occupational and speech therapists; social services and daily activities; and dietary services including special medical diets and feeding assistance as well as a select menu system. All of this is provided in a home-like setting which includes four garden patios, large aquariums and aviaries as well as a pet cat and rabbit.

Although the majority of the residents are in various stages of illness, KMCH provides a positive environment that allows for constructive use of their time. Daily activities range from classes in crafts, music, current events, nutrition and exercise, to bingo, movies and weekly outings to restaurants, museums, parks and ball games.

Three generations of the Hebbel family participate in day-to-day operations.

Special events occur throughout the year, including those which take residents to other times and places such as the annual "Kearny Mesa Railroad Adventure," in which the facility is outfitted to look like a train, and residents and staff take a mock trip around the United States to places like old New England, the deep South and the Wild West. Also annually, the facility magically transforms into a fantasy cruise ship which "travels" to exotic ports such as Greece, the Orient, Africa and the Caribbean. No detail is left untouched during these three-day adventures. The building is decorated from top to bottom, the staff and residents (complete with passports) dress in costumes and the food goes native.

A part of KMCH's community participation involves the Resident Council, a group with elected officers who represent the residents' interests. Once a year, the council sponsors the Rock 'n Roll Jamboree fund-raiser. Similar to a walkathon, only with residents rocking in rocking chairs and rolling in wheelchairs, the proceeds go to a chosen charity. Residents also give to the community by mentoring children who may have no grandparents.

Staff members serve on various community boards, speak at conferences and have received numerous awards. John Hebbel was president of the California Chapter of the American College of Health Care Administrators. Richard Hebbel has been president of the San Diego Health Care Association, has served on the White House Conference on Aging and was honored as California Administrator of the Year in 1987 and for distinguished service in 1998.

To allay the fear that residents will be forgotten by the community when entering a nursing home, every effort is made to bring the community to KMCH. The Volunteer Auxiliary, started in 1967, offers a myriad of opportunities for community members to share the outside world with residents while giving of themselves in service. Some volunteers are family members of current or former residents. Some are youths who have visited the facility to trick or treat and later return as candy stripers. Several local churches hold services in the interfaith chapel on the grounds, affording residents the chance to continue their religious practices.

KMCH furnishes a training site for university students, nurses, physicians, therapists and others in need of training and experience in a clinical environment. The senior Hebbels sponsor a yearly scholarship at San Diego State University for students pursuing an education in gerontology.

As we enter the new millennium, KMCH's goal is to maintain their consistent excellence and to meet the needs of the community. "We've matured with the city of San Diego, but don't have any plans for expansion," Richard explains. "We really enjoy the daily operation of Kearny Mesa and get a great sense of personal satisfaction ... seeing and touching the fruits of our labor. We're proud of what we've contributed to this community and look forward to the challenges of the future."

The relationship between staff and residents is at the heart of what makes Kearny Mesa a special place.

Residents dine in a restaurant atmosphere with a choice of menu items at each meal.

(Left) The homelike one-story brick building is surrounded by four garden patios.

Sharp Rees-Stealy Medical Group

It's 8 p.m. on a Saturday night. A little girl has a fever and is complaining of a sore throat. If she is a patient of Sharp Rees-Stealy Medical Group in San Diego, her family can thank the early health care pioneering efforts of Dr. Clarence Rees and Dr. Claire Stealy for founding the area's first multi-specialty medical group practice. Their bold steps in 1923 were the first of many that focused on delivering high-quality care, convenience and the peace of mind that comes with services such as after-hours pediatric appointments.

Clarence Rees, an internist, and Claire Stealy, a surgeon, believed that patient care would be enhanced if doctors representing multiple specialties worked together. Physicians could obtain immediate access to consultation in other areas of specialization, vastly improving the diagnostic process. This approach allows physicians to collaborate in providing comprehensive, efficient and thorough patient care in a cost-effective manner, all under one roof. The expertise of many disciplines working together produced a new kind of teamwork that revolutionized medical care in San Diego.

The Rees-Stealy office opened at the corner of Fourth Avenue and Grape Street in downtown San Diego in 1923. Soon, they hired an obstetrician, pediatricians, internists, an otolaryngologist, a urologist, a neurologist and a pathologist, as well as another story to their building. A true interdisciplinary approach was forming.

Both physicians were intimately associated with San Diego's growth during the 1920s. Concerned with the health and welfare of civil servants, Dr. Rees served as city fire surgeon, and one of his associates served as police surgeon. The group formed an early partnership for school health projects with the San Diego City School District and developed the Nursing and Physician Services program. Dr. Stealy was instrumental in initiating such innovative programs as the Doctors Service Bureau, a countywide answering and referral service. He was the first organizer of the teaching program at San Diego County Hospital and was the first chairman of the department of medicine.

Recognizing the medical group's unique position in the community as a source for comprehensive medical services, Dr. Rees and Dr. Stealy established the Rees-Stealy Medical Research Fund, the forerunner of the present research foundation. They believed that fundamental biomedical research and its relationship to daily clinical problems would clearly promote the advancement of medical knowledge.

Flagship Rees-Stealy building located downtown at Fourth and Grape streets

In 1938, the Rees-Stealy Research Foundation was formed. That same year, a second structure, built to provide additional space to perform outpatient surgeries, joined the original location. In 1942 Rees-Stealy opened its first on-site pharmacy so patients could receive care and obtain needed medications all at the same location. By 1947 full-service radiology services became available on-site.

Shortly before the onset of World War II, an allergist, ophthalmologist, general surgeon, obstetrician/ gynecologist and another pediatrician were added to the staff. The practice experienced tremendous disruption during World War II. Of the 18 doctors, nine were called into service. Dr. Stealy insisted that the drafted physicians be compensated with the proper share of the group's income to ensure that their families would be provided for while they were away.

In 1954 Rees-Stealy became one of the first medical clinics to use a computer in its practice. The IBM machine filled a 16-by-20 foot room.

Rees-Stealy opened its first satellite medical office in Mira Mesa in 1976.

In 1980, recognizing the unique employee-relations, financial and administrative issues facing employers, and the importance of federal and state regulations relating to employee health and safety, Rees-Stealy developed a specialized, dedicated occupational medicine program. Today, the program is staffed by specially trained physicians and support staff, who serve more than 8,000 San Diego-area employers and register more than 120,000 patient visits annually.

In 1985, Rees-Stealy affiliated with Sharp HealthCare. This venture was the first of its kind and attracted national attention. Sharp HealthCare is San Diego's leader in health care and is well-known for cardiac care, women's services, senior care, rehabilitation, oncology care, diabetes management, and orthopedic joint-replacement programs. A centralized call-center opened in 1995 and each year the friendly and knowledgeable patient-service representatives help patients schedule more that 700,000 appointments.

The Sharp Rees-Stealy San Diego Medical Center opened on the campus of Sharp Memorial Hospital in 1996. In 1998, a week-long series of events commemorated the group's 75th anniversary of caring for generations of San Diegans.

Ever the innovator in the practice of medicine, Sharp Rees-Stealy continues to offer patients quality, service, convenience and choice. Sharp Rees-Stealy meets the needs of its patients' busy schedules by offering such services as same-day primary care appointments, 24-hour-a-day health care advice through Sharp Nurse Connection, pediatric appointments until 9 p.m. daily and five urgent care centers open until 10 p.m. daily.

Nationally known for superior clinical practices and research, the group has been certified — an industry benchmark for quality of care and services — by the Accreditation Association for Ambulatory Health Care. Sharp Rees-Stealy participates in significant collaborative studies with numerous medical institutions and research foundations in such areas as women's health, sinusitis and asthma. Sharp Rees-Stealy's history reflects not only the expansion of medical technology, but also its ongoing mission — to improve the health of the community through a caring partnership of patients, physicians and employees.

Clarence Rees, M.D.
Clair Stealy, M.D.

Thomas Jefferson School of Law

A private, independent law school situated in historic Old Town, Thomas Jefferson School of Law provides an individualized legal education in a supportive environment. Its strong academic program emphasizes newly emerging areas of law.

The law school was founded in February 1969 as the San Diego campus of Western State University College of Law. In its early years, the law school offered only a part-time program. In 1974, however, its commitment to serving the individual needs of its rapidly growing student body prompted it to add a full-time program as well.

In 1983, the law school moved its campus from downtown San Diego to a new facility on San Diego Avenue in Old Town. A little more than a decade later, as a result of continued expansion of the law library, Thomas Jefferson again found itself in need of more space. In early 1996, the law school purchased a second building directly across San Diego Avenue from its existing campus.

For most of its history, Thomas Jefferson served principally a nontraditional student body consisting primarily of working adults. Demand for the student-centered environment offered by the law school was strong and by its 30th year of operation, Thomas Jefferson had graduated more than 4,000 alumni. Its graduates include prominent attorneys, a number of judges, a former president of the California State Bar and a U.S. Congressman.

By the mid-1990s, the composition of the student body had changed. Most students were recent college graduates attending law school full-time. Consistent with its commitment to individualized education, however, the law school continued to offer students considerable scheduling flexibility, allowing students to commence their studies in August or January, to attend full-time or part-time, and to attend class during the day or in the evening.

On January 1, 1996, the law school separated from Western State University and commenced operation as an independent law school known as the Thomas Jefferson School of Law. One week later, it applied for provisional approval by the American Bar Association (ABA), which was granted seven months later. As a result, Thomas Jefferson's graduates are qualified to sit for the bar exam in all U.S. jurisdictions. With approval by the ABA came another dramatic change in the student body. During its first quarter-century of operation, Thomas Jefferson had served a predominantly local population that intended to remain and

Graduation smiles

Old Town-style Spanish architecture

practice law in Southern California. By 1998, nearly 60 percent of the fall entering class was drawn from outside California. The fall class that year included students from 35 states. Virtually overnight, Thomas Jefferson had become a truly national law school.

Rapid growth in the number of applications for admission received by the law school has led to more selective admissions standards and increasingly stronger entering classes. The expansion of the law school's applicant pool also has resulted in a more diverse student body. Fall entering classes typically include students from 20 or more countries; the racial and ethnic diversity of the student body is above the national average for ABA approved law schools.

Thomas Jefferson is distinguished by its commitment to an individualized education in a supportive environment. *The Princeton Review of The Best Law Schools* has ranked Thomas Jefferson fifth in the nation for quality of life, a ranking based on a poll of Thomas Jefferson students that took into account the strong sense of community among students and the high degree of student/faculty interaction. This interaction is made possible by the accessibility of the faculty and by the law school's practice of scheduling small classes.

The Thomas Jefferson faculty includes scholars of national and even international reputation. Members of the faculty have testified before Congress, have been featured on national television news broadcasts and have served as consultants to numerous foreign governments and the United Nations. They also include authors of textbooks used at universities throughout the United States and in several foreign jurisdictions.

The curriculum emphasizes the preparation of students to practice law in the 21st century. New faculty and courses focus on international law and the relationship between law and high technology.

In 1999, Thomas Jefferson established three new academic centers. These are the Center for Law, Technology and Communications; the Center for Global Legal Studies and the Center for Law and Social Justice. All three centers address areas of the law that are critical to the technology-driven process of globalization that will characterize the new millennium. Equally important, these areas of law are inextricably linked to the future of San Diego, a city that rests on the western and southern borders of the continental

Students in the courtyard

United States and that, in the late 1990s, had gained recognition as a center for high-tech industries. Thomas Jefferson's focus on these critical new areas of the law will enable it to prepare its students for professional challenges and, in that way, enrich and enliven the community of San Diego.

Toward Maximum Independence

The strength of a community may be best evident in how it reaches out to support and include its most vulnerable citizens. Like most large, American metropolitan centers, San Diego is comprised of many smaller, diverse communities that celebrate ethnic and cultural differences while seeking a sense of belonging and membership. Toward Maximum Independence (TMI) is a San Diego-based, nonprofit agency that assists people

One of the goals of TMI's Community Living Service is to develop a Circle of Support so that people can live independently.

with developmental disabilities to be included members of the community. Since 1981 the agency has been working with the San Diego Regional Center and the California State Departments of Developmental Services, Rehabilitation, and Habilitation to achieve its mission to support people with disabilities to live and work in the community. TMI provides personalized support to people in their own homes, workplaces, schools, families and neighborhoods.

According to the Lanterman Act, California's progressive legislation which outlines the state's services and support to those eligible, a developmental disability is one that originates before someone's 18th birthday and is expected to continue indefinitely. Included are cerebral palsy, mental retardation, autism, seizure disorders and other conditions that may require similar services or support.

TMI provides services in three broad areas: Community Living, Community Employment and Family Support. All services are based on each participant's Personal Support Plan. Utilizing best practices such as Person-Centered Planning, TMI works with people to achieve their lifelong goals — to live in their own homes in the community, to secure paid employment in real jobs, to maintain family unity or to assure that all children are a part of a family. In years past, people who could not live completely independently were either cared for by family members or placed in group homes, skilled nursing facilities or institutions. Today there are new options.

Community Living Services

In spite of the organization's name, independence is not everyone's ultimate goal. Most people, even without disabilities, rely on others for meeting a variety of their daily needs. TMI assesses a person's need for assistance and together they develop an individualized plan for support. In order to live in a home or apartment in the community, one person with a developmental disability may need live-in support, while another may need only intermittent "come-in" support once or twice a week to help with such things as meal planning, grocery shopping or banking. Providing assistance is only one aspect of TMI's services. There is also an emphasis on skill building and helping people to learn to do things for themselves. The agency also helps people to develop relationships with neighbors or other community members. It assists people to select activities and places where they can meet people, make friends and become productive, contributing participants in the community. It is important for people to learn to pay bills, clean house or advocate for themselves, but it is also important that people are accepted, included and valued as members of their communities.

Community Employment Services

Most adults are defined by the career choices they make — by the role they play in the world of work. Traditionally, people with developmental disabilities were seen as incapable of real work and "sheltered" from the expectations which often accompanied even the simplest of jobs. Today people with disabilities can and do work. Through an integrated work program they are able to achieve meaningful, gainful employment in the community. TMI not only works with individuals to secure and maintain jobs, but also with community businesses to develop job opportunities for adults and high school students with disabilities. The agency also works with a local school district to secure jobs for students in the last year of public education to promote a smooth transition from school to adult life.

Unforgettables, a gift shop operated by TMI, provides a work environment where people with significant disabilities can gain the work experience necessary to make important choices about future employment. The store offers both integrated work and supported employment opportunities as well as an impressive array of gifts, florals and home decor.

Family Support Services

As a licensed Foster Family Agency (FFA), TMI provides alternative family placements for children with significant behavioral challenges. These foster families receive a financial stipend, monthly respite and back-up services, extensive training and the ongoing support of both a social worker and a behavior specialist.

Another aspect of TMI's family support seeks to prevent the need for out-of-home placements. Through Alternatives to Placement, the agency offers support to natural, or birth, families and their children with the goal of addressing support needs before they reach a crisis level. Family preservation is important and even when temporary placement is necessary, the ultimate goal is reunification. In cases where it is not in the child's best interest and the courts have advised against a reunification plan, TMI has been successful in finding long-term, stable alternative families for children where they are loved and nurtured.

The newest TMI venture has lead the agency to develop advocacy services for persons with developmental disabilities who also have a mental health diagnosis or who have been entangled in the criminal justice system. Success Links has been instrumental in working with probation, the public defender's office, juvenile justice, county mental health and other entities to ensure that people with developmental disabilities are able to navigate these complicated systems and to get the services they need.

Toward Maximum Independence has twice been awarded recognition for developing the best new programs in the state for people with developmental disabilities. The agency looks forward to a point in time when all people, including those most vulnerable, will be naturally accepted and included in community life. Until that time, TMI will continue to provide vital support to those whose quality of life depends on it.

People with developmental disabilities work in a variety of jobs including offices, retail stores and manufacturing settings.

TMI's Family Support Services promotes positive parenting in both natural and foster family homes.

University of Phoenix

Dr. John G. Sperling founded the University of Phoenix (UOP) in 1976 to provide high-quality education to working adults. He broke decisively from the high school recruitment process favored at most colleges and universities, and instead, successfully focused on the Phoenix business community where UOP is still based. By targeting individuals with work histories and life experience, Sperling created a blueprint that identified and addressed the previously unmet needs of adults seeking to increase their skills and earn advanced degrees. In the process, he also established himself and the university as independent, pioneering spirits in the nation's educational landscape.

Today, UOP has successfully expanded beyond its original Arizona borders. The university is accredited by the North Central Association of Colleges and Schools. UOP operates in other regions as an accredited institution through reciprocity agreements among the six regional accrediting associations recognized by the Department of Education. The extent of this academic and geographic reach, which includes San Diego, was envisioned by Sperling when he stated, "As we move to meet the educational needs of working adults in a mobile society, our conception of the university must extend beyond place and embrace process. An adult university cannot be campus bound; rather its borders must be defined by the lives of its students."

UOP's continuous goal, to educate working adults better than any institution in the nation, results in a thriving presence in San Diego. UOP understands and respects San Diego as a unique community filled with rich history, tradition and proud ethnic and professional diversity. The students in San Diego embody these unique qualities, while sharing similarities with other UOP students nationwide. Specifically, they are not only active members of the local work force, but many must also balance their professional, family and personal lives. They understand how quickly the world around them changes and that education allows them to be prepared.

In response to the personal and professional challenges faced by its students, the University of Phoenix delivers convenience and career-focused solutions: several campuses throughout San Diego County; evening classes that offer flexibility with students' busy schedules; degree programs structured to logically move students from one course to the next; and the option to begin a program of study any month of the year. UOP offers bachelor's and master's degree programs, as well as professional certificate and custom training programs. Bachelor of science degree programs in business emphasize the key areas that influence modern business environments — administration, management, accounting, marketing and information systems; master's degree programs prepare students

for the most complex level of business administration — global business management, technology management, computer information systems and organizational management; and bachelor's and master's degrees in helping professions programs address the skills of working nurses in areas of general nursing, counseling (marriage, family and child) and health care management.

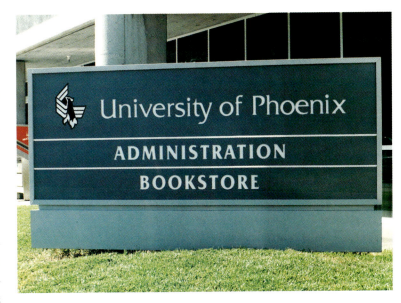

The UOP faculty possesses excellent academic credentials (a doctorate or master's degree is required) and comprises entrepreneurs, managers, directors, consultants and leaders of respective disciplines. The depth and relevancy of its professional knowledge resonates throughout the student body and allows for dynamic student-faculty interaction. Students know that the topics their instructors present are current, insightful and can often be observed or practiced on their jobs the next day. By ensuring that instructors who are active in their field teach every course, UOP eliminates the possibility of a faculty member being distanced from his/her area of expertise. Students can feel confident that each time they attend a class, they are learning from true practitioners.

Students at the university also learn from one another. The classroom is an exciting place where ideas become fully developed theories, and where solutions to problems can be found in one sitting. An urgency and willingness to learn compels students to work in the collaborative spirit of teamwork — in and out of groups — just as the workplace demands. Such intensive classroom instruction and activity is just one way that the university delivers quality education. Another involves distance learning, specifically, the Online Campus, which features computer-based programs that allow students to undertake degree programs from home, work or on the road. The implementation of extensive online learning modules reinforce Sperling's belief that education cannot be "campus bound."

The Online Campus incorporates online computer-conferencing technology, which electronically replicates the group learning experiences found in a physical classroom. The result is a flexible, clearly directed academic environment independent of time and location. Advanced software is made available to students, which allows for communication marked by the finer elements of interactive classroom learning including the lively exchange of thoughts and ideas.

Cutting-edge teaching methods, combined with the depth and diversity of the curricula, are merely a few of the contributing factors in the success story of the University of Phoenix. In San Diego and at campuses across the United States, mature professionals gain career-oriented education in ways that suit their individual lifestyles, schedules and career goals. Back in 1976, this model of education for working adults broke from tradition. Ironically, UOP has now established its own traditions, on its own terms. These include academic excellence and educational integrity, which combined with the university's distinctive level of innovation, has helped thousands of UOP students and alumni — on their own terms —- make their way in the real world.

Digirad Corporation

Pictured is an example of the old-fashioned vacuum-tube technology used in existing equipment today and Digirad's solid-state detector module.

San Diego-based Digirad is a textbook example of how a company paid close attention to market conditions and was able to carve out a unique product opportunity. Digirad's proprietary technology is based on solid-state semiconductor technology, which was developed in-house and originally used in defense technology applications. The company focuses on the medical imaging market and its flagship product is a compact, high-performance, mobile gamma camera for nuclear medicine imaging.

Digirad originally concentrated on defense-related technology. The company was successful in obtaining numerous grants from the Department of Defense, the National Cancer Institute and the Department of Energy, but realized that its core technology could go far beyond just defense-based applications. Digirad developed solid-state detector technology that works at room temperature. This was a major technological advance as crystal sensors used by the military, for example, functioned when supercooled in liquid nitrogen. Digirad developed new ways to enhance the output from the detectors and combine them in large arrays for high resolution. This opened the door to a wide variety of product applications.

The company's innovative technology soon caught the eyes of venture capitalists. In 1994, Kingsbury Associates, a prominent San Diego venture capital firm, invested the first seed money in Digirad. The company has since raised, on its own, more than $33 million in equity financing.

The funds have helped Digirad create the world's first solid-state nuclear medicine gamma camera, known as the Digirad 2020*tc* Imager™, which will be rolled out in 1999. The Food and Drug Administration granted market clearance for the imaging device that only has a 50-pound imaging head. The imaging head attaches to a computer and is mounted on a cart to allow mobility of the imaging system. Since the 2020*tc* Imager™ is portable and lightweight, it allows clinicians to transport it where not previously possible. All other conventional stationary gamma cameras weigh at least 3,000 pounds and use old-fashioned, bulky vacuum tubes; this technology is more than 60 years old! These large vacuum tubes convert the gamma rays to light flashes and then to electrical signals. Digirad's solid-state camera replaces the vacuum tubes with detectors and semiconductors that convert the photons directly to a digital output.

Additionally, Digirad's gamma camera can be moved to locations around the hospital and even to physicians' offices. Because of the camera's size and flexibility, it allows doctors to obtain additional clinical images not possible with the conventional vacuum tube-based cameras.

In nuclear medicine procedures, doctors inject patients with small amounts of radioactive materials that are taken up by body tissues or organs. The Digirad camera images the movement and location of these materials which assist in diagnosing cancer, various types of cardiovascular disease or other abnormalities within the body.

Digirad believes that its products will have a positive impact on the health care bottom line. Currently, after someone has an abnormal mammogram, they are often sent to get a biopsy. About 800,000 breast biopsies are performed each year in the United States — 90 percent of which are negative, at a cost of $3,000-5,000 per biopsy. A nuclear medicine study can detect the breast cancer and provide more direct information to help potentially reduce the number of unnecessary biopsies, which helps reduce health care costs. Cancer specialists, for instance, can detect breast tumors that don't show up on conventional mammograms, especially when breast tissue is very dense.

In addition, cardiologists are using nuclear imaging to determine the extent of heart damage when someone is having, or has had, a heart attack. It's estimated that about 40 percent of the five million Americans who go to emergency rooms each year with cardiac symptoms are not having a heart attack. Conversely, about 50,000 of those having heart attacks are mistakenly sent home. Nuclear imaging can distinguish between these possibilities.

Digirad's ability to evolve and develop new products is not only going to help the company increase sales (the market for gamma cameras in nuclear medicine is more than $700 million a year), but it will also be making a major contribution to medicine and other fields. Health care costs are expected to continue to increase over the next five to 10 years. Digirad's cost-effective solid-state technology can provide faster diagnoses leading to more effective treatment. The company is confident that its core technology will revolutionize the gamma camera market in the same way that other solid-state innovations changed industries such as computers, televisions and radios, and expects the technology can be applied to areas outside the world of medicine. These will not only help produce new sources of revenue, but enable the company to make a significant contribution in a wide variety of markets.

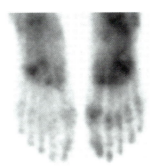

One such area is materials analysis — the detector can be used to look for cracks in airplane engines, oil well logging, nuclear weapons surveying, environmental monitoring and geological surveying, or in industrial X-ray for food processing and for airport baggage scanners for weapons detection. Digirad's core technology could also make it easier to inspect nuclear facilities in countries where access time is limited.

Digirad's solid-state innovations bode well for the company, which is well positioned to enter the 21st century as a leader in this exciting new technology.

(Far left) An example of images (feet) from the 2020*tc* Imager™

The portable 2020*tc* Imager™ can go anywhere!

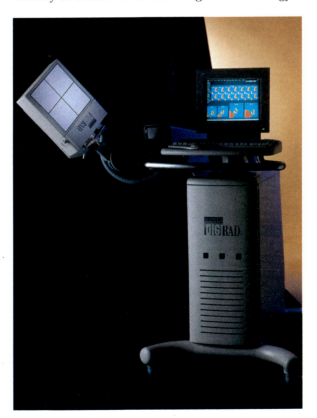

Digirad's 2020*tc* Imager™, the world's first solid-state gamma camera

Big Sister League of San Diego

On the corner of First and Redwood stands a home filled with compassion and care for women the world has forgotten. Since 1942, the Big Sister League has provided temporary housing to homeless women.

The League's origin dates back to World War II, when hundreds of women arrived in San Diego to say goodbye to husbands and boyfriends before they left for military duty overseas. Many, however, arrived after their men had left. Without a place to stay or the funds to return home, their only choice was to live on the streets. The city of San Diego provided overnight housing in the local jail for these women, considered to be vagrants. They became known as "waffle ladies" because of the marks left by sleeping on beds without mattresses.

Concerned about the treatment of the women, Ms. Fannie Anderson Woods established the first Big Sister Home. Located at 1769 Front Street, it became San Diego's first women's shelter. Ms. Woods, then 70, realized these women needed more than a place to sleep. She worked to help each woman find financial assistance, either from family or funds left for them by their husbands.

Eventually, freeway construction forced the League to move to Banker's Hill in 1956. The large brown two-story house was designed by Emmor Weaver, a protege of Frank Lloyd Wright. Due to an increased need for housing, the League acquired another house in Hillcrest in 1996. This house also provides for women with children.

Today, many of the women suffer from abuse and/or mental illness. While the reasons the homeless need assistance have changed over the years, the League's program remains basically the same. The main purpose is to provide physical and emotional care for the women as well as refine the skills they will need to return to an independent state. This can often take more than a year of continued assistance and support.

In 1976, the Big Sister League expanded its programs to assist high-risk girls, ages 6-17, in San Diego. They concluded that a mentor program for girls dealing with issues of abandonment, substance abuse and domestic violence could prevent later problems in life. Interested women are screened and carefully matched with a high-risk girl. These matches often last for years and have made significant differences in both the adult's life as well as the girl's.

A nonprofit organization, the Big Sister League depends on grants and donations to meet its budget. Despite difficult times a few years ago, the organization proudly states that it has never closed its doors. It's been a friend to the military and a resource to hospitals, mental health professionals and law enforcement throughout San Diego County. Perhaps the greatest need met by the Big Sister League is restoring self-esteem and dignity to women and young girls who have lost all hope.

When this original Horton House on Front Street was rezoned to become the middle of Interstate 5, the Big Sister League moved to its second location in Banker's Hill.

A women's libber, Ms. Fannie Anderson Woods dedicated more than 20 years of her life to providing a temporary home for women in San Diego.

Dr. Alan M. Blum, D.C.

Overlooking Interstate 8 in Mission Valley is the office of Dr. Alan M. Blum, D.C., who has practiced chiropractic care in San Diego since 1976. Many of his patients come to him after all other medical options have failed. Dr. Blum wants patients to consider chiropractic care first and bring this 100-year-old profession to the forefront of health care needs.

Upon initial examination of a patient, Dr. Blum will determine the patient's health care needs and utilize natural healing techniques to return the body to optimum performance. Today's environment puts three primary areas of stress on the human body — biochemistry (food, water, toxins); structure (physical traumas to the body); and emotion (reactions to situations). Each component feeds upon its counterparts and eventually impedes the healthy functioning of the body. The positive news is that this interplay also plays a key part in the healing process.

Dr. Blum became involved in Total Body Modification (TBM) while attending a seminar in 1984 on functional physiology, and he has been actively involved with this treatment process ever since. TBM is the brainchild of Drs. Victor Frank and Hal Havlick and operates by treating the body as if it were a computer exposing the potential for the functional maintenance and healing of the body. By finding the "bugs" in the system, Dr. Blum can return the body to its optimum performance. Some of the areas in which TBM has seen positive results include strengthening the immune system, normalizing blood pressure, reducing allergies, and improving blood sugar issues.

Contact Reflex Analysis (CRA) is another curative program for patients that was developed by Dr. Versendaal, D.C. over 25 years ago. CRA is the process of analyzing and correcting deficiencies in the structural, physical and nutritional needs of the body and allows the doctor to use the body's reflexes to determine the root cause of a specific health problem.

CRA targets the 75 known reflex areas on the skin that represent the body's organs, glands and bone structure. CRA shows that many health issues are due to an interruption of energy to the reflexes. The reflex acts as an overloaded circuit breaker impeding the normal flow of energy. Once the area of concern is uncovered, the doctor can create a program of structural and nutritional support to aid the body in the healing process.

Another technique Dr. Blum utilizes in treating the entire patient is Applied Kinesiology (AK), developed by Dr. George Goodheart. Thanks to the work of Dr. Goodheart, the extension of the branches of AK have resulted in such key healing techniques as TBM, RNA (Reflex Nutritional Assessment), NHT (Natural Healing Technique) and CRA — all of which represent the energy healing techniques of the future.

Besides his work with his patients, Dr. Blum has been active in the community since coming to San Diego and was one of the key charter members in the Mission Valley Chamber of Commerce.

To quote Napoleon Hill, Dr. Blum feels that "Anything the mind of man can conceive and believe, it can achieve." The healing techniques that use the body's energy to pinpoint the cause of many health issues are a leap in that direction.

Coleman College

The success of Coleman College and the growth of San Diego have not been mutually exclusive chronicles.

By wisely specializing in an emerging field, implementing an innovative teaching method, and being in the right place at the right time, Coleman College has served as San Diego's educational gateway to the Information Age for more than 35 years.

When husband and wife Coleman and Lois Furr founded the college in downtown San Diego in 1963, they had little idea that their visionary educational model might one day serve as an academic springboard to San Diego's emergence as a major software player. After running their school for several years, in the mid-70s they decided to focus exclusively on computer training. That decision stamped them as pacesetters.

"When you're trying to serve seven or eight curriculums, it's hard to do a truly great job on all of them," says Coleman College President Scott Rhude. "But when you can focus on one, you can really make a statement."

That statement is not only reflected in the school's motto, "Dreams into reality," but achieved through its unique inverted curriculum, in which students take their specialized, skills-oriented courses first so that they can enter the job market quickly and begin earning income. They can return later to fulfill degree requirements in the evening. Coleman was one of the first schools to utilize this now-accepted teaching method. Currently the school is best known for turning out well-trained computer professionals who are able to cope with rapidly changing technology in the workplace. That's because in addition to the 55 full-time instructors, the school employs 50 working professionals as part-time teachers.

"We not only teach fundamentals and concepts," says Rhude, "we also teach them how to learn, so that they can pick up all the emerging technology."

It is an approach that has helped give Coleman College its stellar reputation within the computer industry. Enrollment has flourished, and the school continues to grow. The school moved from downtown San Diego to Old Town, and then to La Mesa in 1982, occupying 70,000 square feet of facilities

on a site which once housed a bowling alley and which the Furrs never thought they would fully utilize. Today, the school is running out of space and is considering expanding or relocating for additional space. In 1986, a branch campus in San Marcos was opened to serve the growing population of San Diego's North County.

An embodiment of Coleman's growth can also be found in the Coleman Foundation, a sister organization to the nonprofit coeducational institution. Still run by Coleman and Lois Furr, the Coleman Foundation supports a wide range of charities in the San Diego area.

Whether it is in the workplace, classroom or community, Coleman College and San Diego are sure to continue their mutually beneficial alliance.

Coleman College's main campus is located in La Mesa in the Coleman Education Center. The College was founded in 1963 and specializes in computer education.

Coleman College provides extensive hands-on training in a wide range of computer languages, applications and equipment.

De Anza Bay Resort

Over 38 years ago, in 1960, Herbert Gelfand, a real estate attorney from Los Angeles, rented a cottage in south Mission Bay for his family's summer vacation. As one summer vacation in San Diego led to another, Mr. Gelfand looked into buying a cottage to rent out when his family was not using it.

In the process, he became interested in De Anza Trailer Harbor. Finally, in 1969, Herb Gelfand and his partner Blaine Quick formed a limited partnership and purchased the mobile home park, beginning what would become a cornerstone of the Mission Bay business community.

De Anza Trailer Harbor was built in 1954 on land leased from the city. At that time, mobile homes were considered mobile and nonresidential. When the partnership bought the lease, the city suggested they change the use to something more appropriate, like a hotel. Since 1972, the partnership has been submitting and revising proposals.

In 1977, the partnership purchased what is now known as Campland on the Bay, an RV park. Herb's son, Michael Gelfand, helped him manage both Campland and the mobile home park, as well as over 40 other properties (valued at over $200 million) that Herb had acquired through his management company, De Anza Group.

Michael Gelfand eventually took on more responsibilities and became the company president in 1990. In 1989, De Anza Group purchased the Mission Bay Golf Course, which is adjacent to the mobile home park. In 1994, the Gelfands sold a portion of the company holdings and Michael formed a new company, Terra Vista Management.

The name Terra Vista, "earth view," reflects Michael Gelfand's focus on an ecological and caring approach toward property management. His most recent hotel proposal for the mobile home park incorporates those ideals. If approved by the city of San Diego, building could begin sometime in the early portion of 2004.

De Anza Harbor Resort Mobile Home Park

Designed with the assistance of an ecological consultant, the 600-room hotel will include a 10-acre public park, and bike and jogging paths running around the entire property. A strong supporter of the ecological balance of the bay, Gelfand's plan is to extend the habitat of the Kendall-Frost Preserve past Campland on the Bay into the hotel and its grounds.

All the newest innovations in energy efficiency, resource conservation and water recycling will be incorporated into the design. All plant life will be indigenous or drought-resistant and compatible with local wildlife. To protect the wildlife, nontoxic materials will be used in the construction and operation of the hotel. Toxic herbicides and pesticides will be eliminated since runoff containing those poisons can harm the flora and fauna of the bay.

It is the partnership's hope that as other Mission Bay businesses renew their leases, they will add similar environmentally friendly changes into their operations. Terra Vista Management operates from the belief that business can be both ecologically as well as economically sound. In this way, it will be doing its part to usher in a healthier future for San Diego.

Campland on the Bay

Peter K. Hellwig, DDS & Associates

Dr. Peter Hellwig and his talented staff are ready to help patients with their dental needs.

Dr. Hellwig is a visionary — one who believes that being a dentist means far more than just cleaning and repairing teeth. This passionate, University of California-trained dentist has established the type of practice he believes should be the standard. Having patients become active parts of the dental care team, rather than passive recipients, allows them to achieve high levels of dental health.

Dr. Hellwig has practiced dentistry in the greater San Diego area since 1969. In 1973, he received a Fellowship in the Academy of General Dentistry. He is a Fellow and Diplomat of the International Congress of Oral Implantologists, and a member of the American Dental Association, the International Association of Orthodontics and the American Association of Implant Dentistry.

His dedication to his art and a passion for continuing education motivates Dr. Hellwig to study new approaches to cosmetic and restorative dentistry, a perfect way for this multitalented man to combine his diverse interests and provide care options. Today, his practice extends from general dentistry to implantology, periodontics and cosmetic reconstruction.

Dr. Hellwig believes a patient's knowledge about the cause, care and prevention of a condition is essential. During dental cleanings, for example, he and his team conduct microscopic screenings for disease-associated bacteria — a valuable, proven procedure used for years. Using this diagnostic tool, plus others, patients are shown hands-on ways to prevent further tooth decay and gum disease.

This proactive approach is the foundation of his nonsurgical treatment regime for periodontal disease. While some dentists routinely cut out infected tissue, when possible, Dr. Hellwig treats the cause rather than the symptoms of dental disease, attaining a more permanent solution to chronic and systemic periodontal disease. Infectious oral bacteria have also been linked to heart disease, premature birth and other systemic conditions as reported in the *New England Journal of Medicine*. While this nonsurgical approach may take more time and more patient involvement, it often prevents disfiguring surgery of the gums and results in a healthy, natural smile and better general health.

Perhaps the most exciting advancement is implantology, in which Dr. Hellwig has become board qualified. Oral implants act as the equivalent of new tooth roots upon which fixed replacement teeth are secured, thus replacing missing teeth with crowns and bridges to eliminate removable partials or loose dentures. All lab work is done by experienced technicians under Dr. Hellwig's strict supervision and control, using the finest porcelains, gold alloys and materials. He has many documented cases with before-and-after photos at his office which have been shown at dental symposiums internationally.

From a routine cleaning to complete oral reconstruction, Hellwig and his highly-trained and experienced staff work with each patient to create a treatment plan that fits the individual's budget, lifestyle and situation. Various forms of sedation (and even general anesthesia) are available to guarantee compassionate, gentle, health-centered care — even for fearful patients.

Dr. Hellwig enjoys designing smiles, and receives great pleasure from the friendships he's cultivated with his local and international patients.

Environmental Health Coalition

Fighting toxic pollution. Protecting public health. Promoting environmental justice.

Founded in 1980, Environmental Health Coalition (EHC) has grown into a high-profile advocacy organization, well known in the San Diego/Tijuana region for its direct and effective approach to confronting and solving tough toxic pollution problems. EHC's success has drawn a substantial local membership base of support and national recognition as a leader in the environmental justice arena.

Whether advocating for a community's right to know, monitoring the actions of government and industry or organizing with communities to speak out, EHC is the passionate voice that promotes solutions to the threat from toxic pollution in the San Diego/Tijuana region.

EHC believes that all people have the right to live, work and play in a safe and healthy environment. The organization operates three distinct campaigns that address the devastating effects of toxic pollution on land, air and water.

Communities of color and low income are disproportionately affected by toxic materials that are used by industry and the military and then discharged into the environment. **The Toxic Free Neighborhoods Campaign** works with affected residents to promote land use and planning reforms, relocation of hazardous industries to industrial zones, reduction of toxic air contaminants released by industry and the abatement of lead hazards in the home.

The Border Environmental Justice Campaign organizes people from both sides of the border to promote all workers' and community members' rights to know about chemicals used by the maquiladoras, to increase their capacity to influence conditions that directly affect their health and to demand the cleanup of abandoned and contaminated sites.

Years of neglect and misuse have taken their toll on the health of San Diego Bay. Pollution from shipyards, naval bases, oil spills and other industrial work has contributed to damaging the bay and devaluing this precious resource. Workers, bayside communities and conservationists are united under the **Clean Bay Campaign** to clean up, restore and protect San Diego Bay as a clean and healthy multiuse water resource capable of supporting a diverse range of activities.

Environmental justice — ensuring that workers, community members and environmental resources are protected from toxic contamination — is not possible without ensuring social and economic justice as well. In every campaign, EHC works in solidarity with social justice groups to guarantee that all aspects of high-quality life — affordable housing, health care, good jobs, effective education — are available to all people. EHC's presence will sustain the voice of the people of San Diego/Tijuana and will demand nothing less than a region that is truly a paradise for all San Diego's inhabitants.

EHC's community organizing stopped the use of toxic pesticides for produce imports and resulted in the nation's first ban on the use of methyl bromide for fumigation by the Port of San Diego.

EHC combined organizing, advocacy and vision to win the establishment of the South San Diego Bay National Wildlife Refuge.

An abandoned U.S.-owned lead smelter in Tijuana is just one of many toxic waste sites EHC is working to clean up.

Loma Alta Children's School

Lewis and Jeanne Sasaran, founders of Loma Alta Children's School, often participate in various holiday activities alongside staff, parents and children.

Loma Alta Children's School offers fun activities such as Camp Amiguitos, a vacation program that makes happy campers out of children.

The history of Loma Alta Children's School begins in 1967, with an enduring philosophy that promotes a developmentally appropriate program for young children, and focuses on the individual's abilities to succeed. For more than 30 years, its founders, Jeanne and Lewis Sasaran, have continually worked to reach goals and set new ones, while maintaining their school's highly acclaimed spot in the educational community. Their philosophy fosters the whole-child concept, respects each child as an individual and stimulates a child's natural interest in learning.

Jeanne and Lewis Sasaran's private school was based on a dream and built on tradition. Living in New Jersey in the 50s and early 60s, the Sasarans recognized a developing need for quality preschools as more families saw both parents enter the work force. A subsequent move to San Diego provided the opportunity for the couple's dream to become a reality and Loma Alta Children's School was born.

The Sasarans believed the school should be located in a quiet, safe, residential neighborhood, away from the hustle and bustle of traffic that comes with commercially zoned locations. Parents feel their children enjoy the homey setting and believe this environment is conducive to better development and learning.

To provide some of the necessary tools, Jeanne enrolled in the Early Childhood Education program at Pacific Oaks College in Pasadena, California. In 1970, she founded the first private, proprietary, infant-toddler program in the state. This program became the subject of her master's thesis in 1972, and the school became accredited in California by the National Association for the Education of Young Children in 1994.

During the 80s, the Sasarans added three buildings to house an expanded preschool, a computer lab that includes The Jump Start Learning System, a music room and kindergarten classrooms. Eight developmental programs were also implemented for infants, toddlers and prekindergarten children, as well as Loma Alta Primary School (K-3).

A vacation program, called Camp Amiguitos, (denoting "little friends" in Spanish) offers swimming, computer classes, art, games, sports, field trips and puppet shows for ages 5 to 12.

Many activities fill this half- to full-day child care center. Programs are planned around the child's developmental abilities. Infants and toddlers enjoy sensory interactive play using puzzles, books, music and art. Verbal and nonverbal communication skills are geared to each child's needs.

The school's mission statement specifies that the program seeks to help each child reach their personal best. The individualized education helps each child become more creative, independent thinkers and it is the Sasarans' hope that children will develop higher moral reasoning skills when exposed to ethics and principles in a warm and caring way.

Loma Alta Children's School offers this day-to-day support for children and their families. It is a commitment to childhood development and education that makes this school seem like home.

San Diego Maritime Museum

Much has happened since the *Euterpe*, now known as the *Star of India*, first slid down the launching ramp of Ramsey, Isle of Man, in 1863. This iron-hulled ship has known collisions and mutiny, a dismasting in the Indian Ocean and entrapment in both the ice of the Bering Sea and on the reefs of Maui. She circumnavigated the globe 21 times carrying both cargo and as many as 416 emigrants per trip, each time rounding Cape Horn, one of the longest and worst climatic sailing routes in history. She later worked as a Hawaiian vessel, carrying coal and sugar, and then in Alaska transporting salmon.

The San Diego Maritime Museum grew out of the acquisition of this graceful, square-rigged ship; the oldest, actively sailed merchant vessel afloat today. In 1926, an ambitious group of San Diegans, led by author Jerry MacMullen, purchased the ship and started to reclaim her from rust and decay. The *Star of India* became a National Historic Landmark in 1966 and her restoration was finished by 1976, in time to sail as part of the bicentennial celebration.

Located on San Diego's colorful and historic Embarcadero, the Maritime Museum transports guests into an almost forgotten era. Along with the *Star of India*, the museum houses the steam vessels *Berkeley* and *Medea*. Each ship is a living museum; collectively they are a tribute to the 19th century shipwright's art.

The *Berkeley* was built at the old Union Iron works in San Francisco and launched in 1898. She quickly became the first successful propeller-driven ferry on the West Coast. Steaming for the Southern-Pacific Railroad, the *Berkeley* shuttled passengers between San Francisco and Oakland with occasional runs to Alameda and Sausalito. Considered the best-preserved 19th century ferry-boat in existence, the Maritime Museum purchased her in 1973. With her original lavish woodwork and beautiful stained-glass clerestory, the *Berkeley* is indeed a treasure.

Built of steel, decked and housed with imported teak and finished inside with quarter-sawn English oak, the steam-driven *Medea* was originally owned by Macalister Hall who used the boat as a yacht. Converted to a warship as needed, *Medea* saw service in both world wars, under three navies and six national flags. She is only one of three surviving examples from the age of great steam yachts.

On the decks of the ships are hundreds of nautical artifacts, a fine collection of marine art, ships-in-bottles and the largest maritime research library in Southern California. Through these exhibits, demonstrations of nautical skills, docent-led tours and interactive activities for children, visitors gain an understanding and appreciation of maritime history: the building of maritime empires in the age of exploration, the rise of the San Diego tuna industry, the hardships of the emigrants packed in steerage on the *Star of India* and the vibration of the *Berkeley's* engines.

Through skilled, adaptive restoration, the San Diego Maritime Museum has given the city a great gift: a chance to celebrate decades of maritime history.

In 1999, the *Star of India* received one of the rarest and most prestigious awards given to ships, the World Ship Trust Award, which was presented by former-President Gerald Ford. This honor has been bestowed on only 11 other ships worldwide since 1980. The *Star of India* is San Diego's most-famed sailing attraction and part of the Maritime Museum.

St. Clare's Home

Children from St. Clare's Home

Sister Claire Frawley founded St. Clare's Home in 1983.

In 1983, Sister Claire Frawley founded St. Clare's Home. Before that time there was no shelter facility for homeless women and children in San Diego's North County. Sister Claire recognized the urgent need when a young pregnant woman with two small children arrived at the door of her youth ministry. They had not eaten in two days and were in despair. Armed with firm resolution and a prayer, Sister Claire took them home with her for the weekend. Shortly thereafter, she rented a house for this little family and another young mother in need. That was only the beginning. As they came to her door — the poor, the tired, the hungry and the hurt — Sister Claire found more beds and more food. And so Saint Clare's Home began.

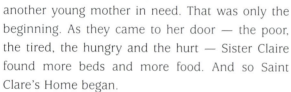

From the very beginning, St. Clare's Home has been a community leader in the prevention of child abuse and domestic violence. Ninety percent of St. Clare's residents have suffered from domestic violence, sexual abuse and substance abuse addiction, as a result of the street life they've endured.

It became the mission of Sister Claire Frawley to provide food, shelter, clothing, alcohol and drug rehabilitation, medical care, transportation, counseling, education and career guidance, legal advocacy, case management, child care, encouragement and unconditional love. Most of St. Clare's young residents have never known unconditional caring or lived in an environment of emotional support. Their emotional response to these acts of kindness is simply overwhelming. Their letters, poems of gratitude, pictures and art decorate Sister Claire's office and the hallways of St. Clare's administrative offices. Even the logo of St. Clare's Home is a loving reminder of a small child who simply drew a picture with the caption "I love my home." One can see this small picture on each piece of letterhead and business card at St. Clare's Home.

Over the years, St. Clare's Home has evolved into a public nonprofit, nondenominational agency serving over 4,000 homeless women and children. Today, St. Clare's operates eight residential shelter homes and four apartments supervised by trained case managers, as well as the Little Angels Learning Center for children's day care, play therapy and counseling services. St. Clare's answers over 1,000 calls for help each year and provides referrals and advocacy for those whose needs cannot be filled. No call goes unanswered; no cry goes unheard.

The Counseling and Resource Center provides the opportunity for homeless mothers to expand their educational horizons, enhances their perspective by broadening their exposure to positive life experiences, and helps motivate their desire for personal growth. The program focuses on sober living, good parenting, goal-setting and achievement while bolstering self-confidence — all steps toward their ultimate objective: emotional and financial independence.

Homeless women and children may stay at St. Clare's Home for two years. Although predicting the time it takes to repair a broken spirit is nearly impossible, St. Clare's Home sets a precedent for program longevity in San Diego County, providing additional aftercare services for up to three years to ensure a successful transition to independence. St. Clare's Home depends upon gifts from generous corporations, foundations, individuals and government grants.

Women's History Reclamation Project

"To change the future we must understand the past." — Lois Wyse

The Women's History Reclamation Project (the Project), established in San Diego in 1983, was the lifelong dream of its founder, Mary B. Maschal. For years, Mary B. Maschal created a living museum of women's history in her own home, filling virtually every room with historic documents, banners, posters and books. In 1995, at the request of family and friends, Mary held an open house to share with the women of San Diego her lifelong passion and dream of establishing a permanent museum of women's history in San Diego. The enthusiasm over Mary's collection generated by the open house, and the obvious need in San Diego for a museum dedicated solely to women and their stories, brought forth the renaissance of the Women's History Reclamation Project.

In 1996, the Project opened its doors to the public in the Art Union Building in Golden Hill. Today, with the help of many volunteers, the Project features a variety of changing exhibits and displays on women's history, a library and research archive, a speaker's bureau, monthly lectures open to the public and a collection of oral histories recording the life stories of women from around the country.

Of the Project's extensive collection of memorabilia from the American women's suffrage movement, one of the most impressive pieces is an original suffrage banner carrying the text of the Susan B. Anthony (19th) amendment to the U.S. Constitution. This amendment secured for women across the nation the right to vote. The banner is immediately visible to visitors and is a constant reminder of the many women and men who fought hard and long to win what should be the most basic political right of all citizens of a democratic nation: the right to vote. This banner represents just one of many diverse pieces owned by the Project which pay tribute to active and assertive women who have changed the world.

Unfortunately, history — as it is traditionally taught — focuses on events of a political, military and economic nature, usually to the exclusion of the historical contributions of women and people of color. While women have made, and continue to make, significant contributions to the more traditional record of "history," they have also been the primary keepers and guardians of culture and should be recognized and remembered in that light too. The Women's History Reclamation Project's mission is to educate and inspire present and future generations about the contributions of women by preserving, sharing and integrating their stories for a more complete understanding of history. This understanding of and respect for the past, and its significance in our lives and actions today, is one contribution that we may give to the world and to all its children for a better future.

"The Fabric of Women's Lives," one of the Project's exhibits, explored the history of women's fashion, including this glitzy saloon hall attire.

A large and diverse group of businesses combine to make San Diego one of the country's leading centers of technology innovation, development, manufacturing and employment.

Partners in
TECHN

San Diego
TECHNOLOGY

The Titan Corporation 408
Interventional Technologies, Inc. 412
Blue Sky Software 415
Dataskill. 416
Edge Semiconductor 418
HNC Software Inc. 420
Inacom Corporation 422
L-3 Communications Conic Division 424
National Decision Systems 426
SSC San Diego 428
Insight Electronics, LLC 430
Prism Lithographic Technologies. 431

The Titan Corporation

The Titan Corporation, established in 1981, is a leading provider of satellite communications, information technology solutions, and sterilization systems and services for commercial and government customers worldwide. The publicly held company (listed under the symbol TTN in the New York Stock Exchange) is located in San Diego and employs more than 2,200 employees. In 1998, Titan's revenues were $304 million.

The driving force behind the explosive growth of Titan has been Dr. Gene W. Ray, founder, president and chief executive officer. Prior to launching Titan, Dr. Ray served in a number of senior executive management positions with leading defense industry companies. He also spent two years as chief of the Strategic Division of the U.S. Air Force.

Titan's core business is defense information and communications systems. The company's strategy continues to focus on markets offering high growth potential and a strong contract backlog. Titan's defense business is focused on two categories: design, development and delivery of specialized information technology products to U.S. and international defense customers; and providing on-site and off-site engineering and technical services requiring an in-depth understanding of defense operations and requirements. Employees frequently work side by side with military personnel providing technical support at locations in the United States and abroad.

Titan has four wholly owned subsidiaries:

Titan Technologies & Information Systems (TTIS) — In 1997, Titan consolidated its defense information technology businesses into TTIS. TTIS provides innovative information technology systems and services to defense-related government agencies via information systems design, engineering and integration services, development of specialized products and prototypes, as well as systems installation, testing and maintenance.

Creative software systems enable businesses to reduce costs and expand capabilities.

Dr. Gene Ray, founder, president, and CEO of Titan Corporation

Titan Scan — This subsidiary focuses on developing and applying electron beam technology to sterilize disposable medical devices. Titan Scan provides turnkey systems and contract sterilization services to customers using SureBeam™, a patented sterilization process. SureBeam is a safe and reliable sterilization alternative to existing radioactive sources and hazardous chemical-based systems. SureBeam uses commercial electrical power to accelerate electrons and is as safe as a microwave oven.

It's anticipated that this technology will soon be used consistently to eradicate food-borne pathogens from foods, particularly for eliminating the E. coli threat in hamburger. Once the United States Department of Agriculture rule-making process is complete, it is expected that Titan's SureBeam process will be widely used for electronic meat pasturization.

Titan Scan also provides other services in the application of electron beam technology. These include product testing and dose mapping, conversion to electron beam processing, project feasibility analysis and system design development. For medical products, Titan Scan delivers turnkey sterilization systems for integration into the production process of the customer's plant and also operates its own contract service facilities.

Titan Software Systems (TSS) — TSS is a systems integrator delivering state-of-the-art technology and business software to commercial and nondefense government clients. Customers include large corporations in the telecommunications and financial areas, the Federal Aviation Administration, and other entities with large and often complicated system integration and data management needs.

TSS focuses on Enterprise Information Portals (EIP), e-Commerce, Enterprise Resource Planning (ERP) and Enterprise Infrastructures. EIP solutions, for example, help unlock information stored in ERP systems and Intranet Web sites, databases, legacy mainframe and client-server systems. Data from multiple sources is aggregated in data warehouses or data "marts," then made available across the enterprise in an organized, secure and searchable fashion. In 1998, TSS also began delivering e-Commerce solutions to companies in the areas of Internet Web site marketing and sales, electronic publishing and call center automation.

Other TSS services include:

Diverse technologies — Provides services for Internet/Intranet/Extranet technologies for PointCast™, electronic commerce and electronic publishing solutions;

Custom software applications — Delivers custom and integrated software solutions, work-flow management, client-server development and executive information systems;

Data management — Offers clients data administration, warehousing, mining, and interface architecture;

Systems management — Provides hosting operation and system administration of mission-critical applications such as network management, data warehouses and software distribution.

Linkabit Wireless — This subsidiary specializes in developing and producing advanced satellite ground terminals, satellite voice/data modems, networking systems and other products incorporating Demand Assigned Multiple Access (DAMA) technology used to provide bandwidth-efficient, cost-effective communications for commercial and government clients worldwide. Linkabit Wireless is a leading provider of DAMA, and a key DAMA product is the mini-DAMA terminal, which provides two channels of UHF satellite communication for up to 16 simultaneous users.

Linkabit Wireless' leading product, Xpress Connection™, provides low-cost voice, facsimile and data services. The product is ideal for remote areas. Linkabit has also joined a consortium led by Alcatel Telspace, a French subsidiary of Alcatel, which is designing a satellite-based alternative to conventional telephone systems. The consortium's Multi Media Asia (M2A) "next generation" system will provide feature-rich telephone, facsimile and high-speed Internet access to homes and businesses in suburban and rural areas at a price competitive with wireline services. Unlike traditional wireline systems, however, these terminals can be quickly installed without the expense and time required to build out wire systems across vast geographic areas.

Linkabit continues to leverage its experience in rural telephony to selectively pursue private networking opportunities in developing countries. In Thailand, for example, Linkabit Wireless provided its multiport DAMA modems for use in a national communications network for the Bank of Agriculture and Agricultural Cooperatives.

In addition to the four core subsidiaries, Titan has an "Emerging Technologies" division that identifies promising Titan technologies that don't immediately fit within the company's core businesses. Titan

Secure military communications in remote areas are made possible by Titan technology.

Digital fingerprint systems and mammography testing are among the high-potential businesses being nurtured.

helps these businesses by either licensing their proprietary technology or creating a new company in which Titan retains an interest. In recent years, a number of these companies have been "incubated" by Titan — these spinoffs continue to provide potential for ongoing revenue streams. Examples include:

Flash Comm, Inc. — Provides a unique system for tracking trucks, cars and trains to follow location, temperature, security and other key parameters.

IPivot — Speeds data flow within Internet environments by reducing computer server blockages. Operating funds for IPivot were raised through venture capital partners.

Tomo Therapeutics — Utilizes X-Ray Needle™ technology developed and patented by Titan to deliver energy from the tip of the needle directly into a tumor without damaging the healthy surrounding tissue. Titan retains an equity stake and receives product royalties.

Wave Systems — Provides specialized electronic product distribution and metering systems embedded in hardware platforms such as set-top boxes and Internet access devices. Wave Systems provides encryption, decoding, usage monitoring and detailed billing information to its users.

In 1998, Titan made a number of key acquisitions:

DBA Systems, Inc. — Founded in 1963, Melbourne, Florida-based DBA is a developer and manufacturer of digital imaging products, electro-optical systems and threat simulation/training systems, primarily for the defense and intelligence communities.

Validity Corporation — An information services technologies company, Validity provides systems engineering and integration, software engineering, network technologies and test and evaluation services. The company maintains significant operations close to customer facilities in Maryland and Arizona.

Horizons Technology, Inc. — Founded in 1977, the company provides systems engineering and program management services, computer systems integration and high-end software. Horizons also developed a commercial software services business, which provides digital map information that can be purchased over the Internet. Principal locations are in Billerica, Massachusetts, and Melbourne, Florida.

VisiCom, Inc. — Established in 1988, the company is a hardware and software product innovator, value-added reseller and systems engineering company dedicated to providing real-time open architecture computing solutions. Products and services are designed to meet the needs of embedded real-time systems for industrial customers and governmental agencies. Company headquarters is in San Diego, California.

Delfin Systems — The Santa Clara, California, company, launched in 1984, provides systems engineering, program management services, computer systems integration and high-end software primarily for the U.S. Department of Defense. Core strengths are in intelligence analysis, computer forensics, information security, and enterprise communications and connectivity.

Transnational Partners II, LLC — Founded in 1995, Transnational Partners provides enterprise infrastructure and ERP solutions for major companies. The company provides the software infrastructure allowing interoperability of ERP system implementations, legacy systems and new software products.

The company entered into a joint venture with Afronetwork, located in Cotonou, Benin. Afronetwork has been engaged by the Office of Post and Telecommunications (OPT) of the Republic of Benin to build a communications system that includes fiber optics, VSAT and wireless local loop solutions.

Titan will be deploying a comprehensive network management and central control center adjacent to the OPT's international satellite earth station complex. The Titan-designed and furnished center will also provide national and international connectivity, interurban capacity as well as telephone, Internet, fax and data services in rural areas for the first time. Installation of personal computers in Benin will further develop the local skills necessary to take maximum advantage of the latest developments in data communications, electronic messaging and Internet-related technologies.

Titan was selected by the U.S. Army Aviation and Missile Command in Huntsville, Alabama, to provide Electro-Optical/Infrared (EO/IR) and Anti-Armor Threat System assessment, modification and enhancement. The contract includes requirements for intelligence analysis/evaluation, design, development, production, testing and deployment of high-fidelity threat simulators and simulations for EO/IR air defense missile systems and anti-tank missile systems.

Titan also works with the National Imagery and Mapping Agency in Chantilly, Virginia. Titan provides engineering development and enhancements for a previously delivered government support system, as well as the continued operation and maintenance of that system.

Titan is furnishing a linear electron accelerator to be used for radiation chemistry research at the Commissariat a l'Energie Atomique (CEA) at Saclay, France. Titan Scan will provide the system, which utilizes a precisely formed electron beam and diagnostic instruments to characterize the beam, to test the radiolytic effects in various media.

In 1998, Titan invested in Sakon, an international telephone service provider and communications company providing "next generation" telephone and Internet services. Sakon is a North Bergen, New Jersey, company specializing in providing telecommunications and Internet services in developing countries of Africa, Latin America, Southeast Asia and other areas where fiber-based systems are not feasible or not yet deployed.

Together, Titan and Sakon will provide carrier, direct dial rural telephony, international fax, conference calling, voice over Internet Protocol (IP), virtual communications centers and virtual private network services to developing nations. Sakon will use Titan's satellite communications technology as its primary international telecommunications infrastructure.

Titan is well-posed for growth in the 21st century. The company's most valuable assets are its employees — their broad array of skills is paramount to meeting current challenges and achieving future growth. The work force expanded from 1,400 in 1997 to 2,200 at the end of 1998. More than 50 employees received commendation letters from various government agencies in 1998. Collectively, Titan's employees have contributed not only to the success of the company, but also the customers they serve. Titan's long-term objective has not changed since the company's inception — to provide growth for its shareholders and employees.

Titan employees work side-by-side with military personnel providing technical support in this country and around the world.

Interventional Technologies, Inc.

Since its inception in 1984, San Diego-based Interventional Technologies, Inc. has been an industry pioneer in developing microsurgical devices and approaches that have improved clinical results at lower overall costs. Chairman and Chief Executive Officer Bob Reiss, a recognized leader in interventional cardiology, cofounded the company along with Carl Hays, a private investor. SMC Corporation of Japan, and two Palo Alto venture capital firms —Sutter Hill Ventures, and Wilson, Sonsini, Goodrich and Rosati — facilitated early venture capital funding. Many of the core executives, including Reiss, participated in the successful evolution of the medical device industry in San Diego. These included companies like Sharp Labs, IVAC, IMED (Alaris) and Advanced Cardiovascular Systems (now part of Guidant).

Reiss has brought together from many of these companies a group of highly qualified, experienced professionals in varied fields that include metallurgy, chemistry, chemical engineering, mechanical engineering and bioengineering. Walk the halls at Interventional Technologies and one is apt to meet employees from Australia, China, Malaysia, Russia, the Philippines, Singapore, Taiwan, Thailand — more than two dozen countries worldwide. This diverse research and development team is reflective of San Diego's burgeoning multicultural biomedical industry.

Cardiovascular disease is the leading cause of death worldwide. In fact, in the United States, it's estimated that cardiovascular disease costs patients and businesses about $350 billion each year.

Although coronary bypass surgery has been a major breakthrough, the procedure has not been without both clinical and financial costs. Doctors began looking for less invasive approaches with better long-term outcomes. The next phase for treating coronary heart disease — interventional cardiology — was made possible with various engineering breakthroughs. Interventional cardiology enables cardiologists to treat the heart and blood vessels from inside the vessels themselves. In 1999, more than one million interventional procedures were performed worldwide.

New medical issues, however, now face doctors — restenosis (the reclosing of the artery after treatment, which about 30 to 50 percent of angioplasty patients experience) emerged as a new threat. This is a direct result of the trauma associated with angioplasty. The challenge is to create effective clinical treatments for cardiovascular disease while containing spiraling health care costs, especially those associated with repeat procedures.

Interventional Technologies' products are helping to combat this. The company's major contributions have been in the field of microprecision fabrication techniques as applied to cardiovascular products. Some of these include: guide catheters, guide wires, microsurgical dilatation catheters, site-specific drug delivery catheters (injecting drugs, gene therapy or radio-pharmaceuticals directly into the coronary artery wall) and a photo-mask-and-etch-on-a-tube chemical milling manufacturing process for cardiovascular stents.

Interventional Technologies has a core group of six patented products:

The Cutting Balloon™ — The company's flagship product, the Cutting Balloon uses microsurgical dilatation to open diseased arteries without provoking the hyperplasia that can lead to restenosis. Longitudinally mounted blades relieve the hoop stress in the artery. The balloon is folded to shield the blades and protect the vessel wall as the catheter is passed to and from the lesion.

The Infiltrator®/Irradiator™ — This product delivers a precisely controlled dose of a therapeutic compound directly into the arterial wall. Its injection ports are less than the diameter of a human hair and are shielded until the target site is reached. The Infiltrator/Irradiator is paving the way for innovative applications such as delivering gene therapy and radiotherapy into the arterial wall.

TEC® (Transluminal Extraction Catheter) System — The only device that simultaneously excises and extracts plaque and thrombi. Studies show lower rates of distal embolization and myocardial injury when TEC is used before angioplasty as compared to balloon angioplasty alone.

LP Stent™ — Stents are tiny metal scaffolds used to prop open diseased arteries treated with balloon angioplasty. While several companies manufacture and sell stents for coronary arteries, Interventional Technologies uses a unique design and patented manufacturing process to give the LP Stent the capability of penetrating and supporting the artery

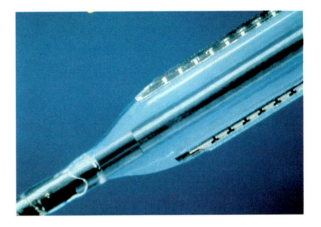

The Cutting Balloon,™ Interventional Technologies' flagship product, has incredibly small surface scalpels which facilitate microsurgical dilatation to open blocked arteries.

with less pressure-trauma, potentially reducing the rate of restenosis. The stent design improves vessel wall penetration and requires less delivery and final placement pressure. The LP Stent also has a much smoother surface finish and higher crush resistance. It is deployed with less pressure than needed to expand first or second generation stents. One version of the LP Stent is a covered stent, which when coupled with TEC atherectomy, represents a state-of-the-art solution to embolization problems associated with treating degenerated saphenous vein grafts.

TrackWire® — This family of guide wires uses proprietary processes and new aerospace materials to provide higher levels of control and support. TrackWire twists and turns to negotiate difficult vasculature at the doctor's command.

FullFlow® — A perfusion dilatation system, FullFlow mechanically dilates arteries without blocking blood flow. It represents one of the most significant improvements in angioplasty since cardiologists started using balloons in the late 1970s, and is opening up opportunities in radiotherapy applications.

The success of Interventional Technologies over the years is due to a number of factors. Seasoned product engineering and manufacturing process development teams have been instrumental in

The TrackWire® family of guidewires use proprietary processes and new aerospace materials to provide the higher levels of control and support.

design breakthroughs. The company provides an array of products that broaden physicians' options and create opportunities for more effective treatments. In addition, physicians are consulted on a regular basis in order to identify clinical needs that might be solved by the company's expertise in design and fabrication. In fact, individual physician input has been integral for most of Interventional Technologies' products.

Interventional Technologies is a true "Pacific Rim" company. About 70 percent of its sales are to Japan. Other key markets are China, Malaysia, Singapore, Korea, India and Taiwan. Many Asian nations don't develop their own medical device products, so Interventional Technologies anticipates a growing market in these areas over the next 10 years. The company also manufactures and distributes its products from Letterkenny, Ireland. The Irish manufacturing and distribution facility supplies customers in Africa, Canada, Europe and Latin America.

Although Interventional Technologies has recorded many breakthroughs, 1998 in particular was a very productive and active year. A St. Paul, Minnesota-based company signed an agreement with Interventional Technologies to provide its pericardial tissue cover on a nonexclusive basis. The company's TrackWire family of guide wires was approved for sale in the United States, Europe and Asia. The company's latest LP Stent product was awarded the CE Mark, facilitating sales in Europe, Canada and certain Asian countries. Finally, the company signed a letter of intention with a German biotech company for a unique gene therapy using the Infiltrator.

The FDA also approved Interventional Technologies' drug delivery catheter for a Phase 1 human clinical trial at the University of Alabama. The Infiltrator will be used to investigate the potential of using intramurally delivered ethyl alcohol to reduce restenosis associated with intracoronary stenting. Because the Infiltrator controls the injection of therapeutic agents directly into the arterial wall, it has advantages over alternative systems, including a reduction of adverse systemic effects, rapid and efficient drug delivery, and increased effectiveness of the therapeutic agent. Interventional Technologies believes the study will usher in a new era of cardiovascular medicine of site-specific drug, gene and radiopharmaceutical delivery and open new pathways for improving the prospects for those suffering from coronary artery disease.

Three other major news events highlighted the year. The company completed its first FullFlow clinical trials in Europe. Interventional Technologies was ISO 9001 certified. The certification applies to the company's operations in both San Diego and Murrieta, California; its operations in Ireland were previously certified. The certification will facilitate international sales efforts, as many countries now require independent ISO 9000 certification for medical device companies. Lastly, the company announced the publication of an important paper that explains the benefits of the Cutting Balloon angioplasty catheter.

As published in *Circulation* magazine (a journal of the American Heart Association), a study conducted by the Dokkyo University School of Medicine in Japan discovered that the Cutting Balloon induced less neutrophil activation, a clinical indicator of less vascular injury and subsequent inflammatory reaction. It suggested that less injury and inflammation might be the explanation for the lower restenosis rate after Cutting Balloon angioplasty as compared to conventional procedures.

Looking ahead into the 21st century, Interventional Technologies will continue to be an industry leader and contribute to the community. Interventional Technologies and its employees support many San Diego cultural activities including the many museums and thematic institutes located here. Interventional Technologies will continue to develop engineering and technology solutions in interventional cardiology that will help medical progress, reduce health care costs, improve the quality of life — and save lives.

The LP Stent™ is deployed with less pressure than needed to expand first or second generation stents. It is manufactured by a chemical milling process.

The Infiltrator® / Irradiator™ Delivery System delivers a precisely controlled dosage of a therapeutic compound or radiopharmaceutical directly into the artery wall.

Blue Sky Software

Blue Sky Software Corporation creates software development solutions that are used by a wide range of computer professionals to create application Help systems and user assistance. Blue Sky Software is an ideal example of a San Diego corporation whose culture and values are not only reflected in its reputation in the industry, but also by its innovative and motivational employee programs. Through monthly bonuses for all employees, annual company-wide "super bonus" awards, stock options, family picnics and team trips, Blue Sky Software makes a concerted effort to ensure that all employees share in the rewards of the company's success and industry leadership.

Founded in a La Jolla home just steps away from its present headquarters adjacent to beautiful La Jolla cove, Blue Sky Software realized early on that the Windows platform would see rapid growth; as a result, it developed WinMaker®, the first C/C++ code generator (a tool that generates computer code, making the programming process for software development faster and easier). Always a step ahead of its competition, Blue Sky Software soon turned its expertise to the development of Help authoring solutions. The birth of RoboHELP® revolutionized the creation of great-looking online Help systems and printed manuals that are highly functional and easy to use.

Since Blue Sky's founding in 1990, over 250 million online Help systems created with Blue Sky Software products such as RoboHELP Office, RoboHELP Classic and RoboHELP HTML, are currently in use, making the company a worldwide leader in Help authoring solutions.

Blue Sky Software has won more than 40 national and international industry awards, competing against industry giants like Microsoft, Oracle, and Sybase. Some of these achievements include winning *PC Week's* Best of Comdex Award and Deloitte & Touche LLP's recognition of Blue Sky Software as one of the 50 fastest-growing companies in Southern California.

As computer operating systems continue to evolve, Blue Sky Software maintains its position on the cutting edge of technology. It was the first company to release a WYSIWYG Help authoring tool specifically designed for the HTML Help standard introduced for online Help files in Windows 98. Blue Sky Software also developed WebHelp — the first full-featured and cross-platform HTML-based Help solution. This Help format is exclusive to Blue Sky Software, and enables Help systems based on HTML or Hypertext Markup Language (the primary language of the Internet) to run on any operating platform in-

cluding Unix, Macintosh, and Windows. WebHelp allows authors to create dynamic Help projects and information systems that can be viewed on almost any computer, using any major web browser.

Blue Sky Software's customer base expands daily as a growing number of users are employing the company's products for the development of intranet information systems and Internet-based user assistance, in addition to their more traditional uses for application Help. With the exciting changes in technology, Blue Sky Software continues to grow in San Diego and serve as an industry success story.

Blue Sky Software is headquartered in the heart of La Jolla, just steps from beautiful La Jolla Cove.

DATASKILL

Every day millions of ordinary-appearing business transactions are routed, recorded, expedited and analyzed using the expertise and complex data systems integrated by a rapidly growing technology solution company named DATASKILL.

Located just a few miles north of San Diego in beautiful Del Mar, this behind-the-scenes company is one of the older organizations in the turbulent field of solutions integration. In the rapidly evolving environment of information management, not many companies can match DATASKILL's two decades of creating successful solutions to data-handling challenges. DATASKILL, one of the country's fastest growing privately-held companies, provides business computer solutions which means they can do anything from taking full responsibility for a systems integration project to deploying the company's computer professionals — programmers, systems engineers, business analysts and project managers — on a contract basis.

President and Chief Technical Officer Nigel Hook (left)

Nigel Hook, originally from Northampton, England, founded DATASKILL in 1981 with the original goal of providing business applications development and cutting-edge technology consulting to companies in the financial sector. Since those early days, the company has broadened and shifted its focus to include a major practice in the retail industry.

In 1984 the company moved its headquarters to Del Mar. "Coming from England, I find the climate in Del Mar particularly appealing," comments President and Chief Technical Officer Hook. "Our location also helps us to attract and hire the best and brightest people in the industry."

DATASKILL's core team of about 85 people includes engineers, programmers, systems analysts, marketing experts and administrators. In addition to the technical and management prowess of its people, the company has a lineup of business partners that reads like a who's who in the data management and information systems industry: IBM (Premier level partner), Microsoft (certified solutions provider), SUN (catalyst developer program), AOL/Netscape (solutions expert), Lotus and Oracle.

With a pool of extraordinary talent and a stack of powerful business alliances, DATASKILL has built an impressive customer base. Clients include LEGOLAND, Holiday Inn Worldwide, Qualcomm, Promus Corporation (Embassy Suites, DoubleTree), San Diego Gas and Electric, Sony, Mazda, Scripps Health Care, Bank of America, Wells Fargo, Union Bank of California, Circle K, Kmart, Marshall's, CSK Auto (Kragen Auto Parts), Nike, Arby's, Foodmaker (Jack in the Box) and Pepsi.

The major portion of DATASKILL's customers look to the company to provide the expert technical and management teams to create software, install hardware, integrate the components with custom interfaces, test every aspect of the system, write operations manuals and train personnel. In other words, DATASKILL provides sophisticated, fully integrated, turnkey business solutions using — and often creating — the most advanced technology available.

With extensive experience in transactional and operational systems employing reusable object technology, scalable three-tier architecture and open Internet standards, DATASKILL continues to achieve excellence in custom integrated and automated systems. DATASKILL's capabilities extend to the specialized skills of EIS, DSS, OLAP and data mining with expertise in many different toolsets including DB2 Universal Database, Oracle, Visual Warehouse and Intelligent Miner. Furthermore, the company has been a pioneer in deploying platform-independent, browser-based applications with 100 percent Java solutions.

In addition to this wide spectrum of services, DATASKILL has the capability of augmenting a customer's technical staffing needs on either a temporary or permanent basis. The firm also sells software and hardware with emphasis on IBM products.

In a recent contract with a large retailer, DATASKILL created an application for warehousing detailed POS data with the capabilities for trending seasonal patterns and customer preferences along with detailed data mining to instantly identify the vital information required for highly competitive positioning. This is typical of the way DATASKILL combines its vast resources with the latest technological innovations to create successful solutions to increasingly complex business challenges. It is, therefore, no surprise that the organization is growing fast. The company is particularly proud of being named to *Inc.* magazine's 500 Fastest Growing Companies in America (ranked number 273 in 1996), one of only six companies in San Diego County to make the list.

DATASKILL has heart as well as brains. The firm plays an important role in the American Red Cross through the direct involvement of one of the company's managers in the San Diego/Imperial counties chapter. One outcome of this involvement is a Red Cross e-commerce Web site created by DATASKILL and IBM where customers are able to order courses, first aid kits and disaster-preparedness packs as well as make donations online. DATASKILL provided their services for this Web site at no cost to the Red Cross.

Symbolic of the company's high performance approach to data and information management, DATASKILL is one of the sponsors of the CITGO Supergard Offshore Powerboat Racing Team. In fact, Nigel Hook, the company's president, founded this team and makes up half the boat's cockpit crew, controlling the throttles of the boat's two 1200 horsepower engines as it races through the waves at over 120 miles per hour. The state-of-the-art epoxy/Baltek-core Scarab prototype race boat incorporates the latest in safety, speed and economy, factors that reflect DATASKILL's approach to business solutions. This is no dilettante weekend racing: in 1997 and 1998 this team won the APBA national and world championships after taking first place in 10 of the 14 races in which it competed. The team works closely with CITGO as a major corporate sponsor of the Muscular Dystrophy Association.

DATASKILL's newest direction represents a leap into the brave new world of Internet commerce. With its proprietary framework, DATASKILL can provide customers with the ability to deploy many of its supply chain and customer service applications by leveraging Internet technology. Enabled by DATASKILL's framework and software from business partner IBM, customers now have access to the unprecedented capability of truly paperless inter-business transactions. Any organization with widely-dispersed multiple operations will obtain particularly strong benefits from such a system.

In the realms of planning, project management, authoring, knowledge transfer and programming support, DATASKILL continues to provide the long-term commitment to its customers to provide a reliable and consistent resource for making the best decisions at all crossroads.

Symbolic of DATASKILL's high-performance approach, the World Champion Offshore Powerboat Team CITGO Supergard throttled by DATASKILL President Nigel Hook.

Edge Semiconductor

Edge Semiconductor, a wholly owned subsidiary of Semtech Corporation, may have begun as an ordinary start-up company, but it wasn't long before it began setting its own standards of excellence.

The semiconductor company was founded in March 1994 by eight employees that had been working in a research and development division of Brooktree in San Diego, a mixed-signal semiconductor supplier. When Brooktree decided it no longer wanted to fund the division, the eight employees decided to band together and branch out on their own. The founders had developed a variety of semiconductor products before they left Brooktree, but some of those products hadn't yet reached production. When they started Edge Semiconductor in Sorrento Valley, the founders began with this handful of unfinished products and some ideas for a few more.

The company's key turning point and big breakthrough came in April 1994 when it launched a product known in the industry as a driver and receiver, which creates a signal with Automated Test Equipment (ATE). In essence, Edge Semiconductor is part of a big food chain. An ATE machine tests other semiconductors' chips before they are placed on the circuit boards of PCs or inside other products. Edge Semiconductor sells the chips to ATE manufacturers, who then sell the tester to a computer chip maker. The semiconductor company proceeds to sell the chips to a PC maker, who then sells the PC to the consumer. The machine can test all kinds of chips, particularly microprocessor and computer chips. The tests performed are designed to detect any defect that can occur during the semiconductor manufacturing process.

While its customers are all over the world, most of Edge Semiconductor's employees are San Diegans. Despite a small semiconductor industry in San Diego, Edge Semiconductor was able to recruit its talented employees from America's Finest City, not

Edge Semiconductor employees pose for their annual Christmas card photo, which is sent out to all customers around the holiday season.

Silicon Valley. And while the semiconductor market is small in San Diego, the ATE market is even smaller. "There are only about three companies in the world that do what we do," explained Wylie Plummer, Edge Semiconductor president and chief executive officer. "It's a very focused, very technical area with specialized products that we create, which was one of the advantages we had starting out. Customer relationships are very important. We brought those over from Brooktree to Edge Semiconductor."

The company's product strategy has been based on the idea that large semiconductor companies tend to have methods of generating chips which cover the bulk of the world's needs but fail to provide solutions for customers with special requirements, such as ATE customers. By the fall of 1994, Edge Semiconductor had raised its first outside financing on a local level, a $400,000 contribution. On its one-year anniversary in March 1995, the company employed 11 people and posted sales of $1.4 million. And unlike many start-up companies, it broke even in its first year of operation. Edge Semiconductor's success continued into 1996, a year in which the company raised an additional $1 million and relocated its operations to Willow Creek Road in Scripps Ranch. On its two-year anniversary, its sales had increased to $4.2 million.

Much of the company's accomplishments were attributed to its eight founding members that included Plummer, John Muramatsu, Stuart Molin and Jeff King. Muramatsu, vice president of engineering, managed the company's vital design and test engineering duties during its infancy. Molin was director of technology development, and King proved instrumental in defining Edge's new products. In October 1997, the company was nominated for an Electronics Industry Recognition Award from the American Electronics Association for emerging growth companies. That same month and year, the company was sold for $50 million to Semtech of Newbury Park, California, an analog semiconductor company. With $15 million in annual sales by then, Edge Semiconductor's employees still owned a large share of the company when it was sold to Semtech.

"The time from start-up to selling was pretty quick. It was a success and didn't take long," Plummer commented. "It was our goal to sell the company or go public; we decided to sell. In the semiconductor business you have to be good at defining products and giving customers what they want. As a start-up company, that was key to our survival and success."

By the beginning of 1999, Edge Semiconductor had grown in five short years from eight employees to 38, selling 25 products. One of the reasons the company has been successful is because its products cater to an extremely specialized market. The products it creates — like the driver and receiver — are particularly unique in that consumers or its competitors can't purchase them anywhere in the world except from Edge Semiconductor. Yet by giving its customers not only what they want, but what they need, the company has played an integral role in helping life-changing products such as PCs function properly because of its contributions to ATE.

In the future, the semiconductor and electronics industry is expected to continue to blossom as the use of chips and technology increases in order to make people's lives better. Chips are being used in everything from shoes to credit cards. The future will also include Edge Semiconductor expanding its horizons by creating new and better products for its industry as well as broadening the appeal of its speciazed chips that have made the company so successful, so quickly.

"Technology changes have caused us to continue improving our products," Plummer said. "PCs get faster every year so these testers get faster. We have to keep up with the new and faster microprocessors and memory chips that are being created and demanded by the world.

"We're doing our part to increase the speed of PCs and the Internet," Plummer added. "We're definitely a piece of the whole puzzle that's required to make communications better."

A specialized, integrated circuit used in Automated Test Equipment

HNC Software Inc.

HNC Software, headquartered in San Diego, is the world's leading provider of Predictive Software Solutions for service industries such as insurance, retail, telecommunications, Internet commerce and financial services. Predictive software accurately predicts the needs and behaviors of individual customers by analyzing millions of transactions in real-time, and helps companies manage customer relationships throughout the entire customer lifecycle.

HNC Software provides companies with the insight they need to succeed by establishing new ways to attract and retain a high-value client base. HNC's Predictive Customer Relationship Management solutions help companies improve business practices by:

- Developing more profitable marketing plans;
- Improving customer service;
- Creating programs that mitigate risk and attrition;
- Optimizing store replenishment activities;
- Detecting fraudulent customer transactions.

History

Like many San Diego-based software companies, HNC Software traces its origins to the defense industry. When the company was launched in 1986, its charter was to develop software and hardware tools that used neural network and related technologies. Its customers were corporate R&D laboratories and U.S. defense and government intelligence agencies. HNC's research on neural networks and other advanced technologies spurred the creation of software that can "learn" and improve its predictive capabilities as its historical database increases in size. In 1990, HNC began adapting these tools to commercial and business applications.

Today, HNC Software is a global market provider of the leading:

- Web-enabled predictive merchandizing solutions for retailers;
- Bill repricing product for workers' compensation insurance;
- Automated e-mail response service;
- Predictive customer profitability management system in the bank card industry;
- Credit card fraud detection solution protecting more than 260 million credit cards worldwide.

Growth

HNC reaps many benefits from being a leader in the rapidly growing software industry. HNC sustained a compound annual growth rate of more than 60 percent for six years leading up to 1998 when annual revenues reached $178.6 million. In 1998, the company was listed among the top 10 most dynamic software companies by *Forbes* magazine, and in that year was also admitted to the Standard and Poors Smallcap 600.

HNC's steady growth is a result of leveraging existing technologies and solutions into new markets through acquisition, and by forming strategic partnerships. International opportunities also fuel growth, and the company sells products around the globe through a direct sales organization and international partnerships.

Customers and Partners

Many of the largest and most successful companies worldwide use HNC solutions, including 20 of the 25 largest U.S. credit card issuers, seven of the 10 largest U.S. insurance carriers, the three largest preferred provider organizations and third party administrators, and the three largest U.S. long distance carriers. In addition, Internet commerce leaders and more than 150 retailers benefit from HNC's software solutions.

As well as providing its customers with complete business solutions, HNC also offers consulting services, applications support and expanded industry expertise, as well as access to several proprietary or consortium databases that provide immediate benefits to its customers. The company has established long-term strategic relationships and technical alliances with leading solution, systems integrator and technology partners.

Predictive Customer Relationship Management

Predictive software solutions are essential to service industries that conduct high volumes of customer transactions, providing the backbone for leading-edge customer relationship strategies, including one-to-one marketing and customer lifecycle optimization. Predictive Customer Relationship Management is the ability to leverage real-time information technology to understand customers at the individual and account level, predict behavior based on that understanding and enable structured actions and strategies so that programs are consistent and profitability-driven across all points of customer contact.

Technology

HNC's proprietary technologies preprocess transaction-level information from various data streams, creating profiles of transaction patterns. In real-time, these solutions look at both linear and nonlinear data relationships to detect specific patterns that are proven to be strong indicators of future customer behavior or needs. The software identifies and analyzes transaction patterns, and "learns" from implementation — improving predictive capabilities as transactional databases increase in size. HNC's predictive solutions interface with real-time production systems and automate customer transaction decisions. They can work in real-time or batch mode to provide customer insight for improved marketing and operational decisions.

HNC's predictive solutions are proven in the most demanding Fortune 100 environments, yet are often scaleable for small- to mid-sized companies. HNC's research and development engineers are forerunners in the fields of neural network, expert rule and Context Vector-based technologies. While some of the company's research is funded by U.S. government defense grants, the primary goal is to leverage innovative technologies into new products that will benefit HNC's current and future customers.

Innovation and extensive research and development have been the hallmarks of HNC since its inception and will continue to be as the company enters the 21st century.

Inacom Corporation

What began as a small company selling personal computers with irrigation software and packaging solutions to farmers in the Great Plains has evolved into a provider of technology management services to businesses worldwide. This Fortune 500 company is Inacom, with corporate headquarters in Omaha, Nebraska.

Inacom was founded in Omaha in 1982 as ValCom, a division of Valmont Industries, which provides center pivot irrigation systems. ValCom began with eight employees, selling computers and specialized agricultural software. The company soon moved away from its agricultural base and into the sale of personal computers, becoming IBM's first value-added reseller for computer products in 1982. Aided by strategic acquisitions, the company gradually opened offices in cities across the United States. In 1986, ValCom added to its services with the creation of Strategic Products and Services (SPS), a subsidiary for marketing telephone systems.

In 1991, ValCom merged with Inacomp Computer Centers to form Inacom Corp. Two years later, Inacom's expansion continued with the acquisition of Sears Business Centers. At this point, all Inacom businesses began operating under the Inacom name. SPS became Inacom Communications.

Inacom expanded into the international market in 1992. In that year, the company became affiliated with ICG, the world's largest systems integrator consortium. Inacom/ICG has a presence in some 40 nations and maintains regional coordination centers in Omaha, Miami, London, Tokyo and Hong Kong. The establishment of Inacom Latin America also occurred in 1992.

By 1995, Inacom had become IBM's number one worldwide customer. Inacom also became the first high-tech provider to achieve ISO 9001 certification. Inacom joined the Fortune 500 in 1997 with record earnings of $29.5 million, approximately 53 percent coming from service sales. In February 1999, Inacom merged with Vanstar, creating the industry's largest manufacturer and independent services company.

Inacom's San Diego office also experienced significant growth during these eventful years. Founded in 1984 in Pacific Beach as a branch of Inacomp Computer Centers, the San Diego office moved in 1988 to University City. With the acquisition of Chaparral Computer Systems in 1994, the office relocated to its present location in the high-tech Sorrento Valley area. Between 1994 and the end of 1998, the San Diego office grew from 20 employees and $10 million in sales to 108 employees and $50 million in sales.

Like many companies in its industry, Inacom's steady growth can be attributed in part to the emergence of advanced technology in everyday business. Inacom is now the industry's largest direct provider of Intel-based products and PC technology for IBM, Compaq and Hewlett-Packard. Inacom is also the recognized leader in system customization. Its highly automated customization centers — in Omaha; Ontario, California; and Swedesboro, New Jersey — are able to integrate up to 8,000 systems per day, reducing order-to-ship times substantially.

Inacom is a global technology management services company.

Inacom's overall commitment to clients, however, takes on a much broader scope. As a global technology management services company, Inacom helps clients design, procure, build, install and manage the costs and efficiencies of their information technology. For these clients, information technology is vital to continued business success. Inacom's job is to keep this information technology up and running so that clients can channel their energies into growing their companies and helping their own customers.

"There is an increased demand to keep up with clients' knowledge and integrate technology into their environment," said Kevin Lawler, general manager of Inacom's San Diego office. "Our job is to allow them to incorporate emerging technologies sooner. As the technology curve is going up, we help reduce their knowledge gap for implementing those technologies through a process called Integrated Life Cycle Services."

Inacom embraces a life cycle services approach that comprises five distinct areas: technology planning, procurement, integration, support and management. While each of the five models is unique, the intent is the same — to make business faster, smarter, leaner, more integrated and more global for each of Inacom's clients.

Inacom not only focuses on its clients' needs but on the community's as well. For example, the San Diego branch has donated personal computers to local elementary, middle and high schools and has participated in charity walkathon events for Muscular Dystrophy and the March of Dimes. The branch has been a member of the Greater San Diego Chamber of Commerce and, since 1984, a member of the Better Business Bureau.

Inacom's community service presence has been particularly influential to Catholic Charities of San Diego. Inacom automated the information technology infrastructure of Catholic Charities, enabling the nonprofit organization to better track and report on San Diego's homeless problem. This, in turn, helps Catholic Charities receive government funding. In its partnership with a local cable company, Inacom has assisted in providing Internet access to local school systems. The cable company offered free Internet access in the classrooms of schools via a cable modem service while Inacom provided the personnel to integrate this technology.

With more than 12,000 employees and the industry's largest customer base, Inacom is uniquely capable of offering its clients unequalled service and support across the full information technology spectrum. "The company is striving to be the dominant technology management services company in every marketplace in the United States," said Lawler. "And this coincides perfectly with our desire to develop and retain Inacom's most valuable asset — our employees."

These employees have made a lasting commitment to the company — indeed, President and CEO Bill Fairfield helped found the original company — and to its clients. Their unbending devotion to exceptional service and client satisfaction are the core of Inacom's ability to assist clients get the most from their technology investments in Omaha, San Diego and around the world.

Inacom offers unequalled service and support across the full information technology spectrum.

L-3 Communications Conic Division

Since its incorporation in 1961, the Conic Division of L-3 Communications has become a pacesetter in the production and engineering of a broad range of telemetry products used in the acquisition, multiplexing and relaying of data from remote locations and satellites. The company's technically diverse product line attracts sales each year from defense, commercial and foreign enterprises.

(Both photos) Pictured is Conic Division's main offices and lobby entrance viewed from Balboa Avenue. The building is one of several structures spread over nearly 17 acres of property in Kearny Mesa.

Interestingly, the corporation's origins trace back to the drive and ambition of five engineers who wanted a company of their own. They quit their jobs, made a small investment and started a business that initially operated from a National City television shop. They named the business Conic.

Among the first products hatched by Conic during the early 1960s was a revolutionary two-watt VHF transmitter. It was the first solid-state, S-band transmitter ever invented. The engineers were then faced with the difficult task of promoting the device, which was initially viewed as merely an interesting novelty. After finally selling the transmitter to Sandia Labs, bigger, more illustrious projects began to emerge.

In 1964, Conic launched itself into the aerospace industry by building a transmitter for NASA for astronaut communications in the Apollo space program. Later, when man began driving on the moon's surface, Conic created and installed a communication relay unit on the Lunar Rover. As a result, the world was afforded direct video images of the Lunar Lander as it left the moon.

During the Vietnam War, Conic's penchant for creating telemetry products soon caught the attention of the U.S. Department of Defense. The company produced the "Twiggy" transmitter, a valuable device capable of detecting troop movements in thick forest areas. The transmitters, camouflaged as trees, used vibration sensors as an alternative eye in the planning of strategic battle maneuvers.

In less than 10 years, Conic had earned a prestigious reputation for the development of airborne and ground-based communication systems.

Conic's product line was further expanded after the 1970 acquisition of Radix Telemetry Company. At this point, the company had successfully evolved into the pulse-coded modulation business. New development encoders, sold to Sandia Livermore, and downlink telemetry encoders for Hughes Aircraft significantly boosted annual sales within a few years.

Another major milestone occurred in 1974, when Conic became a wholly owned subsidiary of the Loral Corporation, a New York-based company registered on the New York Stock Exchange. The transaction reinforced Conic's financial posturing and led to even greater advances in telemetry hardware production.

In the 1970s and 80s, Conic expanded its telemetry product lines. It became a leader in the supply of space products and developed terrestrial HF and microwave radios. The 1990s were marked by the infusion of modern technology and new manufacturing methods.

With an ever-evolving history of expansion, the company changed hands once again in 1996, when Lockheed Martin acquired the Loral Corporation. The well-established Conic name was retained and a year later, Conic and nine other Lockheed Martin divisions throughout the United States became L-3 Communications Corporation.

Today, L-3 Communications Conic Division is a leading competitor in the development, engineering and manufacturing of a diverse line of telemetry, terrestrial communications and satellite products. Based in a modern facility that encompasses nearly 17 acres, the company adheres to strict quality standards dictated through established systems such as ANSI/ASQC Q9001, MIL-S-45208, MIL-Q-9858A and ISO9000. Nearly 30 percent of sales originate from foreign markets and many of the company's existing contracts fall in the multimillion-dollar range.

In addition to making missile, aircraft and ground-based telemetry systems — many of which are tested inside the facility to withstand extreme environmental conditions — the company is highly experienced in ruggedized, miniature product development. Video compression systems used in aircraft surveillance, for instance, or development tools used for building computer circuitry boards aptly reflect the staff's immense talent for finding new approaches to miniaturized designing.

Many of the circuits used in L-3's products are based on past product experience. They represent mature designs that are continually improved to match modern-day technologies and which can be tailor-made to fit the systems of its customers. A complete environmental test lab, located within the facility, is utilized for rigorous reliability analyses and environmental stress screening on all deliverable products.

Software is also developed in-house. The company has produced a menu-driven software package for Windows that allows for total setup and diagnostic capability for a number of product installations and applications. The package allows instrumentation engineers to easily conform to specific formats when configuring a wide range of different systems.

In any given year, L-3 Communications Conic Division remains dedicated to numerous satellite, munitions and launch vehicle programs taking place at the U.S. Department of Energy, NASA, the U.S. Department of Defense, and companies such as AlliedSignal, Hughes Missile Systems Co., McDonnell Douglas, Texas Instruments, Teledyne Ryan, Orbital Sciences and many others.

For Lockheed Martin Corporation, for example, Conic has supplied a number of data acquisition systems for use on the Lockheed Launch Vehicle. The same family of components currently serves several U.S. government agencies and aerospace contractors for ongoing instrumentation programs.

L-3 Communications, Conic's parent company, remains a leading merchant supplier of secure communications systems and products, avionic and ocean systems, microwave components and telemetry, instrumentation, and space and wireless products. Its customers include the Department of Defense, U.S. government intelligence agencies, aerospace and defense contractors, and commercial telecommunications and cellular customers.

With so many innovative projects on its drawing board, the company can be best summed up by one of the original founders when a friend asked him what a typical workday at Conic was like. In his reply, "Lately things haven't been too typical," he intuitively described the enormous impact Conic would have on the electronics industry for years to come.

As communication technology rapidly progresses beyond the vision of the Conic founders, L-3 Communications will continue to play a vital role in future projects that are perhaps as unimaginable today as they were in 1961.

National Decision Systems

Given the million-dollar risks retailers, restaurants and developers face when opening or developing a new site, an advisor with a crystal ball would be a welcome addition to any corporate office. National Decision Systems (NDS) has been helping clients make difficult choices by predicting the success of future sites and merchandise assortments with means a bit more concrete, by utilizing comprehensive

President Bob Nascenzi and CFO Tom Compogiannis are the driving forces behind NDS' success.

marketing data, sophisticated software and custom services tailored to a client's individual needs. Two decades of continual, on-target predictions have made NDS one of the most respected marketing information and target-marketing businesses in the nation, and the company is committed to keeping that stellar reputation intact.

A great deal has changed since NDS entered the desktop market in 1979 as the first company to offer a PC-based marketing workstation. Gone are the days when stand-alone PCs ruled the computer world, replaced instead by the ever-expanding informational universe of the Internet, extranets and company intranets. NDS, a subsidiary of VNU Marketing Information Services since 1997, has helped more than 11,000 clients involved in the real estate, retail, catalog, restaurant, nonprofit and travel industries improve their site selection and target marketing programs.

NDS has stayed in step with the changing needs of such clients as Blockbuster Video, J.C. Penney, Federated Department Stores, McDonald's, CB Richard Ellis, Chevron, Mobil, Levi Strauss and Sears by providing the highest quality data and the best customer service behind its extensive offering of NDS software products and customer applications. NDS also relies on information available from its more than 60 databases containing the most up-to-date consumer, demographic, business and financial data. The company's main focus is helping clients save money by making more accurate marketing, merchandising and site decisions.

NDS recognizes the individual concerns of its clients by avoiding a prepackaged program approach. The complexity of a business or the availability of resources often requires NDS to develop custom projects to address issues of specific importance to the client. This is when NDS makes optimum use of its extensive staff of industry specialists, statistical modelers, demographers, programmers and analysts to provide consultation for specific decision-making needs. NDS feels strongly about providing customers with data that is accurate and timely, along with technology that is fast and flexible, and input from industry experts who know the business inside and out.

NDS provides the answers to its clients by putting the latest technology to work, such as its e-commerce site and *i*MARK, the first truly interactive geodemographic analysis system for a company's Intranet. The e-commerce Web site offers comprehensive demographic reports and maps for any location in the United States. *i*MARK combines NDS' powerful demographic, consumer demand and business databases with a company's own proprietary information (site/store locations, sales, customer records and competitor sites). iMARK enables users to identify and evaluate potential site locations, quantify demand and competitor influence, segment customers by lifestyle, and support marketing and merchandising decisions — all from an Internet browser. iMARK offers a map-centric interface, allowing users to access data by clicking on the map or through dialog screens. The program also has geocoding capabilities, making it possible for users to append latitudes and longitudes and MicroVision lifestyle segmentation codes to customer files. iMARK even makes it possible to zoom in on any address or intersection in the United States and enables the user to produce presentation-quality output in preformatted reports and executive summaries to assist with the interpretation of the data.

In addition to site and market analysis, NDS offers the consumer segmentation system MicroVision, which allows users to identify, locate and target their best customers and prospects. Used in conjunction with iMARK, MicroVision provides clients with the capability of comparing the potential of several markets and locating pockets of high demand within them. MicroVision, which classifies every household in the United States into one of 50 demographically and behaviorally distinct types, makes it possible to profile the client's own customer database. By knowing about their customers' lifestyles, media habits and purchasing behaviors, NDS clients can correlate marketing strategies to effectively target their most profitable customers, plus find prospects that are just like them. NDS clients recognize the necessity of this vital information and know that the data and service they receive is the most current and reliable available.

Despite the demand made on NDS employees to deliver the highest quality service, they still find time to branch out in the community to support causes near and dear to their hearts. The Hands On San Diego United Way campaign is a favorite, as is the Cystic Fibrosis Annual Volleyball Tournament

NDS clients often have to present information and analyses to their own clients. The maps available through NDS help clients add credibility and pizzazz to their presentations.

and the annual Toys for Tots drive. NDS employees also serve meals at St. Vincent de Paul and contribute to Conner's Cause, a nonprofit organization that provides financial assistance to families who have children with life-threatening diseases.

NDS was also proud to be selected as one of *The San Diego Union-Tribune's Computer Link* "Cool 25," an annual list of companies recognized for their impact on technology. Bob Nascenzi, president of NDS, says the honor meant a great deal to the employees, particularly in light of the formidable competition from the high volume of high-tech firms based in San Diego.

Although NDS is keenly aware of the competition in the high-tech world, Nascenzi feels confident of NDS' abilities to stay ahead of the crowd and says, "As technology has changed, our business has changed with it. We create solutions. Our goal is to have our clients grow and to find new and different ways to help them spend less money and make wiser marketing decisions. We can do that because of the quality of our people and their commitment to our customers' satisfaction."

SSC San Diego

The date is May 12, 1906. Shortly after dawn, a Navy chief petty officer and two sailors pull up to the pier in downtown San Diego and load a Massie five-kilowatt transmitter and receiver onto their horse-drawn wagon. It is state-of-the-art communications equipment — known as "wireless radiotelegraphy" — which the Navy later will simply call "radio."

The Navy's first structure on the top of Point Loma was a small wood-frame building housing "Naval Radio Station Point Loma," which began operating in the spring of 1906. *Courtesy San Diego Historical Society*

Many hours later, at 9 p.m., the chief sits down at the radio equipment, now installed in a small wooden structure on Point Loma a few yards from a rutted dirt road that would eventually become Catalina Boulevard, and taps out a hopeful message to the Mare Island Naval Radio Station 500 miles north. He is stunned by the immediate reply; he has just increased the distance record for Navy wireless communication over land by a factor of four. That evening, he commissions the facility as "Navy Radio Station Point Loma."

So begins the nearly century-old legacy of Navy communications on Point Loma. In the years to come, the station would play a key role in major events, exchanging one of the first successful radio voice transmissions as Teddy Roosevelt's Great White Fleet steamed into San Diego harbor in 1909, and also serving for 60 hours on Dec. 7 through 9, 1941, as the only radio link for the ships of the Pacific Fleet in the aftermath of the attack on Pearl Harbor.

Focused efforts to develop substantial improvements in Navy communications began June 1, 1940, with the establishment on the peninsula of the Navy Radio and Sound Laboratory, the Navy's first West Coast laboratory. After six decades of pioneering discoveries and electronic equipment development, and more than a few name changes in between, the facility still thrives on Point Loma, now as the Space and Naval Warfare Systems Center San Diego (SSC San Diego).

In the interim, San Diego residents have known the facility as NRSL, NEL, NELC, NUC, NOSC and NRaD. Generations of highly respected Navy civilian scientists and engineers have passed through the organization, but the focus is still the same as it was on that spring morning in 1906: to support the sailors of the U.S. Navy by meeting their information needs.

SSC San Diego's self-defined vision is to provide an integrated package of information technology to provide U.S. warfighters with a critical edge over potential adversaries — "information dominance"— to assure U.S. forces an early victory in any armed conflict, or before one even begins.

The center has played a major role in developing and improving almost all Navy communications systems — especially satellite systems — as well as the Navy's primary command and control systems for information processing, management and display, and capabilities to collect and analyze information critical to warfighters' needs.

Early innovations included testing of the Navy's first operational radar and development of its first electronic war game, a landmark navigation system, a highly effective submarine communications capability, and a shipboard message handling system in response to urgent requirements from Pacific fleet ships involved in the Vietnam War.

Throughout much of its history, the organization's focus on electronics has been interspersed with other efforts, such as weapons development. The center has developed all the Navy's anti-submarine torpedoes since World War II, beginning with the air-dropped torpedo that helped turn the tide in the Pacific. Testing of the nation's submarine-launched ballistic missiles — Polaris, Poseidon, Trident — was conducted by the center.

Supporting the weapons work was development of the world's first remotely operated vehicle, which was employed primarily to recover weapons underwater after testing, but also during an event that attracted worldwide headlines for the recovery of a lost hydrogen bomb in the Mediterranean.

Other undersea breakthroughs included leadership in Arctic submarine warfare. This included development of under-ice sonar and technical direction of the historic under-ice transit of the USS Nautilus, which in 1958 navigated underneath the icy Arctic Ocean through the North Pole. A year later, these capabilities allowed USS Skate's surfacing at the pole, and in 1960 it made possible the descent of the bathyscaph Trieste to the deepest ocean depth.

More important than these newsworthy events, however, was the center's crucial technology development that allowed U.S. nuclear submarines to operate under (and surface through) the ice of the Arctic Ocean, which was considered essential to countering the threat of Soviet submarines. The center's surveillance efforts provided technology to track those submarines in deep water, a critical requirement during the Cold War when Soviet subs were considered the country's most dangerous threat. Today, using supercomputers, that work continues as warfighters focus on the current formidable threat of potentially hostile and dangerous submarines operating near shore in shallow water.

SSC San Diego also has played a major role in environmental protection. The center has developed capabilities to detect harbor pollution, as well as locate hazardous waste sites on land. It also manages the Navy's Marine Mammal Program, which employs dolphins and sea lions to protect the lives of sailors and marines.

But development of technology for managing information continues to be the focus of the center's efforts. That includes the intelligence, surveillance and reconnaissance technology that employs satellites, ground sensors, at-sea sensors towed by surface ships, and fixed arrays on the sea floor to collect information critical to the needs of the military.

It also includes command-and-control systems and command centers, with interoperable and interconnected networks, to process the information from the sensors and make it available to personnel who must make critical decisions that affect not only the success of any mission but the very survival of American troops. The centerpiece of SSC San Diego's visionary innovation is the command center of the future, which allows center technologists, military decision-makers, and private industry partners to coordinate development of the future technologies that will support the needs of warfighters in the coming decades.

Of course, the center's efforts will continue to include the very first focus of new technology initially brought to Point Loma nearly 100 years ago — communication. SSC San Diego carries on its tradition of improving the ability of Navy ships, submarines, aircraft and shore stations to move the information critical to mission accomplishment and protection of U.S. military forces as they go into harm's way to defend the nation.

SSC San Diego has several hundred buildings on the Point Loma peninsula, where the center was established in 1940. Four major building complexes occupy small areas within a 640-acre ecological reserve the center maintains to preserve endangered plant and animal species and the historic character of the land. *Official U.S. Navy photo*

Insight Electronics, LLC

Insight Electronics, LLC is one of San Diego's high-technology success stories. In 1985, the company's first year of operation, revenues were $1 million. Thirteen-and-a-half years later, Insight Electronics' sales have sky rocketed to $700 million. Insight Electronics has now grown to become the largest specialty distributor of semiconductors in the United States. The company employs 495 people to support its product lines and has 65 divisions in the United States, Mexico, Canada and South America. Since 1993, Insight Electronics has been a wholly owned subsidiary of VEBA AG, a $50 billion distribution conglomerate located in Dusseldorf, Germany.

Insight Electronics' unique organizational structure allows for speed and efficiency. Communication is direct and unfiltered and Insight Electronics' salespeople have the authority to manage and control customer inventories according to the projected needs of their customers.

Paramount to the company's continued success has been providing value-added services to clients. Insight Electronics, for example, offers a single-point-of-trade service center and is one of the top providers of supply-chain solutions worldwide. In addition, Insight Electronics' customers have access to a number of other services, including: auto replenishment, bar coding, bonded inventory, dock-to-stock programs, electronic data interchange (EDI), just-in-time deliveries, labeling and supplements documentation, order fulfillment center, programming services, ISO 9002 certification, special component packaging, damage resistant packaging, and tape and reel service. Another important element to the company's success is its staff of technical sales engineers (TSEs) — experienced digital and analog engineers who understand the complexity of the products and the need to get them to market on time. Every Insight Electronics division has a TSE available to facilitate design efforts — from information and suggestions to software installation and design support.

A key corporate strength is a focused product offering, known in the industry as a "linecard." Over the years, Insight Electronics has assembled a team of suppliers providing comprehensive solutions to various technological challenges. The end product is a linecard featuring five core semiconductor technologies: programmable logic, analog ICs, RF/ wireless, communications ICs, and the "three Ms" — microcontrollers, microprocessors and memory. Key suppliers in these core technologies include AMCC, Atmel, Cirrus Logic, Dallas Semiconductor, IDT, Infineon Technologies, Toshiba and Xilinx.

Insight Electronics believes that educating customers in these technologies is important. Through its Marketing Innovative Products (MIPs) program, Insight Electronics' TSEs conduct analyses for each customer's needs and present the MIPs program to them on-site. The company also offers the "Demand Forecasting Network," a unique program that allows Insight Electronics' account managers to enter what materials a customer requires during the design stage. By anticipating material needs at this phase of the project, customers' time to market is dramatically reduced.

Lastly, as part of its commitment to customer service, Insight Electronics provides seminars on products and software at locations throughout North and South America. Topics cover merged technologies, compatibility, design performance, algorithmic advancements and methodology support. The seminars are tailored to each customer's needs.

Insight Electronics is cognizant that technological advancements occur continuously and rapidly in the semiconductor industry. The company will continue to offer semiconductor solutions that provide a competitive edge via a synergistic combination of semiconductor products, technical design support and advanced logistics technology. This strategy has helped redefine distribution for the industry.

Prism Lithographic Technologies

Prism Lithographic Technologies is the No. 1 dealer of Ryobi printing presses in the United States. Founded in 1991 by three partners, Prism sells and services the "Cadillac of printing equipment" to Southern California printers, publishers, newspapers, advertising agencies and large corporations. The company sells to several branches of the military, city and county offices, and educational institutions who use their printing presses, paper cutters, paper folders and bindery equipment.

Printing has been a part of San Diego since its early history. Ryobi, which has an ISO rating of 9001 (an international standard of manufacturing and service excellence), has been a part of that history since the 1960s. When the company they worked for was sold, Tim Kirby, Ken Williams and Dave Schwarz wanted to carry on the tradition of serving San Diego printers with high-quality products. Prism Lithographic Technologies was born.

Pooling their resources, including a combination of more than 60 years in the industry, the partners started from scratch, building their business on excellent products and service. Many of the companies represented by Prism have been in business more than 100 years. The owners divide the responsibilities of sales, service and support, knowing that the relationship with their clients doesn't end after the sale. "We train our clients to sell the advantages of the quality of the printed product to their customers," says Kirby. "Our greatest satisfaction comes from watching printers we've known for 10 years or more grow…and seeing them become very successful. We like to think we've had a small part in their success." Some of the printers that Prism counts among their clients were trained on Ryobi presses in San Diego high schools and colleges.

Prism is proud to represent Ryobi in Southern California. This Japanese manufacturer, which is world-renowned for product excellence, not only produces printing presses and parts, but with the largest die-casting equipment in the industry, manufactures automobile engines for companies such as BMW and Mercedes-Benz, Craftsman tools for Sears, and Sony stereo components.

The quality of the equipment Prism sells is what sets the company apart. Its printing presses produce heavier solids and finer screen rulings,

Prism Lithographic Technologies, purveyors of finer printing equipment

have the ability to print on heavier stock and run at higher speeds. Keeping up with technology is critical for Prism and its products reflect the latest changes in the printing industry. The digital film and plates in the equipment Prism sells produce the highest caliber printing.

The three partners are active in their churches and are members of the San Diego chapter of the Printing Industry of America and the National Association of Quick Printers. In 1997 the North American Graphic Arts Dealers Association ranked Prism in the Top Five Dealers of a single location.

Prism is committed to continuing its level of quality by carrying only products that meet its high standards. Future plans involve expanding to other geographic areas, as well as continuing its tradition of quality in San Diego. "San Diego has been good to us," claims Kirby. "We plan to be here for the long haul."

San Diego Chronology

(pre-1500 dates approximate)

18,000 B.C.	First human settlement in coastal San Diego; 10,000 B.C., desert settlements.
7500 B.C.	San Dieguito Paleo-Indians.
6000 B.C.	La Jolla culture.
1 A.D.	Yumans move into area, followed by Shoshonean groups, assimilating La Jollans.
1000	Luiseño, Cahuilla, Cupeño, Ipai, Kumeyaay coexist in county area.
1508	New edition of *Amadís de Gaula* published, featuring story of "California," ruled by Queen Calafia.
1535	Hernando Cortés colonizes La Paz, Baja California.
1539	Francisco de Ulloa confirms California is not an island.
1542	Juan Rodríguez Cabrillo discovers San Diego, names it San Miguel.
1602	Sebastián Vizcaíno rediscovers San Miguel, renaming it San Diego, but colonization plans for Alta California are abandoned, 1605.
1697	Jesuits authorized to settle Baja California; mission established at Loreto, the first of 23 established on the peninsula over next 70 years.
1767	Jesuits expelled from all Spanish territories; José de Galvez formulates colonization plan, Gaspar de Portolá appointed governor of California.
1769	Mission San Diego founded, July 16; 1774, mission moved east to present site; 1775, 800 Indians attack, first martyr, Father Luís Jayme; mission rebuilt.
1782	Juan Pantoja y Arriaza, pilot on La Princesa, charts bay and indicates place names on map.
1784	Father Serra, 70, dies at Monterey, having founded nine missions in 15 years.
1786	Two French ships arrive; 1787, American ship, *Columbia*, circumnavigates globe and stirs interest in California.; 1793, 1797, British navigator George Vancouver visits.
1796	Fort Guijarros constructed at Ballast Point.
1798	Mission San Luis Rey established.
1803	Battle of San Diego Bay with American vessel, *Lelia Byrd*.
1810	Fight for Mexican independence begins.
1811	First major flood noted; 1817, Padre Dam completed.
1821	First known home (today's Presidio Hills Golf Course golf shop) built in Old Town; Lieutenant José María Estudillo arrives from Monterey to take command of presidio; flood shifts San Diego River course from False (Mission) Bay to empty into San Diego Bay, causing siltation.
1822	San Diego formally passes into Mexican rule (April 20); 1823, first private rancho granted, Los Peñasquitos, 8,486 acres to Captain Francisco María Ruiz; 33 land grants covering 948 square miles eventually recognized.
1825	San Diego declared capital of California province by first Mexican governor, José Echeandía.
1826	Jedediah Smith, first American to visit San Diego.
1833	Secularization Act leads to closing of missions.
1834	December 21, first pueblo election (13 votes); January 1, 1835, pueblo officials take office, Juan Osuna, first alcalde (mayor); 1838, pueblo status revoked.
1835-36	Richard Henry Dana visits, recounts adventures in *Two Years Before the Mast*.
1845	California divided into two districts; southern district from San Luis Obispo south.
1846	May 13, U.S. declares war on Mexico; October 31, Admiral Robert Stockton arrives aboard *Congress*; December 6, Battle of San Pasqual with General Stephen Watts Kearny in command of "Army of the West"; January 29, 1847, Mormon Battalion arrives.
1848	January 24, gold discovered at Sutter's Fort near Sacramento, setting off gold rush to California; February 2, Treaty of Guadalupe Hidalgo formally ends war.
1850	Census sets non-Indian population at 650 city, 798 county; February 2, San Diego County created; March 18, William Heath Davis purchases 160 acres in "New Town"; June 16, first city election (Joshua H. Bean, mayor); 1851, charter revoked.
1851	Antonio Garra leads last of major Indian revolts at Warner's Ranch.
1852	San Diego votes Whig in first presidential election, Democratic from 1856 to 1868; Indian revolt leader Antonio Garra executed.
1853	Lieutenant George H. Derby begins construction on "Derby Dike" to channel San Diego River back into False Bay.
1856	Thomas Whaley builds first all-brick house in Old Town.
1859	Whaling begins at La Playa; Richard Henry Dana makes return visit.
1861	Earthquake, flood; 1862, Davis wharf burned for army barracks' fuel; smallpox epidemic, drought; 1863, locusts.
1965	Mary C. Walker dismissed as teacher for dining with a black student.
1867	April 15, Alonzo E. Horton arrives; May 10, buys 800 acres for $265 (1869, buys another 160 acres).
1868	City trustees set 1,400 acres aside for Balboa Park; Kimball brothers buy 26,400 acres, founding National City; The San Diego Union founded.
1870	Chamber of Commerce, first local bank, Bank of San Diego, founded; Horton House opens.
1871	County records moved to downtown; Mount Hope Cemetery established.
1872	Old Town fire destroys key buildings; new downtown county courthouse opens.

1873	Thomas Scott of Pennsylvania Railroad sets off brief railroad boom with start of construction of Texas & Pacific Railroad from San Diego east; bond failure in Paris and Wall Street panic halts boom.
1875	Congress funds dike to halt siltation of San Diego Bay (completed 1877).
1882	First public library opens; Russ School (San Diego High School) completed; YMCA organized.
1884	Kate O. Sessions arrives to teach at Russ; founds nursery business, 1885.
1885	November 21, first transcontinental railroad arrives; summer 1886 rate war leads to population boom (2,637 in 1880, about 40,000 in 1887).
1887	John D. Spreckels makes unscheduled stop, begins investing in area; moves permanently in 1906; National City incorporates; *Golden Era* literary magazine moves to San Diego.
1888	Hotel del Coronado opens; boom ends (city population drops to about 16,000); False Bay renamed Mission Bay; Escondido, Oceanside incorporate.
1889	San Diego Flume begins operation; new city charter; Douglas Gunn first mayor elected since 1852; action taken to preserve Torrey Pines forest south of Del Mar.
1891	Coronado secedes from San Diego and incorporates.
1892	400th anniversary of Columbus, 350th of Cabrillo, celebrated.
1893	Wall Street panic leads to lengthy depression; architect Irving J. Gill arrives from Chicago.
1894	Horton sells Horton Plaza park for $10,000.
1896	Katherine Tingley buys Point Loma land for Theosophical Society campus.
1899	Andrew Carnegie donates $60,000 to San Diego Public Library for first of his libraries west of Mississippi, opens in 1902 at Eighth and E; State Normal School, (two-year teaching training) opens in Normal Heights.
1902	Panama Canal authorized in Congress; Samuel Parsons Jr. begins first master plan plan for City Park.
1903	University of California zoologist William Ritter establishes biology lab in La Jolla, precursor to Scripps Institution of Oceanography and UCSD.
1905	Sixty killed as *Bennington* blows up in harbor; Horton House demolished to make way for U.S. Grant Hotel (completed 1910).
1906	Construction begins on Spreckels' $18 million San Diego & Arizona Eastern Railway line to Yuma.
1907	Development of Presidio Park begins; Imperial County secession leaves San Diego with present county boundaries; Marston, Spreckels, Scripps and other investors begin buying presidio property to preserve as a park.
1908	U.S. "Great White Fleet" of naval ships visits offshore; John Nolen completes San Diego's first comprehensive land-use plan.
1909	Panama-California Exposition declared, backed by voter-approved $1.85 million in bonds; Balboa Park named (1910); Horton, 95, dies.
1910	Horton Plaza with fountain, both redesigned by Irving J. Gill, reopens.
1911	Voters approve $1 million in waterfront improvements; Mexican Revolution breaks out; Magonista radicals briefly occupy Tijuana.
1912	North Island aviation base established; International Workers of the World ("Wobblies") riot; Stingaree vice squad raid nabs 138 prostitutes; William Kettner elected to House of Representatives.
1913	Cabrillo National Monument designated.
1915	Panama-California Exposition opens in Balboa Park, extended through 1916.
1916	Paul Hatfield, "rainmaker," hired to end drought; major river valleys flooded.
1917	Banker Louis J. Wilde defeats George W. Marston in "Smokestacks vs. Geraniums" mayoral campaign; World War I prompts area military buildup.
1919	San Diego & Arizona Eastern Railway opens; President Woodrow Wilson seeks support for League of Nations in Balboa Stadium speech.
1920	Edward, Prince of Wales, visits San Diego, Coronado.
1922	Naval Hospital, Naval Training Center opened, followed in 1923 by Marine Corps Recruit Depot.
1924	Creole Palace, "Harlem of the West," opened at Hotel Douglas, popular jazz spot into 1950s, demolished in 1985.
1925	Mission Beach Amusement Center (Belmont Park) opens.
1926	Second Nolen Plan adopted; voters reject proposal to build new San Diego State Teachers College in Balboa Park; Spreckels dies.
1927	Charles Lindbergh completes historic trans-Atlantic flight in plane built by Ryan Airlines; voters approve Lindbergh Field construction; *Star of India* moved to San Diego; Agua Caliente (hotel, casino, spa) opens in Tijuana (1928, golf course, racetrack).
1929	Presidio Park dedicated; Fox Theatre opens; first large tuna boats constructed to serve revived fishing industry; city wins water rights to San Diego River.
1933	Reuben Fleet acts to move Consolidated Aircraft from Buffalo, New York; Natural History Museum completed in Balboa Park.
1935	California-Pacific International Exposition opens in Balboa Park.
1936	Pacific Coast League Hollywood Stars moves to San Diego as Padres, plays at Lane Field at foot of Broadway until 1956.
1938	President Franklin Roosevelt dedicates City-County Administration Center building at foot of Cedar Street.
1941	Pre-war manufacturing orders spark "boom blitz"; notification of Pearl Harbor attack first received at Point Loma navy radio receivers.
1942	Marines acquire Rancho Santa Margarita north of Oceanside and name it Camp Pendleton.
1945	Voters approve $2 million in Mission Bay Park bonds; Day & Zimmerman Report proposes post-war industrial strategy.
1946	San Diego joins Metropolitan Water District, approves $2 million water bonds.
1947	Miramar Naval Air Station 50-year lease to city approved for municipal airport (1953, rescinded).

1948	Palomar Observatory opens after 20 years of planning; U.S. Hwy. 395 (State Route 163) completed through Balboa Park's Cabrillo Canyon; sit-in at U.S. Grant Hotel to protest racial discrimination.
1949	Cedar Street Mall of grouped civic buildings defeated for final time; "Fiesta Bahia" celebrates opening of Mission Bay Park.
1951	Home construction begins in Clairemont neighborhood.
1952	California Western University founded at site of Tingley's Theosophical Society on Point Loma.
1954	University of San Diego founded in Linda Vista; Carnegie Library replaced by Central Library.
1957	Minor League Padres begin playing at Westgate Park in Mission Valley.
1958	Mission Valley rezoned for commercial development.
1959	General Dynamics-Convair employment peaks at 56,400; Lloyd Ruocco founds what will become Citizens Coordinate for Century 3 environmental group.
1961	American Football League Chargers opens first season at Balboa Stadium; Mission Valley (shopping) Center opens.
1962	*Time* magazine article: "San Diego: Bust Town?"
1964	City Administration Building opens at Community Concourse; Sea World opens in Mission Bay Park; first UCSD undergraduates begin classes.
1965	Beatles perform at Balboa Stadium; Mexico authorizes maquiladora "twin plan" factories.
1966	Bob Breitbard completes Sports Arena in Midway area.
1967	San Diego Stadium opens (renamed for San Diego Union sports editor Jack Murphy, 1981, Qualcomm Inc., 1997); Progress Guide and General Plan approved.
1968	Committee of 100 leads successful bond drive for first historic reconstruction in Balboa Park (Casa del Prado completed 1971).
1969	San Diego-Coronado bridge opens; San Diego celebrates its bicentennial; Old Town State Historic Park founded around Bazaar del Mundo; National League Padres begins playing at stadium; Save Our Heritage Organisation launches preservation drive for old Victorian buildings; UCSD philosophy professor Herbert Marcuse reappointed despite community protest over his Marxist beliefs.
1970	Mayor and council members indicted in Yellow Cab scandal; Mexican-American community campaigns for creation of Chicano Park beneath San Diego-Coronado Bay Bridge.
1971	Assemblyman Pete Wilson elected mayor; San Diego State College becomes university.
1972	Republicans move presidential nominating convention to Miami Beach; Tijuana River channel redevelopment project begins; Parkway Plaza shopping center opens in El Cajon; Horton Plaza redevelopment project established in downtown San Diego, followed in 1976 by Columbia and Marina districts, 1982, Gaslamp, and, 1992, balance of remaining downtown.
1974	San Diego City Council designates "swim-suit optional" zone at Black's Beach (rescinded, 1977); Temporary Paradise? report issued; Gaslamp Quarter Association founded.
1975	Vietnamese refugees temporarily housed at Camp Pendleton.
1977	University Towne Centre shopping mall opens near UCSD.
1978	PSA crash, worst air passenger disaster to date nationally, kills 144; Old Globe, Electric Building fires in Balboa Park; state voters approve Proposition 13, throwing local municipal finances into chaos.
1981	San Diego Trolley begins service to border; 1985, East Line; 1990 Bayside Line; 1992, North Line; 1998, Mission Valley Line; voters rejected convention center in mail-ballot election.
1983	Britain's Queen Elizabeth II dedicates rebuilt Globe Theatre; Roger Hedgecock elected mayor (resigns in 1985 over campaign fund-raising scandal); voters approve bayfront convention center; Plaza Bonita shopping center opens in National City.
1984	Padres reach World Series for the first time; first residents move to North City West (Carmel Valley).
1985	Sixty-seven homes destroyed in Normal Heights fire; Horton Plaza shopping center opens; restored U.S. Grant Hotel opens; San Diego Symphony moves into Symphony Hall (former Fox Theatre).
1986	Maureen O'Connor elected as San Diego's first woman mayor; North County Fair shopping center opens in Escondido.
1987	Voters narrowly approve 20-year sales tax increase for transportation improvements.
1988	Four controlled-growth measures defeated at polls; San Diego hosts first football Super Bowl; America's Cup yacht race held in San Diego, again in 1992, 1995.
1989	Soviet Arts Festival held citywide; San Diego Convention Center opens; First San Diego River Improvement Project completed on reclaimed Mission Valley river banks.
1990	California State University, San Marcos, opens.
1991	One America Plaza office tower caps decade-long downtown skyscraper boom.
1992	General Dynamics-Convair begins closing local operations; Susan Golding elected mayor.
1993	Naval Training Center to be closed.
1994	California Center for the Arts, Escondido, opens.
1995	RCO Olympic Training Center opens in Chula Vista.
1996	Chargers appear in their first Super Bowl; Republican presidential nominating convention held in San Diego; fire destroys 54 homes in Carlsbad's Harmony Grove.
1997	"Titanic" opens, largely filmed at soundstage south of Rosarito Beach; Heaven's Gate cult commits mass suicides in Rancho Santa Fe; Hillcrest resident Andrew Cunanan's murders fashion designer Gianni Versace; tainted frozen strawberries shipped from San Diego warehouse; city approves Multiple Species Conservation Program.
1998	Second Super Bowl held in (renamed) Qualcomm Stadium; Coors Amphitheatre opens in Chula Vista; Padres play in their second World Series; voters approve convention center expansion, downtown Padres ballpark, $1.5 billion city school bonds.
1999	Legoland California opens in Carlsbad.

SAN DIEGO COUNTY AND INCORPORATED CITIES POPULATION 1850-1999

Incorporated	City	1850	1860	1870	1880	1890	1900	1910	1920
1850	San Diego		731	2,300	2,637	16,159	17,700	39,578	74,361
1887	National City				248	1,353	1,086	1,733	3,116
1888	Escondido					541	755	1,334	1,789
1888	Oceanside						330	673	1,161
1890	Coronado						935	1,477	3,289
1911	Chula Vista								1,718
1912	El Cajon								469
1912	La Mesa								1,004
1952	Carlsbad								
1956	Imperial Beach								
1959	Del Mar								
1963	San Marcos								
1963	Vista								
1977	Lemon Grove								
1980	Poway								
1980	Santee								
1986	Encinitas								
1986	Solana Beach								
	Unincorporated area	798	3,593	2,651	5,733	16,934	14,284	16,870	25,341
	Total County	798	4,324	4,951	8,618	34,987	35,090	61,665	112,248

Incorporated	City	1930	1940	1950	1960	1970	1980	1990	1999
1850	San Diego	147,995	203,341	334,387	573,224	697,027	875,538	1,110,549	1,254,300
1887	National City	7,301	10,344	21,199	32,771	43,184	48,772	54,249	55,000
1888	Escondido	3,421	4,560	6,544	16,377	36,792	64,355	108,635	125,600
1888	Oceanside	3,508	4,651	12,881	24,971	40,494	76,698	128,398	157,900
1890	Coronado	5,425	6,932	12,700	18,039	20,020	18,790	26,540	28,700
1911	Chula Vista	3,869	5,138	15,92	42,034	67,901	35,490	63,126	166,900
1912	El Cajon	1,050	1,471	5,600	37,618	52,273	73,892	88,693	95,500
1912	La Mesa	2,513	3,925	10,946	30,441	39,178	50,308	52,931	"58,700
1952	Carlsbad				9,253	14,944	35,490	63,126	166,900
1956	Imperial Beach				17,773	20,244	22,689	26,512	28,900
1959	Del Mar				3,124	3,956	5,017	4,860	5,325
1963	San Marcos					3,896	17,479	38,974	52,100
1963	Vista					24,688	35,834	71,872	84,400
1977	Lemon Grove						20,780	23,984	25,700
1980	Poway							43,516	48,400
1980	Santee							52,902	57,200
1986	Encinitas							55,386	60,400
1986	Solana Beach							12,962	14,150
	Unincorporated area	34,577	48,986	136,62	227,386	293,257	480,714	471,000"	367,225
	Total County	209,659	289,348	556,808	1,033,011	1,357,854	1,861,846	2,498,016	2,853,300

Notes: The 1850 census did not list a separate population for the city of San Diego. The city of East San Diego, incorporated from 1912 to 1923, is included in the city of San Diego for the census of 1920. The 1999 figures are estimates by the California Department of Finance.
Source: California Department of Finance

Endnotes

In recent decades, there have been a number of general histories of San Diego that provided guidance in approaching this book. Every author offers a slightly different perspective and I recommend local history readers consult these works, most of which are easily available at many local libraries.

Berger, Dan, Peter Jensen and Margaret C. Berg, *San Diego: Where Tomorrow Begins*, Windsor Publications, 1987

Blair, Tom and Bob B. Yarbrough and Ron Donoho, *San Diego: World-Class City*, Towery Publishing, Memphis, Tennessee, 1998

Brandes, Ray, *San Diego: An Illustrated History*, Rosebud Books, Los Angeles, California, 1981

Engstrand, Iris H.W., *San Diego: California's Cornerstone*, Continental Heritage Press, Tulsa, Oklahoma, 1980

Engstrand, Iris H.W., *San Diego: Gateway to the Pacific*, Pioneer Publications Inc., Houston, Texas, 1992

Grant, Michael Grant, *San Diego Tapestry*, Towery Publishing, Memphis, Tennessee, 1992

McKeever, Michael, *Short History of San Diego*, Lexikos Publishing Co., San Francisco, 1985

Starr, Raymond G., *San Diego: An Illustrated History*, The Donning Company, Norfolk and Virginia Beach, Virginia, 1986

For an encyclopedic-like treatment of San Diego in a question-and-answer format, see:

Kooperman, Evelyn, *San Diego Trivia (1989) and San Diego Trivia II (1993)*, Silver Gate Publications, San Diego

For short biographies of interesting and noteworthy San Diegans, see:

Fuller, Theodore W., *San Diego Originals: Profiles of the movers and shakers of California's first community*, California Profiles Publications, Pleasant Hill, California, 1987

For the history of Tijuana, there is only one work in English that offers a general introduction:
T.D. Proffitt III's *Tijuana: The History of a Mexican Metropolis*, San Diego State University Press, 1994

Prologue

Carrico, Richard L., *Strangers in a Stolen Land: American Indians in San Diego*, 1850-1880, Sierra Oaks Publishing Co., Sacramento, Calif., 1987

Heizer, Robert F., editor, *Handbook of North American Indians, Vol. 8: California*; chapters on the Luiseño by Lowell John Bean and Florence C. Shipek, Cahuilla by Lowell John Bean, Cupeño by Lowell John Bean and Charles R. Smith and Tipai and Ipai by Katharine Luomala

Proffitt Jr., T.D., *Tijuana: The History of a Mexican Metropolis*, San Diego State University Press, 1994

Pryde, Philip R., *San Diego: An Introduction to the Region*, third edition, Kendall/Hunt Publishing Co., Dubuque, Iowa, 1992

Chapter 1

Bancroft, Hubert Howe, *History of California*, Vols. I, II, III, A.L. Bancroft & Co., San Francisco, 1884

Branco, F. Castelo, *Cabrillo's Nationality*, Academia de Marinha, Lisbon, 1987

Carrico, Richard L., *Strangers in a Stolen Land: American Indians in San Diego*, 1850-1880, Sierra Oaks Publishing Co., Sacramento, California, 1987

Case, Thomas, "The Year 1588 and San Diego de Alcala," *Journal of San Diego History*, Winter 1988 (Vol. 34:1), San Diego, 1988

Engelhardt, Fr. Zephyrin, *San Diego Mission*, James H. Barry Co., San Francisco, 1920

Kelsey, Harry, *Juan Rodriguez Cabrillo*, Huntington Library, San Marino, California, 1986

Lavender, David, *DeSoto, Coronado, Cabrillo: Explorers of the Northern Mystery*, U.S. Department of the Interior, Washington, D.C., 1992

Lemke, Nancy, *Cabrillo: First European Explorer of the California Coast*, EZ Nature Books, San Luis Obispo, 1991

Mathes, W. Michael, *Vizcaino and Spanish Expansion in the Pacific Ocean*, 1580-1630, California Historical Society, San Francisco, 1968

Moriarty, J.R. and M. Keistman, *A New Translation of the Summary Log of the Cabrillo Voyage in 1542*, San Diego Science Foundation, La Jolla, California, 1963

Pourade, Richard F., *The Explorers*, Union-Tribune Publishing Co., San Diego, 1960

Pourade, Richard F., *Time of the Bells*, Union-Tribune Publishing Co., San Diego, 1961

Pourade, Richard F., *The Silver Dons*, Union-Tribune Publishing Co., San Diego, 1963

Royal Geographical Society (Great Britain), *Oxford Atlas of Exploration*, Oxford University Press, New York, 1997

San Diego City Schools, *Spanish Colonial Era*, San Diego Unified School District, 1984; prepared for Old Town Historical-Cultural Program by the Community Relations and Integration Services Division

Smythe, William E., *History of San Diego*, The History Co., San Diego, 1908

Sturtevant, William C., general editor, *Handbook of North American Indians, Vol. 8*: California, Smithsonian Institution, Washington, D.C., 1978

Chapter 2

Adams, Charles Francis, *Richard Henry Dana: A Biography*, Houghton, Mifflin and Co., Boston, 1890

Annals of America, "Manifest Destiny," Vol. 7, 1841-1849, Encyclopedia Britannica, Chicago, 1968

Bancroft, Hubert Howe, *History of California*, Vols. II, III, IV, A.L. Bancroft & Co., San Francisco, 1884

Calif. Department of Parks & Recreation, *"Interpretive Program for Old Town San Diego State Historic Park,"* Vol. II: Site Recommendations, for Light-Freeman's San Diego House, GDP 02

Dana, Richard Henry Jr., *Two Years Before the Mast*, Dodd, Mead & Co., New York, 1946

Gale, Robert L., *Richard Henry Dana Jr.*, Twayne Publishers, New York, 1969

Harlow, Neal, *California Conquered: War and Peace on the Pacific, 1846-1850*, University of California Press, Berkeley, 1982

Killea, Lucy Lytle, *Colonial Foundations of Land Use and Society in San Diego, 1769-1846*, doctoral thesis, University of California, San Diego, 1975

Killea, Lucy Lytle, *"Political History of a Mexican Pueblo," Journal of San Diego History, spring and fall 1966 issues*, San Diego Historical Society

Moyer, Cecil C., *Historic Ranchos of San Diego*, Union-Tribune Publishing Co., San Diego, 1966

Pourade, Richard F., *The Silver Dons*, Union-Tribune Publishing Co., San Diego, 1963

Rolle, Andrew, *California: A History*, Harlan Davidson Inc., Arlington Heights, Illinois, 1987

The San Diego Union and *San Diego Union-Tribune*

Smythe, William E., *History of San Diego*, The History Co., San Diego, 1908

State Lands Commission, "Grants of Land in California Made by Spanish or Mexican Authorities," 1982, unpublished draft staff report

Ward, Mary F. and Iris H.W. Engstrand, "Rancho Guajome: An Architectural Legacy Preserved," *Journal of San Diego History*, 1996

Ward, Mary F., "History of Rancho de los Peñasquitos," San Diego County Department of Parks and Recreation, 1998

Chapter 3

Baum, L. Frank, *The Sea Fairies*, 1911, Books of Wonder (reprint), New York, no date

Breed, Clara E., *Turning the Pages: San Diego Public Library History, 1882-1982*, Friends of the San Diego Public Library, 1983

Crane, Clare, "Jesse Shepard and the Spark of Genius," *Journal of San Diego History*, Spring 1987

Fuller, Theodore W., *San Diego Originals*, California Profiles Publications, Pleasant Hill, California, 1987

The Golden Era, 1889-1890

MacPhail, Elizabeth C., *Kate Sessions: Pioneer Horticulturist*, San Diego Historical Society, 1976

MacPhail, Elizabeth C., *The Story of New San Diego and of its Founder Alonzo E. Horton*, San Diego Historical Society, 1979

Marston, Mary Gilman, *George White Marston: A Family Chronicle*, Ward Ritchie Press, 1956

Pourade, Richard F., *The Glory Years*, Union-Tribune Publishing Co., San Diego, 1964

Pourade, Richard F., *Gold in the Sun*, Union-Tribune Publishing Co., San Diego, 1965

Smythe, William E., *History of San Diego*, 1542-1908, The History Co., San Diego, 1908

Starr, Raymond, San Diego State University: *A History in Word and Image*, SDSU Press, 1995

Van Dyke, Theodore S., *The Italy of Southern California*, San Diego Union Co., 1886

Van Dyke, Theodore S., *Millionaires for a Day: An Inside History of the Great Southern California "Boom"*, Fords, Howard & Hulbert, New York, 1890

Chapter 4

Amero, Richard, *The San Diego Expositions*, manuscript, 1996.

Baumann, Thomas, *Kensington-Talmadge, 1909-1997*, Ellipsys International Publications, San Diego, 1997

Branton, Pamela Hart, *The Works Progress Administration in San Diego County, 1935-1943*, San Diego State University, history thesis, 1991

Christman, Florence, *The Romance of Balboa Park*, San Diego Historical Society, 1988

Estes, Donald H. and Matthew T. Estes, "Further and Further Away: The Relocation of San Diego's Nikkei Community, 1942," *Journal of San Diego History*, Winter-Spring 1993

Fuller, Theodore W., *San Diego Originals*, California Profiles Publications, Pleasant Hill, Calif., 1987

Hanft, Robert M., *San Diego & Arizona: The Impossible Railroad*, Trans-Anglo Books, Glendale, Calif., 1984

Hennessey, Gregg Robert. *City Planning, Progressivism, and the Development of San Diego, 1908-1926*, San Diego State University thesis, 1977. (F869 S22H42).

Heilbron, Carl H., *History of San Diego County*, San Diego Press Club, 1936

Higgins, Shelley, *This Fantastic City — San Diego*, City of San Diego, 1956

Joyce, Barry Alan, *A Harbor Worth Defending: A Military History of Point Loma*, Cabrillo Historical Association, San Diego, 1995

Kettner, William, *Why It Was Done and How*, self-published, San Diego, 1923

Killory, Christine, "Temporary Suburbs: The Lost Opportunity of San Diego's National Defense Housing Projects," *Journal of San Diego History*, Winter-Spring, 1993

Life, July 28, 1941

"Long Term Program of Capital Expenditures," City of San Diego, May 2, 1938

Lotchin, Roger W., *Fortress California: 1910-1961 — From Warfare to Welfare*, Oxford University Press, New York, 1992

Marston, Mary Gilman, *George White Marston: A Family Chronicle*, Ward Ritchie Press, 1956

Montes, Gregory, "San Diego's City Park, 1902-1910," *Journal of San Diego History*, Winter 1979; "Balboa Park, 1909-1911: The

Rise and Fall of the Olmsted Plan," *Journal of San Diego History*, Winter 1982

Nash, Gerald N., *The American West Transformed: The Impact of the Second World War*, Indiana University Press, Bloomington, Indiana, 1985

National Geographic, January 1942

Nolen, *A Comprehensive City Plan for San Diego, California*, City Planning Department, 1926,

"Pathfinders Social Survey of San Diego," College Woman's Club, March 1914

Petersen, Martin E, *Second Nature: Four Early San Diego Landscape Painters*, San Diego Museum of Art, 1991; Maurice Braun paintings were exhibited Oklahoma, Mississippi, Utah and North Carolina before returning to San Diego for a show in 1951.

Ports, Uldis, "Geraniums vs. Smokestacks: San Diego's Mayoralty Campaign of 1917," *Journal of San Diego History*, Summer 1975

Proffitt, T.D. III, *Tijuana: The History of a Mexican Metropolis*, SDSU Press, 1994

Pourade, Richard F., *Gold in the Sun, 1965, The Rising Tide, 1967, City of the Dream, 1977,* Union-Tribune Publishing Co., San Diego

Sacks, Benjamin, "The Duchess of Windsor and the Coronado Legend," *Journal of San Diego History*, Fall 1987, Winter 1988

Saturday Evening Post, 19 July 1941

Scott, Mary, *San Diego: Air Capital of the West*, San Diego Aerospace Museum, 1991

The San Diego Union, Evening Tribune,

Smith, Dave, *memo to Assistant Planning Director Mike Stepner,* 17 December 1985

Starr, Kevin, *The Dream Endures: California Enters the 1940s,* Oxford University Press, New York, 1997

Starr, Raymond, San Diego State University: *A History in Word and Image,* San Diego State University Press, 1995

Taschner, Mary, Richard Requa: *Southern California Architect, 1881-1941*, University of San Diego, 1982 thesis

Chapter 5

Breed, Clara E., *Turning the Pages: San Diego Public Library History, 1882-1982,* Friends of the San Diego Public Library, San Diego, 1983

Amero, Richard, *San Diego Expositions*, manuscript, 1996

Day & Zimmerman, "Industrial and Commercial Survey of the City of San Diego and San Diego County," prepared for the San Diego Chamber of Commerce, 31 March 1945

Davis, Susan G., Spectacular Nature: *Corporate Culture and the Sea World Experience*, University of California Press, Berkeley, 1997

Klaus, Arnold, *History of the San Diego Chamber of Commerce, manuscript,* 1970 *San Diego Magazine*

Kimbrough, Jack, *Oral history,* San Diego Historical Society Research Archives, 11 October 1990

Los Angeles Times

Marston, Mary, George White Marston, *A Family Chronicle*, Ward Ritchie Press, 1956

McGill, William J., *The Year of the Monkey: Revolt on Campus, 1968-69*, McGraw-Hill Book Co., New York, 1982

Morgan, Neil, *San Diego: The Unconventional City*, Morgan House, San Diego, 1972

Pourade, Richard F., *City of the Dream*, Copley Books, San Diego, 1977

Revelle, Roger, "The Multiple Functions of a Graduate School," address to seventh conference of the Princeton Graduate Alumni and Graduate College Association, Princeton, New Jersey, December 28,1958

Rick, Glenn A. *San Diego, 1927-1955: Recollections of a City Planner*, published by William Rick, San Diego, 1977

The San Diego Union

The San Diego Union-Tribune

The [San Diego] [Evening] Tribune

Scott Anderson, Nancy, *An Improbable Venture: A History of the University of California, San Diego,* The UCSD Press, La Jolla, 1993

Starr, Kevin, *The Dream Endures: California Enters the 1940s,* Oxford University Press, 1997

Starr, Raymond, *San Diego State University: A History in Word and Image*, SDSU Press, 1995

Time magazine

Chapter 6

Clement, Norris C. and Eduardo Zepeda Miramontes, editors, *San Diego-Tijuana in Transition: A Regional Analysis, Institute for Regional Studies of the Californias*, San Diego State University, 1993

Hahn, Ernest W., *Letter to San Diego Redevelopment Agency,* May 16,1974, Centre City Development Corp. archives

Holle, Gena, *The San Diego Trolley,* Interurban Press, Glendale, Calif., 1990

Morgan, Neil, "San Diego — Where Two Californias Meet," , *National Geographic*, August 1989, p. 196

New York Times, March 19,1986

San Diego Magazine, April 1974

San Diego Sourcebook 1998, San Diego Daily Transcript

The San Diego Union

The San Diego Union-Tribune

The (Evening) (San Diego) Tribune

Scott Anderson, Nancy, *An Improbable Venture: A History of the University of California*, San Diego, UCSD Press, La Jolla, Calif., 1993

Annual Financial Report, 1997, University of California, San Diego

Urban Land, April 1994, Urban Land Institute, Washington, D.C.

Weisman, Alan, *La Frontera: The United States Border with Mexico*, Harcourt Brace Jovanovich, San Diego, 1986

Courtesy San Diego Historical Society

Index

10th Cavalry Regiment (Camp Lockett) 114
Academy of Music 84
African-American 46,50,62,112,132,133
African-Hispanics 29
Agassiz, Louis 64
Agua Caliente Race Track 40,96
Allen, Dennis V. 112
Allen, Frank P. 93
Allen, Marcus 177
Alta California 24,44
Alvarado, Francisco María 41
Alvarado, Juan Bautista 43
Alvarado, Pedro de 20
American Indians 12,29,43,68,109
American Society of Landscape Architects 78
Amero, Richard 110
Anderson, Dr. Albert 130
Anderson, Eddie 112
Anheuser-Busch 128
Anza-Borrego Desert 13
Appleyard, Donald 143,144
Aquarium Society 128
Arbor Day 78
ARCO Olympic Training Center 169
Argüello, Luis 32
Argüello, Santiago 32,41
Arlington National Cemetery 179
Armstrong, Captain James 44
Army Air Corps 108
Army Corps of Engineers 67
Art Walk 164
Atchison, Topeka & Santa Fe Railway 69,96
Atherton, David 175
Babcock, Elisha S. 71
Bacon, Mayor John L. 104
Baja California 10,19,44,151,168
Balboa Naval Hospital 101,176
Balboa Park 59,73,80,91,123,175
Balboa, Vasco Nuñez de 93
Balearic Islands 23
Ballast Point 30,38,66
Bancroft Block 68
Bancroft, Hubert Howe 42
Bandini, Don Juan 41
Bandini, Juan Lorenzo 42
Bandini, Ysidora 42
Batiquitos Lagoon 172
Battle of San Diego Bay 38
Baum, L. Frank 72
Bautista, Juan 28,43
Bean, Joshua H. 48
Benbough, Mayor Percy 110
Benny, Jack 112
Benson Lumber Company 109
Bilbray, Brian 170
Birch, James 50
Black, William Thurston 58

Blevins-Murray, Pat 133
Bohmer, Peter 135
Bonaparte, Napoleon 31,57
Borrego Springs 171
Bouchard, Captain Hippolyte de 31
Boyle, Henry G. 47
Breed, Clara 113,125
Breitbard, Robert 130
Briggs, Henry 27
Brigham, Fro. 133
Britten, Representative Fred 100
Britton, James II 126
Brown Field 115, 169
Brown, Buster 129
Brown, Charles 134
Brown, Governor Edmund G. 131
Brunmark, Walter 126
Buddy, Bishop Charles F. 123
Burgener, Louis 124
Bynon, A. A. 70
Cabrillo Bridge 93,124
Cabrillo, Juan Rodríguez ....19-21; 40th anniversary 75
Cabrillo National Monument 86
Cabrillo, Gerónimo 20
Cahuilla 10,40
Calexico 114
California Institute of Technology 122
California Pacific International Exposition 109
California Southern Railroad 69
California State University 172
California Western University 75,123
CalMat Properties Co. 167
Camp Callan 115,124
Camp Elliott 115
Camp Kearny 100
Camp Kidd 114
Camp Lockett 114
Camp Matthews 115
Camp Pendleton 115,142,145
Camp Pendleton Marine Corps Base 31,115,142,145
Campbell, City Manager O. M. 122,134
Capps, Mayor Edwin M. 76
Carlin, Kari 142
Carlsbad 71,172
Carlson, Mayor William H., ("Billy") 76
Carmel Mountain Ranch 172
Carmel Valley 135,172
Carnegie, Andrew 78
Carrico, Richard 28
Carson, Kit 46
Case, Thomas E. 22
Catellus Development 165
Catherine II 24
Centre City Development Corp. (CCDC) 157-162
Century of Progress Exposition 109
Chacon, Peter 140
Chamber of Commerce, San Diego 52,59,80,92,122

Chapman, Carlton T. 45
Chapman, Charles 28
Chevron Land Development 167
Chico, Colonel Mariano 44
Chula Vista 110,169
Civic Improvement Committee,
Civil Aeronautics Administration 124
Clairemont 123, 124
Cleaver, Eldridge 134
Cleveland, Richard J. 30
Clinton, President Bill 179
Cocopa Mountains 10
Cody, Buffalo "Wild Bill" 72
Coffelt, Beth 158
Coleman Creek 62
Coleman, Frederick 62
Colorado River 12,29,107,125
Columbia University 135
Community Concourse 129,157
Conner, Dennis 177
Consolidated Aircraft (Convair)(General Dynamics) 108,122
Constansó, Miguel 28
Cooper, Walter W. 112
Coors Amphitheatre 170
Copley Symphony Hall (Fox Theater) 162
Copley, Helen 163
Copley, James 123
Copperheads 52
Coronado 82,102,131,170
Coronado Islands 21,58
Cortez Hill 158
Cortez, Hernando 19
Cosmopolitan Hotel 62
Couts, Cave Johnson 42
Coyne, Sheriff Joseph 67
Craven, William 172
Crawford, Superintendent Will C. 112
Creole Palace 132
Crespi, Father Juan 24
Crocker, Charles 64
Cunanan, Andrew 179
Curran, Mayor Frank 129,137,138
Curtiss, Glenn A. 97,107
Dail, Mayor Charles C. 123,157
Damrosch, Walter 97
Dana, Richard Henry 37-40
Davidson, G. Aubrey 91
Davis, Susan G. 128
Davis, William Heath 41,161
Day & Zimmerman 121
Del Mar 14,71,108,131,172
Del Mar Fair 173
Del Mar Racetrack 131
Derby, Lieutenant George H. 49
Deutsches Gasthaus 67
Dickinson, William Green 58
Dominican California 29
Drugan, Frank 109
Duhuat-Cilly, Bernard 32
DuPont, Captain Samuel F. 45
Earp, Wyatt 72
East County 157
East Village 158
Echeandia, Governor José Maria 33,43

Edison, Thomas 94
Edward, Prince of Wales 102
El Cajon 66,98,151,171
El Cajon Boulevard 98
El Cajon Valley 31
El Camino Real 33,42
El Cortez Hotel 158
El Prado 130
Electric Building 143,176
Elizabeth I of England 22
Elizabeth II of United Kingdom 175
Ellington, Duke 132
Embarcadero 91
Emerald Hills 174
Emory, Army Lieutenant William H. 46,47
Encinitas 14, 172
Engelhardt, Zephyrin 29
Ensenada 10,25
Erickson, Arthur 161
Escondido 71,108,172
Estudillo, José María 32,42
Euterpe (*Star of India*) 105
Evenson, Bea 130
Executive Order 8802 (anti-discrimination) 112
Fairbanks, Douglas 96
Fairman, Planning Director James 134
Fashion Valley 130,166
Fenton, H. G. 167
Ferrer, Bartolomé 21
Figueroa, Governor José 43
Fisher Opera House 72
Fitch, Henry Delano 43
Fleet, Reuben H. 108,115
Fletcher, Austin B. 102
Fletcher, Ed 80,102
Flores, Enrique 98
Flynn, Pat 142
Ford Building 109
Ford Motor Co. 109
Ford, Edsel 109
Ford, Henry 94
Forstall, Richard 169
Fort Guijarros 30,38
Fort Rosecrans 86,113
Fort Rosecrans National Cemetery 79
Fort Stockton 87
Franklin House 52
Freeman, Richard 50
Freilich, Robert 139
Frémont, Lieutenant John C. 45
Fuster, Father Vicente 27
Gadsden Purchase 49
Gálvez, José de 23
Garra, Antonio 49
Gaslamp Quarter 48,67,98,131,158,161
Gaslamp Quarter Association 161
Geisel, Theodor (Dr. Seuss) 137,175
Gemological Society of America 172
General Atomics 122
General Dynamics 108,122
Gerichten, Charles P. 67
Giannoulis, Ted 140
Giddings, George H. 50
Gila River Valley 49

Gill, Irving J.	73,93,176
Gillespie Field	115
Glick, Allen R.	140
Goff, James	145
Gold Gulch	109
Gold Rush	48
Goldberger, Paul	159
Golden Eagles	68
Golden Era	70
Golden Hall	157
Golden Hill	132,174
Golding, Mayor Susan	144,165
Goldman, Emma	98
Goodhue, Bertram G.	93
Grady, Don Romera	140
Graham, Peter	139
Grant Club	137
Grant Grill	132
Grant Hotel, U.S.	59,97,132
Grant, Ulysses S.	40
Grant, Ulysses S. Jr.	72
Gray, Andrew B.	48
Great White Fleet	79,100
Greek Theater	108
Gregston, Gene	130
Griffin, John S.	45
Gunn, Douglas	76
Gwynn, Tony	177
Gyzelaar, Captain Henry	38
Haelsig, Harry	126,134
Hahn, Ernest W.	158
Hale, George Ellery	122
Hall, George P.	127
Hamilton, Charles	68
Haraszthy, Sheriff Agoston	48
Harbor Drive	68,86,104,130,149,161
Harbor Island	139
Harcourt Brace Jovanovich	128
Hard Rock Cafe	162
Haro, Jess	140
Harrison, President Benjamin	73
Harrison, James	72
Hatfield, Charles M.	96
Hayes, Thomas J.	71
Hazard Center	166
Hebbard, William S.	80
Hedgecock, Roger	174
Hegland, Sheridan	122
Held, Anna	72
Helix Heights	177
Henfield, John	52
Henshaw, William G.	107
Hensley, George B.	65
Hidalgo, Miguel	31
Higgins, Shelley J.	107
Hillcrest	140,165
Hilton, Barron	130
Hilton, Conrad	130
Historic Shrine Foundation	50
Hitch, Councilman Allen	137
Hoffman, Frederic de	122
Holiday Inn on the Bay	149
Hollister, D. A.	58
Hollywood	103,124
Holmes, Oliver Wendell	37
Homestead	75
Hoover, President Herbert	109
Hopkins, John Jay	122
Horton Bank	61
Horton House	59,157
Horton Library Association	59
Horton Plaza (park)	73,80,97
Horton Plaza (shopping center)	159
Horton Plaza Redevelopment Project	158
Horton, Alonzo Erastus	52,57,79,131,157
Horton, Lydia	78
Horton, Sarah Wilson Babe	58
Hostick, Robert	131
Hot Springs Peak	13
Hotel Del Coronado	170
Hotel Douglas	132
Houston, Texas President Sam	44
Howard, Volney E.	66
Hrdlicka, Ales	94
Hunter, Captain Jesse D.	47
Indian Village	96
Ingalls, Elizabeth	132
Irvine	173
Islas Desiertas (Coronado Islands)	21
Jack-in-the-Box	129
Jackson, Helen Hunt	43
Jackson, Laurence	135
Jackson, President Andrew	44
Jacumba	63
Jahn, Helmut	163
Janssens, Agustin	41
Jayme, Father Luís	27
Jefferson, President Thomas	44
Jerde, Jon	159
Jessop, Arthur	126
Jiménez, Fortún	19
Jobs and Growth Association	134
Johnson, Captain George A.	66
Johnson, Governor Hiram	91
Johnson, Wayman	133
Jones, Commodore Thomas ap Catesby	44
Jones, Dora L.	132
Jones, William	142
Julian	135
Julian Gold Rush	61
Junípero	23
Kahn, Louis	123
Kearny Mesa	122,173
Kearny, General Stephen Watts	45
Keen, Harold	116,131
Keffler, Joe	124
Kelsey, Harry	20
Kennedy, Robert F.	135
Kensington Heights	103
Kensington Park	103
Kent State University	135
Kettner, Congressman William	100
KGB	140
Kidd, Isaac C.	114
Kimball, Frank A.	63,68,69
Kimball, Warren	63
King, Martin Luther Jr.	135
Kino, Father Eusebio	27

Knapp, Lydia Maria 75
Kona Kai Club 137
Kumeyaay 10,25
La Costa Spa 172
La Jolla 71,82,123,167
La Jolla Cove 72
La Jolla Museum of Contemporary Art 176
La Jolla Playhouse, The 175
La Jolla Shores 10,104,131
La Jolla Valley 174
La Jolla-Torrey Pines 122
La Mesa 126,171
Laguna Mountains 13
Lake Hodges 46
Lake Texcoco 20
Lakeside 66
Lancaster, Burt 97
Lane Field 130
Langtry, Lily 72
Las Vegas 140
Lasuén, Father Fermín Francisco de 28
Lawrence, M. Larry 131,170
Leach's Opera House 69
Legoland California 172
Leland, Malcolm 129
Lelia Byrd 30,38
Lemon Grove 174
Levitt, William 124
Light, Allen B. 49
Lincoln High School 133
Lincoln, President Abraham 42,70
Linda Vista 101,123
Linda Vista Federal Housing Project 112
Lindbergh Field 107,108,124,148,163
Lindbergh, Charles A. 107,108
Lipton Tea Company 94
Little Italy 158
Lockling, L. L. 59
Loewes Coronado Bay Resort 170
Long Beach 128
Lopez, Fred J. 133
Lopez, Ignacio 32
Lorwin, Mayor Rosalind 173
Los Angeles 32,40,64,91,122,145,159
Lotchin, Roger W. 100
Louganis, Greg 177
Lucchino, Larry 177
Luomala, Katharine 12
Lyceum Theater 165
Lynch, Kevin 143,144
MacMullen, Jerry 38
MacPhail, Elizabeth 68
Madison, President James 57
Magic Mountain 128
Mahoney, B. Franklin 107
Marcuse, Herbert 134
Marina Park 161
Marine Corps 100,123,148
Marriott Suites 163
Marshall, John 47
Marston Company 68
Marston, George W. 59,67,68,80,91,144
Marston, Hamilton 144
Marston, Mary 144

Massachusetts Institute of Technology 143,144
May Company 126,170
McCartney, Paul 129
McCarty, Arthur 128
McDonald's Restaurant 137
McGill, William J. 134
McKenzie, Flint and Winsby Building 161
McPherson, Aimee Semple 109
Memphis & El Paso Railroad 63
Mendoza, Viceroy Antonio 20,21
Metropolitan Transit Development Board (MTDB) 164
Metropolitan Water District 125
Mexican-American War 42,63
Mexican-Americans 140
Mexico 10,29,31,40,76,96,85,121,159,168
Mexico City 43,76
Meyers, William H. 35
Miami 179
Miami Beach 139
Mickey Mouse 109
Mier y Terán, José 43
Millay, George 128
Mills, Senator James R. 163
Mingei International (Folk Art) Museum 176
Mira Mesa 138
Miramar Marine (Naval) Corps Air Station 100,101,124
Mission Bay 66,72,118,104,124
Mission Bay Park 127,167
Mission Beach 86,115,127
Mission Beach Amusement Center 127
Mission Dam 17
Mission Gorge 32,174
Mission San Diego ....de Alcalá 17,40,104
Mission Trails Regional Park 17,174
Mission Valley 10,68,82,104,110,149,157,166
Modjeska, Helen 72
Moelter, Charles 116
Monterey 22,39,44,102
Montezuma Mesa 105
Montgomery Field 125
Montgomery, John J. 107
Montroy, Martin J. 133
Moores, John 177
Morena Reservoir 96
Morgan, Neil 139
Mormon Battalion 47
Morrison, Harry 30
Morse, Ephraim W. 52,58
Mount Palomar 10,179
Movimiento Estudiantil Chicano 135
Mule Hill 46
Murphy Canyon 176,177
Murphy, Jack 130,166
Murray, James A. 107
Museum of Contemporary Art 164
Museum of Photographic Arts 176
Napa Valley 48
Nash, Gerald N. 115
Nash, Joseph 68
Nash, N. Richard 97
National City 31,58,170
National Geographic 111
National Municipal League 129
National Science Foundation 123

Native Americans	12,29,43,68,109
Nature Interpretive Center	169
Naval Amphibious Base	115
Naval Hospital	100
Naval Station San Diego	100
Naval Supply Center	115
Naval Training Center	100
Navy Field	161
Nay, Don L.	129
New San Diego	48
New York City	78,93
New York Symphony	97
New York Times	159
New York Yankees	177
New Zealand	105,177
Nixon, President Richard	137,139
Nolen Plan	80-87,91,104,144,179
Nolen, John	91,126,179
Normal Heights	75
Normal School	75,105,126
North City West (Carmel Valley)	135,172
North County	10,145,157
North Embarcadero	163
North Island	65,97,125,148
North Island Naval Air Station	100
North Mission Beach	127
North Park	93,143,174
Oakland Raiders	177
Ocean Beach	71,104,135
Oceanside	42,69,96,137,172
O'Connor, Mayor Maureen	164
Ogawa, Louis	113
Ohio National Guard	135
Old Globe Theatre	109,142,175
Old Spaghetti Factory	161
Old Town	42,58,87
Old Town Plaza	45,62
Olmsted Brothers	93
Olten, Carol	129
Orange County	157
Orchids & Onions Awards	173
Ordóñez de Montalvo, Garci	19
Osborne, John B.	79
O'Sullivan, John	46
Osuna, Juan María	43
Otay Mesa	107,151,169
Otay Ranch	41,169
Otay River	174
Otay Valley Regional Park	174
Over-the-Line Tournaments	127
Pacific Beach	71,104
Pacific Coast League Padres	130
Pacific Highway	91,130
Pacific Parachute Company	112
Pacific Rim	121,167
Pacific Southwest Airlines	143
Palomar Observatory	122
Panama-California Exposition	91-99
Pangborn Aircraft Co.	107
Pantoja House	48
Pantoja Park	161
Pardee Construction Company	161
Parrish, John E.	112
Parsons, Samuel	78,80,93
Pathfinders Social Survey of San Diego	98
Pattie, James O.	33
Pearl Harbor	113
Pendleton, General Joseph	115
Pennsylvania Railroad	63
Persian Gulf War	175
Peterson, Clifford	112
Peterson, Robert O.	131
Phelps, Captain W. D.	44
Philip II of Spain	22
Phillips, Harriet	93
Phoenix, John (George H. Derby)	49
Pico, Andrés	35
Pico, Governor Pío	42,44
Pine Hills	80
Pioneer Society	93
Poinsett, Joel R.	44
Point Loma	14,30,37,58,86,92,123,170
Point Loma Nazarene College	75
Polk, President James K.	42
Poole, Charles H.	49
Portilla, Captain Pablo de la	33
Portland	48
Portolá, Governor Gaspar de	23
Pourade, Richard F.	31,41,68
Poway	31,172
Price, Edmund T.	108
Pridemore, Earl	134
Princeton University	122
Prudden, George H.	108
Pryde, Philip R.	13
Qualcomm (San Diego) (Jack Murphy) Stadium	130,166
Qualcomm Corporation	167,177
Queen Calafia	19
Quigley, Rob Wellington	165
Ramona	31,43
Rancho Bernardo	31,169
Rancho Buena Vista	43
Rancho Guajome	42
Rancho Peñasquitos	41,135,139, 172
Rancho San Diego	171
Rancho Santa Fe	10,172
Rancho Santa Margarita	115
Rand, Sally	110
Rand, Tamara	140
Reid, James W.	71
Reid, Merritt	71
Remondino, Peter C.	69
Republican Convention	135
Republican National Committee	139
Requa, Richard	103
Reuben H. Fleet Science Center	176
Revelle, Roger	122,167
Rice, Lilian	104,127
Rick, Glenn A.	105,127
Ridgley, Roberta	131
Ripa, Cesare	20
Ritter, William E.	76
Rivera y Moncada, Governor Fernando de	28
Robeson, Paul	132
Robinson, Alfred	43
Rocha, Juan José	33
Rockefeller Foundation	122
Rockwell Field	108

Rodríguez, Lieutenant Manuel	30
Rogers, Malcolm	10
Rogers, Will	105
Rohr, Fred H.	110
Romero, Don	140
Roosevelt Junior High School	105
Roosevelt, President Franklin D.	94
Roosevelt, President Theodore	79,94,100,109
Rosarito Beach	47
Rose Canyon	50
Rose, Louis	50
Rosecrans, General William S.	63
Rouse, James	158
Royal Inn	149
Royal Presidio	20
Ruiz, Francisco María	32,41
Ruocco, Lloyd	131
Russ, Joseph	71
Ryan Aeronautical Co.	107
Ryan Brougham	107
Ryan, T. Claude	107
Sailor, Michael	179
Salk Institute	122
Salk, Jonas	123
San Andreas fault	13
San Antonio	24
San Bernardino	69,157
San Blas	25,31
San Carlos	24
San Diego & Arizona Railroad	76,78,85,99
San Diegans Incorporated	129,144
San Diego Aerospace Museum	109,143
San Diego Bay	22,38,105,143,170
San Diego Bicentennial	128
San Diego Chamber of Commerce	52,59,80,92,122
San Diego Chargers	130,166,176
San Diego City Council	98,112,122,144,174
San Diego City Hall	78,137
San Diego Convention Center	158,161
San Diego County	48,94,124,172
San Diego County Board of Supervisors	62
San Diego County Courthouse	70
San Diego County Water Authority	125
San Diego Dialogue	168
San Diego Electric Railway Co.	93
San Diego General Plan	134
San Diego Hall of Champions Sports Museum	176
San Diego Herald, The	49
San Diego High School	71,98
San Diego International Sports Arena	130,177
San Diego Land and Town Company	58
San Diego Magazine	124,140,158
San Diego Mission Restoration Commission	104
San Diego Museum of Art	97,175
San Diego Museum of Man	97,176
San Diego Opera	175
San Diego Padres	130,137,166,176
San Diego Park Commission	100
San Diego Philharmonic Society	68
San Diego Police	108
San Diego Public Library	68,81,124
San Diego Race Relations Society	112
San Diego River	17,49,66,127,149,166
San Diego State (College) University	22,75,105,123,133,164
San Diego State College	123
San Diego State Teachers College	105
San Diego Symphony	162
San Diego Trolley	163
San Diego Unified Port District	129,161
San Diego Unified School District	142,175
San Diego Union, The	59,80,93,126
San Diego Union-Tribune Publishing Company	158
San Diego Wild Animal Park	134,176
San Diego Yacht Club	177
San Diego Zoo	97,134,176
San Diego-Coronado Bay Bridge	131,163,171
San Dieguito	10,172
San Dieguito River	10
San Dieguito River Valley	173
San Diego Maritime Museum	107
San Francisco	23,42,57,94,139
San Francisco Bay	23,100
San Francisco Naval Training Station	101
San Gorgonio Pass	64
San Juan Capistrano	28,37
San Luís Obispo	31
San Luís Rey	28,31,33,42,137
San Marcos	43,172
San Miguel	20
San Miguel (San Diego)	21
San Pasqual Battle	31,45
San Pasqual Valley	31,134,176
San Pedro	32,37,92
San Salvador	20
San Ysidro	31,42,103,164,151
Sanchez, Roberto A.	168
Santa Barbara	14,21,39,101
Santa Catalina	21
Santa Cruz (La Paz)	19
Santa Fe Depot	71,161
Santa Margarita	40
Santa Maria de Los Peñasquitos (rancho)	32,41
Santa Rosa Island	14
Santa Ysabel	31,40
Santo Tomás	21
Saturday Evening Post	110
Save our Heritage Organisation	131
Schiller, Marcus	68
Schumann-Heink, Ernestine	97
Schuyler, Howard	66,94
Scott, Colonel Thomas A.	63
Scott, George A.	135
Scripps Institution of Oceanography	76,122
Scripps Ranch	172
Scripps, Ellen Browning	76
Scripps-Howard Newspapers	109
SeaWorld	128
Seaport Village	163
Seau, Junior	177
Sefton, Joseph W. Jr.	110
Serra, Father Junípero (Miguel José)	23,24,75
Sessions, Kate O.	72,73
Seuss, Dr. (Theodor Geisel)	137,175
Seward, Secretary of State William	42
Shapell Housing	161
Shepard, Jesse	72
Sheraton Hotel	139
Shimizu Land Corporation	163

Silberman, Richard T.	131
Smith, C. Arnhold	130,137
Smithsonian Institution	94
Smythe, William E.	47
Solana Beach	135,172
Solar Aircraft	108
Soledad Mountain	86
Sorrento Hills	167
Sorrento Mesa	167
Sousa, John Philip	72
South Bay	115,157
Southern Pacific & Atlantic Railroad Company	49
Southern Pacific Railway	63,163
Soviet Arts Festival	175
Spalding, A. G.	102
Spanish Landing	130
Spencer, Navy Lieutenant Earl W.	102
Spice Islands	20
Spirit of St. Louis	107
Sports Arena	130,177
Spreckels Organ Pavilion	109
Spreckels Theater	97,165,175
Spreckels, John D.	72,93,127,165
Star of India	105
Starbucks	162
Starlight Musical Theater	175
Starr, Kevin	101
State Normal School	75
Stearns, Abel	42
Stevens, George	142
Stockton, Commodore Robert F.	46
Stonewall Mine	64
Strait of Anián	20
Super Bowl XXXII	167
Sweetwater Dam	96
Swing, Phil	107
Switzerland	97,170
Taft, President William Howard	94
Taggart, Charles P.	66
Tavares, Carlos and Claire	124
Teamsters Union	140
Temecula	69,173
Temple Beth Israel	68
Temporary Paradise?	143,144,153
Tent City	171
Texas	44,63
Theater Square	164
Theosophical Society	75
Thorpe, Hartwick	72
Tijuana	13,21,47,75,96,121
Tijuana River	13,31,47,126,151,168,170
Tijuana Trolley	164
Tingley, Katherine A.	75
Torrey Pines	82
Torrey Pines Mesa	104,122,167
Treaty of Cahuenga	46
Treaty of Guadalupe Hidalgo	47
Tribune-Sun	116
Truman, President Harry S.	116
Twain, Mark	72
Tyler, President John	44
U. S. Army Corps of Engineers	166
U. S. National Bank	137
U. S. Small Business Administration	133
U. S. Topographical Engineers	49
U.S. Navy	30,116,124,161
Ubach, Father Antonio	22,79
UC Berkeley	76
Union Bank	131
United States International University	75
University City	167
University Heights	93,126
University of California, San Diego	76,122,126,144,164,167,179
University of San Diego	123
University Towne Centre	164
Urban Outfitters	162
Van Dyke, Theodore S.	69
Van Thieu, Nguyen	142
Vancouver, George	29
Ventura County	128
Vergerano, María	27
Versace, Gianni	178
Victoria, Colonel Manuel	43
Viejas Indian	171
Vietnam War	135
Vila, Vincente	24
Vinson, Joseph	133
Vizcaíno, Sebastián	21
VJ Day	114,116
Wagner, Harrison "Harr"	72
Walker, Mary C.	52
Walker, William	51
Walton, Bill	177
Warfield, Wallis	102
Warner Springs	13
Warner, Charles Dudley	69
Warner, Jonathan	49
Waterman, Governor Robert W.	73
Waterman, Waldo	107
Weede, Lieutenant John	67
Weisman, Alan	169
Weiss, Mandell	175
Wells Fargo	58
Wells, David	177
West, Mae	109
Westfield shopping centers	159
Westgate Hotel	137
Westgate Park	130
Whaley House	50
Whaley, Thomas	50
Wilde, Louis J.	99,102
Wilde, Lucille	102
Williams, Leon	142
Wilson, Mayor (Senator) Pete	75,138,139,158
Wilson, President Woodrow	94
Windansea Beach	129
Winship, Captain Charles	30
Wonderful Wizard of Oz, The	72
World's (Chicago) Columbian Exposition	73
World Progress Exposition	122
World War I	91,115
World War II	107,130,157
Wright Brothers	107
Wright, Frank Lloyd	175
Yellow Cab Company	137
YMCA	68
Zamorano, Agustín	44
ZLAC Rowing Club	127

Partners Index

ABC Veterinary Hospitals	342
American Security Mortgage	226
American Specialty Health Plans	376
Anthony's Fish Grotto	288
Architect Milford Wayne Donaldson, FAIA	214
Arrowhead Group of Companies	226
BFGoodrich Aerospace/Aerostructures Group	252
Babe's, Inc.	266
Baja Duty Free	312
Balloon Flights, LLC	242
Bannister Steel, Inc.	192
Bazaar Del Mundo	280
Bernardo Winery	313
Big Sister League of San Diego	396
Blue Sky Software	415
Borton, Petrini & Conron, LLP	344
Brighton Health Alliance	378
Broadcast Images, Inc.	346
C&B Steel	215
California Closets	194
Casper Company	216
Center for Leadership Studies	348
Center Glass Company	217
Central Meat & Provision Company	267
Cloud 9 Shuttle	328
Coleman College	398
Coles Carpets	314
Collins Plumbing, Inc.	196
D.A. Whitacre Construction, Inc.	198
Daily Marine	268
Dataskill	416
David L. Wolf, M.D., F.A.C.S.	380
De Anza Bay Resort	399
Deer Park Winery & Auto Museum	315
Deering Banjo Company	256
DEFT Companies, Inc.	228
Dewhurst & Associates	200
Digirad Corporation	394
Dr. Alan M. Blum, D.C.	397
Dr. Peter K. Hellwig, DDS & Associates	400
Dutch Growers Nurseries, Ltd.	316
Dyson & Dyson Real Estate Associates	350
Edge Semiconductor	418
El Indio Mexican Restaurant	317
Environmental Health Coalition	401
Erreca's Inc.	218
Falcon West Insurance Brokers	364
FAS-EBA Insurance Services	354
Fireworks & Stage FX America, Inc.	234
Flag Crafters, Inc.	264
Gen-Probe	382
Greitzer Brokers, Inc.	330
Hirsch & Company Consulting Engineers	356
HNC Software Inc.	420
Hovey & Kirby, A.P.C.	358
Inacom Corporation	422
Insight Electronics, LLC	430
Interventional Technologies, Inc.	412
J.P. Witherow Roofing Co.	219
Jakob Gerhardt	292
John Lenore Company	246
Josh Mitchell Photography	294

Karl Strauss Breweries	296
Kearny Mesa Convalescent Hospital and Nursing Home	384
Kenai Construction Co., Inc.	202
"King" Stahlman Bail Bonds	298
Klinedinst, Fliehman & McKillop	365
L-3 Communications Conic Division	424
La Valencia Hotel	300
Logret Import and Export Company	250
Loma Alta Children's School	402
Luchner Tool Engineering Inc.	360
National Decision Systems	426
Newland Communities	204
North County Economic Development Council	366
Orfila Vineyards & Winery	319
Pacific Bell	332
Pacific Messenger Service	324
Pacific Sportswear Co., Inc.	258
Palomar Mountain Spring Water	260
Peaches en Regalia	320
PharMingen	370
Plastic Display Products	270
Port of San Diego	334
Prism Lithographic Technologies	431
Promus Hotels	284
Rancho Valencia Resort	302
Reno Contracting	206
Rhino Linings USA, Inc.	271
RPM Material Handling Co.	254
San Diego Catering Concepts	321
San Diego County Credit Union	230
San Diego Film Commission	236
San Diego Hall of Champions	240
San Diego Historic Properties	188
San Diego Maritime Museum	403
San Diego Office Interiors	304
San Diego Refrigerated Services	306
San Diego Sports Arena	243
Seaport Village	274
Sharp Rees-Stealy Medical Group	386
Sky's the Limit Muralist Co.	308
Solar Turbines Incorporated	262
Southern California Security Services	367
SSC San Diego	428
St. Clare's Home	404
Stanley Steemer	310
Steigerwald-Dougherty Inc., General Building Contractors	220
T&B Planning Consultants	208
Taylor Guitars	265
Techbilt Companies	210
Televideo San Diego	338
The Bedroom Superstore	290
The EastLake Company, LLC	184
The Executive Group	352
The Titan Corporation	408
Thomas C. Ackerman Foundation	374
Thomas Jefferson School of Law	388
Toward Maximum Independence	390
Tower Glass Inc.	221
United Airlines	336
University of Phoenix	392
Urban Systems Associates	362
Warren West, Inc.	212
Warwick's	289
Women's History Reclamation Project	405